The Forgotten Battles

of the

Chancellorsville Campaign

CIVIL WAR SOLDIERS & STRATEGIES
Brian S. Wills, Series Editor

Richmond Must Fall: The Richmond-Petersburg Campaign, October 1864
HAMPTON NEWSOME

Work for Giants: The Campaign and Battle of Tupelo/Harrisburg, Mississippi, June–July 1864
THOMAS E. PARSON

"My Greatest Quarrel with Fortune": Major General Lew Wallace in the West, 1861–1862
CHARLES G. BEEMER

Phantoms of the South Fork: Captain McNeill and His Rangers
STEVE FRENCH

At the Forefront of Lee's Invasion: Retribution, Plunder, and Clashing Cultures on Richard S. Ewell's Road to Gettysburg
ROBERT J. WYNSTRA

Meade: The Price of Command, 1863–1865
JOHN G. SELBY

James Riley Weaver's Civil War: The Diary of a Union Cavalry Officer and Prisoner of War, 1863–1865
EDITED BY JOHN T. SCHLOTTERBECK, WESLEY W. WILSON, MIDORI KAWAUE, AND HAROLD A. KLINGENSMITH

Blue-Blooded Cavalryman: Captain William Brooke Rawle in the Army of the Potomac, May 1863–August 1865
EDITED BY J. GREGORY ACKEN

No Place for Glory: Major General Robert E. Rodes and the Confederate Defeat at Gettysburg
ROBERT J. WYNSTRA

From the Wilderness to Appomattox: The Fifteenth New York Heavy Artillery in the Civil War
EDWARD A. ALTEMOS

Adelbert Ames, the Civil War, and the Creation of Modern America
MICHAEL J. MEGELSH

The Forgotten Battles of the Chancellorsville Campaign: Fredericksburg, Salem Church, and Banks' Ford in Spring 1863
ERIK F. NELSON

THE FORGOTTEN BATTLES OF THE CHANCELLORSVILLE CAMPAIGN

FREDERICKSBURG, SALEM CHURCH,
AND BANKS' FORD IN SPRING 1863

※ ERIK F. NELSON ※

THE KENT STATE UNIVERSITY PRESS
Kent, Ohio

© 2024 by The Kent State University Press, Kent, Ohio 44242
All rights reserved
ISBN 978-1-60635-480-3
Published in the United States of America

No part of this book may be used or reproduced, in any manner whatsoever, without written permission from the Publisher, except in the case of short quotations in critical reviews or articles.

Cataloging information for this title is available at the Library of Congress.

28 27 26 25 24   5 4 3 2 1

To Mary and Thomas

This campaign was to the Sixth Corps a Fredericksburg affair;
but to the rest of the army it was the Chancellorsville campaign.
—*Soldier, Sixteenth New York Infantry*

I respectfully request that the regiments and batteries of the corps
be permitted to inscribe "Fredericksburg" and "Salem Heights" on
their colors. It is an honor they have bravely earned.
—*Maj. Gen. John Sedgwick, Report on the Battle of Chancellorsville*

CONTENTS

List of Maps   viii
Foreword *by Frank A. O'Reilly*   ix
Acknowledgments   xii
Prologue   xv
Introduction   1

1   April 28–29: First Moves   13
2   April 29–30: Waiting   35
3   May 1: First Day of Battle   58
4   May 2: Second Day of Battle   73
5   May 2–3: Night Moves and Action at Deep Run   89
6   Morning of May 3: Fredericksburg   114
7   Afternoon of May 3: The Road toward Chancellorsville   141
8   Late Afternoon of May 3: Salem Church   166
9   May 4: On the High Ground West of Fredericksburg   193
10   May 4: Salem Heights and Smith Run   221
11   May 4–5: Retreat to Banks' Ford   248
12   An Assessment   271

Appendix 1: Order of Battle   281
Appendix 2: Artillery Weapons   291
Appendix 3: The Flag of Truce   295
Notes   302
Bibliography   358
Index   374

MAPS

Map 1   Opening Moves   17
Map 2   Hooker's Plan   44
Map 3   Sedgwick's Bridgehead   54
Map 4   Into Fredericksburg   96
Map 5   Predawn Probes at Marye's Heights   102
Map 6   Action at Deep Run   107
Map 7   Gibbon's Attack at the Rappahannock Canal   119
Map 8   Sedgwick's Attack   130
Map 9   Breakthrough   142
Map 10   Confederates Pull Back   153
Map 11   The Road toward Chancellorsville   162
Map 12   Salem Church (Phase 1)   172
Map 13   Salem Church (Phase 2)   174
Map 14   Salem Church (Phase 3)   180
Map 15   Confederates Close in behind the Sixth Corps   197
Map 16   Sedgwick Repositions on the High Ground   207
Map 17   The Morning Attacks, May 4   210
Map 18   The Afternoon Attacks, May 4   225
Map 19   Early's Renewed Assault at Smith Run   233
Map 20   Federals Flanked at Smith Run   241
Map 21   Banks' Ford   249

FOREWORD

Some people live their entire life in a place and never make a difference. Some people visit a place for only a moment and change it forever. And sometimes, those places alter people forever. Fredericksburg is one such place.

The Fredericksburg area is overflowing with a rich tapestry of history—from Native people to European colonists, from Revolutionary War veterans to modern civil rights activists. But nothing made so indelible an impression on Fredericksburg and its surroundings as the Civil War. Numerous battlefields cover much of its immediate vicinity, attesting to the strategic importance both sides placed on this midpoint between the two opposing capitals. Washington, DC, stood only fifty miles to the north of Fredericksburg; Richmond, the capital of the Confederacy, loomed only fifty miles to the south. Inevitably, the war would come to Fredericksburg. The Federal army desired to use the town and environs as a springboard for operations against Richmond. Confederates needed Fredericksburg and the proximal Rappahannock River to block any Union advance southward.

The Federal Army of the Potomac tried repeatedly to breach the Confederate defensive scheme, resulting in the Battle of Fredericksburg in December 1862, the series of battles associated with the Chancellorsville Campaign in May 1863, and the gruesome bloodletting of the Wilderness and Spotsylvania Court House in May 1864 during the Overland Campaign. For eighteen months, the Fredericksburg area became the most disputed piece of ground on the North American continent. Soldiers forever altered how we consider Fredericksburg, and events there forever changed the people who would go on to shape the nation.

Amid such strife, it was easy to create a selective narrative and focus attention on certain salient features of the struggles around Fredericksburg. Countless battles, great and small, went unheralded in the portrayal of other events. The greatest oversights of them all were the Second Battle of Fredericksburg and Salem Church. History has habitually ignored or glossed over the combatants at these key battles when dealing with the overall narrative of the Chancellorsville Campaign.

Soldiers, students, and scholars have overlooked Second Fredericksburg and Salem Church for numerous reasons. Self-centered commanders like Joseph Hooker narrowly focused the narrative on themselves at Chancellorsville. Most of the troops in the Union and Confederate armies did not participate in the fighting at Fredericksburg or Salem Church, so they elected to center their memory on the part most of them shared in common at Chancellorsville. Historians tended to follow the marquee personalities—Robert E. Lee, Joseph Hooker, and Thomas J. "Stonewall" Jackson—leaving the seeming castoffs—John Sedgwick, Jubal A. Early, and Cadmus M. Wilcox—unconsidered. The results of Second Fredericksburg and Salem Church did not fit neatly into the set narrative of the Chancellorsville Campaign. Federal victory achieved without Hooker, the overall Union commander, went unnoticed, deliberately shunned by the general himself, who set the tone for prioritizing the actions of the campaign and their consequences.

Early, William Barksdale, John B. Gordon, and their Confederate troops performed feats at Fredericksburg and Salem Church, but success eluded their efforts. They could not hold Marye's Heights nor could they prevent the escape of a Union army corps seemingly trapped with its back to a river. Sedgwick and the Federal Sixth Corps had yet to make a name for themselves by 1863. Second Fredericksburg and Salem Church defined both the commander and the command. Yet the results of their efforts did not satisfy either one, they having gone from achieving the campaign's only Union victory to becoming the scapegoats for the Federals' ultimate defeat.

The participants of these battles attempted numerous times to correct misperceptions. They wrote and spoke about these battles often—in the process creating a rich treasure trove of personal accounts—trying to get the public to consider their efforts. They planted monuments on ground where few deigned to memorialize defeat. Unfortunately, theirs was an uphill battle, and even the old veterans grew weary of the struggle. The participants in these battles soon chose to dwell on other aspects of the war, highlighting other accomplishments more in common with their armies and reaping more resounding rewards.

Their chronicles of Second Fredericksburg and Salem Church in the spring of 1863 had all but faded into oblivion—relegated to well-intentioned footnotes at best—by the time of modern studies of the Chancellorsville Campaign. I have been guilty of this in my own articles on Chancellorsville for *Blue & Gray Magazine* during the 2013 sesquicentennial of the Civil War. Erik Nelson has now rescued this vital piece of the Chancellorsville Campaign from obscurity, bringing it back to the prominence it richly deserves.

Erik Nelson is ideally suited to chronicle the actions and exploits of the participants in the Second Battle of Fredericksburg and Salem Church. He has put the fighting in the proper context of the overall campaign and restored the chorus of voices washed out by the droning noise centered on Chancellorsville. I have always admired Erik's abilities as an historian. He has a keen eye for detail, analysis, and making deeper connections. As a veteran, he understands military culture, regimen, expectations, and limitations. As a one-time planner for the City of Fredericksburg, Erik has a brilliant ability for reading terrain and understanding how it shaped and determined military actions.

I have been privileged to prowl the river bottoms and ravines with him, where bygone battlefields lay hidden to all but those with a discerning eye. Armed with a military mind, a topographer's understanding, and a historian's curiosity, Erik Nelson has brought into stark relief and clarity a key component of the nation's past that helped shape its future. Fredericksburg changed Erik Nelson. His book will forever change how we look at Fredericksburg.

Frank A. O'Reilly
Fredericksburg, Virginia

ACKNOWLEDGMENTS

Anyone undertaking historical research must typically travel to a wide range of archives and libraries. In this instance the historians at Fredericksburg and Spotsylvania National Military Park (FSNMP) have done that heavy lifting. Over the decades they have compiled an enviable repository of primary source material related to the battlefields under their stewardship. They have also collected copies of letters and accounts shared by visitors who have come to trace the footsteps of ancestors. This treasure trove of documents extends to the events that occurred beyond the park's boundaries, and I have used this material extensively. I am also deeply indebted to the following individuals.

Robert K. Krick, the park's former chief historian, provided sustained guidance and encouragement as well as important source material. His efforts to preserve Civil War battlegrounds nationwide is a story yet to be properly told. He also initiated the concept of restoring protected battlefield land to its wartime configuration. Park rangers cutting down trees proved a hard sell, but he knew that understanding the landscape is critical to understanding its history.

Noel G. Harrison introduced the City of Fredericksburg's planning staff to unprotected battlegrounds and encouraged us local-government types to consider them as we developed land-use plans. His research is thorough, and he made sure we knew that park historians had created a database for the Second Battle of Fredericksburg. John Heiser compiled and analyzed reports, correspondence, and other documentation. Ed Raus and David Lilley systematically photographed the fields and woodlands around Salem Church and the May 4 battlegrounds before a wave of development in the 1980s began to obliterate their historic integrity.

Frank O'Reilly has written the definitive study of the Battle of Fredericksburg and conducted me over portions of the terrain key in 1862 that loomed large in 1863. He and I also spent several seasons exploring historic sites along stretches of the Rappahannock and Rapidan Rivers. That riparian land is remote from roads and trails, so the effort proved as exhausting as it was rewarding.

Donald C. Pfanz provided reams of archival material from the extensive FSNMP files. Reams may not be the appropriate term for what is contained on electronic disks, but the material collected by park historians is voluminous. He also read an early version of the entire manuscript and provided valuable comments and advice.

Eric Mink does excellent research and is always receptive to rethinking old interpretations. We have tramped battlefields together for years, and he is a knowledgeable companion. He too read early chapters of this work and provided much appreciated assistance to get the manuscript in front of people who might consider its publication.

Steve Stanley took my rough battleground diagrams and skillfully turned them into finished maps. He is a colleague from the early days of the Central Virginia Battlefields Trust.

John Hennessy of FSNMP also passed along primary materials. Mike Ward shared his research on the Salem Church fight. Jeffrey Stocker generously forwarded scores of transcribed primary documents. Joe Rokus read through the entire manuscript with an eye for fine detail and grammatical consistency.

At the local-government level, Fredericksburg Planning Director Jervis C. Hairston made battlefield preservation a prominent part of long-range city plans. We were encouraged in this effort by two city council members, Gordon W. Shelton and Ralph A. Hicks, who had chanced upon the May 4 battlefield as boys. Public policy to preserve and protect Civil War sites resulted in a range of local successes.

Reaching further into the past to days at the University of California, Santa Barbara, Prof. John Talbott guided me through several semesters of study. Jack generously invited me (an older undergraduate) to join his graduate seminars, during which he helped me understand how to evaluate sources and write with clarity. I appreciate his infinite patience as I transitioned from the rough world of a fleet sailor to that of an aspiring scholar.

Finally, the staff at the Kent State University Press have been universally helpful and generous. They constitute a remarkable team that pulled me into their fold.

⇥ PROLOGUE ⇤

In the mid-1960s two Fredericksburg boys, searching a Confederate encampment site for uniform buttons and belt buckles, found smashed bullets and artillery shrapnel. The evidence of hard fighting was distant from any National Park Service holdings in Fredericksburg, to the east, or at Salem Church, to the west. The battleground the boys had stumbled upon appeared to be a place forgotten.[1]

When the federal government set up the Fredericksburg and Spotsylvania National Military Park in 1927, it placed four major battlefields under a single administrative umbrella. A self-guided driving tour invited visitors to see those far-flung battlegrounds in a chronological sequence. In Fredericksburg visitors learned about the winter campaign of 1862. They then drove a dozen miles west to see where the Battle of Chancellorsville took place in May 1863. The tour did not backtrack to the Second Battle of Fredericksburg, which constituted a substantial part of that spring campaign. From Chancellorsville, visitors continued to the 1864 battlegrounds of the Wilderness and Spotsylvania Court House.[2]

The presented sequence of events for the Chancellorsville battle is dramatic. In late April 1863 Federal commander Maj. Gen. Joseph Hooker got a force across the Rappahannock River upstream from Fredericksburg. Under the direction of Gen. Robert E. Lee, the legendary Lt. Gen. "Stonewall" Jackson pulled together a force to stop this advance on May 1. The next day

Jackson got in behind the Federal army and attacked with stunning success but fell wounded in the night from friendly fire. Fighting resumed on May 3 around the historic crossroads, but at Lee's moment of victory, a courier reported that a Union force had broken through the Confederate defenses at Fredericksburg.

The Federal force brought to Lee's attention had done hard fighting to become a threat to the Army of Northern Virginia. Much of the land it fought over, however, remains outside the park boundary. Some of the fighting occurred within the park, but as noted, those holdings are interpreted for December 1862, not May 1863. On the Fredericksburg front the Sixth Corps sustained 26 percent of the overall losses suffered by the Union Army of the Potomac during the Chancellorsville Campaign. Southern losses at Fredericksburg constituted 26–29 percent of Confederate losses for the overall campaign. The fighting at the Second Battle of Fredericksburg, Salem Church, and Banks' Ford was not inconsequential, but the preservation process became skewed by a distorted historic record.[3]

The Confederate loss at Fredericksburg in May 1863 stood in painful contrast to the astonishing victory at Chancellorsville, and many Southerners tried to explain it away by claiming Yankee treachery. They argued that the attackers used a flag of truce to ascertain the strength of the Confederate defenses at Marye's Heights. Brig. Gen. William Barksdale's report made clear that the May 3 assault moved too quickly for reinforcements to respond, but Maj. Gen. Jubal Early did not use Barksdale's submission when writing his own official account. He mistakenly claimed that a flag of truce had been allowed just before the main Federal assault. Lee then used Early's report to develop his own report to Richmond, and Early's mistake became further embedded in the official record. Barksdale died at Gettysburg soon afterward, so Early's and Lee's reports remained uncorrected. Historians have been working with that inaccurate paper trail ever since.[4]

In 1867 Jedediah Hotchkiss and William Allan published *The Battlefields of Virginia: Chancellorsville*. Their work had a decided Lee-Jackson focus, but they did note that the Union army's May 3 assault at Fredericksburg was so rapid that the Confederates had no opportunity to reinforce the points of contact. This sequence of events was entirely consistent with Barksdale's battle report, but the writers still had Early's and Lee's reports to deal with and apparently felt obliged to add a single sentence about a flag of truce during the Federal onslaught. That detail stood out as glaringly inconsistent with the rest of their narrative, but its inclusion gave the misleading story credence.[5]

Three books by Northern writers came out in the early 1880s. Theodore A. Dodge, a Union veteran, wrote *The Campaign of Chancellorsville* in 1881. He referred to the flag-of-truce story as an allegation by Early and made clear that he did not believe it to be a reason for the Confederates loss at Fredericksburg. A historian named Samuel P. Bates published *The Battle of Chancellorsville* in 1882. He also made no reference to a flag of truce and criticized the Southern reports that minimized the intensity of the fighting on May 4. Also in 1882 Abner Doubleday wrote a study called *Chancellorsville and Gettysburg*. A Union veteran, he understood how the Federal attack across a broad front on May 3 made the Confederate lines vulnerable to a breakthrough. He noted the short duration of the Union assault and made no mention of a flag of truce. Doubleday also had the insight to look at Chancellorsville and Gettysburg as a continuum, treating the battle in Virginia as an inconclusive prelude to the decisive confrontation in Pennsylvania.[6]

The Union Sixth Corps's experience during the Chancellorsville Campaign received additional attention in *Battles and Leaders of the Civil War*. Published in 1887–88 by the Century Company, it provided a wealth of firsthand material in four volumes. In an article titled "Sedgwick at Fredericksburg and Salem Church," Huntington W. Jackson focused heavily on the attack on the Confederate center but made no reference to the important supporting attack south of Hazel Run. A quarter century after the fact, significant parts of the Union assault on May 3 were beginning to disappear from histories of the war.[7]

In 1907, twenty years after *Battles and Leaders*, Charles Richardson published a slim volume called *The Chancellorsville Campaign: Fredericksburg to Salem Church*. He described the Fredericksburg battlefield in detail, and his narrative of the combat also included the full scope of the Union assaults. The battle descriptions, however, are very brief, as had been the case with Dodge and Bates. Little original research was being undertaken by anyone, but neither Jackson nor Richardson made any mention of a flag of truce.

Even a Mississippi veteran turned historian could not bring himself to repeat the flag-of-truce story with conviction. Sylvanus J. Quinn had been a captain in Barksdale's Brigade and part of the Confederate defense on May 3. After the war he moved to Fredericksburg, married a local woman, and became active in local affairs. He published a history of the city in

1908, and the considerable detail he provided on the Mississippians at the Second Battle of Fredericksburg is excellent primary source material. Understanding the need for credible documentation, he cautiously noted how "a flag of truce, *it was claimed,* was sent from the town to obtain permission to provide for the wounded."[8]

Historians have had to deal with more than misleading documents. For those who research military operations, battlefields reveal insights not apparent in an archive. The contested landscape helps unravel the inherent confusion of ground combat. By the twentieth century, however, large portions of the Fredericksburg battlefield had been altered by new construction. In 1910 John Bigelow Jr. used the official War Department records (published 1890–1901) to study Hooker's preparations and subsequent campaign. His book, *The Campaign of Chancellorsville,* is recognized as a classic use of the correspondence and after-action reports that are still the cornerstone of Civil War research. What detracts from his work is that he misunderstood the altered terrain around Fredericksburg.

Bigelow's narrative thoroughly recounted the Chancellorsville battle through May 3, but he did not fully understand the action in Fredericksburg. He gave new life to a flag of truce in the middle of the attack sequence, citing official records as well as Hotchkiss and Allan. Bigelow developed a creditable study, but his errors about events at Fredericksburg would appear in subsequent publications.

Civil War scholarship also gravitated toward a focused recitation of Southern valor, evident in Douglas Southall Freeman's biography of Robert E. Lee, published in 1934–35. In volumes two and three (of four), he categorized the Battle of Chancellorsville, fought on May 2 and 3, 1863, as Lee's greatest. He spent little time on the fighting at Fredericksburg and Salem Church since Lee was not there. Where Lee had been present in that area on May 4, Freeman blamed Confederate missteps on subordinate officers who the Southern commander was too much of a gentleman to reprimand or relieve. He intimated that Lee's handling of the Chancellorsville Campaign had been "flawless," a claim that would have become tenuous if he had written more fully of the events of May 3 and 4. Rather than being challenged for a study bordering on hagiography, Freeman's genteel portrayal of war received the 1935 Pulitzer Prize.[9]

Freeman also published a three-volume work titled *Lee's Lieutenants.* In volume two the author examined the fighting at the Second Battle of Fredericksburg, Salem Church, and Banks' Ford using the same methodology as in his Lee biography. He told an immediate story that was said to recreate the fog of war, providing the reader with the information that officers had at the time they were making decisions. Freeman's focus on personalities avoided any military context that might detract from an aura of Southern spirit and bravery. His account of the Second Battle of Fredericksburg included a brief reference to the flag of truce, consistent with Confederate narratives but not with eyewitness accounts. He also explored the battles at Salem Church and Banks' Ford without mentioning that the Union army utterly devastated several Confederate assaults. Historical omission had become a literary device.[10]

In the 1890s the US government preserved expansive landscapes at Chickamauga-Chattanooga, Shiloh, and Gettysburg, where military officers could study the ground and evaluate battlefield decisions. The government had a wealth of data from the *Official Records of the Union and Confederate Armies*. Even better, historians were able to consult the veterans who had been on those fields to address conflicts within the documentation and to confirm details of battle in relation to the terrain.[11]

Battlefields also drew a curious public, which gave preserved land an economic value. Between 1901 and 1904, a dozen jurisdictions petitioned Congress to establish reservations of historic ground. The government responded within tight fiscal constraints and determined that new parks would only need to acquire acreage bearing military features such as earthworks. The intervening land could be left in private ownership because the terrain would surely remain wooded or in agricultural use. That optimistic adaptation to financial reality began at Antietam and continued when Congress authorized other parks, including that for Fredericksburg and Chancellorsville.

A commission studying the Fredericksburg area in 1925 focused on what the visiting public would be able to see from their vehicles. Within that context, only minor areas of land were considered for acquisition at Chancellorsville and Salem Church. A great many earthworks had been filled in, both during the war and afterward, and the surviving trenches at Chancellorsville were hidden in the woods. The minor works on the Salem Church fields had also been obliterated. The tour would have visitors viewing fields and woods in private ownership.[12]

There were other limitations. The War Department still had its collection of archival data, but by 1927, the Civil War generation had passed on. Thus, an outreach to veterans could not be pursued at Fredericksburg.

The Great Depression further reduced funding for land acquisition. Government attention to national parks came from New Deal programs that provided jobs. Constrained funding kept the initial land purchases at the Fredericksburg and Spotsylvania National Military Park to an overall collection of just 2,100 acres, only 110 of which were on the Fredericksburg battleground.[13]

Limited funding also curtailed important research. In 1933 the Interior Department assumed custody of the nation's historic battlefields from the War Department. A solid historic foundation for the Fredericksburg-area battlefields had been initiated, but some investigations never began. A set of maps for the Second Battle of Fredericksburg created in 1935, for instance, stopped short of the march to Salem Church. No maps were developed for the battle there on May 3, 1863, and none for the fighting on May 4. The basis for interpreting battlefields at Fredericksburg had significant limitations from the outset.[14]

Prevailing scholarship influenced initial land acquisition for a park, and subsequent studies perpetuated that limited focus. In 1958 Edward J. Stackpole published *Chancellorsville: Lee's Greatest Battle,* a robust tactical study about the fighting around the historic crossroads. Like Bigelow, his presentation of the action at Fredericksburg, Salem Church, and Banks' Ford proved less useful, although he clearly understood that Maj. Gen. John Sedgwick's swift attack discredited the old flag-of-truce story. In 1991 Ernest B. Furguson published *Chancellorsville 1863: The Souls of the Brave.* He wrote a compelling book based on new material, but he also detailed only a portion of the action at Fredericksburg, Salem Church, and Banks' Ford.[15]

What these twentieth-century historians missed was that the Union attack at Fredericksburg on May 3 was larger than Pickett's Charge would be and extended from the area east of Hazel Run to the ground west of the Rappahannock Canal—an expanse of nearly 4,000 yards. On the day of battle, Sedgwick could see his assault columns from an overlook at the edge of town. Over time, though, only the terrain in front of Marye's Heights has remained discernible as a battlefield. Robert K. Krick, former chief historian of Fredericksburg and Spotsylvania National Military Park, described the challenge of interpreting that painfully small area of a vast battleground: "The Marye's Heights enclave has got to be, by a factor of logarithms, the least preserved, and thus the least interpretable (a poor word, I admit) of any major eastern-theater CW landmark. Akin to interpreting Pickett's Charge with none of the charge and almost none of the defensive line—surround the Copse of Trees and highwater mark with 1910-vintage houses, cheek by jowl, for example."[16]

In 1998 Stephen W. Sears broke the overemphasis on the Lee-Jackson theme in a study simply called *Chancellorsville*. Like Stackpole, he recognized the incongruous flag-of-truce story for what it was—a postbattle attempt to redeem reputations. He placed the actual event well before the assault on Marye's Heights, which is supported by credible documentation. Sadly, that analysis did not get considered in a 2013 study called *Chancellorsville's Forgotten Front: The Battles of Second Fredericksburg and Salem Church, May 3, 1863*. The authors of that work reinserted the incident into the assault on Marye's Heights, reflecting a continuing misunderstanding of the terrain and therefore the battle.[17]

Without concern for historic interpretations, the Fredericksburg community pragmatically figured out how to live on intimate terms with its historic setting. The urban battlefield in downtown Fredericksburg is still a vibrant neighborhood, occupied today as it was in the 1860s by families and businesses. Residents replaced bullet-riddled weatherboards and patched over holes punched by cannonballs. Fredericksburg was also an industrial town when the armies arrived. Some of the large mills, used as hospitals during the war, survived the war and returned to industrial work afterward, some remaining intact and adapted to new uses today.[18]

Immediately after the war, the US government transferred the remains of thousands of Union soldiers to the Fredericksburg National Cemetery. The Ladies Memorial Association of Fredericksburg saw to the reburial of the Confederate dead. Residents found ordnance around their homes, but many of those hazards remained hidden. Intact projectiles could still function and sometimes did, jarred by careless handling or cooked off in building fires. Before the streets were paved in front of Marye's Heights, a good rain would wash Minié balls out of the soil along the edges of hard-packed dirt roads. Workmen unearthed artillery rounds while constructing a state college (now the University of Mary Washington). In the twenty-first century, local gardeners still find bullets, broken weapons, and other debris when planting flowers and tomatoes.[19]

Fredericksburg's growth inevitably cut into the battleground's integrity. A neighborhood of handsome Victorian homes was built along a ridge where Federal artillery once deployed. The open ground Federal troops crossed to attack Marye's Heights also became a neighborhood. North–south highways influence the location of schools, industrial parks, and commercial centers.

But not all change has been destructive, as modern roads directed growth patterns away from other parts of the historic landscape. Riverside canals and portions of trenches and gun pits survive, as do traces of antebellum roads and routes established by Union engineers. Those cuts in the earth can still be found, especially in winter when the leaves are down and a sprinkling of snow provides a contrasting definition that briefly overcomes their fade to invisibility.

With study, the hidden battlefield reveals itself. A few timbers from a mill dam on Hazel Run show exactly where several regiments of Georgians splashed through a mill pond on May 4. A line of cedar trees in an industrial park marks the old road to an antebellum mansion that guided a Federal attack on May 3. An alley behind a row of houses in another neighborhood runs along the top of an embankment that sheltered a brigade of infantry as it waited to launch an attack.

The heavily developed land between Fredericksburg and Salem Church holds the key to understanding Hooker's overall plan. The historic scene, though obscured by commercial construction around an Interstate 95 interchange, extends north across the Rappahannock River into the area where the winter campaign known as the Mud March unfolded in January 1863. At that time, the Federal commander had been Maj. Gen. Ambrose E. Burnside, who had led the Union army to disaster at Fredericksburg the month before. The Mud March has become a symbol of abject failure and led to Burnside's removal from command, yet his plan reflected careful preparation.[20]

Burnside directed his forces toward a crossing of the Rappahannock River near Banks' Ford, which is the first break in the river bluffs above Fredericksburg. After jumping the river, the Federals were to occupy the ground just east of what is now the Interstate 95 and State Route 3 interchange. Occupation of that open plateau would force the Confederate army to either pull back from Fredericksburg or be compelled to attack the strong defensive position that could be established there.[21]

Weather doomed Burnside's effort, but Hooker also made that terrain his campaign objective. It was a place he could occupy in strength and force Lee to either attack his ensconced Federal troops at a disadvantage or retreat south. Hooker never reached that high ground, but on May 4 the Sixth Corps held that terrain and inflicted considerable casualties on the Southern forces that tried to dislodge it. In late 1863 Maj. Gen. George G. Meade, then in command of the Army of the Potomac, would seek authorization to return to Fredericksburg, which could be supplied by rail and become a springboard for the 1864 campaigns. He would be denied that permission, but Lt. Gen. Ulysses S. Grant would shift to that line of communications anyway during his Overland Campaign.[22]

Heavy fighting occurred on the Fredericksburg front on May 3 and 4, 1863, but Hooker took no action when Sedgwick drew off substantial Confederate strength from Chancellorsville. That battlefield negligence left the Sixth Corps to confront an adversary increasing in strength as Sedgwick pushed toward Hooker. Historians have not told that story very well, which has obscured an understanding of the full campaign. This study matches primary documentation to the physical setting in and around Fredericksburg to fill in what previous studies have left out. It thus becomes the missing second volume to existing Chancellorsville studies.

In broad terms, both armies had become used up by the end of 1862. But during the winter of 1862–63, the Union army developed into a force that would be able to fight an extended war. The Southern army made organizational improvements, but its experience that winter revealed that the Confederate government was never going to have enough men or sufficient materiel to support its field forces. The success of the Union army's preparations in the spring of 1863 would become more evident at Gettysburg than at Chancellorsville, but the battles fought at Fredericksburg, Salem Church, and Banks' Ford had been a portent.

INTRODUCTION

On January 27, 1863, Maj. Gen. Joseph Hooker took command of the Army of the Potomac, then in winter quarters. Across the Rappahannock River stood the town of Fredericksburg, held by elements of Confederate general Robert E. Lee's Army of Northern Virginia. The Federals had been severely punished there in a mid-December 1862 battle, an agonizing conclusion to a year that once held great promise for ending the rebellion.

The Union army had become strong in men and materiel, but its leadership had been consistently inept. Pres. Abraham Lincoln had removed Maj. Gen. George B. McClellan from command because he had been unable to prosecute the war with any sense of purpose. Maj. Gen. Ambrose E. Burnside had proved that army command was beyond his capability as well. Lincoln had now turned to Hooker, a man with a problematic reputation but a fighter with a supreme confidence.

The president was trying to fight a war that demanded more of its military leaders than the army had trained them for. During the War with Mexico (1846–48), Maj. Gen. Winfield Scott had landed on a hostile shore with 12,000 men. Fifteen years later McClellan landed on the Virginia Peninsula with an army ten times that size. The nation's industries could arm, clothe, and feed such large forces, but American military men struggled to develop the capacity to organize and administer them and then fight battles that extended beyond their field of vision. Lincoln hoped that in Hooker he had found a man who could handle such daunting tasks.[1]

From his headquarters at the King Farm, Hooker sent out a series of directives to address the army's basic health. The Federal troops benefited from a generous supply system, but scurvy appeared in the camps while fresh food rotted at supply depots. Sick men were dying in hospitals from having only field rations (hardtack) to consume rather than healthful vegetables and soup. Hooker ordered the better distribution of food as well as immediate attention to camp sanitation. He then turned to assessing the army's ability to fight.[2]

Of immediate concern were officers and men absent from their units. The slaughter at Fredericksburg and subsequent exposure to extreme weather during the Mud March of January 1863 had disenchanted once-willing volunteers. A dispirited soldier wrote, "The men in their shelter tents and but poorly supplied with shoes have become disheartened and begin to think they can never succeed." Soldiers had also not been paid, which meant their families suffered. Without confidence in the army, men sometimes just walked away. When Burnside departed, fully 10 percent of the Army of the Potomac could not be accounted for.[3]

Hooker made sure his soldiers were paid, including back pay, but prosecuting massive numbers of men for desertion would be problematic. It was the army that had failed its soldiers, and the effort to bring them back included the commander in chief. Lincoln announced a general amnesty on March 3. Men who returned to their units by April 1 would not be prosecuted for desertion, while those who had deserted and been caught would also have a chance to continue in service. After that date, however, wartime discipline would prevail. Lincoln was famous for his clemency but came to realize that deserters threatened the morale of those who steadfastly stood to their duty. He informed Hooker he would no longer reconsider death sentences for desertion.[4]

As absent men returned, thousands of others prepared to leave. In 1861 Lincoln had called for 300,000 volunteers to serve for three years. Recruiting, however, entailed states raising local regiments, and state officials had to contend with how long men were willing to wear a uniform. Some states had allowed two-year enlistments, and those signed on such terms were coming due for discharge in the spring of 1863.[5]

Events in 1862 added to those manpower issues. McClellan failed to end the war with a decisive battle in Virginia, and horrendous casualties at Shiloh, Tennessee, further shattered illusions of a quick war. Lincoln called for another 300,000 three-year volunteers, but before those troops could be recruited, the Army of Northern Virginia crossed the Potomac River into Maryland. In that acute emergency the president issued a call for 300,000 nine-month militia. With enlistments measured in months instead of years, over 87,000 men responded. The US government would implement a military draft in 1863 to meet its manpower needs, but Chancellorsville and Gettysburg would be fought with the volunteers of 1861 and 1862.[6]

Those recruits had joined regiments that mustered in to service with at least 1,000 men. That number became diminished by battle casualties, contagious diseases, exposure, and exhaustion. In the spring of 1863, average regimental fighting strength stood at 530 men. The amnesty for returning deserters helped fill the ranks, but Hooker also wanted soldiers back from detached duties. He directed that formerly enslaved African Americans be used as teamsters, cooks, and laborers so that fighting men assigned those tasks could return to their combat units.[7]

No matter when men were going to leave the army, training intensified at all levels. Hooker reactivated schools of instruction for both commissioned and noncommissioned officers. Rigorous inspections assessed the readiness of regiments and batteries. Hooker allowed units that met standards of efficiency to release men on furlough. The number of troops allowed to travel home at any one time was never great, but the incentive proved strong. Units not up to standards had furloughs suspended until their capabilities reached acceptable levels.[8]

Inspectors assessed units thoroughly. Were the troops healthy and their camp well ordered? Were wagons in good repair and teams properly cared for? Were weapons and equipment in good condition? Did the appearance and demeanor of the men indicate good discipline? Could they move quickly and efficiently as a formation? Were the men able to judge distances and deliver effective fire? These and other measures of effectiveness were the inspectors' chief concerns. A Pennsylvania soldier described the scrutiny: "Indeed, we were looked after most sharply, especially as to condition of ammunition in cartridge boxes, shelter tents, and shoes." A New York soldier wrote: "The Reg[iment] was inspected this morning, making a very good appearance. Our military discipline is becoming more and more strict. We are held to a more and more strict accountability, for the performance of all our duties. And consequently, our efficiency has been increased."[9]

The spring campaign would open with Hooker executing an extended flank march that put his army on the same side of the Rappahannock River as Lee's. That bold maneuver became possible through the concerted efforts of Federal quartermasters. The sheer size of Civil War armies imposed logistical burdens that hindered their ability to maneuver in the field. A force of 100,000 men consumed 600 tons of supplies a day, including the forage required to feed thousands of horses and mules. The freight capacity of railways and river transport could deliver the necessary beans, bullets, and blankets, but the great challenge was to be able to break away from fixed supply depots and maneuver against an enemy force.[10]

The difficulty of field supply became painfully evident on the Virginia Peninsula. Federal quartermasters managed to keep McClellan's Army of the Potomac fed and ready for battle as it plodded toward Richmond but used 5,000 wagons and 21,000–25,000 horses and mules to do so. Once the fighting began, those thousands of wagons got in the way and hindered operations. Brig. Gen. Montgomery C. Meigs, quartermaster general for the Union army, recognized the great burden supplies and transport imposed. To overcome this problem, he forged a strong working relationship with the Army of the Potomac's chief quartermaster, Maj. Rufus B. Ingalls.[11]

To get the army beyond its supply depots, Ingalls systematically addressed optimizing wagon loads that teams could handle on the South's notoriously poor roads. Operational mobility demanded that fewer wagons accompany the striking columns, which required that their capacity be used for actual supplies rather than the carpetbags and trunks that volunteer soldiers thought they needed on campaign. Ingalls developed standard military loads for wagons as well as for soldier knapsacks.[12]

In March 1863 a board of officers studied how soldiers consumed rations in the field. They found that the standard issue of 100 hard crackers intended as a ten-day supply lasted no more than eight days on the march. Soldiers typically carried three days' rations, but if they became separated from wagons carrying additional food any longer than that, the army lost momentum. After some experimentation, the board established a field load distributed between a knapsack and a haversack. That standardized burden weighed forty-five pounds and included clothing, eight days' rations, weapons, and ammunition.[13]

Soldier loads as well as diligent oversight of wagon loads extended the army's range while reducing the size of its supply trains. Later modifications occurred as quartermasters evaluated what worked and what did not, but in the spring of 1863, the Union army had the ability to maneuver for eight days without resupply. When the Army of the Potomac opened its campaign in April 1863, it would travel faster and farther than the Confederates expected.[14]

Union telegraph signalmen were also not prepared for the army's new range. Flags, torches, and couriers were the traditional means of communications across a battlefield, and the Army of the Potomac had superb signal teams utilizing such equipment. A field-telegraph network held promise for when weather and terrain obscured visibility, but it had technical limitations. The US War Department had asked civilian telegraph companies to provide military communications, using their own skilled operators and supervisors, but Secretary of War Edwin M. Stanton kept the resulting US Military Telegraph under his direct supervision. That political move gave him control over information coming into Washington but did little to support armies on campaign.[15]

In early 1862 George W. Beardslee developed mobile equipment that he grandly called the Beardslee Patent Magneto-Electric Field Telegraph Machine. Instead of heavy batteries, a magneto generated its own current when an operator cranked the device by hand. A dial with the letters of the alphabet and a pointer could be set up at two locations, connected with a wire. The Beardslee stations could potentially function ten miles apart but worked better when separated by no more than five miles. Unfortunately, the system could become unsynchronized, garbling message traffic until recalibrated. Its need for a physical connection also proved a substantial limitation compared with the range and mobility of flag stations.[16]

In addition to logistics and signals, Hooker turned his attention to military intelligence. McClellan had used civilian detective Alan Pinkerton to develop estimates of enemy strength but then succumbed to exceptionally poor analysis. A volunteer soldier named John C. Babcock, with strong engineering and cartographic skills, had worked with Pinkerton and agreed to stay on with Burnside when the detective left with McClellan. Babcock asked to operate as a civilian rather than be subject to an unpredictable military hierarchy, and Burnside agreed. He sent him to work under Brig. Gen. Marsena R. Patrick, the Potomac army's provost marshal general. Hooker inherited Babcock when he assumed command.[17]

To build up the intelligence staff, Dan Butterfield, Hooker's chief of staff, sent over Col. George H. Sharpe to work with Babcock. The new arrival had been a New York attorney before the war, fought at First Bull Run, and subsequently raised the 120th New York Infantry. Hooker knew Sharpe's analytical skills would be more useful at headquarters than in command of a regiment, and Patrick made him deputy provost marshal general, for lack of any intelligence-related title.[18]

The two men worked well together. Sharpe had an organized and keenly systematic mind, while Babcock had become knowledgeable about the Army of Northern Virginia from interrogating prisoners. Their first report providing a view into Lee's army landed on Hooker's desk on March 15, 1863. The team had synthesized information brought in by Union sympathizers as well as data gleaned from scouting reports, newspapers, cavalry observations, intercepted Confederate signals, Confederate deserters, Federal signal stations, and observations from balloons.[19]

Improved intelligence gathering finally integrated the army's use of balloons. Men had ridden into the sky since the 1780s, and enthusiastic aeronauts descended on Washington as America went to war in 1861. Intrigued by the novelty of flight, Lincoln urged the War Department to appoint Thaddeus Lowe to head up an aeronautical service, as he appeared to have developed clear procedures that promised much needed reliability. The army, however, was unimpressed and left its operations to the civilians.[20]

The balloon corps traveled to the Peninsula in 1862 and made aerial observations during the slow advance to Richmond. Both Federal and Confederate balloons were aloft over Gaines's Mill, but the subsequent engagements of the Seven Days unfolded too quickly for cumbersome aerial equipment to be used. Balloons were not used at Antietam because Lowe was ill. At Fredericksburg Burnside held the balloons on the ground until he began crossing the river, relegating their use to simply observing the developing battle.[21]

But Hooker saw balloons as a tool to systematically gather information. He placed Capt. Cyrus B. Comstock in charge of the Aeronautic Corps, which distressed Lowe, but the general intended his intelligence organization to be fully integrated and accountable. He sent up his balloons routinely, both before and during the campaign, but close observers realized that their value had to be weighed against their logistical burden. A more disciplined supply system had increased the range and mobility of the Union army, and aerial reconnaissance seemed to be too cumbersome to keep up.[22]

Specialized functions gave the Union army critical capabilities, and Hooker's training regimen increased its readiness for battle. Less successful were his efforts at reorganization. Within ten days of taking command,

Hooker broke up Burnside's three multicorps grand divisions and directed each corps commander to report directly to him. The grand divisions had comprised two corps each to provide an efficient command structure, but the seniority system had undone the effort. Two of the three grand-division leaders were not up to the task, which contributed to the disaster that was Fredericksburg. While Burnside's reputation has been tarnished by his unsuccessful tenure as head of the Army of the Potomac, his lean command structure had merit. In the Confederate army Lee directed his force through two trusted subordinates—Lt. Gen. James Longstreet and Lt. Gen. Thomas J. "Stonewall" Jackson.

Placing seven corps plus an independent cavalry force under one overall commander reflected a poorly thought-out organization. Hooker was not the first to think he could handle everything, though. In early 1862 McClellan had postponed organizing his army into corps, planning to first evaluate his division commanders in battle. President Lincoln rejected this leisurely approach to the war and organized the Army of the Potomac into four corps himself. After Gettysburg Maj. Gen. George G. Meade retained Hooker's cumbersome command structure, perpetuating the army's struggle to direct its huge field forces.[23]

Hooker's grasp of combined-arms doctrine was also poorly thought through. The general knew that artillery and infantry units often developed bonds of trust that served them well in the heat of battle. Emphasizing such tactical details, however, compromised the army's most powerful battlefield advantage. The Potomac Army's chief of artillery, Brig. Gen. Henry J. Hunt, had proved the concept of marshaling overwhelming firepower on a battlefield, but Hooker assigned batteries to divisions for infantry commanders to direct. He retained an artillery reserve but pulled Hunt away from directing it, reducing his authority to administrative duties.[24]

Lee understood that artillery concentrated on a battlefield could be decisive and reorganized the Army of Northern Virginia's long arm in April 1863. Batteries were grouped into battalions (usually four batteries) and were not to be directed by infantry officers. They were under the charge of a corps's artillery chief, who reported to the army's chief of artillery, who reported directly to Lee. Confederate artillery would dominate the battlefield at Chancellorsville.[25]

Hooker prepared for field operations but did not include his corps commanders in this process. He stole a march on Lee in the opening stages of the spring offensive, but his secretiveness caused problems as the campaign progressed. Lee's lost order during the Maryland Campaign remained a constant reminder that plans committed to paper could be undone through carelessness or bad luck. Thus, Hooker had decided not to share his plan with those who would execute it.[26]

At the time of the Civil War, professional soldiers had studied Napoleon's campaigns, which focused on the so-called decisive battle. McClellan's Peninsula Campaign had been an effort to set up a confrontation outside Richmond that would end the war. He proved to be entirely unprepared for the rapid pace of the Seven Days' Battles that developed instead. In 1846 a young lieutenant named Henry Halleck—in the spring of 1863 a major general and the Union's general in chief—had produced the US Army's standard textbook on strategy and tactics, *Elements of Military Art and Science,* presenting strategy as a war's objective, while tactics related to maneuvering formations on a battlefield. The missing element was a methodology to coordinate separate battles within a larger area of operations, which required the ability to use maps and messages to control events beyond the horizon.[27]

Those few military men who grasped the concept of expanded operations achieved stunning results. In the spring of 1862, for instance, Lee saw very quickly how Jackson's campaign in the Shenandoah Valley affected the action that developed on his own front near Richmond. The famous Lee-Jackson team synchronized its efforts again during campaigns that extended into northern Virginia and Maryland. Maj. Gen. Ulysses S. Grant developed similar operational skills along the Mississippi River, but his eastern contemporaries struggled to effectively coordinate dispersed formations.[28]

Hooker launched a campaign that had every chance of success. Unable to see what was happening beyond the surrounding trees, however, he gave away battlefield advantages daily. On May 1 Federal forces emerged from a gloomy wilderness onto a ridge where Union artillery could have dominated the field. From a distant headquarters, Hooker called his forces back into the woods, and the Confederates moved in to keep him there. On May 2 Hooker became convinced the Confederate army was in retreat while Stonewall Jackson marched a force across his front to launch a surprise flank attack. On May 3 the Union army stood between Jackson's and Lee's separated forces, but rather than standing firm, Hooker pulled back from commanding ground and ensconced himself behind elaborate earthworks.

Hooker's inability to exert command and control on forces beyond sight and sound had an enormous influence on how he interacted with Maj. Gen. John Sedgwick. The Sixth Corps commander remained at Fredericksburg while the main army executed its opening flank march and fought its battle at Chancellorsville. As the campaign progressed, Sedgwick did his best to follow orders but was never entirely sure what his commander wanted him to do. For all his administrative skills and military experience, Hooker was not prepared for the magnitude of the battle he had initiated.

Union odds improved when Lee responded to an apparent threat elsewhere. In March Burnside received orders to take two Ninth Corps divisions to the western theater, leaving one division in Virginia. When the Ninth Corps embarked from Aquia Landing and went ashore at Newport News, Lee sent Longstreet with two divisions to counter what looked to be a threat to North Carolina. Only the one Ninth Corps division marched to Suffolk while the other two headed west, but the Confederate War Department kept Longstreet on the coast, where he had been able to sustain his troops without drawing on Lee's limited resources.[29]

In April preparations for a campaign gathered momentum. On the sixth Lee and his chief of artillery, Brig. Gen. William N. Pendleton, considered how to bring the Southern artillery out of its winter encampments with horses still weak from poor winter feed. That same day President Lincoln reviewed the Army of the Potomac's cavalry, ten thousand strong on well-fed mounts. Over the next few days, Lincoln also reviewed each of the army's seven infantry corps. In between those grand spectacles, he conferred with Hooker about how the war would be prosecuted in Virginia.[30]

On April 13 the Cavalry Corps, under command of Maj. Gen. George Stoneman, departed its camps to raid toward Richmond. A storm in the upper watershed caused the Rappahannock River to rise dramatically, though, and the mounted column stalled on the northern side. Rain fell steadily for the next two days and then intermittently until April 24. By the time the roads had dried enough to handle the passage of troops, the advance elements of Hooker's flanking columns had joined the horse soldiers at Kelly's Ford.[31]

The same day that three Federal corps marched, Capt. Timothy Lubey and a detachment from the Fifteenth New York Engineers traveled from Falmouth to Washington, DC. At the quartermaster depot near the Navy Yard, they secured a pontoon train and ferried it to Alexandria, where stevedores transferred it to railcars for an overnight trip to Bealeton Station. Unlike the cumbersome transfer of bridging equipment to Fredericksburg in November 1862, the Federal army was going to cross the Rappahannock River at Kelly's Ford on the run.[32]

The engineers had benefited from rigorous training under Brig. Gen. Henry W. Benham, who had replaced Brig. Gen. Daniel P. Woodbury. One of Woodbury's subordinates described the gentlemanly officer as "a fine Engineer but not a man to command men in the rough experience of war." The hard-edged Benham had lost a field command due to insubordination during an 1862 campaign on the South Carolina coast, but his engineering skills were a known asset. In February 1863 the army advanced him to brigadier and put him in charge of the Potomac Army's bridge builders.[33]

Benham drilled his engineers relentlessly. He also experimented with having men carry pontoons to get them into position without alerting enemy pickets. Hard experience in December 1862 had shown the difficulty of building a bridge under fire. Benham intended to minimize his casualties by securing the far side of the stream with a waterborne assault before bridge building began. The challenge would be in staging the boats for such a mission. Each pontoon weighed 2,500–3,000 pounds, which a dozen men could unload from a wagon and launch. To carry them any distance, however, the engineers would need additional manpower.[34]

When the Federal flanking columns marched on April 27, 1863, Capt. Samuel T. Cushing, the army's chief signal officer, coordinated his signal teams to provide the anticipated support. He ordered the field-telegraph network extended from Hooker's headquarters to Franklin's Crossing and on to the Scott house, along the road to Banks' Ford. The distances were not far, and both stations were made operational by the morning of April 28. Capt. James S. Hall had charge of the signal operations at the Phillips house but had received instructions to close the station and march with the Second Corps to Banks' Ford. On his own initiative Cushing directed Hall and his signalmen to remain on station, ensuring its immediate availability to whoever had to direct operations on that part of the field.[35]

On April 19 the president, the secretary of war, and the general in chief traveled to Aquia Landing to meet with Hooker. Of particular interest were the 37,200 soldiers nearing the end of their enlistments. The Army of the Potomac could muster 134,800 men but would soon lose strength to time rather than enemy action. The next day Hooker issued General Order No.

44, specifying that service obligations were to be measured from the date of muster into US service. As an example, the Twenty-Seventh New York Infantry had been mustered into state service in April 1861 but was not mustered into US service until May 21, 1861. General Order No. 44 indicated that these troops would not be mustered out until May 21, 1863.[36]

The short-time soldiers discussed Hooker's order with keen interest and sometimes came to poor decisions. On April 25 one company of two-year men in the Thirty-Second New York, believing their military obligation to have ended, refused to continue taking orders. The next day that company remained in its tents when Col. Francis E. Pinto paraded the regiment. Pinto ordered his guard company to load its weapons, and the distinctive sound of ramrods in rifle barrels got the attention of the recalcitrant men. When they emerged from their shelters, the colonel spoke to them of duty, reminded them of their honorable service, and asked them to obey orders until properly mustered out. Called to task by a respected officer, they agreed to continue to serve.[37]

Discipline usually reasserted itself when mutineers were threatened with summary justice, but commanders could not be fully confident that such troops would remain reliable under pressure. As he drafted campaign orders, Butterfield suggested that those whose service was about to expire be considered for rear-echelon duties such as train guards. The short-term regiments, however, were not comprised of poor soldiers; some of them reflected the best of American volunteers. A Vermont soldier watched a nine-month unit vote unanimously to see the campaign through. "They are brave and patriotic fellows," he observed.[38]

Sedgwick's Sixth Corps reflected a solid organization. Only three regiments were nine-month men, while another eight were nearing the end of two-year enlistments. Out of a force of forty-seven regiments and nine batteries, the short-timers constituted approximately 20 percent of the corps. The bulk of Sedgwick's command consisted of veteran troops who had enlisted in 1861 for three years.[39]

The general himself was a dependable commander. Born in 1813, the son of a Revolutionary War soldier, Sedgwick graduated from West Point in 1837. He had fought in the Seminole Wars and in Mexico and gone up against the Cheyenne on the western frontier. On the Peninsula in 1862, Sedgwick led a division and won promotion to major general. He suffered severe wounds at Antietam when ordered into the West Woods without proper reconnaissance. The Confederates cut up his division in just a few minutes, and the general sustained wounds that took him out of action until after the Fredericksburg Campaign.[40]

Sedgwick's men called him "Uncle John," in appreciation of his thoughtful leadership. On the eve of the upcoming campaign, his corps consisted of four divisions. The First, Second, and Third Divisions were led by Brig. Gen. William T. H. Brooks, Brig. Gen. Albion P. Howe, and Maj. Gen. John Newton respectively. All three were professionals. The other division had the specialized designation of Light Brigade and was led by Col. Hiram Burnham, a volunteer officer. With all four division commanders having combat experience, the corps went into battle well trained and confident.

ONE

APRIL 28-29

FIRST MOVES

Hooker planned to steal a march on Lee and grab advantageous ground that would decide the spring campaign. On April 27, 1863, the Fifth, Eleventh, and Twelfth Corps headed toward Kelly's Ford. Two Second Corps divisions were to move up to Banks' Ford the next day, while a third remained near Falmouth, its camp routine visible to Southern observers. The troops in the flanking columns had been instructed not to burn their winter huts or any accumulated trash when breaking camp to avoid announcing their departure with clouds of smoke.[1]

At Fredericksburg on the following morning, Sedgwick met with Maj. Gen. John F. Reynolds, commanding the First Corps; Maj. Gen. Daniel E. Sickles, the Third Corps commander; and the army's chief engineer, Brig. Gen. Henry W. Benham. Sedgwick had orders to provide a diversion below Fredericksburg, which required Benham to have four pontoon bridges across the Rappahannock at two locations by 3:30 A.M. that night. Elements of the First and Sixth Corps would establish bridgeheads and secure the Telegraph Road. If Lee moved forces west to confront Hooker, Sedgwick was to pursue them, while also putting a force on the Bowling Green Road to cut off a Confederate retreat.[2]

Hooker's directive had errors. The road within range of the planned bridgeheads was the Bowling Green Road, not the Telegraph Road (modern Lafayette Boulevard), which ran *behind* the Confederate line. Sedgwick,

Sickles, and Reynolds did not think they were expected to attack where Federal assaults had been repulsed in December, so they pressed ahead with what their orders made clear. They would force a crossing and build up sufficient strength across the river to stay there.

The Sixth Corps would jump the Rappahannock at Franklin's Crossing, where the Army of the Potomac had crossed in December. The First Corps would cross two miles farther downstream near Pollock's Mill Creek. The Third Corps would constitute a reserve. Benham was a precise man and had carefully thought through how to ensure two successful crossings in the middle of the night. He would use approximately one hundred boats to ferry across six thousand fighting men. While the landing force secured the far shore, engineers would hustle the rest of their equipment to the river and float the bridges.[3]

To achieve surprise, Benham wanted to hand carry the boats to the river. Moving pontoons quietly in the dark would keep Southern pickets from knowing the time and place of the assault. During the previous weeks, Capt. Chauncey B. Reese had tested how many men were needed to efficiently get boats to a launching site, determining that thirty-six could carry a boat weighing 2,500–3,000 pounds. To expedite the evolution, a detachment of seventy-two men per boat would provide a double relief.[4]

Sedgwick initially balked at the idea of having troops carry the pontoons. He was not averse to hard marching and even risk. His bold advance over the rickety Grapevine Bridge during the Seven Pines (Fair Oaks) battle had saved the Union army from disaster in June 1862. Setting infantrymen to the hard labor of carrying pontoons and then executing an attack, however, gave Sedgwick pause. He directed that the carrying force should not be used to make the assault. The generals agreed that the Light Division would be the carrying force at Franklin's Crossing and Brig. Gen. William T. H. Brooks's division would constitute the attacking force.[5]

Brooks had spent his life in the army. He had entered West Point's class of 1841 at the age of sixteen. Second Lieutenant Brooks fought the Seminoles in Florida. He was a first lieutenant during the War with Mexico. Captain Brooks saw the onset of the Civil War and soon found himself a brigadier general of volunteers. He led a brigade on the Peninsula and at Antietam, then headed a division at Fredericksburg. Some referred to him as "Bully" Brooks, and a New Jersey officer noted that he "made no gaudy show of dress" but rather "showed by his ability he was a General."[6]

Near Pollock's Mill, Reynolds directed Brig. Gen. James S. Wadsworth to execute the night assault. Wadsworth had been a politically active attorney before the war. He quickly attained the heady rank of brigadier general but had no combat experience when he accepted command of a division in early 1863. On the night of April 28–29, Benham directed Lt. Col. William H. Pettes, a Regular Army engineer, to help coordinate the lower crossing with Wadsworth while he assisted Brooks at the upper crossing.[7]

Benham's plan to quietly get the attacking force into position reflected a willingness to innovate that his contemporaries did not always appreciate. Sedgwick gained some insight when he and Benham met with Maj. Gen. John Newton later that afternoon. While the corps leader conferred with his senior division commander, one of the bridge trains moved out to get into position for the upcoming operation. The iron-bound wheels and hollow pontoons created a rumble and a racket that caused Sedgwick to jump. The startled general now clearly understood how carrying pontoons to the river would help mask the impending assault.[8]

From some of the Union camps, "the spires of Fredericksburg were just visible over the adjoining ridge," a line of sight that worked both ways. Col. Leroy A. Stafford, commanding the Ninth Louisiana Infantry, and Capt. William J. Seymour, a brigade aide-de-camp, climbed into the steeple of St. George's Episcopal Church. On a landing above a clock mechanism, a louvered vent could be removed to reveal a view across the river.[9]

The two Confederates watched what looked to be preparations for a campaign but did not know that a flanking force had already left. Those columns were not only out of sight, but guards were also being posted at homes and farms along the march route to prevent the occupants from slipping away to give warning. As those Union formations closed in on Kelly's Ford twenty-five miles away, bridging equipment was being delivered to a nearby rail station.[10]

By 7:30 A.M. on the morning of April 28, Capt. Timothy Lubey and his detachment of engineers had arrived at Bealeton Station. Comstock met them there with wagons and more engineers to get the pontoons and other material to Kelly's Ford. At the appropriate time they would construct a floating bridge for the approaching infantry to cross the Rappahannock River. The Union force would then press on to the Rapidan River.[11]

One of the flanking columns would uncover United States (or US) Ford, where additional bridges would allow reinforcements to join the march toward Fredericksburg. This crossing, about seven miles west of Banks' Ford, was where the United States Mining Company had been extracting gold since the mid-1830s. Though its mills and mining shafts were temporarily abandoned, related roads provided access to the river through otherwise rough terrain.[12]

The crossing critical to the campaign would be at Banks' Ford. General Hunt arrived there on April 28 to determine where artillery could be placed to cover the anticipated bridge construction. Maj. Alexander Doull, formerly of Britain's Royal Artillery and now Hunt's inspector of artillery, supervised the placement of several batteries and ordered them to create earthworks. The arriving units were Lt. Albert F. Brooker's Battery B, First Connecticut Artillery and Lt. Gustav von Blucher's Twenty-Ninth Battery of the New York Light Artillery. Later that afternoon, Hunt went back downstream to finalize preparations for the diversionary crossing below Fredericksburg.[13]

A brigade of infantry from the Eleventh Corps picketed Kelly's Ford, where the Union cavalry corps had been held up by high water since the fifteenth. Across the river was Brig. Gen. W. H. F. "Rooney" Lee's Virginia cavalry brigade, its headquarters at Brandy Station. Maj. Gen. J. E. B. Stuart, the Army of Northern Virginia's cavalry commander, had his headquarters at Culpeper Court House. Intercepts of deliberately misleading signals had suggested a Federal lunge to the west, so Stuart carefully watched Stoneman to see if he would raid toward the Shenandoah Valley.[14]

The close coordination of three Union infantry corps and two detachments of engineers had come off without a hitch. To get that flanking force across the river, the Fifteenth New York Engineers quietly moved the boats to Marsh Run, which empties into the Rappahannock River five hundred yards downstream from Kelly's Ford. Confederate pickets had become used to the Federal presence, and the blue-clad pickets gave no indication that assault troops were marshaling behind them.[15]

The Federal flanking columns were expected to be at their Rappahannock crossing by late afternoon, Maj. Gen. Oliver O. Howard's Eleventh Corps leading the way. Men making the transition from camp to field, however, were not yet as conditioned physically as they would be in a day or two, especially while carrying more ammunition and rations than in previous campaigns. Howard's lax leadership had also allowed more wagons to be brought along than the newly adopted logistics standards specified. Consequently, his column was moving slowly, much to the disgust of the Twelfth and Fifth Corps behind him.[16]

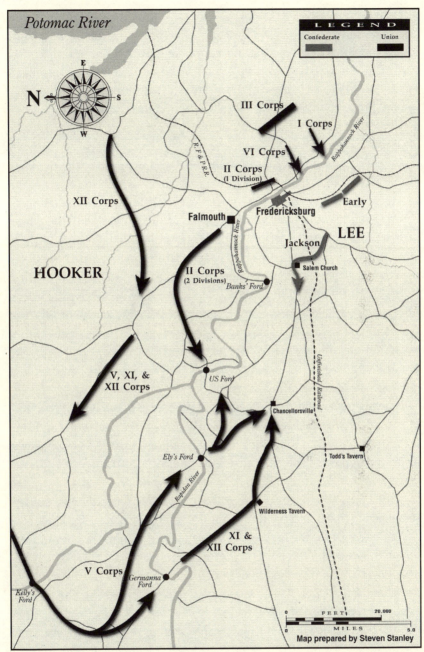

Map 1. Opening Moves. Three Union corps gave the impression of crossing the Rappahannock River downstream from Fredericksburg to distract attention from the bulk of the Federal forces, which had marched far upstream to come in behind the Confederate army.

Hooker rode out from his Falmouth headquarters to personally supervise the flanking columns. He was not pleased to find the leading corps hindering the critical opening move, but the Eleventh Corps reached Mt. Holly Church by 4:30 P.M. Hooker had already established his headquarters there, where he could communicate with Butterfield at Falmouth using the telegraph line running through Warrenton and Washington, DC. The commanding general used that link to issue orders for the next stage of the campaign.[17]

Hooker directed Howard to get his Eleventh Corps across the river that evening. Maj. Gen. Henry W. Slocum's Twelfth Corps would cross in the morning and then take the lead toward Germanna Mills, on the Rapidan River. Howard was pointedly told to make sure his wagon train brought up the rear of his column. Meade's Fifth Corps would march to the Rapidan to cross at Ely's Ford, but he was also to send a force to Richard's Ford to ensure the Confederates there did not try to create any mischief at US Ford.[18]

In that flurry of communications, Hooker modified Sedgwick's orders. The First and Sixth Corps were still expected to get across the river at 3:30 A.M. that morning, but instead of pursuing the Confederates if they withdrew, this move would now be a demonstration only; the corps were to cross just enough troops to hold the bridges. Sedgwick received that message shortly after midnight.[19]

Federal forces jumped the Rappahannock River at Kelly's Ford at 6:00 P.M. Union infantry unleashed a volley toward the Virginia cavalrymen and kept up a covering fire. A landing force, hidden from view in Marsh Creek, shoved off in pontoon boats and paddled across the river. They flanked the Confederate pickets, whose firepower had been diminished by cartridges too damp to ignite. With caps popping but weapons not discharging, the Southerners scrambled to find their horses and get clear of the advancing Federals.[20]

Engineers had a floating bridge ready for use within a few hours, and Union forces began crossing at 10:30 P.M. The Confederate pickets pulled back toward Brandy Station, where Rooney Lee telegraphed a warning to his father, Robert E. Lee. The telegraph link from Brandy Station to Fredericksburg, however, was as circuitous as Hooker's had been at Mt. Holly Church. Any telegram from Culpeper had to go through Gordonsville and Richmond, and along that line of stations, at least one had closed for the night. Confederate headquarters would not receive word of enemy forces across the Rappahannock until morning. By then, the Federals would also be crossing downstream from Fredericksburg.[21]

Lee anticipated a cross-river assault at Fredericksburg but kept an eye on the upriver crossings as well. Brig. Gen. Cadmus M. Wilcox had his Alabama brigade at Banks' Ford, while Brig. Gen. Carnot Posey had his Mississippi brigade in the vicinity of US Ford. Both places were vulnerable, but their distance from Fredericksburg would give Lee time to react if the Federals forced their way across. Any crossing beyond US Ford was surely beyond the reach of units tied to supply depots on the Potomac River.[22]

The Federals engaged in a bit of deception at Banks' Ford. Around 3:00 P.M. on April 28, a detachment of the Fiftieth New York Engineers began cutting trees that had fallen across the approach roads to Scott's Ferry. They worked noisily through the night while the actual threats were developing elsewhere. Upriver, the Eleventh Corps crossed at Kelly's Ford, to be followed by the Fifth and Twelfth Corps in the morning. Downstream from Fredericksburg, the First and Sixth Corps prepared to gain lodgments before dawn.[23]

Three concentrations of artillery were going to support the two crossings below Fredericksburg. At Franklin's Crossing Col. John A. Tompkins, the Sixth Corps's chief of artillery, prepared to deploy forty-six guns. He would place six batteries of rifled weapons on the high ground dominating the waterway and move two batteries of smoothbore Napoleons closer in, putting Confederate infantry across the Rappahannock under a crossfire. Until needed, though, these guns remained hidden. A Virginia artilleryman wrote, "On the night of the 28th we retired as usual, without thinking we were on the eve of a great battle."[24]

Four of the rifled batteries were from the Sixth Corps. Those units were Lt. William A. Harn's Third New York Artillery; Capt. Jeremiah McCarthy's Battery C-D, First Pennsylvania Artillery; Capt. James H. Rigby's Battery A, First Maryland Artillery; and Capt. Andrew Cowan's First New York Artillery. From the Artillery Reserve came two more batteries of rifled guns, consisting of Capt. Franklin A. Pratt's Battery M, First Connecticut Artillery and Capt. Adolph Voegelee's Thirtieth New York Artillery. The two batteries of field guns belonged to the Sixth Corps—Lt. Edward B. Williston's Battery D, Second US Artillery—and the Third Corps—Lt. Francis W. Seeley's Battery K, Fourth US Artillery.[25]

Near Pollock's Mill, Col. Charles S. Wainwright, the First Corps's chief of artillery, had control of forty guns. Four batteries of rifled weapons would be deployed upstream of the mill: Capt. John A. Reynolds's Battery L, First New York Artillery; Capt. James A. Hall's Second Maine Artillery; and two batteries from the First Pennsylvania Artillery, Capt. Frank P. Amsden's Battery G and Capt. James H. Cooper's Battery B. Three batteries with fourteen more rifled weapons would be placed below the mill, consisting of Capt. Frederick M. Edgell's Battery A, First New Hampshire Artillery; Capt. James Thompson's Battery C, Fourth Pennsylvania Artillery; and Lt. R. Bruce Ricketts's Battery F, First Pennsylvania Artillery. Capt. Dunbar R. Ransom would also have six field guns of his Battery C, Fifth US Artillery on hand.[26]

Three more batteries, consisting of sixteen guns, would take position still farther downstream, near a prominent dwelling called Travellers Rest, to protect the downstream flank of the bridgehead. Lt. Col. Edward R. Warner, the Army of the Potomac's inspector of artillery, exercised overall command. The individual batteries were Capt. Elijah D. Taft's Fifth New York, Capt. Charles F. Kusserow's Thirty-Second New York, and Capt. Patrick Hart's Fifteenth New York. Travellers Rest had evolved from a modest colonial-era home to a large brick mansion with a longstanding reputation for hospitality. In the morning of April 28, the only travelers there would be Federal artillerymen.[27]

Deployed weapons as well as those held in reserve totaled 147 artillery pieces available at Fredericksburg. The entire Army of the Potomac had between 325 and 329 guns, so the support for the diversionary crossings would surely give the impression of a major effort. The command structure for Federal batteries, however, was entirely inadequate. Creating powerful concentrations of weapons had become a proven concept, but Hooker had made retention of that capability difficult. Hunt's oversight at Banks' Ford and at the crossings below Fredericksburg ensured that artillery units were deployed effectively at the onset, but Hooker had blithely redefined his duties to be administrative. The overall direction of artillery at Chancellorsville would become painfully inefficient.[28]

During the afternoon of the twenty-eighth, Colonel Tompkins had his headquarters at Capt. John Sands's house. From that open farm two miles from Franklin's Crossing, he directed his batteries to the river line. Earlier that day a young boy who lived at the Sands place had watched the departure of Federal engineers who had camped nearby. Much like English boys in the spring of 1944, the child had been thrilled to have an army near his home. There had been a multitude of horses, exotic equipment, the music of bugle calls, and the purposeful activity of hundreds of men. Many of the soldiers were fathers, uncles, and brothers—easily friendly with a curious youngster. As the troops prepared to march, the boy called out "Good-bye" to the men who had so casually come into his life and were just as casually leaving it.[29]

On the night of April 28–29, a moon nearly 80 percent full would not set until around 2:00 A.M. The Federals could anticipate substantial natural light for the infantry to seize the far shore and for the bridge builders to get their floating spans completed by 3:30 A.M. As it happened, though, rain clouds blocked out the moonlight, masking the gathering host. One New York soldier described how a "cold, drizzling rain fell, and with it came a thick fog."[30]

Like the artillery units, the infantry moved into position in stages. There had been two weeks of anticipated starts, with rations issued, knapsacks inspected, and extra clothing boxed up for storage. Still the army had waited, mostly for the rain to stop and the roads to dry. The troops did not have far to march, but their routes would be circuitous to stay under cover. The day began sunny and bright as the regiments pulled down their tents and threw away what they did not intend to carry into battle.

The good weather did not last. Around midday, dark clouds rolled in and began to drop their heavy contents. For some, the weather reminded them of past failures. A New York artilleryman recalled how "the day assumed the same appearance that characterized the day on which the memorable mud march began, only it was not so cold." Another soldier wrote of their need to stay hidden: "Skirting along behind woods, cutting down through ravines, winding around hills, we found ourselves at sunset bivouacked in the woods not far from the river, with orders to build no fires and make no unnecessary noise."[31]

The infantrymen marched with full loads and felt their burden increase as the rain saturated their clothing and equipment. One New York soldier described the roads as "shockingly bad." The march deteriorated into a maddening series of starts and stops as troops crowded into the staging areas. They would not have an opportunity to dry out either. The First and Sixth Corps massed behind the hills along the river as the day turned cold. A Maine soldier described the ordeal: "Marched at 1:30, raining hard and roads muddy. Moved nine miles to get five and encamped for the night about one mile from the river."[32]

General Brooks had selected Brig. Gen. David A. Russell's Third Brigade as his assault force. After graduating from West Point in 1845, Russell had seen duty on the frontier and in Mexico. He had led a regiment on the Peninsula and in Maryland and had commanded a brigade since Fredericksburg. Once in bivouac on that miserable evening, the experienced brigadier called his regimental commanders together and briefed them on the approaching operation. Well before midnight, officers and noncommissioned officers quietly ordered their infantrymen under arms.[33]

The rain had tapered off when Russell's regiments formed at 11:00 P.M. Officers divided them into companies of forty-five men, and they moved out at midnight to link up with the boats. The timetable began to unravel, however, as muddy roads became clogged by pontoons and groups of men. On the positive side, one soldier noted that the "thick mist and fog completely hid our movements from the enemy." It also negated Hooker's desired balloon observation to determine whether the Confederates were reacting to the flanking columns in Culpeper County. Professor Lowe dutifully went aloft anyway but could not see anything. He suspended operations for the night and moored the balloon in a ravine below the Phillips house.[34]

At twilight engineer troops had brought the bridge trains up to the edge of the woods and unloaded the pontoons. At Franklin's Crossing Chief Engineer Benham provided Col. Hiram Burnham with precise instructions. Burnham's Light Division troops were to begin moving forty-four boats to the river at 11:00 P.M. and be done within an hour. An assault force would have another hour to get across the river and secure the opposite shore. If all went well, the actual bridge building would commence no later than 1:30 A.M., giving the engineers two hours to complete their work.[35]

Burnham assigned the Sixth Maine, the Sixty-First Pennsylvania, and the Fifth Wisconsin to get pontoons to the river. The engineers had finished unloading the boats by 10:00 P.M. The regiments divided into groups of seventy-two men and began carrying them forward at 11:30 P.M. Half of each group held weapons and gear, while the other half carried the heavy boats. The operation began well, but the assault-force detachments did not appear to be ready to follow the pontoons to the river. Benham had wanted to avoid the confusion of stumbling around in the dark, and he became frustrated with this seemingly avoidable lapse.[36]

Brooks was a thoroughgoing professional and had brought his troops to within a half mile of where the pontoons were staged. He had no intention of wearing out his men before they were needed, though. He knew Benham had a reputation of being a thorough soldier but with a significant weakness. As one of his subordinate officers noted, the chief of engineers was an "old school soldier . . . , attending to his business in a most particular manner," but one "exceedingly liable to get malfathomed with drink." Brooks was not sympathetic.[37]

With troops moving pontoons to the river, Benham rode to Sedgwick's headquarters and asked for a staff officer who had the wing commander's authority to coordinate with Brooks. Sedgwick assigned Capt. Richard F. Halsted to help Benham keep his operation in motion. The chief engineer instructed Halsted to notify Brooks that the Light Division troops were hauling boats and directed his own staff officer, Captain Reese, to ensure Brooks's infantrymen joined the pontoons as they were carried to the river's edge.[38]

After making sure that Halsted understood his orders, Benham rode to Pollock's Mill with Col. Charles B. Stuart of the Fiftieth New York Engineers. At First Corps headquarters Benham and Stuart met with General Reynolds. Also present were General Wadsworth, whose division would assault the far shore that night, and Lieutenant Colonel Pettes, whose engineers would get the bridges built. Benham reviewed the planned sequence of events, and Wadsworth readily agreed to let his troops carry the boats to the river. As the time approached 11:30 P.M., Benham rode back to Franklin's Crossing.[39]

There, events were not unfolding to Benham's satisfaction. Getting bridges across a wide river within a few hours required strict coordination, but he did not see the assault force anywhere. As time moved inexorably forward, Benham found Brooks and expressed his displeasure. The division commander, however, had had his troops under arms well before midnight, and Halsted had notified him when Burnham's units began moving pontoons. Several witnesses remarked upon Benham drinking that night, and he appeared to have transitioned from a functioning soldier to someone evidently under the influence. The discussion became heated.[40]

Benham left Brooks in a huff and proceeded to the river to see about staging the boats for the assault. The engineer came to the picket line along a road near the river and found the corporal in charge. The two men moved beyond the pickets to reconnoiter the path by which pontoons could be carried to the riverbank. Light from a nearly full moon seeped through the clouds, but fog now enveloped the ground. Benham and the corporal went back up to the picket line, where they found Captain Reese waiting on the road for Burnham's pontoon carriers. Reese and Benham went back down to the river and quietly discussed where and how to deploy the boats.[41]

When the two officers returned to the road, they found that some of the pontoons had finally arrived. The engineers had determined that two groups of thirty-six men could carry a boat, but Burnham's troops found that ten men on each side of a boat were less likely to trip over one another. Light Division officers thus detailed forty men per boat. The double relief for twenty-man carrying parties moved things along more quickly, but the work was still exhausting. A Fifth Wisconsin infantryman remembered how it affected him and his comrades: "by morning [we] found ourselves pretty much fagged out."[42]

While Reese set up the boats as they were brought down to the river, Benham wanted to move the assault force into place. He found the fighting men nearby but observed that having both the assault teams and the carrying parties on hand crowded the available space and blocked the passage of boats. While trying in the dark to get around one group of men, Benham fell into a ravine and cut his head, which bled profusely (as head injuries will).[43]

Getting bridges across by 3:30 A.M. looked to be increasingly unlikely, and it was an exhausted, disheveled, bleeding, and increasingly frustrated chief engineer who found General Russell on the river road. The brigade commander was himself irritated that his troops appeared to be improperly positioned for the assault. Russell hesitated to let the bleeding and belligerent engineer determine how his infantry would be loaded into the boats, and the increasingly agitated Benham placed him under arrest, ordering the brigadier to report to Brooks.[44]

Benham had long advocated that engineers be authorized to exert overall command during river crossings. Hooker had not seriously considered the concept, which at that point appeared prescient. One of the engineer's staff officers reluctantly observed that "to his dishonor Gen. Benham was tumbling drunk." His inability to function is illustrated by his misguided effort to relieve a brigade commander in the middle of a night operation. When Brooks came down to the river, Benham pointedly asked if the infantry would follow his commands. Brooks apprised the wild-looking engineer that he was not authorized to give orders to his fighting men.[45]

Benham clearly would not have bridges down at the specified hour and knew he would have to answer for it. He hissed at Brooks that the crossing was his problem and then departed. While the generals exchanged contentious words, regimental and company officers continued to work through the confusion and sorted out the assault force as the carrying details moved out of the way. The Eighteenth and Thirty-Second New York Regiments and the Forty-Ninth, Ninety-Fifth, and 119th Pennsylvania units of Russell's brigade moved closer to the boats. During their predawn wait, some wondered who would reach the opposite shore, who would be shot, and who might end up in the river and drown. The anxious men heard activity on the other side of the river, suggesting that the Confederates were ready and waiting.[46]

Fog screened the waiting men, but twilight would begin close to 4:30 A.M. Time had run out for an assault to take place under cover of darkness. Upon someone's quiet signal, the engineers slid pontoons into the river "just as daylight tinged the eastern sky." The waiting infantrymen were eager to get moving, with one of the Pennsylvania soldiers describing how "no sooner were they [the pontoons] afloat than they were filled with living freight." One of the men in a carrying detail observed how "everything was still when they started[,] and as our regiment with others had been at work all night we lay on this side, listening for the first sound of battle."[47]

Twenty-three boats had made it down to the riverbank and now carried the Forty-Ninth, Ninety-Fifth, and 119th Pennsylvania and portions of the Thirty-Second New York. On the water, engineers acting as oarsmen pulled hard to minimize their exposure in the open stream. About halfway across, men crouching in the boats could discern pickets on the riverbank in front of them. The Confederates, in turn, saw the line of boats emerging out of the fog and scrambled back to their rifle pits. A Union soldier on the opposite shore described the initial contact: "All is quiet save the measured dip of the oars in the water; they arrive near the other side, when suddenly comes the bright blaze, then the whistling of balls and the crash of musketry." A New York surgeon observed, "never since I was born, did such a sudden transition from the silence of the tomb to confusion of Babel, fall upon me."[48]

A New York artilleryman, waiting for his role in the unfolding drama to begin, recorded the time as 4:40 A.M. He noted that there were a few scattered shots, then a volley. By then, some of the boats were shoving up against the shore, with Federal infantrymen rapidly disembarking. Skirmishers organized themselves and advanced. The first Confederate volley had passed over the loaded boats and ripped into the troops on the opposite shore. Those waiting men could hear the orders being given to the landing party: "Halt—front. Forward—guide left—March."[49]

Brig. Gen. Joseph J. Bartlett, commanding the brigade that would comprise the second wave, knew the boats were crowded. Russell's first wave needed time, if only a few seconds, to disembark and get sorted out. Without waiting for orders, Bartlett directed the Sixteenth New York to return fire—volleys by battalion—taking care not to hit the troops already across. The New Yorkers were guided in their aim by the muzzle flashes along the Confederate trench line, but the covering fire proved a bit nerve wracking for the troops scrambling ashore. As the Pennsylvanians climbed out of the bottom, some of them yelled back across the river for the New Yorkers to aim higher. Some lost their weapons as they struggled out of the water but found rifles discarded by fleeing Confederates.[50]

The assault troops climbed up the slippery slope, grabbing small trees and bushes for assistance. They were unable to respond to the Confederate fire but pressed on, relying on the cover provided by their comrades across the river. One of them later wrote: "By the time we reached the top we were the maddest set of men the Army of the Potomac ever turned loose, and made very short work of capturing the enemy's works and about all the troops it contained. Very few tried to escape, and those who did had a long level plain to cross, and were exposed all the way to our fire, consequently not many of them got away."[51]

In his after-action report, Bartlett diplomatically noted that there had been "some unaccountable delay connected with the management of the pontoon boats." The different components of the operation continued to mesh when firing began in the growing light. Russell's brigade occupied the Confederate rifle pits at the top of the bluff, while the boats returned to ferry across the rest of the Thirty-Second New York and the Eighteenth New York as well as Bartlett's second wave.[52]

The bridge builders were standing by with their equipment when the fighting started. There was no longer any reason to keep quiet, so they quickly brought wagonloads of bridging material to the riverbank. Captain Reese and his US Engineers began work on the first bridge at 5:50 A.M. Within ten minutes, the Fifteenth New York Engineers began work on the second bridge under the direction of Maj. Walter L. Cassin. The benefits of Benham's strict training program became evident as the New York volunteers exhibited skills and efficiencies comparable to the Regulars. Benham himself paced the riverfront with enough presence of mind to leave his engineers to do their work. Some of the troops thought he appeared a bit drunk, but they appreciated his presence as he exhorted them to "work away my castle boys," referring to the Corps of Engineers uniform insignia.[53]

As the engineers poled pontoons into position and extended their bridges toward the opposite shore, Federal artillery took position. Harn, McCarthy, Rigby, and Cowan brought their rifled weapons into battery on high ground about six hundred yards from the river. Closer in were Williston's 12-pounder Napoleons, slated to cross the river as soon as a floating bridge could handle them. Batteries that had spent the night at the

Sands house moved up and parked on the open ground near the bridges. Upstream, approximately five hundred yards to the right of Williston's guns, were two batteries from the Artillery Reserve, Capt. Patrick Hart's Fifteenth New York Independent Battery and Capt. Franklin A. Pratt's Battery M, First Connecticut Artillery. Around 7:00 A.M., when the Regulars were completing the first bridge, the Union guns opened fire, announcing that the Army of the Potomac had arrived in force.[54]

The Fifteenth New York Engineers were not far behind the Regulars in constructing their bridge. As the artillery fire boomed into the morning air, the volunteers knocked the final pieces into place on the second span. Crews began to stage equipment for a third bridge, its construction to be directed by Col. Clinton G. Colgate of the Fifteenth New York Engineers. With two bridges down, work on the third would not have to be as frenetic.[55]

Russell pushed his skirmishers out toward the Bowling Green Road, giving the bridgehead depth. A picket line extended from the Bernard house ruins on the left to Deep Run on the right. Things were not going so well downstream, though. Just after 7:00 A.M., a courier found Benham as he watched the first bridge nearing completion and informed him that the assault at Pollock's Mill Creek had been repulsed. The chief engineer immediately departed to go see what had gone wrong.[56]

To cover potential crossing sites, the Confederates had strung out two regiments along the river below Fredericksburg. At Franklin's Crossing Capt. James A. Rogers commanded an advance force of the Fifty-Fourth North Carolina. He had his headquarters at Mannsfield, the home of Arthur Bernard. The war had been hard on that attractive setting, with the mansion inadvertently burned down over the winter and nearly 150 Federal soldiers and uncounted amputated arms and legs buried there during its use as a hospital the previous December. The Sixth Corps assault caught the North Carolinians by surprise, and they had pulled back.[57]

The fighting at Franklin's Crossing rippled downriver, where Lt. Col. James B. Terrill's Thirteenth Georgia saw another crossing developing. The action at the river also brought the Confederate camps alive. Drummer boys beat the long roll, and men threw off blankets, grabbed weapons, and found their places in familiar formations. One observer described the camps as being in an uproar, but the insistent summons of the drums quickly imposed order. Regiments took position along the Richmond, Fredericksburg, and Potomac Railroad as their skirmishers moved up to the Bowling Green Road.[58]

Maj. Gen. Jubal A. Early, whose division was becoming engaged, sent his adjutant, Maj. Samuel Hale Jr., to report to his corps commander, Lieutenant General Jackson. The staff officer hurried to Thomas Yerby's home, a place called Belvoir, where the mighty Stonewall had been spending time with his wife and infant daughter. As Jackson hurriedly dressed, he sent his own staff officer, Lt. James Power Smith, to report the Federal activity to Lee. From his headquarters on the Mine Road, Lee had already heard the firing and knew his reliable subordinates would handle things until he could join them.[59]

As the Confederate response gained momentum, the Federals at Pollock's Mill Creek had yet to get across the river. Engineers had staged their pontoons about three-quarters of a mile from the anticipated crossing site, but Wadsworth's division failed to get them to the river for an attack before dawn. Historians have mocked Benham as a drunk, but he had kept the effort at Franklin's Crossing in motion. The First Corps's crossing did not receive the same level of attention. After his meeting with Wadsworth and Reynolds the day before, Benham had suspected those officers were not enthusiastic about an attack in the dark.[60]

Wadsworth's assault troops were the hard-fighting westerners of Brig. Gen. Solomon Meredith's Iron Brigade. Around midnight, Meredith held an officers meeting to brief his brigade and regimental leaders. They understood they would make a waterborne attack at 2:00 A.M. and prepared accordingly. It was the selection of the pontoon carriers that became the weak link in the effort.[61]

The men of the Twenty-Fourth New York had settled down for the night after a march from their encampment near Belle Plain. With little opportunity to rest, they were awakened and mustered as a fatigue party to carry pontoons to the river. The tired troops put the boats on crossbeams, slung their rifles, and began to carry pontoons forward. That they slung their rifles rather than having others carry their weapons suggests they were not prepared for their task. The frustrated men also had no idea how far they had to carry their loads along slippery roads through a disorienting darkness. Their effort became noisy and inefficient.[62]

Whether Reynolds or Wadsworth assigned other regiments to carry pontoons that night is not clear. Reports from the First Corps do not dwell on this failed effort, especially when reporting officers could describe subsequent marching and maneuvering without an embarrassing recounting of what happened on the night of April 28–29. At Franklin's Crossing getting boats to the river had been spread beyond one unit. Some regiments managed to get five of the heavy thirty-five-foot-long pontoons to the river; other units hauled as many as seven. A member of the Fifth Wisconsin recalled the brutal task: "It was the heaviest work we have done yet. We were nearly worn out at the break of day when they [the pontoons] were in the river."[63]

The Fifth Wisconsin was a proud, motivated unit. The Twenty-Fourth New York had refused to march the day before, the men claiming their time in service had ended. Wadsworth handled the developing mutiny with a commendable firmness, and the New Yorkers, who had been willing volunteers in 1861, ultimately chose to march. Coordinating the many moving parts of an entire division for a night assault proved beyond the general's capability, though, and selecting the Twenty-Fourth New York on short notice to move heavy pontoons was a mistake.[64]

With few routes to the crossing site, the assault troops marching behind the pontoon carriers were also delayed in getting into position. Wadsworth could see the plan falling apart and countermanded the orders for hand carrying the boats, instead directing Maj. Edmund O. Beers of the Fiftieth New York Engineers to get them to the river in wagons. Unfortunately, those orders were not going to save time, and the resulting noise and commotion were not going to save lives. Nevertheless, the engineers retrieved the wagons and picked up the pontoons left scattered along the road.[65]

The sweating engineers got their bridging equipment loaded and headed toward the river, as they heard a rooster crowing in the distance. The Confederates had been alerted by the rumbling wagons and the braying mules. One Southerner called out that although the Federals were not yet visible as targets, they soon would be. One Union soldier admitted that "little hope remained of surprising the enemy," but another noted the strange conditions that emerged with the sun: "So thick was the dark river-cloud in which we were enveloped that we could see only a few yards away when the increasing daylight turned its dense darkness to a ghostly white."[66]

Across the river, Georgia pickets heard the approaching wagons and then the sound of materials being unloaded. The dense moisture in the air carried the noise with surprising clarity. A Georgia officer noted how "the river was only 150 yards wide, but so distinct were the sounds made by the movements on the other side, that the distance did not appear to be more than twenty paces." With plenty of warning, his entire regiment stood ready when orders came down the line to open fire. The officer continued his account, noting how "at the first discharge there was a confused sound of screams and imprecations from the other side."[67]

The fog thinned as the sun rose. Initial sporadic fire from Confederate pickets grew in volume as their opponents became visible. The Southerners were in rifle pits on the crest of a bluff, while the Northerners were exposed on the open riverbank. Lt. Howard J. Huntington of the Sixth Wisconsin described how "they opened on us sharply, wounding some of the horses of the pontoon train, setting them to rearing, plunging and running, which added to the disagreeable sensation that invariably comes over men at the opening of a battle."[68]

The Sixth Wisconsin and Twenty-Fourth Michigan had been waiting with the rest of the Iron Brigade behind a ditched fence overlooking the crossing site. The regimental commanders ordered them forward to provide covering fire, and the men ran toward the river, guided by a stone wall. As the fog dissipated, the westerners returned fire, aiming at muzzle flashes. Working parties staging equipment at the river's edge could see the flash of weapons being fired at them and counted themselves lucky if they only heard "the unmusical 'ping' of a Minnie ball."[69]

Federal riflemen could see their targets better when the fog thinned, but they were now without cover on the open bank. The two western regiments pulled back to the shelter of the small rise, where the rest of their brigade waited. The Fourteenth Brooklyn Zouaves, led by Col. Edward B. Fowler, moved up. Officially the Eighty-Fourth New York Infantry, the men had insisted on maintaining their prestigious prewar militia identity. They spread out as skirmishers and opened fire on the Georgians, joined by nearby Federal batteries. While its response grew strong, the First Corps was still being held in place at the river.[70]

As the opposing sides exchanged fire across the Rappahannock, Harrison Wells of the Thirteenth Georgia described the confusion: "The waggoners hallooing to their teams, rattling of planks, splashing of boats as they threw them in the water, hurried commands of officers trying to rally their men, cries of the wounded and shouts of our boys rose in a continued din through the misty darkness." When Benham arrived from the upper crossing, he saw about twenty pontoons at the river's edge. He joined Reynolds and Wadsworth on the heights above Pollock's Mill Creek and learned that the corps commander did not want to launch so few boats in a waterborne assault.[71]

With the First Corps currently immobilized, Reynolds considered sending a force upstream, where bridges were already under construction. If a regiment or two could pass over at Franklin's Crossing, they could flank the Southern skirmishers out of their works and thus uncover the lower crossing site. The idea had merit but would be time consuming and interfere with the Sixth Corps's build up. And Benham, who was supposed to have had bridges in place by 3:30 A.M., was already more than four hours behind schedule.[72]

The Confederate pickets had a slight tactical advantage at the river, but the Federals held a better position within the overall lay of the land. From their vantage point, the three Union generals could see that the Confederate picket line was thin and had no artillery support. The Federal guns on the high ground in Stafford commanded the crossing site and could devastate any Confederate units that tried to move up to help. Benham and Wadsworth prevailed upon Reynolds to let them proceed with the delayed assault.[73]

Twenty boats with oars ready waited at the river's edge. Seven batteries of 3-inch Ordnance Rifles had taken position above Pollock's Mill and on nearby hills. On a rise between the road and the river were 12-pounder Napoleons from Ransom's Battery C, Fifth US Artillery. While there were not as many boats as desired, with artillery backup, an assault could work. When the Federal guns opened fire, the Seventy-Sixth New York would move more pontoons to the Rappahannock.[74]

Benham turned his attention to making sure the engineers had their bridging equipment ready for use. The Iron Brigade's regimental officers went over the attack plan. The Sixth Wisconsin and Twenty-Fourth Michigan would still constitute the first wave. They would be followed across by the Second and Seventh Wisconsin and the Nineteenth Indiana Regiments. As the men removed and stacked their knapsacks, one soldier thought there would probably be "two knapsacks for every man that returns." Another summarized their immediate future when crammed into pontoons: "To be shot like sheep in a huddle and drowned in the Rappahannock appeared to be the certain fate of all if we failed and of some if we succeeded."[75]

More Federal batteries opened up. The Georgians at the river had kept up a steady fire since dawn but were running out of ammunition. An officer sent back to find relief ran into Brig. Gen. Harry T. Hays's Louisiana brigade. Hays ordered Col. William Monaghan to take his Sixth Louisiana forward, but their timing proved tragically bad. The Federal assault began when the Louisianans were still a few hundred yards from the river, and the artillery firing to suppress the Georgians also sent rounds crashing into Monaghan's troops trying to get forward. One artilleryman described the ordeal: "A regiment coming down to relieve or reinforce them [the Georgia skirmishers] was scattered and severely handled by our artillery fire."[76]

Under the covering artillery, Wadsworth ordered the Iron Brigade across the Rappahannock. Col. Edward S. Bragg quietly said to his Sixth Wisconsin men, "Come on, boys," and then gave the formal commands to get them to the boats:

> By the right of companies!
> To the front!
> Double quick!
> March!

The commander of the Twenty-Fourth Michigan did the same. As the first wave charged forward, the Second and Seventh Wisconsin and the Nineteenth Indiana joined the Fourteenth Brooklyn in providing covering fire.[77]

The Wisconsin and Michigan men passed through the Brooklyn skirmish line and piled into the boats. They began taking casualties while pulling oars out for use. Some men partially stood up and returned fire, while others pushed the awkward crafts into the river and climbed in. The incoming fire faded as the Thirteenth Georgia ran out of ammunition but resumed in intensity when the Sixth Louisiana scrambled into the trenches. The Iron Brigade had taken casualties on the riverbank and now began to lose men in the boats.[78]

Wadsworth's staff officers rode up to help but exhibited a painful inexperience. Instead of directing orders to the brigade commander, or even to regimental commanders, they shouted conflicting directions to whoever they saw:

> Cease firing!
> Fire to the right!
> Fire to the left!
> Launch the boats!

Lt. Col. William H. Robinson, commanding the Seventh Wisconsin, collared one of the excited staff officers and learned that Wadsworth wanted the entire brigade to cross immediately. Robinson shouted the necessary orders, and his men sprang forward. Soldiers from regiments slated for the second wave piled into loaded pontoons where there was room for a few more men. They grabbed and launched additional boats as quickly as men of the Second Wisconsin brought them down.[79]

Federal artillery pounded the Confederate pickets, but determined Southern marksmen still fired back. Pvt. Hoel W. Trumbull waded into the water to push off a boat. When he grabbed the gunwale and jumped up to get in, a bullet smashed into his head. In another boat a soldier fell forward, "a stream of blood rushing from his temple down over his face." Capt. William W. Ryan of the Seventh Wisconsin had a hole cut into his hat by a Minié ball as he clambered into a boat. Shortly after, another shot found its mark, piercing his body.[80]

Wadsworth, described by an observer as "eagle eyed and white haired," joined the assault. As division commander, he did not need to be a part of that initial river crossing, but he rode into the water and settled into the rear of a boat occupied by men of the Nineteenth Indiana. He held the bridle as his horse swam across behind the pontoon. One of the assault troops described how "the water fairly boiled" from incoming rounds. As they closed in on the far shore and entered the lee of the bluffs, the Confederate picket fire passed over them. When the boats shoved up against the opposite shore, men jumped over the sides into waist-deep water and mud. They quickly pulled themselves out and raced up a ravine to flank the defenders.[81]

When it became clear the Federal attack could not be stopped, Confederate officers ordered their men to pull back. Some of the Louisianans mistakenly thought those orders were only for those Georgians who had run out of ammunition. They became prisoners when the advancing Federals surrounded those who had not fled. One of the captured men was Lt. Col. Joseph Hanlon, who had been away from the army recuperating from a severe wound received at Antietam (Sharpsburg) and had reported back for duty just the day before.[82]

A Michigan soldier claimed that only seven minutes passed from the time they unslung their knapsacks on one side of the river to when they stood at the top of the bluff on the other side. Wadsworth's men captured more than one hundred prisoners, including three officers. During the attack, some of the Wisconsin men unloaded Captain Ryan from a bullet-riddled pontoon. He looked to be mortally wounded, so they left him on the muddy riverbank. The bullet that tore through his body had missed vital organs, though. When a young soldier later came back to look for his captain's body, he found Ryan still breathing and called for help to get him to a hospital.[83]

Colonel Bragg rallied his Sixth Wisconsin at the top of the hill and moved up to a prominent brick home called Smithfield. In better days Smithfield had been Thomas Pratt's elegant manor house but had become a hospital during the December battle. As at Mannsfield, there were a great many graves of Union dead as well as buried accumulations of amputated limbs. The Federals would later bury the Confederate dead from the morning's action there too.[84]

The Iron Brigade suffered fifty-seven men killed and wounded that morning. The Fourteenth Brooklyn, providing covering fire on the north side of the river, suffered another twenty-three men killed and wounded. The river assaults were a contrast in leadership. Delays and problems at Franklin's Crossing were overcome and the assault made successfully at a cost of twenty men killed and wounded. Command decisions at Pollock's Mill had been less effective, and casualties in the delayed attack had been four times higher.[85]

A man familiar with those surroundings accompanied the Sixth Wisconsin. Fifty-year-old Matthew Bernard, "old Matt" to the young soldiers, had been the human property of Arthur Bernard of the Mannsfield plantation, just three-quarters of a mile upstream. When the Army of the Potomac first came to Fredericksburg in April 1862, the local structure of forced labor quickly collapsed as thousands of enslaved persons freed themselves by making their way to Union lines. Old Matt, like many others, found work with the army, becoming a servant to the officers of Company C. That morning he was back near his old home in the company of a powerful army. His future may have been uncertain, but not his status as a free man.[86]

⫸ TWO ⫷

APRIL 29-30

WAITING

While Reynolds and Wadsworth clumsily executed an overdue assault, the Sixth Corps expanded its bridgehead. Russell's Third Brigade pushed past a burned manor house called Mannsfield and captured a handful of North Carolinians. As the mist dissipated, a Confederate officer on horseback reigned up, startled to see men wearing blue uniforms in the Southern works. Burnham's Light Division crossed over to solidify the enclave. Some men of the Forty-Third New York found $100,000 in Confederate currency in the wrecked mansion, though the value of that cash was probably comparable to the ruined home.[1]

Sedgwick's orders were to engage in a demonstration only, so Brooks crossed the rest of his division into the bridgehead, while the smaller Light Division returned to the north side of the river. The Fifty-Fourth North Carolina had pulled back to the Bowling Green Road, also known as the Richmond Stage Road, and established a line from Deep Run to a ravine between Mannsfield and Smithfield. The Thirteenth Virginia of Brig. Gen. William "Extra Billy" Smith's brigade moved over from the Fredericksburg gas works to maintain contact with the Carolinians.[2]

After daylight the Fifty-Seventh North Carolina moved up and relieved the Fifty-Fourth North Carolina on the Bowling Green Road. The Sixth Louisiana pulled back from its fight at the river and took position to the right of the Fifty-Seventh, while the Fifth Louisiana moved up from the railway to join them. A New York soldier described the Bowling Green Road: "On each side of the road is a ditch and outside of the ditch is a considerable bank of earth, an admirable place for riflemen to defend." The three Southern regiments held a strong position.[3]

Russell's brigade established a skirmish line about one hundred yards from the Confederates on the roadway. The Forty-Ninth Pennsylvania anchored the far right. To its left were the Ninety-Fifth and 119th Pennsylvania and the Thirty-Second New York. Behind them were the division's two other brigades, some units on the uplands and others under the cover of the river bluffs. To bolster the bridgehead, Brooks sent across Lt. Edward B. Williston's Battery D, Second US Artillery. Its six 12-pounder Napoleons dropped trail near the home of Alfred Bernard, a mansion known as The Bend because of its location at a pronounced turn in the Rappahannock River.[4]

At Pollock's Mill Creek the Fiftieth New York Engineers swung into action as the Ninety-Fifth New York got the rest of the pontoons to the work site. Lieutenant Colonel Pettes supervised the construction of one bridge, while Major Beers of the Fiftieth headed up work on the other. They had bridges in place before noon but were more than seven hours behind schedule. A courier found Brigadier General Benham and directed him to report to Hooker. The army commander had been with the flanking columns upriver and had just returned to his Falmouth headquarters.[5]

When Benham rode off to explain the night's delays to Hooker, five bridges were down, and two divisions (over 16,000 men) were on the south side of the Rappahannock. In support were another five divisions with an aggregate strength of nearly 24,000 men; the Third Corps (another 18,000 men) also stood by. This considerable force, however, remained a feint. On April 27 Hooker had briefed Brigadier General Patrick: "Sedgwick and Reynolds are simply to hold their own until the roar of battle is heard on the right—Then there will be a push to the Rail Road."[6]

At the Pollock's Mill crossing, the Twenty-Fourth Michigan anchored the extreme left of the bridgehead on a bluff overlooking Massaponax Creek. To its right was the Nineteenth Indiana and the Seventh, Second, and Sixth Wisconsin. The First Corps lodgment did not yet link up with the Sixth Corps line to their right, so the last unit angled toward the river to secure the flank. No batteries crossed into the bridgehead that day, with long-range support coming from rifled weapons on the north side of the river. Around 10:00 A.M. the Iron Brigade troops came under fire from Confederate artillery.[7]

Capt. Archibald Graham's First Rockbridge Artillery, a Virginia battery from the Shenandoah Valley, had two 20-pounder and two 10-pounder Parrott rifles in gun pits on Prospect Hill. The gunners serving the 20-pounders were ordered to open fire to show there were heavy guns ready to challenge a Union advance. The section fired six rounds in rapid succession. Fifteen minutes later two more rounds went crashing into the Federal position.[8]

General Lee, Lieutenant General Stonewall Jackson, and Maj. Gen. A. P. Hill were on Prospect Hill when the Rockbridge Artillery fired its few rounds. That relatively low knoll did not give much of a vantage point, so Jackson joined the Louisiana skirmishers on the Bowling Green Road. The dour Stonewall surely must have talked with Colonel Monaghan, whose Sixth Louisiana had been to the river's edge and back, but any such exchange did not find its way into subsequent reports. What became remarked upon was that Jackson looked rather resplendent in a new uniform, which was in stark contrast to the threadbare clothes he had worn through the glory days of 1862.[9]

By 10:00 A.M., signal teams had established telegraph connections from the Phillips house to the two crossings. Hooker wanted additional links upriver as well. The Beardslee equipment could handle being extended to Banks' Ford, but headquarters also wanted a telegraph link to US Ford. Hooker's chief signal officer, Captain Cushing, had not been informed of that interim crossing. Instead of rolling out new wire, his signal teams grabbed the eleven miles of wire connecting Belle Plain to Falmouth to make the connection from Falmouth to US Ford. That old wire, however, had become worn out from exposure, and its reuse made for poor connections.[10]

Signalmen at US Ford kept watch for Major General Meade's Fifth Corps, moving downstream to uncover the crossing, but the ability to relay news of its approach to Falmouth suffered another setback. During the afternoon of April 29, a thunderstorm descended on the Rappahannock valley, and lightning caused the Beardslee unit at US Ford to discharge its magnetism. The horrified signalmen worked feverishly to repair their equipment but could not get it working again until 9:00 P.M.[11]

At Fredericksburg the flag stations provided excellent communications. Headquarters received reports about Confederate rail activity at Hamilton's Crossing, observations of Southern troops moving toward the bridgehead, and even a sighting of wagons parked near the "Dahlman" (Downman) house on the Plank Road. A balloon also went aloft, from which Professor Lowe examined the Confederate defenses around the city. In painful contrast to this stream of information, Hooker had no word from his flanking columns. Chief of Staff Butterfield did not receive a message from US Ford until 10:30 P.M.[12]

From captured pickets the Federals at the downstream crossings knew they faced Jackson's Corps. The Confederates, however, were not yet sure what the encroaching Union soldiers were up to. Jackson wanted to find a weak point that might allow him to attack. The Union army had punched through his defenses during the battle in December, and if a stronger, better coordinated effort was coming, he wanted to hit them first.[13]

Major General Early had deployed his main force along the railway, with three regiments from his division on the Bowling Green Road. Jackson placed another division in the existing trenches behind him. He also ordered the troops in winter camps farther away to concentrate at Fredericksburg. The Federal artillery at Travellers Rest opened fire on the units moving up from Moss Neck, forcing them to detour inland, away from the bridge over Massaponax Creek. Federal troops at Franklin's Crossing thought the racket was Confederate artillery firing into the downstream bridgehead.[14]

Early's line extended from Hamilton's Crossing to Deep Run. The open and flat terrain immediately north of Deep Run constituted an awkward gap in the Confederate line that would soon need attention. In the meantime the line remained in the hills. Brig. Gen. William Barksdale held his Mississippi brigade in Fredericksburg.[15]

Fredericksburg itself had a close relationship with Barksdale's troops but suffered the pitfalls of a garrison town. In December 1862 the Mississippi men had been the community's brave defenders. Over the winter young ladies and dashing officers thrilled to new and exciting social interactions. The regiments, however, needed shelter and considerable subsistence, and the inadequate Confederate supply system too often left the Mississippians fending for themselves. Residents then paid the price in lost food and various materials from their homes claimed for firewood. The many hundreds of men also attracted prostitutes and suppliers of ardent spirits.[16]

The Federal crossing below Fredericksburg caught Lee without Longstreet and two of his divisions, which were detached in southeast Virginia, as well as most of the army's artillery, which was not yet available. Around 10:00 A.M. the Southern commander received a dispatch from Culpeper—the long-delayed news of the Federal crossing at Kelly's Ford. That initial message, however, did not convey the strength of the force observed. While the crossing at Fredericksburg looked to be more extensive, Lee could not be sure. The Confederates could see the Stafford hills across the Rappahannock covered with masses of blue-uniformed troops and an array of Federal guns, but the infantry had not advanced beyond its lodgment on the near side of the river. Perhaps the Federal army was coming from the west after all.[17]

Lee telegraphed the War Department in Richmond and asked that Longstreet be allowed to return one of the two divisions redeployed to the coast. Those units had been removed from Lee's direct command, and the Confederate government had to consider this request while also trying to protect North Carolina. Getting artillery out of winter quarters was also more easily said than done. The artillery battalions were camped near Carmel Church, Bowling Green, and Chesterfield Depot, all of them distant from where a battle might be brewing along the Rappahannock.[18]

By chance, one of the battalion commanders, Col. Edward P. Alexander, happened to be at Fredericksburg that morning. After evaluating a new fuzing mechanism in Milford, he had spent the night with friends and been awakened by the Federal incursion on April 29 like everyone else. He noted, "the first thing to be done was to telegraph down to our winter quarters, and to order all the artillery—my own battalion of course included, to march immediately to the front."[19]

General Pendleton, Lee's chief of artillery, had been at the Chesterfield depot getting his batteries ready to move. The Federal crossing made that task urgent. He got Alexander's battalion on the road as well as two batteries of Col. Henry Cabell's battalion. A battery from Lt. Col. John Garnett's battalion also made it out of camp that day. Others would march in the morning. Pendleton also instructed Col. Stapleton Crutchfield, chief of artillery for Jackson's Corps, to get the artillery units at Bowling Green headed north.[20]

At Fredericksburg Confederate mapmaker Jedediah Hotchkiss described how "the plain of the Rappahannock, the former battlefield, presents a beautiful appearance; alas soon to be stained again with blood." A closer look at the seemingly bucolic landscape revealed evidence of that earlier fighting. A Virginia soldier observed that they "could see plenty of old half decayed Yankees, some with their heads sticking out; arms, hands, and feet sticking out." A Georgia soldier noted: "The field is literally covered with graves now. I saw the arm of a dead Yankee sticking out of a grave that had not yet decayed."[21]

Confederate infantry reoccupied this corrupted landscape and waited for their artillery to arrive. The batteries would not move rapidly, though. Shortages of feed during the winter had required that horses be kept alive with corn. That inadequate diet left the teams in poor condition as a new campaign season loomed. The ordeal of Confederate animals was starkly evident around Fredericksburg. Horses and mules had succumbed to exhaustion while hauling supplies during the winter, and their carcasses lay rotting along the roads radiating from Hamilton's Crossing.[22]

When movement orders reached the artillery camps, battery commanders had to determine their combat loads based on the condition of their animals. Certain equipment and even some ammunition had to be left behind. Some batteries were on the road by midafternoon. A cold rain opened on them as they marched into the night. Roads already in poor condition became worse in the downpour. Unwilling to press their horses to exhaustion, some of the batteries stopped to rest, the men camping without tents. They would resume their march at daybreak.[23]

The Union army's flanking force was also in motion on the twenty-ninth. The troops were now becoming field conditioned, and the columns moved along rapidly. Meade's Fifth Corps split off for Ely's Ford as the Twelfth and Eleventh Corps continued to Germanna Ford. Stuart's cavalry units shadowed the Northern columns to figure out their composition.[24]

At Germanna Ford Union cavalry swooped in and captured Confederate pioneers rebuilding a wrecked bridge over the Rapidan River. Federal engineers moved in to adapt the beginning of a trestle bridge into a footbridge, using seized tools and convenient stacks of cut lumber. By late afternoon the Eleventh and Twelfth Corps had crossed that water barrier, continuing toward Fredericksburg. A Pennsylvania officer noted, "By the passage of the Rapidan we were clearly in the enemy's country."[25]

The pontoon bridge used at Kelly's Ford was supposed to have been taken up and hauled to Ely's Ford, but Meade arrived at the Rapidan River well before the engineers. His cavalry had already crossed and scattered a Confederate picket force, and he did not want the army's flank march to lose momentum because of him. Meade decided that his infantry could also wade the river, and his columns pressed on.[26]

Some of the Confederate bridge builders at Germanna Ford managed to escape and report to their respective brigade headquarters, corroborating what Southern cavalrymen had seen at Ely's Ford. Mounted couriers galloped off to relay this news to Lee. Stuart's cavalry had also captured soldiers from each of the three Federal corps. The general dutifully transmitted this news via telegram to Lee, but once again, one of the telegraph stations in that circuitous relay had shut down for the night before the dispatch got through.[27]

In Fredericksburg the Union army had paused since Hooker had ordered only a limited effort below the town. The Northern forces entrenched a forward line about halfway between the Bowling Green Road and the river. On the Confederate side of the lines, Capt. William B. Hurt's Alabama battery had a long-range Whitworth rifle, of English manufacture, on a slight knoll approximately one mile south of Hamilton's Crossing. Around 3:00 P.M., Lt. John W. Tullis directed his gun crew to fire at a signal station he had noticed at the Seddon house, nearly three miles away. A Federal signalman described the result: "One of their heavy bolts pierced the soft earth within ten feet of our flag but without exploding, and it remained there with its ugly nose sticking out during our stay."[28]

Hurt's weapon occupied one of two artillery positions on the east end of Early's front. The other position was Prospect Hill, where Graham's First Rockbridge (Virginia) Artillery had its Parrott rifles in four of fourteen existing gun pits. The other available Confederate weapons deployed north of Deep Run. Capt. Edward S. McCarthy's First Company, Richmond (Virginia) Howitzers took position on high ground overlooking Deep Run and the open plain through which it flows. Capt. John C. Fraser's Pulaski (Georgia) Battery occupied the gun pits on Lee's Hill, near the Telegraph Road. Capt. Basil C. Manly's North Carolina battery and Capt. Henry H. Carlton's Troup (Georgia) Artillery, worn out from struggling up the road, were placed in reserve.[29]

The weather front that dropped a hard rain on the Confederate artillery units en route to Fredericksburg arrived in the Rappahannock valley that afternoon. The hot day turned cold, and the downpour further frustrated Jackson's observation of the bridgehead. Hooker had returned to Falmouth, reassured that the many parts of his army were where he wanted them to be. Butterfield lauded Sedgwick's demonstration at Fredericksburg as "a very strong one."[30]

With the campaign unfolding as desired, army headquarters looked to reinforce the flanking columns through US Ford. Hooker ordered the two Second Corps divisions at Banks' Ford to move to the crossing farther upstream. Engineers with equipment for two bridges would also depart that night. Hooker also ordered one of the observation balloons to relocate to Banks' Ford, which his flanking columns would uncover as they continued toward Fredericksburg.[31]

Just before sunset, at approximately 6:30 P.M., Confederate couriers from upriver found Lee and reported that Federal cavalry, backed up by infantry in unknown strength, had crossed the Rapidan River at both Germanna and Ely's Fords. This news confirmed that Union forces were marching toward Fredericksburg rather than heading south toward Gordonsville, but the Southern commander did not yet know whether these columns were a distraction or the Union army's main thrust. Stuart's dispatch identifying the three Federal corps had yet to arrive.[32]

Lee did not take long to absorb what news he had before responding. The general instructed Maj. Gen. Lafayette McLaws to leave a brigade in Fredericksburg and prepare to take the rest of his division west. He directed Maj. Gen. Richard Anderson to draw in his brigades from the US Ford area and look to his left, where the Federal flanking movement had become evident. Anderson was to concentrate his division at Chancellorsville until the situation could be more fully understood.[33]

Daylight faded on April 29, but few would experience a quiet night. The Federal flanking columns tramped across the floating bridge at Kelly's Ford until well past midnight. One of Lowe's balloons got on the road to Banks' Ford, while the other made an ascent at Fredericksburg. Within the bridgehead, some of the advance units were awakened and repositioned.[34]

Confederate forces also did not get much rest. Anderson's units moved to Chancellorsville that night. A Virginia soldier described how they "marched until day through the muddiest road I think I ever travelled." Confederate artillery units struggled to get their guns forward on poor thoroughfares. Soldiers manning the lines at Fredericksburg had fine shelters to ward off the rain that night, but they remained unoccupied back in the camps the men had left that morning.[35]

Sedgwick's orders had been to get a force across the Rappahannock River and establish a position in front of the Army of Northern Virginia. From an intelligence report delivered the day before, Hooker knew Lee's available troop strength to be around 55,300 men. The Confederates so skillfully accounted for on paper had responded to the Union incursion like angry hornets. Now the question was how much longer would they remain in front of Sedgwick below Fredericksburg.[36]

The hard rain had tapered off to a cold drizzle by the morning of the thirtieth. Daylight revealed that there had been no apparent increase in the Federal host within the bridgeheads. During the December battle, the Union army had forced its way across the river on the eleventh and then spent the entire next day building up an assault force that would attack on the thirteenth. This time after jumping the river, the Federals pushed forward only two divisions of infantry, along with a few batteries but no supply wagons. To Confederate observers, the limited buildup indicated no serious intent.[37]

Instead of reinforcements pouring across the five floating bridges, the only martial activities were picket reliefs. The troops also continued to improve their trenches, emphasizing static defense instead of offensive action. Confederate units used this pause to send details back to their camps to break down tents, gather knapsacks, and retrieve other equipment. The light rain ended midmorning. With the clouds beginning to break around noon, the day warmed up. The Federals were not deploying more troops, but neither were the Confederates showing signs of much activity "save the general disappearance of their tents."[38]

Hooker did not push his formations at Fredericksburg to do much more than they already had. At 8:30 A.M. he ordered Sedgwick to give the impression of an imminent advance at 1:00 P.M. Rather than trying to confuse the Confederates with a show of force, however, Hooker simply wanted to ascertain whether the enemy remained in the area in strength. He instructed his wing commander not to advance beyond his defenses, and if he could see that the Confederate force had not diminished, he need not engage in the demonstration at all. The flanking columns, after all, were supposed to be on the heights west of Fredericksburg the following day.[39]

Sedgwick responded within the hour, notifying Hooker that Reynolds and Brooks had both determined that the Confederates in their front had not been reduced in strength. Both also noted that they did not see much enemy artillery. With the Confederates apparently holding in place, Hooker could get his flanking forces into position for a defensive battle. The weaponry of the day had become overwhelming against troops making a frontal assault—evident at Malvern Hill, Second Manassas, Antietam, and Fredericksburg. When Hooker's army reached the high ground west of Fredericksburg, Lee would be compelled to attack at a disadvantage or to pull back from the Rappahannock.[40]

The Union force coming from the west would uncover two upriver crossings. Control of US Ford would allow reinforcements to reach the flanking columns, but that crossing would only be useful in the short term as the poor roads north of the river could not handle sustained military use. The flanking columns would also need to keep moving to get out of the choked and tangled woodlands. It was Banks' Ford that would provide access to the open ground west of Fredericksburg, the plateau from which

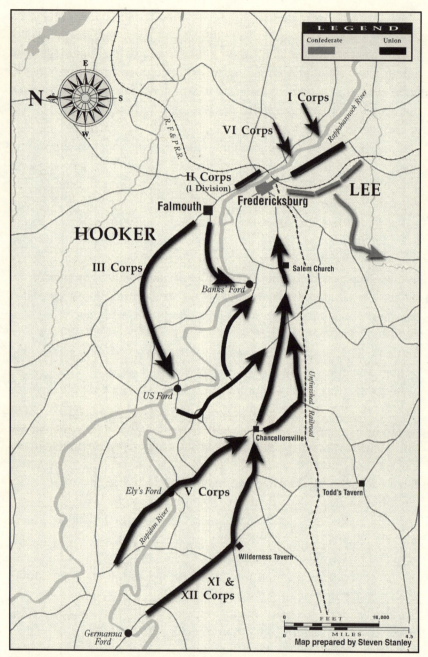

Map 2. Hooker's Plan. Hooker intended to occupy the high ground just west of Fredericksburg, which would leave Lee with two options—attack at a disadvantage or pull back from the Rappahannock River.

Federal forces could dominate the town and its surrounding terrain. Whoever controlled Banks' Ford was going to control the coming battle.[41]

Aeronauts had hauled their observation balloon and equipment to Banks' Ford by around 3:00 A.M. The morning rain obscured any potential visibility, but the unit prepared to make an ascent as soon as the skies cleared. When they got an observer aloft by 10:45 A.M., he could see that the Confederates were not deployed at that crossing in great strength.[42]

Getting troops to US Ford proved more of a challenge. Lt. Col. Ira Spaulding and his men from the Fiftieth New York Engineers found themselves on a primitive, muddy road through a dripping forest. The Potomac Army's chief quartermaster, Rufus B. Ingalls, now a colonel, provided critical assistance with extra teams to keep the bridging equipment moving forward. Soldiers chopped down trees in places where a typical wagon could make a turn, but one with a thirty-one-foot-long pontoon strapped to it could not. The men were utterly exhausted by daylight, when the bridging column finally arrived on the hills overlooking the crossing site. Brig. Gen. Gouverneur K. Warren made a quick inspection of the route to the river and found that a lot more work was going to be necessary before pontoons could be brought down from the uplands.[43]

Warren was Hooker's chief of topographical engineers. An energetic officer, he moved between Fredericksburg and the upriver crossings, effectively becoming the army commander's eyes and ears. Hooker, however, remained strangely passive. Rather than aggressively pushing for every advantage before contact with the enemy, he just let his plan unfold. The general had thought it useful to ride out to Kelly's Ford to supervise three corps commanders. Hooker ordered a demonstration at the Fredericksburg crossings not to throw the Confederates off balance, but to see if Sedgwick was still holding Lee's attention. He then suspended that demonstration at 11:30 A.M., which gave Lee the gift of time to respond to Federal moves.[44]

Hooker planned to rejoin his field forces later that day but first busied himself with General Order No. 47, congratulating the army on the successful flank march:

> Headquarters Army of the Potomac
> Camp near Falmouth, Va., April 30, 1863.

General Order, No. 47:
It is with heartfelt satisfaction the commanding general announces to the army that the operations of the last three days have determined that our

enemy must either ingloriously fly, or come out from behind his entrenchments and give us battle on our own ground, where certain destruction awaits him.

The operations of the Fifth, Eleventh, and Twelfth Corps have been a succession of splendid achievements.

    By command of Major-General Hooker:
    S. Williams
    Assistant Adjutant-General[45]

The ground Hooker meant to claim as his own was the plateau west of Fredericksburg, where a strong force could establish an impregnable defense. The Federal commander's formal boast on April 30, however, was premature as his troops did not yet occupy that critical terrain. Still dithering, Hooker also issued General Order No. 48, which addressed the issue of newspaper stories published under pseudonyms. Injudicious articles too often revealed bits and pieces of information useful to an enemy, but Hooker was still obsessed with keeping his plans secret rather than trying to shape the developing battle.[46]

When Hooker returned to directing his army, he refocused on Banks' Ford. He directed his engineers to take two bridges from the Fredericksburg crossing and stage them upriver. Bridging equipment had already been sent to US Ford, where two Second Corps divisions would cross later that day. Similar equipment was needed at Banks' Ford to support the planned defensive position on the western plateau.[47]

Reynolds bolstered his bridgehead by sending two batteries across the river. Battery B, Fourth US Artillery, under Lt. James Stewart, and Battery C, Fifth US Artillery, led by Capt. Dunbar R. Ransom, rumbled across the floating spans and dropped trail where the infantry held position. Their weapons were 12-pounder Napoleons, excellent guns to counter a Confederate advance against the Federal position.[48]

Lee's artillery continued to dribble in as the general evaluated a growing body of intelligence. At Fredericksburg the limited number of Union troops across the river suggested the main portion of Hooker's army was gathering elsewhere, corroborated by Stuart's delayed telegram from upriver that morning. In addition to this, Stuart's couriers had skirted around the wide-ranging Federal columns to report as well. Lee again asked his War Department to expedite Longstreet's return with at least one division.[49]

The Confederate artillery arrived slowly. Some units, like Capt. William Parker's Richmond Battery and Captain Carlton's Troup Battery, had marched all night, but most units had to stop. Captain Manly, for instance, got his North Carolina battery on the road in the late afternoon. "Soon after we had started," he later reported, "quite a heavy and cold rain began to fall which, in addition to the previous almost impassable condition of the roads, made the marching excessively severe, both on man and beast." The North Carolinians went into camp at dark, without tents, and resumed their trek at daybreak.[50]

Artillery units that started on the morning of April 30 avoided the rain but not the bad road. Each battery, in turn, chewed up the Telegraph Road a bit more, making the journey progressively more difficult for those behind them. The bedraggled artillerymen trying to bring up weapons with weak animals looked more like stragglers than cohesive military units. The Fluvanna Battery, for example, had six weapons that became strung out into a column over six miles long.[51]

Pendleton established an artillery park in a large open area across from Massaponax Church. From that growing concentration of guns, batteries could be guided into position at Fredericksburg or assembled for a march west. By the end of the day, most of the Confederate batteries had managed to straggle in. The artillerymen rested their horses, looked for feed, and prepared their equipment for battle. By late evening the only units still on the road were those of the Washington Artillery, the pride of New Orleans, which had taken a wrong turn along the way and become lost.[52]

The skies cleared as Stonewall Jackson reconnoitered the Federal lines. The formidable collection of artillery on Stafford Heights precluded a counterattack except under cover of darkness or bad weather, and those conditions were disappearing. Jackson found Hotchkiss, his cartographer, and asked him to prepare maps for their potential battle area to the west.[53]

At US Ford a light fog enveloped the Rappahannock River when Lieutenant Colonel Spaulding and his Fiftieth New York Engineers arrived. Warren used the screening mist to cover his inspection of the approach roads, which he found unusable. He would have to spend time getting them into condition for the bridging equipment to be brought to the river. Around 9:00 A.M., as the engineers and a five-hundred-man working party from the Second Corps were getting themselves organized and equipped, the mist thinned out enough to reveal that Federal cavalry occupied the opposite bank. Three squadrons of the Eighth Pennsylvania Cavalry accompanying Meade's Fifth Corps already controlled the south side of the river.[54]

In his postbattle report, Warren indicated that he had been well pleased that Hooker's "grand flanking movement had succeeded." He added, "The work on the road was pushed with all possible dispatch, the men working with the greatest spirit, and by 1 P.M. was made practicable for artillery and pontoon wagons." Butterfield informed Warren, "Until Banks' Ford is uncovered, the route by the United States ford must be understood as our line of operations."[55]

By 3:00 P.M. the engineers had their first bridge in place and immediately began work on the second one. Work also progressed to establish roads on the opposite shore. Union forces ignored the existing US Mine Road, which wound out of the floodplain on a narrow track, and instead leveled the Confederate earthworks in two places. The two Second Corps divisions then pushed straight through the breached trench line to the gentle terrain beyond. Due to the late-afternoon start, the bridges were full of marching infantry well into the evening hours. A near-full moon rose about an hour and a half before sunset, lighting the way as the Federals crossed uninterrupted into the night.[56]

The US Ford bridges provided a way to reinforce the flanking columns headed to Fredericksburg. Hooker, however, gave the crossing more permanence when he directed that telegraph communications be set up there as well. Signalmen unrolled wires across the river to a brick manor house called Forest Hall but were not confident their Beardslee equipment could handle the distance that separated them from Falmouth. Hooker had similar concerns and sought permission to bring in the US Military Telegraph (USMT) service.[57]

The USMT's stronger batteries would provide more reliable service than the Beardslee terminals, but the condition of the wires remained a problem. Cushing had requested fifteen miles of new wire from the Washington depot and was informed that a signals detachment had started south with the requested materiel that afternoon. Colonel Ingalls had a boat and wagons standing by at Aquia Landing to expedite delivery to the Falmouth headquarters.[58]

Around 11:00 A.M. the Union flanking columns converged on Chancellorsville. Meade's Fifth Corps skirmishers pushed into the clearing as the Confederate rear guard faded back into the opposite tree line. When the Twelfth Corps arrived, Meade exuberantly exclaimed: "This is splendid,

Slocum; hurrah for old Joe; we are on Lee's flank, and he does not know it. You take the Plank Road toward Fredericksburg, and I'll take the Pike, or *vice versa,* as you prefer, and we will get out of this Wilderness." Slocum, however, had to tell Meade that he had orders from Hooker to halt at the crossroads. The two Second Corps divisions coming across at US Ford were to reinforce them there, while the entire Third Corps would also be joining them from Fredericksburg by way of US Ford.[59]

At Falmouth Hooker was doing very little to maintain the campaign's momentum. His new logistics capability had allowed his flanking columns to cross two major rivers and then rapidly advance through an area where the Confederate army was not ready to confront them. The men had marched on April 27 carrying eight days of rations; April 30 was only day four. The dynamic of ground combat does not reward hesitation, and Hooker had not given his subordinate commanders the authority to seize opportunity.

Field commanders at Chancellorsville knew that delay risked failure. Meade directed the Eighth Pennsylvania Cavalry toward Fredericksburg to find out what was in front of the infantry. About two and a half miles out, the troopers ran into Confederate cavalry, which "retired very slowly, rendering it evident that they were confident of support." That support, not visible to the blue-clad horse soldiers, were three infantry brigades that had pulled back from Chancellorsville to a ridge near Zoan Church.[60]

Lee sent his engineers to lay out a line along this ridge, and Anderson's infantrymen spent the thirtieth digging. The earthworks north of the Orange Turnpike extended about three-quarters of a mile and then angled toward Banks' Ford. South of the Turnpike, the new works followed the high ground to Tabernacle Church, where it overlooked the Orange Plank Road. The new line of rifle pits thus covered all three roads to Fredericksburg. Colonel Alexander also established strong battery positions along that line even though his artillery had not yet arrived to occupy them.[61]

Meade directed an infantry brigade to push the Confederates a bit more. Two regiments advanced through the trees until they could see the enemy works being dug on a low ridge. The brigade commander wanted to test the strength of what he had found, but Meade called him back to Chancellorsville—Hooker's orders were to wait. The Federal cavalry remained behind to picket a ridge near Motts Run. The Fifth Corps commander's letter to his wife that evening included a note of caution: "We are across the river and have out-maneuvered the enemy, but are not out of the woods."[62]

From Falmouth Hooker had issued a proclamation that characterized a successful approach to a battle as a victory with only two possible outcomes. Lee must either "ingloriously fly" or face "certain destruction." His bombastic declaration reflected an absurd assumption that a dangerous adversary would react as he anticipated. To compound the illusion, Hooker did not plan to join the flanking columns until later that day, not until he had personally ordered the Third Corps at Fredericksburg to further strengthen the gathering forces at Chancellorsville. Hooker continued to constrain his army by trying to handle everything himself.

Major General Sickles, commanding the Third Corps, received his instructions to get across the Rappahannock River at US Ford by early morning on May 1. A Michigan soldier wrote, "About noon the bugle sounds the advance, and the brigade marches in quick time a distance of about twelve miles to within a short distance of United States Ford, and again bivouac for the night." Hunt and the artillery units at Banks' Ford also received orders to get to Chancellorsville via US Ford. At the Fredericksburg crossings, Hooker's general order expounding on the success of the flank march was read to each regiment. Inexperienced troops cheered; veterans were unimpressed.[63]

While Anderson entrenched at Zoan Church, Lee notified him that two of Stuart's cavalry regiments in front of the Federal formations coming from the west were his to use for reconnaissance. He then issued Army of Northern Virginia Special Order No. 121 to position his forces. McLaws was to leave a brigade at Fredericksburg and take the rest of his division to reinforce Anderson. He had already pulled three of his brigades off the line and would move out at sunset. Jackson was to leave a division at the Federal bridgehead and follow McLaws with the rest of his corps the next morning.[64]

Barksdale's Mississippians had moved into the positions vacated by McLaws's Division. Elements of the Thirteenth and Eighteenth Mississippi filed into place behind the stone wall along the Telegraph Road. The remaining companies from the regiments, as well as the complete Seventeenth and Twenty-First Mississippi Regiments, moved up to picket the river. This advance line extended from the Ferneyhough house, near Franklin's Crossing, to Taylor's Hill (modern Fall Hill), overlooking the "reservoir above Falmouth." That reservoir was the slack-water pond backed up behind a stone-and-timber dam across the Rappahannock River, an impoundment that fed into the Rappahannock Canal. At Fall Hill the Mississippi troops linked up with the Tenth Alabama of Wilcox's Brigade, which was picketing the Banks' Ford area.[65]

Jackson and Early knew this would be insufficient force to hold an extended line at Fredericksburg. To bolster that position, Jackson would leave behind a substantial amount of the Confederate artillery. In his memoirs Early noted that he had forty-five guns under his direction, but historian John Bigelow has shown that he undercounted Pendleton's reserve artillery as well as some of the available First Corps batteries. The Confederate defenders left behind at Fredericksburg would, in fact, be supported by fifty-six guns.[66]

Jackson considered Early a capable combat leader. He had held his ground in a tight spot during operations around Cedar Mountain in May 1862, which had earned him Jackson's rare praise. In hard-fought actions at places like Sharpsburg, Early then earned Jackson's trust. An 1837 graduate of West Point, he had been the commonwealth's attorney of Franklin County when the war came. Now Early was a major general, entrusted with an independent command and a daunting responsibility.[67]

McLaws departed Fredericksburg with two batteries from Cabell's Battalion: McCarthy's First Company, Richmond Howitzers and Manly's North Carolina Battery. Cabell himself remained with Early, with Carlton's Troup Artillery and Fraser's Pulaski Battery. Carlton also received temporary direction of Capt. Andrew B. Rhett's guns of Brooks's South Carolina Battery.[68]

Artillery units remaining with Early included Graham's First Rockbridge Artillery on Prospect Hill. Awaiting orders at Massaponax Church were Lt. Col. R. Snowden Andrews's battalion, Lt. Col. William Nelson's artillery battalion, and Lt. Col. Allen S. Cutts's Sumter Battalion. Col. James B. Walton's Washington Artillery had finally arrived following a wrong turn and detour back. General Pendleton was also ordered to stay behind, with Early assigning him to oversee the batteries north of Deep Run. Andrews, Early's own chief of artillery, was to supervise the placement of guns south of that stream.[69]

As Jackson's units made ready to march, Graham's Parrott rifles on Prospect Hill masked their imminent departure with another brief demonstration. Around 5:30 P.M. the Confederate gunners fired into the bridgehead, blasting the infantry at around 2,300 yards. They lifted their aim to target Federal guns on the north side of the river at 3,000–3,400 yards, then concentrated on the two Union batteries south of the river at about 2,000 yards. Those two batteries had smoothbore Napoleons, more suited to killing attacking infantry than engaging in counterbattery fire against rifled weapons.[70]

Three batteries of 3-inch Ordnance Rifles below Pollock's Mill responded to the Confederate Parrotts. Those units were Battery A, First New Hampshire Artillery; Battery C, Fourth Pennsylvania Artillery; and Battery F, First Pennsylvania Artillery. Collectively, they expended 138 rounds. The 3-inch weapons fired the same size ammunition as 10-pounder Parrott rifles, but the Confederates also had two 20-pounder Parrotts on Prospect Hill. The Whitworth gun just beyond Hamilton's Crossing threw over a few rounds as well. Comparing the incoming and outgoing artillery fire, one Federal soldier ruefully noted, "Our batteries were not slow in responding, making some splendid shots, but our metal was too light to be effective at long range."[71]

General Reynolds claimed that faulty ammunition caused the disparity in firepower rather than his decision to send only field guns across the river. He asked Sedgwick for support. At Travellers Rest Lt. Col. Edward R. Warner had command of three batteries. Two units had 3-inch Ordnance Rifles, but the third had 20-pounder Parrott rifles. Warner repositioned a section of those heavier weapons from the Fifth New York Battery, and when they opened fire, the Federal response finally had some heft.[72]

The exchange of metal ended as darkness closed in, and a Union soldier described the reverberating stillness: "The thunder of guns has ceased, but at long intervals like the dying gusts of a storm, the air vibrates with a sullen boom, the sound striking and echoing back from the distant hills." Embarrassed that Confederate guns had the upper hand that day, Colonel Wainwright, the First Corps chief of artillery, pulled the Fifth US Artillery's smoothbore Napoleons off the line, replacing them with the 3-inch Ordnance Rifles of Battery L, First New York Light Artillery. He also moved in the 4.5-inch guns of Battery M, First Connecticut Heavy Artillery. Wainwright kept Battery B, Fourth US Artillery in the bridgehead and moved a section of 12-pounder Napoleons to a position in front of the Smithfield mansion.[73]

Hooker departed Falmouth about an hour and a half before the Confederate demonstration. When he turned off the Warrenton Road to get to US Ford, he was on a crude roadway with severe limitations. His headquarters cavalcade could thread its way through the military traffic, but the fighting units had to proceed in turn. Lt. Joseph W. Martin's Sixth New York Battery spent two days on "the road leading to the ford . . . completely blockaded by the wagon and artillery trains belonging to the Second Army Corps, then en route for the ford."[74]

Sickles and his Third Corps were also on their way to Chancellorsville. They had bivouacked where the US Ford Road branches off from the Warrenton Road, planning to resume their march on May 1. If the Second Corps had cleared the road, they would be across the Rappahannock that morning. At Chancellorsville Hooker contemplated delaying his move toward Fredericksburg until he had more strength on hand. That casual mindset is also evident in Provost Marshal General Patrick's journal entry on the evening of April 30: "So far as we can see, or judge, they [the Confederates] still believe that we are making all our arrangements for a ground attack in front of Sedgwick & Reynolds."[75]

Hooker's insufficient cavalry strength also kept him from knowing what lay ahead. The Eighth Pennsylvania Cavalry had already run into Confederate infantry on the Orange Turnpike. The Sixth New York Cavalry had reconnoitered south, toward Spotsylvania Court House, and run into Confederate cavalry where Catharpin Road crosses the Ni River. The New Yorkers fought well, holding the Confederates at bay until they managed to break out of their predicament and ride north. Both sides exchanged casualties, and the Union horse soldiers realized they had been fighting a brigade of Virginia cavalry. On the battlefield taking shape, the Confederate army had a decided advantage in mounted units.[76]

Yet Hooker remained convinced he had the upper hand and confidently instructed Sedgwick to be vigilant. If the Confederates withdrew, Sedgwick was to put his whole force on the Bowling Green Road and pursue them. Hooker also directed the Sixth Corps to press any withdrawing Confederates down the Telegraph Road, reflecting the same misunderstanding of the roads in Sedgwick's front that he had shown four days earlier. The Bowling Green Road and the Telegraph Road diverge, so advancing on both routes would take the Union forces beyond supporting distance of one another, making each column vulnerable to counterattack.[77]

As before, Sedgwick's questions about what Hooker expected him to accomplish remained unresolved. The army commander again dodged the issue, indicating that he did not really expect much to happen at the bridgehead. Instead, Hooker assured him that he and the army's main body would be on the heights west of Fredericksburg the next day, May 1. If those forces met any opposition, then he might be delayed in reaching that decisive terrain until nightfall.[78]

Hooker anticipated the Confederates would retreat from Banks' Ford rather than face his reinforced flanking column. Benham already had his engineers at work to relocate two spans to Banks' Ford by 8:00 P.M. At Franklin's Crossing men of the Fiftieth New York Engineers dismantled

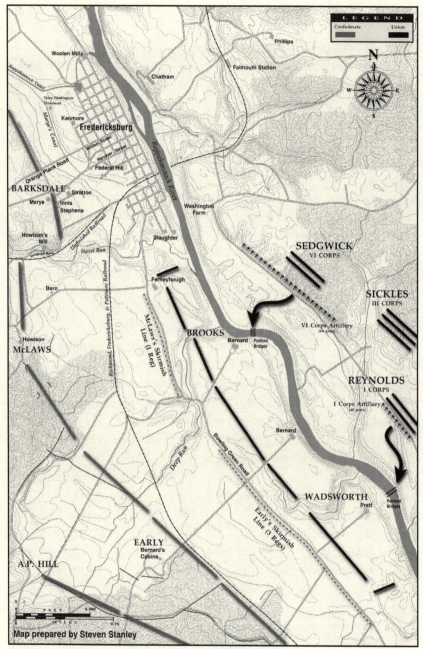

Map 3. Sedgwick's Bridgehead. Hooker wanted a diversion downstream from Fredericksburg while his flanking columns moved into position on May 1 to force the Confederates to retreat.

one of three bridges and loaded its component parts on wagons. At the crossing farther downstream, another detachment of New York engineers removed one of two bridges. Both bridge trains were ready to start for Banks' Ford by midnight. Confederate pickets at these sites reported noises on the north side of the river but could not figure out if the Federals were moving up or pulling back.[79]

Two Sixth Corps units helped the engineers at Franklin's Crossing, while two First Corps units provided manpower at the Pollock's Mill location. But Sedgwick and Reynolds did not want their fighting men to accompany the bridge trains to Banks' Ford. Given Hooker's expectations that they be able to respond to several Confederate moves, the two corps commanders informed Butterfield that they wanted their four regiments to remain in the area after helping dismantle and load the bridging equipment. The chief of staff concurred. The Second Corps division at Fredericksburg was supposed to be headed to Banks' Ford anyway, so Butterfield directed Brig. Gen. John Gibbon to have four of his regiments accompany the bridge trains.[80]

The division commander directed Brig. Gen. Joshua T. Owen to get the bridging equipment upriver. Owen's Philadelphia Brigade, consisting of the Sixty-Ninth, Seventy-First, Seventy-Second, and 106th Pennsylvania Regiments, mustered at sunset and stacked arms. They relieved the First and Sixth Corps units with the bridge trains and prepared for the night's task. Several hours earlier Butterfield had directed Gibbon to have his troops ready to march to US Ford on May 1 to join the rest of the Second Corps at Chancellorsville. The four regiments detached to accompany the bridge trains would either stay at Banks' Ford or return to Falmouth, the decision to be clarified by future orders.[81]

In addition to the manpower of four infantry regiments, the engineers were again supported by the Potomac Army's chief quartermaster. Ingalls loaned them horse teams from the reserve artillery, as he had done to help get bridging equipment to US Ford. The engineers thus had twelve horses for each pontoon. Even then, the ten-mile trek from the Fredericksburg crossings to the staging area at Banks' Ford proved a difficult haul.[82]

Col. Charles B. Stuart of the Fiftieth New York Engineers led the march that night. A bright moon initially lit the way, but the roads were washed out and rutted in many places. This caused several wagons to overturn, but the accompanying troops pushed them back upright and quickly made any necessary repairs. Twilight began to lighten the sky at 4:45 A.M., and sunrise came a half hour later. The engineers established a wagon park on the uplands above the planned crossing site, the last wagon rolling into that holding area by 6:15 A.M. Benham's demanding training regimen and Ingalls's conscientious support had ensured that the army's operations were not going to be held up by the bridge builders.[83]

At Fredericksburg three floating bridges remained in place. The engineers at the uppermost bridge kept watch that night for fire rafts or waterproof explosive devices called torpedoes. No such weapons drifted into the bridges, but the engineers did find a less warlike craft. Along the riverbank they discovered a small wooden boat, described by a soldier as fifteen inches long, five inches wide, and three inches deep. There was a place carved out in the middle to hold trade goods, and lead bullets had been nailed to the bottom, to act as ballast. Penciled on the side were the words "John Butternut, 24 Va, Co K." Its owner was a member of Maj. Gen. George E. Pickett's division, then in North Carolina with Longstreet.[84]

The night appeared quiet. Professor Lowe had taken his balloon back up at around 7:00 P.M. to see whether the Confederates were moving west in response to the Federal flanking columns. Around 8:30 P.M. he reported numerous fires beyond the heights composing the Southern line, with more fires behind Fredericksburg. What the aeronaut did not realize was that behind that screen of campfires, McLaws would depart shortly after midnight. Jackson was to depart at dawn.[85]

Lt. James Power Smith of Jackson's staff described the night march: "By the light of a brilliant moon, at midnight, that passed into an early dawn of dense mist, the troops were moved, by the Old Mine road, out of sight of the enemy." Jackson did not know that Hooker had held up his forces at Chancellorsville and had concerns that the Federals might close in on Anderson's position at Zoan Church before reinforcements were on hand. Instead of waiting for daybreak, he decided to move out at 3:00 A.M. to be within supporting distance of Anderson's outpost shortly after the sun broke the horizon.[86]

When Jackson departed, Early's units repositioned themselves and dug more trenches. When the Ninety-Sixth Pennsylvania went on picket at the end of the day, the Confederate picket line was a strong one and only about forty yards away. The next morning the Pennsylvanians saw that the Southerners had pulled back across a ravine to the Bowling Green Road.[87]

When May 1 dawned, the bulk of Lee's army was on its way west. The Confederates remaining at Fredericksburg consisted of approximately 7,500 men in Early's Division and another 1,500 men in Barksdale's Brigade, a grand total of 9,000 infantrymen. There were, however, fifty-six guns on hand to support them. On the Federal side Sickles had marched his Third Corps away, but Reynolds and Sedgwick remained, with a combined force of 40,000 troops plus artillery.[88]

May 1 was the day Hooker planned to be on the heights just west of Fredericksburg. As Butterfield had relayed to Sedgwick, "the army now at [Chancellorsville] will assume the initiative to-morrow morning, and will advance along the line of the Plank road, uncovering what is called Banks' Ford, where bridges will be at once thrown across the river, which route will become the shortest line of communications between the two wings of the army." The army commander added that Sedgwick was to watch how the Confederates at Fredericksburg reacted to the Union advance. If the opposing force dropped its guard at some point and offered an opportunity for an assault, Sedgwick was to "attack him in full force and destroy him."[89]

THREE

MAY 1

FIRST DAY OF BATTLE

Banks' Ford, a shallow-streambed crossing, was not suitable for the rapid passage of troops, but an antebellum ferry landing just downstream was an excellent place for a pontoon bridge. Confederate pickets kept watch along a three-mile line beginning near Banks' Dam, extending around a deep bend in the river, and ending at Fall Hill, overlooking Fredericksburg. During the night, they heard the rumble of iron-bound wheels on the north side of the river. Federal engineers were staging pontoons and bridging material, but the Southerners thought the noise might be from wagons and artillery.[1]

The Confederates had dug extensive earthworks and adapted some of them to provide shelter. On the lower slope, where the sun reaches only briefly, they created roughly ten-by-ten-foot spaces in the rear of the trench that could be covered to provide protection from foul weather. While on picket, those sheltered places allowed soldiers to get warm as they rotated between vigilance and rest.[2]

Military trenches were not the only earthworks around Banks' Ford. Gold had been discovered in Spotsylvania County in 1806, and the antebellum years saw mining operations throughout the area. To get at the precious metal, miners dug into the quartz veins, creating trenches long before the armies arrived. Extracting gold from the quartz was a laborious process that required heavy equipment and scores of laborers. Related infrastructure included a road network as well as a navigation canal.[3]

The Rappahannock Navigation had not been constructed as a continuous waterway like the Chesapeake and Ohio Canal. Instead, a series of stone-and-timber dams created slack water ponds for boat passage. Connecting canal sections fed by those reservoirs carried boats around the unnavigable parts of the river. Between Banks' Ford and Fredericksburg, there were two sections of the river flooded by dams.[4]

Wilcox's Brigade guarded Banks' Ford. Cadmus Marcellus Wilcox, West Point class of 1846, had entered Confederate service as colonel of the Ninth Alabama Infantry. Within a few months, he was a brigadier general in command of a brigade. He fought well on the Peninsula and in the subsequent battles that took the Army of Northern Virginia to Maryland and back. The competent Wilcox remained in brigade command, however, while West Point classmates such as Jackson and Pickett led a corps and a division, respectively. Lee may have held Wilcox back for missteps as an acting division commander at Second Manassas, when two brigades under his temporary command had not been effective during an attack on the Federal flank.[5]

At Fredericksburg a heavy fog obscured visibility along the river, although its moisture carried farther the noise of soldiers in motion. On May 1 moonset occurred at 3:41 A.M., and the sun would not break the horizon until 5:14 A.M. The Confederate forces slated to reinforce Major General Anderson pulled away under cover of darkness. Federal units holding the bridgehead formed in line of battle after the moon disappeared and remained in that posture of readiness until 6:00 A.M., listening to the slight rumble of wagons and artillery and the occasional clanking of equipment. The troops relaxed slightly when no dawn attack occurred but remained vigilant.[6]

When the fog lifted, the opposing lines got a good look at one another. The Federals could see that the Confederate lines were thinner. The Southerners noticed that Union pickets were closer than the day before. One of those units had moved up too far. Sent forward for picket duty, the Seventy-Sixth New York cautiously pushed out in the darkness. When the fog dissipated, the men found themselves "within a few rods of the rebel army!" The New Yorkers fell flat as the Confederates unleashed a volley and would spend an uncomfortable day sheltering in shallow folds of ground or in whatever holes they could dig without getting themselves killed.[7]

On the cusp of battle, the army command addressed its intermittent electrical communications. Experienced US Military Telegraph (USMT) operators with strong lead-acid batteries replaced army signalmen with hand-cranked Beardslee magnetos. Worn-out connecting wires, however, remained a weak link.[8]

Replacements were coming. As Federal units deployed in the fog and darkness, six signal officers arrived in Falmouth. They had with them a detachment of signalmen and fifteen miles of new communications wire. Capt. Samuel T. Cushing informed the Falmouth headquarters that the coveted men and materiel were on hand, and Major General Butterfield gave verbal instructions for the entire detachment to proceed to Chancellorsville, where they were to report to Capt. Benjamin F. Fisher.[9]

Directing all the signal wire to Chancellorsville reveals that Butterfield did not really understand Hooker's plan to uncover Banks' Ford. The US Ford crossing, with its circuitous and poor approach road, was not supposed to have been anything more than a temporary link as the flanking columns tramped across Spotsylvania County. At the Falmouth headquarters, however, telegraph reliability had superseded the Union army's hard-won freedom of movement. Cushing suggested that some of the newly arrived signal assets be sent to Banks' Ford. Butterfield acquiesced, sending five miles of wire to Chancellorsville and another five miles to Banks' Ford while holding the remaining wire at Falmouth.[10]

But Cushing had second thoughts about keeping the reserve group of signalmen and the last five miles of critically needed wire at headquarters. He thought the additional signal teams would be more useful backing up the USMT detachment at Banks' Ford as the battle developed south of the river. Later that morning, the captain directed Lt. Ephraim A. Briggs and Lt. Isaac S. Lyon to take the remaining men and equipment to Banks' Ford.[11]

While Cushing sorted out signals assets, Butterfield became confused about how Brigadier General Gibbon's division was to deploy. The four Pennsylvania regiments of Brigadier General Owen's Philadelphia Brigade had helped move pontoons to Banks' Ford the night before, but Butterfield directed that three of the four regiments return to Falmouth. Owen directed Col. Dennis O'Kane to hold his Sixty-Ninth Pennsylvania Infantry at the crossing site.[12]

Signal delays and poor signal procedures hindered coordination. Hooker's dispatch to Butterfield indicated that Gibbon was to cross "tomorrow." The chief of staff, however, claimed not to know if "tomorrow" meant May

1 or May 2. He suspected that the directive from Hooker called for Gibbon to be ready to cross the river by 9:00 A.M. on the first, but he sought confirmation. Butterfield's focus on telegraph communications through US Ford had distracted him from helping maintain the momentum of the flank march. The confusion had still not been clarified when the Sixty-Ninth Pennsylvania at Banks' Ford and the three regiments waiting at Falmouth heard heavy firing upriver.[13]

Hooker's secretiveness about his operational plans relegated Butterfield to operating the Falmouth headquarters as a message-relay center rather than an integral part of a leadership team directing a campaign. The chief of staff compounded his slide toward ineffectiveness by passing along rumors and speculation. At 5:30 A.M. Butterfield informed Hooker that a deserter revealed Jackson's Corps to be waiting at Fredericksburg. He also relayed intercepted Confederate camp gossip that Longstreet had arrived in Culpeper. Both observations were inaccurate.[14]

Hooker had an intelligence team that evaluated new information. The day before, Col. George H. Sharpe had interrogated prisoners captured at Fredericksburg, probing for details that might corroborate information from other sources. Sharpe first learned there were no reinforcements coming from Richmond, consistent with messages from Union forces at Suffolk. Longstreet had *not* departed from southeast Virginia. Sharpe also noted that the Confederate infantry had not seen their artillery arrive from its winter camps.[15]

As Butterfield tried to keep Hooker informed that morning, the army commander explained his orders to Sedgwick. On April 28, prior to the river assault, Hooker had directed his wing commander to pursue any retreating Confederates down the Bowling Green Road as well as the Telegraph Road. The problem was that these two roads headed in different directions. On May 1 Hooker clarified those three-day-old instructions by having Butterfield relay to Sedgwick that he was "to throw [his] whole force on the Bowling Green Road and no other." About twenty minutes later the chief of staff sent another dispatch to ensure Sedgwick understood that the previous telegram had been sent in response to his query.[16]

As it happened, Sedgwick did not receive that explanation until early afternoon. Both Hooker and Butterfield were busy sending messages, but they were talking past one another. By the time Sedgwick received the morning message at 1:00 P.M., Hooker had run into Stonewall Jackson's Confederates on the Orange Turnpike, which changed everything.[17]

Around 8:30 A.M. at Fredericksburg, Federal signalmen saw Southern troops in motion. Looking at the artillery in the columns, they saw that some of the guns were being pulled by eight horses. But four pairs of animals hauling a single weapon did not indicate a large gun, as Confederate equines had not yet regained their strength from fresh grass after a season of poor winter feed. Capt. James S. Hall had a powerful telescope at the Phillips house, and through an opening in the hilly terrain, he saw bayonets and the tops of wagons on the Plank Road near the Guest and Downman houses. Those dwellings were prominent landmarks on the high ground that Hooker was supposed to reach that afternoon.[18]

Hall deduced that the Confederates had been on the march long before they became visible through the haze. After careful observation he reported two Confederate corps in motion, accompanied by artillery. Butterfield, however, informed Hooker that no more than 10,000–15,000 Confederates had been seen since the fog cleared, ignoring the hours of obscured visibility. Hall noted that the reported forces had passed his point of observation by 11:30 A.M., headed toward the fighting that had erupted to the west.[19]

Anderson had marshaled three brigades at Chancellorsville but pulled them back out of the woods. On more defensible open terrain, they had dug a line of rifle pits around a dilapidated wooden church with the name of Zoan. Before the war, a small group of congregants had embraced temperance as a moral imperative and split from Salem Church, two miles to the east. The new church had clearly struggled. A Confederate soldier noted that "its boards were paintless, weather-beaten, storm-stained, and its shingles wore the moss of age."[20]

Around 5:00 A.M. on May 1, twenty-four hours after Confederate soldiers began turning dirt, McLaws arrived from Fredericksburg with three of his brigades. The laboring soldiers welcomed reinforcements, but Confederate artillery had yet to arrive. Not until around 8:00 A.M. did Colonel Alexander see his battalion coming up on a road south of the Orange Turnpike. With artillery on hand, the line could be held.[21]

A sense of anticipation rippled through the Confederate formations when Stonewall Jackson arrived. Lee's second in command had left Fredericksburg around 3:00 A.M. with three divisions. His columns stretched back to the town, but his lead division, combined with Anderson's and McLaws's Divisions, were enough men to press forward and spoil a Federal advance from the west.[22]

"Immediately we knew that all our care & preparation at that point was work thrown away," Alexander later wrote. "We were not going to wait for the enemy to come & attack us in those lines, we were going out . . . after him." Amid those preparations, Jackson also directed Anderson to call in Wilcox's Brigade from Banks' Ford and Brig. Gen. E. A. Perry's Brigade from Falmouth. They were to proceed to the Orange Turnpike, where soldiers were turning in their entrenching tools and beginning to check weapons and ammunition.[23]

Around 10:30 A.M. elements of Anderson's Division pushed west on the turnpike. Scattered small-arms fire erupted as the advance units ran into the Eighth Pennsylvania Cavalry, which had probed the Confederate line the day before. As the attack developed, Lee rode up from Fredericksburg and met with Jackson. Unlike Hooker, the Confederate commanders were looking to shape the unfolding events to their advantage and had 48,000 troops hustling to get within striking distance of the advancing Federals.[24]

At Chancellorsville the Federal flanking force had grown to a powerful 72,000 men and thirty-one batteries. Their objective was to control the high ground west of Fredericksburg. With Union forces about to consolidate at Fredericksburg, other elements of the Army of the Potomac began to execute their own parts of Hooker's plan. Chief Quartermaster Ingalls alerted Col. William W. Wright, superintendent of the US Military Railroad, to be ready "on short notice" to begin rebuilding the railroad bridge across the Rappahannock River. Banks' Ford would support the flank columns, but Fredericksburg would become the principal route for meeting the army's logistics needs.[25]

Hooker had assured Sedgwick that the flanking forces would be on the Fredericksburg heights by 2:00 P.M. but then casually waited at Chancellorsville for the Third Corps to cross the river at US Ford. He finally pushed forward around 10:30 A.M., deploying two corps in three columns. The trees would initially hinder communications, but the Federals pushing forward on three parallel roads would be able to link up when they were in open country. Major General Slocum headed east on the Orange Plank Road with two of his Twelfth Corps divisions, a force of 13,400 men. Two of Meade's Fifth Corps divisions, numbering 13,450 men, took River Road toward Banks' Ford. The third Fifth Corps division, under Major General George Sykes and numbering 5,000 men, followed the Orange Turnpike.[26]

Hooker had been informed of the Confederate earthworks on a ridge not quite four miles to the east. Delaying his advance to wait for the Third Corps, however, assumed that his adversary would wait for him there. The modest force he sent against an entrenched position on the Turnpike also suggests that Hooker anticipated that his forces to the north and south of Sykes would outflank the Confederate works and cause the defenders to pull back. The combined Union advance consisted of just 32,000 men and a handful of batteries with twenty-six guns. The Federals had squandered several hours of daylight waiting for reinforcements, and an overconfident Hooker then moved forward with only half of his available strength.[27]

The Federals at Chancellorsville occupied a wilderness of dense secondary growth, the consequence of a colonial-era iron industry. A single ton of raw iron required approximately five cords of wood smoldered into charcoal. The iron enterprise consumed thousands upon thousands of trees to produce thousands of tons of pig iron. Year after year, with virtually all organic matter getting burned up in furnaces instead of replenishing the soil, Spotsylvania County devolved into a sterile landscape where vegetation struggled to reestablish itself. By the time of the Civil War, a huge swath of Spotsylvania County had become a snarled woodland that had come to be called the Wilderness. Hooker's dithering risked having to do battle in the stunted growth.[28]

On the Orange Turnpike Sykes got his division into open ground. To the south on the Plank Road, Slocum's advance fell behind in the dense woods, leaving Sykes's right flank uncovered. North of the Turnpike Meade's two divisions followed River Road, which swung away to the north and thus put them beyond supporting distance of Sykes's Regulars. Aggressive Confederate infantry barreled down on the smallest of the three Federal columns.[29]

As fighting erupted on the Turnpike, Jackson saw the opportunity for a flank attack. He directed a brigade to engage and hold Sykes while he pushed two other brigades against Slocum on the Plank Road. After running into the Twelfth Corps, Jackson saw a way to develop yet another surprise attack on the Union right. In the 1830s a railroad company had cleared and graded portions of a thirty-mile route from Fredericksburg to a community called Orange. This cleared roadbed extended through the Wilderness trees, conveniently providing a level, unobstructed route unknown to the advancing Union forces. Jackson diverted a brigade to this unfinished railway to get in behind Slocum.[30]

From the vantage point of a balloon at Banks' Ford, Aeronaut Ezra S. Allen saw Confederate columns moving west. Wilcox's Alabama regiments could see the Union observers aloft but not what they were observing. Rumors had spread through the camps that the Yankees had crossed the river upstream, and now the Alabamans heard fighting on the Orange Turnpike. As the sounds of battle drifted through the trees, Anderson's orders arrived directing them to join the fight.[31]

Combat on the Turnpike moved back and forth across modest farmsteads. Jackson's brigades continued to come up from Fredericksburg and deployed both north and south of the main road. Perry's small brigade arrived from Falmouth and extended the Confederate line toward River Road. When Wilcox arrived, McLaws directed him to take position on Perry's right, effectively fronting the gap between Meade and Sykes.[32]

Without anyone except Confederates to his right and left, Sykes needed help. Brigadier General Warren, who had accompanied the attack formations, rode back to Chancellorsville to seek reinforcements. At headquarters, though, Hooker remained comfortably connected by telegraph to his rear echelons and did not exert himself to venture toward the battle. To compound his isolation, the Federal commander would not let anyone exercise initiative at the point of contact.[33]

When Warren reported that Sykes needed assistance, the army commander decided to end the confrontation. Couriers galloped toward all three of the Federal columns with orders to break contact and withdraw. On the Plank Road, Slocum pulled back reluctantly, unknowingly thwarting the Confederate forces looking to outflank him by way of the unfinished railway. On River Road, Meade's vanguard had Banks' Ford in view and could see an observation balloon in the air, indicating a friendly presence on the north side of the river. The sound of gunfire, however, suggested a need to respond quickly, so Meade turned his column around and left Banks' Ford under Confederate control.[34]

Hooker sent a division from Maj. Gen. Winfield Scott Hancock's Second Corps to the Turnpike to help extricate Sykes. Hancock, accompanying the division, established a strong line on a ridge where Union artillery would be able to dominate the rolling open ground. Holding such favorable position, Hancock, Warren, and Sykes thought it a mistake to abandon the advance. They had plenty of daylight to adapt to Confederate moves, and with a few more troops and artillery, their position could be consolidated to give Hooker tactical options. The army commander, however, did not ride out to examine the ground before insisting that his orders to withdraw were peremptory. A disgusted Meade exclaimed, "My God, if we can't hold the top of a hill, we certainly can't hold the bottom of it."[35]

It did not take long for the Confederates to realize they were receiving an astonishing gift of terrain. Alexander remembered: "In about two miles of Chancellorsville, we got into an extensive open country & at the far side of it we saw a great display of Hooker's force, & I brought up more guns, & more infantry was deployed, which we move moved steadily forward towards them. But they soon began to disappear in the woods & we recognized that they were being withdrawn."[36]

Upon reflection, Hooker directed his second in command, Second Corps commander Maj. Gen. Darius Couch, to hold his position until 5:00 P.M. The army commander may have wanted more time to consider his next move, but Couch sent back word that the withdrawal had moved too far along to be reversed. The powerful Union force south of the Rappahannock River and west of Fredericksburg held every advantage in men and materiel, but the bold flank march of more than sixty miles across two rivers fell apart in the early afternoon of May 1 when the Potomac Army's commander hesitated to fight.[37]

Hooker had established the US Ford crossing to consolidate his forces before pushing toward Fredericksburg, knowing there was no other way across the Rappahannock River until he reached Banks' Ford. With a usable crossing at his back, however, Hooker too quickly decided to fight a defensive battle where he was—tangled woodlands of no strategic value. The army's quartermasters had given his columns the capability to operate for eight days without resupply. Only four of those days had been used up by May 1, theoretically leaving four more days to get to Banks' Ford and Fredericksburg. Yet by holding the Army of the Potomac at Chancellorsville, Hooker ceded control of the battle.

The troops at Fredericksburg "heard the first shots come rumbling down the river." If Hooker's plan held, he would be on the high ground west of Fredericksburg in a few hours. Yet with the Third, Fifth, Eleventh, and Twelfth Corps, plus two divisions of the Second Corps at his disposal, the Union commander hesitated. At 2:00 P.M. Hooker informed Butterfield that, due to the nature of the intelligence received at Chancellorsville, he had suspended his attacks. He added that Sedgwick was to "keep a sharp lookout, and attack if it can succeed." The "intelligence" appears to have been the reports from Fredericksburg of Confederates headed west.[38]

When Union forces ran into opposition on the Orange Turnpike, Hooker directed General Hunt, then at Chancellorsville, to prevent a Confederate incursion into his rear by way of Banks' Ford. Hunt immediately ordered Lt. Albert Brooker to take his heavy 4.5-inch rifled weapons of Battery B, First Connecticut Artillery back to his former position at Banks' Ford. From US Ford Hunt wired Butterfield to send him another twenty-two guns from the reserve batteries at White Oak Church as well as two batteries of field guns. If 12-pounder Napoleons were not available from the Artillery Reserve, then two batteries of 3-inch Ordnance Rifles from Sedgwick would do, if he could spare them.[39]

Some of the batteries at the Fredericksburg crossings became part of this redeployment. Capt. Patrick Hart's Fifteenth New York Independent Light Artillery pulled out of the line at Travellers Rest and headed toward Banks' Ford. Capt. Frank P. Amsden's Battery G, First Pennsylvania Light Artillery took their place, but General Reynolds had asked that heavier guns be made available to him after the Confederate artillery had so thoroughly embarrassed him the day before. Hunt now responded by sending the six 20-pounder Parrott rifles of Lt. Gustav von Blucher's Twenty-Ninth New York Independent Light Artillery to Travellers Rest.[40]

Most of the batteries making their way to Banks' Ford that evening consisted of 3-inch Ordnance Rifles. Lt. Robert Clarke's Battery M, Second US Artillery was an unusual ten-gun battery. Lt. Lorenzo Thomas Jr.'s Battery K, First US Artillery had the more standard six weapons. Hart's Fifteenth New York Artillery was on the road as was Lt. Henry Meinell's Battery C, Third US Artillery. Lt. David H. Kinzie's Battery K, Fifth US Artillery would bring up its 12-pounder Napoleons, the requested field guns.[41]

Supporting infantry was also needed at Banks' Ford, but getting Owen's Philadelphia Brigade there had become a painful lesson in miscommunication. The four regiments had helped move pontoon trains to that area the night before, but only the Sixty-Ninth Pennsylvania had remained behind, with the others returning to Falmouth to retrieve their knapsacks. The 106th Pennsylvania had then marched back to relieve the Sixty-Ninth to allow the men to return and retrieve their gear. On the morning of May 1, the Seventy-Second Pennsylvania had relieved the 106th. The regiments were moving back and forth instead of remaining and occupying Banks' Ford at full strength.[42]

Around midmorning Lee returned to Fredericksburg and met with Pendleton on Lee's Hill. While discussing artillery dispositions, he informed his artillery chief that two US Navy gunboats were reported to have steamed up the Rappahannock River to Port Royal. Lee asked Pendleton to send a battery there, and Lt. Col. Allen S. Cutts detached Capt. Hugh M. Ross's Battery A, Sumter Artillery to confront the waterborne intruders with its 10-pounder Parrott rifles.[43]

Lt. Col. R. Snowden Andrews had charge of the batteries deployed south of Deep Run. Captain Graham's Rockbridge Artillery already occupied the south end of Andrews's line with four Parrott rifles. Across Massaponax Creek, Lieutenant Tullis still had a Whitworth rifle in battery. Capt. William D. Brown brought the Fourth Maryland Battery, known as the Chesapeake Artillery, from the artillery park at Massaponax Church to the existing gun pits on Prospect Hill. When the fog dissipated, one of the Marylanders noted what "a splendid position it is." About a quarter mile south of the Hamilton's Crossing–Prospect Hill area, Capt. Joseph Carpenter placed his Alleghany Artillery into battery.[44]

Federal signalmen had reported earthworks under construction between Prospect Hill and Deep Run, about two hundred yards behind the railway. Maj. Joseph W. Latimer had charge of two batteries in that area. Latimer's units consisted of Capt. William Dement's First Maryland Battery and Capt. Charles J. Raine's Lee Battery. From his experience in December, the major knew the position to be exposed and ordered works dug behind the battery line to protect the limbers and horses from incoming rounds.[45]

Pendleton was responsible for the batteries north of Deep Run. Captain Carlton had three 10-pounder Parrott rifles in his Troup Artillery. He placed two of them on a hill overlooking Deep Run and directed the third weapon into earthworks behind Braehead, a Greek Revival mansion built in 1859 by John Howison. He held his fourth weapon, a 12-pounder howitzer with limited range, in reserve. Capt. George M. Patterson positioned three 12-pounder field guns of his Battery B, Sumter Battalion on Howison Hill as well. Extending toward the Telegraph Road (modern Lafayette Boulevard) was Lee's Hill, where Capt. John C. Fraser and his Pulaski Battery had been in place for several days with three rifled weapons.[46]

There was additional artillery on Marye's Heights. Two 10-pounder Parrott rifles occupied gun pits on Willis Hill, just north of the Telegraph Road. That section came from Capt. Andrew B. Rhett's South Carolina battery. They had been left behind on outpost duty at Fredericksburg when the rest of Alexander's Battalion had gone into winter quarters at Carmel Church. Detached duty is made difficult without a unit's usual logistics and administrative support, and Rhett made things worse by absenting himself more often than he saw to the welfare of his troops.[47]

By spring, the readiness of Rhett's section had deteriorated to the point that Colonel Alexander wanted to get rid of the underperforming captain. General Pendleton had avoided that decisive remedy until the morning of May 1. With battle imminent near Zoan Church, he directed Alexander to detach the personnel from a section in Capt. William Parker's Richmond Battery and send them back to man Rhett's two guns on Marye's Heights. Alexander sent Lt. J. Thompson Brown Jr. and thirty men to Fredericksburg. The Virginia artillerymen arrived on Willis Hill at 10:00 A.M. Rhett was not happy about being relieved but relinquished his weapons without argument.[48]

Major General Early remained anxious about his artillery. He was left to hold a line with a severely diminished force, and the Washington Artillery had yet to arrive. That famous battalion had been built around a state militia battery organized in New Orleans in 1838. It mustered into Confederate service as a trained, battle-ready unit and had fought in many engagements since First Manassas. Its several batteries were going to be a welcome addition to the Fredericksburg defenses—if only they would show up.[49]

Early appreciated that Marye's Heights should be properly manned but thought the Federals opposite Prospect Hill posed a more serious threat. Since Cutts had sent his Parrott rifles to Port Royal, Early made sure Pendleton understood that Andrews was now short a battery. When Col. James B. Walton finally turned up with his Washington Artillery, Pendleton directed him to send four Napoleons to Early's far right. The Louisiana officer detached Capt. John M. Richardson's battery, but the tired horses, without any opportunity to rest after their extended time on the road, moved slowly in hauling their guns farther. Richardson did not report to Andrews until 11:00 P.M. that night. The rest of the Washington Artillery would spread out across Marye's Heights the next morning.[50]

Federal signalmen had observed and reported on Confederate activity all day. In the morning they saw strong columns of infantry headed west. Later they watched enemy soldiers constructing earthworks and rifle pits. Finally the observers reported artillery being moved into place. One of the late arrivals was the Fluvanna Artillery of Lt. Col. William Nelson's battalion. This battery, led by Capt. John L. Massie, consisted of three 12-pounder Napoleons and one 3-inch Ordnance Rifle and took position in the Confederate center.[51]

As Hooker advanced his columns from Chancellorsville, he tried to coordinate the two wings of his army. In a message to Butterfield at 11:30 A.M., he asked that Sedgwick provide a demonstration "as severe as can be, but not an attack." When Confederates blocked his way and Hooker retreated, however, a demonstration by Sedgwick and Reynolds became meaningless. Yet neither general was informed that Hooker's plans were not unfolding as anticipated. They continued to wait for the army's main body to reach the heights behind Fredericksburg. Hooker's orders for a demonstration at 1:00 P.M., sent before noon, arrived at the Falmouth headquarters after 5:00 P.M. Sedgwick and Reynolds executed those orders immediately. The First Corps units formed up as if preparing for an advance. Major General Newton moved his Sixth Corps division downstream, making a show of reinforcing Wadsworth's division.[52]

At Franklin's Crossing Colonel Burnham's Light Division marched to the bridges, and crossed over. It moved up in support of Brooks's division, which was also giving the impression of an imminent advance. Some Confederate pickets pulled back, but others saw that no Federal wagons were in motion, unaware that the Union army's new supply standards allowed it to operate for several days without a wagon train. To them, since the Union army's late-afternoon activity did not include supply wagons coming across the bridges, it must not be a serious development.[53]

When the Federals did not advance beyond their own lines, the Confederates raised a shout of defiance. A Southern soldier described how the "yells would commence on one end of the line, and it would go as fast as men could hoop along the lines till it would reach the other end." The Federals noisily responded in kind. Another distraction added to the atmosphere of diminishing danger. Three horses got loose from the Union line and galloped into the open ground between the armies. Sgt. William L. Strickler caught one of the horses when it trotted into the Rockbridge Artillery's position. He named him "Sedgwick" and rode him for the rest of the war.[54]

At sunset the crossing sites became further removed from martial violence when musicians broke out their instruments. A Confederate band played "Yankee Doodle." A Federal band responded with "Dixie." To one Federal soldier the whole affair "was a strange sight and the sun going down at the moment made a deep impression on everyone." Another Confederate demonstration began, with Barksdale's Mississippians raising tents and lighting a great many fires to give the impression of a much larger force than was present. The Federals were not fooled. As night settled in, Confederate deserters scrambled across the lines to give themselves up to Union pickets.[55]

Butterfield had fired off a message to Hooker, confirming that the demonstration would proceed as ordered. At 8:45 P.M. the commander responded that the demonstration had come too late and that he had suspended his advance. He also informed his chief of staff that his flanking columns were establishing defenses with clear fields of fire. The Potomac Army's commander had clearly called it a day.[56]

The Federal command had become especially aggravated by the delayed telegraph communications. The problem remained worn-out wires, but inattentive troops were also clumsily damaging the lines without realizing it. Col. Francis E. Heath received orders for his Nineteenth Maine Infantry to post guards along the telegraph wires from Falmouth to Banks' Ford and then up to US Ford. His instructions bluntly directed him to shoot anyone damaging the wires. Heath marched out at 9:00 P.M. and left small detachments at intervals along six miles of communications line before going into bivouac. His unit would resume its task at first light. Butterfield reassured Hooker that he had placed "patrols on the telegraph lines, with directions to put to death instantly any person found tampering or interfering with them at all."[57]

The telegraph between Falmouth and Banks' Ford did not have as many issues as the link to the distant US Ford station. Consequently, Hunt was able to contact Butterfield without incident when he arrived at Banks' Ford that evening. The artilleryman asked that several batteries be sent to that crossing from the Artillery Reserve as well as from the Sixth Corps if they could be spared. He also reminded the chief of staff that he had only six hundred of Brigadier General Benham's engineers on hand because Owen's brigade was still in Falmouth. Butterfield's indecision had kept the Philadelphia infantry from getting on the road until 10:00 P.M.[58]

Despite Hooker's concern, Hunt did not think he faced any immediate danger. The Confederates more likely feared an attack rather than planned to make one. By morning the Philadelphia Brigade would finally be on hand to support a total of thirty-four Union guns. The pontoon train remained in park, the USMT team had been assigned to that location, and new communications wire would soon be available. Everything appeared to be coming together at what was supposed to become the Union army's primary river crossing.[59]

At Fredericksburg not all was well with Gibbon's division, from which the Philadelphia Brigade had come. The Thirty-Fourth New York Infantry, two-year men whose term of service would expire in June, had refused to march on April 30. A disgusted Gibbon relieved the brigade commander, Brig. Gen. Alfred Sully, for being unable to enforce discipline. Gibbon personally got the mutinous New York men to reconsider their actions by deploying the veteran Fifteenth Massachusetts around them and letting them know he would have them shot dead if they refused to follow orders. The New Yorkers were convinced to return to duty, but the affair did not end there.[60]

Sully requested that a court of inquiry review his actions. After the campaign a group of three general officers convened for that purpose. The episode suggests a failure of regimental leadership, which the court appears to have realized. Acknowledging that Sully had been unsure of his authority under those unusual circumstances, the tribunal exonerated him. The army then sent him west to fight Native Americans on the Great Plains. But for the time being at Fredericksburg, Col. Henry W. Hudson of the Eighty-Second New York Regiment assumed brigade command.[61]

Back on the Orange Turnpike and Orange Plank Road, Southern forces had moved up after the Federals pulled back. On the Confederate far right were Wilcox's Alabamans. One of them wrote the following in his diary: "Have had us trotting around pretty well all day, and I can't see the beauty in being a reinforcing brigade." At 10:00 P.M. orders came for the brigade to move back to the Turnpike, and three and a half hours later they had worked their way out of the trees and taken position behind the line facing west. Someone must have realized that perhaps Banks' Ford ought to be reoccupied, because Wilcox then received new orders to return there and "hold it at all hazards."[62]

The tired Alabamans were five miles from that crossing. Marching on the Turnpike, they could see where they were going under the remaining bit of moonlight. The trek became more tiresome when the column had to take a lesser road to get back to the river. After the moon had set and before the sun rose, the tired Southerners stumbled along in total darkness. The Ninth Alabama had the farthest to go to get back to its old position at Dr. Taylor's home (Fall Hill). Its men lay down to sleep when they got reasonably close, then climbed the hill in the morning. At daylight Wilcox's units filed into their old lines, exhausted but positioned where the Confederate command wanted them to be.[63]

FOUR

MAY 2

SECOND DAY OF BATTLE

"There was hard fighting up the river yesterday," observed a New York soldier at the Fredericksburg bridgehead. He and his comrades knew little else. A Vermont soldier noted how the "roar of artillery at the west of Fredericksburg told us that there was a great battle being fought at Chancellorsville, and our anxiety to know the result grew more and more as the day went away."[1]

The night before, Hooker had taken up a position that Lee described as "remarkably favorable." From the Chancellorsville crossroads, the Federal left extended to the Rappahannock River. The Union right extended west along the elevated corridor of the Orange Turnpike. To confront the gathering Federal host, Lee had five divisions. After the fighting ended on May 1, he had directed Early to join him if he thought he could diminish his force at Fredericksburg without undue risk.[2]

In a grove of trees south of the Orange Turnpike, Lee and Jackson considered ways to overcome the Federal advantage in manpower and position. They waited while Stuart's cavalry probed the Union line. From south of the Turnpike, Confederate horse soldiers pushed their way toward the probable location of the Union line until pickets fired from the darkness. They repeated these rapid probes down the line. Maj. Gen. Oliver O. Howard called it "'a rolling reconnaissance,' evidently to determine . . . the position of our flank."[3]

Stuart eventually reported that the Union right extended as far west as Wilderness Church. The Southern command knew the terrain in that sector to be less severe than on the Union left. Furthermore, the Union army might not anticipate an attack so far from where the fighting had ended on May 1. The challenge would be to get enough strength into position to make the effort.[4]

Both Lee and Jackson were determined to attack and came up with a daring plan. Jackson would march west with his entire corps, fully 31,700 men and 112 guns, to get around the Union flank. Lee would remain with McLaws's and Anderson's Divisions, a force of less than 15,000 men with 24 guns, to hold the Federals' attention.[5]

While the Confederates split their forces, Hooker continued to concentrate his. The three corps in the flanking columns had been joined at Chancellorsville by the Third Corps and two divisions of the Second Corps. At 1:55 A.M. the Federal commander directed the First Corps to march from Fredericksburg to Chancellorsville as well. The worn-out telegraph wires had yet to be replaced, though, and those orders became delayed for several hours.[6]

Hooker held a strong position with a strong army and gained another advantage when he learned the size of his adversary's force. Colonel Sharpe, his deputy provost marshal, had a spy in Richmond who confirmed that rations for 59,000 men had been assembled for Lee's army. Whether Hooker would use such good intelligence to advantage remained to be seen.[7]

Jackson and his veterans were used to marching well before dawn, but on May 2 sunrise found the Confederates still waiting to depart. As they formed up around 5:15 A.M., Confederate artillery on the Orange Turnpike opened a probing fire, to which two Union batteries responded. Artillery rounds crashed through the woods for approximately an hour. Two long hours after sunrise, Jackson reined up at Lee's bivouac. The two warriors chatted briefly before Jackson rode on with his hustling foot soldiers.[8]

The two wings of the Confederate army became widely separated, but the two generals coordinated all day through couriers. Lee probed the Federal line in his front to give the impression of an imminent attack, keeping Hooker's attention focused on the road to Fredericksburg. Both he and Jackson fed troops into a fight that developed at the Catherine Furnace, which further distracted Hooker. Jackson sent Lee a brief report when he was nearly in position, and in a final show of trust and coordination, Lee opened his own attack when he heard Jackson's guns.

The Federal crossing at Banks' Ford had yet to be established. Chief Engineer Benham had joined his bridge builders on the uplands during the night. Just before sunup a signal team reported to him with miles of new telegraph wire. The signal troops and bridge builders could do little more than stand by, though, because the Federal advance had come to a halt. A signal officer explained that their goal "was to open communication with the advance forces of General Hooker when he should succeed in driving the enemy down the river. This object was not effected, by reason of our forces under General Hooker not advancing as was anticipated."[9]

While waiting for Banks' Ford to be uncovered, signal detachments unspooled the rolls of new wire to replace the worn-out connection to Falmouth. A crew also ran a line from the uplands down to Scott's Ferry. Downstream from Fredericksburg, flag stations continued to keep all components of the left wing in close contact, and a detachment of flag signalmen waited at Banks' Ford to integrate a new station into that functioning network.[10]

Around 6:00 A.M. General Owen's Pennsylvania regiments finally arrived at the crossing. A bemused observer noted that the single brigade was a painfully small command to be overseen by three general officers (Owen, Benham, and Hunt). Less amused were the Alabamans across the river. "Our stay in the ditches [trenches] was not at all comfortable," an uneasy soldier remembered. The Federal guns, "to all appearances, were capable of cleaning out the ditch that the Tenth Alabama Regiment occupied at one well directed shot." From about 5:15 to 6:30 A.M., artillery had been audible at Chancellorsville. Around 7:30 A.M. the troops at Banks' Ford heard artillery at Fredericksburg.[11]

At daybreak the First and Sixth Corps had three divisions south of the Rappahannock. The Third Corps had left the day before to join Hooker at Chancellorsville, and General Reynolds soon received orders to take his First Corps upriver as well. Once Reynolds departed, Hooker wanted Sedgwick to take up the three pontoon bridges below Fredericksburg, apparently forgetting that the Union forces at Fredericksburg held a bridgehead on the other side. Sedgwick recognized that if he abandoned the south shore, the Confederates being held in place at Fredericksburg would be free to depart and reinforce Lee.[12]

Within the bridgehead, General Wadsworth received orders to withdraw around 7:00 A.M. Hooker had wanted that move to take place under cover of darkness, but his instructions to Reynolds were three hours in transmission and further delayed when the orderly carrying the message got lost. The two

First Corps divisions on the north side of the river moved off immediately, but Wadsworth's troops had to break contact and cross the river before getting on the road. A few regiments had crossed over the single pontoon bridge without incident when the Confederates opened fire.[13]

Early held the Fredericksburg line with his division plus Barksdale's Brigade. The weakened defense had been a calculated risk to gain advantage at Chancellorsville, but Early had standing instructions to join Lee if he could do so without endangering the town. The high riverbank screened the main Union force from view, so he decided to probe its lines with artillery. If the Federal response proved weak, he would detach two brigades and send them west.[14]

Early had already given instructions to Lieutenant Colonel Andrews for another bombardment on May 2. He also directed General Pendleton to open with his Parrott rifles "if there was anything within their range." As Pendleton rode off to see to these matters, he heard Confederate guns commence firing behind him. The reconnaissance by fire had begun, and it happened to coincide with the Union First Corps's withdrawal.[15]

Between 7:30 and 8:00 A.M., Captain Graham's Rockbridge Artillery and Captain Brown's Chesapeake Artillery on Prospect Hill blasted the Federals. Their heavy Parrott rifles, a total of six guns, ranged their fire across the lower bridgehead. To their left, Major Latimer directed Captain Raine to open fire with his two rifled weapons. The First Maryland Battery held position alongside Raine, but Captain Dement's 12-pounder Napoleons were not suitable for long-range work and remained silent.[16]

The Confederates could not see the single bridge at the Pollock's Mill crossing, as it was hidden by the river bluffs. By chance, an exploding round landed on one of the pontoons, killing or wounding several men. The regiment caught on the bridge stampeded across to get clear of the incoming fire. Federal engineers quickly floated another pontoon into place and repaired the slender escape route, but a concerned Reynolds thought to halt Wadsworth's withdrawal, worried it was now impractical in daylight. But the New Yorker prevailed upon his corps commander to allow the crossing to continue.[17]

Veteran troops at the Sixth Corps crossing could see and hear the Confederates directing their attention to the First Corps's sector. A Federal paymaster found himself with the Thirty-Sixth New York Infantry when the shooting began. He did not have the same practiced ear for the sounds of a battlefield as the veterans around him and thought it might be a good idea to get clear of the danger. Lt. Col. James J. Walsh, the regimental commander, thought otherwise. As guns boomed menacingly, he made sure that every one of his men received their pay before he let the nervous paymaster depart.[18]

The Thirty-Sixth New York, the men now with money in their pockets, was a two-year regiment due to be mustered out in July. While the actions of some of the two-year units caused concern about their reliability in battle, no one had any doubts about Walsh's Empire State troops. They had a well-regarded brigade commander, Col. William Browne, described as "a very firm officer and brave as a lion." Good brigade and regimental leadership had made the regiment a solid force.[19]

The artillery firing may have been distant, but the picket line unexpectedly came alive. After Burnham's Light Division crossed the river during the demonstration the day before, the Fifth Wisconsin had been moved up to the advance line. When artillery boomed across the landscape, a zealous soldier took a shot at his Southern counterparts, who responded with a volley. The Federals scrambled to dig their slight picket works deeper with spoons and tin plates. An unsympathetic soldier in the main line remarked, "there was not a shot fired until those Wisconsin fellows went out."[20]

While picket firing flared up in the Sixth Corps's sector, artillery fire continued at the lower crossing. Having been outgunned two days earlier, Colonel Wainwright, the First Corps's chief of artillery, had redeployed several batteries. On May 2 three of them responded "with much better effect than on the 30th ultimo." Still, the eight Confederate Parrott rifles, both 10- and 20-pounders, were powerful and well served. They concentrated much of their fire on six 3-inch Ordnance Rifles within the bridgehead, which belonged to Battery L, First New York Light Artillery, Capt. John A. Reynolds commanding.[21]

The Confederate guns fired slowly and deliberately for about an hour and a half. A New York artilleryman described the action: "Then crash came a ball, right in the midst of one of the limber teams, and down fell two horses, shot dead. Thicker and hotter the iron missiles came, plowing up the earth all about the battery, lodging in the earthworks in front of us, striking under the limbers, breaking an axletree and disabling a wheel, wounding horses, creating a panic among them, so that several times some of the teams came very near running away and dashing down the bank and into the river."[22]

Casualties mounted. An incoming round took off the legs of Pvt. Charles Carpenter and then struck the earth, throwing rocks and dirt into Pvt. John

Grogan's face, causing a severe wound and temporary blindness. Its kinetic energy far from spent, the projectile disabled two horses as it ricocheted to the other side of the river. Pvt. William E. James, one of the battery's ammunition carriers, felt a round scratch his neck as it whizzed past. The accompanying concussion knocked him off his feet. Pvt. Charles Husted, detailed to the battery from the 141st New York Infantry, had his arm shattered by an incoming round. From across the river General Reynolds remarked: "If that battery continues to stand such a fire, as it is receiving, it will stand anywhere."[23]

The Twenty-Ninth Battery, New York Light Artillery on Stafford Heights also brought the Confederates under fire. Wainwright reported how "Lieutenant Blucher did good service with his 20-pounders after he had ascertained the range and got his men quieted down." One of the Confederate guns had been forced to stop firing after about twenty-five rounds because of a sprung vent piece. From across the way the Union artillerymen concluded their fire had disabled it. The Federal guns kept shooting for another half hour to cover the withdrawing infantry.[24]

Battery L, First New York Light Artillery kept up its fire until Wadsworth's infantry had cleared the bridgehead, or around 10:00 A.M. An artilleryman later wrote, "We keep firing and then move off, one piece at a time, firing retiring and covering the infantry, until we are across the river." Federal engineers dismantled their floating bridge and pulled pontoons from the river but left boats on the south shore for the last men coming out. There were no trains on hand to haul the bridging equipment away, so the Ninety-Eighth and 102nd Pennsylvania helped the engineers remove the pontoons from the floodplain, stacking the material near the road.[25]

When skirmishers finally received orders to fall back, officers ran along the picket line to tell their men it was time to leave. The troops filtered back as rapidly as possible. Soldiers of the Twenty-Fourth Michigan remembered Lt. William R. Dodsley making sure every one of his men got out, becoming the last man to leave the collapsed bridgehead. At 11:05 A.M. Reynolds reported to Sedgwick that all of his troops were across and moving up the road to US Ford.[26]

Wadsworth's units passed near General Gibbon's headquarters near Falmouth. Gibbon had trained and led the First Corps's Iron Brigade through the summer and fall of 1862. Its members had their baptism by fire at Second Bull Run and had since proved themselves a consistently reliable formation. The western regiments and their old commander exchanged the greetings of men who have shared the experience of war and regarded each other as comrades and professionals.[27]

Butterfield thought that Reynolds might be able to shorten his march if he crossed the First Corps at Banks' Ford. That suggestion indicates a disturbing lack of knowledge about the upriver terrain. Following the chief of staff's advice, Reynolds rode to the crossing but found no bridges down, which was just as well. If the First Corps had crossed at Banks' Ford instead of US Ford, it would have found itself unable to join Hooker without fighting its way through the Confederate army.[28]

In Fredericksburg Pendleton met with Colonel Walton to finally place the guns of his Washington Artillery, deploying them along Marye's Heights to the left of the two guns manned by Lt. J. Thompson Brown's section of Parker's Richmond Battery. Capt. Charles W. Squires placed two 3-inch Ordnance Rifles in front of the Willis Cemetery. Lt. Andrew J. Hero brought two guns into battery in the redoubt just north of Hanover Street. On the north side of William Street, Lt. George E. Apps positioned two guns in existing gun pits. The additional earthworks extending along the ridge remained empty.[29]

Shortly after sunrise at Chancellorsville, Hooker rode out to inspect his lines. Sickles, newly arrived with his Third Corps, joined him at Hazel Grove. The Federal position looked strong, but confidence turned to concern when the two generals reached Howard's lines. The Eleventh Corps constituted the army's westernmost reach, but its line had not been anchored on any terrain feature, and there were few earthworks evident. Hooker directed Howard to correct those deficiencies but also knew that the First Corps would soon be on hand to bolster that flank. He did not realize that poor communications had delayed Reynolds's departure from Fredericksburg.[30]

When Hooker returned to Chancellorsville around 9:00 A.M., he learned that Confederate columns were visible south of his lines and moving west. He decided they were getting into position for an assault and instructed Howard to look to his flank. Hooker remained content to await an attack, but Sickles directed a battery to open fire and also sent a brigade toward the Catherine Furnace to harass the marching troops. Howard reassured headquarters that he was preparing to receive an attack, but Hooker had already witnessed his lax discipline and inattention and would have done well to check on those assertions. When Jackson's column reached the Orange Turnpike around 2:30 P.M., Federal attention remained focused on the fighting around the Catherine Furnace.[31]

Union forces confronting Jackson's rear guard near Catharine Furnace saw the Southern columns turn south. Sickles reported the Confederates to be in retreat, and Hooker concluded they were headed toward Orange Court House and Gordonsville. At 2:30 P.M. he directed his corps commanders to replenish their supplies and prepare to follow the retreating Southern army. At 4:00 P.M., while Jackson's divisions were spreading out in line of battle, Hooker ordered Howard to lend a brigade to support the fight at the Catherine Furnace.[32]

Hooker's initial instructions for the Eleventh Corps commander to prepare to receive an assault still stood when a courier then asked him to detach a brigade to support the Third Corps. Howard refused to give up his reserve force, but the subsequent orders to prepare for a pursuit indicated that the danger had passed. When Hooker's courier returned, a reassured Howard detached the requested brigade.[33]

While the Union army suffered from misdirection at Chancellorsville, the Confederate defense at Fredericksburg was thrown into disarray by a member of Lee's staff. Early's reconnaissance by fire that morning had been followed by Union forces withdrawing from a portion of their bridgehead. Barksdale joined Early and Pendleton on Lee's Hill to watch the First Corps divisions pass through Falmouth. Around 11:00 A.M. Col. Robert H. Chilton rode into this meeting and informed the generals that the Fredericksburg position had to be relinquished. Early's Division, less a brigade, and Barksdale's Brigade, less a regiment, were needed for the main battle developing to the west.[34]

Chilton insisted that Lee needed men but not the batteries so painstakingly brought to Fredericksburg. A good portion of the Reserve Artillery was to return to its winter camps, which had to have struck the gathered officers as lunacy. Chilton had been a professional soldier for a quarter of a century but not a very good one. He had handled his staff duties poorly on the Peninsula and does not appear to have improved much since. When his verbal orders were met with skepticism, the colonel pointed out that he had seen Union troops moving west on their way to reinforce Hooker. Early needed to pull his units out of the line and march them toward Lee as well.[35]

Early explained that when the Federals saw the Confederates abandoning their defensive works, they would surely depart to reinforce Hooker.

He further noted that his forces could hold more troops at Fredericksburg by remaining in place than they could actively engage if they were to join Lee. Displaying an acute lack of strategic acumen, Chilton ignored the general and said that the troops left behind should be instructed to hold for as long as possible and then retreat to Spotsylvania Court House. The Army of Northern Virginia could come back and retake Fredericksburg later. Lee's orders were peremptory.[36]

Early dutifully said he would comply with Lee's instructions and directed General Hays to remain at Fredericksburg with his Louisiana brigade. Barksdale would notify Col. Benjamin Humphreys that his Twenty-First Mississippi Regiment would also be staying behind. Around 2:00 P.M. Early rode off Lee's Hill to issue the orders that would put his units into motion. Barksdale left shortly thereafter to pull his Mississippi regiments out of the line and to see that the Twenty-First Mississippi deployed to cover their front. Pendleton remained at that central post to direct some of his batteries back to Chesterfield.[37]

Confederate forces began to pull away on the right, where the Federal First Corps no longer posed a threat. He directed Lieutenant Tullis to remove his Whitworth gun and report to Lt. Col. William Nelson of the Reserve Artillery. He sent Captain John B. Richardson's battery to join the rest of the Washington Artillery in Pendleton's sector. Lieutenant Colonel Andrews was to see that Graham and Brown pulled their Parrott rifles off Prospect Hill. Raine and Dement were also to prepare their batteries to pull away and follow Early's infantry west.[38]

North of Deep Run Pendleton kept just fifteen guns in position. He retained eight weapons on Marye's Heights, four on Lee's Hill, and three on Howison Hill. All other units pulled out of the line. He ordered the three batteries of Nelson's Battalion as well as Captain Rhett's South Carolina Battery to return to the rear. With horses somewhat recovered and without heavy rain to deteriorate the roads, by late afternoon those units were back in their old winter camps. They sat out the rest of the campaign there.[39]

Other batteries did not get away as quickly and did not go as far. Colonel Cabell noted that most artillery units withdrew only a few hundred yards to nearby Telegraph Road. From there they would be able to move back into the line if needed but could also retreat farther if the Union army broke through. Captain Carlton held his three Parrott rifles and one 12-pounder howitzer at the Leach house, where there was plenty of room for artillery units to assemble, replenish ammunition chests, and let their teams find fresh grass. A water pump could be seen from the road, so the Leach house was often called the "pump house." Farther south, Confederate forces also marshaled around a farmstead owned by the Cox family.[40]

Pendleton's fifteen guns would have only the Twenty-First Mississippi and Hays's Brigade for support. Humphreys had to deploy his few hundred men from the Ferneyhough house just south of Hazel Run, through the Fredericksburg riverfront, to the industrial buildings opposite Falmouth, and on to Fall Hill. On that prominent hilltop he linked up with the pickets from Wilcox's Brigade, which still held Banks' Ford.[41]

As Barksdale departed he gave advice to the man who already knew he was being left in a precarious position. "Watch your flanks," the general told Humphreys. "Hold the picket line as long as you can, then fall back along the Spotsylvania Court House Road, and hunt for your brigade." Col. William D. Holder of the Seventeenth Mississippi took a lighter approach, perhaps to bolster his friend's confidence with humor. In his relayed message Holder said: "Tell the Colonel farewell; the next time I hear from him will be from Johnson's Island," referring to a Union prisoner-of-war pen.[42]

Hays was a Mexican War veteran and a New Orleans lawyer. He was also a solid leader who could handle the nerve-wracking task he now faced. He moved the Sixth and Ninth Louisiana onto the heights behind Fredericksburg, giving some depth to the position held by the Mississippians. The Fifth and the Eighth Louisiana took position along the railway, from the area behind the Ferneyhough house to Prospect Hill. The Seventh Louisiana relieved the North Carolina skirmishers on the Bowling Green Road. Some of the Louisianans moved up to the Pratt house (Smithfield), where a broken wheel and some dead horses indicated the former position of a Federal battery.[43]

The troops the Louisiana men relieved were from Brig. Gen. Robert Hoke's brigade. The North Carolinians pulled back by 4:30 P.M. and reached the Plank Road "about dark," which would have been around 7:00 P.M. Early's other two brigades had also pulled out and headed west by that time. Barksdale's Brigade, however, was not an integral component of Early's Division, having been detached from McLaws's Division. Barksdale halted his Mississippians about two and a half miles out on the Plank Road, ostensibly to wait for some of his men to catch up. More likely he thought to minimize the incapable Chilton's error in misdirecting forces away from Fredericksburg.[44]

The Confederates tried to mask their activity but did not escape detection. Conditions were too windy for balloon observations, but signalmen with telescopes saw a great deal. They reported enemy artillery heading west and infantry pulling back. Gibbon also reported seeing Southern forces withdrawing. Butterfield passed on these observations to Hooker, which may have reinforced his belief that Lee had begun a retreat. The signal troops also received orders to upgrade the telegraph link between Banks' Ford and Chancellorsville, reflecting Hooker's diminished interest in using that crossing.[45]

Butterfield reminded his commander that the Fifth, Eleventh, and Twelfth Corps had consumed four days' worth of their field rations and that supply trains had been diverted from Banks' to US Ford. Convinced that the Confederate army had begun a retreat, Hooker issued orders for his army to replenish to eight days' rations and be ready for a pursuit in the morning.[46]

Pressing Lee's retreating army had become the Army of the Potomac's new objective. At 4:10 P.M. Hooker ordered Sedgwick to cross the river, capture Fredericksburg, and pursue the withdrawing Confederates. The Sixth Corps commander received these new instructions at 5:50 P.M. but still did not know in which direction he was to move. A few days earlier, when Hooker had claimed he would be on the heights west of Fredericksburg, his orders were to follow the Bowling Green Road. The commanding general had not executed his plan, though, and Sedgwick needed to know if he was to move west instead of south.[47]

Some historians have suggested that Sedgwick had lost some of his nerve after a horrific experience on the morning of September 17, 1862. Then in command of a division, he had been ordered to advance into the West Woods at Antietam. Without any proper reconnaissance beforehand, those hasty orders led to the loss of more than 2,000 men in a brutal fifteen-minute ordeal without discernible gain. Sedgwick had also been severely wounded that day.[48]

A commander must have confidence his orders will be vigorously executed, but experienced leaders try to avoid getting men killed through neglect or carelessness. A signal officer said of the Sixth Corps commander that "no representations would be sufficient to induce him to overlook an order." Sedgwick's caution in the spring of 1863, therefore, can be seen as a commander unwilling to waste lives executing poorly conceived instructions. Men under his command appreciated his thoughtful leadership and defended his professionalism.[49]

Compounding poorly written orders, Fredericksburg remained a place where the terrain stymied military maneuvering. Federals advancing across the open ground had to move away from their artillery support and into the teeth of Confederate guns. No one had orders to drive the Southerners from their main line, but seizing the Bowling Green Road, with its sheltering embankments, was a logical first step. The Confederate withdrawal on May 2 broke the rough equilibrium that had held since the river crossing on April 29.[50]

Colonel Burnham, commanding the Light Division, ordered Col. Frank Jones to probe the Confederate position with his Thirty-First New York. The Federals moved up the Deep Run ravine and swiftly cracked the picket line of the Seventh Louisiana. On the New Yorkers' left the Sixth Maine, Fifth Wisconsin, and Sixty-First Pennsylvania expanded the lodgment toward Mannsfield. The Seventh Louisiana fought back, but the Light Division rushing its line was too much. Federal casualties were eight men wounded. A New York soldier exulted that they had finally been able "to obtain possession of a road that had served as a shelter for the enemy for some days."[51]

Brigadier General Brooks also advanced his division. A Pennsylvania soldier wrote how they welcomed orders for "the whole line to advance and drive the 'Rebs' into their rifle pits." Once on the Bowling Green Road, the Federals pushed pickets out to the slightly elevated ground to control the terrain overlooking the Confederate position along the railway. Behind them "the remainder of the corps immediately began to cross the river."[52]

Officers of the Twenty-First Mississippi observed the Federal advance from the upper floor of the Ferneyhough house. They sent a report back to Humphreys, who had his own vantage point in the cupola of a three-story house called Hazel Hill. From Lee's Hill, Pendleton saw the two Federal divisions already across the Rappahannock as well as two other divisions preparing to cross. Unlike the previous demonstrations, the advance to the Bowling Green Road expanded the bridgehead so that additional units could jump the river.[53]

Chilton's incompetent staff work had pulled three brigades and most of the Confederate artillery from Fredericksburg. From Hazel Hill Humphreys redeployed some of his pickets to cover the south end of town. Using Hazel Run as a barrier, two companies stretched a line from the municipal gas works to the railway. Pendleton directed Carlton's Troup Artillery to return to Howison Hill. These actions were minor but might give the impression that the Confederate line remained more intact than it was.[54]

A worried Hays met up with Pendleton on Lee's Hill, and they quickly decided to wait until dark before abandoning Fredericksburg. The fifteen guns the artillery chief had retained for defense would be brought off first. The half-dozen guns from the Washington Artillery and the section of Parker's battery could withdraw quietly down the back slope of Marye's Heights. Next would be the guns on Lee's and Howison Hills, which could reach the Telegraph Road by moving to their rear. Hays's infantry would pull back once the artillery was clear.[55]

A staff officer from Humphreys's Twenty-First Mississippi joined the two generals on Lee's Hill. He said he was on his way to report to Barksdale, not too far away on the Plank Road, and offered to carry any message the officers had for his brigade commander. Pendleton asked the subaltern to let Barksdale know they planned to withdraw that night. Getting clear of Fredericksburg would keep the lone Mississippi regiment from being captured.[56]

Barksdale had withdrawn as ordered but had not gone too far. When the courier from the Twenty-First Mississippi brought word of the Federal advance, the general immediately ordered his brigade to turn around, which elicited a hearty cheer. Such blatant insubordination could result in a court-martial, but Barksdale sent a courier to let Early know his Mississippi units had turned back to try to stave off disaster at Fredericksburg.[57]

Early had also withdrawn from Fredericksburg against his better judgment. His misgivings were vindicated when a courier from Lee found him on the Orange Plank Road and delivered a message indicating that it had been left to Early, the on-scene commander, to determine if he needed to retreat from Fredericksburg. The division commander now had to decide whether to return to his lines, which may have already been overrun, or continue west to fight with Lee. He had decided that he had passed the point of no return and to continue west when Barksdale's courier caught up with him. The rider reported that the Federals were advancing, that Pendleton thought his artillery would be captured, and that Barksdale had already turned his column around to forestall disaster.[58]

In Early's column Hoke had gone as far as Salem Church, followed by "Extra Billy" Smith's brigade and Brig. Gen. John B. Gordon's. On his way west Barksdale's rider had informed Gordon that the Federals were breaking out of their bridgehead, and the Georgian had taken it upon himself to turn his regiments around to follow the Mississippian back to Fredericksburg. What the West Point–trained Early thought of volunteer commanders taking matters into their own hands is not recorded. He was the most recently appointed major general in Lee's army, which may have influenced Gordon and Barksdale to still think of him as a peer rather than as their superior officer. Whether irritated or relieved, Early pragmatically decided to keep his command intact and turned all his units back to Fredericksburg. He sent his adjutant to inform Lee.[59]

Barksdale ran into Pendleton on the Telegraph Road. The artillery officer noted he was complying with orders to abandon the town, so the two generals rode to the Marye house to consult with Hays. Barksdale urged everyone to return to their defensive positions, adding that Gordon was also on his way back. Thoroughly confused, Pendleton sent his assistant adjutant general to find Early and ask what he wanted done. He and Hays agreed to wait until 11:00 P.M. before continuing to pull back from Fredericksburg.[60]

The miscommunications at Fredericksburg aggravated Early, but reports of Confederates in retreat thoroughly misled Hooker. Around 5:30 P.M. Jackson's troops came crashing out of the dense woods, striking the Union army's right flank. The action at the Catherine Furnace had pulled the Third Corps out of position as well as a brigade from the Eleventh Corps. In addition, Howard had assumed he faced no danger and accompanied his detached troops to Hazel Grove. The Eleventh Corps fell back from the Confederate onslaught without leadership and without reserves.

The Confederate flank attack devastated both the Eleventh and the Third Corps. The First Corps, finally getting across at US Ford, marched through panicked troops to report to Hooker. From Fredericksburg a New York soldier wrote that he and others could hear the artillery "and sometimes when the wind was favorable, the sound of musketry would reach us."[61]

At Franklin's Crossing Newton's and Brig. Gen. Albion P. Howe's divisions crossed the pontoon bridges in turn. When the sun went down, a nearly full moon lit the way for the marching columns while creating shadows where embankments or trees blocked its reflected light. A New Jersey soldier watching the buildup noted that the "men of the Corps moved quickly to the river, crossed and passed us marching towards a ravine where we lost sight of them in the darkness."[62]

Not yet apprised of the disaster unfolding at Chancellorsville, Butterfield clarified Sedgwick's orders shortly after 7:00 P.M. The Sixth Corps was to cross the Rappahannock "as soon as indications will permit," capture Fredericksburg, and "pursue the enemy on the Bowling Green road." Hooker's relayed message indicated his excitement about Lee's supposed withdrawal, noting that Third Corps troops were even then among the Southern trains near the Catherine Furnace. Sedgwick's orders to seize Fredericksburg were logical because quartermasters and railroad men were standing by to establish the army's supply lines through that river town. Pursuing retreating Confederates on the Bowling Green Road, however, would take him in the wrong direction.[63]

Sedgwick would get his corps across the river that night but wait for daylight before going farther. Brooks continued to hold the Bowling Green Road as Newton moved his division to the left. The Seventh Louisiana had fallen back to the railway, and its commander decided to test the Federal advance, which proved to be a bad idea. Union troops drove the Confederates back, capturing two companies of Louisiana men, including a major. Skirmish firing continued into the night.[64]

Sedgwick reported to Butterfield that he would have his entire corps in motion at daylight. The chief of staff responded: "Dispatch received. Can't you take Fredericksburg to-night, so we can commence railroad and telegraph and pontoon bridge by daylight?" Butterfield was pursuing the campaign objective of getting Fredericksburg set up as a logistics base.[65]

To the west there occurred a pause in the Southern assault. While Union troops rallied and prepared defenses, Stonewall Jackson rode forward to determine how best to continue his advance. He presented a dark silhouette against a full moon on his way back, and a jumpy North Carolina regiment shot him from the saddle. At 9:00 P.M., as the Union lines stabilized, Hooker ordered Sedgwick to march west to Chancellorsville. He sent an identical telegram to Butterfield and ordered Capt. Valerian Razderichin to Falmouth with a written dispatch. Hooker had five corps on hand and another arriving, yet he thought Sedgwick needed to get his Sixth Corps to Chancellorsville and "attack and destroy any force he may fall in with on the road." Gibbon's division would hold Fredericksburg while the railway was reestablished across the Rappahannock.[66]

But Gibbon had only two brigades at Falmouth, his third brigade remaining at Banks' Ford, the place Hooker had been neglecting since halting the army's advance on May 1. Owen's Philadelphia Brigade remained there with Benham's engineers and their bridging equipment. The Potomac Army's chief of artillery, Henry Hunt also remained in that quiet sector. Opposite these Federal forces, Wilcox's Confederates continued to man their works.[67]

Sedgwick received his orders at 11:00 P.M. On his fifth day across the river, his new assignment was to save Hooker and the bulk of the Army of the Potomac. He could not wait until morning either. Sedgwick had to reorient his corps from a pursuit on the Bowling Green Road toward an attack on Fredericksburg. At Chancellorsville Hooker expressed concern to General Warren that Sedgwick would be too far away for him to direct. Warren replied that he knew the area's roads and asked if he could act as a guide. The army commander concurred, and Warren headed to US Ford for the long ride to Fredericksburg.[68]

At the Marye house Pendleton and Hays had been trying to determine the best time to evacuate Fredericksburg, but new developments suggested they might be able to avoid that decision. Barksdale had already turned his brigade around, and they learned that Gordon's Brigade would also be returning. Finally, around 10:00 P.M., one of Early's staff officers brought word that the entire division was on its way back. When the Southerners filed back into their lines, though, they would find that the Sixth Corps had moved up in their absence.[69]

FIVE

MAY 2-3

NIGHT MOVES AND ACTION AT DEEP RUN

During the evening of May 2, Sedgwick consolidated his corps on the south side of the Rappahannock River. General Brooks moved his First Division to where the First Corps had been, while Colonel Burnham moved his Light Division to the right. General Newton's Third Division and General Howe's Second Division funneled into the bridgehead behind them, the last troops getting across around 11:00 P.M.[1]

Newton moved into position on Brooks's left and used Brig. Gen. David A. Russell's Third Brigade to anchor his line on the river. The rest of his division occupied the Bowling Green Road, Col. Henry W. Brown's First Brigade on the left and Brig. Gen. Joseph J. Bartlett's Second Brigade to the right. Howe's division took position to Brooks's right, Col. Lewis A. Grant's Second Brigade on the left and Brig. Gen. Thomas Neill's Third Brigade on the right; the Second Division had no first brigade. Maj. J. Watts de Peyster brought the division's artillery across and placed Capt. Andrew Cowan's First New York Independent Light Artillery in front of Neill. He directed Lt. Leonard Martin's Battery F, Fifth US Artillery to drop trail in front of Grant.[2]

The buildup made the bridgehead a crowded place, but the Sixth Corps stood ready to execute whatever orders came its way. Hooker's next instructions, however, were written after Jackson's attack had exploded out of the trees near Wilderness Church. At 11:00 P.M. Sedgwick found out that he was expected to cross the river and link up with the main army at Chancellorsville—by morning. There were at least a dozen miles between the Sixth Corps and the rest of the Union army across an unfamiliar landscape controlled by Lee's forces. Hooker's absurd order reflected a headquarters in panic.[3]

There were more crisis-driven directives. Butterfield instructed Sedgwick to seize a local citizen, perhaps even the mayor, to guide him through town. The chief of staff added that the chosen individual should know that any misinformation would result in "pain of death." A tired Butterfield was suggesting that the Sixth Corps commander be ready to murder the mayor of Fredericksburg or some other hapless citizen.[4]

In the field Sedgwick reoriented his divisions to push west instead of south. Whether he was going to save the main army at Chancellorsville remained to be seen, but he was going to keep his corps intact and able to protect itself en route. Brooks, already familiar with the bridgehead terrain, would hold his division in place as the corps's rear guard. Newton would join with Burnham's Light Division to lead the drive into Fredericksburg. Howe would follow Newton.[5]

Communications across US Ford had been consistently bad. By comparison, the connections between Banks' Ford, Falmouth, and Sedgwick's corps had been excellent, and the signalmen meant to keep it that way. Captain Cushing, the Potomac Army's chief signal officer, sent three miles of new telegraph wire to Lt. Fountain Wilson, the man charged with providing signal support to the Sixth Corps. Three miles of wire would provide a link between the Falmouth headquarters and signal stations established on the road west by Capt. Seymour Pierce and Lt. George J. Clarke. Cushing sent two other signal officers, Capt. James S. Hall and Lt. Peter A. Taylor, to Falmouth, where two of General Gibbon's brigades were finally going to become part of the unfolding campaign.[6]

Before midnight Butterfield directed Gibbon to take Fredericksburg, although with more drama than clarity. The division commander had to ask if he would have a pontoon bridge available or if he should prepare to wade the river at the Falmouth Ford. Getting two brigades across that boulder-ridden crossing in the dark would be an arduous task. It would be significantly delayed if there was any opposition.[7]

Shortly after midnight Butterfield sent Gibbon another message: "Push everything to get that bridge over. If you are likely to fail with the bridge, keep your ammunition dry, and push over the ford, if practicable. You must cross tonight."⁸

Urging an experienced combat officer to keep his powder dry was gratuitous, but Butterfield could not help himself. An hour later he sent another rambling message: "If it is found to be entirely impracticable to lay a bridge or cross at the fords near Falmouth, you can go via Sedgwick's crossing; where the two bridges remain. I learned about dark that the Twenty-first Mississippi Regiment had been left in the town and were trying to get out. They may be there still. If so, you can easily capture them by sending a brigade via Sedgwick's crossing."⁹

The above message indicates a severe lack of coordination. The anxious Butterfield had already called on Maj. Edmund O. Beers to retrieve the dismantled bridge at Pollock's Mill Creek, which he had done with a detachment of the Fiftieth New York Engineers. The Second Corps infantry units had mustered near Chatham, and the engineers had let Gibbon know that a bridge was on its way well before Butterfield did. The division commander thus knew to keep his troops nearby rather than follow the chief of staff's suggestion to find another place to cross.¹⁰

While the engineers staged their equipment, Gibbon noticed that Col. Henry W. Hudson, newly assigned to command his First Brigade, had quite obviously been drinking. He placed the intoxicated man under arrest and reached into the Thirty-Fourth New York to assign Col. Byron Laflin to brigade command. Some of the Thirty-Fourth's men had recently mutinied, but the uncompromising the general must have seen something in Laflin that gave him confidence. Gibbon's forces continued to wait for a bridge to be floated.¹¹

Colonel Chilton had single-handedly disrupted the Confederate defenses at Fredericksburg, but Sedgwick needed a few hours to reorient his command for the march west. That interval provided time for Southern units to recover from their misguided orders and reoccupy their lines. Around midnight General Gordon's Georgians filed back into their old position along the railway at Hamilton's Crossing.¹²

Generals Hoke and Smith were six to seven miles out, near Salem Church, when Early directed them to return to Fredericksburg. They arrived back a few hours later and joined Gordon on the railway. Smith's Virginians took position to Gordon's left, with Hoke's North Carolinians on Smith's left. The Southerners sought to reclaim the Bowling Green Road, but in their absence the Federals had taken position there.¹³

While Early had been headed west, Generals Hays and Pendleton had been directed to avoid becoming prisoners. When it looked like the advancing Sixth Corps might capture their commands whole, they had left. Hays had marched out no more than a few miles, though, when he ran into the rest of Early's Division heading back to Fredericksburg. As the Southern units reoccupied their old positions, Hays and Barksdale rode to see Early at Hamilton's Crossing to find out what orders were still applicable for their respective brigades. The major general still expected the Federals to attack his lines where they had broken through in December, but Fredericksburg proper also remained vulnerable. He directed Barksdale to keep his Mississippians in position behind the town and directed Hays to move his Louisianans over to back him up.[14]

Pendleton also sought out Early that night and found him exasperated with Lee's incompetent staff officer. He was further angered that Barksdale and Gordon had ignored his explicit orders when they turned back to Fredericksburg from the Orange Plank Road. His independent command confronted an increasingly difficult assignment, and the challenge to his authority did not bode well in a situation that demanded discipline. Early insisted on sharing Lee's written message with Pendleton, which made clear that the Army of Northern Virginia's commander had left it up to him to determine if it made sense to abandon the Fredericksburg position.[15]

Some of the artillery units had also cautiously ignored orders. Like Barksdale, Colonel Cabell's command was not a component of Early's Division, and he held his battalion close after pulling off the line. Captain Carlton kept his guns at the Leach house and returned to Howison Hill when the Federals advanced in the late afternoon. Around the same time Captain Fraser brought his Pulaski Battery back into position on Lee's Hill.[16]

At the south end of the line, Captain Dement's First Maryland Artillery of Andrew's Battalion returned in the middle of the night, moving onto the knoll north of Prospect Hill. The battery commanders were unsure what the Federals had done in their absence, so two men volunteered to find out. Instead of locating a Southern picket line to their front, they walked into Federal skirmishers and were hustled away as prisoners.[17]

Colonel Walton brought back his Washington Artillery to Marye's Heights. Early, however, remained concerned his right would become the Federal target that day and directed Pendleton to divert Captain Richardson's battery of four 12-pounder Napoleons to report to Lieutenant Colonel

Andrews. Early's artillery commander placed the Napoleons to the left of Captain Carpenter's Allegheny Battery.[18]

Captain Graham brought his Rockbridge Artillery back to Prospect Hill, redeploying its two 10-pounder and two 20-pounder Parrott rifles. They were joined again by the two 10-pounder Parrotts from Captain Brown's Chesapeake Artillery. Captain Raine joined Dement with two rifled weapons from his Lee Battery. Before daybreak the guns anchoring the Confederate right were prepared for the Federal advance.[19]

Like Dement's two captured artillerymen, the returning Confederate infantry did not realize how far the Federals had advanced. Two regiments of Neill's brigade and two regiments from Brooks's First Division had moved up to the Bowling Green Road. One Federal observed that "about midnight we could hear the rebels talk quite plainly." The listening Northerners heard a Southern officer incautiously giving loud orders, and when the approaching Confederates became visible in the moonlight, the waiting pickets unleashed a sharp volley. The startled Southerners quickly withdrew.[20]

Nearer to Fredericksburg, Barksdale remained unhappy about his brigade having to cover an extended line from Taylor's Hill, across Marye's Heights, to Howison Hill. As he settled down to get some sleep, Colonel Humphreys of the Twenty-First Mississippi came to look for him, hoping to find out what he had learned about their plans. He called out in the darkness: "Are you asleep, General?" The tired brigade commander responded: "No sir. Who could sleep with a million of armed Yankees all around him?"[21]

Humphreys and Barksdale took a few moments to talk through the brigade's dispositions. The Thirteenth and Seventeenth Mississippi Regiments held a line east of the Telegraph Road on the ridge behind the Howison house. Upon Hays's return, one of his Louisiana regiments would extend that line farther south to the end of the high ground, where it drops off to the flat terrain of the Lansdowne valley. The Eighteenth Mississippi sheltered behind the stone wall at the base of Marye's Heights. Humphreys was to use his Twenty-First Mississippi to extend the brigade line to the Plank Road. Both men were uneasy about the strength of their position, and to Humphreys's expressed concern, Barksdale replied: "Well sir, we must make this fight whether we hold it or are whipped."[22]

The Federals were already in motion. Brooks maintained the Sixth Corps's bridgehead perimeter, while Newton moved his division from the downstream end of the line to the Bowling Green Road. Burnham's Light Division joined up with Newton, and their combined force pressed toward Fredericksburg. Howe's division prepared to follow behind Burnham.[23]

Newton put Col. Alexander Shaler's First Brigade at the head of his column, followed by Burnham's Light Division. Lt. John H. Butler followed the Light Division troops with his Battery G, Second US Artillery. Brig. Gen. Frank Wheaton's Third Brigade marched behind the US artillery, followed in turn by Capt. Jeremiah McCarthy's Battery C-D, First Pennsylvania Light Artillery. This odd unit designation came from two depleted batteries having been consolidated into one. The last formations in Newton's column were the regiments of Col. William H. Browne's Second Brigade.[24]

An African American man came into the lines with information about Confederates occupying the heights behind Fredericksburg as well as cutting a canal to flood the streets. There were two canals that diverted water from the Rappahannock River to provide power to local industries, but the topography is such that neither one could have been made to inundate any streets. The reference to flooding would have to have been to a drainage that locals knew as Marye's Canal, which soldiers had referred to as the Canal Ditch. Manipulating the control gates for this waterway could have made the surrounding terrain wetter, but the only road it would have affected would have been lower Charles Street.[25]

The advancing Federals had no way to know if flooding posed a real threat, but the road to Fredericksburg had already proved quite miserable. A Rhode Island soldier described their march as being "through ravines filled with water, and roads too muddy for comfort." There existed a strong potential to be ambushed along the way, but orders were to get into Fredericksburg quickly. A Massachusetts soldier observed how "the long dark columns of troops moved off with the moonlight flashing from the bright barrels and bayonettes of the guns."[26]

The Sixty-Fifth New York Infantry, also called the First US Chasseurs, led the column. Like Zouaves, Chasseurs were light infantry trained to move swiftly on a battlefield. These New Yorkers, led by Lt. Col. Joseph E. Hamblin, wore standard Union blue rather than anything colorful, as typically favored by Zouaves. Sgt. Samuel S. Kissinger described how skirmishers advanced one hundred yards in front of the regiment. A handful of scouts were another fifty yards in front of them. The 122nd New York Infantry followed the Chasseurs, with flankers out beyond the roadway. A soldier remembered, "we felt our way along a strange road and near the enemy expecting every moment we should catch a fire from an unseen foe."[27]

Although a stage road for decades, the Bowling Green Road had no bridge across Deep Run. On the night of May 2-3, that stream ran about forty feet wide and over knee-high as the infantrymen waded across. Beyond it the Federals began to receive the occasional shot fired from the shadows. One of Newton's staff officers described the march: "The night was dark and the road made darker by the foliage of the trees on either side. The progress was necessarily slow. Frequent short halts were made while the skirmishers were feeling their way. There were men out there, whether close by or far away no one knew, but they made themselves known." He noted that "nothing broke the deep silence of the night except an occasional shot followed by the never-to-be-forgotten *ping* of the minie-ball."[28]

Not quite a mile beyond Deep Run, the Federals approached the Ferneyhough house on the east side of the road. Officers of the Twenty-First Mississippi had directed their picket line from there, but it now stood empty. The building occupied a prominent hilltop overlooking Hazel Run, which flows into the Rappahannock River a few hundred yards to the north. The Mississippians had pulled back to Fredericksburg, but the advancing Federals were about to collide with two companies of riflemen left behind to impede their approach.[29]

The Bowling Green Road dropped fifty feet in elevation across the five hundred yards between the Ferneyhough house and Hazel Run. Like the road at Deep Run, there was no bridge here, with the stream running sixty feet wide that night. The First US Chasseurs descended through the open bottomlands, which were flat and marshy along the waterway, with hills to the front and to either side. On elevated ground to the right was a neighborhood of houses, but no lights shown from the windows.[30]

Two companies of the Twenty-First Mississippi waited on that high ground. As the Chasseurs crossed Hazel Run, the Southerners unleashed a volley. To the left of the Federal column, one company of Mississippi riflemen had spread out along a low ridge in front of the railway. The other company occupied the high ground where Princess Anne Street began, its line including the Slaughter family home called Hazel Hill.[31]

The Confederate fire went high over the Union soldiers on the left but slammed into the troops who were on the right. In that hail of projectiles, Maj. Henry G. Healy dropped, shot in the abdomen. With the moon in the

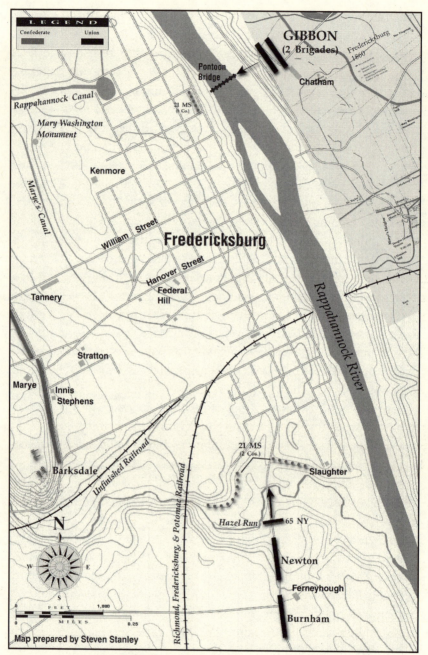

Map 4. Into Fredericksburg. During the night of May 2–3, Sedgwick's Sixth Corps approached the lower end of Fredericksburg, first running into Confederate opposition at Hazel Run. Gibbon's Second Corps division prepared to cross the Rappahannock into the upper end of town.

western sky, the Confederates remained in the shadows, while the advancing Federals were caught in its reflected light. The New Yorkers could not be sure of their targets, and their return fire proved ineffective.[32]

The Mississippians had chosen their ground well. Back in the column General Newton became concerned that his division was not pushing into Fredericksburg with enough energy. He sent Lt. Huntington W. Jackson to urge Colonel Shaler to move more aggressively, the staff officer riding forward while working his way through waiting soldiers. He reported to Shaler, who was then conferring with Lieutenant Colonel Hamblin about how best to knock the Confederates out of the way. Rather than pushing up skirmishers as infantry tactics suggested, Hamblin massed his regiment and launched his entire unit in a sudden charge. The time was about 2:00 A.M.[33]

Lieutenant Jackson remembered the action that followed: "In a moment there was the noise of hurrying feet, the troops quickly disappeared in the dark; a shout, a bright, sudden flash, a roll of musketry followed, and the road was open." The swift lunge caught the Confederates by surprise. The Mississippians fired a ragged volley and hastily withdrew, but fourteen Union soldiers were killed or wounded. The Chasseurs carried the injured men to a nearby tenant cottage, then pressed on. They were not familiar with the town proper but had heard stories. Advancing through streets closed in by seemingly empty buildings, each man anticipated a bullet in the back from a dark window.[34]

As the Northern soldiers felt their way forward through the narrow streets, Sedgwick received messages telling him to hurry. His initial orders to march west had been received at 11:00 P.M. About thirty minutes later Capt. Valerian Razderichin arrived from Chancellorsville and briefed Butterfield on the confusion inflicted by Jackson's flank attack. Around midnight he then carried a message from Butterfield to Sedgwick, "it seems to be of vital importance that you should fall upon Lee's rear with crushing force." Hooker's chief of staff sent another courier around 1:45 A.M. to explain "how necessary it is that you should push through every obstacle in your path."[35]

At the Falmouth headquarters Butterfield and Razderichin heard the fighting that flared up briefly at Hazel Run. Shortly thereafter, the chief of staff sent a message to Chancellorsville, noting that Confederate forces were still in Fredericksburg. He added that the developing resistance would keep Sedgwick from reaching Hooker by daylight. He then fired off another message to the corps commander, "Everything in the world depends upon the rapidity and promptness of your movement." If there were going to be repercussions about the night's activities, Butterfield would conveniently have a record of urgent dispatches.[36]

General Warren had also ridden from Chancellorsville to Fredericksburg that night. He found Sedgwick around 3:00 A.M. and provided a welcome update that did not include breathless directives to get to Chancellorsville by morning. Intelligence reports suggested that Confederate forces at Fredericksburg had been diminished in strength, but there had been audible sounds of rail traffic near Hamilton's Crossing. Warren thought the Sixth Corps should press on as quickly as possible, but Sedgwick had been receiving delayed and conflicting messages for several days and knew he would have to rely on his own experience and instincts in the hours ahead.[37]

In the darkness and on unfamiliar ground, the Sixth Corps needed a guide to get through town to the Plank Road. Butterfield informed Sedgwick that he had sent him a local African American man who knew the area; apparently he had backed away from his idea to seize and threaten the mayor. He also let him know that Gibbon would be crossing the river into Fredericksburg that night.[38]

Sixth Corps signalmen skillfully maintained effective communications, but Butterfield soon interfered, fearing the Confederates had figured out the Federal ciphers. Shortly after 2:00 A.M., without notifying the chief signal officer, the chief of staff instructed Sedgwick to quit using signal torches. For the next two hours, Captain Cushing became increasingly exasperated that his signal team south of the Rappahannock appeared to be neglecting its duties. Not until an orderly from across the river found him at the Phillips house did he learn that Butterfield had ordered the men to cease signaling. An angry Cushing instructed his signalmen to use their new ciphers and resume work.[39]

While the Sixth Corps moved into Fredericksburg on the Bowling Green Road, Gibbon's Second Corps division prepared to enter the town from its upper end. The general had received the information that only a single Confederate regiment held the whole of Fredericksburg, and he took a calculated risk to get a bridge down without first seizing the edge of town. The engineers needed a working party, and Gibbon reached into the 127th Pennsylvania to provide a three-hundred-man detail.[40]

Between 2:00 and 3:00 A.M., the engineers began floating pontoons to extend a span to the foot of Fredericksburg's Hawke Street. As would have been expected, this activity drew the attention of Confederate pickets. A Federal soldier described the scene:

The work of making the bridge commenced,—the handling of the boats and timber made ominous sounds in the still air. The men were pushing the first boats into the water,—the General and Staff were upon the bank near the workmen, watching the progress of matters,—Not a sound had come from the sombre town,—not a twinkle of light, when all at once, a small stream of flaky fire, a sharp report, and the hiss of a bullet startled the senses,—then a volley, of like appearance, and from the same source, spattered in among us from across the river.[41]

A single company of the Twenty-First Mississippi had fired on the bridge builders. Gibbon responded to its show of defiance by having his artillery blast the town with canister, sending dozens of iron and lead balls to blow apart men rather than houses. The Confederate company's commander reported being subjected to a "shower of shell and shrapnel." After just a few rounds, the Mississippians withdrew, and the bridge builders resumed work.[42]

Gibbon had two storming parties ready to launch boats into the night. At the bridge site one hundred volunteers from Laflin's brigade stood by. The Nineteenth Maine had been detached to guard telegraph lines, but the Fifteenth Massachusetts, the First Minnesota, and the Thirty-Fourth and Eighty-Second New York provided twenty-five men each. Eighteen of the volunteers from the Thirty-Fourth were soldiers who had previously refused to serve beyond May 1. In Colonel Laflin Gibbon had found a brigade commander who could motivate troops. Capt. George W. Ryerson of the Eighty-Second New York took charge of this combined force.[43]

Hall's brigade provided another storming party, fifty men strong, to constitute a flanking force. Lt. Thomas M. McKay led twenty-five men from the Twentieth Massachusetts up a riverside road, taking a pontoon with them on a carriage. Lt. John J. Ferris led another twenty-five men from the Nineteenth Massachusetts with another pontoon on wheels. The combined force stopped opposite a large mill and slid their two boats into the water. The looming structure was the Washington Woolen Mills, a substantial, four-story brick building.[44]

There had been Confederate pickets across the way earlier that evening, but they had departed by the time the Massachusetts men floated their pontoons. Under pressure from a force coming up from the south and Union artillery blasting the town with canister, Colonel Humphreys had ordered his Mississippians to fall back after first destroying the bridge over the millrace fed by a mill pond at the end of the Rappahannock Canal.

There were two bridges, though, and the Southerners wrecked only the one near a mill pond. They missed the one at the end of Princess Anne Street only a few blocks away.[45]

At daylight McKay's and Ferris's men heard skirmishing in Fredericksburg. They piled into their boats and pulled into the stream but soon saw blue uniforms among the buildings—Sixth Corps men from the lower end of town. The fifty-man flanking force floated downstream to the bridge site and turned their two pontoons over to the engineers. The bridge builders completed their floating span in short order, and the united one-hundred-man storming party crossed as well. By 6:00 A.M. Laflin's and Hall's brigades were in Fredericksburg and had moved up to Princess Anne Street.[46]

Batteries B and G, First Rhode Island Artillery had spent the night near the Lacy mansion. A staff officer brought orders to Capt. George W. Adams, commanding Battery G, directing his unit to join Gibbon in Fredericksburg. Adams took his artillerymen forward immediately, glad to be the first battery across the river. He casually saluted Battery B's officers as he passed, mocking them for having to follow. The staff officer then delivered the same orders to Lt. T. Frederick Brown, commanding Battery B.[47]

Lieutenant Brown knew this ground from December. While Adams followed the road that angles across the slope, Brown ordered the wheels of his limbers and caissons locked and then took his battery straight down a crude road directly to the pontoon bridge. Battery B thus beat Battery G to the crossing, and Adams had to halt and wait for the route to clear. Brown saluted him as he passed, crossing the river first as he had done in December. Once in town both batteries turned right onto Water Street (modern Sophia Street), then left at Pitt Street, and moved up to the edge of town.[48]

After the brief action at Hazel Run, Shaler's brigade, followed by Burnham's Light Division, had cautiously moved along Princess Anne Street between closed and shuttered houses. At the railway the ground to the northwest became more open, and Marye's Heights stood silhouetted to the west about eight hundred yards distant. Shaler formed his brigade to find out whether those heights were held in strength or had been abandoned. Newton rode up as the near-full moon was dropping toward the western horizon, lengthening the night's shadows. After a few moments the division commander ordered Shaler to press farther into town instead; he would use Wheaton's brigade to reconnoiter the dark hills.[49]

In addition to losing the moonlight, fog had filled in the low ground. A Pennsylvania soldier observed that the troops "could see no distance."

To overcome the fading visibility, skirmishers and flankers kept their intervals "by a low whistle to one another." Wheaton's units took position past a brickyard, north of the railway and west of Marye's Canal. Browne's brigade remained in column behind them.[50]

If Confederates were present, they would likely be on the Telegraph Road (modern Sunken Road) at the base of Marye's Heights. Stone walls lined that route, and a gentle slope dropped about thirty feet in elevation over an expanse of about 250 yards. A swale ran across the terrain at that distance, and another 200 yards of open ground extended beyond it before dropping off to Marye's Canal. The Federals moved up on the west side of that drainage and took position below the rise, sheltered from direct fire.[51]

Wheaton and Shaler reconnoitered different sections of Marye's Heights. Shaler had entered Fredericksburg with Col. Nelson Cross's Sixty-Seventh New York leading the way, but he directed Col. John Ely to take his Twenty-Third Pennsylvania, a light infantry unit known as Birney's Zouaves, toward the heights. These men advanced in open order just south of Hanover Street. When they had approached within 30–40 yards of the stone-lined road (near modern Freeman Street), waiting Mississippi infantrymen rose with a yell and fired. The muzzle flashes briefly illuminated the advancing Federals, including Wheaton's probe with the Zouaves to the left. Consequently, the Confederate volley rippled down the Telegraph Road, from Hanover Street to where it bends around the end of Marye's Heights.[52]

Wheaton had sent Lt. Col. Theodore B. Hamilton's Sixty-Second New York to reconnoiter the heights, supported by Col. Joseph M. Kinkead's 102nd Pennsylvania. Like the Zouaves, the New Yorkers advanced in open order. They were about 250 yards from the stone wall when the Confederate fire ripped through them. Confederate muzzle flashes coming down the line lit the night and made the unfolding volley increasingly deadly. Subjected to the initial fire 30–40 yards from the enemy position, Birney's Zouaves had eight of their number shot down. The Sixty-Second New York, 250 yards from the Mississippians, lost sixty-four men killed or wounded. A New York soldier wrote, "it was just dark enough to make every flash distinct, and the sight was beautiful but terrible."[53]

For good measure, Confederate artillery opened fire. As the Federals came tumbling back, Sedgwick sent two of his staff officers to rally them. He was under orders to get his corps headed west, but an undetermined number of Confederates blocked his way. He rode out into the open to see

Map 5. Predawn Probes at Marye's Heights. Two Federal probes across the old 1862 battleground were quickly repulsed by Confederates on Marye's Heights.

the terrain for himself. His adjutant general, Lt. Col. Martin T. McMahon, noticed that the general was drawing fire and suggested they pull back out of range. "By heavens," Sedgwick responded, "this must not delay us."[54]

Hearing the Confederate guns, Captain McCarthy immediately rode forward. He saw the Sixty-Second New York and 102nd Pennsylvania falling back and the brigade's three other regiments—the Ninety-Third, Ninety-Eighth, and 139th Pennsylvania—moving up into a line on their left. In town a Rhode Island soldier observed, "At daylight the Rebels opened their guns from the forts on the hills and the shot and shell came crashing through the houses sounding like volleys of musketry." Newton directed McCarthy to bring the Confederate position under fire with canister.[55]

The division commander also ordered up the three artillery units in his column. Troops standing in the roadway moved to the side as the guns rumbled into Fredericksburg. The Third Battery, New York Light Artillery, under Lt. William A. Harn, brought its six 10-pounder Parrott rifles into battery between a railway cut to its front, graded but without tracks, and an active railway behind them.[56]

Across the unfinished railway, approximately one hundred yards to the right of Harn's battery, McCarthy had his Battery C-D, First Pennsylvania Light Artillery. Its 10-pounder Parrott rifles occupied a slight knoll. Newton's other artillery unit, Battery G, Second US Artillery, under Lt. John H. Butler, deployed 12-pounder Napoleons to McCarthy's right.[57]

McCarthy opened fire from behind Wheaton's brigade, as did Butler. Shooting over infantry can be risky, though, and an outgoing Parrott round exploded prematurely over the 102nd Pennsylvania, killing two men and wounding others. The infantrymen then moved farther down the sheltering slope. Casualties from friendly fire are always troubling, and in this instance Pennsylvanians had killed Pennsylvanians.[58]

Seeking a clear field of fire, McCarthy advanced his guns onto the open plain in front of the stone wall and continued to pound the Confederate line. His gunners got off fourteen rounds of canister under a hail of musketry before pulling back. From a less-exposed position, the artillerymen elevated their barrels to bring the Confederate guns on top of the hill under fire.[59]

As the artillery fire intensified, Newton directed Colonel Browne to bring his brigade into town. From the Bowling Green Road, the regiments ascended the hill to Princess Anne Street at double-quick time. One soldier described Fredericksburg as a place "battered to pieces and used up."

A Massachusetts soldier described a "street with rifle pits on both sides connecting the houses and every little ways crossing the streets."[60]

After its unsuccessful probe of the Confederate stronghold, Shaler's brigade had spread out through the town to gather up Confederate stragglers, capturing about a dozen. After turning the prisoners over to the provost marshal, the units were directed to prevent Union stragglers from finding places to hide as the Sixth Corps prepared for the next stage of the developing fight.[61]

At the upper end of town, Gibbon's two brigades moved up from the river to higher ground. The main streets of Fredericksburg run parallel to the Rappahannock River, each progressively higher in elevation. The third street in is Princess Anne Street, which occupies the edge of a plateau that stretches to the west. The Second Corps troops advanced to that urban avenue, characterized by churches, banks, and government buildings. They found a line of Confederate rifle pits linking buildings and extending along the edge of the plateau to the area overlooking the Rappahannock Canal. Beyond Princess Anne Street were a scattering of houses not yet constituting full city blocks.[62]

Two batteries of the First Rhode Island Light Artillery took position near a turning basin at the end of the Rappahannock Canal. The basin had become a mill pond that fed a millrace to the woolen mills. Union artillerymen could see the heights crowned by defensive works, but the only enemy in view was artillery to the left covering the Plank Road. Gibbon directed Lieutenant Brown to move his Battery B to the ridge in front of them. The six 12-pounder Napoleons went into battery next to an unfinished monument to Mary Washington.[63]

Within the bridgehead, waiting troops listened to their comrades advance into Fredericksburg. Fighting flared up at Hazel Run around 2:00 A.M. They heard small arms and artillery around 3:00 A.M. from the crossing opposite the Lacy house. More shooting occurred as the Federals probed Marye's Heights just before dawn. Gibbon observed how "the army fought at intervals nearly all night by moonlight."[64]

· Brooks's division remained south of Deep Run as the Sixth Corps's rear guard. Early that morning Confederate batteries opened fire from the knoll across the railway. Two Federal batteries galloped forward to respond. Capt. James H. Rigby brought his Maryland Light Artillery into battery across the Bowling Green Road. His six 3-inch Ordnance Rifles brought the enemy guns under fire at a range of approximately 1,000 yards. On Rigby's left, about 150 yards farther down the road and also on its west side, Capt. William H. McCartney positioned his Massachusetts Light Artillery. His six 12-pounder Napoleons were about 1,300 yards from the Confederate guns across the railway.[65]

Fighting resumed at Chancellorsville, where the Union army still stood between the Confederate assault columns to the west and Lee's blocking force to the east. The previous day Lee and Jackson had boldly divided their forces, but that calculated risk had not yet fully paid off. Exhausted Confederates had laid down to sleep in line of battle and were thus already deployed upon awakening. Colonel Alexander noted: "I have seen many actions ordered to commence at daylight, but this is one of the very few which was punctual to the minute." Firing rose to a roar and losses became heavy as the Confederates confronted Federals behind earth-and-log breastworks.[66]

As Rigby's and McCartney's batteries opened fire below Fredericksburg, Bartlett's brigade prepared for action to their right. The Fifth Maine and the Sixteenth and 121st New York occupied the roadway, but the Twenty-Seventh New York and the Ninety-Sixth Pennsylvania were in the shelter of the Deep Run ravine where it runs parallel to the road. Lt. Augustus N. Parsons took a supporting position with his Battery A, New Jersey Light Artillery on the Mannsfield plantation. Lt. Edward B. Williston held his Battery D, Second US Artillery in reserve near the ruins of the manor house.[67]

General Howe also had his divisional artillery nearby. Capt. Andrew Cowan's First New York Independent Light Artillery had dropped trail on the west side of the road, opposite the Ferneyhough house. His six 3-inch Ordnance Rifles would be able to reach the Confederate guns on the heights overlooking the Lansdowne valley. Howe's second battery was Lt. Leonard Martin's Battery F, Fifth US Artillery, which had four 10-pounder Parrott rifles and two 12-pounder Napoleons. It came into battery roughly midway between Cowan's guns and Deep Run.[68]

In the light of day, General Early could see that the opposite side of the Rappahannock River had become devoid of Federal infantry. The Sixth Corps now had its full strength on the south side of the waterway, and the heaviest buildup appeared to be at Deep Run. A Mississippi officer noted that Sedgwick's "troops could be seen in every portion of the city; and his lines stretching off down the turnpike for a mile below the Bernard House. The position of the enemy seemed to justify the suspicions of General Early, that the real attack would be made at Hamilton Station."[69]

The relatively open Lansdowne valley was a mile-wide gap along the Confederate line. Southern infantry had dug earthworks across that intervening space, and artillery supported both flanks. Carlton's Troup Artillery had two 10-pounder Parrott rifles and one 12-pounder howitzer covering that interval from the north. The Georgia battery also had two 6-pounder howitzers, but those did not have the range to do anything useful. Under the direction of Major Latimer, Dement's First Maryland Battery and Raine's Virginia Battery covered the gap from the south, positioned on a knoll just beyond Deep Run and west of the railway. Farther south on Prospect Hill stood Graham's Rockbridge Artillery and Brown's Chesapeake Battery. Anchoring the far right were Richardson's Washington Artillery battery and Carpenter's Alleghany Battery.[70]

In support of these guns, Early had three brigades along the Richmond, Fredericksburg, and Potomac Railroad. Gordon's Georgians anchored the line in front of Prospect Hill. Smith's Virginians were to his left. Hoke's North Carolinians continued the line to Deep Run and occupied the trenches across the Lansdowne valley. Hays's Louisiana brigade had been sent to support Barksdale on the hills behind Fredericksburg.[71]

On the Confederate right and across the railway, a skirmish line followed a low rise that angled across the open landscape. Pickets from the Twenty-First North Carolina were on the left, and men of the Thirteenth Virginia on the right. On the extreme right three companies of Virginians pushed out as far as the Bowling Green Road, putting them about one hundred yards east of the Federal line.[72]

When artillery could be heard firing in Fredericksburg, several batteries south of town opened up as well. Rigby's Maryland Battery and McCartney's Massachusetts Artillery targeted Latimer's two batteries. The Federal guns filled the air with solid shot as well as explosive rounds. The Confederate guns returned fire only briefly, conserving their ammunition for the expected infantry assault.[73]

Between 6:00 and 6:30 A.M., Brooks ordered Bartlett to advance a regiment to the railway. The Ninety-Sixth Pennsylvania received the assignment, and its commander, Maj. William H. Lessig, examined the ground from horseback before riding back to his waiting regiment. Dismounting, he directed his men to unsling their knapsacks and to fix bayonets. The Pennsylvanians then advanced up the Deep Run ravine "nearly concealed from view by the trees along its banks."[74]

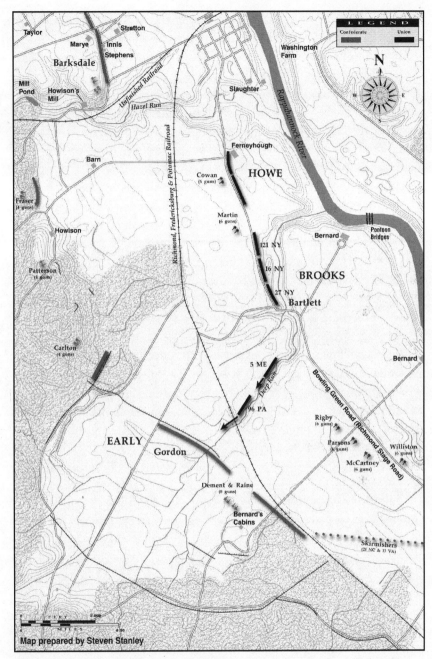

Map 6. Action at Deep Run. As Sedgwick's Federals advanced from their bridgehead into Fredericksburg, elements of the Union rear guard pushed up Deep Run.

The Confederates were startled when the Union troops emerged from the ravine. Latimer, however, finally had his targets and directed Dement and Raine to fire grape and canister. Hoke's North Carolina infantry also opened fire as the Pennsylvanians charged forward with a cheer. Lessig's right quickly pressed the Confederates back from the railway. Trees provided cover for the Southerners defending against his left, however, and they managed to hold for a brief period. But the Pennsylvanians did not back away and soon drove on to the railway. The North Carolina skirmishers fell back to their main line.[75]

Southern troops had dug a strong trench line that tied in with the railway where it bent toward Fredericksburg. The Pennsylvanians sheltered against the east side of the railway embankment as Confederates occupied these newly established earthworks. The two sides were as close as 250 yards on the south end of their lines and as far apart as 500 yards on the north end.[76]

The Pennsylvanians exchanged fire with the North Carolinians and endured Latimer's artillery fire. Raine's two rifled weapons enfiladed portions of the meandering Deep Run ravine. A Federal soldier caught in that murderous place wrote how the Confederate fire "swept the ravine tearing trees down and kicking up thunder generally." To support his beleaguered Pennsylvania unit, Bartlett moved the Sixteenth, Twenty-Seventh, and 121st New York regiments up to its left to bring the Confederate line under fire. He also ordered the Fifth Maine Infantry to move up the ravine in direct support. Federal batteries kept up a steady fire, as did the Confederate artillery.[77]

Col. Clark S. Edwards, commanding the Fifth Maine, moved up behind the Sixteenth New York. A tributary stream entering Deep Run where it intersects the Bowling Green Road offered a break in the tree cover, which gave the artillerymen of Carlton's battery a clear view of the advancing Federals. One of the Maine men described how they ended up "in plain sight of the rebel battery in our front [which] raked us terribly." The experienced soldiers jumped that deadly gap one by one and pressed on, causing their brigade commander to exclaim in quiet admiration, "Noble men, noble men."[78]

The Maine men continued up the ravine, once again hidden from Carlton's guns in the hills but now exposed to Latimer's two batteries on the knoll across the railway. Capt. Frank L. Lemont wrote: "While filing into a ravine the enemy opened upon us from a battery distant 300 yds. Their shots fell among us with merciless precision. The 2nd shot they fired swept two men from my side killing one instantly and wounding the other." The intense fire kept the Maine men from getting to the protection of the railway embankment. They "halted under cover of the bank of the ravine," unable to get farther forward. Latimer's guns were just two hundred yards away.[79]

Unlike the Ninety-Sixth Pennsylvania, the Fifth Maine soldiers had advanced with their knapsacks on, which increased each man's silhouette. The shrapnel from an exploding shell tore the blanket from the top of one man's knapsack, the kinetic energy throwing it into the air and spreading it over a tall tree "as neatly as a house-wife hangs her clothing on the line." A round tore through another man's knapsack, scattering its contents but leaving him unhurt. Sgt. James M. Evans had a bullet pass through his rolled rubber blanket and later counted forty-two holes in it, which his regimental commander helpfully pointed out made it "no longer water tight."[80]

The Ninety-Sixth Pennsylvania had held its advanced position for about a quarter of an hour when the Fifth Maine tried to join it. Both regiments remained in their respective positions within a deadly crossfire for close to another hour before pulling back. The Pennsylvanians suffered five men killed and another eighteen wounded, while the Maine men had four of their number killed and seventeen men and one officer wounded. To cover their withdrawal, Bartlett moved up the Twenty-Seventh New York into the area south of Deep Run. The New Yorkers brought the Confederate line under fire so the Fifth Maine and Ninety-Sixth Pennsylvania could filter back from a position that had no hope of being expanded.[81]

During this fighting, Brooks directed Battery A, New Jersey Light Artillery and Battery D, Second US Artillery into position between Rigby's and McCartney's batteries. From Prospect Hill Andrews saw the two additional Union batteries advancing and decided to replace Dement's field guns with longer-range weapons. He ordered Carpenter to take his two 3-inch Ordnance Rifles to the left and then asked Graham to redeploy his two 20-pounder Parrott rifles to Latimer's sector as well. Brown also received instructions to take his two 10-pounder Parrott rifles to the left.[82]

The artillerymen pulled their respective sections back to the military road. The travel distance to Latimer's position was approximately a mile and a half, but the trees thinned out near the railway, which made the approach over the last 400–500 yards exceedingly dangerous. Carpenter's section arrived first and joined Raine in keeping up a constant fire while Dement prepared to retire. Graham's and Brown's sections arrived next. Sgt. James P. Williams later wrote: "I rode at the head of my piece in a gallop; Captain Brown was about 10 yds. ahead of me & the shell & shrapnel were flying under & over us as thick as hail. I saw three or four solid shot pass right between his horse & mine & I was just expecting every minute for my horse to roll from under me."[83]

When the long-range weapons arrived, both the arriving and departing artillerymen unhitched the horse teams that had brought up Graham's and Brown's guns and hitched them to the caissons that would pull Dement's guns away. Three horses were killed during that frantic period. The steady work under pressure did not go unnoticed. Andrews, who had once commanded the Fourth Maryland Artillery, met the unit coming off the line and informed them that Early had watched them in action and sent his compliments "for their gallant and noble conduct."[84]

Back in the battery position, Latimer directed his newly arrived weapons to concentrate on each Union battery in turn. The Federals furiously returned fire. McCartney's Massachusetts guns sent over 600 rounds into Latimer's position, while Rigby's Marylanders fired 450 rounds. Parson's New Jersey battery fired 300 rounds once it moved up in to battery. Williston's US Artillery did not become engaged but did endure Latimer's converging fire. The Thirty-Second New York Infantry, behind them in support, also took casualties. One of the rounds smashed into Cpl. William Fieldhouse, and "his head was blown to atoms."[85]

On the Union far left, McCartney's battery kept up a steady fire as Brown's New Jersey brigade took position on the Bowling Green Road. The Fifteenth New Jersey, whose men had been under arms since 2:00 A.M., was on the extreme left of the Union line, within eight hundred yards of Latimer's guns. The Twenty-Third New Jersey took position on its right.[86]

Skirmishers from the Thirteenth Virginia were just beyond the far end of the Federal line. In his later reports Lieutenant Colonel Andrews stated that Smith's Brigade counterattacked that morning, but he did not witness the action and overstated the effort. An artillerymen in the Rockbridge Artillery described what actually happened: "While the cannonade was going on the 13th Va. Reg. charged a battery and silenced it. They charged across a bottom unprotected and were at least one mile from support. They did not mind the canister."[87]

The seemingly impetuous gallantry had a dimension not apparent to the distant observer. Lt. Samuel D. Buck of the Thirteenth Virginia described how three companies of his unit were on the road while the rest of the regiment stretched across the terrain to connect with the Twenty-First

North Carolina's skirmishers to their left. Buck had been asked to describe their situation to Lt. Col. James B. Terrill, who commanded the regiment but was quite nearsighted: "After close examination I reported line of battle and several pieces of artillery in our front. We were well protected and from our position could look over an enbankment [sic] in our front and see the enemy laying in [the] road not over a hundred yards to the left."[88]

Terrill wanted his entire command to have the protection of this road embankment. With his poor eyesight, though, he could not see that the Federals were deployed in the place he wanted to occupy. Terrill stood up and ordered the left of his regiment forward in a right wheel, but when the Virginians stood up to comply, a volley from the Fifteenth New Jersey slammed into them. Without waiting for orders, the quick-thinking Buck called to the three companies on the right to follow him. They quickly moved onto the road and delivered an oblique fire into the Jersey men as they were reloading. The lieutenant's quick response to his commander's error is what the distant observers called a counterattack.[89]

Once committed, the Virginians pushed hard to gain some level of success and maintained a rapid fire to put pressure on the exposed Union battery. McCartney, whose guns they shot at, described those few moments of intense action: "The enemy advanced so near that we could hear the officers rally the men, but we poured the canister into them with such effect that they were forced to retire. Had it not been for a ridge in front of us which answered as a breastwork, our loss would have been very heavy."[90]

The New Jersey troops found themselves between the Confederates and their own artillery and hustled to their right to get out of the way. McCartney subsequently turned his two left guns on the Confederate infantry. He fired canister rounds into the aggressive Virginians as his other four guns continued to blast away at the enemy batteries across the railway. His pieces had made it extremely difficult for the Confederates to bring up their longer-range weapons, and now the two guns facing the Virginia infantry at seventy-five yards kept them in check as well.[91]

During the Fifteenth New Jersey's back-and-forth movements, Lt. Edmund Halsey had been hit in the leg and tumbled into a ditch full of water. When his unit moved out of the artillery's field of fire, he heard Southern voices nearby and lay still. No Confederates found him, but he was not alone. "I heard the groans of one of our men," he remembered, "growing less and less audible in the ditch south of the road till they stopped altogether." The lieutenant lay there, exposed to stray rounds, until Lt. Col. Edward L. Campbell came looking for him and got him back to the regiment. Whatever had struck Halsey's leg did not penetrate his boot, and he resumed his duties.[92]

With the Confederate infantry on his flank, McCartney's position had become very exposed. His Massachusetts battery had exhausted its long-range ordnance and pulled off the line around 10:00 A.M. to replenish its ammunition chests. The Thirteenth Virginia did not pose a threat that the Fifteenth New Jersey could not handle, but the Southerners were quite sure they had caused the Federal guns to retire.[93]

In Bartlett's front the Twenty-Seventh New York covered the withdrawal of the Fifth Maine and Ninety-Sixth Pennsylvania under intense artillery and small-arms fire. One man who pressed himself as close to the earth as possible died with a bullet in his head. Another man stood up to move and took a bullet in the chest. Near the Bowling Green Road, Brooks and Bartlett observed the action through field glasses. An appreciative soldier wrote, "To the coolness of such leaders may be attributed the bravery and steadiness of many a regiment in the division."[94]

As the action along Deep Run came to an end, the Sixth Corps began moving beyond its bridgehead. Two bridges were dismantled when the First Corps departed, but two other floating spans remained. Butterfield now ordered both moved to Fredericksburg. Shortly after 9:00 A.M. the Fifteenth New York Engineers began to separate them into rafts of several pontoons each and float them upstream. There was no danger from sharpshooters, but they did take fire from the rifled Whitworth weapon near Prospect Hill. An anxious observer thought that "the taking of the Ponton up to the city was the most risky thing he ever saw done."[95]

Maj. Walter L. Cassin had orders to get another span in place where Major Beers and the Fiftieth New York Engineers had established a bridge near the Lacy house. The engineers poled and pulled their rafts of pontoons past wrecked bridges and other obstructions along the town waterfront to that upper crossing. They had that second span in place by midday.[96]

Capt. Chauncey B. Reese moved the second bridge from Franklin's Crossing to the area below a line of stone bridge piers, where Union railway men were staging equipment to rebuild the wooden superstructure. The engineers knocked the rafts of pontoons together with diligent speed. One of the bridge builders proudly noted, "60 minutes from the time when it was in condition to be crossed at the old place, it could be crossed at the new."[97]

General Barksdale scrambled to deploy his limited forces effectively from Howison Hill to the Marye house. He had directed Humphreys, bringing his Twenty-First Mississippi out of Fredericksburg, to extend the brigade line to the Taylor house on the north side of the Plank Road. As the colonel pulled back his pickets before dawn, a courier informed him he was needed on the other side of the Telegraph Road (modern Lafayette Boulevard). He dutifully reported to Barksdale, and the brigade commander realized the orders to the Twenty-First Regiment had been issued in error. He apologetically directed Humphreys to move his unit back to the Confederate left. The Mississippi men hustled across the length of Marye's Heights as the Federal probed the line in the dark.[98]

Looking around after daylight, Humphreys realized that Federal columns were approaching Fredericksburg from two directions. He heard the fighting at Deep Run but began to suspect that the main Union effort could come directly from Fredericksburg.[99]

SIX

MORNING OF MAY 3

FREDERICKSBURG

There were three roads out of Fredericksburg. The Telegraph Road (modern Lafayette Boulevard) ran south to Richmond. River Road (modern Riverside Drive and Fall Hill Avenue) ran adjacent to the Rappahannock River and over Fall Hill, with a connection that arced back to the Orange Plank Road (modern State Route 3). The Plank Road coursed west to Chancellorsville, intertwined with a parallel route called the Orange Turnpike. On the hills around Fredericksburg, Major General Early had 9,000 men on hand, although most of them were getting back into position after a night of pointless marching and countermarching. Generals Sedgwick and Gibbon had a combined Union strength of 27,000 troops to punch through the Confederate position.[1]

William and Hanover Streets crossed over Marye's Heights and connected to Plank Road. Those heights remained a Confederate stronghold, confirmed by two Federal probes before dawn. The stone-lined Telegraph Road provided solid protection for Southern infantry, and artillery occupied the hilltop. Hundreds of dead Federals from the December battle lay in two mass graves in front of that position. The southern end of the heights, called Willis Hill, forms a salient. One thousand yards from the edge of town, it was the closest point troops could approach under cover.[2]

At daylight Sedgwick set up his headquarters at 406 Hanover Street, the home of local businessman John G. Hurkamp. They were both established men in their forties and appear to have developed a respectful friendship.

The house stood in a neighborhood of large brick homes near Prince Edward Street, which was then the edge of town. To the west stood a large two-story home called Federal Hill, which overlooked the open ground toward Marye's Heights.[3]

Newton joined Sedgwick on Hanover Street, and the two commanders walked out to Federal Hill to study the terrain. Marye's Canal cut across the open ground, which would hinder any advancing force. Beyond the canal was a relatively clear approach, with a few houses here and there. The December battle had been a disaster, but if an assault could be launched from across the intervening drainage canal, it might close in on the heights before it could be obliterated by concentrated firepower.[4]

The predawn probes of Marye's Heights had resulted in casualties, and their presence became evident when the sun came up. Around midmorning a Union officer sent forward a flag of truce, seeking permission to recover several dozen wounded men. Col. Thomas M. Griffin, commanding the Eighteenth Mississippi, granted the protection of the white flag, and a detail emerged from the Northern lines to gather in the injured men.[5]

On the Chancellorsville front, the Confederate assault columns, now under command of Major General Stuart, resumed their advance. Small-arms fire rippled through the woodlands. By 7:30 A.M. the roar of gunfire carried to the soldiers at Fredericksburg. Hooker pulled back from Hazel Grove and redeployed into a tighter defensive perimeter around Chancellorsville. The Confederates seized this opportunity and deployed twenty-eight guns on the abandoned promontory.[6]

When Federal batteries depleted their ammunition chests, there was no one in authority to reach into reserve formations for fresh batteries. Hooker had blithely relegated his chief of artillery, Brigadier General Hunt, to administrative tasks at Banks' Ford. When the volume of Federal artillery fire diminished as batteries used up their ordnance, exhausted Confederate attackers managed a final surge that finally broke through.[7]

At the Chancellor house Hooker had been leaning on a porch column when an artillery round smashed into it. The post splintered and knocked him senseless, but the stunned general did not relinquish command of the army to the next senior man. Instead of letting Second Corps commander Darius Couch stabilize the Union line, the injured Hooker decided to retreat yet again.[8]

The Chancellorsville position, held by several corps and an array of artillery, collapsed from misdirection and used-up ammunition supplies.

By 10:00 A.M. Confederate forces had cleared the Federals from south of the Orange Turnpike, and the two wings of the Southern army reached around to link up. A better Federal commander would have punished Lee for dividing his forces, but against Hooker, the Army of Northern Virginia merged back into a unified fighting force. Lee's gamble had paid off.[9]

At 10:00 A.M. in Fredericksburg, Sedgwick prepared to force his way beyond the hills that hemmed him in. At 8:42 A.M. Butterfield informed the Sixth Corps commander that a deserter had apprised him of the Confederate march out to the Plank Road and back. He intimated that Sedgwick could have carried the heights during the night without significant opposition.[10]

Passing on new information allowed the chief of staff to gloat but hardly constituted useful intelligence. Since receiving orders to get to Chancellorsville, Sedgwick had reoriented his corps for an advance west. An immediate assault into the hills beyond his bridgehead would have occurred in the dark, across unknown terrain, and without a clear objective. Butterfield had no way to know if a night attack would have put the Sixth Corps in a tenable position at dawn. Confederate forces had pulled out of the line due to botched orders, but they had then moved back as intact, battle-ready formations.

Hooker had called on Sedgwick to be at Chancellorsville by morning, and Butterfield kept him apprised of the Sixth Corps's progress:

5:45 A.M. . . .
Heavy cannonading in Sedgwick's front for the last twenty minutes, apparently in front of Fredericksburg. No reports yet.[11]

6:08 A.M. . . .
Balloon reports the enemy reappearing on heights in front of Sedgwick's crossing. Sedgwick, judging from the sound, is meeting with strong resistance. I have no reports from him yet.[12]

6:20 A.M. . . .
Sedgwick reports himself at Sumner's old battleground at 5:30 A.M., hotly engaged, and not sanguine of the result.[13]

6:45 A.M. . . .
Sedgwick's prospects here look unfavorable, from reports. He is not out of Fredericksburg.[14]

7:05 A.M. . . .
Sedgwick still in front of Fredericksburg, as far as I can judge. Trains were running up all night to vicinity of Hamilton's Crossing. It may be that the enemy were re-enforced.[15]

8:30 A.M. . . .
Our skirmishers just occupied rebel rifle-pits on Hazel Run. Gibbon moving to right, with prospect of flanking the enemy. Enemy resist desperately.[16]

8:45 A.M. . . .
Sedgwick at 7:40 o'clock reports about making combined assault on their works. Gibbon right; Newton center; Howe on left. If he fails, will try again.[17]

There were constant rumors of Longstreet's units coming back from the Atlantic coast, but interrogation of prisoners revealed none had arrived through Hamilton's Crossing.[18]

At 9:05 A.M. Butterfield informed Sedgwick he had suspended signal communications during the night, asserting that the Confederates knew their codes and could have learned the army's movements. (As noted earlier, the signal teams had new codes in hand and were miffed the chief of staff had curtailed their important work.) Ten minutes after this signals message, Butterfield informed Sedgwick that Confederate forces were exposed and vulnerable at Chancellorsville. The two Federal forces were still a dozen miles apart, so one wonders what the expectation was when the chief of staff also directed Sedgwick to "attack at once."[19]

At 10:00 A.M. Butterfield again directed him to attack. Hooker had a powerful army at Chancellorsville but proved unable to direct it very well. His artillery had been overwhelmed, not by better guns, but by an adversary who was better organized. Federal infantry formations were solid, but too many had run out of ammunition. A well-led Confederate army had exploited Hooker's poor leadership, and the Federal commander's response was to call on the distant Sixth Corps for help.[20]

Newton's division occupied Fredericksburg while he and Sedgwick planned the Sixth Corps's breakout. Colonel Shaler's regiments looked for stray Confederates and prevented straggling from Federal units. Brigadier General Wheaton's formations were still arrayed in front of Marye's Heights, under shelter on the west side of the drainage. To their right Colonel Browne's brigade extended the line, its right anchored by the Seventh Massachusetts Infantry in "a defensive position in a cemetery on the west side of town."[21]

The Fredericksburg Cemetery Company had a three-acre burying ground enclosed by brick walls. In 1851 the Fredericksburg and Valley Plank Road Company had lowered the grade of William Street in front of the sandstone entry gate to give wagon teams an easier haul upon arrival into town. Along the cemetery's west wall were several rows of buried Confederates, many of them young men who had succumbed to camp illnesses in 1861. The Seventh Massachusetts spread out along the rows of Confederate graves, where they were only six hundred yards from Marye's Heights.[22]

As Sedgwick prepared to move west, Captain Cushing moved additional signal teams into Fredericksburg. Lt. James B. Brooks and Lt. William H. Hill climbed up into the cupola of the courthouse, where they had a clear view across the town's rooftops to the heights. Two blocks to their right, Lt. Frank W. Marsten and Lt. Joseph Gloskoski clambered into the steeple of the Fredericksburg Baptist Church, where they could observe and report on Gibbon's two Second Corps brigades to the north.[23]

That morning Sedgwick had ordered Gibbon to take his forces to the right. The area looked to be lightly held, and a concerted rush might knock things loose and open the road to Chancellorsville. The two brigades on Princess Anne Street constituted a force of approximately 3,500 men. At the far end of the street stood an intact bridge over the millrace fed by the Rappahannock Canal, which the company of Mississippi troops had missed in the darkness.[24]

Upon receipt of Sedgwick's orders, Generals Gibbon and Warren reconnoitered the terrain beyond the canal bridge. They were on relatively flat ground as they approached the hills around the town. The prominent Stansbury mansion, called Snowden, stood on a hilltop to their front. The heights appeared undefended except for two Confederate guns visible where William Street cuts through the rising ground. Gibbon could cross into the open ground from Princess Anne Street but would have to cross the Rappahannock Canal a second time to get onto the Confederate left flank.[25]

At its downstream end, the Rappahannock Canal created a turning basin that fed a millrace to the Washington Woolen Mills. About four hundred yards upstream from the turning basin, a secondary drainage called Marye's Canal blocked Federal forces from being able to skirt around the outside edge of the larger canal barrier. Without bridging equipment, Gibbon had to negotiate the larger waterway over existing spans. He also needed to move quickly. When Confederate forces saw what he was up to, they would surely deploy to block his way.

Gibbon and Warren concluded their reconnaissance and returned to the bridge at Princess Anne Street. Gibbon rode on to get his troops in motion, while Warren waited at the span. Col. Norman J. Hall brought his Third Brigade out first, and Warren directed the troops across the open

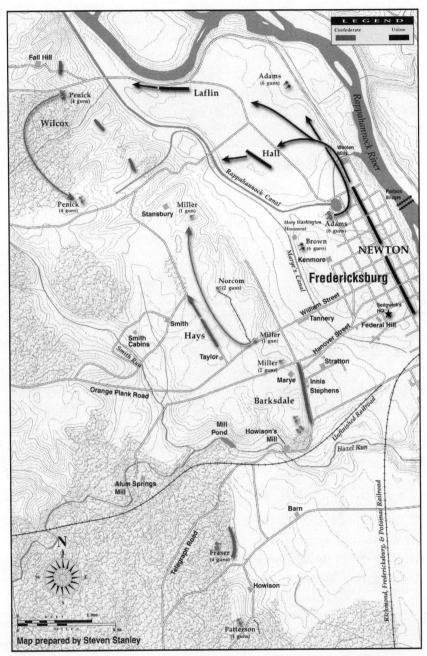

Map 7. Gibbon's Attack at the Rappahannock Canal. Two Union brigades from Gibbon's Second Corps division crossed the millrace formed from the Rappahannock Canal to flank the defenders on Marye's Heights, which pulled Confederate attention away from Fredericksburg.

plain. Battery B, First Rhode Island held position near the forlorn and uncompleted Mary Washington monument to support them. Battery G First Rhode Island waited in reserve near the turning basin.[26]

The Nineteenth Massachusetts led the way across the canal bridge. Warren galloped toward the next one, riding past a partially sunken road bordered by stone walls (modern Fall Hill Avenue). From that stone-lined travel way he followed a lesser road toward a small bridge that crossed the Rappahannock Canal in front of the Stansbury house. Barksdale's Mississippians had pulled off the bridge deck the night before but had no tools to damage the underlying frame.[27]

Warren later wrote: "Not a man or a gun was at that moment there to resist us." A lone Confederate horseman rode forward on the other side of the waterway, but Warren ignored him. The Nineteenth Massachusetts hustled forward, and the engineer directed the infantrymen to pull off the siding from a nearby house. If they could lay down enough boards across the stringers, their combined thickness could become a usable bridge deck.[28]

Colonel Humphreys saw Gibbon's troops on the move. Earlier that morning he had left three companies of his Twenty-First Mississippi to reinforce the Eighteenth Mississippi on the Telegraph Road and deployed the rest of his regiment into existing rifle pits between Hanover and William Streets. Capt. Merritt B. Miller had two 12-pounder Napoleons in battery from his Third Company, Washington Artillery. One gun occupied a redoubt across Hanover Street from Brompton, and the other was placed in a gun pit adjacent to William Street. He saw the Federal units moving to the left as a growing threat.[29]

Newton's division had occupied the town that morning, and Sedgwick directed him to detach two regiments to support Gibbon's two batteries. Colonel Browne received that assignment and detached the Tenth Massachusetts, Col. Henry L. Eustis commanding, and the Second Rhode Island, led by Col. Horatio Rogers Jr. The two regiments hustled toward the elevated ground occupied by Battery B, First Rhode Island Artillery.[30]

The Confederates moved over reinforcements as well. General Pendleton deployed Lt. Joseph Norcom's detachment of two guns from Eschleman's Fourth Company, Washington Artillery. The gun crews brought their weapons into battery in partially completed earthworks. Their first round whistled toward the men of the Nineteenth Massachusetts taking apart a house for material to lay across the canal-bridge framing. Work stopped as the Federals ducked for cover, but another of Hall's regiments invited attention by getting bunched up. Gibbon described how "a bad place in the road caused the 20th Massachusetts to become somewhat massed, and the enemy almost immediately opened fire."[31]

Hall's entire brigade went to ground. In addition to the Nineteenth and Twentieth Massachusetts, the Seventh Michigan, Forty-Ninth and Fifty-Ninth New York, and the 127th Pennsylvania were on the field. The Confederate artillerymen fired spherical case shot into the prone Federals. Caught in the open, the Union troops rushed to the shelter of the stone-lined road, leaving behind several blue-clad forms in the grass.[32]

One of the men under fire that morning was Lt. Oliver Wendell Holmes Jr. of the Twentieth Massachusetts. He watched in helpless disgust as the Confederate gun crews kept loading and firing. A piece of case shot sliced into his heel, the young Harvard man's third wound of the war. He later pursued a career in the law that ultimately led to a seat on the US Supreme Court.[33]

Gibbon shared Holmes's irritation. He later wrote, "I was perfectly powerless to advance and had to take the artillery pelting in silence." The Confederates had halted the Federal advance but kept feeding troops into the fight. Barksdale directed Captain Miller to redeploy the 12-pounder Napoleon posted on William Street. He apparently thought the danger on the left to be more immediate than anything that might come out of Fredericksburg. But Pendleton did not know that an infantry officer had pulled Hero's gun from its critical location, leaving William Street unguarded.[34]

Lt. Andrew J. Hero commanded that weapon, and his orders were to move beyond Norcom's guns, which were blasting the Tenth Massachusetts and Second Rhode Island as they moved to Gibbon's support. A Massachusetts infantryman described how he and others "ran the gauntlet of this infernal fire for a mile and the enemy having obtained a perfect range, exploded every shell within the most deadly distance; the ragged fragments flying, howling and screeching, into our midst with terrible effect."[35]

Warren saw Confederate infantry now taking position on the heights overlooking the canal. Hays's Louisiana brigade had arrived back at Fredericksburg by 7:00 A.M., and Early sent it to support the Mississippi brigade. Barksdale directed the Sixth Louisiana, Colonel Monaghan commanding, to his far right to support Captain Carlton's Troup Artillery overlooking Deep Run. He sent the Fifth, Seventh, Eighth, and Ninth Louisiana Regiments to bolster the Confederate left.[36]

The arriving Louisianans filed into existing trenches along the heights. Across the canal, Gibbon directed Colonel Laflin to bring up his brigade.

Laflin moved the First Minnesota, the Fifteenth Massachusetts, and his own Thirty-Fourth New York past Hall's units sheltering in the road and hustled farther to the right. Gibbon wanted them "to attempt the passage of the second canal by the bridge near Falmouth."[37]

Laflin's brigade immediately took fire. A New York soldier described how "over us, and all around us screamed and burst the rebel shells." The Federals could also see the Louisiana units keeping pace as they extended the Confederate line along the hills past the Stansbury house. Federal artillery on the heights around Falmouth weighed in at long range. Battery G, First Rhode Island Artillery, waiting near the turning basin, prepared to move into the open ground west of the canal. Battery B, First Rhode Island Artillery, remained in place near the unfinished monument.[38]

Captain Adams immediately realized he was taking his battery into a bad place. As his gun crews carefully moved over the well-used canal bridge at the end of Princess Anne Street, a Confederate round smashed into one of his caissons, knocking it into the water. Out on the plain they found a somewhat protected area "in a hollow by the roadside, behind a fence ridge." The Rhode Island artillerymen brought their guns into battery but still found themselves at a disadvantage. Three Confederate guns were on the high ground to their front, sheltered in earthworks, and delivering a plunging fire. Casualties mounted. The Federals returned fire but without apparent effect.[39]

The Tenth Massachusetts and Second Rhode Island also crossed the canal to support Gibbon. They too took shelter behind the stone walls lining the road as Laflin pressed on to the right. On the heights additional Confederate artillery moved into position. The arriving guns were a section of 3-inch Ordnance Rifles from Lewis's Pittsylvania Battery, brought over from Banks' Ford by Lt. Nathan Penick.[40]

At Banks' Ford General Wilcox had discretionary orders to reinforce Lee if he could do so without compromising the army's security. Observing the Federals opposite him, he "found that the enemy had reduced very much (apparently) his force." Wilcox also noted that the "sentinels on post had their haversacks on, a thing unusual." They looked to be ready to march. The brigade commander heard the artillery fire at Chancellorsville as well as the firing at Fredericksburg.[41]

With no Federal preparations evident at Banks' Ford, Wilcox decided to get his Alabama infantry and two Virginia artillery units back into the fight. He detailed fifty men and two field guns of Capt. Joseph D. Moore's Norfolk Battery to remain at the ford, a force sufficient to warn of an attack rather than confront one. As the rest of the brigade formed up to march to the Orange Turnpike, a soldier ran in with news from Fredericksburg. Catching his breath, he reported that pickets on Fall Hill had seen a Federal force "advancing up the road between the canal and the river."[42]

Wilcox rode to Fall Hill, where he could assess this latest news. He saw three Federal regiments (Laflin's units) near the canal bridge that the Nineteenth Massachusetts had tried to repair. They were moving past it toward another bridge, which crossed the canal at River Road (modern Fall Hill Avenue). There were fewer than twenty skirmishers of the Tenth Alabama on hand, and the general realized he needed reinforcements. He directed the picket force into existing earthworks before riding away.[43]

Wilcox hurried back to bring up his regiments and two batteries. Penick had the four guns of his Pittsylvania Battery limbered up for the march to Chancellorsville. Wilcox directed him to take two 3-inch Ordnance Rifles to a set of lunettes on Fall Hill across the road from Dr. Taylor's house. He ordered Moore to take his 10-pounder Parrott rifle and a 3-inch Ordnance Rifle to the Fall Hill gun emplacements as well. The Alabama foot soldiers would follow.[44]

By the time Penick and Moore brought their long-range weapons into battery, Laflin's brigade was approaching the River Road canal bridge. The Confederate guns opened fire, and Laflin's lead regiment, the First Minnesota, sought the shelter of Confederate rifle pits near the river. Following behind the Minnesotans, the Thirty-Fourth New York and Fifteenth Massachusetts lay down in the road, protected by its stone walls.[45]

Gibbon's infantry found itself well protected but unable to advance. Their position became tenuous as Confederate reinforcements arrived. Hays's Louisiana units moved into the trenches near the Stansbury house. Now Wilcox's Alabama units took position "in the ditches at Dr. Taylor's and to the right." The Alabama pickets who had nervously watched the approaching Federals rejoined their unit.[46]

This buildup of Confederate infantry was daunting, but it had been artillery that had halted the Union advance. Norcom's two howitzers had interrupted efforts to repair the canal bridge below the Stansbury house. Hero's additional gun had helped drive the advancing infantry into the shelter of the road. Penick's and Moore's guns had then subjected the Federals to a crossfire. After his initial burst of shooting, Penick pulled his guns out of position on Fall Hill and backtracked on River Road to a narrow trace that brought them to a double lunette on a hill behind the Stansbury mansion. Guns in those works were better positioned to cover the canal bridge.[47]

The two 3-inch Ordnance Rifles of Moore's battery remained on Fall Hill. In addition to shooting at Gibbon's units, they engaged Federal batteries across the river. From that vantage point Wilcox saw a group of officers at the Stansbury house and rode to confer with them. He found Barksdale and Hays, and the three brigade commanders from three different divisions quickly discussed what to do now that the Federals had advanced into Fredericksburg. Wilcox had intended to march to Chancellorsville but said he would bring his units over to Fredericksburg instead.[48]

Following the trace that Penick's artillerymen had used to get to the double lunette, the Eleventh Alabama moved toward Hays's Louisianans to link up their two lines. As they marched behind the earthworks occupied by the Virginia battery, the hard-pressed Battery G, First Rhode Island Artillery brought them under fire. Incoming Federal rounds tore through the Alabamans, and Wilcox ordered his units not manning trenches to find cover in nearby ravines.[49]

Barksdale and Hays rode off to their respective brigades. In short order a Mississippi staff officer found Wilcox and reported that Barksdale had become hard pressed in Fredericksburg and needed a regiment. Wilcox immediately ordered Col. William H. Forney to take his Tenth Alabama to the right. The brigade commander also rode toward town and saw Louisiana units pulling back. He could not yet be sure, but it looked like the Confederate position had collapsed.[50]

In December Northern attacks on Marye's Heights had been launched within a relatively narrow front, constrained by Hazel Run and the Rappahannock Canal. Confederate defenders had blunted every advance, and Federal troops never managed to close with the enemy. Sedgwick would need to overcome that constricted battleground. He had sent Gibbon to probe the Confederate left, searching for vulnerabilities on that flank, but the effort had been halted at the Rappahannock Canal. An assault against Marye's Heights could not be avoided, so Sedgwick directed Newton to develop a plan.[51]

Gibbon had extended the Union line to the right. Sedgwick and Newton extended their front to the left, directing Brigadier General Howe to prepare for an attack beyond Hazel Run. Howe's division had spent the night on the Bowling Green Road, listening to the small-arms fire that punctuated Newton's advance into Fredericksburg. At daybreak they watched artillery fire intensify in Fredericksburg. To their left Brooks's units probed the Confederate defenses at Deep Run.[52]

Maj. J. Watts de Peyster, commanding Howe's divisional artillery, placed his two batteries west of the Bowling Green Road. Capt. Andrew Cowan's First New York Independent Artillery took position where the ground begins to drop toward Hazel Run. Lt. Leonard Martin's Battery F, Fifth US Artillery dropped trail on Cowan's left. They could hear Newton's two batteries and Burnham's single battery slow firing in Fredericksburg. Directly in front of them, about 1,800 yards away, were low hills crowned by Confederate artillery.[53]

Sedgwick had informed Howe that he was to leave the fighting at Deep Run to Brooks and be ready to advance across the open ground toward the hills. When the division commander examined the fields in front of him, he could see a railway cutting across his front about five hundred yards out. From the Ferneyhough house, a farm road extended toward a large barn beyond the tracks to the right. After crossing the railway, that crude trace turned to the south, bending toward a break in the hills near the Howison house.[54]

The men Howe would send across that ground waited under cover east of the Bowling Green Road. The ground dropped away there, extending toward the Rappahannock River seven hundred yards away. They watched casualties from the fighting at Deep Run being carried on stretchers or making their way on their own toward Fredericksburg, the pontoon bridges at Franklin's Crossing then being dismantled.[55]

Howe's two brigades prepared to advance. Brigadier General Neill detailed three of his regiments as the first line of an assault column. Col. Lewis A. Grant would have three of his regiments in the second line. The reserve line included units from both brigades. Within those battle-tested commands were the Twenty-First and the Twenty-Sixth New Jersey, both of which would be nine-month regiments.[56]

The leadership of the Twenty-Sixth New Jersey provided reason for concern about both units. Col. Andrew J. Morrison worked hard to give the impression of being an experienced soldier of fortune. The thirty-four-year-old had presumably run away from home at the age of sixteen to fight in the War with Mexico. He also claimed to have been in Cuba in 1851 with Narcisso de Lopez, in Nicaragua in 1856 with William Walker, and with Giuseppe Garibaldi in Italy in 1860. Whatever his story, preparing troops for battle was not a skill he had picked up along the way. After seven months of service, his nine-month New Jersey regiment remained poorly trained.[57]

Howe's first two lines of battle comprised 2,850 men. At the appropriate time they would filter through their artillery, form up quickly, and advance to the hills. While listening to the fighting at Deep Run, the men stacked their knapsacks and waited. A Vermont soldier wrote how that "Sunday, we had to lay all the fore noon under the fire of Reb batteries, their shells passing over us and the hot Virginia sun pouring down on us."[58]

In Fredericksburg Burnham's Light Division had moved up in the dark and crossed Marye's Canal, getting that obstacle behind them. By 6:00 A.M. his units were sheltered behind an embankment about five hundred yards from the base of Marye's Heights. A Wisconsin soldier wrote how the troops formed "in line of battle directly to the rear of Fredericksburg, and in front of the stone wall and fortifications on which Gen. Hancock's Irish Brigade made the famous but unsuccessful charge last fall." An attack would need to unfold quickly, so Burnham's men stacked their knapsacks. They had also been two days without sleep, and many of them fell into a sound slumber, so tired that they remained oblivious to the booming artillery. A Maine soldier wrote,"[for] three long weary hours under the Virginia sun lay the men, tired, impatient, and not overconfident, yet determined."[59]

Five companies of Col. Thomas S. Allen's Fifth Wisconsin prepared to deploy as skirmishers. Allen had come from the Second Wisconsin, and there was talk that he had usurped a position that might have gone to one of the Fifth's own officers. The new commander sought to dispel those hard feelings by sharing the danger of the most exposed places his men occupied. To the left of the Fifth Wisconsin, Lt. Col. Benjamin F. Harris had his Sixth Maine. Col. Frank Jones had his Thirty-First New York to Harris's left. Birney's Zouaves (Twenty-Third Pennsylvania), Colonel Ely commanding, had taken casualties in the early morning probe but remained nearby to support any subsequent attack. The rest of the Fifth Wisconsin waited behind the Thirty-First New York.[60]

To the left of the waiting assault troops, a portion of Wheaton's brigade continued to hold a line in support of the division's artillery. Burnham was under orders not to engage, but Wheaton had no such constraints. Col. Joseph M. Kinkead sent two men of his 102nd Pennsylvania to reconnoiter along the unfinished railway. The two riflemen moved up to where the cut tapered off to open ground. A force there could remain under cover but still partially enfilade the "stonewall rifle pit." When the two soldiers reported back, Kinkead sent a company forward to annoy the Confederates until the planned attack crossed their field of fire.[61]

The area in front of Marye's Heights did not provide sufficient space for anything more than an assault in brigade strength. But Sedgwick would launch a larger attack. While Howe's two brigades completed their preparations south of Hazel Run and Burnham continued his preparations north of that stream, two more assault columns were deployed to Burnham's right. The attack in the center could not be made overwhelming but might succeed with enough peripheral support.[62]

On Burnham's immediate right, Hanover Street extends out of Fredericksburg to Marye's Heights. It had been the primary avenue of advance in December, but this time only two regiments would use it. Once across Marye's Canal, they would not spread out in line of battle but continue in column in coordination with Burnham's assault. The road column came from Colonel Browne's brigade. Col. Thomas D. Johns brought his Seventh Massachusetts over from the Fredericksburg Cemetery, accompanied by the Thirty-Sixth New York under Lt. Col. James J. Walsh.[63]

The Hanover Street assault would have to advance two blocks from Princess Anne Street to Prince Edward Street, where Sedgwick had his headquarters. Once past the sheltering buildings, they would be 420 yards from Marye's Canal and exposed to Confederate artillery. Once across that drainage, they would still be 430 yards from the stone wall where Mississippi riflemen waited. To reach that objective, they had to cross a daunting 850 yards of open ground.

There was one bright spot in the Hanover Street approach. Observers could see that the Confederates had left the bridge over Marye's Canal undamaged. In December Union attackers had found the bridge decking removed, forcing them to cross single file on the stringers. The bridge had since been repaired, and the Confederates had done nothing to preclude its use by Sedgwick's troops.

At their point of departure along Princess Anne Street, the assault troops stacked their knapsacks, loaded weapons, and fixed bayonets. They were directed not to cap their rifles. Once the attack began, men stopping to fire would slow the column. There was likely going to be only one opportunity to punch through the Confederate defenses, and victory was going to rely on momentum and cold steel.[64]

The Federal command put together a stronger assault on William Street. At the head of this column would be two of Burnham's Light Division units.

Col. George C. Spear's Sixty-First Pennsylvania would take the lead, followed by Col. Benjamin F. Baker's Forty-Third New York. From Shaler's brigade the Sixty-Seventh New York (also known as the First Long Island Regiment) and the Eighty-Second Pennsylvania, led by Col. Nelson Cross and Maj. Isaac C. Bassett respectively, would add their weight to the attack.[65]

Colonel Spear took a moment to brief his sergeants, something he had not done previously. The view up William Street looked daunting, and there was every possibility that many officers would be killed in the attack. Spear made sure his noncommissioned officers were prepared to carry on without them, concluding his briefing with a quick "God bless you." All four regiments stacked their knapsacks and other gear on Princess Anne Street, retaining only weapons and ammunition.[66]

The William Street advance had to cover nearly seven hundred yards to Marye's Canal. As on Hanover Street, there was an intact bridge over that drainage. These spans were described as "bridges of the ordinary width," which meant they were wide enough to handle a common wagon. That basic standard also accommodated a column of troops four abreast. Once across the waterway, however, the attackers had another four hundred yards to go before crossing bayonets with Confederate infantry and another two hundred yards beyond that to the artillery positions on the hilltop.[67]

While the Hanover Street column would link up with Burnham's line of battle, the William Street attackers would be on their own in a narrow road corridor. Ponds and tannery buildings on the other side of the drainage would keep them in a tight formation. The hills beyond the tannery would force the attack into a narrow front. Confederate artillery on these heights would be able to fire down the full length of the files, every round able to kill and cripple large numbers of men.

General Early expected the main Federal assault to occur south of Deep Run, where a Federal breakthrough had occurred in December. The activity on his front that morning reinforced his anticipation, and he retained three brigades and twenty-six guns in that sector. Those assets were more than half of his available strength.[68]

Early had sent Hays's Brigade to reinforce Barksdale's Mississippians, and Barksdale had sent most of them to confront Gibbon's two brigades at the Rappahannock Canal. Those Louisianans had also been reinforced by Wilcox's Alabama regiments. The growing Confederate strength confronting Gibbon, however, had become a misapplication of force. The Rappahannock Canal effectively hindered a strong Federal effort, but a sizable number of Confederates remained in that sector while the Sixth Corps prepared to launch attacks elsewhere.[69]

Marye's Heights and Howison Hill were held by Barksdale's Brigade and a single Louisiana regiment. Artillery would be critical to hold a line that thinly manned. On the heights overlooking Deep Run and the Lansdowne valley, three 10-pounder Parrott rifles of Carlton's Troup Artillery had the range to blast Howe's artillery near the Ferneyhough house. On Howison Hill Patterson's Battery B, Sumter Artillery had four 12-pounder smoothbores in battery, which would be effective when the infantry attack came. On Lee's Hill Capt. John C. Fraser had in place his Pulaski Battery, consisting of a 10-pounder Parrott rifle, a 3-inch Ordnance Rifle, and a 12-pounder howitzer.[70]

North of Hazel Run, two 10-pounder Parrott rifles from Rhett's South Carolina Battery, manned by crews from Parker's Richmond Battery, were on the shoulder of Willis Hill. Also on those heights were six guns from Colonel Walton's Washington Artillery. Those sons of New Orleans had two 3-inch Ordnance Rifles in front of the Willis Cemetery, Captain Squires commanding. To their left Capt. Merritt B. Miller had deployed a 12-pounder Napoleon on either side of William Street, although one of them had been pulled out of position to confront Gibbon's advance to the Rappahannock Canal.[71]

Confederate infantry had also reoccupied the line. Colonel Monaghan's Sixth Louisiana occupied Howison Hill. Col. James W. Carter's Thirteenth Mississippi extended toward Lee's Hill, where Col. William D. Holder's Seventeenth Mississippi was deployed. Across Hazel Run, at the base of Marye's Heights, Griffin's Eighteenth Mississippi and three companies of Humphreys's Twenty-First Mississippi were on the Telegraph Road, protected by a stone wall. The rest of the Twenty-First Mississippi extended the line to William Street. There were no reserves.[72]

Sedgwick sent Maj. Thomas W. Hyde, his assistant inspector general, out to the Bowling Green Road to coordinate Howe's attack with Newton's overall plan. Upon his return, as he rode up Hanover Street, a Confederate shell burst over its intersection with Prince Edward Street, where a 12-pounder Napoleon of Lt. John H. Butler's Battery G, Second US Artillery was firing. The exploding round killed three horses and wounded five artillerymen and a staff officer. To his great surprise, Hyde remained unscathed. As he dismounted to report to Sedgwick, one of the Federal storming columns came toward him from Princess Anne Street.[73]

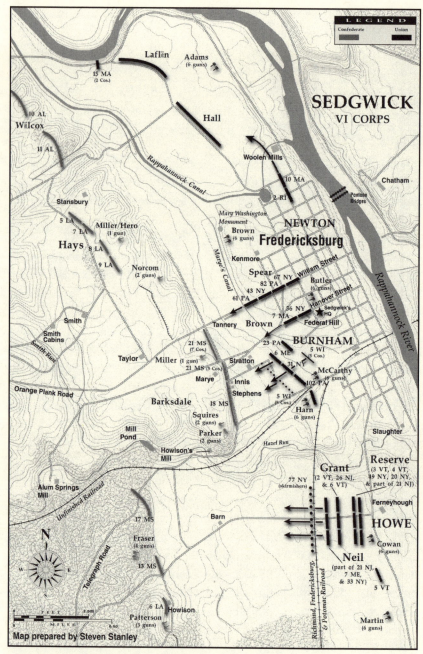

Map 8. Sedgwick's Attack. The Sixth Corps advanced across a broad front, with columns on William and Hanover Streets, a line of battle on the 1862 battleground, and a division-strength attack south of Hazel Run.

Federal artillery kept up a steady but measured fire, which sometimes made the infantry nervous. A Maine soldier remembered: "From behind, across the river, our heavy artillery was pounding away at the enemy's works on the heights in front of us. As the shells screamed over our heads, it sometimes happened that one with the fuse [sic] cut too short burst over our heads, varying none too pleasantly the monotony of lying close under cover. The enemy replied but seldom, choosing to save his ammunition for fighting at closer range."[74]

Around 10:30 A.M. the volume of Federal artillery fire tapered off, which increased the tension. At 11:00 A.M. the report from a single gun signaled the attack.[75] Edwin Buckman, the Ninety-Eighth Pennsylvania's surgeon, described the renewed cannonade: "[The] batteries opened with increased vigor not leaving a moments cessation from the continual tremendous pounding going on in every direction—this was soon joined by the opening of the 32 pounders from the other side of the river throwing their shot and shell right over our heads.... These shots come with a crushing force and shock nearly equal to the sharp thunder following close the flash of lightning."[76]

Colonel Spear's column came out from behind the cover of the Princess Anne Street buildings and turned onto William Street. The men moved at the double-quick, a rapid and steady pace that would keep their formation intact. Those in the front ranks could see down the long, straight road to the Confederate position, a hilltop three-quarters of a mile away.

Buildings hemmed in the road corridor, but when the advancing troops crossed over Charles and Prince Edward Streets, they could see the Hanover Street assault column two blocks to their left. The houses along Prince Edward Street constituted the edge of town, and as the men pressed on into a more open landscape, an unkempt cemetery, enclosed by a low brick wall, stood to their left. Up ahead were large wagon yards and a few more buildings along the roadway. Another cemetery, also enclosed with a brick wall, became visible on the right. Union skirmishers were arrayed along its east side as well as inside the enclosure behind its west wall.

The William Street column had the strength of a brigade but had a long way to go to bring that force to bear. The road dropped toward Marye's Canal, and the men hustled down the cut created by the Turnpike Company in front of the cemetery. They were now roughly halfway to the heights. But there was something going on to their right because Confederate cannons were shooting there instead of into the regiments on William Street.

As Spears crossed the bridge over the drainage canal, the Confederates finally caught the Federals in what one soldier described as "the most murderous fire that you can imagine . . . principally spherical case shot and musketry, with some shells." Norcom's two howitzers had been shooting up Gibbon's forces but now turned their attention to this new target, which was in a choke point at the canal bridge. Miller's 12-pounder Napoleon, still in position in a redoubt south of William Street, also opened fire. The storming column found itself in a crossfire.[77]

About half of the Sixty-First Pennsylvania had cleared the bridge when the incoming rounds slammed into them. Dead and wounded men fell into the watery ditch, where those too injured to stand up drowned. Colonel Spear fell in that initial fire, and his men began to falter. Many went to ground in a depression between the road and a brick tannery. That industrial complex belonged to John Hurkamp, whose house had become Sedgwick's headquarters.[78]

Immediately behind the Sixty-First Pennsylvania, the Forty-Third New York had to break stride, which made it a stationary target. The Sixty-Seventh New York and Eighty-Second Pennsylvania also paused involuntarily, their way forward blocked by the confused mass of men getting hit by Confederate artillery. Because of the drainage ditch, there was no way to go around the stalled units in front of them.[79]

Colonel Shaler had accompanied his lead regiments as they moved toward the bridge. He intercepted some of the scared men, reassured them the setback could be overcome, and then led them back to where regimental officers were rallying their stalled formations. In the Forty-Third New York, Capt. Douglas Lodge had been knocked down by a shell fragment, and Colonel Baker had collapsed, exhausted. Lt. Col. John Wilson and Maj. John Fryer tried to bring order from the chaos. Lt. George R. Koonz was killed trying to do the same. Pvt. James Robb grabbed the Forty-Third New York colors from a wounded sergeant, and Baker, having caught his breath, used him to rally the regiment.[80]

Major Bassett moved up his Eighty-Second Pennsylvania in support. His men had not yet been hit by the incoming fire, and he pushed through with his colors, rallying men from the Forty-Third New York and Sixty-First Pennsylvania along the way. Captain Lodge had not been incapacitated by the piece of shell that knocked him down, and he resumed his place with his regiment. The William Street column began to move forward again.[81]

On Hanover Street the Seventh Massachusetts, followed by the Thirty-Sixth New York, came forward at the double-quick in column of fours, their weapons at the right shoulder. Houses along the street and a bend in the road kept the advancing men from seeing their objective, but they still caught glimpses of the William Street column two blocks to their right. When these veterans crossed Prince Edward Street, however, they broke into the open and could finally see where they were headed. Confederate artillerymen could also see them.[82]

The panorama of the December battleground opened up as the attack column hustled past Federal Hill. About four hundred yards away was a canal drainage, with a blue line of infantry on its far side to the left. Some wrecked houses lined the road on the east side of that ditch, while others appeared intact on its west side. On top of the heights, still over eight hundred yards away, stood a brick mansion with artillery visible nearby. Johns guided his Massachusetts men from horseback, while Walsh led his Thirty-Sixth New York forward on foot, giving orders and steadying the men in his heavy Irish brogue.[83]

Thanks to an undamaged bridge, the Federals crossed Marye's Canal without losing momentum. To their left the Light Division troops waited behind an embankment. On the right stood a large house (801 Hanover Street) and a scattering of outbuildings. The troops briefly found themselves in defilade, and Colonel Johns dismounted. Beyond the house the ground leveled off, and advancing troops would soon become visible to the waiting Mississippi riflemen.[84]

A few minutes earlier Burnham had called the Light Division to attention, and all talking had ceased. Word came down the line to remove the caps from loaded rifles, as the attack would be a rush to close with the enemy as quickly as possible. Colonel Allen knew his men would have to traverse the open ground where troops had been slaughtered in December, and he took a few moments to steel them for the coming shock: "Perhaps you think you cannot take them; I know you can. When the signal forward is given, you will start at the double quick. You will not fire a gun and you will not stop until you get the order to halt. You will never get that order."[85]

In the Sixth Maine's line, Lt. Charles A. Clark and Maj. Joel A. Haycock shook hands and said "God bless you" to each other. The waiting men observed the column on Hanover Street. A Maine soldier wrote, "it was truly a time of suspense to see these two regiments marching up, and all around was still no sound except the steady tramp of the men before they came up with our right."[86]

After his words of encouragement, Allen led his Fifth Wisconsin skirmishers forward a few yards, where a stone retaining wall provided shelter (along modern Weedon Street). When the Seventh Massachusetts came abreast of them, Allen waved his sword and the company commanders shouted: "Charge!" Lt. George E. Bissell recalled the agony of ordering men to almost certain death: "It is impossible to describe my feeling when I gave the order, but give it I did."[87]

Unlike the street columns, Burnham's regiments were in line of battle. At his signal they burst out of the declivity that had sheltered them and broke into a full run. A Maine soldier remembered, "We all came to our feet with a tiger, and soon caught up with the skirmishers." Their world exploded as the Mississippians opened fire. Major Haycock became one of the first casualties, shot in the head. The first volley also decimated the skirmishers of the Fifth Wisconsin.[88]

A Wisconsin soldier described the frenzy of their ordeal:

We rose to our feet and with a yell charged in line of battle for the heights. The line of earthworks and the flanking batteries were a blaze of living fire, and men were falling fast among us before we cleared the little crest which sheltered us. Across the "Slaughter Pen" we rushed while grape-shot and shrapnel and bullets tore through our ranks, while officers and men were dropping on every hand. It was a race with death, but with all this terrible tension we were under we kept our formation, the lines closing up as they were thinned by the firing.[89]

The Hanover Street column staggered as Confederate lead tore into them. One of the Massachusetts men later wrote, "The road and gulch was filled with the dead, wounded, and dying." They pressed on, however, trying to keep pace with the line of battle to their left. Another Massachusetts soldier remembered how "the cries and groans of the wounded are lost in the huzzas and shouts of those who, unhurt, press madly forward."[90]

Behind the Wisconsin skirmishers the Sixth Maine and the Thirty-First New York advanced side by side. The Twenty-Third Pennsylvania joined the assault as well. The five remaining companies of the Fifth Wisconsin followed directly behind the battle line. But those five companies serving as skirmishers had taken the initial volley full on. As they sprang toward the sunken road, incoming fire stripped away nearly a hundred of their number, strewing them out in the wake of the charging line.[91]

Unable to handle the barrage, the Twenty-Third Pennsylvania fell back. The regiment had meant to join the assault, but eyewitnesses seldom mention it. The Thirty-First New York also faltered. Its members dropped to the ground in a swale halfway to the stone wall, just as units had done in December. The Wisconsin men behind the New Yorkers ran through the prostrate troops and extended the front presented by the Sixth Maine. Those two units together numbered around 850 men rushing forward. Capt. Lewis A. Strong of the Fifth Wisconsin took a bullet in his mouth but continued running forward. He fell when another bullet tore through his chest. One of his men shouted, "God bless you, Captain," as he ran past the dying man.[92]

The stone wall along the Telegraph Road provided solid protection for the Confederate defenders until close to Hanover Street, where the roadway fell below grade and it became a retaining wall, unusable as a barrier against attacking troops. The Maine and Wisconsin men charged "on a full run" and reached the stone wall with considerable momentum. At the sunken portion of the Confederate position, the attackers jumped into the roadway and ran defenders through with bayonets. To their left, where the stone wall stood above ground, a screaming Maine soldier vaulted over the barrier without touching it. Twenty-five to thirty men scrambled over behind him.[93]

The Mississippians fought hard, but the Federals piled in on them. The close combat proved bloody, brutal, and brief. One of the Maine men described a comrade who "bayoneted two rebels in succession, and then, as the resistance was obstinate, he brained a third with the butt of his musket." A Wisconsin soldier wrote how "our boys dashed forward furiously into the rifle pit [sunken road] and bayoneted many of the rebels where they stood and taking nearly all the rest prisoner."[94]

There was one man in the road glad to see the arriving Federals. Pvt. Charley Smallwood had been wounded several hours earlier when his Twenty-Third Pennsylvania (Birney's Zouaves) had probed the Confederate line in the darkness. He had crawled to a small dwelling (probably the Ebert house), where some Confederates made him a prisoner. Smallwood's captors did not bother to evacuate him, and he was still there when the Maine and Wisconsin men surged over the stone wall.[95]

On Hanover Street the Seventh Massachusetts and Thirty-Sixth New York were momentarily halted by the intense fire from the defenders. Colonel Johns fell wounded, hit twice. Lt. Col. Franklin P. Harlow rallied his men at a cluster of small buildings around a brick house at the bend in the road. In that temporary shelter they were still about 160 yards from the Confederate riflemen but could see that the stone wall ended well short of the street. The terrain in front of them was open, and they were further encouraged by the supporting artillery rounds crashing into the Confederate positions on top of the hill.[96]

One of Harlow's troops remembered him calling out, "Forward, boys!" Another recalled someone shouting, "Massachusetts colors to the front." The regiment sprang forward and "struggled over and through the stone wall, bleeding at every step." A shot in the stomach knocked Harlow down, but the column surged up the road, moving past the sunken part of the Telegraph Road to their left. They poured an enfilading fire into a trench across the lower slope of the hill to their right.[97]

Sound leadership kept the William Street regiments in motion as well. A Pennsylvania soldier wrote: "Gen. Shaler's advance on horseback . . . was a great exhibition of coolness under fire. The road, and especially the bridge, was strewn with killed and wounded. The rider and the horse seemed equally careful to avoid further injury to the prostrate men, the noble animal being permitted, regardless of danger, to pick his steps while slowly advancing amid the din of conflict."[98]

As the troops moved up the hill, the narrow William Street corridor shielded them from enemy artillery on both flanks. As one soldier described it, "Beyond the tannery the road ascended toward the rebel works through a cut." The Eighty-Second Pennsylvania surged ahead, with remnants of the Sixty-First Pennsylvania and Forty-Third New York in tow; the Sixty-Seventh New York Regiment followed in reserve. The end of the column remained exposed, and the troops "got jammed together in a sort of gulch, through which the enemy were pouring a murderous fire."[99]

This incoming fire staggered the Union column, but there was no Confederate artillery in front of them. The Napoleon that should have been at the top of the hill and shooting down the road was gone, moved to the left to confront Gibbon's force. That error had been perpetrated by Barksdale, but an exhausted Pendleton had failed to ensure the integrity of his artillery screen. Pushing beyond the fields of fire of the guns on either side, the Federals had a fair chance of breaking the Confederate line.[100]

Union troops leapfrogged forward. The Eighty-Second Pennsylvania had moved through the stalled Sixty-First Pennsylvania and Forty-Third New

York, followed by the Sixty-Seventh New York. After this reshuffle, those men rallied and followed in support of the other two regiments. The Eighty-Second Pennsylvania then faltered in turn, and Colonel Cross led his Sixty-Seventh New York (First Long Island) through the struggling line. When it surged into the open ground on top of the hill, the New Yorkers saw the flag of the Sixth Maine to their left.[101]

The Sixth Maine and Fifth Wisconsin had lunged into the road in front of Marye's Heights and overwhelmed the Mississippians. Fleeing Southerners raced down the road toward Hazel Run as well as up the draw between Willis Hill and the Marye house. The Federals swarmed after them. One of the pursuers wrote that they rushed ahead "with a wild and indescribable frenzy."[102]

Burnham's two regiments advanced to the hilltop, but only the Maine men had their colors. The Fifth Wisconsin men rushing onto Willis Hill were the skirmishers who had been in advance of the line when the attack began. Their colors were with the other half of the regiment advancing behind the Thirty-First New York. The Sixth Maine thus claimed the honor of being the first to plant its flag on the Confederate works.[103]

A clerk at Sedgwick's headquarters had taken out his watch to time the attack. When he saw the Federal colors flying over Marye's Heights, he noted that the assault had lasted all of six minutes. What he had timed, however, was the attack launched in line of battle from behind the embankment. As noted, the assault columns on Princess Anne Street had stepped off shortly after 11:00 A.M. A half hour later a Wisconsin soldier noted how his unit and the Sixth Maine broke onto the heights "precisely as the city clock struck." That single strike marked the time as 11:30 A.M. Events were still moving quickly, though. A second set of colors went up almost immediately, planted by men of the Sixth Vermont Infantry of Howe's division—from across Hazel Run.[104]

Major Hyde's visit to Howe had been Sedgwick's means of coordinating his overall attack. The columns in town could see and keep pace with one another, but Howe's forces were south of Hazel Run. They had been waiting "behind a bank of the road" since the early morning, having also stacked their knapsacks and haversacks to go in with just weapons and ammunition.[105]

As Hyde departed Howe's headquarters, Neill ordered the Seventy-Seventh New York Infantry to advance toward the Confederate-held hills just over a mile away. They were to advance in skirmish order and "occupy, if possible, a house and rifle-pits in the possession of the enemy's skirmishers and covered by their artillery." The New Yorkers moved up toward the railway five hundred yards out. As the Southern skirmishers pulled back, the Northerners ensconced themselves in the vacated position.[106]

Howe heard the Federal artillery open with a resounding fury on his right and prepared to advance. Neill's brigade formed the first line, with a portion of the Twenty-First New Jersey on the left, the Seventh Maine in the center, and the Thirty-Third New York on the right. The second line consisted of the Second Vermont, the Twenty-Sixth New Jersey, and the Sixth Vermont from Grant's brigade. While forming up, the men could see the attack columns to their right preparing to start forward, and they ran to get into position. The last of them were barely in place when the order came to advance.[107]

Howe's division moved forward with a steady pace, the hills in front of them quiet. As the line of battle approached the railway, the Seventy-Seventh New York skirmishers moved ahead. Guiding on the road that led to the Howison house, the New Yorkers veered slightly to the left. To prevent a gap from opening in the battle line, the Thirty-Third New York moved up to extend the skirmish line to the right.[108]

When the Federals were about halfway between the railway and the heights, Confederate artillery came alive. From Carlton's Troup Artillery on the far left to Fraser's Pulaski Battery on the right, Southern guns pounded the Federal lines. Fraser's guns had been shooting at the Federals approaching Marye's Heights but now turned their fire to blast the attack in front of them.[109]

Howe's two batteries redirected their fire to support the infantry advance. On the west side of the Bowling Green Road, Cowan's First New York Independent Artillery and Martin's Battery B, Fifth US Artillery had been firing at Willis Hill to the right. They now shifted their fire to the Confederate guns on Lee's and Howison Hills.[110]

Lt. Col. Winsor French, leading the Seventy-Seventh New York, described the effect of the Southern guns: "I saw the concentrated fire, the havock [sic] it was making, the rattling of the grape, the shrieking of shells, and the earth plowed up around that brave and beautiful line, almost hiding them from my view.... I expected they would be annihilated. Still on they pressed till they came upon the line of skirmishers." The shelling began to break up the attack formation, causing the Seventh Maine and

Thirty-Third New York to veer to the right. The Sixth Vermont, in the second line, followed them.[111]

Moving to the left, behind the Seventy-Seventh New York, the Twenty-First and Twenty-Sixth New Jersey had inadvertently become the main line of battle. The New Jersey soldiers were good men but not prepared for the firestorm in which they found themselves. Colonel Morrison, commanding the Twenty-Sixth, had found a way to get drunk and rode along the line giving conflicting orders. Lt. Col. Edward Martindale stepped in to take charge, but the regiment had lost cohesion. The men scattered, many of them gravitating toward the seeming shelter of nearby hay and tobacco barns.[112]

The Twenty-First New Jersey also broke. Col. James H. Walbridge's Second Vermont charged forward to fill the gap, coming up between the two wings of the Seventy-Seventh New York. These veterans knew that survival hinged on closing in on the hills. They scrambled to the foot of Lee's Hill, where they found a wide ditch filled with muddy water. Some of the Jerseymen made it to the ditch as well, willing soldiers gravitating toward troops who knew what they were doing.[113]

Grant had accompanied the Second Vermont and found himself pressing his attack with that one regiment and the more stalwart men of the Twenty-Sixth New Jersey. He moved the Vermonters to the right, kept the New Jersey men on the left, and then let everyone catch their breath. French also held his Seventy-Seventh New York in place while the other units closed up.[114]

In the meantime the Seventh Maine and Thirty-Third New York, followed by the Sixth Vermont, had split to the right. They rushed across what one soldier described as "a deep ravine, full of brush, logs, and vines and briars, with a creek [Hazel Run] at the bottom, some twenty feet in width and two or three feet deep." These wayward units splashed across the stream, which put them on the flank of the Willis Hill salient.[115]

The three regiments reached the shelter of the unfinished railway embankment, about two hundred yards to the left of where the 102nd Pennsylvania occupied the railway cut. The Maine men and the New Yorkers paused in that defilade, but the Sixth Vermont followed the sheltering earth farther to the left. They then cut over to Howison's Mill, where a road ascended the west side of Willis Hill. Elements of the Fifth Wisconsin on the Telegraph Road had pushed around to that area as well. The Vermonters, with the Thirty-Third New York close behind them, ran past the mill and followed the road up the hill. Some of them scrambled up a gravelly draw to the right of a house just uphill from the mill. Bursting onto the hilltop, behind the Confederate guns, they confronted a scene of overwhelming confusion.[116]

SEVEN

AFTERNOON OF MAY 3

THE ROAD TOWARD CHANCELLORSVILLE

Sedgwick and Newton watched their attacks unfold from the vicinity of Federal Hill. Anxious about the potential for failure, the Sixth Corps commander dispatched staff officers to follow the assault columns and help rally them if they broke. As it turned out, the line officers maintained the momentum of their attacks without assistance.[1]

To preserve precious ammunition, Southern artillery typically avoided counterbattery fire while waiting for an infantry assault. When the Union attack began, though, the Confederate cannoneers had their targets. The gunners kept track of their fuzing as the Federals advanced. "There goes our 5," Cpl. James M. Tyler called out, as the rounds with five-second fuzes exploded among the advancing columns. The artillerymen, however, did not have much time before the attack formations closed in.[2]

The Mississippians in the Telegraph Road lost about forty men bayoneted and clubbed to death in a frenzy of hand-to-hand combat. Many surrendered by lying down on their faces. Others sprinted down the road to get around the end of Marye's Heights or raced up the hill and down the other side, dodging Union soldiers as they headed toward Lee's Hill. Federal infantry pursued the fleeing Confederates and ultimately captured over two hundred Mississippi infantrymen and more than fifty Louisiana artillerymen.[3]

Elements of Howe's division came up the reverse slope and swarmed around the brick walls of the Willis Cemetery. To their front the Sixth

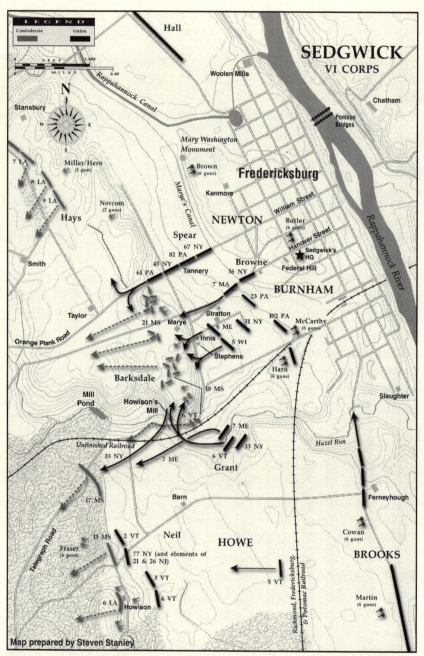

Map 9. Breakthrough. With Confederate attention drawn to the Rappahannock Canal to the north and to Deep Run to the south, Federal forces crashed through the center in a matter of minutes. Part of Howe's attack column crossed Hazel Run and helped seize Marye's Heights.

Maine's color bearer planted the national flag on one of the gun pits. Captain Squires surrendered his two guns, but Cpl. Thomas J. Lutman held the lanyard of a loaded piece. Ignoring calls to surrender, he fired the gun and was immediately shot dead. A disgusted Union soldier later wrote down the circumstances of Lutman's death in the Confederate's own diary, concluding with the statement that he "had his brains blown out as a consequence of his wilfulness."[4]

A similar scenario unfolded for Captain Brown's Virginians. As the Union attackers closed in, Sgt. William B. Cogbill ordered his gun crew to wheel their weapon out of the gun pit and make ready to fire at the enemy troops emerging onto the hilltop. They hurriedly loaded double rounds of canister, but when all was ready, the cannoneer hesitated to pull the lanyard. Cogbill screamed, "Fire!" and the outgoing blast tore through the Federal infantrymen. Even as their weapon blew men to oblivion, Pvt. Sam Duffey waved a meal sack as a white flag.[5]

Some Southern accounts claim surrendering soldiers were killed by drunken Union troops. Such stories are similar to the indignant complaints about the supposed flag of truce and suffer from the same dearth of evidence. Surrendering in close combat is always risky. Some men who did not give up quickly enough surely paid for their hesitation with their lives. Given the circumstances, it is surprising that more men of Parker's Battery were not cut down. Twenty-five to twenty-eight men were captured from Brown's gun crews that day, and only Edward T. Martin did not survive the ordeal. Perhaps Brown's Virginians were ultimately captured by soldiers of the Sixth Vermont coming up behind them rather than by the troops from the Fifth Wisconsin and Sixth Maine, who suffered from the battery's last discharge.[6]

Scrambling up the draw opposite the Stevens house on the Telegraph Road, elements of the Fifth Wisconsin had turned toward the brick mansion overlooking the landscape. They were returning fire by then. The Southerners there found themselves between troops coming up from the Telegraph Road and the assault column on Hanover Street.[7]

On William Street the Forty-Third New York had planted its colors on the hilltop. The other units were right behind but intermingled and disorganized. Colonel Shaler knew better than to lose momentum, however, and forged ahead. Colonel Cross took a portion of his Sixty-Seventh New York and some of the Eighty-Second Pennsylvania to the left to roll up any Confederates between them and Hanover Street. Other members of those units, plus men of the Sixty-First Pennsylvania and the Forty-Third New York, pushed ahead and to the right.[8]

On the edge of the hill, Miller's two howitzers had hindered Gibbon's brigades at the Rappahannock Canal and then blasted Shaler's column on William Street. With Federal troops closing in, it was time to get away, but a gully cut the terrain behind them. To pull back the cannoneers needed to move their wheeled weapons toward William Street, but blue-clad skirmishers were already between them and the road.[9]

Pvt. M. Keegan, one of the Confederate drivers, grabbed a team of horses and rode in front of the advancing skirmishers to get to the rear. The Federals ignored him as they concentrated on capturing the guns. Pvt. Robert Brown of the Sixty-First Pennsylvania shot down the lead horse on one of the limber teams, and his comrades closed in to capture the two weapons.[10]

Colonel Humphreys, commanding the Twenty-First Mississippi, had only seven companies to rally. The other three of his regiment had been with the Eighteenth Mississippi and been killed or captured in the Telegraph Road. He recognized that his troops were not panicking but simply needed to get away and reorganize farther back. One of his men killed and left behind was Pvt. Frank Ingraham, the nephew of Union general Meade.[11]

Confederate doctrine was to respond to a breakthrough with a counterattack, to push back victorious troops when they were tired and disorganized. The Sixth Corps, however, had no intention of being shoved off Marye's Heights. At William Street Shaler had his staff officers hold the regimental colors of the Sixty-First and Eighty-Second Pennsylvania as rally points. Colonel Ely of the Twenty-Third Pennsylvania noted how unit commanders gave orders for "speedily forming line of battle without regard to companies or regiments, as one thousand resolute men that might possibly be rallied behind the hill, would have swept us back from the heights."[12]

Wheaton brought up fresh troops. His Sixty-Second New York and the Ninety-Third, Ninety-Eighth, 102nd, and 139th Pennsylvania Regiments followed the attacking columns up to the high ground. As the general described it: "After forming on the crest beyond the works now abandoned by the enemy, I received orders, through a staff officer, to form all troops as soon as they reached the heights in two lines of battle. This was rapidly done, and they were sheltered as much as possible from the fire of the enemy's guns, which was kept up with some vigor on our left." The Sixth Vermont had charged up Willis Hill as part of Howe's attack; Wheaton deployed them as skirmishers.[13]

Two Federal batteries moved up to support the infantry. Lt. William A. Harn brought his Third New York Independent Light Artillery up Hanover Street and went into battery behind the Marye house. Captain McCarthy advanced his Battery C-D, First Pennsylvania Artillery to the open plain in front of Marye's Heights, where he had blasted the enemy line that morning. Both units sent rounds into the Confederates on Lee's Hill.[14]

On Lee's Hill Fraser's Pulaski Battery had targeted Howe's attack south of Hazel Run. When the Confederate position on Marye's Heights collapsed, Generals Barksdale and Pendleton authorized the captain to bring Willis Hill under fire. Fraser ordered his 12-pounder howitzer crew to deliver an oblique fire into the Federals swarming over what had once been a Southern stronghold.[15]

Fraser's two rifled weapons continued to blast Howe's advancing regiments. A New Jersey chaplain watched the Federal attack in awe: "They closed up the ranks broken by shot and shell and moved with a slow and majestic tread until quite near and then at the double quick with a voice like 'the voice of many waters,' in defiance of a most sweeping storm of grape."[16]

Captain Carlton's Troup Artillery also directed its fire against Howe's advance. Before the attack it had engaged Lieutenant Martin's Battery F, Fifth US Artillery and Captain Cowan's First New York Artillery at the Ferneyhough house. Both sides had inflicted casualties and destroyed equipment. There had also been close calls. At Carlton's Battery a Federal shell landed on a gun-pit parapet, its burning fuze still sputtering. Lt. Thomas A. Murray saw the hot round and shouted a warning. Pvt. Richard W. Saye shoved the projectile outward, so it tumbled down the outside of the redoubt and exploded in the dirt. The Confederate gun crew owed their lives that day to a quick-thinking comrade.[17]

As noted, the Sixth Vermont, Thirty-Third New York, and Seventh Maine had approached Willis Hill behind an unfinished railway embankment, described as a "strong covered way leading from the first works on Marye's Heights to Hazel Run." The Sixth Vermont and the Thirty-Third New York had charged up the back slope of the hill, while the Seventh Maine encountered men of the Fifth Wisconsin clearing the Telegraph Road. General Wheaton kept the Sixth Vermont with him on the hilltop while the Thirty-Third New York raced back down to join the attack on Lee's Hill. The Seventh Maine heard the renewed gunfire and hurried through the battle smoke to support the New Yorkers.[18]

When three of his regiments rushed over to Willis Hill, Howe's first line of battle had been reduced to the Seventy-Seventh New York (its left and right wings separated), the Second Vermont, and elements of the Twenty-First and Twenty-Sixth New Jersey. While they rested at the base of Lee's Hill, Colonel Grant pushed up two Second Vermont companies as skirmishers. To their left Lieutenant Colonel French also paused with half of the Seventy-Seventh New York, noting, "I halted the line in a ditch which afforded some protection from the fire of the enemy & waited a few moments for the Vermont Brigade."[19]

Some of the Confederate skirmishers had scrambled away, but many surrendered. The main force of the Thirteenth and Seventeenth Mississippi Regiments waited farther up the slopes on Howison and Lee's Hills respectively. To their right Colonel Monaghan's Sixth Louisiana constituted Barksdale's flank. The brush had caught fire in places, and smoke drifted into the ravines through which the Federals would soon advance.[20]

As Confederate guns destroyed the large barn where some of the New Jersey troops had taken shelter, Colonel Walbridge reorganized his Second Vermont at the foot of Lee's Hill. Lieutenant Colonel Martindale did the same with the men of the Twenty-Sixth New Jersey who had kept up with the assault. Grant saw a regiment near Hazel Run, Col. Robert F. Taylor's Thirty-Third New York, and sent an aide to guide it forward. When the New Yorkers were within supporting distance, Grant put his hand on Walbridge's shoulder and asked: "Are you ready, colonel?" "I am," came the reply. Both officers mounted their horses, and Grant called out, "Up now, my brave boys and give it to them."[21]

The Federals began to climb. On Lee's Hill over three hundred men of the Seventeenth Mississippi had taken shelter behind a ridge of dirt thrown up where a road ran up toward the Confederate gun pits. Fallen trees impeded the Federal advance, and the brushfires hindered visibility. Farther south the Thirteenth Mississippi and the Sixth Louisiana waited for the Seventy-Seventh New York.[22]

When the Mississippians opened fire, the Federals realized they needed support. Walbridge reassured his tired Vermonters that reinforcements were on the way, and the Thirty-Third New York soon moved up on their right. The Federals found the rough road (still evident within the national park) and unleashed a sharp flank fire into the Confederate forces using its shelter. The Seventh Maine also came up to extend the line even farther.[23]

The Federal units curling around the Confederate stronghold forced the Mississippi infantry to pull back, which exposed Fraser's artillery. His Pulaski Battery had kept up a steady fire as Howe's attack closed in, but he risked the loss of his guns if he stayed much longer. The advancing Federals had been a visible target as they crossed the open ground but were in defilade once they reached the base of the hills. The troops were now advancing uphill within the shelter of several ravines.[24]

The Southern artillerymen had already expended their supply of canister. Since shell and solid shot would not be effective in close fighting, Fraser ordered his guns to retire. His Georgians rushed to bring up their horse teams and limbers from a sheltering ravine. Amid those preparations, an incoming projectile took off the back of Lt. Frederick A. Habersham's head, killing him instantly. The stricken officer came from a prominent Savannah family; his horrified comrades lashed his mangled corpse to a caisson. Most of the other artillerymen escaped with the guns, but some of the Georgians were made prisoners by the fast-moving Union infantry.[25]

On the high ground overlooking Deep Run, Carlton had to decide if he too needed to pull back. His Georgia battery had kept up a rapid fire on Howe's attacking force, but when the Federals reached the hills, the gunners lost sight of them. Union infantry might slip around behind them, so the Troup Artillery limbered up and pulled back to the Leach house.[26]

On top of Lee's Hill, the Second Vermont paused to reorganize. Through the battle smoke the Vermont men saw Confederate officers, about one hundred yards away, trying to rally their shattered infantrymen. If successful, they might soon be ready to make another stand, perhaps even counterattack. The Vermont soldiers lunged forward and crashed into the Seventeenth Mississippi with as much force as tired men could muster. The Confederates held briefly, but they too were exhausted and left the hilltop to the Vermonters.[27]

Federal casualties were strewn on the hillside and around the Confederate gun emplacements. One of them, his jugular nicked by a Minié ball, knew he had only moments to live and asked his comrades to tell his family that he had been a good soldier. As the fighting subsided, elements of the Twenty-First New Jersey came up. They were not conditioned for the rigors of combat but still added weight to the advance. One of them wrote: "I never was so tired as then, my mouth became parched, and by the time I got to the bottom of the first hill I had to stop for breath. I then started on again and kept up and when I arrived at the top of the hill I fell down from exhaustion, but I was bound not to be behind hand at that time—I kept with the company. I have never straggled on the march and I did not want it to be said that I was behind at that time of need."[28]

To the right of the Vermont and New Jersey men, the Thirty-Third New York and the right wing of the Seventy-Seventh New York captured remnants of the Eighteenth Mississippi trying to escape the onslaught that had overrun Marye's Heights. The Federals gathered in several dozen prisoners, including three officers. They also grabbed the regiment's flag. Colonel Griffin, commanding the Eighteenth Mississippi, was captured in front of Willis Hill. With this success, the right wing of the Seventy-Seventh New York moved south to find the rest of its unit.[29]

On Howison Hill the left wing of the Seventy-Seventh New York also advanced. French recounted that once the Vermont Brigade "came within supporting distance I rallied the men on the colors and we charged the heights." The New Yorkers closed in on the four guns of Captain Patterson's Battery B, Sumter Artillery. The Southerners pulled two guns back to the Telegraph Road, but the Federals captured a howitzer and a 12-pounder Napoleon. While the New Yorkers paused to regroup, their other wing caught up with them and reestablished the regiment's integrity. Colonel Grant rode up and congratulated them on their prizes.[30]

The Confederates had fought well, but the Union attacks had been too much for them to contain. A Vermont soldier assessed the defenders in a letter to his wife: "I must say that their artillery men was gritty. They did not abandon their guns until our men had shot nearly all of them down and when they was a loading the last time our men shot the one from the gun before he could have time to fire. The rammer was left in the gun."[31]

Farther to the left, Howe's third line had also closed in on the Confederate position. Colonel Thomas O. Seaver's Third Vermont had the lead, with Colonel Charles B. Stoughton's Fourth Vermont right behind them. They followed the farm road that coursed across the open ground between the Ferneyhough house and the Howison house. Seaver saw Confederates in line of battle and ordered his troops to open fire. Coming from Lee's Hill, Grant warned them that the troops to their front might be Federals, but then the line under observation opened fire. Seaver gave the order to charge, and his regiment rushed forward. The Confederates disappeared into the woods.[32]

When Marye's Heights fell, General Pendleton had directed Fraser's battery on Lee's Hill to concentrate its fire on the Federals as they reformed. When two guns of Patterson's battery fell back from Howison Hill to the Telegraph Road, the general directed Fraser to open fire on Willis Hill as well.[33]

Captain Richardson also reported to Pendleton with his Second Company, Washington Artillery. He had only three 12-pounder Napoleons that day, the fourth undergoing repairs in depot. They deployed as Federal batteries opened fire from Marye's Heights as well as from the open ground in front of the Telegraph Road. The Second Vermont and the Thirty-Third New York were also closing in. Richardson's artillerymen limbered up to withdraw but lost one gun when the Union infantry shot down its horses.[34]

Howe's units pressed up against the Confederate line south of Hazel Run. The Thirty-Third New York gained Lee's Hill, with the Seventh Maine on its left, while the Second Vermont had secured the hilltop to their left. The Fifth Vermont, which had been protecting Martin's and Cowan's batteries on the Bowling Green Road, joined the Seventy-Seventh New York and the Third and Fourth Vermont on Howison Hill.[35]

As the Federals grew in strength, the Confederates rallied on the Telegraph Road. Seaver halted his advance at the tree line and rode into the woods to reconnoiter. He came galloping back and ordered his troops to lie down. Through the trees he had seen a Confederate battery in the clearing where the Leach house stood. A Vermont soldier described what came next: "We expected something was coming, and in a minute it came, in the shape of grape and canister from a battery concealed in the bushes. We dug our noses into the ground while the storm whistled over us." Within minutes, Confederate attention shifted away from the infantry in the woods, as Federal artillery pushing past Lee's Hill on the Telegraph Road posed a more immediate threat.[36]

From Prospect Hill Early's attention had been focused on the substantial Union strength evident on the Bowling Green Road and at Deep Run. Around 10:30 A.M., however, when enemy artillery opened a heavy fire concentrated in Fredericksburg, the Confederate commander knew something was up. He sent Lt. William Calloway to Lee's Hill to find Pendleton and Barksdale and learn what was happening.[37]

After Calloway left, Early decided to ride toward Fredericksburg himself. A courier intercepted him on the military road and reported the loss of Marye's Heights. The general hurried on. A courier from Pendleton reined in and reported Confederate forces holding their position, which was clearly a message out of sequence. Shortly thereafter, Calloway found Early and confirmed that the Federals had broken through.[38]

The Leach farmstead stood on the east side of the Telegraph Road (where modern Longstreet Avenue intersects Lafayette Boulevard). Three-quarters of a mile farther south was the Cox house. Early tried to deploy Richardson's two surviving guns as they fell back, but they had no ammunition. He then called back Carlton's and Fraser's batteries, which were headed down the road to the Cox house. The tired Georgians swung their caissons and weapons around to take position at Leach's.[39]

Pendleton found Early at the house as the two batteries arrived. He suggested that the guns move back since there were Federals of unknown strength moving through the woods on their right. Early, however, had already sent orders to General Gordon to bring up three of his Georgia regiments. A stand would be made at the Leach house.[40]

As Fraser and Carlton went into battery, two of Barksdale's Mississippi regiments appeared. Colonel Holder spread out his Seventeenth Mississippi on the west side of the road, while Colonel Carter deployed his Thirteenth Mississippi on the east side. Barksdale's two other regiments were not available, the Eighteenth Mississippi and three companies of the Twenty-First Mississippi having been scattered by the Federal assault while the seven remaining companies of the Twenty-First Mississippi were cut off. The Sixth Louisiana was also on hand to bolster the developing line.[41]

The rallying Confederates watched Federal artillery swing into battery. McCarthy's Battery C-D, First Pennsylvania Artillery had already pumped forty rounds into the Southerners from the plain in front Marye's Heights. The two batteries that had supported Howe's attack from the Ferneyhough house had quickly made their way to Fredericksburg and were directed to support the ongoing advance. Cowan's First New York Artillery joined Lt. William Harn's battery on the heights behind the Marye house. Martin took his Battery F, Fifth US Artillery out the Telegraph Road and "was in position on the crest of the hill only a few seconds after its capture." McCarthy's battery followed "with all possible speed."[42]

Colonel Tompkins mistakenly reported that Harn took his battery up the Telegraph Road, followed by McCarthy. Harn's report, however, indicates that he did not advance beyond the Marye house. Howe's artillery commander, Major de Peyster, also noted in his report that it was Martin's battery that advanced on the Telegraph Road. Both Harn and Martin had 10-pounder Parrott rifles, so their units would have looked similar, whether in battery or in column.[43]

Carlton and Fraser opened fire on the two Union batteries at around six hundred yards. The Federals responded with a rapid fire, during which McCarthy expended seventy-five rounds. A Georgia soldier wrote that it was "one of the fiercest artillery fights of the war." The Confederate fire diminished when Carlton's battery exhausted its ammunition. As the cannoneers prepared to pull out of the line, a round struck one of the gun carriages, and sweating artillerymen hurried to replace a smashed wheel.[44]

Pendleton had two of Patterson's guns on hand but knew they were "not the most efficient." He ordered up Colonel Walton's Washington Artillery, but it soon became evident that the Federals were disengaging. The Sixth Corps's objective was to the west, toward Chancellorsville, rather than south on the Telegraph Road. With that unexpected respite, the Confederates also pulled back to the more defensible terrain around the Cox house.[45]

Early had brought up three of Gordon's Georgia regiments to take a blocking position on the Telegraph Road and decided he needed to redeploy his other brigades as well. Riding toward Prospect Hill, he ran into Colonel Andrews, his artillery commander, looking to see if his guns would be more useful elsewhere. Early directed him to move his weapons to the ridge overlooking the Lansdowne valley.[46]

Confederate troops on the right had not been able to see the Federal attack in Fredericksburg, but they certainly heard it. They were confident their comrades would hold the line, so orders to withdraw were unexpected. A North Carolinian wrote, "Ther was right smart cannonading and picketing don until about 12 o'clock and then for sum cause we was all ordered to fall back about a half of a mile to our last breastworks."[47]

The attack on Marye's Heights had been executed with stunning speed, but casualties had been high. With dead and dying troops scattered along the attack route, an officer in the Sixth Maine recalled, "I hardly dare look about me, But was forced to face it and gather the company together." On William Street a soldier in Shaler's brigade wrote: "The dead of the enemy were mingled with our own in ghastly profusion. Each ditch, ravine, trench, pit and tree had its quantum of dead and dying."[48]

Lt. George E. Bissell of the Fifth Wisconsin faced the consequences of having to give orders for an attack: "I cried like a child upon going over the field, to see my old Company lying stretched all over the ground. There are only 13 men left for duty; no prisoners and none missing—all the rest were either killed or wounded." Another Wisconsin soldier claimed, "our Regiment had had the hardest fight this campaign that we have ever had before." A New York chaplain commented, "What a business for God's holy day of rest."[49]

On the heights the victors counted ten captured weapons, including a 3-inch Ordnance Rifle, four 12-pounder Napoleons, three 12-pounder howitzers, and two 10-pounder Parrott rifles. A New York soldier noted that the captured guns were the "very best kind." He could not similarly brag about the captured teams, noting how "the horses that were hitched to them look like shadows." Abandoned haversacks, blankets, and knapsacks also attested to the assault's swift violence.[50]

The Federal breakthrough cut off the Confederates north of Fredericksburg. The Louisiana troops overlooking the Rappahannock Canal heard cheers to their right. Thinking they were the triumphant whoops of comrades who had held back the Yankee assault, they took up the shouts with their own rebel yells. The enthusiasm petered out, though, when they received orders to abandon their works. The jubilant shouting had come from Federals atop Marye's Heights.[51]

During the assault, a courier reported to General Wilcox that the Mississippians needed help. With the left flank secure behind the canal, Wilcox led the Tenth Alabama past the Stansbury house but soon saw Louisiana units hustling to get away. The Confederate line had been broken. General Hays found him and shared that he had orders to rejoin the division on the Telegraph Road. He suggested that Wilcox also bring his brigade to the rally point. But Wilcox had not been assigned to Early's command, his Alabama brigade being a part of Anderson's Division, then fighting at Chancellorsville.[52]

Wilcox suggested to Hays that their two brigades could probably contain the Federal breakthrough, at least for a while. They would not be able to hold back a Federal corps, but their effort might buy time for Lee to respond to the unfolding disaster. Hays considered the idea but said he must follow orders. Getting to the Telegraph Road had challenges enough, because the Louisianans would have to get around enemy forces surging on to the high ground.[53]

General Gibbon received orders to leave the Rappahannock Canal behind. Lieutenant Penick's Virginia guns were still in battery behind the Stansbury house, so the Union infantry withdrew "under a heavy artillery fire." The

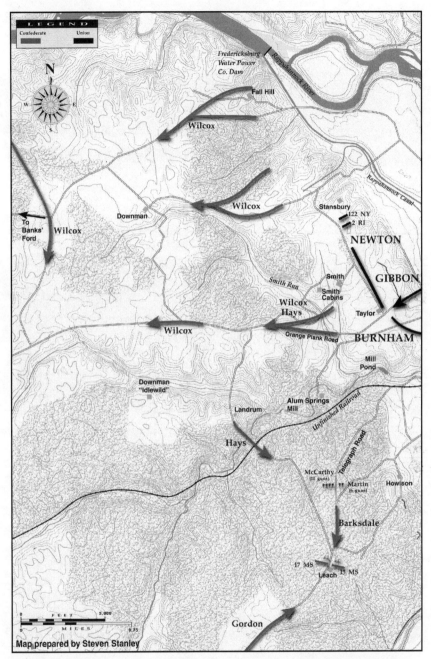

Map 10. Confederates Pull Back. Hays's and Barksdale's units retreated south to join Early on the Telegraph Road. Wilcox headed west to establish a blocking position and give Lee time to respond to the Union breakthrough.

Second Rhode Island and the Tenth Massachusetts from Newton's division pulled away first, followed by Colonel Hall's and Colonel Laflin's brigades. At William Street a New York soldier observed: "Through avenues of the dead and dying we pass. Here are a lot of cannon that could not get away in time. . . . And here are a lot of prisoners." Gibbon's casualties had been comparatively light. Hall had lost three men killed, fifty-six wounded, and eight men missing. Laflin had sixteen men wounded and four missing.[54]

From the edge of the Fredericksburg plateau, near Mary Washington's grave, Lieutenant Brown's Battery B, First Rhode Island had kept up a rapid fire in support of the William Street assault. Captain Adams joined him there with his Battery G, First Rhode Island, which had lost five men killed and eighteen wounded while across the canal. The Federals turned their fire on Norcom's and Hero's artillerymen, then bringing up teams to pull away their weapons. Brown personally sighted one of his guns "and hit the ammunition chest on the limber, taking the men off as if with a stroke of lightning." As the Confederates hastily departed, the lieutenant received orders to send a section of guns to join in the pursuit.[55]

Following William Street, Gibbon's two brigades finally gained the heights that had loomed over them all morning. In front of them Newton and Burnham had pushed their divisions past the Confederate earthworks and formed on a road that ran along that high ground (modern Augustine Avenue). From there the Federal troops looked across Smith Run to a higher ridge where Confederate troops were taking position. Farther forward, skirmish fire rippled through the air.[56]

While Newton and Burnham waited on the heights, Howe pulled his units off the hills they had just seized. Before heading west, the men needed to retrieve their knapsacks, haversacks, and canteens, which had been stacked and left under guard on the Bowling Green Road. Division commanders often had to figure out how their men could best retrieve gear left behind. Howe had his units go back themselves to get their equipment, which took time. Newton had his quartermasters retrieve stacked knapsacks for later delivery to the fighting men. The less-experienced Burnham did not think to do either, and a New York soldier remembered the consequences of that inattention: "We left our knapsacks behind when we charged the heights, and that was the last we saw of them, so that I lost everything belonging to me, grub and all."[57]

Howe's men picked up their knapsacks and took time to brew coffee and grab something to eat. Abandoning the bridgehead, General Brooks's units passed through their scattered cooking fires alongside the road. After a hasty meal, Howe's soldiers also donned their packs and followed Brooks toward Fredericksburg.[58]

Confederate forces hurried to reposition themselves. From Early's Division, Gordon and Hays marshaled their brigades on the Telegraph Road, joined by Barksdale's surviving Mississippians. Hoke's and Smith's Brigades abandoned their line along the railway and pulled back to a second line near the Military Road before returning to the Telegraph Road as well.[59]

Hays looked to join Early on the Telegraph Road, but Federal forces blocked his way. There was a potential escape route, though, recently used by a Mississippi regiment. The Twenty-First Mississippi had been cut off when the Federals seized Marye's Heights, and Humphreys had thought his best option was to join the main army at Chancellorsville. On the march west, however, he discovered a farm road that led south from the Orange Plank Road.[60]

The Mississippians followed the trace downhill past the deteriorating Landram house. To get to the Telegraph Road, they scrambled across Hazel Run and then over a graded railroad embankment. Hays likely followed the same route to get his four Louisiana regiments to where the Confederates were regrouping at the Cox farm.[61]

Wilcox, meanwhile, deployed his forces where the Plank Road cuts through the hills overlooking Fredericksburg. Smith Run inconveniently bisected his thin line, but he had the Pittsylvania Artillery's four rifled weapons on hand to anchor his flanks. Two guns were still in a redoubt six hundred yards behind the Stansbury house. Penick placed the other section on a rise just north of the Plank Road. Captain Moore's Norfolk Battery had also occupied the gun pits on Fall Hill. To emphasize his presence, Wilcox ordered Penick to open fire.[62]

Sedgwick had pulled his attention away from the Telegraph Road and was preparing to push west from Marye's Heights. Wheaton's and Browne's brigades occupied the ground south of William Street. Shaler had deployed his brigade to the north, along a road that intersected the street just east of the Taylor house (Rose Hill). Gibbon's two brigades extended the line farther to the right.[63]

The artillery units attached to Newton's, Burnham's, and Howe's divisions were on Lee's Hill and Marye's Heights. On William Street Lt. William Perrin brought a section of Battery B, First Rhode Island Artillery up the hill at a trot, and Gibbon directed it into a position in front of his infantry in the road across the open plateau. Perrin's two guns swung into battery and opened fire. The rest of Battery B was ordered to join them, and soon six guns were pounding Wilcox's blocking force.[64]

The two guns from Penick's Virginia battery had kept firing from the redoubt west of the Stansbury house. To overcome that annoyance, Shaler ordered Col. Silas Titus to take his 122nd New York and drive them off. Titus spread out his command in skirmish order and moved off. The Second Rhode Island and the Tenth Massachusetts were then coming up onto the heights, and Newton sent the former to support the New Yorkers.[65]

Capt. George W. Clark's skirmishers of the Eleventh Alabama exchanged fire with the advancing New York and Rhode Island men. He lost nine men wounded, and the swift-moving Federals also gathered in some prisoners. Moore's Norfolk Battery on top of the hill pulled away. Penick's artillerymen also brought off their weapons but lost a caisson in the rush to get clear.[66]

Gibbon pushed out on Plank Road, where Penick's two other guns had taken position. His vanguard comprised Laflin's one-hundred-man storming party, led by Capt. George W. Ryerson of the Eighty-Second New York. Hall's brigade followed in line of battle. When Wilcox saw these Union forces curling around his flank, he directed his units to withdraw.[67]

The general identified Salem Church as his brigade's rally point. Union batteries were still shooting at them, and an Alabama soldier recalled how "the shells and shot were pouring into us in such a style as to become murderous. Quickly the order was passed to each regimental commander to make his way to the Brick Church." Moore's section of guns and the Alabama infantry on Fall Hill would have to move quickly to get clear before the Union advance on Plank Road cut them off.[68]

Col. Hilary Herbert, commanding the Eighth Alabama, remembered, "never were legs more valuable than when we were making a straight line for a point on the plank road some three-quarters of a mile beyond where were our friends, the enemy." Gibbon's advancing troops gathered in nearly one hundred prisoners as they pushed west. Casualty returns make clear that in addition to Alabama men, the Federals came across tired Louisiana soldiers who had been unable to keep up with their units headed for the Telegraph Road.[69]

Wilcox had on hand forty to fifty troopers from the Fifteenth Virginia Cavalry, led by Maj. Charles R. Collins. To give his infantry time to regroup at Salem Church, he directed the cavalrymen to deploy about a mile and a half to their front, where the Plank Road passed near a pine thicket. The Confederate horse soldiers watched the powerful Union force approach, but the Federals paused at the Guest plantation, about a half mile short of where they waited.[70]

With that unexpected reprieve, Wilcox ordered Lt. James S. Cobbs to take his section of the Pittsylvania Battery to a rise of ground where, in better times, a tollgate had once welcomed those who would use the Plank Road.[71]

Sedgwick has been criticized for holding up his march, but his objective was Chancellorsville, not the Salem Church ridge. Early's Division remained on his flank, fully capable of cutting his line of communications. Further, the artillery fire coming from Chancellorsville had diminished. Sedgwick was no longer moving toward the sound of guns, but into a silent landscape where he could potentially run into the entire Confederate army. In that hostile setting the Sixth Corps commander took the time to bring his units within supporting distance of one another.

Compounding the lack of information, Hooker had not been in communication for several hours. The last message Sedgwick had received had been sent at 10:00 A.M., and that had simply been a repeat of an earlier message to "attack at once." Butterfield continued to pester Sedgwick with messages urging him forward and repeatedly asking about his progress without passing on anything useful. He did note, around midmorning, that Confederate forces might be abandoning Banks' Ford.[72]

General Lee had won a stunning victory at Chancellorsville, but for a while, the Union command had believed it had been winning. The Federals began May 3 behind solid entrenchments. The Confederates had occupied Hazel Grove as early as 6:45 A.M., but Union artillery at Fairview continued to hold. North of the Orange Plank Road and Orange Turnpike, a counterattack had pushed the Confederates back to the captured Union trenches from which they had started their morning advance.[73]

Colonel Ingalls, the chief quartermaster, sent Butterfield a confident message from the US Ford signal station: "A most terribly bloody conflict has raged since daylight. Enemy in great force in our front and on the right, but at this moment we are repulsing him on all sides. Carnage is fearful. General Hooker is safe so far. [Maj. Gen. Hiram G.] Berry is killed. I return to the front, but will keep you advised when in my power. Our trains are all safe, and we shall be victorious. Our cavalry has not come up."[74]

With this message in hand, Butterfield wrote a quick dispatch to President Lincoln at 8:50 A.M.: "Though not directed or specially authorized to do so by General Hooker, I think it not improper that I should advise you that a battle is in progress."[75]

The seeming good news did not last. Some ordnance officers failed to get ammunition to their units, forcing them to subsequently withdraw. Without anyone in overall command of the Union artillery, batteries that had expended their ammunition came off the line to replenish and were not replaced. The Confederates pushed hard where Federal fire diminished, and the Union line eventually collapsed. Hooker pulled away from the Chancellorsville crossroads between 11:00 A.M. and noon to dig new defensive works.[76]

Incoming artillery fire by then had become relentless, and not only was the Chancellor house burning but so too were the surrounding woods. To the horror of nearby troops, wounded men unable to move were consumed by the flames, their screams piercing the smoky air.[77]

Hooker, with nearly the entire Army of the Potomac at his disposal, had been acting as if he commanded a beleaguered garrison. Before daylight he had called on Sedgwick for help. A message sent at 2:35 A.M. stated, "everything in the world depends upon the rapidity and promptness of your movement." Another, sent at 4:55 A.M., suggested that "any force in front of General Sedgwick must be a small one." As his battle grew in intensity, Hooker sent orders to Sedgwick at 9:15 A.M. and 10:00 A.M. to "attack at once."[78]

Hooker had not responded to Butterfield's updates from Fredericksburg. He had also become incapacitated when a cannonball hit the porch post he was leaning against. His headquarters staff, however, continued to call on Sedgwick for relief. At midday Ingalls sent the following dispatch to Butterfield: "General Hooker is doing well. We have plenty of fresh troops still left, but have gained no ground to-day, yet our lines are strong; but no doubt another desperate effort will be made to force our position. We feel confident that Sedgwick must press them fast. Answer me here. I will take it to General Hooker. He wants Sedgwick to press them."[79]

Butterfield responded with yet another update: "Sedgwick is by this time (12 m.) probably free from all obstructions of earthworks. He has carried the heights on right of Telegraph road. Two lines of his troops have disappeared in the woods, on the hills, and all seems going well. Will advise you further as soon as I can get word from Sedgwick."[80]

At 12:45 P.M. Ingalls again contacted the chief of staff: "I think we have had the most terrible battle ever witnessed on earth. I think our victory will be certain, but the general told me he would say nothing just yet to

Washington, except that he is doing well. In an hour or two the matter will be a fixed fact. I believe the enemy is in flight now, but we are not sure."[81]

This dispatch sounded optimistic, so Butterfield took it upon himself to send another message to Lincoln at 1:30 P.M.: "From all reports yet collected, the battle has been most fierce and terrible. Loss heavy on both sides. General Hooker slightly, but not severely, wounded. He has preferred thus far that nothing should be reported, and does not know of this, but I cannot refrain from saying this much to you. You may expect his dispatch in a few hours, which will give the result."[82]

Secretary of War Stanton responded to the general: "The President thanks you for your telegrams, and hopes you will keep him advised as rapidly as any information reaches you." Butterfield had taken it upon himself to communicate with Washington while he continued to apprise Hooker of events at Fredericksburg, relaying General Warren's 1:00 P.M. report at 2:30 P.M.:

> We have advanced with Newton's division on the Plank road as far as Guest's house. The heights were carried splendidly at 11 A.M. by Newton. Howe immediately afterward carried the heights to the south of Hazel Run. We have been waiting to get his division behind us before advancing, to get up batteries and stragglers, and get the brigades straightened out, which were a little disorganized by a successful charge and pursuit. Our loss, though honorable proof of a severe contest, is not very severe. The Sixth Corps is in splendid spirits. We captured several guns. General Howe reports a force yet in his front.
>
> P.S.—Brooks' division were kept by the enemy's fire in position on our left, and after the heights were carried he had 3 miles to march to join us. He is not up yet.[83]

Warren's suggestion of light casualties was a disservice to the Sixth Corps. It had seized its objectives at a high cost in blood, but the impression passed on to Hooker implied minimal opposition. Butterfield's message of 3:25 P.M. relayed yet another report: "Brooks' division has just moved ahead again, and [the] other two divisions will follow shortly. Sedgwick says loss heavier than he expected, having lost several colonels and many field officers. Warren thinks 1½ miles beyond this the enemy have halted and will make a stand. The men show much fatigue, but Sedgwick intends to push vigorously. No report of where he was exactly."[84]

Hooker was clearly being kept abreast of Sedgwick's progress, but he did not use that information to advantage. His powerful Army of the Potomac, more than double the size of the Army of Northern Virginia, apparently could not prevail without the Sixth Corps's help. Acting as if the campaign had ended, the commanding general sent a message to Washington at 1:15 P.M., which Lincoln received at 4:00 P.M.:

> We have had a desperate fight yesterday and to-day, which has resulted in no success to us, having lost a position of two lines, which had been selected for our defense. It is now 1.30 o'clock, and there is still some firing of artillery. We may have another turn at it this P.M. I do not despair of success. If Sedgwick could have gotten up, there could have been but one result. As it is impossible for me to know the exact position of Sedgwick as regards his ability to advance and take part in the engagement, I cannot tell when it will end. We will endeavor to do our best. My troops are in good spirits. We have fought desperately today. No general commanded a more devoted army.[85]

Following this series of optimistic messages, news of disaster did not sit well with the commander in chief. At 4:35 P.M. Lincoln tersely responded: "Where is General Hooker? Where is Sedgwick? Where is Stoneman?" Shaken from his casual condescension, Butterfield responded within five minutes: "General Hooker is at Chancellorsville. General Sedgwick, with 15,000 to 20,000 men, at a point 3 or 4 miles out from Fredericksburg, on the road to Chancellorsville. Lee is between. Stoneman has not been heard from. This is the situation from latest reports, 4.30 P.M."[86]

Sedgwick at this time had the only Union force still active on the field. Having broken out of Fredericksburg, he continued to press on, unaware that Hooker had withdrawn from the fight. Butterfield continued to send updates to his commander at roughly half-hour intervals. His dispatch sent at 5:30 P.M. revealed that Lee was responding to the Sixth Corps's action even if Hooker was not.

Butterfield to Hooker, 5:30 P.M.: "The signal telescope discovers about several thousand troops due west from this point, about 8 miles. Counts seven colors—rebel battle-flags. This would locate them at 5 P.M. near Tabernacle Church by the photograph map. Is not this a column marching to meet Sedgwick and away from your front? Will get further information if I can."[87]

The Confederates observed moving east were units from McLaws's Division that Lee had detached after receiving news of the Union breakout from Fredericksburg. Butterfield reported the following to Hooker at 6:50 P.M.: "Sedgwick's column reported at 4.15 P.M. advanced three-quarters of a mile beyond Guest's house. Sedgwick tells my staff officer he is getting along very well. He is moving in two columns on either side of the Plank road, a line of a half mile deployed. Warren thinks the enemy will made a stand half a mile beyond their then position."[88]

Butterfield's message at 7:15 P.M. detailed when fighting began at Salem Church. "General Sedgwick was attacking the enemy on a ridge at Salem Church, 6 1/2 miles from Chancellorsville, the enemy making a stand at that point. Infantry fire heavier than hitherto, and our men fall back a little in center. Heavy infantry fire reported. Time, 6.05 to 6.15 o'clock."[89]

These communications were not proving to be of much use to anyone. Washington officials had become frustrated with the dearth of any real information. Hooker had no use for the stream of messages about Sedgwick's progress because they only revealed that the Sixth Corps had not yet reached him. He had also pulled back from Chancellorsville to fortify a strong defensive position yet never thought to modify Sedgwick's instructions. The Sixth Corps pressed on under orders issued the night before.

On the Chancellorsville field, Lee had also been informed when Sedgwick's troops seized Marye's Heights. Lt. Andrew L. Pitzer took the initiative to ride west and warn Lee without pausing to let General Early know where he was going. About an hour after the Southern line collapsed at Fredericksburg, Pitzer rode into the Chancellorsville clearing, where the tavern still burned and long rows of dead bodies lay covered with canvas shelter halves.[90]

Amid the detritus of battle, Pitzer reported to Lee. The Southern commander wanted to attack the Union army in front of him, but the lieutenant's news required immediate attention. Without hesitation Lee ordered Mahone's Brigade toward Fredericksburg and directed McLaws to send Brig. Gen. Joseph B. Kershaw's brigade with him. He soon directed the division commander to follow with the brigades of Brig. Gen. Paul J. Semmes and Brig. Gen. William T. Wofford. Lee's ability to adapt to rapidly changing circumstances stood in sharp contrast with Hooker's inability to imagine battlefield dynamics beyond what he had planned.[91]

The Union and Confederate troops deploying for battle west of Fredericksburg and east of Chancellorsville had been marching and fighting all day under a hot sun. Some of the Alabamans hurrying back to Salem Church were so tired they fainted from exhaustion. The retreating troops on the

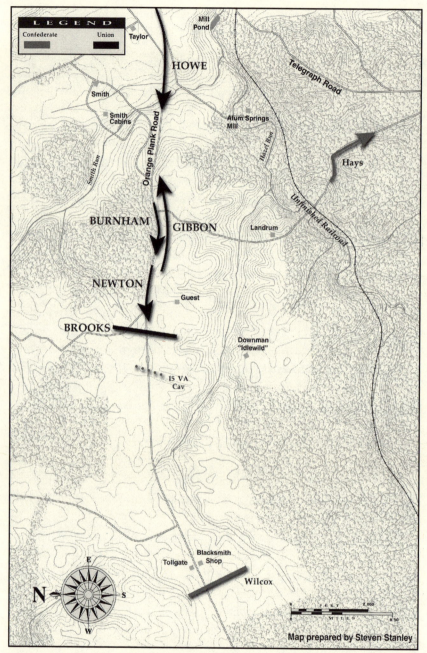

Map 11. The Road toward Chancellorsville. The Sixth Corps halted at the Guest house to concentrate its far-flung divisions before continuing west. Wilcox held his brigade on the Salem Church ridge. Gibbon's Second Corps division returned to Fredericksburg.

Plank Road occasionally formed a line and fired on the approaching Federals but then quickly hustled away. The pursuing troops were also beat. A New York soldier wrote, "We are driving the enemy as fast as we can for tired men, for we have not slept but a few hours at a time for the last six days."[92]

At the Guest house Sedgwick and Newton waited for Brooks and Howe to arrive, while the troops there took the opportunity to rest. Back in Fredericksburg, Federal construction crews began work to reconstruct the railroad bridge. From their perspective the campaign had moved into its next phase, which was to establish a logistics base on the south side of the Rappahannock River for whatever came next on the road to Richmond.[93]

From the bridgehead south of town, Brooks had his division on the road to join the rest of the Sixth Corps. Howe's men followed, having grabbed something to eat and gathered their equipment. A five-mile trek separated Deep Run from the Guest house, and Brooks marched his troops without stopping. As the columns approached Sedgwick's headquarters, the soldiers could see a sharp-angled Gothic Revival dwelling south of the roadway, more reminiscent of New England than a Southern plantation.[94]

Sedgwick allowed Brooks to rest his men for fifteen minutes before pushing west in battle formation. Looking up the road, Brooks could see Confederate cavalry deployed near a pine thicket. Behind them were a few artillery guns. He instructed Colonel Brown to take the lead with his New Jersey brigade. Brown's men had started the day the farthest east in the Fredericksburg bridgehead; now they were the farthest west. Bartlett's and Russell's brigades would follow.[95]

Gibbon's two Second Corps brigades had no orders to join the Sixth Corps's march west, so Sedgwick sent them back to occupy Fredericksburg. State regiments often had close ties to one another, and sometimes those connections could be acknowledged during active operations. The Thirty-Fourth New York of Laflin's brigade, while moving east, encountered the 121st New York of Bartlett's brigade headed west. The two regimental commanders halted their columns next to each other, and for a few brief moments brothers had a chance to see one another, and men could ask about friends. The units then pressed on to their respective destinies.[96]

Once they reached Fredericksburg the Second Corps troops had orders to get captured artillery across the river, move prisoners to the rear, and gather up the rifles and ammunition scattered across the battleground. Hall's brigade also spent time burying the dead and forwarding Sixth Corps stragglers back to their units. The 127th Pennsylvania drew the assignment of provost guard. Under orders not to enter houses, the Pennsylvanians established their camp on Sophia Street, adjacent to the Rappahannock.[97]

While Hall's regiments went to work in Fredericksburg, Laflin's brigade recrossed the river and deployed to guard the floating bridges. The two Second Corps artillery units joined them. Adams guided his Battery G, First Rhode Island to what had once been the Washington farm and took position overlooking the pontoon bridge. The First Minnesota deployed in support, the troops watching construction crews work on the railway bridge. Brown took his Battery B, First Rhode Island to the high ground at the Lacy house. About that time the Nineteenth Maine rejoined the brigade, relieved from its detail to guard the telegraph lines between Falmouth and US Ford.[98]

General Hunt had remained at Banks' Ford while the battle unfolded. Around 2:00 P.M. Butterfield informed him that Gibbon and Sedgwick were moving west. General Benham had seen the Confederates at Banks' Ford move off and thought it might be time to finally get a pontoon bridge down. His original orders had been to float a span on May 1, when Federal forces uncovered the crossing. As far as Hunt and Benham knew, those orders were still in effect, and the engineers proceeded to execute them.[99]

Col. Charles B. Stuart of the Fiftieth New York Engineers had led the night march that brought the pontoon trains to Banks' Ford. He now followed behind Company E, Seventy-First Pennsylvania, led by Lt. Robert S. Seabury, as it splashed across the ford to secure the far shore. Stuart left the infantry to fulfill its responsibilities while he moved downstream to confirm that the floating bridge could be built to the old ferry landing opposite Scott's Mill. He verified that there were good roads to the uplands, and the engineers, under the direction of Lieutenant Colonel Pettes, began work to float a bridge.[100]

The Banks' Ford crossing had always been critical to the overall campaign. Instead of being opened by Hooker's main forces moving east, however, it was about to be made operational by the Sixth Corps moving west. Back at the Guest house, Sedgwick watched Brooks pushing out the Plank Road, followed by Newton. When Howe arrived his troops would cover the approaches south of that roadway. Early still had a division down there somewhere, and Sedgwick needed to be sure that it did not catch him unaware. The Southern general, in turn, was anxious about what the Federals were doing. He rode across Hazel Run to a point where he could see the columns headed west. They were moving slowly, indicating that something up ahead blocked their way.[101]

On the Telegraph Road Lt. Col. Allen S. Cutts had reconnoitered toward Lee's Hill. Upon his return he claimed there were Federals in the woods and ordered the waiting artillery to fire. The guns blasted away from one end of the line to the other. General Gordon had also scouted ahead but had seen no Union soldiers. He yelled for the artillery to cease fire, but the cannoneers ignored him. Gordon found Cutts and prevailed upon the artilleryman to order his guns to cease fire.[102]

Early's Division remained at the Cox house for the rest of the night. A minor incident showed how vulnerable the Sixth Corps's rear echelon would be as it moved west. During the fighting that morning, one of the weapons in Cowan's First New York Artillery had suffered a broken axle tree. The captain had instructed Lt. Theodore Atkins to take the inoperative piece back to camp and get it repaired. He was to return with the mended weapon as well as the battery wagon, the mobile forge, and the unit's baggage wagons.[103]

Later that afternoon Atkins recrossed the river with the now-serviceable gun and the requested wagons and forge. By then the Sixth Corps had moved beyond the town, and the roads were clear. The lieutenant mistakenly led his collection of wagons down the Telegraph Road instead of the Plank Road. About a mile past Lee's Hill, Atkins and Quartermaster Sgt. William Sears came upon a Confederate picket post. The guards had watched their approach but thought the column consisted of friendly forces with either a recovered or a captured gun. The Federal artillerymen were upon the Southerners before any of them recognized their error, and the startled pickets ran back toward a Confederate battery, shouting a warning.[104]

During the few moments when the fleeing pickets were within their own artillery's field of fire, the teamsters hurriedly turned their wagons around and whipped their teams to get away. When the Confederate guns finally opened fire, at a range of only six hundred yards, exploding shells panicked the mules. The teamsters struggled to keep their animals under control, but one of the wagons swerved to avoid a fallen tree and overturned. Two other wagons and the forge found their escape route blocked. Under the pressure of a few more artillery rounds, the drivers unhitched horses and mules and mounted them to escape; the man who had wrecked his wagon fled on foot. Atkins and Sears managed to bring off the repaired gun and the battery wagon, but they had lost their forge and the baggage wagons. They belatedly found the Plank Road and headed west to rejoin the First New York.[105]

EIGHT

LATE AFTERNOON OF MAY 3

SALEM CHURCH

By punching through Marye's Heights and pressing west on the Plank Road, Sedgwick had forced Lee to respond to a new threat. The Southern commander had pulled four brigades away from the Chancellorsville front, a move that should have given Hooker an opening to attack a substantially weakened adversary. Since May 1, however, the Union commander had consistently avoided doing anything aggressive, and Lee anticipated little interference when he sent Brigadier Generals Mahone and Kershaw with their respective brigades to confront Sedgwick, followed by Brigadier Generals Semmes and Wofford.[1]

Hooker's inaction remained inexcusable. He had close to 90,000 troops, approximately 35,000 of whom had not yet been fully engaged. Rather than renew the fight with those battle-ready forces, he held fast behind earthworks, a stronghold of no strategic value that could only be supplied through the remote US Ford. Hooker was doing little more than sitting on an escape route.[2]

The Army of Northern Virginia stood between two portions of the Army of the Potomac, but Hooker held his forces in check. A staff officer observed, "His dash, promptness, and confidence as a division and corps commander were gone." His pathetic message to President Lincoln, sent at 1:15 P.M., lamented that Sedgwick had not "gotten up." A few miles away at the home of George Guest, the Sixth Corps commander no longer heard any fighting at Chancellorsville and must have wondered if Hooker was still there.[3]

Lee had only 34,000 men left on the field and had just sent away four brigades. While redirecting forces toward Fredericksburg, he sought to deter any Federal initiative that might test his weakened lines. He sent Brig. Gen. Raleigh E. Colston's division up the US Ford Road to probe Hooker's left flank, anchored on the Rappahannock River. The Union line in that sector had been occupied since May 1. Around 3:00 P.M., when Colston's column came into view, an entrenched grand battery of thirty guns shot up the Southern infantry. The point of the move had been to keep the Federals within their defenses, however, and that goal was attained.[4]

Sedgwick waited at the Guest house for his scattered divisions to assemble. The old tollgate on the knoll was about 2,500 yards down the road. Another 950 yards past it stood the brick sanctuary called Salem Church. A Pennsylvania soldier described the terrain beyond the tollgate, noting "a large plain with a belt of woods running through the center about 100 yards in width—on our side a range of hills descending to these woods, at the bottom a small swampy bushy meadow, running parallel with the woods (and just knee deep as we found out when we retreated across it)." Another soldier observed, "This woods is, as many others down here, a long narrow belt of timber & generally clogged by underbrush & fallen limbs and trees."[5]

Brigadier General Brooks marched his First Division from the bridgehead to the Guest house without stopping to rest. His arrival brought each Sixth Corps division within supporting distance of the others. After Brooks's men took a few minutes to catch their breath, they pushed on toward the Confederate brigade blocking the Federals' way. Sedgwick would use Brigadier General Howe's Second Division, the last one coming up from Fredericksburg, to watch the flank to keep Early's Division from threatening the Federal advance from the south.[6]

On the Orange Plank Road, Brooks placed Colonel Brown's New Jersey brigade north of the road and Brigadier General Bartlett's regiments on the south side. Brown and Bartlett were short a regiment each, those absent units still hustling forward from Fredericksburg. Brooks augmented them with two regiments from Brigadier General Russell's brigade, the Ninety-Fifth and 119th Pennsylvania. Russell had served as the division's rear guard, so his three other regiments had not yet arrived. Elements of

Brooks's three brigades constituted a two-brigade front for the advance to Salem Church.[7]

Brooks's vanguard would be in column of brigades, able to deploy quickly if it ran into trouble. Major General Newton followed with his Third Division in column of march—Colonel Browne's brigade in front, followed by Brigadier General Wheaton's brigade, and then Colonel Shaler's brigade. Colonel Burnham's Light Division followed Newton.[8]

The advancing Federals could not see the Confederates through the intervening trees or in the man-made barriers along the farm roads that intersected the Plank Road. These fieldworks were mounds of dirt topped by cedar or pine trees, much like the tree-lined barriers along the Bowling Green Road. More common, though, were wattle fences, constructed by driving stakes into the ground and interweaving pine or cedar boughs through them, which were then beaten down tight with a maul to create an impenetrable barricade. One such barrier extended eight hundred to one thousand yards north of the Plank Road, running along a road leading to Banks' Ford (modern Featherstone Drive). South of Plank Road another brush fence bordered the east side of a trace through the woods.[9]

Brigadier General Wilcox had spread out his Alabama brigade on the Salem Church ridge. When the Union columns paused at the Guest house, he took his regiments back down the hill to the area near the tollgate. The Alabamans established a line in the woods, while Lt. James S. Cobb deployed two 3-inch Ordnance Rifles from Penick's Pittsylvania Battery in the road. Farther forward were the forty to fifty troopers of the Fifteenth Virginia Cavalry, under Major Collins.[10]

Wilcox got the first hint that Lee was sending support when Capt. Basil C. Manly's North Carolina battery approached from Chancellorsville. His guns went into battery adjacent to Penick's section but had arrived with depleted ammunition chests.[11]

Colonel Brown shook out six companies of the Second New Jersey as skirmishers. Its other four companies had been part of the rear guard and had not yet rejoined their command, so Brown added two companies from the Third New Jersey to the skirmish line. The rest of his brigade formed a line of battle two hundred yards behind them. The First New Jersey and the remainder of the Third New Jersey extended to the right of the road, under overall command of Col. Mark W. Collet. Brown used the Ninety-Fifth and 119th Pennsylvania, led by Col. Gustavus W. Town and Col. Peter C. Ellmaker respectively, to extend his brigade line to the north. The

Twenty-Third New Jersey, led by Col. E. Burd Grubb Jr. and known as the Yahoos, straddled the Plank Road as Brown's left flank. Bartlett's brigade advanced south of the road, with three regiments in line and two on the road behind the Yahoos.[12]

Collins's horse soldiers unleashed several volleys toward the advancing Federals, then withdrew. When the cavalry passed the tollgate, the Confederate cannoneers opened fire. A staff officer riding with Brooks felt the rush of a shell shrieking past his head before it tore off the arm of Capt. Theodore Read riding behind him. A second round crashed into Battery A, Maryland Light Artillery, severely injuring Sgt. John Wormsley. A Federal signalman heard the booming of those guns and noted the time as 3:25 P.M. Sedgwick had about three and a half hours of daylight to break the Confederate line and get to Chancellorsville.[13]

The two artillery units behind the New Jersey brigade rushed forward and brought their guns into battery. Capt. James H. Rigby placed one gun of his Maryland battery to the left of the Plank Road and deployed his other five weapons to the right. Lt. Augustin N. Parsons rushed his New Jersey Light Artillery into battery as well but only had room to deploy three weapons.[14]

The nine Federal guns opened a rapid fire and sent nearly one hundred explosive shells against the Confederate guns. Short of ammunition, Manly's North Carolina Battery fired twenty rounds and pulled back, as did Penick's section. When the Confederate guns withdrew, Rigby's and Parson's batteries jumped forward, taking position on both sides of the Plank Road where the road to Banks' Ford (modern Bragg Road) branches off. Wilcox knew his regiments could handle a brief holding action at the church while he himself waited near Five Mile Fork (where the Plank Road and the Orange Turnpike diverge) for reinforcing infantry to come up.[15]

Maj. Samuel P. Hamilton of Cabell's Battalion tried to coordinate the arriving artillery. Manly had fired off everything except a dozen rounds of canister and pulled back behind the ridge. Capt. Edward S. McCarthy arrived from Chancellorsville with his company of Richmond Howitzers, but he too was low on ammunition. He paused at the William Perry house, where he found Captain Moore and his Norfolk Battery resting after their hasty retreat from Fall Hill. There were no ordnance wagons on hand to replenish ammunition chests. Now only Penick's section remained on the Salem Church ridge.[16]

The sound of renewed fighting carried to Banks' Ford as the Fiftieth New York Engineers began sliding pontoons into the stream. Benham informed

Major General Butterfield that work had commenced, but the chief of staff responded that "the commanding General does not see the necessity of a bridge at Bank's Ford." Engrossed with events at Chancellorsville, Hooker wanted a third bridge at US Ford instead. With the fighting south of Banks' Ford growing in intensity, however, Benham was not going to leave Sedgwick stranded by pulling the newly constructed bridge. He also knew a single span would be militarily irresponsible.[17]

Benham addressed his dilemma by holding back some of the bridging equipment directed to US Ford. A standard pontoon-bridge train consisted of twenty-two boats and material to construct 240 feet of bridge. Benham's engineers had needed only fourteen boats at Scott's Mill, which left eight boats unused. When Col. Clinton E. Colgate harnessed up his teams to move the only available bridge train to US Ford, the chief engineer held back six of its pontoons. When added to those left over from the first bridge's construction, he would have fourteen boats to float a second span at Banks' Ford. Surely sixteen boats would be plenty for another bridge upstream.[18]

Events on the Plank Road were gathering momentum. The two Federal batteries blasted the Confederates ensconced in the woods in front of Salem Church. When those guns fell silent around 5:00 P.M., blue-clad skirmishers trotted forward. A tired soldier noted: "Pretty soon we began to hear our skirmishers firing. I began to think we were not done fighting yet. Our skirmishers kept advancing and we kept following within supporting distance."[19]

While keeping Hooker apprised of the Sixth Corps's progress, Butterfield thought he might get additional information through Banks' Ford. He had informed Brigadier General Hunt that the Federal forces at Fredericksburg were moving toward Chancellorsville and asked that he send a scout to find out where they were. Hunt directed Maj. Alexander Doull, a former British soldier on his staff, to contact Sedgwick and report back. Doull swam his horse across the Rappahannock downstream from the ford. When he rode past elements of the Seventy-First Pennsylvania, he saw that they had captured some Alabama men. As the major directed his horse beyond the pickets, he did not know how many other Confederates might be between him and Sedgwick's forces on the Plank Road.[20]

When the pontoon bridge had been made ready for the passage of troops, Hunt directed Brigadier General Owen to extend troops from his Philadelphia Brigade toward Sedgwick's force and find a good place for a picket line. The Seventy-First Pennsylvania, led by Col. R. Penn Smith, joined its advance elements on the south side of the river, and the full regiment advanced about three-quarters of a mile onto the uplands, pushing past some modest farmhouses occupied by women and children.[21]

Federal signal teams were also looking to establish a connection between Banks' Ford and the Union force on the Plank Road. While the bridge builders knocked together a floating span, signalmen swam across the river with telegraph wires. Lt. Aaron B. Jerome and the rest of his team brought the rest of their equipment across in a pontoon and set up an electrical signal station. Benham ordered Lt. Martin Denicke to link the Sixth Corps with Lt. Brinkerhoff N. Miner's flag station at the Scott house, which stood on a highly visible hilltop two and a half miles downstream from the developing pontoon crossing.[22]

Denicke and his men made their way on foot to the Plank Road and reported to Sedgwick. He tried to establish communications with Miner, but the developing action at Salem Church kept them from doing so before dark. Jerome's electrical signal team on the south side of Banks' Ford managed to open a line to the Falmouth headquarters, but that link had no immediate use. The signal team shut down its station after dark and recrossed the river.[23]

Owen's infantry did not make contact with the Sixth Corps either. The brigade commander sent one of his adjutants to try to reach Sedgwick, but that officer did not return. The Federals had seen Confederates (some of Wilcox's Alabamans) moving across their front, and Owen requested a section of guns to help defend his position. Benham put the request to Chief of Artillery Hunt before he departed to report to Hooker. Hunt had placed his artillery on the high ground north of the river to cover Banks' Ford. After some hesitation, he released a section of guns to Benham.[24]

On the Plank Road Wilcox greeted Mahone when his brigade reached Five Mile Fork around 4:00 P.M. The initial orders for the Virginia brigade and Kershaw's South Carolinians had been to set up a blocking position on the Zoan Church ridge, but new instructions kept them moving to reinforce Wilcox. Semmes and Wofford followed with their respective Georgia brigades. When Mahone approached the Salem Church ridge, Wilcox directed him to form on his left, extending toward Banks' Ford.[25]

Withdrawing from the tollgate, the Tenth Alabama redeployed along a narrow trace near Salem Church. The break in the trees made an attack

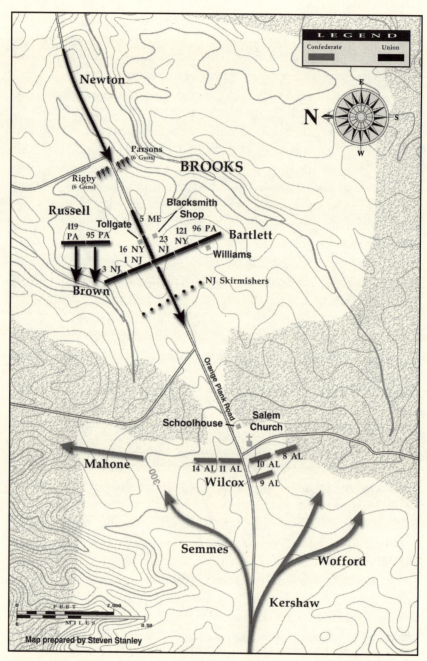

Map 12. Salem Church (Phase 1). As the Federals pushed a two-brigade front toward Salem Church, four Confederate brigades arrived from Chancellorsville to reinforce Wilcox.

up the road the most likely avenue of advance, so Wilcox stacked the Ninth Alabama behind it. One company of the Ninth also occupied the sanctuary, where it could shoot from upper-story windows. Another company ensconced itself in a log schoolhouse approximately sixty yards in front of the main line. Soldiers secured the door and knocked out some of the chinking between the logs to create loopholes.[26]

To the right of the Tenth Regiment, the Eighth Alabama extended the brigade line farther south. The Eleventh Alabama took position north of the Plank Road, and the Fourteenth Alabama extended the line to its left. An interval of about eighty yards across the roadway separated the Eleventh and Tenth Alabama, providing space for supporting artillery. Unfortunately, the Confederate batteries were low on ammunition. Only Penick brought his guns into battery on the ridge, in line with the Alabama infantry.[27]

Unlike the artillery, the arriving infantry had drawn ammunition back at Chancellorsville. As Mahone's Virginians deployed, Maj. James M. Goggin, from McLaws's division staff, galloped up and informed Wilcox that there were three more brigades on their way. Kershaw's was the next to arrive, and Wilcox directed it south of the road. When Semmes approached with his Georgia brigade, Wilcox asked Mahone to slide to the left. Rather than having the Georgia units force their way through the woods, it would be more expedient for the Virginians to extend to the left and let the Georgians fill in the interval. Wilcox would soon stand in Sedgwick's way with the strength of a division instead of his single brigade.[28]

This attention to speed proved prescient because the Federals were coming on strong. Wofford's Georgians were the last brigade to arrive and heard gunfire getting closer as they hurried up the road. Semmes's Georgians were already hustling toward the gap Mahone had left for them. With the Northerners so close, there was no longer any time for brigade movements. Semmes's regimental commanders saw where they needed to be and rushed their troops into position without confusion or delay.[29]

Even so, they were not quite quick enough. A soldier in the Tenth Georgia later wrote, "Before our lines could be formed the enemy was upon us, and the Fiftieth and Fifty-Third Georgia Regiments, not yet having taken position, suffered severely." Semmes reported that his two units "took position under a storm of bullets." Another officer later wrote, "then began one of the hardest contests I ever witnessed." The Georgians hastening to get into position, however, did not know that a skirmish line of Virginia troops was deployed in front of them.[30]

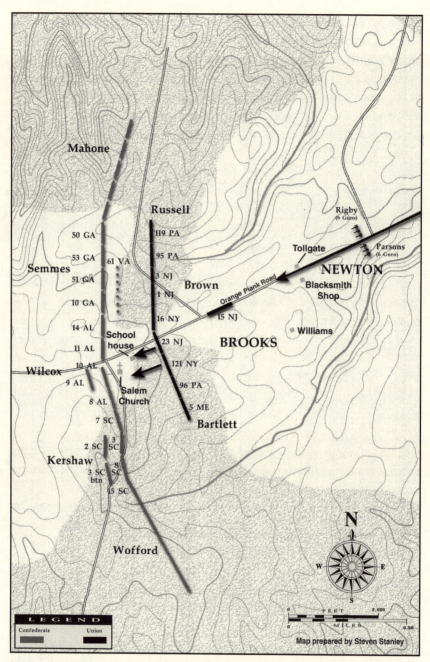

Map 13. Salem Church (Phase 2). The Federals advanced toward the Confederate-held ridge through a tangled woodland. The Twenty-Third New Jersey and the 121st New York charged across the open ground in front of Salem Church.

Col. Virginius D. Groner's Sixty-First Virginia, having been Mahone's vanguard unit, was directed to form a skirmish line as the rest of the brigade deployed for battle. The men hurriedly pushed about one hundred yards into the tangled woodland and spread out in open order. When the First and Third New Jersey came into view through the trees, the Virginians fired a volley and pulled back. Semmes's Georgians, however, had filled in the line where Mahone's units had been. When the Federal skirmishers opened fire, so too did the Georgians.[31]

A Virginia sergeant described the confusion:

As we came out we saw a musket pointed at us and a man shouted, "a minute later and I would have shot you." As soon as we got over the fence, behind which our troops were in position, horror of horrors! one whole brigade opened upon our skirmishers. I stood horror stricken for an instant, but as soon as I recovered my self-possession, I ran along the line, begging the men for God's sake to cease firing, they were murdering our own men; but as the Yankees had gotten up and their balls came flying over, it was some time before we could convince the men that they were firing on their own skirmishers.[32]

The Federals advanced relentlessly. The front line would fire a volley and drop to the ground to reload. The next line advanced through them, fired a volley, and dropped down to reload. A third line advanced through them both to do the same. By then the first line had reloaded and the sequence continued. The Virginia skirmishers found protection behind an embankment but scrambled out of the woods when the firing momentarily diminished. The sergeant remembered that "they all appeared indignant but not panic stricken." Eventually, the Sixty-First Virginia managed to rejoin its brigade.[33]

South of the Plank Road, Bartlett's brigade advanced slightly behind Brown's brigade. Lt. Francis W. Morse, adjutant in the 121st New York, had carried Brooks's orders to the assault columns. It appears he delivered them to Brown first and then to Bartlett before rejoining his regiment in the latter brigade. That sequence accounts for Brown's units north of the Turnpike stepping off first and getting ahead of Bartlett's line.[34]

In Bartlett's brigade the Fifth Maine, Col. Clark S. Edwards commanding, guided on the road. To its left Col. Emory Upton advanced with his 121st New York. On the far left Major Lessig brought up his Ninety-Sixth

Pennsylvania. These units had marched from Deep Run to the Plank Road with full knapsacks, which the men still wore. Brown's New Jersey units had stacked their knapsacks before advancing toward Salem Church, but Bartlett's troops had not. As a consequence, the brigade's advance consisted of tired men in full marching gear.[35]

The Fifth Maine adjusted its facing to get around the Twenty-Third New Jersey and into the line of battle. Edwards oblique marched his unit to the left, executing a 45-degree change of direction that kept moving forward as it traveled across the rear of the advancing brigade to come up on its left flank. The Ninety-Sixth Pennsylvania, however, moved into the woods before the Fifth Maine came up on its left. The Pennsylvanians did not know they had support on that flank when they began taking fire.[36]

At the edge of the woods, New Jersey skirmishers let Bartlett's units know that Confederates were among the far edge of the trees. The Federal assault troops stepped through the skirmishers, and the New Jersey men pulled back to rejoin their unit north of the Plank Road. Colonel Seaver's Sixteenth New York remained behind the Twenty-Third New Jersey on the Plank Road. The time was around 5:30 P.M.[37]

Sedgwick knew his circumstances were becoming precarious. He was no longer marching to the sound of guns but pushing into an ominous silence. The last artillery heard from upriver had been around 3:00 P.M., which was when Union guns had blasted Colston's probe. Early's Division remained intact on the Telegraph Road and a threat to communications through Fredericksburg. A bridge had been put down at Banks' Ford, but an advance too far west would cut him off from that crossing and potentially leave his corps isolated and open to attack and destruction. It was also getting late—sundown would come at 7:03 P.M., less than two hours away.[38]

The terrain at Salem Church broke up the Federal advance. Lt. H. Seymour Hall of the 121st New York described how the troops "advanced through the almost impenetrable thicket, across deep ravines that impeded our progress and broke our alignment, exposed to a destructive fire of musketry and artillery, from which the tangled bushes did not protect us . . . and as we came out on the opposite side of the thicket, the steep bank, the church, the school house, the enemy's line of rifle pits fringed with fire were before us."[39]

Wilcox's Alabamans saw their targets emerge from the trees and unleashed a volley. That initial blast, at eighty yards, did not inflict many casualties, and the next volley did not have its full effect either. A New

York lieutenant remembered why: "We marched up directly in their front, when they opened a volley on us, that would have killed every man in our brigade, had they not fired so high, all of their balls going over our heads." Kneeling to return fire, the Union troops got off a couple of rounds each, then pressed forward into enemy fire becoming increasingly accurate.[40]

The 121st New York overran the log schoolhouse, which was occupied by a company of the Ninth Alabama. A lieutenant foolishly shouted, "Show them no quarter," indicating that the Union troops were not taking prisoners. The Confederates inside redoubled their fire, shooting between the logs as Union soldiers crowded behind its seeming shelter. Casualties mounted. An Alabama soldier later wrote, "The rash command of that lieutenant cost him his life and many of his squad."[41]

Upton pushed his New Yorkers forward against the Tenth Alabama. They were new to combat but well trained. When the colonel gave the command to charge, the regiment advanced without hesitation into a withering fire. To its left the Ninety-Sixth Pennsylvania kept up a steady fire, but its soldiers had been more cautious, as described by one of their officers: "Our orders were to advance. I told my men to take plenty of room and leave a pace between each file (which was the cause of my losing so lightly). We passed on and when within 30 paces of the field on the other side of the woods, suddenly I saw two lines of Battle of the 'Rebs' rise to their feet."[42]

The Pennsylvanians were ready for quick action and fired first. Their volley riddled the ranks of the Eighth Alabama and injured its commander, Col. Young L. Royston. The survivors, however, immediately returned fire, punishing the advancing Federals with a concentrated crossfire.[43]

The Ninety-Sixth Pennsylvania men appear not to have emerged from the trees, which limited their field of vision. They did not see the Fifth Maine to their left and thought that their regiment constituted the brigade's flank. Battle smoke further obscured visibility. A soldier later described the disconcerting experience: "Soon these hitherto quiet woods rolled up dense volumes of sulphurous smoke and seemed almost rent asunder by the crack and crash and rattle of small arms."[44]

To the right of the 121st New York, the Twenty-Third New Jersey should have advanced simultaneously to strengthen the assault. Without battle experience, however, the New Jersey men opened fire too soon. They stopped to reload, lost momentum, and were blasted by the Tenth and Eleventh Alabama. Penick's Pittsylvania Battery also sent what few rounds it had into the advancing Federals. The battery commander reported pulling his guns off the line after firing one round, but Union attackers reported multiple rounds of incoming artillery fire. Penick likely meant that each of his guns fired a round before pulling back.[45]

When the Fifth Maine obliqued to the left, Seaver's Sixteenth New York continued to advance behind the Twenty-Third New Jersey. The few artillery rounds that crashed through the Yahoos also smashed into the New Yorkers. Seaver decided to maneuver to the right and soon inserted his unit into the New Jersey Brigade's line. A severe fire came from the hedgerows ahead. Through clouds of powder smoke, Salem Church loomed up on the left, Confederate riflemen at the upper-story windows.[46]

The Sixteenth New York was a two-year regiment, its men within days of mustering out. They had not tried to avoid this last campaign and now rushed forward to close with the enemy. One soldier described how they "found the rebels behind a dirt fence which was a fine brest [sic] works for them and when we came in range they pored [sic] a terrible fire in us and we being in so thick brush that it was impossible to go through in order."[47]

Being out of the woods had its own challenges. Upton's 121st New York found itself in the eye of the storm, taking fire from the log schoolhouse, the brick church, and the road behind the church. Capt. Nelson O. Wendell, commanding Company F, staggered and fell from a Minié ball in his shoulder. When he managed to get back to his feet, another bullet struck him in the head, killing him. Bullets smashed into Upton's horse, causing it to bolt toward the Confederate line. The colonel jumped off quickly and thereafter led his unit on foot. Six color bearers would be killed in that maelstrom of flying lead, but the 121st continued to press forward.[48]

Confronting the New Yorkers were Col. William A. Forney's Tenth Alabama and the Eighth Alabama, now commanded by Lieutenant Colonel Herbert. Their firepower proved insufficient to hold back the determined Union infantry, who slammed into the Tenth Alabama. The Southern regiment crumpled and fell back on the Ninth Alabama. The Eighth Alabama, however, did not get knocked out of position. Herbert deflected the Federal surge by shifting his three left companies backward in a half wheel. This maneuver kept his unit intact and allowed those three companies to fire into the flank of the advancing New Yorkers.[49]

About thirty yards behind the Tenth Alabama, Maj. Jeremiah H. J. Williams had eight companies of his Ninth Alabama, Wilcox's only reserve formation. Williams had kept his troops lying down, awaiting their call to action. When they stood up to confront the oncoming Federals, they rose into a storm of flying lead. Men fell dead before having a chance to enter the fight. Those Alabamans who had not stepped into a bullet rushed forward and crashed into the 121st New York. The Federals were taking fire from their left and front, and without the Twenty-Third New Jersey moving up on their right, they took fire from that quarter as well. The New Yorkers gave way.[50]

Lessig's Ninety-Sixth Pennsylvania had kept up a steady fire from within the trees. When Upton's troops fell back, the Eighth Alabama poured a heavy fire into the Pennsylvanians' right flank. At the same time, the Third South Carolina of Kershaw's Brigade opened fire on the Ninety-Sixth's left. With the 121st falling back on the right and no supports visible to the left, Lessig ordered his regiment back as well.[51]

Even if Lessig had known the Fifth Maine had taken position on his left, the Pennsylvanians were too exhausted to hold. Their commander reported that "the men were entirely worn out and without spirit, having been nearly sixteen hours under arms, the greater portion under a burning sun." The soldiers became disordered in retreat, and Alabamans following closely behind called on them to surrender.[52]

When Edwards led his Fifth Maine to the far left of the brigade line, he thought he was getting on to the Confederate flank. Kershaw, however, had deployed his South Carolina troops on Wilcox's right, unseen by the attacking Federals. The Third South Carolina had already made its presence known to the Ninety-Sixth Pennsylvania. The Fifth Maine soon found itself under a severe fire and lay down, its forward progress ended. The colonel described the tense action: "As we lay there, we could distinctly hear the rebel forces running to get around our left flank. Realizing the great danger of this movement, we gave the order, 'Up! Fire low! Ready! Fire!' A deafening volley was discharged. The next order was 'Load and fire as fast as possible.'"[53]

Bartlett watched his brigade come tumbling back through the trees, but he could not see the Fifth Maine. He sent his adjutant, Lt. Robert P. Wilson of the Sixteenth New York, to find the regiment. Wilson located the endangered troops and shouted, "For God's sake, Colonel, get your men out of this as quickly as possible, for you are nearly surrounded." Before he could ride back out of the woods, incoming fire killed his horse; the adjutant continued back on foot. In the desperate fighting to avoid capture, some of the exhausted men forgot to withdraw their ramrods before firing, leaving their rifles ineffective until they could find another one.[54]

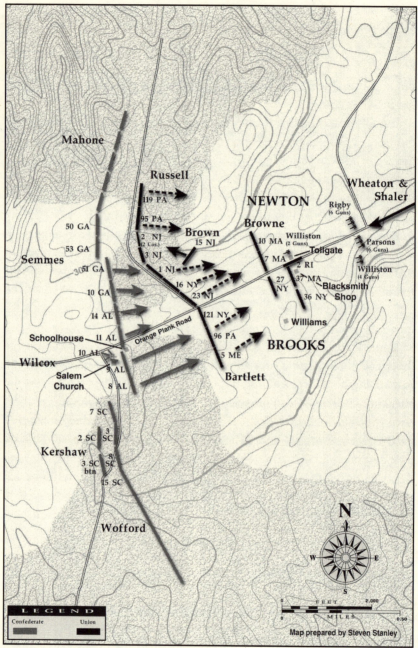

Map 14. Salem Church (Phase 3). A Confederate counterattack pushed back the Federals along the road and in the area to the south. Fighting continued in the woods north of the road. Federal reinforcements deployed to hold the line.

Pvt. George Hamilton recounted the tired Fifth Maine's ordeal: "The rebels got out of the woods on the right of our regiment before we did. Gen. Bartlett thought we were captured sure. We gave them two or three volleys and were ordered to fall back as fast as we could. So we had to take our legs for it. We had to run across an open field for some distance, the bullets flying around us in every direction."[55] The New Englanders rallied at a house that belonged to a William S. Williams before falling back farther. The Fifth Maine had lost twenty-three men in the assault at Marye's Heights; at Salem Church they lost another seventy-four men.[56]

When the Ninth Alabama pushed back against the 121st New York, the men impetuously pressed beyond the brigade line. Under the impression that someone had ordered a counterattack, other units joined in. Wilcox later reported: "Our line was lying impatiently waiting for orders to charge and whether the order was given or not, I cannot say. Almost before I knew it several officers charged, among whom I recognized Lieutenant [Woody] Dozier of Company D as he hallooed out, 'Come on boys, we'll get our blankets back.' Officers and men went over the brush fence with a shout that echoed for miles along the Rappahannock."[57]

Confederate doctrine called for a swift counterattack when ground had been lost, and the Alabama troops certainly anticipated being directed to charge. They had lost their blankets and other gear earlier in the day during a precipitous retreat, hence the somewhat domestic battle cry. Some of the units reported receiving orders to advance, but the brigade commander did not give them. Except for the shattered Tenth Alabama, Wilcox's Confederates surged forward with a yell.[58]

The Tenth and Fifty-First Georgia sprang forward with the Alabamans. They had been in position for only a few moments when the Federal attack came. In that immediate crush of fighting, Lt. Col. William C. Holt, leading the Tenth Georgia, informed General Semmes that Wilcox's Brigade had launched a counterattack. Semmes immediately gave orders for his brigade to charge, but only his Tenth and Fifty-First Regiments jumped the fence and rushed forward.[59]

The Georgia brigade's left wing, consisting of the Fiftieth and Fifty-Third Regiments, was still moving up when the Federals opened fire. They suffered severely when a volley ripped into them at 150 yards. Maj. Oliver P. Anthony had assumed command of the Fifty-Third Georgia when both its colonel and lieutenant colonel became casualties at Chancellorsville; Lt. Col. Francis Kearse led the Fiftieth Georgia. Rather than pursuing a retreating foe, the Georgians confronted a stubborn Federal force that was not going anywhere.[60]

The two Georgia units formed line of battle under fire from the Federal infantry now just sixty yards away. At that range the Confederates "poured a volley into the enemy's ranks that seemed . . . to sweep their first rank entirely out of existence. Every twig and bush for nearly three hundred yards to our front was cut off knee high, while the woods in front was covered with blue coats, lying dead in every conceivable form." The two regiments maintained a united front but lost contact with the Fifty-First Georgia to their right.[61]

Opposite the Georgians, the First and Third New Jersey Regiments pushed through the trees. The Sixteenth New York was to their left and the Ninety-Fifth and 119th Pennsylvania Regiments of Russell's brigade extended the line to the right. The Ninety-Fifth, known as Gosline's Zouaves, had worn out their colorful uniforms and now wore standard-issue blue uniforms. They did, however, retain their distinctive, red-trimmed jackets.[62]

The Pennsylvanians advanced cautiously but steadily. A few rounds of Confederate artillery fire had come from their left front but passed overhead without causing them harm. Near the woods Colonel Town gave orders for the two regiments to lie down behind a brush fence. After a few moments the men pushed on to the edge of the woods and paused again. When they advanced into the trees, the Confederates unleashed a volley that killed Town as well as his second in command, Lt. Col. Elisha Hall. Maj. Thomas J. Town, the colonel's brother, briefly took command until he too fell wounded.[63]

With the Confederate line overlapping the two Keystone State regiments, the Federals became heavily engaged but with little chance of doing more than exchanging volleys with a well-positioned adversary. When the Confederate counterattack rippled along the line at Salem Church, the Pennsylvanians were on the far right without apparent support. Both regiments fell back.[64]

The New Jersey regiments, meanwhile, stubbornly held their position as the small-arms fire on their front intensified. To their left the Sixteenth New York and the Twenty-Third New Jersey Regiments, each from a different brigade, did not have the cohesiveness to withstand the pressure, and they began to falter. One of the New Yorkers described what came next: "Reg of Jerseys [the Twenty-Third] broke on our left and we could not do anything else than but fall back for the Rebels following up the Jerseys were geting [sic] round us. We got the order to fall back and the rebels followed and killed many while we were falling back."[65]

South of the Plank Road, Bartlett's attack had failed. As the Fifth Maine, Ninety-Sixth Pennsylvania, and Sixteenth and 121st New York Regiments came tumbling back, they were pursued closely by Wilcox's screaming Alabamans. In his report Colonel Sanders, commanding the Eleventh Alabama, described how his men "charged through the wood, an open field, across a lane and into the field beyond, driving the enemy before us. . . . The guns, knapsacks, accoutrements, &c., strewn over the field told that the enemy had been routed."[66]

North of the road the First New Jersey had been knocked loose from its brigade with the departing New Yorkers and started to retreat as well. The Third New Jersey (with two companies from the Second New Jersey) reeled but had held thanks to a brief period of support from the Ninety-Fifth and 119th Pennsylvania on its right. The Keystone State men had also pulled back but not precipitously, as had occurred south of the road. Because the New Jersey troops held firm, the battle in the wooded terrain north of the Plank Road began to turn into a slugging match.[67]

The Third New Jersey pulled back through the woods a bit, but from the edge of the trees, they could see that help was on the way. Sedgwick had intercepted Col. William H. Penrose's Fifteenth New Jersey as it came up the road and directed it toward the desperate fighting. There was no time to lose, so the arriving unit deployed from column into battle line as it crossed the open ground toward the woods. The Third New Jersey had taken shelter along an old rail fence, and one of the arriving soldiers noted that beyond that line of blue-clad men "the woods was full of smoke and the firing was continuous."[68]

The Fifteenth New Jersey was not combat experienced, and the veteran Third New Jersey soldiers shouted to them: "Throw off your knapsacks. You don't want them here." The men dropped their packs without breaking stride, jumped the low fence, and advanced into the tangled secondary growth. They pressed forward until they were within thirty to fifty yards of the Confederate line and received a blast of musketry from troops who looked to be sheltered in a ditch.[69]

Only two men of the Fifteenth New Jersey fell dead, both shot in the head. Minor casualties from an initial volley indicated the Southerners were firing high. Penrose gave the command to "fire by file, commence firing," which would have been a measured response that rippled down the line of battle. The excited Federals, however, fired all at once. The musketry became steady, and both sides quickly found the range. Casualties mounted as the Georgians and the New Jersey men pounded away at each other. The Third New Jersey moved back into the trees to help hold the line with the Fifteenth.[70]

Newton's division came up behind Brooks, pushing through scores of wounded men to bolster what was left of the Federal line. Colonel Browne's brigade led the way. The Thirty-Seventh Massachusetts moved to the south of the road, and the Thirty-Sixth New York extended the line to its left. The Seventh Massachusetts deployed adjacent to and north of the road. The Tenth Massachusetts extended its line to the right. The Second Rhode Island followed the New England regiments as a reserve.[71]

The Federals had run into heavier Confederate strength than anticipated. Major Tompkins brought up Williston's Battery D, Second US Artillery, with 12-pounder Napoleons. The battery commander directed two sections into position south of the road, to join the gun line comprised of Rigby's and Parson's batteries. Williston personally took charge of the third section and dashed forward another three hundred yards to the rise at the tollgate. Before charging into harm's way, he had instructed his next in command to keep an eye on him. If the Confederates overran the forward section, he was to blast the position with the other four guns.[72]

While going into battery, Williston's gunners saw there were still Federal troops between them and the approaching Confederates. They turned their attention to the threat north of the road, where the Georgia regiments had advanced farther than Wilcox's Alabamans. Williston's artillerymen enfiladed them with spherical case shot. With fuzes set to burst at 1.75 seconds, the rounds exploded among the advancing formations, and the Southern pursuit wavered. That slight pause allowed Williston's alert gunners to rapidly fire sixteen more rounds with the same fuze setting. The Georgians broke, with some of them moving across the road to get clear. Williston's two Napoleons positioned on the road then fired solid shot directly up its straight, hard-packed surface, their position "peculiarly suited for ricochet firing."[73]

Under the cover of considerable battle smoke, the Confederates rallied south of the road. After a few quiet minutes, they pressed forward again, but the Federal guns now had a clear field of fire. Williston's artillerymen fired double canister and decimated the advancing ranks. Above the smoke they saw a large Confederate battle flag go down twice. Union infantry, lying prone on either side of the road, added their firepower. Still, casualties mounted among the Northern gun crews, and Williston jumped in to help serve the left gun. He remained at that post until an incoming round struck the rammer he had just removed from the barrel, the kinetic energy knocking him down. When the counterattack collapsed and the firing stopped, a great many Confederates crawled forward and surrendered.[74]

Bartlett used Browne's arriving infantry to create a bulwark against which his retreating units could rally. Col. Alexander D. Adams spread out his Twenty-Seventh New York to intercept the fleeing soldiers, and the Fifth Maine, Ninety-Sixth Pennsylvania, and the Sixteenth and 121st New York were able to reform in front of them. The Thirty-Sixth New York and Thirty-Seventh Massachusetts of Browne's brigade took position to help check the Confederate counterattack.[75]

North of the road the Seventh and Tenth Massachusetts moved up toward the Third and Fifteenth New Jersey. Smoke hung heavy in the trees, and the noise of combat remained incessant. Browne directed his Massachusetts men to lie down. Before long the First New Jersey came tumbling back, the Confederates right behind them. When the retreating men were clear, the New England regiments stood up and opened fire. The pursuing Southerners fired back, and the two lines blasted at each other only fifty feet apart. Colonel Browne fell wounded almost immediately, and Col. Henry Eustis assumed command.[76]

When Eustis stepped up to lead the brigade, Maj. Dexter F. Parker assumed command of the Tenth Massachusetts. In the heat of battle, Parker ended up in front of his regiment rather than behind it. One of his men called out, "You'll get hit, major." The new commander called back: "Fire away boys, fire away. Never mind me." The firing intensified as the Confederates tried to hold on to their gains, but the Southerners fell back under the pressure. Eustis moved the Seventh and Tenth Massachusetts up and stabilized a line in the woods.[77]

Without the First New Jersey on its left, the position held by the Third New Jersey became tenuous. The Ninety-Fifth and 119th Pennsylvania were no longer on its right, and the Fifteenth New Jersey was not yet within supporting distance. The men were on their own and running low on ammunition. The Confederates had also found the Third's exposed flank and were curling around it.[78]

Newton had Wheaton's brigade coming up the road and decided he could send in Browne's reserves. He rode over to Col. Horatio Rogers Jr.

and inquired: "What regiment, colonel?" Rogers replied, "The Second Rhode Island, sir." The general ordered it forward: "Move your regiment at once to the right, beyond the house." Rogers remembered him adding, "We are being badly driven; hurry up and help them."[79]

The Second Rhode Island moved across the open ground east of the woods. The First New Jersey's precipitous retreat disrupted its advance along the way, but the men soon came up to the right of the Tenth Massachusetts, near a frame house. Rogers used three companies to connect to the New Englanders and led his remaining seven companies to the right of the house and across a ravine, looking for the Fifteenth New Jersey.[80]

In the woods Rogers saw a flag and blue uniforms to his front, a sighting confirmed by an officer who ran across the field to report that the Third New Jersey stood in danger of being cut off. When the Rhode Islanders emerged on the far side of the ravine, they saw that they overlapped the Confederates who had pushed beyond their own lines. His men needing more firepower, Rogers sent back for his three companies near the house, although he did not wait for them. The colonel moved toward the beleaguered Third New Jersey, warning his Rhode Islanders to avoid shooting into friendly troops. Even with care, though, the Jerseymen still "suffered unmistakably from the Federal fire."[81]

The Third New Jersey pulled back with its regimental colors, but just barely. In hand-to-hand fighting a Georgia soldier had seized their flag; a Union soldier grabbed it back. As men clubbed, shot, and bayoneted each other, the Federal with the flag yanked it from its staff and stuffed the banner under his shirt. The Confederates captured only a bare flagstaff, which was little to show for the brutal fighting in the tangled trees. The Georgians lost three of their own color bearers that day. Veterans compared the fighting at Salem Church to what they had experienced in June 1862 at Gaines's Mill.[82]

With the Third New Jersey saved from capture, Rogers turned his attention to the Fifteenth New Jersey. The Rhode Islanders formed behind them, and the relieved troops fell back through their ranks. The New Jersey men continued back out of the woods and picked up the knapsacks they had flung off earlier. They were not out of danger, though, and some were killed while picking up their provisions. The Second Rhode Island remained in the trees, where hard fighting continued.[83]

Rogers had been new to command as his unit approached Salem Church. His Rhode Island troops had been watching him closely to assess whether he was the type of leader who could make good decisions under pressure. The colonel had been quick thinking and cool that day, continuously aware of changing battlefield conditions. When the regiment later pulled back and reformed, the hard-bitten infantrymen knew they had a regimental commander they could trust.[84]

Semmes's Georgia regiments that charged with Wilcox's Alabamans advanced to within one hundred yards of the Federal's reserve line. They had paid dearly for their impetuousness. One Georgian remembered, "Sedgewick [sic] had sturdy fighters and they mowed our men down by scores." When the Southerners fell back, though, they brought off a great many prisoners they had snagged in their pursuit.[85]

Semmes's other two regiments continued to slug it out on the Salem Church ridge. They had been resupplied with ammunition before marching east but were using it up fast. They also had to contend with their rifle barrels becoming fouled to the point that ramming home a cartridge required banging the ramrod with a rock or pushing it against a tree. Failing to seat a round risked a burst barrel.[86]

Lieutenant Colonel Kearse, standing among his men of the Fiftieth Georgia, became frustrated at the lack of support from Mahone's Brigade to his left. He also cursed the sun for not setting fast enough and exclaimed, "I shall have no regiment left." The Georgians had already been picking up rifles and ammunition to use from the dead and wounded. Kearse sent his litter bearers back to find more cartridges.[87]

Semmes did not know that his Fiftieth and Fifty-Third Regiments were thus engaged, realizing only that they had not counterattacked with the Tenth and Fifty-First Regiments. It was McLaws who thought to support the two hard-pressed Georgians on the ridge. Grabbing the last two regiments of Wofford's Brigade coming up the road, he redirected them to support Semmes's two units as well as Mahone's Virginians.[88]

The Fiftieth and Fifty-Third Georgia took heavier casualties fighting in the woods than what the Tenth and Fifty-First Georgia sustained during the counterattack. Semmes had thought his left wing sheltered in the woods instead of attacking but later realized his mistake, writing an accurate official report. Making amends in person proved more difficult. In a postbattle formation the general raised his hat in salute, but the survivors of that grueling fight, angry at his momentary lack of confidence in them, expressed their ire by remaining silent.[89]

Semmes instructed his units to keep fighting until their ammunition was gone and then retire behind the Virginia brigade to their left. With the heightened chance for error or mistaken identity in the smoke-filled woods, Kearse sent a staff officer to inform General Mahone that the Georgia troops would soon be moving behind his troops. When the Georgians fired their last rounds, they pulled back about thirty yards to a position behind the Virginians' right flank and found a relatively sheltered place to reform.[90]

Mahone's Brigade held the extreme Confederate left, and its fight had been entirely within the woods. The Virginians had received small-arms fire from an unseen foe but held their position as men fell dead and wounded. To the north only a few hundred yards away, Owen's Philadelphia Brigade held the high ground overlooking Banks' Ford, but a stream valley separated the two forces, and they appear not to have engaged one another. When the Fiftieth Georgia pulled back to Mahone's right, the Virginians executed a right wheel—at least as best they could in the dense woods—and fired into the Federal flank. The sudden storm of lead from an unexpected quarter devastated the Union force, and the Southerners "gathered those in they didn't kill."[91]

Newton continued pushing up reinforcements. Wheaton brought up his brigade behind Browne's, now being led by Eustis. His Sixty-Second New York and Ninety-Eighth Pennsylvania deployed south of the road and rushed forward but were knocked back. They joined the line of infantry forming behind the artillery near the tollgate. The Ninety-Third and 102nd Pennsylvania spread out north of the road, staying out of the woods, but supporting the Seventh and Tenth Massachusetts and the Second Rhode Island. Wheaton held the 139th Pennsylvania in reserve.[92]

Wheaton's Ninety-Third and 102nd Pennsylvania continued moving to the right, crossing the ravine and pressing toward the ridge beyond. On that fluid battleground Semmes's Georgians aggressively pushed down the ravine behind the Federal infantry. One of the Pennsylvania soldiers remembered: "Our regiment went into action on the right of our lines, and was soon under a terrible fire, but held its position. Soon heavy firing was heard directly in our rear. Our lines had been broken further to the left, and the enemy had possession of the ground over which we had a short time passed."[93]

As the Ninety-Third and 102nd Pennsylvania tumbled back, Wheaton sent in Col. Frederick H. Collier's 139th Pennsylvania. Some of the men streaming to the rear called out that there were still some of their men in the woods, but events moved too quickly to spare stray soldiers. The 139th met a heavy fire and was immediately engulfed in close fighting. As one of the men remembered: "Two old regiments broke and were being pursued by the enemy. The confusion was terrible. The flying regiments rushed through our boys, breaking our ranks, and I said to myself, 'Its all up with us.' But not so. The boys rushed into the 'rebs' and drove them back into the woods, faster than they came out."[94]

Sunset would come at 7:03 P.M. Until then, however, the fighting continued, and casualties kept mounting. Wheaton had every one of his units engaged and concluded, "To sustain this line many minutes was evidently impossible, and I immediately dispatched a staff officer to the rear to bring up troops, with which to form a second line."[95]

Colonel Shaler's brigade came up the Plank Road and filled a gap that had developed on Wheaton's left. Lieutenant Colonel Hamblin brought up the Sixty-Fifth New York (First US Chasseurs) alongside Colonel Titus's 122nd New York. They moved in behind the Seventh and Tenth Massachusetts. Having run out of ammunition, the New Englanders heard Titus shout welcome words: "Git out o' here, you Tenth Massachusetts fellers. You've fit long enough."[96]

The Salem Church battle was not ending well for the Sixth Corps. Troops south of the Plank Road had been forced into a precipitous retreat. The fighting north of the road remained inconclusive. Having gained no advantage, General Brooks remarked to his aide, "Twenty-five years in the army, Mister Wheeler, and ruined at last." Mr. Wheeler was Lt. Daniel D. Wheeler of the Fourth Vermont, assigned to the division staff. He spent the evening of May 3 helping stabilize the Federal line amid hundreds of dead and dying men on the slope in front of Salem Church.[97]

Near sundown, General Russell arrived on the field with the Eighteenth and Thirty-Second New York and Forty-Ninth Pennsylvania. His other two regiments, the Ninety-Fifth and 119th Pennsylvania, had fought with the New Jersey brigade and suffered 282 casualties between them. As the Forty-Ninth Pennsylvania moved up, it passed remnants of the 119th Pennsylvania. Lieutenant Colonel Hughes greeted Colonel Ellmaker, his fellow regimental commander, and asked how they had fared; Ellmaker responded "All gobbled up." Hughes remembered that his friend's "voice was coarse and sounded very funny."[98]

Darkness finally ended the fighting. Southern skirmishers remained in the open field, with the covering woods behind them. When the Forty-Ninth

Pennsylvania took position between the Plank Road and the ravine just to the north, its skirmishers could hear wounded men on the ground in front of them.[99]

Sixth Corps units continued to arrive, taking position to hold their gains on the Plank Road. As night descended, those who had their knapsacks took in some food. Newton had made sure his quartermasters retrieved the stacks of knapsacks his men had dropped on the Bowling Green Road and delivered them to his fighting men that evening. The less-experienced Burnham had not done the same. Most of Howe's units had gone back to the Bowling Green Road to pick up their gear, though not all of them. An irritated New Jersey soldier said they got little rest that night "as our blankets were gone and the night cold and damp."[100]

Federal artillery units needed relief. Three of Major Tompkins's batteries were in position near the tollgate, and his fourth battery had come up just after the Confederates struck. At dusk Rigby pulled his Maryland Light Artillery back, and Harn's Third Battery, New York Light Artillery took his place. Lieutenant Butler, commanding Battery G, Second US Artillery, came up after dark and relieved Williston's Battery D, Second US Artillery. After a hard day Parsons anticipated being able to pull his New Jersey battery off the line, but his relief had not yet arrived.[101]

Following the Federal breakthrough at Marye's Heights, Cowan's First Battery, New Jersey Independent Light Artillery had been placed in reserve. He was one gun short since the axle tree for one of his weapons had been damaged and taken across the river for repairs. At 9:15 P.M. Cowan received orders to relieve Parsons. While going into battery north of the road, his men could see Confederate skirmishers in the moonlight approximately seven hundred yards in front of them.[102]

Lieutenant Atkins finally brought up the New Jersey battery's repaired gun. He was supposed to have returned with the battery wagons and a mobile forge but had taken the wrong road out of Fredericksburg and run into Confederates on the Telegraph Road. With Atkins's return, the artillery changeover had replaced three batteries with the same number and mix of weapons—12-pounder Napoleons, 3-inch Ordnance Rifles, and 10-pounder Parrott rifles.[103]

Colonel Grant's Vermont Brigade of Howe's division came out of Fredericksburg as the fighting raged at Salem Church. Instead of continuing toward the sound of guns, they were directed to the left, to guard against a potential attack from the south. Grant's five regiments established a line "considerably beyond the brick house on the south side of the creek." Four of the Vermont units pushed out to the edge of the plateau, overlooking Hazel Run; the Second Vermont remained behind in reserve. Forbidden to build fires, the brigade enjoyed the luxury of cold hard tack without coffee.[104]

Howe established his headquarters in the "brick house," a Gothic Revival mansion called Idlewild. One of his batteries had already moved up toward Salem Church, but the second, Battery F, Fifth US Artillery under Lt. Leonard Martin, deployed six weapons on the open ground around the house. Its occupants, William Downman and his wife and children, nervously watched the war close in on their home.[105]

Within the Chancellorsville entrenchments, Brig. Gen. Alpheus S. Williams observed how they "could distinctly hear the artillery combat between Sedgwick's corps and the Rebs, toward Fredericksburg, and yet no attack began on our side." As late as 7:00 P.M., Butterfield reported heavy infantry fire on the Sixth Corps's front to Hooker.[106]

Butterfield also kept President Lincoln informed. At 8:00 P.M. he sent the following update to Washington: "I have had no time to advise you. We have to-day here over 800 prisoners; six guns handsomely taken, at the point of the bayonet. I can give no general idea of how affairs stand. Last reports all quiet in front of Chancellorsville, and Sedgwick fighting at 6:15 P.M."[107]

As had occurred in front of Marye's Heights, the battlefield terrain around Salem Church limited the numbers of troops that could be brought to bear, no matter the size of the overall forces. The equivalent of two Federal brigades had pressed forward along the Plank Road. At the point of contact, they fought a Confederate force of similar size. Brooks attacked with around 4,100 men and engaged around 4,000 Confederates.[108]

The casualty figures show who held the better position. Federal forces lost 1,523 men at Salem Church. Bartlett's brigade went into the assault with 1,500 men and lost 580. Within that brigade Upton's 121st New York suffered the highest loss. Of 453 men who stepped off into their first battle, 276 were killed, wounded, or captured.[109]

Casualties on the Confederate side are more difficult to determine. Semmes's Salem Church casualties, for instance, were not reported separately from his losses over the entire three days at Chancellorsville. His brigade losses at Salem Church were probably comparable to those sustained by Wilcox's Alabamans. Wilcox lost 535 men that day, although some of them fell near the Stansbury house and others were captured on the Plank Road. The sustained fighting experienced by Semmes probably cost nearly

550 men. Overall Confederate losses at Salem Church appear to have been close to 1,100 men.[110]

Scouring the battleground, Confederate soldiers took weapons, shoes, haversacks, and canteens from dead and wounded Yankees. An Alabama soldier in the process of pulling the boots off a Federal officer was startled to hear a distressed voice asking him to stop. He sat down and quietly smoked a pipe, staking his claim to the footwear while waiting for the man to die.[111]

May 3 finally came to an end. A Massachusetts soldier wrote: "It was a warm spring night, and the mournful notes of the whippoorwill were mingled with the cries of the suffering.... We slept very little."[112]

NINE

MAY 4

ON THE HIGH GROUND
WEST OF FREDERICKSBURG

The tangled growth south of the Orange Plank Road ignited in places to add a horrifying new dimension to the plight of wounded men. A Union soldier wrote home a week later: "Just after the battle closed near Salem Tabernacle on Sunday night, the underbrush in the woods to the left in front were soon in flames. In these woods were hundreds of rebel and Union wounded, who were so badly injured that they could not escape the awful destruction that threatened them. No flags of truce from either side were respected."[1]

A letter home to a New York woman contained shocking details: "It pains me to be obliged to inform you of the death of your brother Henry who fell in the heat of battle. . . . Alass Dear Calista I do not know but he was burned alive or before he died for our forces retreated and the engagement was so hot that it set the woods on fire where he was. Do not tell this to anyone."[2]

Away from those horrors, units prepared for the next day. General Wheaton's brigade pulled back to where the road to Banks' Ford branched off from the Plank Road. "Here we bivouacked," he reported, "filled our ammunition boxes, received our knapsacks, sent by train from Fredericksburg, and rested, after having fought two battles in twelve hours and skirmished all day."[3]

Close to midnight, Major Lessig of the Ninety-Sixth Pennsylvania reported to General Bartlett, who invited him to have something to eat. "Our supper," the tired major remembered, "consisted of hard tack and coffee, and it was the first thing I had tasted since 4 o'clock in the morning." His chance to rest, however, proved short. An orderly shook him awake at 3:00 A.M. with instructions that his unit draw ammunition and be under arms by daylight. The sun would break the horizon shortly after 5:00 A.M.[4]

Preparations for May 4 included recovering wounded men. One man noted: "All night long we could hear the grinding of the ambulance wheels on the roads, as they moved back and forth, filled with their bleeding, suffering loads of wounded. The dead were left unburied on the field." Despite best efforts, a few hundred wounded men remained between the lines, unreachable.[5]

Ambulances were not the only conveyances on the road that night. Over four hundred mules brought up small-arms ammunition for the Sixth Corps's forty-eight regiments. Wagons delivered ordnance to its nine batteries. A pontoon bridge was across at Banks' Ford, but it was not yet clear how that crossing would be used. General Hunt had directed that forty wagon loads of artillery ammunition be sent to the batteries protecting that new crossing. The ordnance officers were not to wait until daylight but to get that ammunition train moving by midnight.[6]

General Warren decided to return to Hooker's headquarters. The chief topographer had been with Sedgwick for nearly twenty-four hours, and the end of the fighting at Salem Church appeared to be a good time to report back to army headquarters. He used the pontoon bridge at Banks' Ford to shorten his journey but still had a long ride to get to US Ford. Though quite tired when he finally arrived, Warren took the time to get off a message to Sedgwick.[7]

While Brigadier General Wilcox handled the fighting at Salem Church, Major General McLaws, as senior officer, needed to figure out what would happen next. Wilcox had informed him that Major General Early had his division on the Telegraph Road, so McLaws sent Maj. Ellison L. Costin to report to him there. At the Cox house Early recommended that his division retake Lee's Hill and Marye's Heights to cut off Sedgwick from Fredericksburg. He would then extend to his left to link up with McLaws, and their combined forces would attack the isolated Union corps.[8]

McLaws sent Costin to relay the tentative plans to General Lee. The major reported to the army commander near the smoldering Chancellorsville house while the sounds of fighting at Salem Church rumbled in the distance. At 7:00 P.M. Lee sent back a message to Early. He lamented the loss of Fredericksburg, noted having sent five brigades east, and urged him to work with McLaws to regain the lost ground. Actually, only four Confederate brigades had been detached from the Chancellorsville front, as Lee was also counting Wilcox's Brigade.[9]

Wilcox continued to exert tactical control of the Salem Church battle, but as the fighting ran its course, McLaws gradually took over direction of Confederate forces there. The Federals would likely renew their assaults on May 4. He had already strengthened General Mahone's front with two of General Wofford's Georgia regiments. McLaws now directed General Kershaw to close to his left to strengthen the Confederate center on the Plank Road.[10]

Sedgwick sought similar guidance from his army commander. He had shoved aside the Confederate force at Fredericksburg, which drew off substantial enemy strength from Hooker's front. The Sixth Corps had run into those redeployed formations at Salem Church. Sedgwick had also been required to leave a Confederate division in his rear as he raced west to relieve the army's main body. During the night, he sent the following to Hooker: "We were checked here last night and held until dark. I believe the enemy have been re-enforcing all night and will attack me in the morning. How do matters stand with you? Send me instructions." At daylight on the fourth, Sedgwick still waited for a reply.[11]

Before dawn soldiers of the Thirty-Second New York peered into the dark woods and saw an indistinct line to their front, possibly a regiment of Confederates preparing to attack. As the sun emerged, a line of abandoned knapsacks became discernible. White lettering painted on the black waterproof fabric indicated they had been left there by the 119th Pennsylvania. Dead and wounded men also became visible in the shattered woods and across the open fields. A Union soldier described how "some of the wounded could be seen holding up their caps, as signals for assistance, but none came."[12]

Leaving wounded men to die became a cold calculation. Col. Francis E. Pinto, commanding the Thirty-Second New York, gave permission to Capt. William Wyckoff to approach the Confederates with a flag of truce. A Southern officer came out to meet him but refused to accept his flag. The wounded would remain where they lay.[13]

Cowan's First New York Artillery observed Confederates building earthworks with bayonets and tin plates. The Southerners drew attention to themselves when they started pulling up planks from the road to reinforce their feeble defenses. Cowan's gunners opened fire around 6:00 A.M. at a range of about 1,200 yards. They were joined by Lt. John H. Butler's Battery G, Second US Artillery, and Lt. William A. Harn's Third Battery, New

York Light Artillery. The guns fired intermittently for the next few hours, keeping the Confederates from establishing usable barriers.[14]

South of Fredericksburg Early prepared to sever the Sixth Corps's line of communications. General Gordon's Georgia brigade would lead the advance up the Telegraph Road, while Generals Hays and Hoke crossed their brigades over Hazel Run and prepared to extend west to connect with McLaws's Division. General Barksdale would advance behind Gordon on the right side of the Telegraph Road. Brig. Gen. "Extra Billy" Smith would advance on the left. Lieutenant Colonel Andrews stood ready to follow with his battalion of artillery and take position on the heights overlooking Fredericksburg.[15]

To ensure coordination with McLaws, Early accompanied Hays and Hokes. The Louisiana and North Carolina troops scrambled across the unfinished railway and Hazel Run but remained under cover in the woods near the ruins of the old Alum Springs Mill. Screened from view, the men checked weapons and ammunition. Early returned to the Telegraph Road and found that Gordon had misunderstood his instructions and already launched his advance.[16]

Gordon had been a twenty-nine-year-old attorney when the war came, soon discovering that he had an aptitude for field command. Grievously wounded at Sharpsburg in September 1862, he had returned to duty in April 1863 and received command of a brigade of Georgia regiments. He and his men had never been in battle together, but the lawyer-turned-warrior knew how to get men to follow him into harm's way.[17]

Around 7:00 A.M. Gordon called his troops to attention. The new brigade commander assured the hardened veterans that he would not ask them to go beyond where he was willing to lead. He then raised his hat and shouted that those who were willing to come with him should raise theirs. A soldier of the Twenty-Sixth Georgia described the thrill to action that rippled down the line. "Every hat was in the air," he remembered, "and with a shout we followed him."[18]

Spread out as skirmishers, the men of the Thirty-First Georgia trotted into the open ground of the Leach farm. The Thirteenth, Twenty-Sixth, and Thirty-Eighth Regiments followed in line of battle. No shots came from the woods to their front. Entering the trees, the skirmishers found the battery wagons and battery forge from the Federal detachment that had lost its way the evening before.[19]

Pressing toward Lee's Hill, the Georgians saw Federals on the high ground beyond Hazel Run. Wagons and mules were moving up supplies

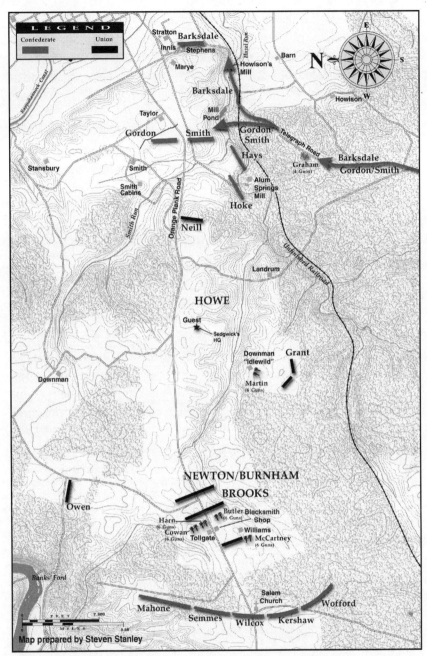

Map 15. Confederates Close in behind the Sixth Corps. Late on May 3 Early's Division regrouped, while Sedgwick pushed west toward Chancellorsville. The next morning the Confederates cut between the Sixth Corps and its line of communications through Fredericksburg.

on Hanover Street, while ambulances moved back toward Fredericksburg on the Plank Road. The skirmishers rushed down the slope, crossed the unfinished railway embankment, and came to a large mill pond on Hazel Run. The millrace extended to their right to Howison's Mill, but they needed to go straight ahead, where the pond looked to be about fifty yards wide. One man jumped in to test its depth and found he could wade across. The remaining skirmishers plunged in behind him and splashed their way forward.[20]

When Gordon's line of battle reached Lee's Hill, they too saw the Federals on the heights as well as the Thirty-First Georgia skirmishers wading across the mill pond. Regimental commanders passed the word to fix bayonets. When the Georgia line bristled with steel, the Southerners "went down the hill like an avalanche and into the mill pond where the water on the right of the regiment reached to our waist." Ahead of them the wet skirmishers scrambled up the slope toward Hanover Street.[21]

Gordon's Brigade's relentless advance became a wedge between the Federals to the west and those left in Fredericksburg. Capt. Archibald Graham brought his First Rockbridge Artillery into battery on Lee's Hill. His gunners could see Federals around the Guest and Downman properties and opened fire, announcing to the Union forces that the Confederates had got in behind them.[22]

The targeted Federals were elements of Howe's division south of the Plank Road. To a disgusted Vermont officer, the whole campaign began to look like a wasted effort. As he remembered: "I don't know whether I was most grieved, angered or indignant. All we had gained was lost." A New York soldier described how the Southerners taunted them with "one of their characteristic yells so much resembling a wolf howl."[23]

Atop Marye's Heights, Union troops mounted a brief defense from behind a low stone wall along Hanover Street. They were not an organized unit, though, and scattered as the Southern infantry surged into them. The swift-moving Confederates also captured the battery train of Battery G, Second US Artillery, which Gordon later presented to Andrews.[24]

Signal men at the Phillips house saw the Confederate advance emerge from the trees and immediately notified Gibbon and Butterfield. On Marye's Heights Capt. Paul H. Babcock ordered the wagon with his signals equipment to get away to Fredericksburg. With Confederate skirmishers rapidly approaching, he and Capt. Joseph Gloskoski mounted up and galloped away to the west. Capt. William H. Hill and Lt. Frank Marsten made their way back to Fredericksburg. Hill went to the signal station in the steeple of the Baptist church, while Marsten continued across the Rappahannock and reported to Captain Cushing. The chief signalman sent him to headquarters to relay the morning's events to Butterfield. With Confederates on the surrounding heights, Cushing realized the Fredericksburg station no longer had any use and directed Hill to dismantle it and bring the equipment across the river.[25]

Riding west on the Plank Road, Babcock and Gloskoski ran into Brigadier General Neill. They reported to him what had unfolded on Marye's Heights and then continued on to the Guest house. Neill had four of his six regiments on hand and hustled them back toward Fredericksburg. Thoroughly disgusted to have to retake ground that had been hard won, the Thirty-Third and Forty-Ninth New York, the Seventh Maine, and the Twenty-First New Jersey pushed their way through stragglers and wagons.[26]

On Lee's Hill, Graham's artillerymen saw Neill's units approach the edge of the plateau overlooking Smith Run. At a range of about 1,200 yards, the Virginia battery opened fire, and the Federals spread out as skirmishers. The Thirty-First Georgia tried to push forward, but even with artillery support, they were outnumbered and went to ground.[27]

There were no Union guns near at hand to help Neill's infantry, but Capt. Leonard Martin's Battery F, Fifth US Artillery opened fire on Graham's battery from the Downman house. At 2,600 yards the distance was beyond the effective range of Martin's weapons, but the experienced gunners elevated their tubes as needed. The Virginia artillery, however, had two 20-pounder Parrotts as opposed to the Union battery's 10-pounders and responded with heavier metal. Some of the Confederate rounds clipped away portions of the dwelling, still occupied by the Downman family.[28]

Andrews wrote that the Confederate fire silenced the Federal guns, which then "limbered up and ran off to the rear." Martin's guns had not effectively countered the incoming fire, but they did not head for the rear. Instead they pulled back to the Guest house and then redeployed farther east, going into battery to support Howe's infantry. The Confederate artillerymen on Lee's Hill could also see a second battery behind and slightly to the right of the Downman house. At about 4,100 yards the range was extreme but reachable if the Parrott tubes were fully elevated. Graham's Virginians opened fire on that distant battery as well.[29]

The targeted field guns belonged to Capt. William H. McCartney's Battery A, Massachusetts Light Artillery, positioned on the left end of the Federal line facing Salem Church. The Virginia artillerymen opened fire on a section of his guns visible from Lee's Hill. McCartney's weapons did not have the range to respond, but the Confederate Parrott rounds were not exploding. While the Southern gunners may well have been using their rounds as solid shot at extreme range, there had been ongoing problems with Confederate fuzes.[30]

Fuzing for rifled weapons had always been problematic. Prior to the spring campaign, the Confederate Ordnance Department had introduced a fuze igniter to try to make the rifled rounds more reliable. On smoothbore guns the propelling charge engulfed the cannon ball when the weapon fired and ignited a powder train in the fuze. Ammunition for rifled weapons, however, fit more tightly in the bore, and the close tolerance reduced the amount of burning propellant that enveloped the shell to ignite the fuze. The fix consisted of a small wooden component with a striker and powder charge pressed into place over the fuze. When the round was fired the striker recoiled, which struck and ignited a small charge that lit the powder train in the fuze.[31]

The fuze igniter has been blamed for the high dud rate endured by some of the Confederate artillery at Chancellorsville. The problem may have been with the fuze installation during the loading sequence. In the time fuze the powder train consisted of fine gunpowder, called meal powder, that burned in a groove for the selected time. The procedure was to seat the fuze on a round with two slight taps with a mallet. Under the strain of combat, it appears that some artillerymen tapped too hard, knocking the meal powder loose.[32]

When outgoing rounds were assembled with care, the fuze igniter increased the reliability of the Confederate ordnance. If the device got pounded into place in such a manner as to knock the meal powder out of the groove, however, the igniter would function but not have anything to ignite. An explosive round without a functioning fuze became nothing more than solid shot, effective only in the event of a direct hit. We do not know whether the Rockbridge Artillery fired at that maximum range without fuzes or simply did not take sufficient care in assembling rounds while loading and firing. On the receiving end McCartney reported that as "none of his shells burst, they did no harm."[33]

Back at his Gothic Revival mansion, William Downman decided it was time to get his family to safety. As the Federal units deployed for an imminent fight, the Downmans followed the lane from their home to the Guest house and the Plank Road. A soldier described seeing them: "The regiments were in motion and as we crossed a field below the house its fleeing occupants went by us. I was near enough to see them closely: an intelligent-looking man with his fair, pale wife and two little children. They were friends of our foes, but every heart ached for them and we let them pass in respectful silence. I noticed that the man's face bore the same set, despairing expression that I had seen the day before in the faces of the wounded men."[34]

When Early returned to the Telegraph Road and saw that Gordon had launched his advance, he directed Barksdale and Smith to get their brigades moving as well. The Mississippians reoccupied their old position at the base of Marye's Heights. Smith's Brigade pushed straight ahead, crossed Hazel Run below its confluence with Smith Run, and then paused, its line roughly parallel with the Plank Road.[35]

Gordon's advance had gone as far as it could. It had swept away rear-echelon soldiers and teamsters but now faced frontline infantry. To the left, on the other side of Smith Run, Hays and Hoke realized they were not positioned well to be useful and pulled their brigades back. Early had cut Sedgwick off from Fredericksburg, but further damage to the Sixth Corps required a coordinated assault with additional brigades.[36]

McLaws had indicated a willingness to attack the Federal line as part of a larger effort. He launched a minor probe of the position around 9:00 A.M., advancing Kershaw's and Wofford's Brigades. The three Union batteries near the tollgate turned their fire on those advancing Confederates and quickly convinced McLaws that he lacked sufficient strength to continue without help. He hesitated and then pulled the two brigades back.[37]

When the Federals in Fredericksburg awakened to picket firing on the surrounding hills, Colonel Hall's brigade transitioned from rear-echelon duties to an active frontline defense. The day before, his men had gathered up equipment and weapons scattered across the battleground and provided manpower to hospitals. The Twentieth Massachusetts, Seventh Michigan, the Forty-Second and Fifty-Ninth New York, and several companies of the 127th Pennsylvania now took position south of William Street. The Nineteenth Massachusetts moved up from its bivouac south of the Plank Road. Seeing Confederate forces rushing from Lee's Hill to Marye's Heights, one Bay State soldier noted, "Where they came from we could not tell, but they were there."[38]

In addition to the Georgians spreading across Marye's Heights, Barksdale's Mississippians appeared at the base of the hills. Without realizing a Federal brigade still occupied Fredericksburg, Early had directed Barksdale to seize the pontoon bridges. A Pennsylvania soldier described how the Confederates "deployed skirmishers, who rushed boldly on until they came within easy range of our guns. This was the decisive moment. . . . We now poured a terrible volley into them almost at the same instant, which had the desired effect, for it caused them to skedaddle back to their rifle pits on the double quick, and they did not again venture from them the entire day."[39]

Hospitals established in Fredericksburg had taken in the casualties of the May 3 assaults. During the night, ambulances had also brought in shot-up men from the Salem Church battlefield. With Confederate forces closing in, the medical men thought it a good idea to expedite evacuation of the wounded. Over two thousand casualties could be relocated, but about two dozen men would have to be left behind, their wounds too life threatening to survive being transported.[40]

Sedgwick needed guidance. He had not yet received Warren's late-night message nor any instructions from Hooker and was still operating under orders to get to Chancellorsville. At 6:20 A.M. Sedgwick sent another message to Butterfield: "I am anxious to hear from General Hooker. There is a strong force in front of me, strongly posted. I cannot attack with any hope of dislodging them until I know something definite as to the position of their main body and ours. I have sent two or three messengers to Banks' Ford, but none have returned, nor have I heard from the general since yesterday."[41]

On the morning of May 4, army headquarters had lost contact with the Sixth Corps. Believing the ciphers had become compromised, Butterfield had issued instructions in the early hours of the third to avoid flag and torch signals. The signal teams had new ciphers, but the restrictive orders stood. Hooker and Butterfield could send messages back and forth via telegraph, but messages to the Sixth Corps had to go by courier across hostile ground.

In a message that went out at 6:00 A.M., Hooker's staff asked about the Sixth Corps's disposition: "The general commanding desires you to telegraph to him your exact position. What information have you respecting the force of enemy in front and rear? What is your own strength? Is there any danger of a force coming up in your rear and cutting your communications? Can you sustain yourself acting separately or in co-operation with us?"[42]

It does not appear that this message reached Sedgwick before 8:30 A.M., around the time that signal connections were being reestablished. The Sixth Corps commander sent a brief response: "I am occupying the same position as last night. The enemy made an attack on Howe; did not amount to much.

I think I have made secure my communications with Banks' Ford. I think they will attempt to drive me back. I await instructions." Sedgwick knew there was no point in dislodging the Confederates from the Salem Church ridge unless there was a plan for what would come next.[43]

Driven from Marye's Heights, Babcock and Gloskoski had made their way to Sedgwick's headquarters at the Guest house. On that open plateau they broke out their flags and tried to contact the signal team at the Phillips house. Within four minutes alert signalmen at the station across the river had picked up the waving flags far out on the Plank Road. They were still under strict orders not to use flags but knew they needed to reestablish communications without delay.[44]

Cushing would claim in his after-action report that Babcock and Gloskoski were unaware of the chief of staff's directive. It is unlikely that the two officers remained uninformed of the prohibition on using flags, but no official report from that tightly knit group was going to say that. At the Phillips house, Hall noted, "those who had ordered the signals not to be used were the first to avail themselves of our ready means of communications."[45]

The signal stations at the Guest and Phillips houses were in contact for the rest of the day, sending messages over the heads of the Confederate forces between them. Butterfield would claim he had only meant to curtail nighttime communications with torches but his instructions, issued at 2:05 A.M. on May 3, read: "I don't want any signal. It will betray the movement for miles. The enemy read our signals." At 8:55 A.M., with those orders still in place, the chief of staff informed Hooker: "Have opened flag signal communications with Sedgwick."[46]

The signal teams at Banks' Ford also worked to set up a link to Sedgwick. At the Scott house Lt. Brinkerhoff N. Miner had a telegraph connection to the Phillips house. Lt. Martin Denicke and Lt. Isaac S. Lyon crossed the pontoon bridge at Scott's Mill and found a house about a mile from Banks' Ford that was visible to both the Guest house and the Scott house. They soon had a flag relay set up to link the two stations. In the event Confederate forces interfered with Babcock's flag station, the Banks' Ford signal team had created a backup.[47]

At 9:00 A.M., with communications reestablished with Falmouth, Sedgwick responded again to Hooker's queries:

> I am occupying same position as last night. I have secured my communications with Banks' Ford. The enemy are in possession of the heights of

Fredericksburg in force. They appear strongly in our front, and are making efforts to drive us back. My strength yesterday morning was 22,000 men. I do not know my losses, but they were large, probably 5,000 men.... It depends upon the condition and position of your force whether I can sustain myself here. Howe reports the enemy advancing upon Fredericksburg.[48]

Sedgwick's casualties were closer to 3,000 at that point, but an overestimate under field conditions was not unusual. An accurate accounting would not be feasible until after the fighting ended. Around the same time as this message went out, Sedgwick received Warren's dispatch sent to him the night before from Chancellorsville.

Warren described Hooker's contracted and entrenched line as "snug," a place where the army commander wanted to receive an attack rather than to make one. He also made clear that Hooker no longer expected the Sixth Corps to attack on its own. Further offensive action by the Federal forces would only take place with one wing of the army working in concert with the other. This dispatch from army headquarters formally released Sedgwick from having to press on to Chancellorsville.[49]

The conscientious Warren carefully provided additional guidance: "He [Hooker] says you are too far away for him to direct. Look well to the safety of your corps, and keep up communication with General Benham at Banks' Ford and Fredericksburg. You can go to either place if you think it best. To cross at Banks' Ford would bring you in supporting distance of the main body, and would be better than falling back to Fredericksburg."[50]

With Sedgwick's orders to march to Chancellorsville rescinded and Confederate forces astride the road to the east and west, the Sixth Corps had no discernible reason to remain on the south side of the Rappahannock River. Sedgwick reported to Hooker at 9:45 A.M.: "The enemy are pressing me. I am taking position to cross the river whenever necessary." Unlike his commander, Sedgwick did not have the luxury of being able to delay a decision. He faced an enemy who had already broken his line of communication and stood capable of doing more. At 10:20 A.M. Butterfield warned Hooker, "Heavy force of enemy reported advancing on Fredericksburg."[51]

Hooker had done nothing to challenge the Army of Northern Virginia since retreating into his new position. Safely ensconced behind earthworks and without any immediate plans, he was not sure what the Sixth Corps should do either. At 10:30 A.M. a staff officer sent Sedgwick the following dispatch: "The commanding general directs that, in the event you fall back, you reserve, if practicable, a position on the Fredericksburg side of the Rappahannock, which you can hold securely until to-morrow P.M. Please let the commanding general have your opinion in regard to this by telegraph from Banks' Ford as soon as possible."[52]

This communication would not have given anyone confidence. In the first place, orders do not use the word "please." Second, the message started out as a directive but then became a plea for Sedgwick's opinion. The vague reference to waiting until the next day suggested Hooker was trying to figure out what to do.

A message sent a half hour later tried to give Sedgwick some direction but again without reference to any overall plans or objectives. At Antietam the general had led a division forward under ill-advised orders and had lost hundreds of good men, all slaughtered because the man directing the battle could not see or understand the prevailing circumstances. This follow-up message also appeared to come from a superior with little idea of the situation Sedgwick faced: "The major-general commanding directs me to say that he does not wish you to cross the river at Banks' Ford unless you are compelled to do so. The batteries at Banks' Ford command the position. If it is practicable for you to maintain a position south side Rappahannock near Banks' Ford, you will do so. It is very important that we retain position at Banks' Ford. [Brigadier] General [Robert O.] Tyler commands the Reserve Artillery there."[53]

Before receiving this second message, Sedgwick had already responded to the first one in a dispatch to Butterfield: "I hold the same position. The enemy are pressing me hard. If I can hold until night, I shall cross at Banks' Ford under instructions from General Hooker, given by Brigadier-General Warren."[54]

He sent a similar message at 11:15 A.M. directly to Hooker. In response to being ordered to hold a position south of the river, the general pointedly asked if he could expect support:

> The enemy threatens me strongly on two fronts. My position is bad for such attack. It was assumed for attack and not for defense. It is not improbable that bridges at Banks' Ford may be sacrificed. Can you help me strongly if I am attacked?
>
> P. S. My bridges are 2 miles from me. I am compelled to cover them above and below from attack, with the additional assistance of General Benham's brigade alone.[55]

Hooker's headquarters responded to Sedgwick at 11:50 A.M.: "If the necessary information shall be obtained today, and if it shall be of the character he anticipates, it is the intention of the [commanding] general to advance tomorrow. In this event the position of your corps on the south bank of the Rappahannock will be as favorable as the general could desire. It is for this reason he desires that your troops may not cross the Rappahannock."[56]

With Hooker directing him to hold his position, Sedgwick oriented the Sixth Corps into a defensive stance. Brooks kept Russell's brigade facing Salem Church, its left anchored on the Williams house, where Captain McCartney had positioned his six 12-pounder Napoleons of Battery A, First Massachusetts Light Artillery. They were about one thousand yards from a tree line to their south and six hundred yards from the woods where the Salem Church battle had been fought.[57]

From the Williams house, Brooks used Bartlett's brigade to form a line facing south, parallel to the Plank Road. Roughly one thousand yards east of McCartney's battery position, a ravine extended toward the Union line. Lt. Augustin N. Parsons deployed a section of his First New Jersey Light Artillery to cover that potential approach. He placed his two other sections on a knoll farther east, facing the Downman house. The New Jersey brigade, now commanded by Col. Samuel L. Buck, extended Brooks's line along the Plank Road. The Twenty-Seventh New York pushed out as skirmishers across the brigade front.[58]

Newton held the line to Brooks's right, extending the line facing Salem Church toward the river. His artillery support consisted of the three batteries near the tollgate: Butler's Battery G, Second US Artillery and Cowan's First Battery and Harn's Third Battery, New York Light Artillery. Two additional batteries were on a rise of ground just west of the road to Banks' Ford. Lt. Edward B. Williston's Battery D, Second US Artillery stood ready on the right of that hilltop. To his left Captain McCarthy had deployed his Battery C-D, First Pennsylvania Light Artillery.[59]

Beyond Newton's division, Colonel Burnham's Light Division held the line. The Forty-Third New York secured the Union right flank on high ground overlooking Banks' Ford. That natural crossing stood outside the Sixth Corps's perimeter but had never been considered militarily important. It was the pontoon bridge downstream at Scott's Mill that constituted Sedgwick's line of communications.[60]

The Light Division troops, without knapsacks and probably quite hungry, did not appear to face serious opposition that morning. Around midday the

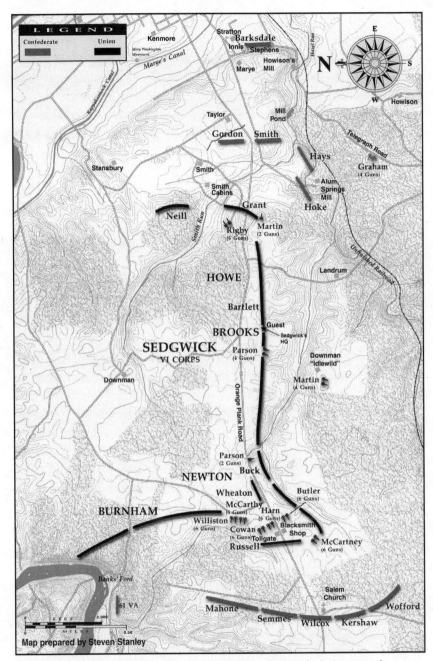

Map 16. Sedgwick Repositions on the High Ground. The Sixth Corps took position against Confederate forces to the west and to the east.

Sixty-First Virginia moved into position on the hills south of the road that descended to Banks' Ford. Elements of the Sixty-First Pennsylvania and the Forty-Third New York had deployed as pickets north of the road. Skirmishing flared up and continued throughout the day, but neither side tested the other by trying to advance across the ravine that separated them.[61]

The Union line facing toward Fredericksburg looked to be the weak link in the position. Neill had already hurried his brigade into position near the Plank Road to stop Gordon's morning advance. Colonel Grant's Vermont Brigade arrived from the Downman farm to join him. Their combined strength of 6,000 men was not sufficient to cover a front of nearly one and a half miles. They could not actually extend a solid line from Brooks's left flank to the river and would have to concentrate on holding a series of hilltops.[62]

Howe had two batteries to try to cover the intervals between his major infantry units. Captain Rigby's Battery A, Maryland Light Artillery took position on the right of Howe's line on a hilltop north of the Plank Road. Lieutenant Martin had placed a section of his Battery F, Fifth US Artillery in two gun pits south of the Plank Road. His other two sections were still back at the Downman house.[63]

On the Confederate side of the lines, Early and McLaws had yet to apply real pressure. After probing the Fredericksburg defenses, Barksdale's Brigade settled into its old position at the base of Marye's Heights. Gordon's Brigade confronted the Federals to the west but on ground dominated by the Union-held plateau to their front. Smith held his brigade nearby, south of and parallel to the Plank Road. McLaws had made only a halfhearted advance that morning.[64]

None of Early's brigade commanders were professionals, but most had grasped the art of combat command. Gordon had a way of inspiring men to follow him into battle. Hays had fought in Mexico and had become an effective brigade commander. Hoke had also developed into a solid soldier. Among this group of reliable brigadiers, William Smith stood apart. He was an older fellow who had served in both the US Congress as well as the Confederate Congress. He was decidedly unimpressed with military doctrine and disinclined to believe that professional expertise counted more than his own innate ability.[65]

Early had his doubts about Smith but needed a probe to determine if opportunity beckoned. The Virginia brigade had once been Early's own and stood in a position where it could test the Federal line. He ordered the Thirteenth Virginia to advance in skirmish order. Smith suggested the

Forty-Ninth Virginia be used as the advance element since the Thirteenth had been engaged in skirmishing for the past two days. Early made clear he had more confidence in the Thirteenth Virginia.[66]

Smith reoriented his brigade toward the west, forming up perpendicular to the Plank Road. Lt. Col. James B. Terrill's Thirteenth Virginia came up on the left of the Thirty-First Georgia, which had led Gordon's advance and essentially cleared the heights upon which they stood. Looking at the steep hill to their front, where some trees had been cut to create obstacles, some of the Virginians called on the Georgians to advance with them. But Gordon's men were quite sure there were solid Union formations on top of the ridge and responded to the Virginians "in language more forcible than polite."[67]

Around 11:00 A.M. the Thirteenth Virginia stepped off, descending the hill to Smith Run. The advancing troops found shelter from Union small-arms fire on the far side of the streambed, and Terrill had to use up time to get them moving again. Smith's Brigade also began to spread out. Col. Francis H. Board brought his Fifty-Eighth Virginia up behind the Thirteenth, while Lt. Col. Jonathan C. Gibson and Col. Michael G. Harman moved their Forty-Ninth and Fifty-Second Virginia Regiments to the left. Ahead of the Confederates, Union artillery remained silent.[68]

Smith's Virginians approached Neill's four regiments. Two companies of the Forty-Ninth New York had been pushed out as skirmishers. When it looked like the Confederates were becoming active, Neill sent a company from the Seventh Maine to reinforce them. The waiting Federals had a clear view of the approaching Southerners. The section of Fifth US Artillery 12-pounder Napoleons south of the Plank Road opened fire. The experienced artillerymen created a deadly curtain of metal in front of the Union skirmishers, who also fired away. The Confederate probe faltered.[69]

The Thirteenth Virginia made several attempts to move forward but could not come to grips with the Federal line. Graham's Rockbridge Artillery tried to provide support from Lee's Hill, about 1,600 yards away, but the combined effort had little cohesion. The probing advance essentially had the strength of a single regiment because the Forty-Ninth and Fifty-Second Virginia did not engage on the left. One soldier of the Fifty-Second Virginia would later admit that the regiment did not fire its weapons during the entire campaign. Board finally got his Fifty-Eighth Virginia moving and came up behind the Thirteenth, but it could not return fire with Terrill's unit to its front. Federal artillery continued to play havoc with the exposed Confederate infantry.[70]

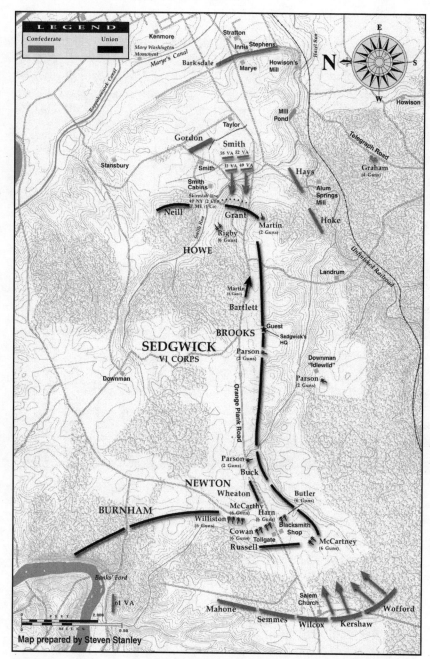

Map 17. The Morning Attacks, May 4. Union artillery easily pushed back a minor Confederate advance from the Salem Church line. Closer to Fredericksburg, the Federals quickly repulsed a poorly executed probe by Smith's Brigade.

Smith ordered the Fifty-Eighth Virginia to lie down so the Thirteenth Virginia could fall back through them. The Fifty-Eighth then opened fire once they cleared, but any opportunity to advance farther had faded. The Federal skirmishers maintained a heavy volume of fire, and the field guns continued to tear into the Confederate formations. A Maine soldier described how it all ended: "As they came up the hill their lines became more and more unsteady until as they came within about twenty yards, our men charged upon them with a cheer and drove them back." The Forty-Ninth and Fifty-Second Regiments were already in retreat when Board ordered his Fifty-Eighth Virginia back as well.[71]

Martin's 12-pounder Napoleons had devastated the Virginians, and no more than three companies of skirmishers had been needed to hold the line. Those Union riflemen and the rest of the Forty-Ninth New York now advanced. Smith Run remained an obstacle in retreat as it had been during the advance, and some of the Confederates jumped down into the eroded streambed to rest a moment. A few hundred feet beyond the creek, other tired and wounded Southerners paused at a cluster of three white-washed slave cabins and a barn.[72]

At the waterway Capt. Samuel D. Buck stood on the open ground to rally his men. A private passing in front of him to take his place in the line was shot and fell into the creek bed. Convinced the bullet was meant for him, Buck jumped down to minister aid, reflecting later that he "for the first time and only time, left my post to help a wounded man." There was little he could do; the man was dead. When the young officer looked up, he saw Federals closing in and had to run to avoid capture. Union infantry overtook the Virginia troops who rested too long behind the stream embankment or among the slave cabins. Squads of men from both Maine and New York gathered in over 150 prisoners. Near the barn Sgt. French W. Fisher of the Forty-Ninth New York shot the color-bearer for the Fifty-Eighth Virginia, and Cpl. John P. McVean grabbed the regimental colors.[73]

The Federals were surprised that the Confederate advance fell apart so rapidly. A soldier remarked how "the enemy now retreated to their rifle pits and remained very quiet for several hours." Another participant observed, "We killed quite a number of them before they got out of reach." The failed effort provided Early with little information, but Smith's political background kept him from suffering any consequences for being inept. In a few days he would be elected governor of Virginia, and a governor-elect was not going to be reprimanded or reassigned.[74]

Early sent his aide-de-camp, Lt. Andrew L. Pitzer, to apprise McLaws of the morning's events. He told his fellow division commander that he could send two brigades, reliably led by Hoke and Hays, to establish a strong front for a combined assault. McLaws, however, had decided he did not have strength enough to attack and had requested reinforcements from Lee. Pitzer returned and informed Early that Anderson's Division was on its way from Chancellorsville and that they should wait for the arrival of those additional troops.[75]

At noon Sedgwick informed both Hooker and Butterfield of the abortive Confederate attack on Howe's position. He included the details that his troops had captured over two hundred prisoners as well as a regimental battle flag. The Federal counterattack reaped other rewards. Some men from the Twenty-First New Jersey recaptured an abandoned wagon that turned out to be well stocked with food belonging to a division headquarters. The hungry troops ate well that morning. They also brought in several mules packing boxes of small-arms ammunition.[76]

On the morning of May 4, Hooker developed a renewed interest in Banks' Ford. He directed Chief Engineer Benham to get a balloon up and send scouting parties across the river. At 1:20 P.M. the commanding general sent the following message to Sedgwick: "I expect to advance to-morrow morning, which will be likely to relieve you. You must not count on much assistance without I hear heavy firing. Tell General Benham to put down the other bridge, if you desire it." Hooker had provided neither clear direction nor useful information. He *might* advance. Sedgwick should *not* count on assistance. He could get down another bridge, forgetting that he had ordered the second bridge train at Banks' Ford to be sent to US Ford.[77]

Benham's initiative to hold back enough pontoons for a second bridge at Banks' Ford would now pay dividends. High bluffs and a canal prevented its installation adjacent to the one at Scott's Mill, but there was another break in the river bluffs farther downstream. That location, however, stood at the upper end of a slack-water pond behind an antebellum dam related to the river navigation system. Fourteen pontoons were not going to be enough to span the reservoir. The engineers would have to build an abutment on the south shore to fill in the gap between dry ground and the available reach of the floating bridge. The bridge became ready for use around 3:30 P.M., but work continued on the fixed extension so it could withstand sustained use.[78]

Hooker had not kept Washington informed of the battle's progress. Colonel Ingalls had taken it upon himself to send an occasional message, and General Butterfield of course had done the same. At 3:10 P.M. Lincoln sent a telegram to Hooker indicating he had heard that Confederates had retaken the heights behind Fredericksburg. He pointedly asked, "Is that so?" Hooker confirmed the report but dismissed it as inconsequential. He then obscured his own failures by complaining to Lincoln that his campaign might have been successful if only Sedgwick had arrived to assist him.[79]

By May 4 Sedgwick's position on the high ground west of Fredericksburg had become the Union army's only battlefield success. The problem was that Hooker did not know what to do next. The opportunity for a joint operation had long passed. At 1:40 P.M. Sedgwick outlined his circumstances for the army commander:

> I occupy the same position as yesterday, when General Warren left me. It is not a strong one. I have no means of judging of the enemy's force about me; deserters say 40,000. I shall take a position near Banks' Ford and the Taylor house, at the suggestion of General Warren. Officers have already gone to select a position.
>
> It is believed that the heights of Fredericksburg are occupied by two divisions of the enemy.

Sedgwick's estimate of there being two divisions at Fredericksburg is likely based on balloon observations. Aloft over Falmouth, an aeronaut reported 15,000 Confederates to be visible. Sedgwick knew he had faced Early's Division for the past few days, but another division (Longstreet's men?) may well have arrived at Hamilton's Crossing.[80]

Hooker responded with a message more persuasive than directive:

> It is of vital importance that you should take a commanding position near Fredericksburg, which you can hold to a certainty till to-morrow. Please advise me what you can do in this respect. I inclose substance of a communication sent last night. Its suggestions are highly important and meet my full approval. There are positions on your side commanded by our batteries on the other side I think you could take and hold. The general would recommend as one such position the ground on which Dr. Taylor's is situated.[81]

The specified enclosure is a copy of what Warren had sent to Sedgwick earlier that day, although there is no time noted. The referenced morning attack appears to have been Brigadier General Colston's probe of the Federal left flank.

> I have reported your situation to General Hooker. I find that we contracted our lines here somewhat during the morning, and repulsed the enemy's last assault with ease. The troops are in good position. General H. says you are separated from him so far that he cannot advise you how to act. You need not try to force the position you attacked at 5 P.M. [Salem Church]. Look to the safety of your corps. You can retire, if necessary, by way of Fredericksburg or Banks' Ford. The latter would enable you to join us more readily.[82]

Sedgwick responded at 2:15 P.M.: "I shall do my utmost to hold a position on the right bank of the Rappahannock until to-morrow."[83]

Hooker did not have a plan, but Lee did. The Southern commander had arrived on the field with the rest of Anderson's Division, and he fully intended to hurt Sedgwick's isolated corps. The loss of Marye's Heights the day before had been demoralizing, but Lee's presence renewed confidence that this day would be different.[84]

The arriving Confederate formations consisted of Brig. Gen. Ambrose R. "Rans" Wright's Georgia brigade, Brig. Gen. Carnot Posey's Mississippi Brigade, and Brig. Gen. Edward A. Perry's small brigade of three Florida regiments. Lee arrived at Salem Church somewhere between 10:00 and 11:30 A.M., around the time Smith was getting roughly handled near Smith Run.[85]

McLaws had asked Lee for reinforcements, but when help arrived in the form of three brigades, he was not ready for them. The general had suspended his operations that morning and then done nothing to prepare for a renewed assault. Lee thus had to take on duties that would have been handled already by a more competent subordinate. Colonel Alexander described the situation:

> About ten o'clock, Gen. Lee in person with his staff came up to where I was on the line, & for the first time . . . I saw him in a temper. I could not comprehend at the time whom it was with, or what it was about. . . . But the three ideas which his conversation with myself & others in my presence seemed to indicate as uppermost in his mind were as follows. 1st. That a

great deal of valuable time had been already uselessly lost by somebody, some how, no particulars being given. 2nd. Nobody knew exactly how or where the enemy's line of battle ran & it was somebody's duty to know. 3rd. That it now devolved on him personally to use up a lot more time to find out all about the enemy before we could move a peg.[86]

Sedgwick's corps occupied the plateau across which the Plank Road ran. The Confederates could move laterally across that front on the cleared and graded roadbed of an unfinished railway, but beyond that covered way, they had to contend with the rugged terrain of the Hazel Run valley. Getting into position was going to take time. The assault itself would also be uphill. If any Confederates saw any advantages in their deployment that day, no one bragged about them.[87]

Lee found Early, who shared his plan of attack. They agreed that the three additional brigades from Anderson's Division would take position along Hazel Run, filling in the interval between Early and McLaws. As these troops came into the line, Early would pull Hoke and Hays to the right, placing them in position to concentrate on a corner of Sedgwick's line. The two brigades would converge on that potentially vulnerable apex, Hoke on the left and Hays on the right. When they hit the Union position, Hays would forge straight ahead, while Hoke moved left to expand the breakthrough.[88]

In support of that assault, Gordon was to bring his brigade up to Smith Run and be ready to cut diagonally toward the Taylor house on Fall Hill, sweeping the crest of the heights on the east side of the stream. Smith's Virginians would constitute a reserve for Early's advance to the west as well as the reserve force for Barksdale's Brigade, which would remain facing east toward Fredericksburg. Giving Smith's Brigade that conflicting double duty was a calculated risk but made full use of the available forces. Lee approved the plan and left to check on his other forces preparing for an attack.[89]

Early proceeded to get his assault troops into position. Hays moved back to where he and Hoke had been deployed that morning, at the foot of the hill near Alum Springs Mill. A Louisiana soldier described how his "brigade was conducted by a circuitous route through a deep ravine to the foot of an enormous hill." The regiments stretched out in line of battle across the rough terrain, keeping within the woods that screened them from view.[90]

Hoke moved his brigade farther west to constitute Early's left. The North Carolinians crossed to the north side of Hazel Run and then deployed near the stream. They were on the rear slope at the lower end of the ridge upon which the Downman house stood. In their immediate front stood the neglected Walker Landram farm. The brigade arrayed itself with the Sixth Regiment on the right and the Fifty-Fourth, Twenty-First, and Fifty-Seventh Regiments extending to the left. The First Battalion North Carolina Sharpshooters was on the far left.[91]

Anderson's three brigades continued the line from Early's left. Wright's Georgia regiments connected with Hoke's North Carolinians. They too deployed "on the slope of the hills in rear of Downman's farm." A ravine extended up the slope to their left. Coming from Chancellorsville, these were tired men, as expressed by a soldier in the Third Georgia: "We had been engaged for three successive days and thought it was over, but there was more fighting yet to be done."[92]

Posey brought his Mississippi brigade into position to Wright's left. Perry extended the developing line of battle with his three Florida regiments. They would have to climb the slopes out of the Hazel Run bottomland through recently abandoned winter encampments, where hut holes and crude chimneys dotted the landscape. Perry did not have enough troops to fully close the gap between his units and Wofford's Brigade on the Salem Church ridge, but he scouted the terrain and thought that the Confederate advance would still be able to drive the Federals.[93]

The troops on the Salem Church line had been fortifying their position, although hindered by a lack of tools and Union batteries sending the occasional round crashing into them. An Alabama soldier noted that the Federal guns were "knocking our frail works to pieces." Remembering the impetuous counterattack the day before, he worried that someone among the annoyed Alabamans would yell "charge, and away would go the brigade." Another Southerner remarked upon their enemy's skills: "Before we advanced on Monday we received some of the closest shelling we ever had."[94]

In addition to the well-served Federal guns on the Plank Road, the Union guns at Banks' Ford posed a significant danger to the Confederate position. On the high ground north of the river, Federal batteries could enfilade the left flank of any Confederate advance that took place along the axis of the Plank Road. While Anderson's three brigades deployed in the Hazel Run valley, only Wofford's and Kershaw's Brigades were going to be able to support them.[95]

The terrain also limited their use of artillery. In Fredericksburg Confederate batteries could dominate the town from Marye's Heights. On the east side of Sedgwick's position, Lee's Hill also provided a vantage point with good fields of fire. To the west, though, there were few opportunities for artillery to support an advance out of the Hazel Run valley or from the Salem Church ridge.[96]

There were similar limitations on the Chancellorsville field. Hooker's heavily fortified position north of the crossroads had been made formidable. A frontal attack had little hope of success, so Lee looked elsewhere to inflict damage. He directed Maj. Robert A. Hardaway to shell the US Ford crossing during the night of May 3–4.[97]

Hardaway pulled sections of guns from several batteries to put together a battalion of long-range weapons. In the moonlight Capt. Samuel R. Johnston guided the artillery into position on the bluffs overlooking US Ford. The roads were crude, so Hardaway held some guns back rather than risk them getting stuck and unable to be pulled free by weak animals. Ten of thirteen weapons went into battery.[98]

Around 3:30 A.M. the Confederate guns fired fifteen rounds each into the densely packed supply wagons and ambulances on the north side of the river. According to a Federal commissary officer, those 150 projectiles landed in a herd of cattle, into a cavalry camp, among some Confederate prisoners, and into ammunition trains. Hardaway could hear wagons splintering, but there were no secondary explosions. The Confederate artillerymen may have rushed their fuze installation. Still, when they pulled away from the bluffs, they left a satisfying chaos behind them.[99]

In the light of day, Hardaway's battalion joined Anderson's column headed toward Fredericksburg. Colonel Alexander greeted them when they came up into the open ground west of Salem Church. He thought the arriving weapons might be able to counter the Federal guns overlooking Banks' Ford that could enfilade infantry advancing beyond the Salem Church ridge. The colonel asked Hardaway to wait while he scouted the area for suitable battery positions.[100]

While Alexander was away, Lee directed Anderson to get his brigades into position south of the road. Anderson ordered Hardaway to follow the infantry, but the artilleryman let him know that his guns were needed elsewhere. The division commander knew his own inaction had made Lee testy, so he sent Hardaway to clear up matters on his own. The major explained to Lee that Alexander wanted his rifled weapons to counter the Federal artillery at Banks' Ford. He suggested that some nearby batteries of 12-pounder Napoleons would be more suited to Anderson's needs. Lee understood the issue at once and ordered Maj. Frank Huger to accompany

Anderson with the field guns. Hardaway's weapons were to remain available to Alexander.[101]

Upon his return, Alexander directed Hardaway to take his thirteen-gun battalion to the Smith farm, across the river from the Banks' Ford uplands. He reinforced the major with eight additional weapons, creating a formidable concentration of firepower. It took more time than anticipated, however, to get them all into battery. The gun crews spent the day identifying fields of fire, cutting through fallen trees to get weapons into position, and digging earthworks. Under a hot sun and without rations, strong men fainted from exhaustion, but by late afternoon the artillerymen on Smith Hill were reasonably ready. Alexander reported that they had also "marked points of direction" for firing toward Banks' Ford after dark.[102]

Newton's Federals watched the Confederate infantry moving into position in the Hazel Run valley. One of the skirmishers in the Twenty-Seventh New York Infantry described the ominous activity: "All the A.M. they were massing their troops and placing batteries in positions and their commands could be distinctly heard. The troops had evidently come from a distance, and are thought to be a part of Longstreet's command, as their movements indicated exhaustion and fatigue from long marches."[103] In dispatches and reports there are constant references to Longstreet's arrival on the field. Two of his divisions had been detached for duty on the Virginia–North Carolina coast, and the potential for these troops to reappear as reinforcements loomed large at Union headquarters. Longstreet's two other divisions, led by McLaws and Anderson, had remained with Lee and were present on the battlefield. The Confederates observed by the waiting Federals were indeed part of Longstreet's Corps, but they were worn out not from a trip up from the coast, but from several days of fighting around Chancellorsville.

The Southerners moved through the woods as quickly as tired men could manage. The coming assault was not planned as a surprise, and an occasional rebel yell echoed up from Hazel Run. Once in place, the Confederates waited with the casual fatalism of veteran troops. A Louisiana soldier observed how "the men spent the interval in snatching a hasty supper (for many of them their last) of crackers and bacon, chatting, smoking and jesting as if danger were the last thing in their minds." The waiting Federals also remained confident. They held the better ground and were supported by artillery posted in strong positions. They would not be easily shoved aside.[104]

On the line facing Fredericksburg, Howe recognized that his 6,000-man division would be stretched thin, so he decided to hold critical areas in depth. To this end Howe anchored his line on the high ground just south of the Plank Road, tying in with Bartlett's brigade, which was facing south. Lt. Col. John R. Lewis's Fifth Vermont held the interval between the two divisions.[105]

Extending north from the Plank Road, Neill's brigade angled along a series of low hills on the east side of Smith Run. The rest of Grant's Vermont Brigade established a line that followed the high ground on the west side of that stream. About 250 yards north of the Plank Road, Rigby had positioned his Battery A, Maryland Light Artillery, supported by Col. Elisha L. Barney's Sixth Vermont on its left. A Vermont soldier observed: "We had a good position. Our batteries occupied the most advantageous points; and we waited on our arms the bursting of the storm which seemed inevitable."[106]

On the skirmish line the occasional rifle shot punctuated what passed for silence. On the west side of the Federal perimeter, Lt. William H. Terrill of the Forty-Third New York wrote: "A few moments ago, a captain near me, of my regiment, exposed himself, and in a moment a bullet from a Rebel picket went through his head. He is now dying." On the east side of the perimeter, two lines of skirmishers had deployed in front of Neill's brigade. The Twenty-First New Jersey lay in front, backed up by the Seventy-Seventh New York. Under the tension of waiting, a fidgety New Yorker accidentally shot a Jerseyman in the back.[107]

Southerners waiting to attack also felt the tension. Many of them had been through hard fighting at Chancellorsville, and another impending attack proved too much for some. A man in Wright's Brigade swallowed tobacco to make himself sick. Another soldier, more desperate to avoid the fight, shot himself in the foot.[108]

By May 4 the Union army's plans to establish supply depots in Fredericksburg had been overtaken by events. Headquarters directed Chief Quartermaster Ingalls and Brig. Gen. Herman Haupt, in charge of military railroads, to pull back their assets. The railway bridge would not be rebuilt, and supplies would not be stockpiled south of the Rappahannock. Instead, the time had come to prepare to abandon the river town. At 10:27 A.M. Butterfield directed that the pontoon bridge at the wrecked railway bridge be removed. Once the bridging equipment had been hauled away, the bridge builders were to stand by to pull the two bridges at the upper end of town.[109]

To hold Fredericksburg until ordered to leave, Gibbon reinforced Hall's units holding the line at the edge of town. Capt. William Plumer's First Company of Massachusetts Sharpshooters and Maj. George C. Joslin's Fifteenth Massachusetts, known as the Andrew Sharpshooters, reported to Hall and spent the rest of the day skirmishing with Barksdale's Mississippians.[110]

North of William Street, Lt. Col. Max A. Thoman's Fifty-Ninth New York established a stronghold in the Fredericksburg Cemetery. A soldier remembered how the men "fought all day behind the wall walking over the graves of hundreds of Rebels we killed last fall when we took the city before." Lt. Col. Arthur F. Devereux deployed his Nineteenth Massachusetts and four companies of the 127th Pennsylvania from the cemetery to the unfinished Mary Washington memorial. Five other companies from the 127th were on the other end of the line with Hall's skirmishers.[111]

The Nineteenth Massachusetts had also taken charge of about 225 Sixth Corps men cut off from their units. Maj. Edmund Rice organized those scattered troops and used them to help evacuate the town. By the end of the day, they had removed over 2,500 wounded men and large numbers of wagons and ambulances. Sometime before 6:00 P.M., Federal engineers at the pontoon bridges at the foot of Hawke Street heard firing to the west.[112]

On the Sixth Corps line, a Vermont soldier remembered how "the day was fast wearing to a close in comparative silence and inactivity." A Maine officer conversing with a staff officer noted: "'It's five o'clock now, Major; if the rebs want anything to-night, it's time for them to commence.' Hardly were the words out of my mouth when they did commence, charging our whole line in overwhelming force."[113]

TEN

MAY 4

SALEM HEIGHTS AND SMITH RUN

About an hour and a half before sundown, probably between 5:30 and 6:00 P.M., Captain Graham's Rockbridge Artillery fired three rounds in rapid succession. His guns were adjacent to the Telegraph Road on Lee's Hill, where the battery had supported "Extra Billy" Smith's attack at midday. Its ordnance had been replenished from another battery's ammunition chests, which allowed the well-positioned guns to remain where they had already worked out the range to various targets. Their late-afternoon signal sent three Confederate divisions against the isolated Sixth Corps.[1]

The daylight hours had been stressful for the men on the ground. For the Federals, some of the unease dissipated when friendly cavalry came across the Rappahannock on the bridge downstream from Scott's Ferry. The horse soldiers were the Eighth Pennsylvania Cavalry, and one of them described their arrival on the uplands: "The infantry were ignorant of the existence of a bridge, and all manner of questions were eagerly asked, such as, 'where did you come from;' 'how did you get here;' 'how is Hooker making out;' etc." Sedgwick directed Maj. Pennock Huey to take his troopers and report to Howe. They moved over behind Neill's and Grant's brigades.[2]

The boom of Captain Graham's 20-pounder Parrott rifles reverberated over thousands of waiting troops. A New York soldier wrote that "a death-like stillness rested upon the scene for a few minutes." That quiet lasted while the Confederates sprang to their feet, dressed their lines, and stepped off with a shout. A Federal officer observed, "The rebel yell broke from the woods far in front and the whole hillside was alive with men." From another soldier's perspective, "the inevitable came at last."[3]

Lee had deployed 23,000 men against Sedgwick's corps, which by then numbered fewer than 21,000. The odds were marginal, but this had become the best option for the aggressive Southern commander to damage his adversary. The terrain, however, made coordinated attacks difficult.[4]

A three-quarter-mile gap still separated McLaws's formations on the Salem Church ridge from Anderson's three brigades extending Early's line from Fredericksburg. When the attack signal came, Wright's Brigade, on Anderson's left, advanced out of the Hazel Run valley. One of the Georgians described emerging from cover: "Our portion of the battlefield was a series of ravines and corresponding eminences. As the head of the column made its appearance a Yankee battery opened."[5]

The guns were Captain McCartney's Battery A, Massachusetts Light Artillery, posted on the knoll occupied by the Williams house. A section from Lieutenant Parsons's Battery A, First New Jersey Light Artillery was also in battery at the Downman house (Idlewild). Federal skirmishers from the Twenty-Seventh New York extended across the area, reinforced by two companies of the Sixteenth New York.[6]

McCartney's battery opened fire at about 1,500 yards with solid shot, which crashed through the Confederate ranks. To their left front, Parsons's New Jersey guns blasted the advancing Georgians with shell and case shot at a range of 700 yards. The attackers recoiled when the artillery rounds slammed into them. They scrambled into a ravine, quickly rallied, and continued under cover toward the Downman house. A soldier described how "Gen. Wright advanced us in column through a ravine until the regiment on the right debouched on the rising ground in front, when we were wheeled into line at a double quick and thus advanced through the open field."[7]

Emerging from the sheltering earth, the Confederates had closed the distance to Idlewild to just over 400 yards. When they came into view, the New Jersey gun crews limbered up and pulled back to the Orange Plank Road. Seeing the two guns retreating, General Brooks rode to the battery position at the Williams house, calling out to McCartney that "everything depended upon [his guns] keeping those fellows back." With the other section no longer to their front, the Massachusetts artillerymen switched from solid shot to exploding case shot.[8]

The Union guns poured out a relentless storm of metal. A Georgia soldier recounted how he could hear the battery commander shouting: "God damn them, pour the grape into them." Another observer described the artillerymen at their work: "The men blackened by powder smoke, worked like demons, the guns belched forth a flood of fiery death, and the hill seemed to rock under the terrific thunder of the battery; great gaps were opened in the enemy's lines, by the tornado of shot and shell."[9]

The Georgians charged through a wheat field toward the Downman house and developed enough momentum to scatter the Federal skirmishers. Under the unrelenting artillery fire, however, Wright's troops gravitated toward some wooded ground northwest of the mansion. General Anderson ordered them to wait in the relative shelter of the trees because the rest of his division's attack had not unfolded as anticipated.[10]

Anderson would later report that Wright drove away a battery, but there were only two guns at Idlewild when the attack signal came. The Fifth US Artillery had been in place near the house that morning, where its six 10-pounder Parrotts attempted to take on the heavier Confederate guns on Lee's Hill. Those Regular Army artillerymen had since departed to support Howe's line facing Fredericksburg. A section of 10-pounder Parrotts from the First New Jersey Artillery was all that was deployed at the Downman house when Wright attacked, and they pulled back to Sedgwick's main line safely.[11]

The Confederates tried to bring up their own artillery to the open ground at Idlewild. Captain Carlton's Troup Artillery deployed two field guns, but the Georgia cannoneers were overwhelmed by McCartney's six 12-pounder Napoleons. A Massachusetts artilleryman described how "a rebel battery in our front with the same kind of pieces as ours, opened a rapid fire upon us. We returned the compliment in the shape of a few solid shot, and after a few rounds we heard no more of them."[12]

But what of the rest of Anderson's assault? General Posey had formed his Mississippi brigade on Wright's left. To Posey's left, General Perry awaited the attack order with his Florida brigade. The two commanders had dutifully scouted the terrain across which they would advance. They had planned to capture the battery section at the brick manor house (Idlewild) by getting behind it to cut off its route to the Plank Road.[13]

As Wright's Georgians moved forward, they had dropped into a ravine to avoid the intense artillery fire and then used its cover to advance farther. In doing so they had cut in front of Posey's and Perry's Brigades, preventing them from moving ahead. Consequently, the expected attack by three brigades became an advance by just the one. The botched attack also gave Federal troops the impression that this advance had been a feint; Major Tompkins called it a "demonstration." When the Southerners hesitated to advance farther, some of the Twenty-Seventh New York skirmishers taunted them, calling out, "Come on Johnnie, do come over and see us."[14]

Along the Salem Church ridge south of the Plank Road, two of McLaws's brigades waited for their attack orders. A courier brought word that Anderson and Early would strike soon, and Generals Wofford and Kershaw were to advance their regiments when they heard fighting to their right. The two brigade commanders mounted up when they heard the distant signal guns and orders rippled down the line: "Attention battalion! Fix bayonets! Right shoulder shift! Forward March!" The rebel yell echoed through the trees.[15]

As soon as Wofford and Kershaw emerged from the woods, Lt. John H. Butler's Battery G, Second US Artillery opened fire with spherical case shot. The two brigades obliqued to the right to close the gap between them and Anderson's Division, but Anderson's attack by then had fallen apart, Federal artillery forcing Wright's Georgians to grind to a halt. Wofford and Kershaw consequently encountered an enfilading fire. Their troops slowed their advance and sought shelter in wooded terrain. The Thirty-Sixth New York soon after reestablished its skirmish line, reinforced by the Thirty-Seventh Massachusetts.[16]

When the Confederate assaults began, Colonel Alexander directed the batteries arrayed on Smith Hill to open fire. Two hundred yards west of the Smith house were two 3-inch Ordnance Rifles from Captain McCarthy's First Company, Richmond Howitzers, and two 10-pounder Parrott rifles from Capt. Edward A. Marye's Fredericksburg Artillery. Nearby were two more 3-inch Ordnance Rifles from Capt. William P. Hurt's Alabama battery as well as his Whitworth rifle.[17]

The above seven weapons were in the open, but five more guns near the Alabama battery had the benefit of gun pits. The entrenched weapons were two 3-inch Ordnance Rifles from Lieutenant Penick's Pittsylvania Battery and three guns (probably 3-inch Ordnance Rifles as well) from Capt. William W. Parker's Richmond Battery. This overall collection of twelve weapons occupied ground west of a narrow road that dropped down from the Smith farm to the Rappahannock River.[18]

On the east side of that road stood another concentration of artillery. Capt. William P. Carter's King William Battery had brought a section of

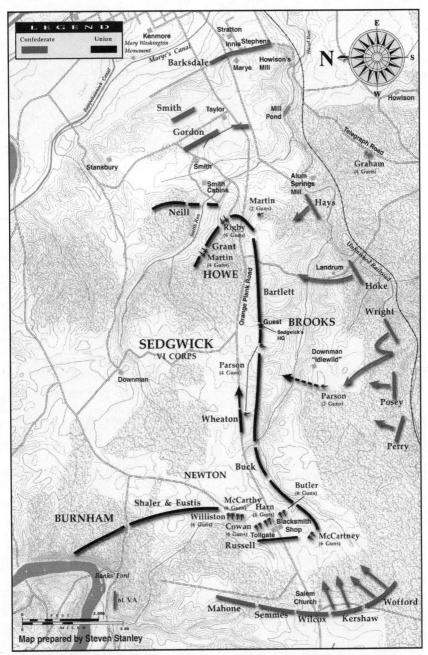

Map 18. The Afternoon Attacks, May 4. Confederate formations in the Salem Church line and newly arrived brigades from Chancellorsville attacked the Sixth Corps but were easily pushed back. The brigade attacks by Hoke and Hays were executed with more vigor but also failed to break the Union line.

10-pounder Parrott rifles into position. They were joined by a section from Capt. Charles W. Fry's Orange Battery, either 10-pounder Parrotts or 3-inch Ordnance Rifles. These weapons were also protected by earthworks. Another cluster of guns was on a hilltop farther east, about a half mile from the Smith house. Capt. Tyler C. Jordan's Bedford Battery had dropped trail there and dug protective earthworks for its four 3-inch Ordnance Rifles.[19]

Looking across to the ground above Banks' Ford, Major Hardaway reported eight Federal guns entrenched near an old white house as well as two guns two hundred yards upriver and two more guns four hundred yards downriver. General Hunt, the Potomac Army's chief of artillery, had an artillery park at Banks' Ford but appears to have deployed only three batteries. One of those units was Lt. Albert F. Brooker's Battery B, First Connecticut Heavy Artillery, with four 4.5-inch rifled weapons. The other two were Lt. Lorenzo Thomas Jr.'s Battery K, First US Artillery, with six 3-inch Ordnance Rifles, and Capt. Alexander C. M. Pennington's Battery M, Second US Artillery, which also had six 3-inch Ordnance rifles and was supplemented by two additional sections for a total of ten weapons.[20]

These were the batteries that returned fire and pounded the Confederates on Smith Hill. Their targets were initially the guns west of the Smith house without protective earthworks. As the Federals poured in an accurate fire, Hardaway observed that the guns on the east end of his line were not putting much pressure on the enemy. He rode over to order Carter, Fry, and Jordan to increase their rate of fire and stayed to gauge their shooting.[21]

As had occurred at US Ford that morning, the outgoing Confederate rounds were not exploding. A frustrated Hardaway reported:

> I took position over in front of our rifle pits in the abatis, where I had full view of the effect of our shot. I found our fuses were very defective, although it was reported to me that we were using the fuse-igniter. I estimated that one of our shell out of fifteen exploded. I must think that the meal-powder was knocked off the fuse by the mallet while inserting the fuse. I prepared a few myself, which answered very well. I was compelled to watch closely the effect of all the projectiles, as if we were using entirely solid shot.[22]

Overall, the Confederate attack against the western part of the Union line had not gone well. Five brigades from McLaws's and Anderson's Divisions had been held back by Federal artillery along the Plank Road. The other three brigades on the Salem Church ridge did not advance, presumably to avoid being enfiladed by the powerful Union guns on the Banks' Ford uplands. Confederate success was going to depend entirely on Early's Division.

Early had joined the Rockbridge Artillery on Lee's Hill to oversee his assault. Directly to his front General Hays had moved up his Louisiana brigade past the Alum Springs Mill and across Hazel Run. To his left General Hoke's North Carolina brigade also waited on the north side of Hazel Run. On the right some of General Gordon's Georgia regiments waited in reserve, while others engaged Federal troops in Fredericksburg from rifle pits on Marye's Heights.[23]

Hays had five regiments in line and took charge of his brigade's left wing, consisting of Col. Davidson B. Penn's Seventh Louisiana on the left and Col. Leroy A. Stafford's Ninth Louisiana on the right. His senior colonel, Henry Forno, directed the brigade's right wing. Col. Trevanian D. Lewis's Eighth Louisiana stood to the right of the Ninth, with Forno's Fifth Louisiana to its right, and finally Colonel Monaghan's Sixth Louisiana on the brigade's right.[24]

When the signal guns fired, Hays and Forno shouted, "Forward—double-quick!" The Louisiana men surged forward "with a yell that sounded like a legion of 50-ton locomotives." But the slopes between Hazel Run and the uplands were covered with brush and fallen trees, which disrupted the advancing formations. One soldier described how the ground was "broken by defiles, and covered with the stunted post oak that seems to grow in that part of Virginia where nothing else is planted."[25]

The onrushing Confederates pushed their way through the tangled vegetation as Federal skirmishers at the edge of the plateau kept up a steady fire. A Louisiana soldier admitted that "an orderly ascent was utterly impossible." The attack formations lost coherence as they struggled forward. But when the Southerners crested the hill, the weight of numbers prevailed. They drove back the skirmishers but then paused to reform while musketry and artillery fire slammed into them. A soldier described how the incoming fire "seemed to make the very air boil." The Southerners pressed on, maintaining a disciplined momentum, to close with the Union defenders "as yet unseen but manifestly not far off."[26]

When Hays's troops reached the uplands, they became visible to Union artillery across the river. There were two Federal batteries on the hills above Falmouth supporting the western end of Sedgwick's lines. Capt. Elijah D. Taft had four 20-pounder Parrott rifles of the Fifth New York Light Artillery there, along with Lt. George F. Gaston's six 3-inch Ordnance

Rifles from Capt. Charles Kusserow's Thirty-Second New York Independent Light Artillery. The records are not clear as to which battery occupied which hilltop, and although the range was extreme, those ten weapons brought fire down on the Confederates threatening Sedgwick's left.[27]

In addition to the guns at Falmouth, Battery G, First Rhode Island Artillery occupied the hilltop at the Washington farm, just south of Fredericksburg's railway bridge. Its six 3-inch Ordnance Rifles could deliver rounds into the attacking Confederates as well, although at the extreme range of three thousand yards. The necessary precision for time fuzes would have been difficult to achieve, but the kinetic energy of solid shot caused horrible damage. One Louisiana Tiger saw a round crash through his regiment that killed and wounded seventeen men.[28]

As the Union guns on Stafford Heights opened fire, the few Confederate batteries supporting Early's attack stopped shooting because the infantry had advanced into their fields of fire. When artillery rounds slammed into Hays's assault columns from the right, the Louisiana men instinctively veered left. As a result they did not hit the Fifth Vermont on the far left of the Plank Road line. Without the pressure of a head on assault, the Federals poured a heavy fire into the flank of the charging enemy.[29]

Meanwhile, Hoke closed in on the Plank Road on Hays's left, with Maj. Rufus W. Wharton's First Battalion North Carolina Sharpshooters on his far left. That special unit advanced with seventy-five experienced soldiers and one civilian. A fellow named Samuel Lyons had come down from Maryland to visit his soldier-brother and decided to join his sibling on the firing line.[30]

The sharpshooters linked up with Col. Archibald C. Godwin's Fifty-Seventh North Carolina on their right. Next in sequence along the line were Lt. Col. William S. Rankin's Twenty-First North Carolina, Col. James C. S. McDowell's Fifty-Fourth North Carolina, and Col. Isaac E. Avery's Sixth North Carolina.[31]

Hoke's Tar Heels had swept over the Landram farm, where they became visible crossing over the hill between Hazel Run and a tributary called North Hazel Run. Incoming rounds fell short, though, kicking up rocks and sending ricochets through the ranks. Some of the men stopped to shoot back, but officers shouted for them to keep moving. Federal artillery began to find their range from the Plank Road. Under an increasingly intense fire, the brigade dashed down the slope, splashed across North Hazel Run, and began to climb out of the ravine toward the uplands.[32]

Like the Louisiana men to their right, Hoke's North Carolinians suffered severely trying to close with the enemy. The Federal skirmish line poured out a high volume of fire from the edge of the plateau. Colonel Avery reported how these forward troops, "from their naturally strong position, fought with unusual stubbornness, occasioning considerable loss to the Brigade." The attacking Tar Heels were also receiving a disturbing amount of fire from their left.[33]

Wright's Brigade was supposed to have advanced on Hoke's left, but these Georgians were nowhere in sight. As previously noted, Wright's troops moved up a ravine that took them away from their axis of advance. With no support evident on their flank, Hoke and Early concluded that Wright had not advanced at all. Hoke's units endured what one officer described as a "murderous enfilading fire," which threw the North Carolina regiments into disorder. The veterans managed to rally and reform, but then they collided with Hays's Brigade on the wide plateau, the Louisiana regiments losing cohesion under the intense fire.[34]

The North Carolinians forced back the Federal skirmishers but then came under fire from a section of 10-pounder Parrott rifles on their right. These guns of Battery A, New Jersey Light Artillery were not the best weapons for close-in work but blasted away from where the Federal line turned north from the Plank Road. A New York soldier described the aggressive Confederate advance: "Our artillery poured in a raking fire, which mowed them down fearfully. They fell in heaps, but they quickly filled up the gaps and pressed on. Twice they were thrown into utter confusion, but as quickly rallied and moved forward."[35]

The regimental chaplain of the Fifty-Fourth North Carolina later wrote that "being unsupported at the time, they were ordered to fall back a short distance to a place of safety." Safety, however, is a relative term on a battlefield. One Tar Heel described how the troops remained stationary only "until our boys had sufficiently rallied to renew the charge, which being accomplished in a little less time than I can write it." In that place of seemingly reduced danger, Colonel McDowell, leading the Fifty-Fourth North Carolina, fell dead with a bullet in his head. Lt. Col. Kenneth M. Murchison assumed command of the regiment.[36]

Regimental officers were not the only high-ranking casualties. An incoming bullet mangled General Hoke's shoulder, and responsibility for continuing the assault devolved upon Colonel Avery of the Sixth North Carolina. Hoke, however, had not briefed his regimental commanders on the attack plan. The North Carolina brigade was supposed to turn to its left when it hit the Plank Road to expand the anticipated gap opened in the Union line by the Louisiana brigade. Unaware of that tactical imperative, Avery led the North Carolinians straight ahead and into the startled Louisianans. Battle smoke obscured the field, and some of the Tar Heels fired into Hays's formations. Trying to get out of the way, some of the hard-pressed Louisiana units moved to their left, intermingling the brigades.[37]

Screaming Confederates closing in on the Plank Road also encountered a brush fence and had to quickly decide if they were going to jump over it or halt their forward progress at its line. Like the Federals advancing on the stone wall at Marye's Heights the day before, many of the swift-moving Southerners leaped over the obstacle to close with the enemy. In midstride they were surprised to find that the fence stood at the edge of a road cut. Men cleared the fence but tumbled down an embankment and bowled into Union soldiers in the road. Some surprised Federals thought they were being overwhelmed and surrendered. Others took advantage of the turmoil and scrambled away to the other side of the cut.[38]

The Confederates pressed forward but continued to lose cohesion. A Louisiana soldier noted: "All semblance of military order had been totally lost. Captains lost their companies, and companies and regiments were so intermingled that the brigade formed simply a howling, rushing and firing mob, without pretense of organization or authority."[39] Taking advantage of the confusion, Lt. Col. John R. Lewis advanced several companies of his Fifth Vermont into a line perpendicular to the Confederate advance. "Standing and firing rapidly," the Federals got off about seven rounds each, a relentless flanking fire that cut into the right wing of Hays's Brigade.[40]

A Louisiana soldier observed how their attack "had lost its momentum, and, so far as offense was concerned, we were powerless from confusion and lack of organization." Opposite the exhausted Southerners, the Federals were comparatively thin on the ground. But the open plateau had few advantages for the attackers, and the defenders were able to shove them back. The Louisiana men gave way—individually at first, then in groups. The broken formations looked for a place to rally.[41]

Within their defensive perimeter, the Federals had the advantage of interior lines. Near the Guest and Downman houses, only a single brigade (Wright's Georgians) had pushed up against the Union position, an attack so poorly executed that Union observers assumed it to be a sham. Sedgwick had little concern, then, about directing Newton to reinforce Howe.[42]

upper bridge at Scott's Ferry had good approach roads and was strongly anchored at the ferry landings. That span became the route for wagons and artillery. The lower bridge, by contrast, had required construction of a trestle to fill a space left after every available pontoon had been used. That crossing would be used primarily by the infantry.[64]

Other commands in the Banks' Ford area also dutifully reported. Thirty minutes past midnight, Brig. Gen. Robert O. Tyler, in charge of the artillery on the uplands, sent the following message to Butterfield: "Communication with General Sedgwick is at present full and open by two bridges and by messenger or telegraph. His main body is, however, below the crest of the hill, opposite the ford, under full fire of artillery. I consider his command in great danger."[65]

Sedgwick knew the risk to his corps but understood that Hooker expected him to be able to support other operations. In addition to his and Benham's message, he had tried to reassure the army commander that he would be available if needed: "I shall hold my position, as ordered, on south [bank] of Rappahannock."[66]

At 1:00 A.M., May 5, Hooker received the Benham-Sedgwick communication from 11:50 P.M., May 4. Sedgwick's later message arrived shortly thereafter. By then it appears that army headquarters had responded to the first message. Shortly before 2:00 A.M. an aide rode down from the Scott house signal station and reported to Benham with clear orders from Butterfield to retreat. The chief engineer immediately relayed them to Sedgwick:

> Dispatch this moment received. Withdraw. Cover the river, and prevent any force crossing. Acknowledge this.
> By command of Major General Hooker[67]

Sedgwick replied to the chief of staff: "General Hooker's order received. Will withdraw my forces immediately."[68]

The Sixth Corps units had waited patiently for orders to cross. On the uplands the delay fed rumors that a bridge had been damaged by the Confederate artillery. The bridges remained intact, though, and supply wagons had been making their way across the floating span at Scott's Ferry. A New York soldier remembered that "it was not one of Sedgwick's habits to leave any of his supplies in the hands of the enemy." Still, the wait seemed endless. The New Yorker further described how time passed: "Too weary to walk about to warm myself, and too cold to sleep, I could only lie and listen to the shriek and whir of the shells from a Whitworth battery that was shelling us from the left."[69]

Medical teams were able to get seventeen ambulances across the river. Getting those specialized conveyances beyond the floodplain, however, proved impossible. The flow of batteries and regiments moving toward the river blocked the few roads to the uplands. The ambulances would only be able to transport injured troops who had been brought to the crossing by others. A great many wounded had to be left behind because of inadequate means to evacuate them.[70]

During the evening, some soldiers broke away from their commands and crossed the river individually in between the wagons and ambulances. Benham stationed a company of engineers to curtail unauthorized use of the bridges. A colonel of a New Jersey regiment overcame this obstacle by forming up his men and marching them across. The startled engineers did not believe they had the authority to halt a regiment in formation. The identity of this unit is not known, but it could well have been one of the nine-month regiments nearing the end of its enlistments and not too concerned with repercussions in an army they would soon leave behind.[71]

Sedgwick's disciplined forces crossed the river in about an hour, getting clear of the area where the Confederate artillery rounds had been dropping. They would still be within range on the uplands, but the Southerners would not see them there until daylight. Benham asked for permission to dismantle the bridges, but Sedgwick asked him to wait. There were still units unaccounted and small groups of soldiers filtering in.[72]

While waiting for wayward troops to find their way to the crossing, the general received another message from Hooker. It had been sent at 1:20 A.M. in response to his communication stating he would hold his position on the south side of the river. It had clearly been delayed somewhere in delivery. It read: "Yours received, saying you should hold position. Order to withdraw countermanded. Acknowledge both."[73] Sedgwick responded immediately at 3:20 A.M., but Hooker would not receive the reply until two hours later. The Sixth Corps commander wrote: "Yours just received, countermanding order to withdraw. Almost my entire command has crossed over."[74]

Hooker did not actually have a plan to continue the campaign. In the formidable earthworks north of Chancellorsville, he remained in a position of no military value with an extended supply line. He had three bridges behind him, though. During the night of May 3, Colonel Colgate and a con-

Newton tapped Brigadier General Wheaton to send a regiment to reinforce the line being assailed by Early's Division. He sent the Ninety-Eighth Pennsylvania. While Lt. Col. George Wynkoop led his regiment down the Plank Road at the double-quick, Newton determined the situation on the Union left to be more serious than he initially thought. He ordered Wheaton to take his other units to reinforce Howe as well.[43]

Wheaton would not be able to reposition his entire brigade. The 139th Pennsylvania still held a position facing the Salem Church ridge and would not be able to pull away without being relieved. In addition, Maj. Wilson Hubbell had four companies of the Sixty-Second New York in the line opposite Confederate pickets north of the Banks' Ford Road; they too would not be able to move elsewhere. Wheaton's reinforcing column would consist of a respectable four and a half regiments, but Newton now looked for additional units to send to the endangered sector.[44]

The division commander pulled Butler's Battery G, Second US Artillery away from the tollgate area to follow Wheaton's infantry. He also reached into Colonel Burnham's Light Division for two more regiments to move east. These were the Sixty-First Pennsylvania, now led by Maj. George W. Dawson (replacing Colonel Spear, who had been killed at Marye's Heights), and Col. Thomas S. Allen's Fifth Wisconsin.[45]

On the road east the Ninety-Eighth Pennsylvania saw Southerners already north of the Plank Road. Wynkoop ordered his regiment into position along a brush fence. The Pennsylvanians deployed in line of battle without breaking stride and raised a shout as they neatly flanked the advancing Confederates. The rest of the brigade was right behind them. The remaining six companies of the Sixty-Second New York, led by Lt. Col. Theodore Hamilton, took position on Wynkoop's immediate left. The Ninety-Third Pennsylvania, Capt. John S. Long now commanding, extended the line further, and Col. Joseph M. Kinkead brought his 102nd Pennsylvania to the Ninety-Third's left to anchor the new line.[46]

In addition to running into reserves on the north side of the Plank Road, the Confederates encountered thick underbrush and trees with low limbs. Units already disorganized became more confused. When the newly redeployed Federals opened fire, the disordered and tired Twenty-First, Fifty-Fourth, and Fifty-Seventh North Carolina Regiments were in no condition to fight back. The First North Carolina Sharpshooters was off to the left somewhere, and the Sixth North Carolina appeared to have obliqued to the right. The three regiments in front of Wheaton began to pull back, but by then some of them were too exhausted even to flee. The arriving Federals gathered in several hundred prisoners as the North Carolinians tumbled back across Plank Road.[47]

Wheaton's hastily established line had disrupted Early's left flank. When the situation looked to be under control, the brigade commander went to find General Howe to report his arrival and availability. But in the turmoil of the Louisiana brigade's onslaught, Wheaton could not find the division headquarters and returned to his brigade.[48]

On the right of Hoke's Brigade, the Louisiana troops had also run into wooded terrain that slowed their advance. To maintain momentum both General Hays and Colonel Forno were on the Plank Road on horseback, exhorting troops who might pause in its shelter to keep moving. Terrain and fatigue continued to slow the Confederate advance, however, and the Federal units waiting in the woods halted it completely. One Louisianan observed how the attacking units had become scattered: "Beside me, as I lay on the ground, I found the Lieut. Col. of my regiment, but most of the men in my neighborhood were total strangers, belonging to other regiments of the brigade."[49]

Both Avery and Hays tried to reform their units, but the situation remained fluid. Colonel Godwin of the Fifty-Seventh North Carolina fell wounded, and command of the regiment devolved upon Lt. Col. Hamilton C. Jones Jr. When Avery had taken command of the brigade, Maj. Samuel M. Tate assumed command of the Sixth North Carolina. That unit was on the far right of the brigade front when a portion of the Fifth Vermont pushed out to enfilade the Confederate line. Tate marched his regiment to the right, moving around behind the Federals who were devastating the Southern battle line.[50]

By virtue of maneuver instead of firepower, the major and his Sixth North Carolina had put themselves in a position that compelled the Fifth Vermont men to pull back. The Tar Heels thus managed to relieve a considerable amount of pressure on the attacking Confederates, but they were now separated from their brigade. They heard firing to the east but did not know that it came from Confederates taking position to support the attack. The North Carolinians moved back to their left.[51]

General Early had committed two brigades and now directed a third one to join the fight. Gordon's Georgians had spent the day on the high ground overlooking Fredericksburg, skirmishing with the Federals ensconced in the shelter of houses on the western edge of town. When Hays launched

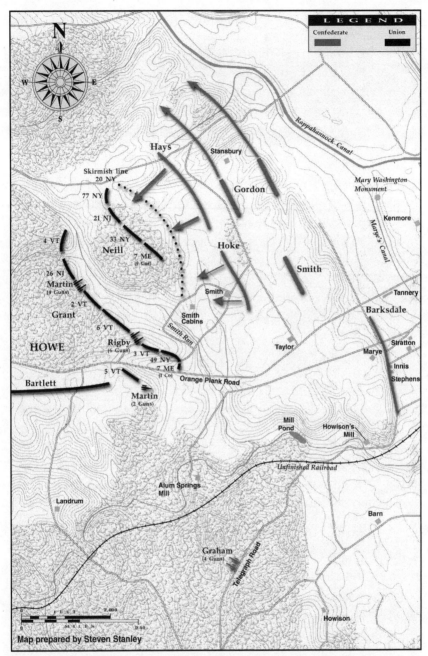

Map 19. Early's Renewed Assault at Smith Run. Hays and Hoke moved around the apex of the Union line and renewed their attacks. Gordon pushed north to get around the Federal flank. Smith remained in reserve, and Barksdale hemmed in Gibbon's division in Fredericksburg.

his brigade attack, Smith's Brigade moved to relieve Gordon's units so the Georgians could prepare for an advance in support. Just getting out of the earthworks, however, proved an ordeal.[52]

The men of the Thirty-Eighth Georgia left their trench at a run, knowing that alert Federals would not let them escape unscathed. Sure enough, when they scrambled away from the line, a volley ripped into them, and twenty men staggered and fell. Leaving those dead and wounded behind, the regiment kept running to get beyond the crest of the heights, where they could reform and move on to support Hays's Louisianans.[53]

The Union fire had come from Colonel Hall's brigade, aggressively skirmishing while medical troops evacuated the Union wounded from Fredericksburg. The Federals could hear the attacks on the Sixth Corps and thought they too would soon become more heavily engaged. Instead of receiving an assault, however, they saw the Georgians pulling out of the line, apparently to fight elsewhere. Other Southern units slid into the trenches being abandoned, however, and the faceoff continued. At dusk the Second Corps men heard cheering from the Confederate works, suggesting a triumph against their Sixth Corps comrades.[54]

Gordon's Brigade deployed in line of battle to the right of Hays's Brigade but found themselves under artillery fire from the Washington farm. Battery A, First Rhode Island Light Artillery had been sending rounds into Hays's and Hoke's formations since they charged toward the Plank Road. Once aligned, Gordon's Georgia regiments faced right and marched by the flank to look for an opening in the Union line.[55]

The Georgia units moved beyond the field of fire of the guns at the Washington farm but entered the range of two batteries at Falmouth. On hilltop positions overlooking that river community were Taft's Fifth New York Independent Light Artillery and Gaston's Thirty-Second New York Independent Light Artillery. The distance from those guns to where Gordon's units were becoming visible was over three thousand yards, beyond their effective range but still within their extreme range. The Union batteries opened fire.

When Hoke's assault tumbled back, the First North Carolina Sharpshooters on the brigade's flank became isolated. Major Wharton pushed his battalion through a dense thicket, which caused it to lose cohesion by the time its men found the Union line. The waiting Federals, under no pressure from their front, directed their fire into the riflemen emerging from the trees and wounded twenty of their number. Unable to do anything useful, Wharton withdrew back into the woods, with Mr. Lyon still among them.[56]

From Lee's Hill, Early could see Anderson's units halted well short of the Plank Road. His own attack had penetrated the Union line but then faltered. The division commander descended the hill and rode on to the battlefield as Hays and Avery fell back. He helped to reform the shattered brigades and ordered Smith to send him the Forty-Ninth and Fifty-Second Virginia Regiments as reinforcement. Those units had not made serious contact during their attack earlier that day and presumably remained ready for action.[57]

Early's attack had dented the Union position, but reinforcements from Newton had bolstered the enemy line. To launch his division into another attack, the Virginian decided to move his troops around to his right, where Gordon's Brigade could provide support. The North Carolina and Louisiana regiments rallied, reformed, and then faced right to push around the edge of the hill, where the Union line turned north from the Plank Road. The ground in front of the Federal far left was cut by ravines, which attacking infantry would be able to use to advance under cover. Once in position to exploit the terrain, the regiments moving by the right flank could halt, face left, and immediately advance.[58]

Neill's brigade constituted Howe's first line of defense. Its right occupied a hill just west of Smith Run, where the Forty-Ninth New York and part of the Seventh Maine had helped repulse the Confederate attack that morning. The rest of the brigade line extended to the north, east of Smith Run. Grant's Vermont Brigade held the second line, extending along a series of hills west of the waterway. His Fifth Vermont, however, still held the end of the Plank Road line just south of that road.[59]

East of Smith Run, the Thirty-Third New York and the Twenty-First New Jersey deployed on a broad hilltop with the rest of the Seventh Maine. They were screened by a skirmish line made up of the Twentieth New York. Neill's overall position would have been stronger if he could have established a cohesive line extending to Fall Hill, but the paucity of men available required General Howe to focus on holding a series of hills and being ready to adapt as any Confederate attack developed. A soldier in the Thirty-Third New York described how the "regiment was thrown forward as a forlorn hope, trusting that by desperate fighting we might hold the enemy in check until the left could be strengthened."[60]

In his official report Sedgwick described the left end of his line as being attacked in echelon, with Early shifting his formations to his right and continuing the attack. Two of Early's brigades already had tried to break open the Plank Road front. When that assault had failed, they regrouped and hustled around the hills east of Smith Run to renew their attack, this time against Neill's line. The Federals thus had to continually change front to prevent a breakthrough.[61]

The Louisiana and North Carolina veterans first tangled with the skirmishers of the Twentieth New York, a nine-month regiment led by Col. Ernst von Vegesack, a Swedish officer come to fight in the American war. Neill had only another nine-month regiment, the Twenty-First New Jersey, to call on if the shaky New Yorkers needed help. The Forty-Ninth New York remained out of reach on the other side of Smith Run, holding the shoulder of the hill just north of the Plank Road. The Seventy-Seventh New York anchored the north end of his line across Smith Run on the next hill over, separated by a ravine from the hilltop held by the Thirty-Third New York and Seventh Maine.[62]

Neill had too few troops for his position to be tenable. The hilly ground he occupied provided too many places where Confederate formations could get through. The best he could do would be to hold long enough for Grant's brigade to consolidate a better defensive line on the west side of the waterway. The Confederate advance pushing up against the New York skirmishers quickly found the gap between the Thirty-Third New York–Seventh Maine position and the Seventy-Seventh New York to their left. As firing rippled along the line, von Vegesack fell wounded, and his Twentieth New York began to waiver.[63]

With no other option, Neill directed Col. J. Gilliam Van Houten to meet the Confederate advance with his Twenty-First New Jersey. Van Houten ordered his men to fix bayonets, the distinctive rattle of steel on steel echoing down the line. As the regiment pressed on, a horrified staff officer watched as it "smashed itself to pieces against ten times its numbers." The crash of musketry rose to a crescendo, and Van Houten dropped wounded, his leg shattered by a Minié ball.[64]

Under the pressure exerted by the Confederate advance, the wobbly Twentieth New York skirmishers gave way. The broken troops fell back through the Thirty-Third New York and Seventh Maine. Trying to stem the retreat, Capt. Henry F. Hill of the Seventh Maine shot one of the Twentieth New York men dead. This panicked attempt to impose discipline had little effect, and the Union line continued to unravel. The Thirty-Third New York and the rump Seventh Maine sustained a rapid fire, but Confederate forces were curling around them. Major Hyde of the Seventh Maine looked around his regiment's position and saw where "near a hundred of the poor fellows lay in their blood."[65]

The New Yorkers and the Mainers kept shooting but faced new dangers in getting away. A fence behind the battle line remained standing, and men trying to get over it rather than through it became ready targets. Rallying his brigade, Neill escaped being hit, but his horse did not. The wounded mount fell and slammed the general to the ground, leaving him momentarily stunned. Col. Robert F. Taylor of the Thirty-Third New York took temporary command of the brigade and rallied a new line with the help of officers from the Seventh Maine.[66]

North of the ravine, where the Twenty-First New Jersey had been halted, the Seventy-Seventh New York anchored the end of Neill's line. The Confederate attack lapped up against this unit but did not push too hard. The Southerners also had their limits. Still, the Seventy-Seventh fell back through the woods when the Thirty-Third New York and Seventh Maine retreated. As one of the Maine soldiers put it, "Three regiments could not hold the ground which should have been occupied by a whole Division."[67]

During the retreat, many injured Federals were left behind. Hungry and footsore Confederates often looked for food, shoes, and greenbacks on the bodies they encountered, friend or foe. A soldier from the Thirty-Third New York had been knocked down by a bullet that penetrated his belt and clothes but not his skin. Temporarily stunned and unable to move, he described the experience of being looted: "The next thing I knew, two fellows in grey clothes were rolling me over and exploring my wounds and pockets at the same time."[68]

With the collapse of Neill's line, the Federals on the west side of Smith Run prepared for an onslaught. Captain Rigby had his Maryland Light Artillery in battery on a hilltop north of the Plank Road. Colonel Barney deployed his Sixth Vermont to the left of the Maryland guns. Col. Thomas Seaver's Third Vermont stood to the right of the battery, extending toward the Plank Road. Lieutenant Colonel Lewis pulled his Fifth Vermont away from the Plank Road and skirted around Rigby's guns to find another position in the brigade line.[69]

Neill had lost hundreds of men killed, wounded, and captured, but the Confederates were still coming. Major Hyde thought to warn Rigby that his battery was about to be overrun, fearing that the battle smoke hid its imminent danger. The smoke also obscured the staff officer, however, who foolishly approached the battery from the front. Luckily, the gunners saw him riding into the muzzles of their weapons, and Hyde belatedly realized he had spent a few moments on the edge of oblivion.[70]

Grant tried to slow the Southerners as his Vermonters solidified their line. The Twenty-Sixth New Jersey held a position on the left, on the shoulder of a hill overlooking a tributary to Smith Run. It was arrayed, as one of its members later wrote, "in a depression along a ditch dug by a farmer to drain his land." As Neill's units were forced back, Grant ordered the Twenty-Sixth to push down into the ravine. He did not expect to restore Neill's line, but he needed the Jersey men to delay the Confederates until his brigade could better establish its position.[71]

Lt. Col. Edward Martindale advanced his Twenty-Sixth New Jersey down the stream valley, described by one soldier as a "deep hollow covered with trees, mostly low pine." Colonel Walbridge slid his Second Vermont to the left to fill the gap where the regiment had been. In turn, Seaver moved the Third Vermont to its left to fill the position vacated by the Second Vermont. One soldier described their swift redeployment: "'Attention, left face, forward, double quick!' and away we went, perhaps three times the length of the regiment, halted and came to the front." The Vermonters became engaged almost immediately.[72]

While the Thirty-Third New York and Seventh Maine had struggled to hold Neill's line, the Twentieth New York streamed to the rear. Grant's regiments tried to corral some of the fleeing men to add to their firepower. One of the New Yorkers ordered to lie down in the second line of a Vermont regiment accidentally fired his weapon. The bullet passed between the ground and the soldier lying flat in front of him. No one was hurt, but the Vermont men thought it safer "to let the skedaddlers run."[73]

Neill's other units succumbed to the relentless Southern assault but did not panic. The Seventh Maine and Thirty-Third New York filtered back through the line west of Smith Run and rallied. A Mainer recounted how they "reformed the brigade while the Vermont Brigade attended to the enemy." While Neill's regiments moved back, the Fifth Wisconsin and Sixty-First Pennsylvania of the Light Division moved up from the west.[74]

To the right of the Vermont Brigade, Col. Daniel B. Bidwell's Forty-Ninth New York had lost contact with its own brigade (Neill's). When the Confederates fell back from their attack on the Plank Road, the New Yorkers had watched them reform and march by the right flank across their front. When the Southerners attacked the Smith Run line, the Forty-Ninth became exposed. The New Yorkers and the detached company of the Seventh Maine pulled back to some woods, where they held their pursuers in check. The loss of daylight, however, promised new challenges.[75]

As Neill's line collapsed, Lieutenant Butler's Battery G, Second US Artillery arrived from the Union right. Traveling along the Plank Road past the Guest house, the battery had turned on to a road angling off to the north and followed it through the woods to an open area along Smith Run. Emerging from the trees, Butler saw where he could bring his six 12-pounder Napoleons into battery, about two hundred yards from where Rigby's battery was keeping up a steady fire from a hilltop position.[76]

The newly arrived field guns were excellent weapons for stopping infantry. Confederate troops were visible across the stream, and the Regulars dropped trail and opened fire with spherical case shot. The guns, however, had begun shooting without an adequate understanding of the battleground. A sergeant from the Third Vermont came up to the battery to warn that their rounds were cutting into friendly infantry. Butler adjusted his fire but still put nearby Federals in danger. A lieutenant colonel directed the artillerymen to wait until the Third Vermont could get clear of their target area.[77]

A few hundred yards to Butler's left, Lieutenant Martin had two sections of his Battery F, Fifth US Artillery in place. Lt. Charles R. Hickox had charge of two 10-pounder Parrott rifles and Lt. Alexander J. McDonald commanded two 12-pounder Napoleons. The Napoleons were the better weapons for close-in fighting and had kept up a sustained covering fire. That section was close to depleting its ammunition, though. Colonel Grant needed Butler to get his guns into action before Martin pulled away.[78]

The Twenty-Sixth New Jersey advanced across the front of the Vermont units on the west side of Smith Run as the Confederates closed in. The Second Vermont hustled to fill the gap in the line left by the Jersey men. Once in place, the Granite State men opened fire using a new type of waterproof cartridge that minimized misfires. One of the Vermont men observed how they "could not see the end of our rifles through the smoke."[79]

Southerners poured across the ground being relinquished by Neill's brigade. When the Twenty-Sixth New Jersey cleared the Third Vermont's front, that unit also opened fire, helping the Second Vermont repulse the Confederates who had shoved aside the Twenty-First New Jersey. The Third Vermont then moved to the left of Butler's Battery G, Second US Artillery, finally giving his 12-pounder Napoleons an unobstructed field of fire.[80]

Lt. Col. Samuel E. Pingree of the Third Vermont described the action:

As soon as our first lines had broken and got out of the way our cannon opened in splendid style, in good grape and canister range. The infantry held fire. Each discharge of the Napoleon battery knocked their columns open, but they gathered in and moved on. Their steadiness was the admiration of all of us. As they gained the little valley before us our line opened.... Our position was the best possible; theirs the worst possible. We were losing at the rate of hundreds a minute, the enemy more.[81]

The Twenty-Sixth New Jersey pressed on as bravely as any veteran unit, but its senior leadership did not have the experience to overcome the developing situation. Martindale saw where the Forty-Ninth New York had pulled back its left wing to take advantage of the terrain but had thereby created a gap in the line. He could not come up with the appropriate tactical response, however, and issued orders that momentarily confused his troops.[82]

Oncoming Confederates blasted through the misdirected Twenty-Sixth New Jersey, which broke to its right. Some of them rallied under their own officers; others found places with Vermont regiments. Part of the Sixth Vermont, for instance, occupied the sunken lane that Butler's artillery had used to get into position. The Vermonters there called out, "Rally on us, boys," and about two dozen Jersey men dropped down beside them.[83]

Not all of the retreating troops had the presence of mind to slip back through infantry units. Some of them ran back through the Maryland battery's field of fire, with tragic results: "The captain rushed out in front and swung his saber and shouted to them to turn to the right, or left, so as to give him a chance to fire, without firing through them, but they paid no attention, and finally he dropped back and gave the order to fire. I have no doubt that many of the Jersey men were killed here by our own fire."[84]

The relentless Confederate attackers sought a weak point to tear open the defending line. The gap between the Second Vermont and Fourth Vermont held promise, as the terrain along a tributary stream separated those

Facing page: **Map 20.** Federals Flanked at Smith Run. Hays and Hoke overwhelmed Neill's line east of Smith Run and moved toward Grant's line west of the stream. The Twenty-Sixth New Jersey moved up to support Neill but was shattered by the Confederate onslaught. The Second Vermont moved over to fill in the gap where the Twenty-Sixth had been, and the Third Vermont moved over to fill in where the Second had been. The Fifth Vermont abandoned the Plank Road line to stabilize the Vermont brigade's left flank. A Federal counterattack later pushed back Hays and Hoke, but Gordon continued north to outflank the Union line.

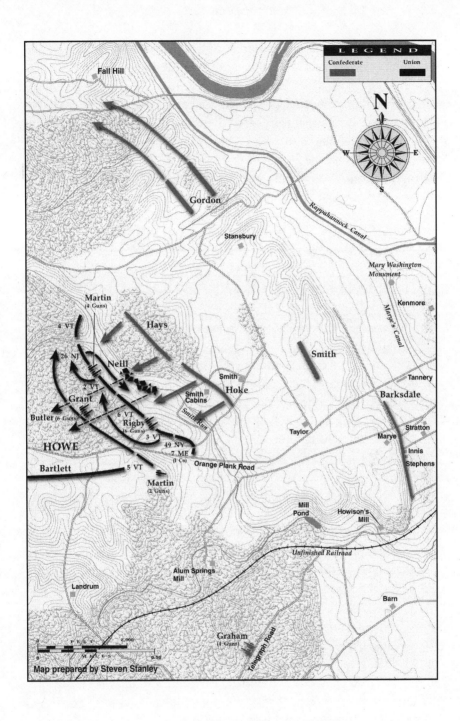

two regiments by about two hundred yards. It is not clear which Southern regiments probed Neill's line, but reports of captured prisoners indicate that both Louisiana and North Carolina units moved across the stream.[85]

The Fourth Vermont had positioned itself on the shoulder of a hill north of Smith Run. Its commander, Col. Charles B. Stoughton, observed the Confederates approaching at an angle. When he pulled back his right wing and opened fire, some of the flagging attackers rushed forward to gain shelter in defilade. Another Southern force appeared to their right, pushing up against the Third and Second Vermont. The Fifth Vermont moved up behind them to provide support, but the two regiments held their own. Lewis and his Fifth Vermont continued across the small branch to reinforce the Fourth Vermont instead.[86]

Two units from Colonel Burnham's Light Division also moved up to support Howe's line. Dawson's Sixty-First Pennsylvania and Allen's Fifth Wisconsin moved into position behind the Fourth Vermont as the fighting became intense. Confederate Minié balls ripped through them before they were able to lie down. Eighteen Wisconsin men fell wounded; the record is not clear on casualties suffered by the Sixty-First Pennsylvania.[87]

Stoughton's Fourth Vermont brought the Confederate advance in his sector to a halt. The Fifth Vermont moved across the ridge to the left of the Fourth, spreading out to anchor the brigade's flank, but the Confederate assault had reached its limit. Grant's brigade had been pressed but not driven. The colonel later wrote, "At this time the enemy had a large force in front of our entire line, attempting with desperate vigor to force or turn it; but the Vermont regiments remained firm and unbroken, closely hugging the crest and literally presenting a wall of fire."[88]

The weak end of the Federal line appeared to be along the Plank Road, where both the Fifth and Third Vermont had disconnected from Bartlett's brigade facing south. The Sixth Vermont, however, remained intact on the left of Rigby's Maryland battery, protected by a swell of ground. Colonel Barney, commanding the regiment, wore a black raincoat, and a soldier noted that it gave him the appearance of a Methodist preacher. The veteran troops gauged how close the Confederates were by the fuze settings called out by the gunners. Orders came for two-second fuzes, then one second, then a half second. As the Southerners closed in, a young New Jersey officer thought he needed to see what was going on and cautiously rose up to take a look. A bullet smashed into his head.[89]

Rigby's outgoing fire had become compromised by the confused mass of retreating infantry around his battery position. When the Confederates were within eighty yards, he ordered his artillerymen to limber up and get away. One set of horses bolted, taking a limber with them. The Marylanders quickly hooked up their other weapons and rushed them through openings cut into a brush fence. One of the artillerymen called out to the Vermont infantry, "Stand fast, boys, you are our only hope now."[90]

The Confederates pressed on, pulling down their hats to block the setting sun in their eyes. The remaining gun crew prepared to haul its weapon off by hand. Rigby grabbed retreating infantrymen to help with that desperate task, striking the scared men with the flat of his sword to keep them focused. By the time they unwound the prolong, a stout rope attached to the gun carriage, the Confederates were upon them, calling out: "Hold on. Hold on, boys. You are too late."[91]

The Maryland artillerymen used their rammers and other battery equipment to dispute the Southern claim to the gun. A Sergeant Cummings of the Twenty-Sixth New Jersey rallied some infantrymen to fight hand to hand with clubbed muskets against the Confederates swarming the gun. Some of the Sixth Vermont men to their left shot into the approaching attackers. With the enemy assault upon them, Barney shouted to his regiment: "Up and fire boys! Charge!" A Vermont soldier described how they "waited until the enemy were within twenty feet of our guns, then rose, fired and at once charged with level bayonets."[92]

The Confederates had endured more than an hour of combat since climbing out of the Hazel Run valley. When the Sixth Vermont and remnants of the Twenty-Sixth New Jersey counterattacked, the Southern formations broke and reeled back across the ground they had just paid for in blood. The Federals drove them back across Smith Run to the hill where Neill's line had been. They captured men from the Seventh, Eighth, and Ninth Louisiana as well as from the Twenty-First, Fifty-Fourth, and Fifty-Seventh North Carolina. The counterattack also freed some Twenty-Sixth New Jersey soldiers who had been captured just minutes earlier.[93]

Colonel Grant would report that his brigade captured more than one thousand prisoners, including two dozen line officers. Among the Confederate officers taken were Col. Leroy A. Stafford and Maj. Henry L. N. Williams of the Ninth Louisiana. Lieutenant Colonel Lewis of the Eighth Louisiana also became a prisoner, along with Maj. Aleibiades DeBlanc. From the Seventh

Louisiana, Lt. Col. Thomas M. Terry became a captive. A single Union regiment, however, could not bring off so many prisoners, and large numbers of them slipped away as darkness descended. In the end the Sixth Vermont reported a prisoner count of 237 enlisted men and twenty officers.[94]

While many would-be prisoners avoided a trip to a Northern stockade, the counterattack devastated the Confederate formations. A Vermont officer boasted in a letter, "The Colonel and I, and many of the line officers now wear rebel swords." A Vermont soldier wrote, "Some of our prisoners say they never saw men come out of the ground before." In the abandoned battery position, Rigby's artillerymen used the prolong to pull their last gun off the hilltop. About two hundred yards to the rear, they came upon the limber with the wayward horses, which were standing patiently in their harnesses. The sweating men gladly relinquished their burden.[95]

The Union counterattack effectively ended the fighting along Smith Run, but only the Sixth Vermont, with some of its Twenty-Sixth New Jersey comrades, had advanced. They now found themselves where Neill's line had been, far in front of Grant's line. No organized Confederate resistance appeared evident, and some of the troops thought the rest of the brigade should move up so they could hold the position. Colonel Barney even pushed out a skirmish line.[96]

Hays's and Hoke's Brigades had been torn apart by both artillery and small-arms fire, but Gordon's Brigade remained intact. As the sun dropped toward the horizon, the Georgians moved around the flank of the overextended Vermont line. Federal guns on Falmouth heights tried to cover the gap between the Vermont Brigade and the river, but Grant could see the Confederates were getting around his flank. His entire line needed to pull back or risk capture, so he recalled the Sixth Vermont from its advanced position. Recrossing Smith Run, one of the men noted, "The ground was covered with one commingled mass of rebel knapsacks, haversacks, canteens, muskets and equipment, besides the dead and dying."[97]

Gordon's regiments maintained their lines of battle as they marched by the right flank past the fighting at Smith Run. Half of the Georgia units moved between the Rappahannock Canal and the line of hills upon which the Stansbury house (Snowden) stands. The other half pressed forward across the ground between the house and the hills where Neill's line had been overrun.[98]

In front of Gordon's columns, skirmishers trotted across the terrain, firing occasionally at Union soldiers in their path. At Fall Hill the men eagerly headed into the shelter of a ravine, finally putting them beyond observation of the Union gunners at Falmouth. Gordon gave his troops time to catch their breath and to ensure they would head in the right direction in the gathering darkness. He then exhorted them to clear the woods to their front of Yankees.[99]

The Georgians pressed on "with yells and whoops that almost shook the earth." In the gathering gloom they clawed their way through tangled undergrowth in the sheltering ravines. They were no longer taking fire from across the river but moving toward Union skirmishers on the uplands. Advancing toward muzzle flashes, Gordon's men saw artillery awaiting them as they emerged onto the hilltop. As darkness enveloped them, soldiers from both sides guided their movements by the momentary flashes of light that accompanied cannon fire.[100]

With Gordon threatening the Federal left, some of the more steadfast Louisiana and North Carolina troops rallied. First Sgt. Luke W. Kendall of the Fourth Vermont underscored the urgency of their retreat when he wrote a family about the death of their son Henry Bush: "He was killed Monday night, shot through the body near the heart. He never spoke after he was hit and as we were drove from the field we had no chance to bury him. The rebs occupied the ground in less than 15 minutes after he was shot."[101]

The Vermonters regrouped briefly at a house and barn about three-quarters of a mile from the Smith Run line. It belonged to another family named Downman, not to be confused with the Downman house Idlewild south of the Plank Road. Some of the Twenty-First New Jersey men had brought their wounded Colonel Van Houten there. Without medical attention he was not doing well, and Sgt. Maj. George W. Fielder volunteered to stay behind to care for him. Other wounded men carried back from the Smith Run line were made as comfortable as possible before their unhurt comrades continued on.[102]

Pursuing Confederates were not far behind, and the Federals who remained at the Downman place became prisoners. The Vermont units took position on Fall Hill, where the embankment along River Road provided some semblance of protection on the flat upland terrain. The Twenty-Sixth New Jersey also arrived there in good order. The Vermont veterans were impressed enough to note that their New Jersey comrades "left the conflict a victorious and compact regiment."[103]

The Eighth Pennsylvania Cavalry had formed a reserve line behind the Vermont Brigade but had not been needed. Rigby had already retreated, and Butler received orders to get his Regular Army battery to River Road. The Confederates briefly pressed Martin's two sections on the left of the Smith Run line. The Federal artillery met this last push with a few rounds of grapeshot before limbering up and pulling back.[104]

Forming on River Road, the Sixth Vermont extended across the uplands to the bluffs overlooking the Rappahannock. The left end of Sedgwick's line was now finally anchored on the river as Gordon's Georgians came up onto Fall Hill. Some of the artillery from the Smith Run line took position on River Road. Butler's US battery dropped trail on either side of the road that descended from the uplands to where the pontoon bridges were floating.[105]

At the Plank Road the Forty-Ninth New York and a company of the Seventh Maine had rallied inside a tree line and used that cover to hold back pursuing Confederates. When the rest of their division pulled back as the sun disappeared, they were left very much on their own. Straining their eyes and ears, the men heard sticks breaking as the Confederates tried to move up stealthily in the dark. Capt. Thomas Cluney passed the word for his troops to wait for orders and then called out: "First Battalion! Ready! Fire!" About one hundred men let loose a volley, but the captain's noisy commands suggested a much larger Union force. The contingent of Seventh Maine troops and the Forty-Ninth New York had little ammunition and no orders. A replying volley of musketry passed over their heads, convincing them to head toward the river.[106]

The rest of Neill's brigade had worked its way back to River Road. One New York soldier remembered that "though no panic prevailed, there was the utmost confusion." Rumors spread that Confederate artillery had destroyed the pontoon bridges, and some tired men considered sitting down to rest and await capture. Military discipline, however, kept most going.[107]

When Gordon's regiments reached the uplands, a battery opened fire. A Vermont infantrymen likened the sound of grapeshot striking trees to "pebbles against the side of a building." Exposed to artillery in their front, a member of the Sixtieth Georgia described how they ended their day: "They throwd Grape shot & Canister & shells among us. I don't think ther Batterys was 300 yards from us But it was so dark we had no Chance to Charge it so we just laid as flat to the ground as ever you saw a flying squirrel lay to a tree. . . . [T]her was sevrl men's heads tore off."[108]

Gordon could not be sure what lay ahead and had his troops lie down on the edge of the woods. In the period of dark between sunset and moonrise, the Federal battery withdrew. The rumble of iron-bound wheels on the hard-packed roadway carried to the waiting Confederates, and Gordon directed the Thirty-Eighth Georgia to investigate. The soldiers pressed forward to the abandoned battery position, then halted.[109]

Throughout the campaign there had been a consistent undercurrent of Hooker's disdain for his Sixth Corps commander. Sedgwick did not move quickly enough. He faced only minimal opposition. He had not reached Chancellorsville. Hooker even fingered Sedgwick as the man responsible for his defeat. Shortly after sunset Chief of Staff Butterfield relayed a message to Sedgwick: "The general directs a full report of your position, the number of the enemy's forces opposed to you, and your dispositions. He wishes this report as soon as possible, that he may act advisedly." Hooker's assistant adjutant general, Brig. Gen. Seth Williams, reported from Sedgwick's front that small-arms fire had diminished as daylight faded, but artillery fire remained heavy. He also noted that the battle smoke was too thick for signal officers to be able to see anything.[110]

For his part Sedgwick did not have the time to respond to Hooker's message. Fighting may have ended along Smith Run, but the onset of night provided cover for Confederate forces to push forward again. An almost full moon would rise at 8:38 P.M., leaving about an hour of absolute darkness for the Southerners to advance into the Union positions that had repulsed them in daylight.[111]

ELEVEN

MAY 4-5

RETREAT TO BANKS' FORD

The fighting along Smith Run had lasted until Gordon's Brigade coiled around the north end of the Union line and made it untenable. The moonless period between sunset and moonrise would be the best time to pull away, as articulated by a Vermont soldier: "Darkness was what we loved this night, not because our deeds were evil, but because it would hide our movements from the rebels."[1] Moving about without being able to see anything, however, sometimes resulted in opposing forces stumbling upon one another. A New York soldier described how "the rebels came so close upon us, or we upon them, they could not tell whether we were friends of foes."[2]

When the time came, retreating troops would need to move to the Guest house and then take one of two roads leading north to the river crossing. The first usable way ran through a farm marked on various maps as Alsop, Donnegan, and even Downman. The other was the Banks' Ford Road (modern Bragg Road), which became the most heavily used route that night. Russell's brigade drew the task of covering the intersection of the Orange Plank Road and the Banks' Ford Road. Newton bolstered that critical position with the Thirty-Sixth New York and the Thirty-Seventh Massachusetts of Eustis's brigade. This combined force would hold the crossroads open while the rest of the Sixth Corps got clear.[3]

Bartlett's brigade had blunted the Confederate attacks on the Plank Road line, but men prepared to depart when Howe's units pulled back from Smith

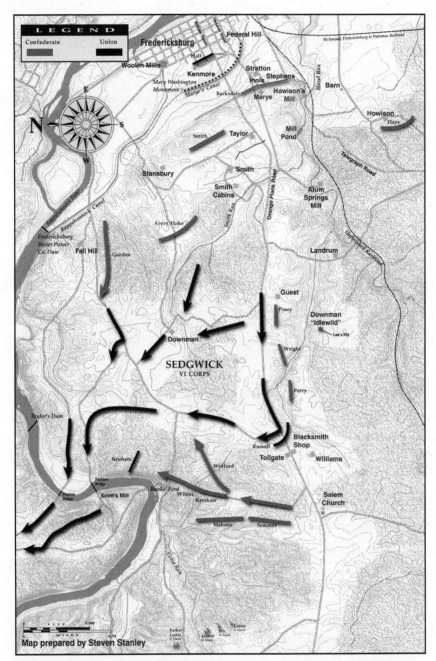

Map 21. Banks' Ford. During the night of May 4–5, the Sixth Corps withdrew to pontoon bridges downstream from Banks' Ford. Howe's two brigades at Smith Run pulled back cross-country. Brooks and Newton were able to use the roadways. Confederate artillery on Smith Hill blindly bombarded the pontoon bridges throughout the night.

Run. The Twenty-Seventh New York, Col. Alexander D. Adams commanding, was the farthest out, constituting a skirmish line. As those men peered into the enveloping darkness, Col. Joel Seaver sent out two companies of his Sixteenth New York to give the skirmish line more weight.[4]

Farther west, Colonel Edwards's Fifth Maine had moved over to support Lieutenant Parsons's Battery A, First New Jersey Light Artillery. Just over 200 Maine infantrymen pushed out as skirmishers, their unit having started the campaign with 320 soldiers. Pvt. William H. Morse described how "the rebs advanced so near that we could hear them swearing." The wait proved nerve wracking, but at long last orders came for them to pull back.[5]

The New York skirmishers, to the left of the Fifth Maine, also received orders to pull back. Rather than trying to depart silently and hope the Confederates did not rush them, the New Yorkers fired into the night and reloaded as they filtered back through another line behind them. Once the next line had a clear field of fire, the waiting men also fired a volley and withdrew in turn. On the Plank Road only Major Lessig's Ninety-Sixth Pennsylvania remained in position along the brigade line. Around 7:00 P.M., with the skirmishers in, the Keystone State men also joined the retreat.[6]

Seaver deployed his Sixteenth New York in the brigade line above the crossing, then rode back to the Plank Road to look for his detached skirmishers. Amid scores of retreating troops, he called out, "Where are my men." A voice in the darkness quietly responded, "Here, Colonel." Reassured, Seaver warned the assembled soldiers that the brigade had pulled back and that they needed to get out of there quickly. Some of the tired men dropped their knapsacks, unwilling to risk capture for a week's worth of rations and a change of underwear.[7]

Sedgwick departed his Guest house headquarters as the sun dropped to the horizon. He could hear the fighting on Howe's front when he stopped to talk to Captain Cowan and the men of the First Battery, New York Independent Light Artillery. The general told them they would need to provide cover for General Brooks as his division marched west to the Banks' Ford Road. To Cowan's left Lieutenant Harn's Third Battery, New York Independent Light Artillery would also remain in place until the infantry had passed.[8]

Major Tompkins made sure his other batteries retreated immediately. He pulled McCartney's First Massachusetts Light Artillery back from the Williams house knoll. With the loss of daylight, that exposed site could not be maintained without infantry. Tompkins also directed Lieutenant Williston to pull his Battery D, Second US Artillery out of the line. Both units were to make their way to the Banks' Ford bridges.[9]

After their hair-raising escape at Smith Run, Captain Rigby reported to Major Tompkins with his Battery A, Maryland Light Artillery. Newton's artillery chief placed the tired Marylanders north of the Plank Road in front of a grove of trees opposite the Guest house. From that vantage point they too would cover the roads and fields to the south as Brooks's units pulled away.[10]

In the darkness Cowan heard Confederates to the left of his New York battery, possibly infiltrating into the area behind them. The Forty-Ninth Pennsylvania Infantry to their front also heard distant firing, seemingly behind them. Lt. Col. Thomas M. Hulings sought to reassure his Pennsylvania troops while they awaited orders to withdraw, but something triggered a volley. A soldier described the result: "It is quite dark, and the skirmish line is a sheet of fire, and we see by the flash that our men are falling back."[11]

What the Federals could see, the approaching Confederates could see also. Hulings assigned a dozen men to hold their position while the skirmish line fell back. The dozen soldiers had their knapsacks on, ready to get away quickly. When the Confederates were within fifty yards, the skirmish line peeled away. After a few agonizing minutes, two officers rode back to order the twelve-man detachment back. The Confederates rushed forward with a shout, and the dozen Pennsylvanians took off running.[12]

With no infantry in his front, Cowan's gun crews discharged their weapons from right to left. As each gun fired in turn, its crew limbered up and moved out to the right, heading west on the Plank Road. An artilleryman remembered, "Before the shell from the left piece had reached the point aimed at, the entire battery was on the road to Banks' Ford." The other Union batteries on the Plank Road also pulled back without losing a gun or any battery equipment. The Plank Road line soon stood entirely abandoned.[13]

Colonel Buck's New Jersey brigade had held that line on Bartlett's right. The only Confederates they had seen that day were prisoners, described by one New Jersey soldier as "all very saucy and impudent." Once Brooks's units had passed, they too would slip back. While the Federals used the darkness to screen their movements, the Confederates did not. Lt. Edmund D. Halsey of the Fifteenth New Jersey observed, "As we marched along we could hear the rebels yelling in our rear."[14]

General Wheaton held a position north of the Plank Road, where his units had helped repulse Early's first assault. At dark the brigade commander reached into the Sixty-Second New York to establish a forty-five-man picket line south of the Plank Road. Wheaton and his adjutant then rode west to make sure his right regiment tied in with Brooks's left. The two officers did not find anyone. They did, however, hear the rumble of artillery wheels on a road to their north. They also heard distinctly Southern voices carrying across the dark stillness.[15]

Wheaton hastily got his brigade headed toward Banks' Ford, but word did not reach the 102nd Pennsylvania at the end of the line. When Colonel Kinkead found his unit isolated, he tried to contact units on the Plank Road. His patrols found two wounded men where the Sixty-Second New York had been and a New York soldier who had captured a Confederate prisoner. The captive claimed to be from Anderson's Division, which he said hovered nearby with 40,000 troops. The fantastic number likely did not fool anyone, but there were certainly Confederates to their front who had gobbled up the Sixty-Second New York skirmishers.[16]

Kinkead sent a patrol to find an escape route through the forest behind them. The Confederates closing in were moving slowly, taking time to rifle through abandoned knapsacks and joking about what to keep. Unable to wait for the patrol to return, the colonel quietly ordered his 102nd to cross over a fence behind them and make their way north. The Confederates heard sounds and let loose a volley. The Pennsylvanians returned fire and then hustled away, stumbling into swampy ground that slowed their progress. Wheaton rode ahead to determine their destination and found Newton near River Road. The division commander directed him to position his unit in the roadway.[17]

The 102nd Pennsylvania Infantry ran into videttes of the Eighth Pennsylvania Cavalry. Some of the startled horse soldiers opened fire, but the infantrymen shouted out who they were, and the hasty shooting died down. Once Kinkead saw that his troops had begun to reach the gathering Union force on River Road, he rode back into the swamp to guide his other soldiers to safety. Still, nearly one hundred of his men were captured that night.[18]

In the confusion the 102nd Pennsylvania also lost its colors, the only Sixth Corps unit to experience that indignity during the entire campaign. The regiment did not lose its flag to enemy action but to fatigue and inattention. A corporal from the color guard reported that when the regiment came out of the swamp, the flag bearer gave the colors to an Eighth Pennsylvania cavalryman, a fellow Keystone State soldier.[19]

On the uplands above the pontoon bridges, the Ninety-Eighth Pennsylvania and the remainder of the Sixty-Second New York established a defensive position. They were screened by Colonel Collier's 139th Pennsylvania, which had remained behind when the rest of Wheaton's brigade hurried east to reinforce Bartlett's hard-pressed units. They heard troops moving about to their front, so Collier sent a man forward to determine if they were Federals looking for the pontoons. The scout had not returned by daybreak, when the Pennsylvanians pulled back and crossed the river. The man left behind, a fellow named James M. Stevenson, came back six months later as an exchanged prisoner. He dryly reported that the troops in front of them that night had been rebels.[20]

On Newton's line Colonel Eustis had command of a brigade of New York and New England regiments. Unlike Wheaton's units to its left, Eustis's brigade withdrew without firing a shot. The Tenth Massachusetts acted as rear guard, but farthest out were the pickets of the Thirty-Seventh Massachusetts. Eustis and his staff waited in the darkness to ensure their men closest to the enemy got clear. Realizing the Federal line was being evacuated, the Confederates raised a shout and surged forward. The Thirty-Seventh Massachusetts ran for nearly a mile and a half, its disciplined soldiers keeping their heavy knapsacks. The exertion proved too much for one man, though, who dropped dead along the way. When the Northerners gained the shelter of wooded terrain, the Confederates declined to follow them farther.[21]

Colonel Shaler, also commanding a brigade of Newton's division, had positioned his units on the edge of a woods, an open field to their front. The 122nd New York stood on the west side of the road that would take them back to the crossings. The Sixty-Fifth New York took position on Shaler's left. In between were the Sixty-Seventh New York and the Twenty-Third and Eighty-Second Pennsylvania. Shaler brought his units back in successive lines. One of his soldiers remembered "Through all this seeming disorder, there was a great deal of method, and the advance of the rebels was very slow."[22]

The terrain west of Eustis and Shaler consisted of high bluffs overlooking the river. Colonel Burnham had three regiments from his Light Division there to anchor the Sixth Corps's far right. Atop the high bluffs the Sixth Maine constituted the end of the Federal line. The Thirty-First and Forty-Third New York Regiments were to their left. The Fifth Wisconsin and Sixty-First Pennsylvania, sent to reinforce other sectors earlier in the day, had not yet returned.[23]

Under the cover of darkness, Union formations continued to pull back toward the pontoon bridges. The Confederate pursuit proved inconsistent. Anderson's brigades on the Confederate left moved up very cautiously. Posey got his Mississippi brigade up to the Plank Road and halted. Wright's Brigade took position on his left. Perry did not advance his Florida regiments at all. Sometime after 8:30 P.M., when the rising moon illuminated the terrain, Wright pushed beyond the Plank Road. Posey waited until after midnight before moving his brigade over to the Banks' Ford Road but did not advance much farther.[24]

At dark McLaws sought to get his division moving again. After the fighting along Smith Run died down, he could hear the rumble of wagon wheels on a pontoon bridge. After a frustrating day of losses on his own front, McLaws put Wofford's and Kershaw's Brigades into motion. They had been held up in their late-afternoon advance by a punishing artillery fire but pressed forward again under the cover of night before the moon rose. Unlike Anderson's units to their right, McLaws's two brigades continued beyond the Plank Road.[25]

From Kershaw's Brigade, Col. John D. Kennedy pushed his Second South Carolina through a thicket of pines that one of his soldiers thought to be as "dark as Egypt." They did not know if anyone stood in their way, so Kennedy ordered his men to fire a volley. A lieutenant colonel and over one hundred Union troops immediately surrendered. Emboldened by their initial success, the Confederates continued forward, moving northeast of a tributary that flows west to Golin Run. Near the road to Banks' Ford, Federal cavalry dashed in among them, causing a flurry of shooting and a pause in the Confederate advance.[26]

On the Plank Road General Kershaw rode west to the tollgate, where Federal artillery had blasted away at the Confederates earlier in the day. There were no dead horses or broken artillery equipment there, as might have been the case if the Confederate counterbattery fire had been anything other than negligible. The brigade commander asked Kennedy to send a detachment to contact whatever unit from Anderson's Division was on their right. The colonel directed Lt. R. S. Brown to take ten men east on the Plank Road to establish contact between the two divisions.[27]

General Lee and his staff followed behind Major Generals Anderson and McLaws and set up headquarters in the empty Downman house. Without experienced corps commanders on the field, Lee had been coordinating the late-afternoon attack himself. From Idlewild he continued to monitor some of the night's operations. He informed McLaws that Early had met with success against the Union left flank and his units were pressing the Union perimeter from the east. Lee ordered McLaws to press the Federals from the south.[28]

Kershaw reported back to McLaws that he was on the Plank Road. General Wilcox joined him there. Capt. G. B. Lamar, from McLaws' staff, found them and delivered new orders. They were to seize the redoubts overlooking Banks' Ford and bring up artillery to shell the massed Union troops retreating toward the pontoon bridges. Wilcox sent forward Lieutenant Colonel Herbert's Eighth Alabama. By then the moon had made its appearance, as described by Lt. Edgar P. Alexander of the Second New Jersey: "The moon rose at eight and a half or thereabouts and looks down mournfully upon the still disputed ground."[29]

Herbert deployed his regiment between Embrey Mill, on Golin Run, and the Banks' Ford Road, then his troops advanced toward the river. The tangled secondary growth broke up their formation, and the men became increasingly noisy as they moved forward. Luckily, the Federals in front of them were scattered and unorganized, more intent on finding a way across the Rappahannock than seeking to hold a line. The Eighth Alabama captured scores of these stragglers in their push toward River Road.[30]

The Alabamans captured so many prisoners that they needed the entire regiment to get them away from the front lines. After gathering them together near the river, the Southerners marched their captives back to Salem Church. The long column of blue-clad prisoners and their Eighth Alabama escorts encountered the rest of Wilcox's Brigade on the east side of the Banks' Ford Road, moving forward in battle formation. Back at the church the Southerners counted their prisoners and found they had gathered in 1,020 men.[31]

The rest of Wilcox's Brigade advanced cautiously, taking over an hour to advance from the Plank Road to the high ground south of River Road. Kershaw followed in its wake, moving up his Third, Seventh, and Fifteenth South Carolina Regiments. Wilcox realized there were Federals about three hundred yards in front of them, and he suggested to Kershaw that they wait for artillery before proceeding farther. Kershaw agreed, and Wilcox directed Captain Manly to bring up his North Carolina battery. The Tar Heel artillerymen soon dropped trail on the high ground south of River Road. Having been able to replenish ammunition chests, they now shelled the woods that Wilcox identified for them. After half an hour the Alabama and South Carolina units pressed forward. The time was close to 11:00 P.M.[32]

On the bluffs overlooking Banks' Ford, the Sixth Maine knew the Confederates were closing in. Lt. Col. Benjamin F. Harris and his adjutant, Lt. Charles A. Clark, heard muffled voices and the soft rattle of arms and equipment to their left, where the Thirty-First and Forty-Third New York were in position. The Light Division regiments had become exposed when the unit on their left pulled back, and the Confederates had found that opening. Looking into the bright moonlight from the edge of the woods, the two Maine officers saw Confederate troops swarming into the line and hustling away several companies of New Yorkers as prisoners.[33]

The Thirty-First New York had engendered ill feelings on May 3 when it went to ground during the attack on Marye's Heights. It and the Forty-Third New York both endured the loss of prisoners that night. Apparently the men were simply worn out from hunger and lack of sleep, having been obliged to leave their knapsacks in Fredericksburg the day before, which left them without rations for nearly two days. As Harris and Clark watched, the Southerners also looked to be forming up for an attack on their own regiment. The two officers quickly realigned their troops to meet the approaching danger.[34]

Alabama and South Carolina men from Wilcox's and Kershaw's Brigades had captured thirteen officers and nearly two hundred New York men without firing a shot. They now unleashed a volley at the Sixth Maine. The Federals responded in kind, and the two sides exchanged fire for nearly a quarter of an hour. The woods, the moonlight, and the shadows made for a confusing battleground. Harris decided he needed to get instructions from Burnham and rode toward the pontoon crossing. He just missed being captured by the Confederates working their way around the regiment's left.[35]

The Sixth Maine's leadership had been decimated in front of Marye's Heights. The surviving officers in the chain of command were good men but hesitated to step up and take charge of the regiment in Harris's absence. With the enemy closing in, the situation became urgent. Clark, as the adjutant, took control. When a Southern voice from the darkness demanded their surrender, the lieutenant roared back in defiance. He then quickly called the company commanders together and informed them that he would lead them out.[36]

Marching along the top of the bluff was the most direct to get to the pontoon crossing. It was the way Lieutenant Colonel Harris had gone, but as Clark formed up the nervous troops, he began to suspect that Confederate infantry now blocked the way. He needed another plan quickly. As he later described it, "I rode along the line, cautioned the men to maintain perfect silence and not rattle their canteens or accouterments [sic], then left facing the regiment I led them over the bluff."[37]

The terrain in this area is precipitous, and a person needs to hang on to trees and bushes to descend to the river. Clark tried to go down on horseback, but his mount lost its footing and both horse and rider fell. The young adjutant got caught in the branches of a tree. He climbed down and made his way to the bottom, where he found his horse waiting for him. Clark described how the other Maine men "came over the bluff helter-skelter, but as silent as possible." Behind them the Confederates attacked an empty position. Their rifle fire covered the inevitable noise of the Union infantrymen scrambling down the bluff. At the river the Sixth Maine gathered in the shelter of deep shadows and filtered downstream toward the bridges.[38]

At the Scott's Ferry site, Colonel Burnham waited for his scattered units. The Fifth Wisconsin and Sixty-First Pennsylvania, detached to reinforce Howe, were not yet back. His old regiment, the Sixth Maine, may well have been captured like substantial portions of the Thirty-First and Forty-Third New York had been. Back in 1861 Burnham had turned a rough bunch of lumberjacks and laborers into the solid soldiers comprising the Sixth Maine Infantry. He had then led his troops through battles on the Peninsula, at Antietam, and around Fredericksburg. When he was a boy, his drunken father had murdered his mother, so a sentimental home life was not likely a tangible memory. When told that his old regiment, his wartime family, had reached the crossing, tears of relief rolled down his cheeks.[39]

The two detached Light Division regiments were also working hard to avoid capture. The Fifth Wisconsin and Sixty-First Pennsylvania had come under fire near Smith Run. They also endured a brief spate of friendly fire from a Union battery while extricating themselves from the encircling Southern forces. Lt. George E. Bissell of the Fifth Wisconsin remembered that when the Confederates discovered the Federals had pulled out, they responded "with a yell that made my blood turn cold." The two units followed a rough trace through slashed timber and up steep embankments. Shots rang out when the moon broke from behind the clouds and lit them up, but the Federals did not pause to respond. They eventually made it to the bridgehead and crossed the river in the early morning.[40]

After dark General Wofford moved his Georgia brigade across the Plank Road and pushed north to the east of Semmes's and Mahone's Brigades. He advanced to River Road and fired a rocket to let McLaws know his position.

The division commander sent forward an order for him to wait where he was, but Wofford purportedly became furious, claiming the Yankees were being allowed to escape. The halt McLaws insisted upon, however, was meant to keep his infantry out of the Southern artillery's field of fire.[41]

Confederate batteries on Smith Hill had temporarily ceased firing at dusk. Captain McCarthy reported that his Richmond Howitzers had expended their ammunition, and Major Hardaway ordered them off the line to replenish. He moved in Lt. George A. Ferrell's section of Captain Hurt's Alabama battery, bringing the Whitworth rifle into battery on that high ground.[42]

Earlier Confederate artillerymen had pounded stakes into the ground or set out some other tangible feature on Smith Hill to delineate their fields of fire when darkness fell. Capt. Frederick M. Colston described those preparations as "points marked for night firing." The staff officer earlier had enjoyed a cup of coffee, a luxury that "had come from the haversack of one of the dead soldiers of the enemy lying around us." While the batteries waited for orders, Colston lay down to grab a quick nap. The many days without sleep immediately caught up with him, and he dropped into a deep slumber that remained uninterrupted even when the nearby guns opened fire later that night.[43]

Lee wanted Early to get the Federals to quit the south side of the river so he could concentrate his forces at Chancellorsville. He directed him to use two brigades to confront the Sixth Corps north of the Plank Road and to send two brigades to reinforce General Barksdale. Early held Gordon's Brigade on Fall Hill and directed Avery, commanding Hoke's Brigade, to establish a line to his left. Hays and "Extra Billy" Smith were to array their brigades facing Fredericksburg. Smith's Forty-Ninth and Fifty-Second Virginia showed up to reinforce the late-afternoon attacks, though after the fighting had ended. Early sent them back to their brigade. Smith occupied a position north of the Plank Road, and the two arriving regiments extended his brigade line along Marye's Heights. Hays took position in the trenches south of Hazel Run between Lee's Hill and Deep Run.[44]

The Federals had planned to establish a logistics base on the south side of the Rappahannock, but the failed campaign rendered such plans moot. All the staged equipment and construction material had been removed from the Fredericksburg area. The field engineers dismantled the floating bridge that had spanned the river just downstream from the railway bridge piers. As May 4 ended, the two bridges at the Lacy house became the only intact crossing in Fredericksburg. Those floating spans had been in constant use, as described by a Pennsylvania soldier: "All the hospitals, army wagons, ambulances, and in short anything and everything belonging to Uncle Sam was removed to this side of the river during the day."[45]

Union artillery protected the floating escape route. Near the Lacy house, six 12-pounder Napoleons of Lieutenant Brown's First Rhode Island Artillery overlooked the two pontoon bridges. The two batteries of long-range weapons that had pounded Early's assault troops from the Falmouth heights remained in position overlooking Falmouth Ford. Chief of Staff Butterfield decided he also needed field guns there, and Brown sent Lt. Joseph S. Milne's section of Napoleons. About an hour before midnight, the First Minnesota Infantry returned to the vicinity of the Lacy house and occupied rifle pits under the bright moon.[46]

In Fredericksburg General Gibbon prepared defenses to cover his division's eventual withdrawal. The Federals dug ditches across the Plank and Telegraph Roads. Closer in they barricaded streets and loopholed buildings. Provost Marshal General Patrick rounded up some of the Sixth Corps stragglers, gave them each a rifle and sixty rounds of ammunition, and deployed them on the perimeter as skirmishers. With clear direction and purpose, the wayward men acquitted themselves well.[47]

Troops also wrecked bridges across the waterways running through town. Maj. Edmund Rice of the Nineteenth Massachusetts had a working party of around thirty Sixth Corps men who thoroughly wrecked the bridges across the Rappahannock Canal. Turning to Marye's Canal, the Federals destroyed the wooden bridge at William Street but were unable to do the same at the Hanover Street bridge because Confederate infantry could bring that crossing under fire. They removed the decking but decided that destruction of the framing was not worth the casualties.[48]

The Federals on the Second Corps's perimeter kept a watchful eye on the enemy forces hemming them in. At the pontoon bridge Capt. Newton T. Hartshorn of the US Engineers described the evening: "The dismal howl of the dogs in its [Fredericksburg's] deserted streets and the town clock which some straggler has wound up slowly tolling the hour of the night causes strange feelings to creep over me. The moon is shining bright. Every few moments the growls of distant guns fall upon the ear."[49]

The rising moon lit up the landscape, and an outbreak of musketry near Banks' Ford awakened Hardaway on Smith Hill. That small-arms fire may have been the brief fight between Wilcox's troops and the Sixth Maine. Captain Carter's King William Battery and Captain Fry's Orange Battery had been deployed to the right of the Confederate concentration of guns, and the major now pulled them back. He did not want them in anyone's field of fire when he turned the artillery's attention to the pontoon bridges to the northeast.[50]

Batteries on Smith Hill, at three hundred feet of elevation, would be able to shoot over the Banks' Ford uplands, which are at an elevation of two hundred feet. The bend in the river, however, blocked the bridges from view. Southern artillerymen would have to guess the location of their targets but had made some initial calculations of range and trajectory during the day. Colonel Alexander warned Hardaway that there were two Confederate brigades on the uplands in the line of fire.[51]

Hardaway rode down to the river along the road west of Golin Run. Pickets from the Forty-First Virginia had extended a line along the river, and Capt. Charles R. McAlpine joined the major on his reconnaissance. They moved downstream past Golin Run and Banks' Dam. With the sound of water flowing over the stone-and-timber dam behind them, the two officers tried to discern what might be going on downstream. They heard Federal artillery and wagons crossing the river, the hollow pontoons amplifying the sound of their passage.[52]

After determining the direction of the pontoon bridge, Hardaway returned to his battalion. His two batteries on the right had been pulled out of the way, and he now cautioned his battery commanders to be careful not to send rounds short into Confederate infantry on the river bluffs. The major ordered each battery to fire a round every twenty minutes within its predetermined field of fire. Between the several batteries on Smith Hill, Hardaway later estimated that there was an outgoing projectile in the air every minute from 10:00 P.M. until about a half hour after sunrise.[53]

The Confederate artillery's rate of fire meant that over a seven-hour period, more than four hundred rounds crashed into the river or within the Federal bridgehead. The gunners, however, could not see their targets to adjust their fire. Certainly the shells dropping around the bridges caused some anxiety, and some rounds exploded along the roads to and from the crossings. Still, there were limitations, as Alexander admitted: "I got the range & direction of Banks' Ford, where they were evidently to recross the river during the night; & I marked it in a gunpit I had built on a high wooded point, and I sat up there all night long firing shell[s] at that ford. The country is hilly & banks were far too high for me to see the water, but my shell[s] would curve over the hills & their fragments would all find the ground somewhere."[54] When Wilcox and Kershaw advanced into Burnham's sector, they uncovered a set of gun pits north of River Road overlooking Banks' Ford as well as the area downriver. From that vantage point Confederate artillerymen could see the pontoon bridge established at the Scott's Ferry landing, just over one thousand yards away.[55]

Captain McCarthy moved his Richmond battery into the existing earthworks. He had two 6-pounder howitzers as well as two 3-inch Ordnance Rifles. The floating bridge lay just outside the effective range of the howitzers, but the rifled weapons would be able to reach the span very nicely. A soldier in the Twelfth Virginia described the scene: "On a high bluff overlooking their ford, Col. Alexander was present and ordered one of the guns loaded and to aim at a certain number of degrees which was properly done. The shot had [the] desired effect as it struck the line moving on the bridge and we could distinctly hear the horses tramping on the wood bridge in wild confusion."[56]

A Federal soldier wrote how "a rebel battery from a contiguous bluff shelled us constantly during the entire passage of the army." Luther C. Furst of the 139th Pennsylvania noted that some units crossed the bridges at intervals, trying to avoid the artillery fire as much as was possible. About an hour after Hardaway's guns began dropping rounds onto the Union bridgehead, Wilcox ordered Manly to also shell the bridges with his North Carolina battery. The artillerymen likely remained in position on the hill just south of River Road, where they could shoot down the open river corridor. The guns on Smith Hill did not have that view. Manly's gun crews kept up their fire until a few hours past midnight, when use of the pontoon bridge slowed.[57]

The Union forces had a reasonably intact perimeter, and the Confederates coming from two directions were not yet ready to test it. Gordon's Brigade had halted at dark on Fall Hill. Avery's North Carolina brigade pulled up on Gordon's left. Units from McLaws's Division came across the Plank Road but halted, with Wilcox's Brigade on the bluffs overlooking the ford. When Early's two other brigades turned back toward Fredericksburg, they left a gap between the two divisions through which Union troops continued to escape.[58]

At the Banks' Ford bridges, Sedgwick met with his division commanders on the slope between the uplands and the river. The Sixth Corps commander also asked General Benham to join them to provide information on their line of communication. The chief engineer picked his way across the nearly completed bridge to respond to Sedgwick's summons. He knew there were many Irishmen among the bridge builders and called out the Irish Brigade's motto, "Faugh a Ballaugh (Clear the Way)." From the sweating soldiers came several responses in Gaelic. History has not recorded whether those retorts reflected the pride of being engaged in a critical task or were muttered curses from exhausted men.[59]

Sedgwick and his officers were discussing whether to leave a division on the south shore when the rest of the corps withdrew when Benham arrived. The chief engineer and the corps commander had been classmates at West Point, and the two old friends drew aside to confer in private. Sedgwick first asked whether the bridgehead could be kept secure. Benham reported that the Confederates had a concentration of artillery behind the Decker house (the guns on Smith Hill). While the current bombardment was not of great concern, it might become more effective when observers were able to correct their fire.[60]

Benham strongly advised against crossing just a portion of the command. He also cautioned Sedgwick not to move without authority. Messages from Hooker had been mixed. Headquarters appeared to have accepted Sedgwick's determination that he risked his command if he did not withdraw, but Hooker had also hinted at operations that involved the Sixth Corps remaining on the south side of the Rappahannock. Benham and Sedgwick talked through the wording of a message they would send to Hooker for clarification, and the engineer left to get it to the Scott house signal station.[61]

To keep Butterfield apprised of the Sixth Corps's operations, Benham had been sending messages to the Falmouth headquarters and then to Chancellorsville, after the chief of staff had been summoned upriver. At 10:00 P.M. he had reported having direct communications with Sedgwick. Twenty minutes later he conveyed that two pontoon bridges were down, that the crossing was taking artillery fire, and that Confederate infantry looked to be closing in.[62]

After meeting with Sedgwick, Benham sent the following message from the Scott house to Hooker's headquarters at 11:50 P.M.: "My army is hemmed in upon the slope, covered by [Federal] guns from the north side of Banks' Ford. If I had only this army to care for, I would withdraw it tonight. Do your operations require that I should jeopard it by retaining it here? An immediate reply is indispensable, or I may feel obliged to withdraw."[63]

Benham sent a copy back to Sedgwick and directed an aide to wait at the signal station for a reply while he continued monitoring the crossing. The tingent of the Fifteenth New York Engineers had brought a bridge train up from Banks' Ford, minus the pontoons that Benham had held back, and had floated a third span at US Ford before noon on May 4.[75]

At Banks' Ford the Federal artillery positioned to support Hooker's march to Fredericksburg on May 1 would now be used to cover the Sixth Corps's retreat. There were already thirty-four guns on the Banks' Ford uplands, although most of them were being held in reserve. Captain Graham had had his Battery K, First US Artillery in place since May 3. During the crossing on the night of May 4–5, he engaged McCarthy's Richmond battery on the bluffs overlooking the ford.[76]

Individuals and small groups of soldiers were swept up in the moonlight by the advancing Confederates. Surgeon Daniel Holt of the 121st New York tried to lead a contingent of men to safety and stumbled into a Southern line of battle. The surgeon loudly called out, "Halt!" His own troops stopped and so did the Confederates. As the command to halt rippled down the line, an outraged officer stormed toward the doctor and his party. Cursing mightily, he placed the Federals under guard and got his line moving again.[77]

Skirmishers felt especially vulnerable as their units departed. Capt. John S. Long, in charge of the picket line for the Ninety-Third Pennsylvania, waited anxiously for orders to pull back while the regiment retreated by companies. Just before daylight those isolated men, still without orders, broke away and reached a bridge that engineers had already begun to dismantle.[78]

Some stragglers had to swim or be captured. Elements of the Eighth Pennsylvania Cavalry found themselves at the river without a bridge in sight. Lt. Henry H. Garrett ordered his detachment to swim their horses across. Capt. John B. Cook of the Seventh Maine Infantry also found himself cut off from the bridges. He too escaped by swimming.[79]

With a few warnings about keeping the Confederates at bay, Butterfield allowed Gibbon the discretion to retire from Fredericksburg when he thought it appropriate. In the same message the chief of staff also thought it useful to disparage Sedgwick: "Make your dispositions so that no confusion or panic ensues. Three regiments of enemy kept Sedgwick out of town for several hours. You ought to be able to manage the position so as, if compelled to retire, to do so gracefully and sound." The difference in tone between this communication and messages to Sedgwick is striking. Gibbon was given the respect due a professional. Sedgwick continued to receive curt orders from a headquarters determined to delegate blame.[80]

A heavy fog enveloped Fredericksburg between midnight and dawn. The thick weather provided cover, but the moisture in the air also carried sound. Colonel Hall began to pull back his regiments as quietly as possible. One man described how the pickets loomed up like "a ghostly parade as they stealthily marched along." Jumpy nine-month men enveloped in the mist added to the challenge of getting away. Elements of the 127th Pennsylvania fired into a New York regiment.[81]

As those regiments pulled back, alert Confederate skirmishers let out a rebel yell, signaling that the Federals were leaving. The Southerners followed closely to cut off and capture anyone who dawdled. One by one, Hall's regiments made their way through the town to Hawke Street, where the pontoon bridge waited.[82]

The last regiment out was Lt. Col. Arthur F. Devereux's Nineteenth Massachusetts, which made use of the rifle pits already dug in the urban blocks. One company of skirmishers took position in a trench that cut across a road. The Confederates following them were familiar with the town and knew where the pontoon bridge would be. They came running in the fog, but upon rounding a corner they found themselves in full view of the waiting skirmishers, who unleashed a volley.[83]

The Bay State men scrambled back and rushed across the floating span. Maj. Edward Rice and Lt. Harmon Donath, also of the Nineteenth Massachusetts, had a working party of a half-dozen men standing by to cut the bridge loose once their comrades were clear. They used axes to chop through the heavy cables holding the bridge in place, and the current took the floating span toward the north shore. The two officers and their working party coolly stepped into a spare pontoon and poled across. From the heights around the Lacy house, Battery A, First Rhode Island Artillery opened fire, covering the men on the river until they reached safety.[84]

At Banks' Ford the Federal engineers dismantled their two bridges. Lt. Col. William H. Pettes of the Fiftieth New York Engineers had charge of removing the bridge established at Scott's Ferry. His superior, Col. Charles B. Stuart, took charge of dismantling the bridge farther downstream. The fog that rolled in during the night protected the working parties from observation, although Confederate artillery continued to drop ordnance around them.[85]

Just before dawn, the Second and Sixth Vermont, their division's rear guard, came down the ravine that led to the upper bridge. The engineers had already cut away the span but left one pontoon still connected to the south shore. A dozen men ran along stringers that had supported the bridge decking, but in their haste the soldiers did not properly distribute their weight in the pontoon. A corner of the boat dipped, causing water to pour in and rendering the craft useless. A Vermont soldier described their circumstances: "The pontoon floated out into the stream, the stringers drifted away, guns went to the bottom, knapsacks spilt their 'eight day ration' where only fishes will be likely to eat them, and several men took a bath in the Rappahannock."[86]

Engineers on the north shore shouted across to the stranded infantrymen that another bridge remained in place downstream. The Vermonters rushed across the floodplain toward the second span, about a third of a mile away. They hustled across the trestle that had anchored the bridge to the shore and then onto the floating bridge itself. One of them later wrote: "No sooner had the last man stepped on the bridge than the fastenings on the south shore were cast off, and the bridge swung round to the north shore, and the Chancellorsville Campaign, so far as the Sixth Corps was concerned, was ended."[87]

At 5:00 A.M. Sedgwick reported to headquarters that his efforts on the south side of the Rappahannock were complete: "The bridges at Banks' Ford are swung and in process of being taken up. The troops are much exhausted. The dispatch countermanding my movement over the river was received after the troops had crossed."[88]

Back at the river, the 139th Pennsylvania helped the engineers at the Scott's Ferry landing pull pontoons from the river and carry them back into the trees. All of them had been hauled clear when Confederates emerged from the uplands and debouched onto the floodplain.[89]

In the growing daylight the infantry closed in. Scouts from Early's and McLaws's Divisions linked up. The soldiers had known all night that there were other troops nearby, but each thought the other to be Federals. Their caution proved justified. A group of around seventy blue-clad troops approached with a white flag, having lost their way during the retreat and being unable to reach the bridges.[90]

Continuing toward the river, Southerners captured additional men and gathered in horses and mules. A Georgia soldier remarked, with a certain sense of relief: "About four hundred prisoners were picked up in the woods and along the river's bank. Arms were scattered everywhere. The morning sun shone beautifully upon the dew spangled blades of wheat and the bursting buds of spring."[91]

Wilcox's Brigade also moved up. The Confederate artillery on Smith Hill had ceased firing, and without the threat of artillery rounds dropping on them, the Alabama troops approached the crossing sites. One of them found the colors of the 102nd Pennsylvania Infantry, the only battle flag lost by the Sixth Corps during the entire campaign.[92]

Confederate forces had already closed in on Fredericksburg. At daybreak near Lee's Hill, Hays's Louisiana units found two 12-pounder Napoleons, which they thought were Federal guns. In fact, they were captured Confederate cannons that had been abandoned when the Federals pulled back. Meanwhile, Barksdale's Mississippians cleared the town, capturing about forty Northerners who had fallen asleep or been delayed in getting out.[93]

General Lee turned his attention back to the main body of the Union army. To reinforce an attack on Hooker, he ordered Anderson and McLaws to march west. Those orders included Wilcox, while Barksdale was to remain in Fredericksburg. Early was to also march his division west but had not cleared Salem Church before orders came to return to Fredericksburg. Around 4:30 P.M., during the return march, a hard rain began to fall.[94]

While Early's brigades resumed their positions at Fredericksburg, the other Confederate divisions continued west. Wilcox's units were halted near Chancellorsville and went into bivouac. The troops made themselves relatively comfortable under canvas, but orders soon arrived to get back to Banks' Ford. Like their trek to the battleground on May 1, this trip out and back produced no benefits except to wear out already tired men. Robert T. Harper of the Jeff Davis Battery in Carter's Battalion stepped over to the road as Wilcox's units passed. He called out to the bedraggled column, asking if anyone knew his brother, Lt. Matthew Harper of the Tenth Alabama. A fellow named William Smith spoke up and informed the artilleryman that his brother had been killed and lay buried at Salem Church.[95]

In the relentless rain the Union army abandoned its Chancellorsville defenses and crossed the Rappahannock at US Ford. The rushing river threatened to wreck the bridges there, but the engineers skillfully pulled one bridge from the raging stream and used its pontoons and other materials to strengthen and extend the two remaining spans. By 8:00 A.M. on May 6, the US Ford crossing had served its purpose. The Fifteenth and Fiftieth New York Engineers pulled up the floating spans without hindrance and loaded all of the bridging material on wagons for the return trip to Falmouth.[96]

Back in the Sixth Corps's area of operations, one more pontoon bridge needed to be recovered. The bridge components at Scott's Ferry had been concealed in the nearby ravine until the engineers could bring down wagons to remove them. Downstream, the second bridge swung clear of the south shore but had not yet been recovered. Two companies of the Second Rhode Island had been assigned to pull the boats from the water, but Confederates on the other side stood ready to inflict casualties. The two sides agreed not to shoot at one another, but that meant the pontoons remained in the stream.[97]

The Federals waited until night to continue their work. Under the cover of darkness, the Rhode Island men secured a line to the pontoons and, one by one, floated them downstream to the vicinity of Taylor's Dam. That stone-and-timber structure created a slack-water pond in the river channel, where the Ninety-Sixth Pennsylvania was on hand to help remove the boats from the water. Getting the second bridge out of the river did not go entirely unnoticed. Boats scraping on gravel or rocks drew fire, which the working parties ignored. They were handling their task in complete darkness and avoided pinpointing their location by shooting back. By the time the Confederates could see the other side of the river in moonlight, the boats had been hauled out of sight and staged for retrieval by the engineers.[98]

Somewhere along the river a Federal soldier about to be mustered out shouted in the general direction of the Confederate pickets: "Good bye, boys, I am going home. I never expect to fight you again." Over the course of the next few weeks, many of the two-year and nine-month units would head north to their home states. Some of them had gained the respect of the three-year men who had been with them under fire. On the march back to camp, some of the veterans had called out, "Bully for the two-years' men."[99]

The Sixteenth New York Infantry was one of those solid and dependable units, and General Brooks mentioned them prominently in his after-action report: "The conduct of the officers and men of the two-years' regiments, on the eve of the expiration of their term of service, has excited universal admiration, and as pre-eminent among them I beg leave to call attention to the Sixteenth New York Volunteers, Colonel [Joel J.] Seaver." Those New Yorkers had lost nearly two hundred men killed, wounded, and missing at Salem Church alone. Some of those missing soldiers were now under guard and marching south. Instead of going home, they were headed to Libby Prison in Richmond.[100]

Dr. Holt, the surgeon of the 121st New York, had technically been a prisoner, but the Confederates allowed him to return to his own lines after the transfer of wounded had been completed. There is a suggestion that the captive and his captors were all Freemasons and thus inclined to overlook inconveniences such as prisoner exchanges. It appears that others also knew that Holt would soon be departing. Lieutenant Patterson of the Ninth Alabama, himself a native of Ohio, planned to write a letter to his family as soon as he came off picket duty. He hoped the doctor would be able to take it back across the river and mail it.[101]

Confederate soldiers remained supremely confident in Lee and he in them, their victory at Chancellorsville giving the impression they were unbeatable. Union troops, however, were also buoyed by clear successes. They had fought well in the tangled woodlands of Spotsylvania County and had shown tactical skill and leadership against long odds in Sedgwick's breakout from Fredericksburg. A member of the Sixth Vermont Infantry articulated their faith: "With all our indecisive battles—no defeats—there is a peculiar honor which attaches to this fated old army, a glory yet to be."[102]

TWELVE

AN ASSESSMENT

The confident Southerners that Robert E. Lee led into Pennsylvania in June and July 1863 sustained punishing casualties at Gettysburg. What the Confederates had missed was that between January and June of that year, Joe Hooker had transformed the Army of the Potomac from a failing organization into a force that could win the war.

What clouds Hooker's accomplishment is his painfully mismanaged fight at Chancellorsville. Some writers suggest that "Fighting Joe" was a hard drinker who curtailed his intake of spirits during the campaign and thereby lost his equilibrium if not his nerve. Others are more tolerant of Hooker's performance and side with him in blaming subordinate commanders for his loss. The army commander had also been incapacitated when a shell struck a porch post he was leaning on, which knocked him senseless for a period.

The Union commander's physical condition is a distraction. Hooker simply did not have the capacity to lead an army. As a corps commander he had been able to see and control his forces from horseback. At the head of an army comprising multiple corps, Hooker had to fight a campaign with maps and messages, but he had neither the training nor the temperament to fight a battle under those strictures. He was not alone. Historians studying Meade, his successor, at Gettysburg have realized that his victory masked similar command disorganization resulting from trying to direct large forces in the field.[1]

Casualties

The Sixth Corps began the campaign with a strength of 23,667 men. During the operations at Fredericksburg, it lost 4,611 men killed, wounded, or captured. Over 1,000 of them fell in just a few minutes during the assault on Marye's Heights. To this number must be added the casualties of the accompanying First Corps and Second Corps units. Gibbon's division lost 87 men killed, wounded, or captured. Reynolds's corps lost 300 men at the river crossings below the town. Total losses at Fredericksburg, from April 29 through May 5, came to 4,998 men, which constituted 28.8 percent of the Army of the Potomac's casualties overall.[2]

Opposite the Union forces, Confederate losses were also high. Early's Division lost 1,548 men, while Barksdale's and Wilcox's Brigades lost 592 and 535 men respectively. Total losses sustained by those Southern forces came to 2,675 men killed, wounded, or captured. Sedgwick also caused Lee to detach several brigades from the Chancellorsville front and send them east as reinforcements. On the afternoon of May 3, four brigades arrived at Salem Church and were part of the late-afternoon fighting there. The day after the Salem Church fight, Lee diverted three more brigades to Fredericksburg, where those units also lost men in combat.[3]

The reinforcements from Chancellorsville came from Anderson's and McLaws's Divisions, but their losses east of Salem Church are difficult to determine. With one exception, the after-action reports filed by the brigade commanders reported casualties for the campaign overall. Estimates of their casualties at Fredericksburg suggest a combined total of about 1,000 men killed, wounded, or captured. That number puts the Confederate losses at Fredericksburg, Salem Church, and Banks' Ford at 3,675 men, or approximately 27 percent of the Army of Northern Virginia's casualties for the campaign.[4]

Federal Successes—Real and Imagined

Though he did not reach Chancellorsville, Sedgwick provided significant support to the main body of the Potomac Army. His operations on May 3 and 4 pulled seven Confederate brigades from the Chancellorsville front, although Hooker never acknowledged that substantial contribution. Instead, he disparaged Sedgwick at every opportunity, avoiding any questions about why he took no action after Lee weakened his already thin lines to confront the Sixth Corps's advance from Fredericksburg.

Sedgwick and his troops knew they had done well. James H. Leonard, a noncommissioned officer in the Fifth Wisconsin, confidently wrote, "We do not consider ourselves whipped by a considerable." The fighting had been intense, and the Federals had inflicted serious damage on their adversaries. Looking toward the future, Lt. William H. Pohlman of the Fifty-Ninth New York reflected on the hard fighting and noted that "two or three more such victories, as they claim, will completely use up Lee's army."[5]

Hooker, however, continued to reveal that army command was beyond his capabilities. On May 6 he issued General Order No. 49 congratulating the army "on its achievements of the last seven days." To deflect blame he took a swipe at the Eleventh Corps by stating that if his command had "not accomplished all that was expected, the reasons are well known to the army." He further admitted that the Federal host had left "before delivering a general battle to our adversaries." The thousands of men who had fought for their lives across those several days must have been thoroughly confused.[6]

Lincoln, Halleck, and Hooker

On May 7, President Lincoln and Major General Halleck traveled by steamer from Washington, DC, to Aquia Landing. Upon arrival, Lincoln offered his full support to Hooker and promised not to interfere with any ongoing planning. Privately, however, he recognized he might have to appoint a new commander of the Army of the Potomac yet again.[7]

Hooker assured the president that he was prepared to resume active campaigning. "I do not deem it expedient to suspend operations on this line," he stated with unjustified bravado. The army commander also attributed unforeseen circumstances for his defeat, confirming that he lacked the ability to adapt to enemy actions: "If in the first effort we failed, it was not for want of strength or conduct of the small number of the troops actually engaged, but from a cause which could not be foreseen, and could not be provided against. After its occurrence, the chances of success were so much lessened that I felt another plan might be adopted in place of what we were engaged in, which would be more certain in its results. At all events, a failure would not involve a disaster, while in the other case it was certain to follow the absence of success."[8]

The commanding general admitted that he had withdrawn rather than risk battle but then reassured Lincoln that the next time "the operations of all the corps, unless it be part of the cavalry, will be within my personal supervision." Hooker still did not understand that he could not micromanage his way to victory. He needed to rely on subordinate commanders to handle the fight beyond his field of vision.[9]

During that trip, Halleck had a frank discussion with the Potomac Army's corps commanders. Able to speak freely within the chain of command, Hooker's lieutenants heatedly expressed their concerns with their commander. There was a growing consensus that George Meade ought to be given command of the army, even though three of the army's generals were senior in rank to the Fifth Corps commander.[10]

To Gettysburg and Back

In late May Lee reorganized his Army of Northern Virginia for a march north. He knew the Union army was losing its nine-month and two-year men, so his odds might never be better for a decisive fight. In early June he began to draw forces away from Fredericksburg. As the Confederate army marched into Pennsylvania, Hooker became increasingly indecisive and decidedly unable to develop a strategy to address the rapidly developing crisis.

On June 28 Lincoln gave Meade charge of the Army of the Potomac. The collision in Pennsylvania came three days later. The Hooker era had ended, but while the Army of the Potomac fought under a new commander at Gettysburg, its pride, professionalism, and readiness for battle were a direct result of Hooker's tenure.[11]

Meade pursued Lee's army back to Virginia after the battle. By the end of July, the two armies were back in the Rappahannock valley. Subsequent maneuvers accomplished little. Once again Confederate authorities detached Longstreet's Corps to reinforce armies elsewhere, turning the tide of battle at Chickamauga in September. Fearing the loss of Chattanooga, Washington authorities reinforced the western armies with the Army of the Potomac's Eleventh and Twelfth Corps.[12]

Back in the Rappahannock valley in early November, Meade proposed a march to Banks' Ford and a rapid river crossing to seize the high ground west of Fredericksburg. Burnside and Hooker had identified that terrain as the key to holding the town, and Sedgwick had demonstrated its inherent strength on May 4. Now Meade proposed to take advantage of it, recognizing that the railway through Fredericksburg would be needed to supply a campaign in the spring of 1864.[13]

Unfortunately, neither Lincoln nor Halleck wanted to authorize a change of base. Instead the Potomac Army moved into Culpeper County, and minor fighting occurred while Federal railroad men repaired the tracks of the Orange and Alexandria Railroad to Brandy Station. From that base of supply, Meade launched a late-season advance across the Rapidan River, which resulted in the inconclusive Mine Run Campaign. In the spring of 1864, Lt. Gen. Ulysses S. Grant launched the Overland Campaign from Culpeper County but quickly reestablished a supply route through Fredericksburg.[14]

The Joint Committee on the Conduct of the War

Over the winter of 1863–64, the congressional Joint Committee on the Conduct of the War convened to investigate the Army of the Potomac's leadership during the Chancellorsville and Gettysburg Campaigns. Summoned from Tennessee, Hooker continued to blame three of his former corps commanders for his defeat at Chancellorsville. Sen. Benjamin W. Wade and Sen. Zachariah Chandler were friendly to the general and solicited testimony to corroborate his version of events.

Under oath, Hooker characterized his cavalry commander, Maj. Gen. George Stoneman, as ineffective. In the spring of 1863, Hooker had ordered his Cavalry Corps to interrupt Lee's communications with Richmond, but the horse soldiers were delayed by weather and never quite managed to strike a decisive blow. For his part, Hooker kept back too few mounted units in the immediate battle area, and Southern cavalry shoved them aside to discover the information that gave Lee the opportunity to smash the Eleventh Corps. No matter, the joint committee absolved Hooker of any blame for mismanaging his cavalry.[15]

Hooker called Maj. Gen. Oliver O. Howard inattentive. That charge had weight because it had been his unprepared and poorly deployed Eleventh Corps that collapsed under Stonewall Jackson's assault on May 2. Howard's negligence was inexcusable, but Hooker had set the stage by placing the army in a bad position when he halted his advance on May 1. He had then focused on creating a line of communications across US Ford rather than thinking through the potential moves a dangerous adversary might make to undo his plans.[16]

The third commander to incur Hooker's wrath was Sedgwick. In his correspondence while the campaign was still in progress and in his after-action reports, Hooker all but called the Sixth Corps commander incompetent. After being blindsided by a Confederate attack on May 2, Hooker had pleaded for Sedgwick to come to his rescue. The Sixth Corps—on its own—was to break through strong defenses that had repulsed the entire Union army in December 1862, then march a dozen miles through Confederate-controlled country to Chancellorsville. The committee explored these expectations with several witnesses.

Hooker had given Sedgwick an impossible task, yet the Sixth Corps still provided significant support. Its advance out of Fredericksburg drew seven Confederate brigades away from Hooker's front, but the army commander never even tested the weakened enemy lines. Rather than acknowledge Sedgwick's effort, he disparaged a corps commander he did not like. The joint committee heard consistent testimony about Hooker's inaction at Chancellorsville, which revealed his claims against Sedgwick to be flawed. Nevertheless, its report backed up the former army commander and called out Stoneman, Howard, and Sedgwick as culpable in the Union defeat.[17]

Senators Wade and Chandler obtained additional testimony to support Hooker. Wade, for instance, questioned Brig. Gen. Albion P. Howe to elicit statements critical of his corps commander. Sedgwick had given Howe high praise for his leadership along Smith Run but had also been compelled to pull his division back to prevent its capture. Howe thought his corps commander had not fully appreciated the position his division held after repulsing the Confederate attacks and suggested that the Sixth Corps's retreat on the night of May 4 had been premature. None of Sedgwick's other division commanders was called to provide observations and assessments for a larger context.[18]

Wade and Chandler also questioned a regimental commander who had known Hooker in California before the war. Col. Thomas D. Johns commanded the Seventh Massachusetts Infantry, a regiment from the general's home state. He testified that Sedgwick had been too slow to attack at Fredericksburg. The regimental commander's limited perspective was of dubious value. Of the fifty-six fighting units in the Sixth Corps on May 3, 1863, the committee summoned the one commander who knew Hooker personally and could be counted on to tell the two senators what they wanted to hear.[19]

Maj. Gen. Dan Butterfield's testimony also supported Hooker's version of events. He discounted the strength of the Confederate forces in Fredericksburg and stated that Sedgwick ought to have seized Marye's Heights on the night of May 2–3. That suggestion, made in hindsight, took no account of the orders Sedgwick had in hand nor the conditions the Sixth Corps faced at the time. The former chief of staff's testimony was entirely protective of his and Hooker's reputations.[20]

In his after-action report, Brig. Gen. Gouverneur K. Warren carefully avoided criticism of his commander. His private correspondence, however, had been brutally frank. In a letter of May 11, 1863, he wrote: "We went forward with high hope and courage [;] we grappled with the foe; already the dread of destruction had begun to shake him and I thought the great victory that was to close the war was ours. . . . But that steady purpose was wanting in the controlling power. We halted, we hesitated, wavered, retired."[21]

A circumspect after-action report kept Warren in Hooker's good graces, and less than a week after the campaign, he was promoted to be the Army of the Potomac's chief engineer. In front of the joint committee in 1864, however, he was no longer in Hooker's chain of command. Consequently, Warren managed to get in critical details regarding Hooker's inactivity as the Sixth Corps fought its battles on May 3 and 4.

Question: Considering your situation and the situation of the enemy, what would have been the effect of an attack by General Sedgwick, in conjunction with the main army, on the enemy's lines provided he had been there at daylight, according to his orders?

Warren: I think we ought to have destroyed Lee's army. But it would depend a great deal upon how hard the other part of the army fought, for General Sedgwick, with his 20,000 men, was in great danger of being destroyed if he became isolated.

Question: I am inquiring upon the hypothesis that he reached there at the time ordered.

Warren: If he had got over there, and the other part had fought as they might have done, I think we should have pretty nearly destroyed General Lee's army.[22]

The committee's questions were not getting Wade and Chandler to an unimpeachable criticism of Sedgwick, so they tried harder. Warren, however, kept stating that it was Hooker who had not done his part, although carefully avoiding any mention of him by name.

> Question: Then, if I understand you, it would seem that if the 6th corps under General Sedgwick had vigorously and energetically attempted to comply with the order of General Hooker, in your judgment the result of that battle would have been very different from what it was?
>
> Warren: Yes, sir; and I will go further, and say that I think there might have been more fighting done on the other end of the line. I do not believe that if General Sedgwick had done all he could, and there had not been harder fighting on the other end of the line, we would have succeeded.
>
> Question: Why did not they fight harder on the other end of the line?
>
> Warren: I was not there, and do not know. All I know is that the 1st corps did not fight at all. And from the time we made this advance under General Sedgwick, we kept firing pretty heavily, and whipped that division of the rebels all to pieces. There was a little slowness afterwards. In the after-noon, about 6 o'clock, we met an attack from a division that General Lee sent down. The battle at Chancellorsville stopped at 1 o'clock, when we were beginning down below, so General Lee turned around on us.[23]

Warren's statements were guarded, but the committee's ranking members from the House of Representatives, Rep. Daniel W. Gooch of Massachusetts and Rep. Moses F. Odell of New York, made sure to get a more reasoned analysis into the record. Brig. Gen. John Gibbon's testimony was characteristically blunt.

> Question: What would you say, as a military man, was the duty of the general commanding at Fredericksburg—that is, General Sedgwick—in case he had received an order on Saturday at 10 or 11 o'clock, directing him to advance immediately towards Chancellorsville, so as to be there at daylight the next morning?
>
> Gibbon: I should think his first duty would be to inform his commanding general that before he could do that he must take some very strong positions in front of him. And the next thing to do would be, of course, to attempt to take those heights, and I take it he would take them just as

speedily as he possibly could; and until he did take them, of course any advance in the direction of Chancellorsville was out of the question.

Question: In your opinion, would a judicious military commander deem it a practicable thing to attempt the taking of those heights in the night?

Gibbon: I should think not.

Question: Then you would regard the order as one not possible to be executed?

Gibbon: I do not consider that an order sent to General Sedgwick on Saturday night, to be at Chancellorsville at daylight on Sunday morning, was a practicable one.[24]

The above questions were posed by Gooch. Odell followed up with additional queries to maintain continuity in the developing public record.

Question: Will you assign the reasons?

Gibbon: In the first place, the distance. In the second place, the opposition which he had to encounter on those heights, which, we all know were exceedingly strong, and which were pretty well defended. In the third place, Lee's army, or that portion of it between Fredericksburg and Chancellorsville.

Question: What was the distance?

Gibbon: About twelve miles. But it is a very difficult thing for any man to put himself in another man's shoes after the thing is over, and then say what was the best thing to be done. These things can only be decided with any propriety by the men themselves.[25]

Sedgwick had known Hooker would blame him for the failed Chancellorsville Campaign, evident in a letter he penned to his sister on May 15, 1863: "I wrote to you that I apprehended the General would attempt to throw an undue share of the failure on the 6th Corps." With the help of political cronies, Hooker managed to do just that. The joint committee reported its findings as if there had been no testimony supporting Sedgwick's actions and declared Howard, Stoneman, and Sedgwick to have been negligent. It also noted that Hooker's injury incapacitated him at a critical juncture. The committee had not only ignored Hooker's loss of nerve on May 1 but also neatly justified his lack of leadership on May 3.[26]

Assessing Hooker

During a postwar visit to the Chancellorsville battlefields, Hooker rode across the high ground west of Fredericksburg with the historian Samuel P. Bates. The open plateau had been his objective on May 1, 1863, and the civilian noted what the former commander of the Army of the Potomac said to him about that expansive terrain: "Upon our arrival at the broad, open, rolling fields opposite Banks's Ford, some three or four miles up the stream, General Hooker exclaimed, waving his hand significantly: 'Here, on this open ground, I intended to fight my battle.'"[27]

As Hooker had known, the position was a good one, but he did not get there. On May 1, 1863, he recoiled when the Confederates pushed back just east of Chancellorsville, and Lee thereafter dictated how and where the rest of the battle would be fought. Not until Sedgwick broke out of Fredericksburg with his single corps did Lee have to back off from trying to destroy Hooker and respond to that developing threat in his rear. David H. Strother, a war correspondent turned soldier, described Hooker's failure as follows: "He was a dashing and brave leader of an army corps. His organization and discipline of the Army of the Potomac held at Gettysburg. He failed to command the army successfully because it was perhaps over his strength."[28]

The Sixth Corps compelled Lee to detach nearly two divisions from Hooker's front. That tremendous effort, however, had no effect on how Hooker fought his battle in the woods. Frozen into inactivity after Jackson's flank attack, he remained quiescent as the fight at Fredericksburg pulled away Confederate strength to confront the Sixth Corps at Salem Church and Banks' Ford.

The successful operations of the Sixth Corps at Fredericksburg became overshadowed by Stonewall Jackson's dramatic attack and Lee's eventual victory. During the march into Pennsylvania, a British observer with the Army of Northern Virginia noted that "the universal feeling in the [Southern] army was one of profound contempt for an enemy whom they had beaten so constantly, and under so many disadvantages." The Confederate army had every right to be confident, but the pride of victory at Chancellorsville eclipsed what Union forces had accomplished at Fredericksburg and what their army had become by the spring of 1863. A few weeks later Southern arms paid a high price for that inattention.[29]

APPENDIX 1: ORDER OF BATTLE

This compilation of forces engaged at Fredericksburg, Salem Church, and Banks' Ford is taken from the Order of Battle developed by Stephen W. Sears for his book *Chancellorsville* (1996) with some minor corrections.

Army of the Potomac: Maj. Gen. Joseph Hooker
    Chief of Artillery: Brig. Gen. Henry J. Hunt
    Engineer Brigade: Brig. Gen. Henry W. Benham
        15th New York Engineers: Col. Clinton G. Colgate
        50th New York Engineers: Col. Charles B. Stuart
        US Engineers Battalion: Capt. Chauncey B. Reese
    Provost Guard: Brig. Gen. Marsena R. Patrick
    Signal Corps: Capt. Samuel T. Cushing
    Topographical Engineers: Brig. Gen. Gouverneur K. Warren

    First Corps: Maj. Gen. John F. Reynolds
        Chief of Artillery: Col. Charles S. Wainwright
        First Division: Brig. Gen. James S. Wadsworth
            First Brigade: Col. Walter Phelps Jr.
                22nd New York
                24th New York

30th New York
84th New York

Second Brigade: Brig. Gen. Lysander Cutler
7th Indiana
76th New York
95th New York
147th New York
56th Pennsylvania

Third Brigade: Brig. Gen. Gabriel R. Paul
23rd New Jersey
29th New Jersey
30th New Jersey
31st New Jersey
137th Pennsylvania

Fourth Brigade: Brig. Gen. Solomon Meredith
19th Indiana
24th Michigan
2nd Wisconsin
6th Wisconsin
7th Wisconsin

Artillery: Capt. John A. Reynolds
   1st New Hampshire Light: Capt. Frederick M. Engell
   Battery L, 1st New York Light: Capt. John A. Reynolds
   Battery B, 4th US: Lt. James Stewart

Detached from Second Division
  Artillery: Capt. Dunbar R. Ransom
   2nd Maine Light: Capt. James A. Hall
   5th Maine Light: Capt. George F. Leppiana
    Lt. Edmund Kirby
    Lt. Greenleaf T. Stevens
   Battery C, Pennsylvania Independent Light: Capt. James Thompson
   Battery C, 5th US: Capt. Dunbar R. Ransom

Detached from Third Division
  Artillery: Maj. Ezra W. Matthews
   Battery B, 1st Pennsylvania Light: Capt. James H. Cooper
   Battery F, 1st Pennsylvania Light: Lt. R. Bruce Ricketts
   Battery G, 1st Pennsylvania Light: Capt. Frank P. Amsden

Detached from Second Corps
  Second Division: Brig. Gen. John Gibbon
    First Brigade: Brig. Gen. Alfred Sully
        Col. Henry W. Hudson
        Col. Byron Laflin
        19th Maine: Col. Francis E. Heath
        15th Massachusetts: Maj. George C. Joslin
        1st Minnesota: Lt. Col. William Colville Jr.
        34th New York: Col. Byron Laflin
          Lt. Col. John Beverly
        82nd New York: Col. Henry W. Hudson
          Lt. Col. James Huston
    Second (Philadelphia) Brigade: Brig. Gen. Joshua T. Owen
        69th Pennsylvania: Col. Dennis O'Kane
        71st Pennsylvania: Col. Richard P. Smith
        72nd Pennsylvania: Col. De Witt C. Baxter
        106th Pennsylvania: Col. Turner G. Morehead
    Third Brigade: Col. Norman J. Hall
        19th Massachusetts: Lt. Col. Arthur F. Devereaux
        20th Massachusetts: Lt. Col. George N. Macy
        7th Michigan: Captain Amos E. Steele
        42nd New York: Col. James E. Mallon
        59th New York: Lt. Col. Max A. Thoman
        127th Pennsylvania: Col. Frederick H. Collier
    Artillery
        Battery B, 1st Rhode Island Light: Lt. T. Frederick Brown
        Battery G, 1st Rhode Island Light, Capt. George W. Adams
    Sharpshooters
        1st Company, Massachusetts: Capt. William Plumer

Sixth Corps: Maj. Gen. John Sedgwick
  Chief of Artillery: Col. Charles H. Tompkins
  First Division: Brig. Gen. William T. H. Brooks
    First Brigade: Col. Henry W. Brown
        Col. Samuel L. Buck
        Col. William H. Penrose
        1st New Jersey: Col. Mark W. Collet

> Lt. Col. William Henry Jr.
> 2nd New Jersey: Col. Samuel L. Buck
> > Lt. Col. Charles Wiebecke
> 3rd New Jersey: Maj. J. W. H. Stickney
> 15th New Jersey: Col. William H. Penrose
> > Lt. Col. Edward L. Campbell
> 23rd New Jersey: Col. E. Burd Grubb Jr.
>
> Second Brigade: Brig. Gen. Joseph J. Bartlett
> > 5th Maine: Col. Clark S. Edwards
> > 16th New York: Col. Joel J. Seaver
> > 27th New York: Col. Alexander D. Adams
> > 121st New York: Col. Emory Upton
> > 96th Pennsylvania: Maj. William A. Lessig
>
> Third Brigade: Brig. Gen. David A. Russell
> > 18th New York: Col. George R. Myers
> > 32nd New York: Col. Francis E. Pinto
> > 49th Pennsylvania: Lt. Col. Thomas H. Hulings
> > 95th Pennsylvania: Col. Gustavus W. Town
> > > Lt. Col. Elisha Hall
> > > Maj. Thomas J. Town
> > > Capt. Theodore H. McCalla
> > 119th Pennsylvania: Col. Peter C. Ellmaker
>
> Artillery: Maj. John A. Tompkins
> > Battery A, Massachusetts Light: Capt. William H. McCartney
> > Battery A, New Jersey Light: Lt. Augustin N. Parsons
> > Battery A, Maryland Light: Capt. James H. Rigby
> > Battery D, 2nd US: Lt. Edward B. Williston

Second Division: Brig. Gen. Albion P. Howe
> Second (Vermont) Brigade: Col. Lewis A. Grant
> > 2nd Vermont: Col. James H. Walbridge
> > 3rd Vermont: Col. Thomas O. Seaver
> > > Lt. Col. Samuel E. Pingree
> > 4th Vermont: Col. Charles B. Stoughton
> > 5th Vermont: Lt. Col. John R. Lewis
> > 6th Vermont: Col. Elisha L. Barney
> > 26th New Jersey: Col. Andrew J. Morrison
> > > Lt. Col. Edward Martindale
>
> Third Brigade: Brig. Gen. Thomas H. Neill

        7th Maine: Lt. Col. Alexander Shaler
        21st New Jersey: Col. Gilliam Van Houten
            Lt. Col. Isaac S. Mettler
        20th New York: Col. Ernst von Vegesack
        33rd New York: Col. Robert F. Tayler
        49th New York: Col. Daniel B. Bidwell
        77th New York: Lt. Col. Winsor B. French
    Artillery: Maj. J. Watts de Peyster
        1st New York Independent Light: Capt. Andrew Cowan
        Battery F, 5th US: Lt. Leonard Martin
Third Division: Maj. Gen. John Newton
    First Brigade: Col. Alexander Shaler
        65th New York: Lt. Col. Joseph E. Hamblin
        67th New York (1st Long Island Regiment): Col. Nelson Cross
        122nd New York: Col. Silas Titus
        23rd Pennsylvania: Col. John Ely
        82nd Pennsylvania: Maj. Isaac C. Bassett
    Second Brigade: Col. William H. Browne
        Col. Henry L. Eustis
        7th Massachusetts: Col. Thomas D. Johns
            Lt. Col. Franklin P. Harlow
        10th Massachusetts: Col. Henry L. Eustis
            Lt. Col. Joseph B. Parsons
        37th Massachusetts: Col. Oliver Edwards
        36th New York: Lt. Col. James J. Walsh
        2nd Rhode Island: Col. Horatio Rogers Jr.
    Third Brigade: Brig. Gen. Frank Wheaton
        62nd New York: Lt. Col. Theodore B. Hamilton
        93rd Pennsylvania: Capt. John S. Long
        98th Pennsylvania: Capt. John F. Ballier
            Lt. Col. George Wynkoop
        102nd Pennsylvania: Col. Joseph M. Kinkead
        139th Pennsylvania: Col. Frederick H. Collier
    Artillery: Capt. Jeremiah McCarthy
        Battery C-D, 1st Pennsylvania Light: Capt. Jeremiah McCarthy
        Battery G, 2nd US: Lt. John H. Butler
Light Division: Brig. Gen. Calvin F. Pratt
    Col. Hiram Burnham

6th Maine: Lt. Col. Benjamin F. Harris
31st New York: Col. Frank Jones
43rd New York: Col. Benjamin F. Baker
61st Pennsylvania: Col. George C. Spear
    Maj. George W. Dawson
5th Wisconsin: Col. Thomas S. Allen
3rd New York Independent Light Artillery: Lt. William A. Harn
Reserve Artillery: Capt. William M. Graham
Brig. Gen. Robert O. Tyler
Battery B, 1st Connecticut Heavy: Lt. Albert F. Brooker
Battery M, 1st Connecticut Heavy: Capt. Franklin A. Pratt
5th New York Independent Light: Capt. Elijah D. Taft
15th New York Independent Light: Capt. Patrick Hart
29th New York Independent Light: Lt. Gustav von Blucher
30th New York Independent Light: Capt. Adolph Voegelee
Battery K, 1st US: Lt. Lorenzo Thomas Jr.
Battery C, 3rd US: Lt. Henry Meinell
Battery G, 4th US: Lt. Marcus P. Miller
Battery K, 5th US: Lt. David H. Kinzie

Army of Northern Virginia: Gen. Robert E. Lee

Detached from First (Longstreet's) Corps
  Anderson's Division: Maj. Gen. Richard H. Anderson
    Mahone's Brigade: Brig. Gen. William Mahone
      6th Virginia: Col. George T. Rogers
      12th Virginia: Lt. Col. Everard M. Field
      16th Virginia: Lt. Col. Richard O. Whitehead
      41st Virginia: Col. William A. Parham
      61st Virginia: Col. Virginius D. Groner
    Posey's Brigade: Brig. Gen. Carnot Posey
      12th Mississippi: Lt. Col. Merry B. Harris
        Maj. Samuel B. Thomas
      16th Mississippi: Col. Samuel E. Baker
      19th Mississippi: Col. Nathaniel H. Harris
      48th Mississippi: Col. Joseph M. Jayne
    Perry's Brigade: Brig. Gen. E. A. Perry
      2nd Florida: Maj. Walton R. Moore

  5th Florida: Maj. Benjamin F. Davis
  8th Florida: Col. David Lang
 Wilcox's Brigade: Brig. Gen. Cadmus M. Wilcox
  8th Alabama: Col. Young L. Royston
   Lt. Col. Hilary A. Herbert
  9th Alabama: Maj. Jeremiah H. J. Williams
  10th Alabama: Col. William H. Forney
  11th Alabama: Col. John C. C. Sanders
  14th Alabama: Lt. Col. Lucius Pinckard
 Wright's Brigade: Brig. Gen. Ambrose R. Wright
  3rd Georgia: Maj. John F. Jones
   Capt. Charles H. Andrews
  22nd Georgia: Col. Joseph Wasden
  48th Georgia: Lt. Col. Reuben W. Carswell
  2nd Georgia Battalion: Maj. George W. Ross
 Garnett's Artillery Battalion: Lt. Col. John J. Garnett
  Maj. Robert A. Hardaway
  Norfolk (VA) Battery: Capt. Joseph D. Moore
  Pittsylvania (VA) Battery: Lt. Nathan Penick
McLaws's Division: Maj. Gen. Lafayette McLaws
 Kershaw's Brigade: Brig. Gen. Joseph B. Kershaw
  2nd South Carolina: Col. John D. Kennedy
  3rd South Carolina: Maj. Robert C. Maffett
  7th South Carolina: Lt. Col. Elbert Bland
  8th South Carolina: Col. John W. Henagan
  15th South Carolina: Lt. Col. Joseph F. Gist
  3rd South Carolina Battalion: Lt. Col. William G. Rice
 Semmes's Brigade: Brig. Gen. Paul J. Semmes
  10th Georgia: Lt. Col. Willis C. Holt
  50th Georgia: Lt. Col. Francis Kearse
  51st Georgia: Col. W. M. Slaughter
   Lt. Col. Edward Ball
   Maj. Oliver P. Anthony
  53rd Georgia: Col. James P. Simms
 Wofford's Brigade: Brig. Gen. William T. Wofford
  16th Georgia: Col. Goode Bryan
  18th Georgia: Col. S. Z. Ruff
  24th Georgia: Col. Robert McMillan

   Cobb's Georgia Legion: Lt. Col. Luther J. Glenn
   Phillips's Georgia Legion: Lt. Col. E. S. Barclay Jr.
 Barksdale's Brigade: Brig. Gen. William Barksdale
   13th Mississippi: Col. James W. Carter
   17th Mississippi: Col. William D. Holder
   18th Mississippi: Col. Thomas M. Griffin
   21st Mississippi: Col. Benjamin G. Humphreys
 Cabell's Artillery Battalion: Col. Henry C. Cabell
  Maj. S. P. Hamilton
  1st Company, Richmond (VA) Howitzers: Capt. Edward S. McCarthy
  Manly's North Carolina Battery: Capt. Basil C. Manly
  Pulaski (GA) Battery: Capt. John C. Fraser
  Troup (GA) Artillery: Capt. Henry H. Carlton
First Corps Reserve Artillery
 Alexander's Battalion: Col. E. Porter Alexander
  Maj. Frank Huger
  Ashland (VA) Battery: Capt. Pichegru Woolfolk Jr.
  Bath (VA) Battery: Lt. Osmond B. Taylor
  Bedford (VA) Battery: Capt. Tyler C. Jordan
  Madison (LA) Battery: Capt. George V. Moody
  Richmond (VA) Battery: Capt. William W. Parker
 Washington (LA) Artillery: Col. James B. Walton
  1st Company: Capt. Charles W. Squires
   Lt. C. H. C. Brown
  2nd Company: Capt. John B. Richardson
  3rd Company: Capt. Merritt B. Miller
  4th Company: Capt. Benjamin F. Eshleman

Detached from Second (Jackson's) Corps
 Detached from Hill's Light Division
   Fredericksburg (VA) Artillery: Capt. Edward A. Marye
 Detached from Rodes's Division
  Carter's Artillery Battalion: Lt. Col. Thomas H. Carter
   Jeff Davis (AL) Battery: Capt. William J. Reese
   King William (VA) Battery: Capt. William P. Carter
   Morris Louisa (VA) Battery: Capt. R. C. M. Page
   Orange (VA) Battery: Capt. Charles W. Fry

Early's Division: Maj. Gen. Jubal A. Early
- Gordon's Brigade: Brig. Gen. John B. Gordon
  - 13th Georgia: Col. James M. Smith
  - 26th Georgia: Col. Edmund N. Atkinson
  - 31st Georgia: Col. Clement A. Evans
  - 38th Georgia: Col. James D. Mathews
  - 60th Georgia: Col. William H. Stiles
  - 61st Georgia: Col. John H. Lamar
- Hoke's Brigade: Brig. Gen. Robert F. Hoke
  - Col. Isaac E. Avery
  - 6th North Carolina: Col. Isaac E. Avery
    - Maj. Samuel M. Tate
  - 21st North Carolina: Lt. Col. William S. Rankin
    - Col. William W. Kirkland
  - 54th North Carolina: Col. James C. S. McDowell
    - Lt. Col. Kenneth M. Murchison
  - 57th North Carolina: Col. Archibald C. Godwin
  - 1st Battalion North Carolina Sharpshooters: Maj. Rufus W. Wharton
- Smith's Brigade: Brig. Gen. William Smith
  - 13th Virginia: Lt. Col. James B. Terrill
  - 49th Virginia: Lt. Col. Jonathan C. Gibson
  - 52nd Virginia: Col. Michael G. Harman
  - 58th Virginia: Col. Francis H. Board
- Hays's Brigade: Brig. Gen. Harry T. Hays
  - 5th Louisiana: Col. Henry Forno
  - 6th Louisiana: Col. William Monaghan
  - 7th Louisiana: Col. Davidson B. Penn
  - 8th Louisiana: Col. Trevanian D. Lewis
  - 9th Louisiana: Leroy A. Stafford
- Andrews's Artillery Battalion: Lt. Col. R. Snowden Andrews
  - 1st Maryland Battery: Capt. William F. Dement
  - 4th Maryland Battery (Chesapeake Artillery): Capt. W. D. Brown
  - Alleghany (VA) Battery: Capt. Joseph Carpenter
  - Lee (VA) Battery: Capt. Charles J. Raines

Second Corps Reserve Artillery
- Detached from Brown's Battalion
  - 1st Rockbridge (VA) Artillery: Capt. Archibald Graham
  - Warrenton (VA) Battery: Capt. James V. Brooke

Detached from McIntosh's Battalion
    Hurt's Alabama Battery: Capt. William P. Hurt

Army Reserve Artillery: Brig. Gen. William N. Pendleton
  Sumter Battalion: Lt. Col. A. S. Cutts
    Battery A: Capt. Hugh M. Ross
    Battery B: Capt. George M. Patterson
  Nelson's Battalion: Lt. Col. William Nelson
    Amherst (VA) Battery: Capt. T. J. Kirkpatrick
    Fluvanna (VA) Artillery: Capt. John L. Massie
    Milledge's Georgia Battery: Capt. John Milledge Jr.

APPENDIX 2: ARTILLERY WEAPONS

Union Artillery

The number and types of weapons for Union artillery units are taken from the *Official Records* as well as from the research done by National Park Service historian Eric J. Mink in "Armament in the Army of the Potomac during the Chancellorsville Campaign" (May 2018).

Unit	Number of Weapons	Weapon type
1st Connecticut Heavy Art., Battery B	4	4.5-inch Siege Rifles
1st Connecticut Heavy Art., Battery M	4	4.5-inch Siege Rifles
2nd Maine Light Artillery	6	3-inch Ordnance Rifles
5th Maine Light Artillery	6	12-pounder Napoleons
1st Maryland Light Artillery, Battery A	6	3-inch Ordnance Rifles
1st Massachusetts Light Artillery, Battery A	6	12-pounder Napoleons
1st New Hampshire Light Artillery	6	3-inch Ordnance Rifles
1st New Jersey Light Artillery, Battery A	6	10-pounder Parrott Rifles
1st New York Independent Light Artillery	6	3-inch Ordnance Rifles
1st New York Light Artillery, Battery L	6	3-inch Ordnance Rifles
3rd New York Independent Light Artillery	6	10-pounder Parrott Rifles
5th New York Independent Light Artillery	4	20-pounder Parrott Rifles
15th New York Independent Light Artillery	6	3-inch Ordnance Rifles
29th New York Independent Light Artillery	4	20-pounder Parrott Rifles

Appendix 2

Unit	Number of Weapons	Weapon type
30th New York Independent Light Artillery	6	20-pounder Parrott Rifles
Pennsylvania Independent Light Artillery, Battery C	4	3-inch Ordnance Rifles
1st Pennsylvania Light Artillery, Battery B	4	3-inch Ordnance Rifles
1st Pennsylvania Light Artillery, Battery C-D	10	10-pounder Parrott Rifles
1st Pennsylvania Light Artillery, Battery F	4	3-inch Ordnance Rifles
1st Pennsylvania Light Artillery, Battery G	4	3-inch Ordnance Rifles
4th Pennsylvania Light Artillery, Battery C	4	3-inch Ordnance Rifles
1st Rhode Island Light Artillery, Battery B	6	12-pounder Napoleons
1st Rhode Island Light Artillery, Battery G	6	3-inch Ordnance Rifles
1st US Artillery, Battery K	6	3-inch Ordnance Rifles
2nd US Artillery, Battery D	6	12-pounder Napoleons
2nd US Artillery, Battery G	6	12-pounder Napoleons
2nd US Artillery, Battery M	10	3-inch Ordnance Rifles
3rd US Artillery, Battery C	6	3-inch Ordnance Rifles
4th US Artillery, Battery B	6	12-pounder Napoleons
4th US Artillery, Battery G	6	12-pounder Napoleons
5th US Artillery, Battery C	6	12-pounder Napoleons
5th US Artillery, Battery F	6	Two 12-pounder Napoleons Four 10-pounder Parrott Rifles
5th US Artillery, Battery K	4	12-pounder Napoleons

Confederate Artillery

Weapons in Confederate batteries as determined from the *Official Records* and other primary sources. There are gaps in the data, though. The Army of Northern Virginia reorganized its artillery several times, and the changing type and number of weapons is not consistently specified in available records.

The following chart is as complete as possible.

Unit	Number of Weapons	Weapon Types
Alabama		
Hurt's Alabama Battery	4	Two 3-inch Ordnance Rifles Two 2.75-inch Whitworth Rifles
Jeff Davis Battery	4	Two 3-inch Ordnance Rifles Two 12-pounder howitzers
Georgia		
Milledge's Georgia Battery	4	One 10-pounder Parrott Rifle Three 3-inch Ordnance Rifles
Pulaski Battery	3	One 10-pounder Parrott Rifle One 3-inch Ordnance Rifle One 12-pounder howitzer
Sumter Artillery, Battery A	4	Three 10-pounder Parrott Rifles One smoothbore field gun
Sumter Artillery, Battery B	4	Two 12-pounder Napoleons Two 12-pounder howitzers
Troup Artillery	4	Three 10-pounder Parrott Rifles One 12-pounder howitzer
Louisiana		
Madison Battery	4	Two 3-inch Ordnance Rifles Two 24-pounder howitzers
Washington Artillery, 1st Company	2	3-inch Ordnance Rifles
Washington Artillery, 2nd Company	4	Three 12-pounder Napoleons One in depot
Washington Artillery, 3rd Company	2	12-pounder Napoleons
Washington Artillery, 4th Company	4	Two 12-pounder Napoleons One 12-pounder howitzer One weapon in depot
Maryland		
1st Maryland Battery	4	12-pounder Napoleons
4th Maryland Battery (Chesapeake Artillery)	4	Two 10-pounder Parrotts Two smoothbore field guns

Appendix 2

Unit	Number of Weapons	Weapon Types
North Carolina		
Manly's North Carolina Battery	4	Two 12-pounder Napoleons Two 3-inch Ordnance Rifles
Virginia		
1st Rockbridge Artillery	4	Two 10-pounder Parrott Rifles Two 20-pounder Parrott Rifles
Alleghany Battery	4	Two 12-pounder Napoleons Two 3-inch Ordnance Rifles
Amherst Battery	4	Combination of 12-pounder Napoleons and 3-inch Ordnance Rifles
Ashland Battery	4	Combination of rifled weapons and smoothbore field guns
Bath Battery	4	12-pounder Napoleons
Bedford Battery	4	12-pounder Napoleons
Fluvanna Artillery	4	Three 12-pounder Napoleons One 3-inch Ordnance Rifle
Fredericksburg Artillery	4	Two 12-pounder Napoleons Two 10-pounder Parrott Rifles
King William Battery	6	Combination of rifled weapons and smoothbore field guns
Lee Battery	4	Rifled weapons
Morris Louisa Battery	6	Smoothbore field guns
Norfolk Battery	4	One 10-pounder Parrott Rifle One 3-inch Ordnance Rifle Two smoothbore field guns
Orange Battery	4	Two 10-pounder Parrott Rifles Two 3-inch Ordnance Rifles
Pittsylvania Battery	4	Two 10-pounder Parrott Rifles Two 3-inch Ordnance Rifles
Richmond Battery	2	10-pounder Parrott Rifles from Rhett's Battery
Richmond Howitzers, 1st Company	4	Two 3-inch Ordnance Rifles Two 6-pounder howitzers
Warrenton Battery	4	Two 12-pounder Napoleons Two 12-pounder howitzers

APPENDIX 3: THE FLAG OF TRUCE

When the sun rose on May 3, 1863, several dozen blue-clad soldiers lay dead or wounded on the ground in front of Marye's Heights. In the predawn darkness two separate probes in regimental strength had advanced to reconnoiter the Confederate defenses. The infantrymen got caught in the open, and both approaches were halted by a volley of gunfire that rippled down the Confederate line. The Federals hastily pulled back, and sometime after sunrise, a Union officer sent forward a flag of truce to request a brief ceasefire to retrieve wounded men.

Col. Thomas M. Griffin, commanding the Eighteenth Mississippi, granted the protection of the proffered flag, and Union infantry details then came forward to recover their injured comrades. A few hours later the Sixth Corps launched an assault and overran the Confederate position at Marye's Heights in a matter of minutes. It was a stunning success on a field where the Union army had met disaster the previous December.[1]

Four days later, on May 7, Brig. Gen. William Barksdale submitted his official report, wherein he recounted a clear sequence of events, beginning with the initial reconnaissance: "The battle commenced at daylight. A furious cannonade was opened from the enemy's batteries in town, and along both banks of the river. Two assaults were made upon Marye's Heights, but both were signally repulsed."[2] These two advances were the two probes to determine if the Confederates held their position in strength.

Barksdale then noted the activity that occurred about three hours later, around 8:00 A.M.: "A heavy column of the enemy were seen moving up the river, evidently for the purpose of getting possession of Taylor's [Fall] Hill, which, if successful, would have given him command of the position which I held."[3] The heavy column was Brig. Gen. John Gibbon's advance toward the Confederate right. Barksdale noted how Brig. Gen. Harry Hays moved to the threatened sector with four of his Louisiana regiments. He also described the arrival of Brig. Gen. Cadmus Wilcox with at least three of his Alabama regiments. While waiting for an assault coming out of Fredericksburg, Barksdale asked Wilcox to be ready to send him a regiment if needed.[4]

When the main Federal attack came, shortly after Gibbon's foray, it moved too quickly for any reinforcements to come to anyone's aid. Barksdale explained how he had been responsible for an "extended" front with only a "small number of forces at my disposal." Furthermore, there had been "uncertainty as to the point against which the enemy would hurl his immense force he had massed in town." The general described additional challenges:

> The distance from town to the points assailed was so short, the attack so suddenly made, and the difficulty of removing troops from one part of the line to another was so great, that it was utterly impossible for either General Wilcox or General Hays to reach the scene of action in time to afford any assistance whatever. It will thus be seen that Marye's Hill was defended by but one small regiment, three companies, and four pieces of artillery. A more heroic struggle was never made by a mere handful of men against overwhelming odds.[5]

Barksdale specified the disparity in forces as twenty to one, which was not accurate but reflected his impression. He also tried to convey the intensity of the fight by doubling the casualties his troops inflicted. Barksdale went from "1,000 killed and wounded" gleaned from Northern newspapers to 2,000 "according to statements from intelligent citizens." Following the recitation of the fighting that day, he also reported the flag of truce as a possible mitigating factor in the Confederate defeat: "Upon the pretext of taking care of their wounded, the enemy asked a flag of truce after the second assault on Marye's Hill, which was granted by Colonel Griffin, and thus the weakness of our force at that point was discovered. It is proper to say that Colonel Griffin, who is a brave and gallant officer, granted this flag of truce without consulting me."[6]

According to the sequence of events in Barksdale's report, the second assault described was one of the predawn probes. The main assault, the third attack in his sector, moved swiftly and overwhelmed his position before help could arrive. He did not describe the flag of truce as occurring in the middle of that final attack.

Maj. Gen. Jubal Early wrote his own report on May 7 and did not request Barksdale's report until the fourteenth. Barksdale's Brigade was a component of Maj. Gen. Lafayette McLaws's division, so the Mississippian's official report presumably went up the chain of command to McLaws instead of to Early. Without a report in hand from the on-scene commander, Early did not understand how the action unfolded in Barksdale's sector and wrote a hurried and inaccurate account.[7]

From Hamilton's Crossing Early had heard the predawn fighting at Fredericksburg. The two Federal advances described by Barksdale had been repulsed at the same time, though, which meant that the division commander heard what sounded like one sustained burst of firing. Early described the action on his own front and then included what he had heard from four miles away. He incorrectly stated that "one attack on Marye's Hill was repulsed" instead of two.[8]

When Early recounted the flag-of-truce story, he said it occurred just before the main Federal attack. As noted above, however, the flag of truce came out after the two morning probes that Barksdale described as "two assaults." Early's official statement got the sequence of events wrong, as did so many others who did not witness the events in question: "The enemy, however, sent a flag of truce to Colonel Griffin, of the Eighteenth Mississippi Regiment, who occupied the works at the foot of Marye's Hill with his own and the Twenty-first Mississippi Regiment, which was received by him improperly, and it had barely returned before heavy columns were advanced against the positions, and the trenches were carried and the hill taken."[9]

The next day, May 4, Early retook Marye's Heights, cutting off the Sixth Corps from Fredericksburg. He then fought aggressively against the Union lodgment without a commensurate effort by Maj. Gen. Richard H. Anderson and McLaws. Early did most of the fighting that day and came to harbor ill feelings toward the divisions that had not fought as hard.

As a division commander in Jackson's Corps, Early also became self-conscious about the successful Union assault at Fredericksburg, which stood apart from the dramatic flank attack executed by his peers and comrades at Chancellorsville. A Federal breakthrough should not have been construed as a shameful occurrence, but he apparently needed to delegate blame. Deciding that official channels were insufficient to tell his side of the story, the general turned to private newspapers to supposedly set the record straight.

In a letter dated May 11, 1863, Early addressed alleged claims that Barksdale had not had enough support to be able to prevent the Federal victory. He described the reinforcements he had sent before adding, "Barksdale's brigade occupied the position which was strongest in natural and artificial defences [sic] and was better guarded by artillery than any other." Following that misleading statement, Early then took a swipe at a subordinate officer. Barksdale's Brigade was a part of McLaws's Division but had been detached and placed with Early's command at Fredericksburg. Ignoring his military responsibilities, Early tried to absolve himself with unseemly pettiness: "I will state that my division did not lose Marye's Hill, but one of my brigades (Gordon's formerly Lawton's) recaptured it before 9 o'clock on the next morning."[10]

Barksdale had been an attorney, a politician, and a newspaper man before the war, and he also knew how to submit letters to a newspaper. On May 13 he responded to Early's letter of May 11 with a measured recitation of facts already submitted in his official report. He detailed how he had been given responsibility for a line that extended across miles of terrain instead of just the Marye's Heights sector. He readily acknowledged support from Hays and Wilcox but reiterated that when the Federal attack came against Marye's Heights, it was too sudden for any reinforcements to be able to help.[11]

Early would not let things go. In a letter dated May 19, again published in a Richmond newspaper, he said he merely sought to correct the record rather than impugn Barksdale and his brigade. He then proceeded to do just that. Early said he was only defending the actions of his brigade commanders, neglecting to recognize that the Mississippi brigade had also been under his direction. He then took a final jab: "When Marye's Hill was recaptured by Gordon's brigade, General Barksdale with his brigade was some distance in the rear and not in sight."[12]

Letters sent to newspaper editors for public consumption reflect a self-conscious effort to handle the sting of a personal defeat amid celebrations of a resounding Southern victory. In this mix, however, was a letter that should have been the standard rather than an outlier. When Barksdale responded to Early's May 19 correspondence in a letter dated May 31, he refuted the Virginian's statements about what the Mississippian had said during and after the battle. He closed with the following statement: "If Gen.

Early's first publication had been written in the style and spirit of the following letter addressed to me, no reply would have been deemed necessary."[13]

In its June 15, 1863, edition, the Richmond newspaper printed Early's letter of May 14, which was considerably more professional than his public outbursts.

Camp Near Hamilton's Crossing
May 14th, 1863

General: You will please send to me, as early as practicable, a detailed report of the operations of your brigade from the time you reported to me on the night of the 30th to the close of the operations at Fredericksburg, and the return of the different commands to their positions, as it is necessary for me to make a full report of all the operations in the vicinity of Fredericksburg during that time, and I wish to do full justice to your brigade.

Having seen in the papers statements to the effect that your brigade had been left unsupported on the line in rear of Fredericksburg, and it being known that I was left in charge of the whole line, I have felt it incumbent on me to make a correction according to the facts in justice to myself by a brief statement in the papers, which I did without attempting or designing to cast any blame on your command. There is no need of any conflict in our views at all. The whole line was exposed for want of reserves, and the enemy made his most determined and desperate effort against the part defended by your brigade, and while it may be true that the enemy's attack may have been facilitated by the advantage he took of the flag of truce received by Col. Griffin, I am satisfied that the carrying [of] Marye's hill could not well have been avoided. It was an unavoidable consequence of the length of the line to be defended by a comparatively small force, and the difficulty of moving from one part of the line to another. Had a large force been concentrated in rear of Marye's hill, the enemy could have easily penetrated other parts of the line and thus accomplished his object. These are the views I entertain and I wish, therefore, to get all the facts of the case, so that I may show in my report that all our troops, including yours, did their duty under the trying circumstances in which they were placed.

Yours respectfully,
(Signed) J. A. Early
Major General commanding

Brigadier General Barksdale
   commanding brigade[14]

Early knew his report had been poorly composed. He admitted as much to Robert E. Lee after the war. In a letter dated November 20, 1868, he confessed that he "wrote a hasty and imperfect sketch" and claimed he had meant to submit "the detailed report" later. Early never followed up on his cursory after-action report of May 7, 1863.[15]

Before the Confederate army's march into Pennsylvania, Barksdale tried to address Griffin's actions with his letter of May 31. Camp talk had consistently blamed the colonel for accepting the white flag, implying that Confederate defeat at Fredericksburg had been his fault. To overcome this tendency to assess blame for lost battles rather than engage in actual analysis, Barksdale finally extended support to his subordinate: "It is proper for me to say in justice to a gallant officer, that I am satisfied from his statement, that the enemy gained no advantage from the flag of truce which was granted by Col. Griffin."[16]

The day after Barksdale's May 31 letter appeared in a June 15 Richmond newspaper, the Army of Northern Virginia began crossing the Potomac River into Maryland. Barksdale did not survive the fighting at Gettysburg, thus removing the highest-ranking eyewitness to the events being so publicly debated. The misunderstanding about the flag of truce in Early's May 7 report remained uncorrected, Lee using this report to complete his own. Thus, ranking Confederates gave the flag-of-truce story an official imprimatur.

A basic timeline discredits the notion of a flag of truce in the middle of an assault comparable in size to Pickett's Charge, yet the claim persisted. A narrative of Yankee duplicity instead of Confederate errors became solidified through repetition in countless letters and accounts by persons who heard about but did not actually witness the attack. The preponderance of that so-called evidence, backed up by Early's and Lee's official reports, influenced a great many writers.

In his 1910 Chancellorsville study, John Bigelow inserted the flag of truce into his description of the main Federal assault at Fredericksburg. Forty-eight years later Edward Stackpole made no reference to a flag of truce in his popular Chancellorsville study, but he did have other errors in his narrative because he did not understand the terrain at Fredericksburg, Salem Church, and Banks' Ford. Ernest B. Furgurson wrote a campaign study in 1992 and reinserted the flag of truce into the main attack, citing Bigelow. In his 1996 campaign study, Stephen Sears placed the white-flag incident where it belonged, well before the main attack. When Chris Mackowski and Kristopher White published their 2013 account of the May 3 battles, they discussed the ambiguity of various sources but then decided the flag of truce belonged in the attack sequence after all.

The loss of the battlefield context probably accounts for the persistence of a demonstrably improbable battle sequence for the Second Battle of Fredericksburg. Confronted with a problematic official record and a large collection of Confederate claims, writers have had to figure out how the flag of truce fit into their studies. Too many of them ended up placing it in the middle of the attack on Marye's Heights. Such conclusions might have seemed logical when standing among the later houses and trees that blocked views of the overall battlefield, but their purported sequence of events remained entirely unsupported by Barksdale, the man who had stood in the path of the Union assault that day and described how he saw it unfold.

The indignity that Early visited upon Barksdale and his command never diminished. The Virginian died in 1894, but his memoirs, published in 1912, described Barksdale's report not as it had been written, but as Early had interpreted it. In a footnote Early wrote the following: "General Barksdale informed me that just before this final attack was made the enemy sent a flag of truce to Colonel Griffin, commanding the force behind the stone wall, asking permission to take care of his wounded lying in front under our fire, which permission was imprudently granted by Colonel Griffin, without his knowledge, and that the weakness of the force at that point was thus discovered, and immediately afterwards the assaulting columns advanced."[17] This passage is not at all consistent with what Barksdale had reported. But with the Mississippian no longer around to say otherwise, Early decided not to correct what he had reported to Lee.

❧ NOTES ☙

Abbreviations

In citing works in the notes, short titles have generally been used. Works frequently cited have been identified by the following abbreviations:

Birney's Zouaves	*History of the Twenty Third Pennsylvania Volunteer Infantry, Birney's Zouaves, 1861–1865* (1903–4; repr., Salem, MA: Higginson Book, 1998)
FSNMP	Fredericksburg and Spotsylvania National Military Park, Fredericksburg, VA
HCWRT	Harrisburg (PA) Civil War Round Table Collection
LC	Manuscripts Collection, Library of Congress, Washington, DC
OR	*The War of the Rebellion: A Compilation of the Official Records of the Union and Confederate Armies*, 128 vols. (Washington, DC: Government Printing Office, 1890–1901); all citations to series 1 unless otherwise stated.
OR Supplement	Hewett, Janet B., Noah Andre Trudeau, and Bryce A. Suderow, eds., *Supplement to the Official Records of the Union and Confederate Armies*, 4 pts. in 100 vols. (Wilmington, NC: Broadfoot, 1994–2000); all citations to part 1 unless otherwise stated.
SHC	Southern Historical Collection
UNC	Univ. of North Carolina at Chapel Hill
USAMHI	US Army Military History Institute, Carlisle Barracks, PA
UVA	Manuscripts Department, Univ. of Virginia Library, Charlottesville
WHS	Wisconsin Historical Society, Madison

Prologue

1. Ralph A. Hicks, interview by author, Fredericksburg, VA, Jan. 15, July 29, 2015. Hicks hunted the Confederate camps for years before Interstate 95 cut through them. The Hazel Run valley accommodated large encampments, and many of the hut holes are visible today. Near Smith Run Hicks found evidence of the May 4, 1863, battle in the form of fired bullets, fragments of artillery rounds, bayonets, and an eagle breastplate damaged by shrapnel.
2. Zenzen, *Crossroads of Preservation and Development*, 44.
3. Sears, *Chancellorsville*, 475–501. Sears has done an extensive analysis of casualties sustained during the Chancellorsville Campaign. The Federal casualties on the battlefields east of Salem Church are mostly confined to the Sixth Corps. There were also some few hundred casualties sustained by the First Corps at the river crossing south of Fredericksburg between April 29 and May 1, before Hooker called that unit to Chancellorsville early on May 2. Confederate casualties from the units detached to confront the Sixth Corps are readily calculated, but several formations that fought at Chancellorsville and then marched to Salem Church only reported losses for the overall campaign. A reasonable estimate of their losses east of Salem Church is 3,500–4,000 men, or about 26–29 percent of overall Confederate losses for the entire campaign.
4. OR, 25(1):801, 839–40, 1001.
5. Hotchkiss and Allan, *Battlefields of Virginia*, 81.
6. Dodge, *Campaign of Chancellorsville*, 176–77; Bates, *Battle of Chancellorsville*, 155, 185; Doubleday, *Chancellorsville and Gettysburg*, 57–59.
7. Jackson, "Sedgwick at Fredericksburg and Salem Heights," 224–32.
8. Quinn, *History of the City of Fredericksburg*, 97 (emphasis mine).
9. Freeman, *R. E. Lee*, 3:2–3. Freeman is artfully passive in asserting that Chancellorsville was a "flawless" victory. He states that Lee himself would never have dreamed of describing his victory in such terms but that military critics had done so, which neatly absolves both Lee and his biographer from any responsibility for that conclusion.
10. Freeman, *Lee's Lieutenants*, 617–35.
11. Smith, *Golden Age of Battlefield Preservation*, 64, 102, 130, 160, 198.
12. Zenzen, *Crossroads of Preservation and Development*, 36; Blackford, *Memories of Life in and out of the Army in Virginia*, 2:167; Fredericksburg and Spotsylvania County Battle Fields Memorial Commission, *Report on Inspection of Battle Fields in and around Fredericksburg and Spotsylvania Court House, Virginia*, Dec. 1, 1935, copy at FSNMP. The report's associated maps show both the Antietam Plan and Gettysburg Plan land-acquisition options for the Fredericksburg battlefield. The Chancellorsville map shows not only extremely limited acquisitions but also the potential to be able to interpret the full battle, from Chancellorsville to Fredericksburg. These maps are available at the Special Collections Library, Pennsylvania State Univ., University Park.
13. Zenzen, *Crossroads of Preservation and Development*, 36, 43.

14. Zenzen, 32, 36–37, 59–60, 158. The park's interpretive panels are handsome cast-aluminum signs with an identifying circular logo for each of four battlefields. They appear to have been designed by park historian Ralph Happel in the 1930s. As additional signs were placed on newly acquired lands, the park's staff maintained the same cohesive look. Robert K. Krick, interview by author, Fredericksburg, VA, Oct. 26, 2015; Library of Congress, *Report of the Librarian of Congress, for the Fiscal Year Ending June 30, 1934,* 105–6. The National Park Service's chief historian at the time was Verne E. Chatelain, and the staff working in the Division of Maps consisted of Col. Thomas L. Heffernan, Maj. Joseph Mills Hanson, Mr. Edward Steere, and Miss Ruth Graham. This group developed a set of detailed maps that track the Sixth Corps's movements from April 29 through midday of May 3, 1863.

15. Furgurson, *Chancellorsville 1863,* 263.

16. Robert K. Krick, email to author, Sept. 15, 2014.

17. Sears, *Chancellorsville,* 353; Mackowski and White, *Chancellorsville's Forgotten Front,* 200–201.

18. Franklin Powell, interview by author, Fredericksburg, VA, Feb. 2, 1997. Powell was a local contractor who renovated numerous buildings in downtown Fredericksburg. While working on a house at the corner of Caroline and Hawke Streets, where extensive urban fighting had occurred on December 11, 1862, he found interior walls riddled with bullet holes that had been neatly wallpapered over. While the owners had made the outer walls and the roof of the house weathertight, replacing the interior walls would have been extravagant. The wallpaper worked very well to hide the evidence of violence. Another aspect of extant battle damage in Fredericksburg is the prevalence of shattered roof trusses. Prof. Gary W. Stanton of Mary Washington College (now the University of Mary Washington) measured and documented numerous buildings in town and was surprised to find that severe damage to roof framing had not been fully repaired. Again, it was expedient to simply nail a board to the broken member so the roof could be made whole and keep out the weather. Stanton's notes are on file at the Department of Historic Preservation, Univ. of Mary Washington, Fredericksburg, VA.

19. "Civil War Shell Makes Big Noise," *Winchester (VA) Evening Star,* Jan. 19, 1915; "Woolen Factory Costing $128,000 Destroyed by Fire," *Virginia Herald* (Fredericksburg), Oct. 25, 1875; Amy Satterthwaite, "Civil War Shot Found in Kenmore," *Fredericksburg (VA) Free Lance–Star,* Feb. 22, 1989; "Burst Up at Hunter & Frost's Foundry," *Virginia Herald* (Fredericksburg), Apr. 29, 1872. Fredericksburg residents have seen more ordnance collected and disposed of than just the rounds referenced in these various newspaper stories. Jean Rayman's family owned a small property north of the Chancellorsville clearing, where they routinely found bayonets, bullets, grapeshot, and cannonballs, some of which were unexploded. Her father was not sentimental about the old metal in the ground and was happy to let relic hunters search the property and haul away what they found. He also worked at Mary Washington College in Fredericksburg and encountered numerous Parrott shells. Jean Rayman, interview by author, Fredericksburg, VA, June 23, 2015. The author's neighbor, Mrs. Othello Hayden, recounted how heavy rains would wash out Minié balls in the ditches along the edges of the properties before the city installed curbs and gutters and paved the

streets. Fredericksburg resident and relic hunter Ralph A. Hicks remembered that a Mrs. Gordon found a rare Mississippi belt buckle while gardening at her home on Washington Avenue. Ralph A. Hicks, interview by author, Fredericksburg, VA, May 31, 2016. Gardening stories are legion, including within the author's own experience.

20. Patrick, *Inside Lincoln's Army*, 202–3.
21. Greene, "Morale, Maneuver, and Mud," 194–97.
22. O'Reilly, *Fredericksburg Campaign*, 473–74; Bates, "Hooker's Comments on Chancellorsville," 217; OR, 29(2):409.

Introduction

1. Sears, *To the Gates of Richmond*, 24.
2. OR, 25(2):57–59, 239–40; Krick, *Civil War Weather in Virginia*, 83. Hooker's headquarters at the King Farm was located near the intersection of White Oak Road and Ferry Road.
3. OR, 25(2):58; Marjorie Kaschewski, ed., "Diary of Edmund D. Halsey," Feb. 2, 1863, *Morristown (NJ) Daily Record*, Sept. 1973; Lonn, *Desertion during the Civil War*, 145, 151; White, *Civil War Diary*, 65–66.
4. OR, 25(2):58, 149; Burlingame, *Abraham Lincoln*, 2:493–94.
5. Weigley, *Great Civil War*, 233–36, 307–8; McPherson, *Battle Cry of Freedom*, 600; Fox, *Regimental Losses*, 476.
6. Weigley, *Great Civil War*, 232–33; OR, ser. 3, 2:2–3, 202; Geary, *We Need Men*, 10, 81.
7. OR, 25(2):119; Fox, *Regimental Losses*, 49; Livermore, *Numbers and Losses*, 68.
8. OR, 25(2):120.
9. Inspection report for the Light Division, Sixth Corps, Apr. 25, 1863, copy at FSNMP; Donaldson, *Inside the Army of the Potomac*, 217; Rush P. Cady (97th NY Infantry) to Gustavus Palmer, Apr. 25, 1863, American Civil War Collection, Digital Collections, Hamilton College Library, https://litsdigital.hamilton.edu/collections/letter-written-rush-p-cady-lieutenant-97th-new-york-volunteer-infantry-regiment-47.
10. Weigley, *Quartermaster General of the Union Army*, 268.
11. Hagerman, *American Civil War and the Origins of Modern Warfare*, 45.
12. Nelson, "'Each Man His Own Supply Train,'" 48–52.
13. OR, 25(2):562.
14. After the experience of Chancellorsville, the amount of ammunition carried by individual soldiers was reduced from a standard of sixty rounds to one of forty cartridges.
15. Thompson, "Civil War Signals," 188, 194; Fortescue, *Service with the Signal Corps*, 6, 11–12.
16. Thompson, "Civil War Signals," 194.
17. Fishel, *Secret War*, 257–58.
18. Fishel, 287–89; OR, 25(2):167; Tsouras, *George H. Sharpe*, 50.
19. Fishel, *Secret War*, 297.
20. Evans, *War of the Aeronauts*, 25, 62, 81.

21. O'Reilly, *Fredericksburg Campaign*, 285; Evans, *War of the Aeronauts*, 229, 232, 258–59, 264.

22. Evans, *War of the Aeronauts*, 274.

23. OR, 25(2):51.

24. OR, 25(2):51; Hebert, *Fighting Joe Hooker*, 174; Naisawald, *Grape and Canister*, 214–18.

25. Alexander, *Fighting for the Confederacy*, 104–5.

26. Fishel, *Secret War*, 325.

27. Weigley, *Great Civil War*, xx, xxiii.

28. Weigley, xxiii.

29. Bigelow, *Campaign of Chancellorsville*, 53–54, 57, 114; Welcher, *Union Army*, 1:424–25.

30. OR, 25(1):883, 25(2):709.

31. OR, 25(2):265; Krick, *Civil War Weather in Virginia*, 94; Bigelow, *Campaign of Chancellorsville*, 145.

32. Henry W. Benham, "Gen'l H. W. Benham's Report No. 3, being Part 1, of Report of Services with Army of the Potomac from March 1863, until March 1864, Brigadier General H. W. Benham; including Benham's Report to Major General Joseph Hooker, May 20, 1863," June 22, 1876, National Archives, M1098, Roll 6, typescript at FSNMP (hereafter Benham, "Report to Major General Joseph Hooker, May 20, 1863"); OR, 25(2):264.

33. Brainerd, *Bridge Building in Wartime*, 134, 137; "Benham, Henry Washington," in Boatner, *Civil War Dictionary*, 58–59.

34. Benham, "Report to Major General Joseph Hooker, May 20, 1863."

35. OR, 25(1):217–18, 223–24, 229; "Myer, Albert James," in Boatner, *Civil War Dictionary*, 576.

36. OR, 25(2):233; Burlingame, *Abraham Lincoln*, 2:497. John Bigelow incorrectly states that Hooker traveled to Washington, DC, on April 19 and that Lincoln, Stanton, and Halleck later visited the army for several days. See Bigelow, *Campaign of Chancellorsville*, 168. The latter meeting was for one day and occurred at Aquia Landing.

37. Francis E. Pinto, "History of the 32nd Regiment, New York Volunteers in the Civil War, 1861 to 1863, and Personal Recollections during That Period," Brooklyn, NY, 1895, WHS, 135A–35B, copy at FSNMP.

38. OR, 25(2):262, 267; Fisk, *Hard Marching*, 76.

39. OR, 25(2):239.

40. Winslow, *General John Sedgwick*, 1–3, 46–47, 54.

1. April 28–29

1. Soldier (124th NY Infantry) letter, May 7, 1863, *Newburg (NY) Telegraph*, May 14, 1863; Bigelow, *Campaign of Chancellorsville*, 173, map 7.

2. OR, 25(1):205, 213; Benham, "Report to Major General Joseph Hooker, May 20, 1863."

3. OR, 25(1):205, 213; Gilbert Thompson, "My Journal, 1861–1865, U.S. Engineer Battalion, Army of the Potomac," Apr. 29, 1863, copy at FSNMP.

4. OR, 25(1):205.

5. OR, 25(1):206; Benham, "Report to Major General Joseph Hooker, May 20, 1863."

6. "Brooks, William Thomas Harbaugh," in Boatner, *Civil War Dictionary*, 89; "Brooks, William Thomas Harbaugh," in Faust, *Historical Times Illustrated Encyclopedia of the Civil War*, 81–82; Lucian A. Vorhees letter (15th NJ Infantry), *Flemington (NJ) Hunterdon Republican*, June 5, 1863.

7. OR, 25(1):206–7; "Wadsworth, James Samuel," in Boatner, *Civil War Dictionary*, 882–83; "Wadsworth, James Samuel," in Faust, *Historical Times Illustrated Encyclopedia of the Civil War*, 795.

8. Benham, "Report to Major General Joseph Hooker, May 20, 1863."

9. Thomas M. Crowder, "One Month in the Northern States: The Civil War Diary of Lieutenant Colonel Thomas M. Crowder, 1863," trans. and ed. Sebastion N. Page, copy at FSNMP, 5; Seymour, *Civil War Memoirs*, 47; Mann, *Bells and Belfries*, 56–61.

10. Seymour, *Civil War Memoirs*, 47. The prominent churches in Fredericksburg are on a plateau about sixty feet in elevation. The louvered openings in St. George's steeple, through which the Confederate officers observed the Union camps, are another eighty feet above that. From that vantage point, the vista extends for miles.

11. OR, 25(2):275; Benham, "Report to Major General Joseph Hooker, May 20, 1863."

12. Sweet and Trimble, *Virginia Gold—Resource Data*, 2, 182; OR, 25(1):196; OR Supplement, 4:557.

13. OR, 25(1):246.

14. Sears, *Chancellorsville*, 151; Fishel, *Secret War*, 367.

15. OR, 25(2):276; Sears, *Chancellorsville*, 152.

16. Sears, *Chancellorsville*, 146–47; Donaldson, *Inside the Army of the Potomac*, 228.

17. Sears, *Chancellorsville*, 147.

18. OR, 25(1):506.

19. OR, 25(2):273, 276, 278.

20. Sears, *Chancellorsville*, 152; Quiner Scrapbooks: Correspondence of Wisconsin Volunteers, 1861–1865, comp. Edwin B. Quiner, WHS, 8:272, copy at FSNMP.

21. OR, 25(1):774, 783; Sears, *Chancellorsville*, 152–53.

22. OR, 25(1):849.

23. OR, 25(2):277; Brainerd, *Bridge Building in Wartime*, 138.

24. OR, 25(1):246; Soldier (Rockbridge Artillery) letter, May 9, 1863, William McCauley Papers, SHC, UNC, copy at FSNMP.

25. OR, 25(1):246, 309.

26. OR, 25(1):247.

27. OR, 25(1):247. Travellers Rest served travelers to and from the Northern Neck. According to Works Progress Administration reports from the 1930s, it had distinctive corner fireplaces but was built on soil that was too sandy, which eventually caused its foundation to fail. The house did not survive this flaw, and the site is now part of a sand-and-gravel operation.

28. OR, 25(1):247, 252; Naisawald, *Grape and Canister,* 186. In addition to a lack of artillery coordination in battle, Federal battery commanders did not have opportunities for promotion and quite often transferred to the infantry, where good combat leaders could rise above the rank of captain. The artillery in general thus lost experienced leadership.

29. OR, 25(1):596; Thompson, "My Journal," May 1, 1863, FSNMP. The house occupied by Capt. John Sands and his wife, Pina, had been built in 1832. It remains a single-family home at what is now 6 Purvis Lane.

30. US Naval Observatory, Astronomical Applications Dept., Sun and Moon Data for Apr. 28, 1863, https://aa.usno.navy.mil (accessed May 28, 2014); Morse, *Personal Experiences,* 21.

31. "From the Second Regiment," *Orleans (VT) Independent Standard,* June 5, 1863; Fisk, *Hard Marching,* 74; George D. Breck (1st NY Light Artillery) letter, Apr. 29, 1863, *Rochester (NY) Daily Union and Advertiser,* May 4, 1863; "From the 16th Regiment," *Malone (NY) Palladium,* May 7, 1863.

32. Holt, *Surgeon's Civil War,* 103–4; Soldier (6th VT Infantry) letter, Apr. 29, 1863, *Burlington (VT) Times,* May 6, 1863; Soldier (7th ME Infantry) letter, May 20, 1863, *Bangor (ME) Daily Whig and Courier,* May 22, 1863; George D. Breck (1st NY Light Artillery) letter, May 4, 1863, typescript at FSNMP.

33. Francis E. Pinto, "History of the 32nd Regiment, New York Volunteers in the Civil War, 1861 to 1863, and Personal Recollections during That Period," Brooklyn, NY, 1895, WHS, typescript, 136, copy at FSNMP; Smith, *Seventy-Sixth Regiment New York Volunteers,* 208–9.

34. OR, 25(2):277; OR ser. 3, 3:311; Soldier (6th VT Infantry) letter, Apr. 29, 1863, *Burlington (VT) Times,* May 6, 1863; Fisk, *Hard Marching,* 75. The balloon site is still intact but is now on private property within a wooded area of a modern subdivision. The old road is now paved and named Ridge Pointe Lane. The site was identified by National Park Service historian Noel Harrison in 2009.

35. OR, 25(1):205, 213; OR Supplement, 4:639.

36. OR, 25(1):206; Benjamin R. J. Thaxter (6th ME Infantry) letter, May 21, 1863, USAMHI, typescript, copy at FSNMP.

37. OR, 25(1):206; Benham, "Report to Major General Joseph Hooker, May 20, 1863"; Thompson, "My Journal," May 1, 1863, FSNMP.

38. OR, 25(1):206.

39. OR, 25(1):206–7; OR Supplement, 4:645; Soldier (6th ME Infantry) letter, Apr. 28, 1863, *Bangor (ME) Daily Whig and Courier,* May 25, 1863.

40. OR, 25(1):206–7; Pinto, "32nd Regiment, New York Volunteers," 137; Sewell Gray (6th ME Infantry) diary, Apr. 28, 1863, Maine State Archives, typescript, copy at FSNMP; Thompson, "My Journal," Apr. 29, 1863, FSNMP.

41. OR, 25(1):207.

42. Brewer, *Sixty-First Regiment Pennsylvania Volunteers,* 52; Soldier (5th WI Infantry) letter, May 14, 1863, *Grant County Witness* (Lancaster, WI), May 28, 1863.

43. Benham, "Report to Major General Joseph Hooker, May 20, 1863."

44. OR, 25(1):207, 211.

45. OR, 25(1):207, 212; Thompson, "My Journal," Apr. 28, 1863, FSNMP.

46. Westbrook, *49th Pennsylvania*, 143.

47. US Naval Observatory, Astronomical Applications Dept., Sun and Moon data for Apr. 28, 1863 (civil twilight at 4:49 A.M., sunrise at 5:17 A.M.), https://aa.usno.navy.mil (accessed May 28, 2014); Westervelt, *Lights and Shadows of Army Life*, 39; Swinfen, *Ruggles' Regiment*, 19.

48. OR, 25(1):566, 591; William A. Lessig, "The Ninety-Sixth Reg., P.V., in the Late Battles," *Pottsville (PA) Mining Journal*, June 6, 1863; Holt, *Surgeon's Civil War*, 104; Westbrook, *49th Pennsylvania*, 144.

49. William P. Wright (1st NY Independent Artillery) diary, Apr. 29, 1863, Osborne Family Papers, Dept. of Special Collections, Syracuse Univ. Library, typescript, copy at FSNMP; "From the 16th Regiment," *Malone (NY) Palladium*, May 7, 1863.

50. OR, 25(1):580, 585, 591; John F. L. Hartwell (121st NY Infantry) diary, Apr. 29, 1863, LC, typescript at FSNMP; Westbrook, *49th Pennsylvania*, 144; Pinto, "32nd Regiment, New York Volunteers."

51. Westervelt, *Lights and Shadows of Army Life*, 39.

52. OR, 25(1):580, 591.

53. OR, 25(1):208, 215; Thompson, "My Journal," Apr. 29, 1863, FSNMP.

54. OR, 25(1):563; OR Supplement, 4:659; Wright diary, Apr. 29, 1863.

55. OR, 25(1):208.

56. Benham, "Report to Major General Joseph Hooker, May 20, 1863."

57. Lt. Col. Kenneth M. Murchison (54th NC Infantry) report, May 13, 1863, Alphonso Calhoun Avery Papers, SHC, UNC; Harrison, *Fredericksburg Civil War Sites*, 2:76–80.

58. Urbanus Dart (26th GA Infantry) letter, May 13, 1863, *Brunswick (GA) News*, May 4, 1963; "From a Soldier in the 6th Louisiana Regiment," *Richmond (VA) Sentinel*, May 14, 1863; Malone, *Diary*, 32; Francis L. Hudgins (38th GA Infantry) article, *Atlanta Journal*, Sept. 28, 1901.

59. Seymour, *Civil War Memoirs*, 48; Robertson, *Stonewall Jackson*, 698; Early, *Lieutenant General Jubal Anderson Early, C.S.A.: Autobiographical Sketch and Narrative of the War between the States*, 194 (hereafter Early, *Autobiographical Sketch and Narrative*).

60. OR, 25(1):209; Benham, "Report to Major General Joseph Hooker, May 20, 1863."

61. OR, 25(1):273; Dawes, *Service with the Sixth Wisconsin*, 136; Curtis, *Twenty-Fourth Michigan*, 125.

62. Haight, "Among the Pontoons at Fitzhugh's Crossing"; Smith, *Seventy-Sixth Regiment New York Volunteers*, 208–9.

63. Capt. David Burhans (43rd NY Infantry) letter, May 5, 1863, *Albany (NY) Evening Journal*, May 12, 1863; Quiner Scrapbooks: Correspondence of Wisconsin Volunteers, 8:293, copy at FSNMP.

64. Virgil W. Mattoon (24th NY Infantry) letter, May 1, 1863, Connecticut Historical Society, copy at FSNMP; Dawes, *Service with the Sixth Wisconsin*, 129, 135; Earl M. Rogers (6th WI Infantry), "A Stubborn Regiment: How General Wadsworth Saved Some Soldiers from Disgrace at Chancellorsville," *Philadelphia Weekly Times*, July 1, 1882.

65. OR, 25(1):209, 212.

66. Dawes, *Service with the Sixth Wisconsin*, 135; Haight, "Among the Pontoons at Fitzhugh's Crossing."

67. Soldier (13th GA Infantry) letter, May 17, 1863, *Savannah (GA) Daily Morning News*, May 29, 1863.

68. Haight, "Among the Pontoons at Fitzhugh's Crossing"; Curtis, *Twenty-Fourth Michigan*, 125; Matrau, *Letters Home*, 53; Cheek and Pointon, *Sauk County Riflemen*, 62; William Speed (24th MI Infantry) letter, May 10, 1863, Schoff Civil War Collection, Clements Library, Univ. of Michigan, copy at FSNMP.

69. Cheek and Pointon, *Sauk County Riflemen*, 62; Dawes, *Service with the Sixth Wisconsin*, 135; Curtis, *Twenty-Fourth Michigan*, 125; Smith, *Seventy-Sixth Regiment New York Volunteers*, 209.

70. Cheek and Pointon, *Sauk County Riflemen*, 62; Dawes, *Service with the Sixth Wisconsin*, 136.

71. OR, 25(1):208–9, 253; Harrison Wells (13th GA Infantry) letter, May 9, 1863, Harrison Wells Papers, UNC, copy at FSNMP.

72. OR, 25(1):209; David D. Davies (11th NY Artillery) diary, Apr. 29, 1863, copy at FSNMP.

73. OR, 25(1):209.

74. OR, 25(1):247; Smith, *Seventy-Sixth Regiment New York Volunteers*, 209.

75. OR, 25(1):209; Sullivan, *Irishman in the Iron Brigade*, 77; Cheek and Pointon, *Sauk County Riflemen*, 64; Dawes, *Service with the Sixth Wisconsin*, 136.

76. Col. William Monaghan (6th LA Infantry) report (partial), *Daily Richmond (VA) Enquirer*, May 25, 1863 (report is not in the OR nor in the OR Supplement); Seymour, *Civil War Memoirs*, 48; "Letter from the Sixth Louisiana," *Mobile (AL) Advertiser and Register*, June 4, 1863; Weymouth, *Civil War Letters*, 102–6; OR, 25(1):247, 258.

77. Dawes, *Service with the Sixth Wisconsin*, 136–37; Cheek and Pointon, *Sauk County Riflemen*, 64. These accounts differ slightly in the exact wording of the commands given.

78. Cheek and Pointon, *Sauk County Riflemen*, 64; Dawes, *Service with the Sixth Wisconsin*, 137; Haskell, *Haskell of Gettysburg*, 68.

79. OR, 25(1):273; Curtis, *Twenty-Fourth Michigan*, 125.

80. Sullivan, *Irishman in the Iron Brigade*, 77; Cheek and Pointon, *Sauk County Riflemen*, 65; Margaret Ryan Kelley, "A Soldier of the Iron Brigade," *Wisconsin Magazine of History* 22, no. 3 (Mar. 1939): 300–301.

81. Sullivan, *Irishman in the Iron Brigade*, 78; Haight, "Among the Pontoons at Fitzhugh's Crossing"; Curtis, *Twenty-Fourth Michigan*, 128; Uberto A. Burnham (76th NY Infantry) letter, Apr. 29, 1863, Uberto A. Burnham Papers, Special Collections, New York State Library, copy at FSNMP.

82. Seymour, *Civil War Memoirs*, 48–49; Monaghan (6th LA Infantry) report (partial), *Daily Richmond (VA) Enquirer*, May 25, 1863; Soldier (Hays's Brigade) letter, May 13, 1863, *Mobile (AL) Advertiser and Register*, May 21, June 4, 1863.

83. Curtis, *Twenty-Fourth Michigan*, 126; Monaghan (6th LA Infantry) report (partial), *Daily Richmond (VA) Enquirer*, May 25, 1863; *Wisconsin Magazine of History* 22, no. 3 (Mar. 1939): 300–301.

84. Cheek and Pointin, *Sauk County Riflemen*, 65; Harrison, *Fredericksburg Civil War Sites*, 2:95–97. Smithfield is one of the few riverside plantation houses that have survived. It is a part of the Fredericksburg Country Club and surrounded by a golf course.

85. Cheek and Pointin, *Sauk County Riflemen*, 66; Sullivan, *Irishman in the Iron Brigade*, 78; Fox, *Regimental Losses*, 215; Nolan, *Iron Brigade*, 214; Smith, *Seventy-Sixth Regiment New York Volunteers*, 210–11.

86. Lloyd G. Harris (6th WI Infantry), "Forward into Line," *Milwaukee (WI) Sunday Telegraph*, Apr. 8, 1883; Dawes, *Service with the Sixth Wisconsin*, 110; Blight, *Slave No More*, 45.

2. April 29–30

1. Westbrook, *49th Pennsylvania*, 144; Marshall B. Stull (15th NJ Infantry) letter, May 1, 1863, *Sussex (NJ) Register*, May 22, 1863; Fairchild, *27th Regiment N.Y. Vols.*, 165; "The 43d Makes a Big Haul," *Albany (NY) Evening Journal*, May 13, 15, 1863.

2. OR, 25(1):566; David Burhans (43rd NY Infantry) letter, May 5, 1863, *Albany (NY) Evening Journal*, May 12, 1863; Lt. Col. Kenneth M. Murchison (54th NC Infantry) report, May 13, 1863, Alphonso Calhoun Avery Papers, SHC, UNC; Samuel D. Buck (13th VA Infantry), "At and around Fredericksburg," *Richmond (VA) Times Dispatch*, June 25, 1864.

3. Lt. Col. H. C. Jones Jr. (57th NC Infantry) report, n.d., Avery Papers, copy at FSNMP; Seymour, *Civil War Memoirs*, 49; Uberto A. Burnham (76th NY Infantry) letter, Apr. 30, 1863, Uberto A. Burnham Papers, Special Collections, New York State Library, copy at FSNMP; Bradwell, "31st Georgia at Chancellorsville." The Fifty-Seventh North Carolina report was filed in response to a brigade directive, which the Fifty-Fourth North Carolina's report notes was dated May 13, 1863.

4. OR, 25(1):247, 563, 566; OR Supplement, 4:624–25; Westbrook, *49th Pennsylvania*, 144; Lucian A. Vorhees (15th NJ Infantry) letter, Apr. 29, 1863, *Hunterdon (NJ) Republican*, May 8, 1863; Harrison, *Fredericksburg Civil War Sites*, 2:71.

5. OR, 25(1):204–5, 215; Soldier (95th NY Infantry) account, *Rockland County Messenger* (Haverstraw, NY), May 21, 1863.

6. OR, 25(1):384; Patrick, *Inside Lincoln's Army*, 239.

7. OR, 25(1):247, 254; Curtis, *Twenty-Fourth Michigan*, 127.

8. Soldier (Rockbridge Artillery) letter, May 9, 1863, William McCauley Papers, SHC, UNC, copy at FSNMP; David E. Moore (1st Rockbridge Artillery) report, John Warwick Daniel Papers, UVA, copy at FSNMP.

9. Seymour, *Civil War Memoirs*, 49; Memoirs of Eli S. Coble, Apr. 28, 1863, Greensboro (NC) Historical Museum Archives, copy at FSNMP.

10. OR, 25(1):217–18, 225, 226–27, 229, 233, 238–39; Plum, *Military Telegraph during the Civil War*, 364.

11. OR, 25(1):227–29.

12. OR, 25(1):217–18, 227, 238, 288–91.

13. Francis E. Pinto, "History of the 32nd Regiment, New York Volunteers in the Civil War, 1861 to 1863, and Personal Recollections during That Period," Brooklyn, NY, 1895, WHS, typescript, 138, copy at FSNMP.

14. OR, 25(1):1000; OR Supplement, 4:691; Early, *Autobiographical Sketch and Narrative*, 195; Jacob W. Haas (96th PA Infantry) letter, May 12, 1863, HCWRT, USAMHI, copy at FSNMP.

15. OR, 25(1):849; Early, *Autobiographical Sketch and Narrative*, 195.

16. Caldwell, "'It Does Appear as if Our Soldiers Were Made Altogether of Patriotism,'" 33; Douglas H. Gordon letters, Jan. 30, Mar. 2, 1863, FSNMP; John McDonald (13th MS Infantry) letter, Apr. 11, 1863, copy at FSNMP.

17. OR, 25(1):756–57, 796; Fishel, *Secret War*, 379; Early, *Autobiographical Sketch and Narrative*, 194.

18. OR, 25(1):757–60; Wise, *Long Arm of Lee*, 450.

19. Alexander, *Fighting for the Confederacy*, 194.

20. OR, 25(1):809; Robert E. Lee to William N. Pendleton, Apr. 28, 1863, SHC, UNC.

21. Hotchkiss, *Make Me a Map*, 136; Adam W. Karsh (52nd VA Infantry) letter, May 24, 1863, typescript at FSNMP; Marion H. Fitzpatrick (45th GA Infantry) letter, Apr. 30, 1863, Civil War Misc. Collection, USAMHI, typescript, copy at FSNMP.

22. Smith, *A Savannah Family*, 144–48; Hotchkiss, *Make Me a Map*, 133.

23. OR Supplement, 4:672; James P. Williams (Chesapeake Artillery) letter, May 7, 1863, UVA, copy at FSNMP; Smith, *Richard Snowden Andrews*, 81.

24. Donaldson, *Inside the Army of the Potomac*, 230; Sears, *Chancellorsville*, 163.

25. Sears, *Chancellorsville*, 164–65; Donaldson, *Inside the Army of the Potomac*, 230.

26. Sears, *Chancellorsville*, 165–66.

27. Sears, 167.

28. OR, 25(2):343; Wise, *Long Arm of Lee*, 452; Fortescue, *Service with the Signal Corps*, 226–27; Early, *Autobiographical Sketch and Narrative*, 194.

29. OR, 25(1):844, 848; Memoirs of Eli S. Coble, Apr. 28, 1863 Greensboro (NC) Historical Museum Archives, copy at FSNMP; Soldier (Rockbridge Artillery) letter, May 9, 1863, William McCauley Papers, SHC, UNC, copy at FSNMP. Hurt's artillery position appears to have been a low rise of ground fortified over the winter of 1862–63. Those earthworks are preserved on a twelve-acre parcel of land acquired by the Central Virginia Battlefields Trust in 2003.

30. OR, 25(2):292; George D. Breck (1st NY Light Artillery) letter, May 4, 1863, typescript at FSNMP; Newell, *"Ours,"* 202.

31. OR, 25(1):197, 25(2):291; OR, ser. 3, 3:310–11.

32. OR, 25(2):757, 796.

33. OR, 25(2):759–60.

34. Newell, *Annals of Tenth Regiment Massachusetts Volunteers*, 202; Smith, *Seventy-Sixth Regiment New York Volunteers*, 210–11; Fairchild, *27th Regiment N.Y. Vols.*, 165–66; Smith G. Bailey (5th ME Infantry) diary, Apr. 30, 1863, Rauner Special Collections Library, Dartmouth College, copy at FSNMP.

35. Sgt. J.H.B (61st VA Infantry) letter, May 8, 1863, *Savannah (GA) Republican*, May 20, 1863.

36. Fishel, *Secret War*, 375.

37. George D. Breck (1st NY Light Artillery) letter, May 4, 1863, typescript at FSNMP; Fairchild, *27th Regiment N.Y. Vols.*, 166.

38. Malone, *Diary*, 32; Soldier (13th GA Infantry) letter, May 17, 1863, *Savannah (GA) Daily Morning News*, May 29, 1863; Sewell Gray (6th ME Infantry) diary, Apr. 30, 1863, Maine State Archives, typescript, copy at FSNMP.

39. OR, 25(2):306.

40. OR, 25(2):305, 310, 313.

41. The US Ford crossing is only four and a half miles from the Warrenton Road (modern Route 17), but the approach road had seen only limited use before the Civil War, as the US Mining Company had been served by better roads south of the river and by the Rappahannock navigation system. The neglected road north of the river ran straight enough across the open ground near the Warrenton Road, but as the route approached the river, it twisted and turned through dense woods. Today, earthworks remain on the west side of Horsepen Run that appear to have been created to deter Confederate raiders approaching the Union outpost at the river.

42. OR, ser. 3, 3:311.

43. OR, 25(1):197; Sears, *Chancellorsville*, 183.

44. OR, 25(2):306–7.

45. OR, 25(1):171.

46. OR, 25(2):316; Bates, "Hooker's Comments on Chancellorsville," 217.

47. OR, 25(2):307, 309.

48. OR, 25(1):258, 25(2):309–11.

49. OR, 25(1):760–61, 796, 845.

50. OR Supplement, 4:672; Krick, *Parker's Virginia Battery*, 121–22.

51. Martin, *Fluvanna Artillery*, 70–71.

52. OR, 25(1):810. A year later, on May 21, 1864, Timothy O'Sullivan would expose a series of photographs of Massaponax Church when the Union high command paused there briefly during the Overland Campaign. The Confederate artillery park of 1863 had been located directly across the road from the church.

53. Hotchkiss, *Make Me a Map*, 136.

54. OR, 25(1):196–97, 780.

55. OR, 25(1):196–97, 25(2):306.

56. OR, 25(1):197; Cole, *Under Five Commanders*, 136; US Naval Observatory, Astronomical Applications Dept., Sun and Moon data for Apr. 30, 1863 (moonrise at 3:03 P.M., sunset at 7:00 P.M.), https://aa.usno.navy.mil (accessed May 28, 2014). The US Mine Road that the army bypassed had a parallel trench that created a killing ground on the road itself. A gun pit at the top of the hill also had a clear field of fire down the road. Ultimately, three pontoon bridges spanned US Ford, and the bank was altered in three places by the engineers to accommodate the floating spans. A transcontinental pipeline (from Texas to New York), placed underground, has obliterated portions of one of those sites, but the spacing of the bridges in proximity of the historic roads is clear. The pipeline required modification of one of the roads on the north side of the river, but a second road remains intact. On the south side of the river just east

of a modern dirt road is a severely eroded draw, which was one of the wartime roads prepared by the Federal engineers. Traces of a second wartime road are to the east of the eroded remnant.

57. Plum, *Military Telegraph during the Civil War*, 363. Forest Hall is approximately three-quarters of a mile from the pontoon-bridge site. The stately building suffered from several decades of neglect but has since been refurbished, serving once again as a comfortable family home.

58. OR, 25(1):218–19.

59. Bigelow, *Campaign of Chancellorsville*, 221; Donaldson, *Inside the Army of the Potomac*, 232.

60. OR, 25(1):514–15, 780, 850.

61. OR, 25(1):850; Alexander, *Fighting for the Confederacy*, 196.

62. OR, 25(1):515; Meade, *Life and Letters*, 370, Patrick, *Inside Lincoln's Army*, 232.

63. OR, 25(1):248, 305, 384, 25(2):305, 308; Newell, *Annals of the Tenth Regiment, Massachusetts Volunteers*, 203.

64. OR, 25(1):578, 585, 761–62, 25(2):308–10, 314; William A. Lessig, "The Ninety-Sixth Reg., P.V., in the Late Battles," *Pottsville (PA) Mining Journal*, June 6, 1863; Curtis, *Twenty-Fourth Michigan*, 127.

65. OR, 25(1):833, 839, 25(2):312; "Memoir of Genl. Benjamin Grubb Humphreys" (21st MS Infantry), Mississippi Dept. of Archives and History, typescript, chap. 13, copy at FSNMP; Soldier (13th MS Infantry) letter, May 6, 1863, *Mobile (AL) Advertiser and Register*, May 22, 1863; Oden, "End of Oden's War," Apr. 30, 1863, 80.

66. Bigelow, *Campaign of Chancellorsville*, 268n.

67. Early, *Autobiographical Sketch and Narrative*, 5, 81, 102–6, 116.

68. OR, 25(1):842, 848; Anderson W. Reese (Troup Artillery) letter, May 11, 1863, *Athens (GA) Southern Banner*, May 27, 1863.

69. OR, 25(1):793, 810, 842, 1000; Early, *Autobiographical Sketch and Narrative*, 197.

70. OR, 25(1):254, 258, 25(2):311; OR Supplement, 4:552; Isiah Fogleman (8th LA Infantry) diary, Apr. 30, 1863, typescript copy at FSNMP.

71. OR, 25(1):258, 25(2):310–11, 334; Newell, *Annals of the Tenth Regiment, Massachusetts Volunteers*, 203; William I. Bishop (10th MA Infantry) letter, May 6, 1863, *Hampshire (MA) Gazette*, May 19, 1863.

72. OR, 25(1):258, 25(2):310–11.

73. OR, 25(1):254, 258; Soldier (5th WI Infantry) letter, Apr. 30, 1863, *Burlington (VT) Times*, May 6, 1863; Quiner Scrapbooks: Correspondence of Wisconsin Volunteers, 1861–1865, comp. Edwin B. Quiner, WHS, 8:297, copy at FSNMP.

74. OR, 25(1):786.

75. OR, 25(2):314; Patrick, *Inside Lincoln's Army*, 239.

76. OR, 25(1):777. The Federals reported being attacked near Louisa Run. Most likely, they ran into Confederate cavalry where Catharpin Road crosses the Ny River, which has a tributary called Lewis Run.

77. OR, 25(2):306–7, 312.

78. OR, 25(2):306–7, 311–12.

79. OR, 25(1):213, 25(2):308–9; Benham, "Report to Major General Joseph Hooker, May 20, 1863"; William L. Fagan (8th AL Infantry) account, *Philadelphia Weekly Times*, July 7, 1883.

80. OR, 25(2):311–12.

81. OR, 25(2):312; Banes, *Philadelphia Brigade*, 159.

82. Benham, "Report to Major General Joseph Hooker, May 20, 1863."

83. OR, 25(1):213; Ward, *One Hundred and Sixth Regiment Pennsylvania Volunteers*, 163.

84. Gilbert Thompson, "My Journal, 1861–1865, U.S. Engineer Battalion, Army of the Potomac," May 1, 1863, copy at FSNMP.

85. OR, 25(1):824; OR, ser. 3, 3:312; OR Supplement, 4:516.

86. Robertson, *Stonewall Jackson*, 703; Smith, "Stonewall Jackson's Last Battle," 203.

87. Jacob W. Haas (96th PA Infantry) letter, May 12, 1863, HCWRT, USAMHI, copy at FSNMP; Westervelt, *Lights and Shadows of Army Life*, 40.

88. Bicknell, *Fifth Regiment Maine Volunteers*, 213.

89. OR, 25(2):306–7.

3. May 1

1. McClelen, *I Saw the Elephant*, 35. The Banks' Ford area is remote from modern intrusions, and one can still find remnants of the old roads as well as stone dam abutments, stone-lined canal sections, and stone mill foundations. The Rappahannock River routinely floods, so the wartime roads in the floodplain have been obliterated over the decades.

2. Bailey G. McClelen (10th AL Infantry) memoir, Feb. 1863, typescript copy at FSNMP. Most of the Civil War earthworks around Banks' Ford, both Union and Confederate, are on land owned by the City of Fredericksburg and are under an open-space easement held by the Virginia Outdoors Foundation.

3. Palmer C. Sweet, *Gold in Virginia*, Publication 19 (Charlottesville: Virginia Division of Mineral Resources, 1980). The relationship between gold mining and the canal project in the Rappahannock valley is not explicitly stated, but documentary evidence suggests a strong link. The Fredericksburg Common Council voted to invest public funds in the canal project in 1829, 1832, 1836, and 1846. Those votes were overwhelmingly positive and were preceded by equally strong referendums. When those political actions are correlated with gold-production statistics, it appears that the community was responding to the promise of gold in the upstream valley, where a canal would facilitate the movement of the necessary heavy equipment and other materials. Ibid., table 1.

4. Donald S. Callaham, "The Rappahannock Canal" (Master's thesis, American Univ., 1967), 33.

5. Freeman, *Lee's Lieutenants*, 141; Hennessy, *Return to Bull Run*, 359, 412.

6. US Naval Observatory, Astronomical Applications Dept., Sun and Moon data for May 1, 1863, https://aa.usno.navy.mil (accessed May 28, 2014); Fairchild, *27th Regiment*

N.Y. Vols., 166; Malone, *Diary*, 32; John P. Carter (15th NJ Infantry) diary, May 1, 1863, copy at FSNMP; Smith G. Bailey (5th ME Infantry) diary, May 1, 1863, Rauner Special Collections Library, Dartmouth College, copy at FSNMP.

7. Smith, *Seventy-Sixth Regiment New York Volunteers*, 213–14.
8. OR, 25(1):219.
9. OR, 25(1):219.
10. OR, 25(1):219, 25(2):335.
11. OR, 25(1):219.
12. Ward, *One Hundred and Sixth Regiment Pennsylvania Volunteers*, 163.
13. OR, 25(2):322–23, 343–44; Bigelow, *Campaign of Chancellorsville*, 238–39.
14. OR, 25(2):322.
15. Fishel, *Secret War for the Union*, 384.
16. OR, 25(2):322, 339–40. The Bowling Green Road, modern-day Route 2/17, was also known as the Richmond Stage Road. The Telegraph Road, modern-day Lafayette Boulevard, became US Route 1.
17. OR, 25(2):339.
18. OR, 25(2):323–26, 336; OR, ser. 3, 3:313.
19. OR, 25(2):325.
20. OR, 25(1):849; Harrison, *Chancellorsville Battlefield Sites*, 24.
21. OR, 25(1):850; Alexander, *Fighting for the Confederacy*, 196.
22. OR, 25(1):850; Robertson, *Stonewall Jackson*, 704.
23. Alexander, *Fighting for the Confederacy*, 196; OR, 25(1):850.
24. Sears, *Chancellorsville*, 199. The exact time of each side's advance is not obvious from the historic record. On the Union side John Bigelow notes that verbal instructions must have preceded the written directives because the advance began before orders were drafted. Bigelow, *Campaign of Chancellorsville*, 241. On the Confederate side there also remains a level of ambiguity. Lafayette McLaws reported that he pushed forward at 11:00 A.M., but Stephen Sears has determined that the actual time was closer to 10:30 A.M.
25. OR, 25(2):326; Sears, *Chancellorsville*, 202.
26. OR, 25(1):507, 25(2):306–7, 311–12; Sears, *Chancellorsville*, 202; Bigelow, *Campaign of Chancellorsville*, 240.
27. Sears, *Chancellorsville*, 202.
28. Spotsylvania County is named after colonial-era lieutenant governor Alexander Spottswood, who established an iron furnace on a tributary of the Rappahannock River in 1720. He had acquired considerable land grants from the Crown so he could claim ownership of both the deposits of iron as well as vast tracts of forests to provide fuel. He initially began operations with a group of paid German workers who ultimately left, but Spotswood sustained his operation with slave labor. Industrial slavery was quite viable and gives lie to suggestions that slavery would have died out on its own. Rappahannock iron production ended only when the trees ran out. Richmond eventually became the center of large-scale iron operations because it had a better port and could obtain both iron ore and anthracite coal from the interior of the colony by way of the James River Navigation Canal. James Roger Mansfield, *A History of*

Early Spotsylvania (Orange, VA, 1977); Kathleen Bruce, *Virginia Iron Manufacture in the Slave Era* (New York, 1931).

29. OR, 25(1):507.

30. OR, 25(1):825. The unfinished railway would be completed in 1877, initially with a narrow-gauge track but later with a standard gauge. The modest line struggled economically, though, and could not sustain itself past 1938. The company removed and sold first its tracks, then its land. J. William Mann, *A Most Unusual Railroad* (Fredericksburg, VA, 2007). Several areas of the railway right of way have been compromised by new development, but much of the route remains a linear earthen feature cutting across the landscape, looking very much like it did during the Civil War.

31. OR, 25(1):337, 825, 854–55, 874; Isiah Fogleman (8th LA Infantry) diary, May 1, 1863, typescript copy at FSNMP.

32. OR, 25(1):507, 854–55, 874; McClelen, *I Saw the Elephant*, 35; Charles Richardson, "Fredericksburg to Salem Church," *Richmond (VA) Times Dispatch*, June 3, 1906.

33. OR, 25(1):197.

34. OR, 25(1):507; Sears, *Chancellorsville*, 203, 213.

35. Bigelow, *Campaign of Chancellorsville*, 254; Sears, *Chancellorsville*, 220–21.

36. Alexander, *Fighting for the Confederacy*, 198.

37. Couch, "Chancellorsville Campaign," 159.

38. OR, 25(2):325–27, 329; Bruce, *Twentieth Regiment of Massachusetts Volunteer Infantry*, 249; Fishel, *Secret War*, 391.

39. OR, 25(1):248, 25(2):327.

40. OR, 25(1):248.

41. OR, 25(1):248, 563; OR Supplement, 4:550.

42. OR, 25(1):258.

43. OR, 25(1):810; Allen S. Cutts (Sumter Artillery Battalion) letter, May 6, 1863, *Sumter (GA) Republican*, May 22, 1863.

44. Smith, *Richard Snowden Andrews*, 81–82; James P. Williams (Chesapeake Artillery) letter, May 2, 1863, UVA, copy at FSNMP.

45. Smith, *Richard Snowden Andrews*, 81–82. The earthworks for the two batteries under Latimer's control have been obliterated by postwar agriculture. The secondary works behind them survive within the Fredericksburg and Spotsylvania National Battlefield Park.

46. OR, 25(1):845; Harrison, *Fredericksburg Civil War Sites*, 2:229; Charles Richardson, "Fredericksburg to Salem Church," *Richmond (VA) Times Dispatch*, June 3, 1906.

47. Krick, *Parker's Virginia Battery*, 122.

48. OR, 25(1):820, 842; Krick, *Parker's Virginia Battery*, 122; Edward S. Duffey (Parker's VA Battery) diary, May 1, 1863, Virginia Historical Society, copy at FSNMP.

49. OR, 25(1):810–11; "Washington Artillery of New Orleans," in Boatner, *Civil War Dictionary*, 893–94.

50. OR, 25(1):811.

51. OR, 25(2):328–29, 341–42; Martin, *Fluvanna Artillery*, 71.

52. OR, 25(1):254, 558, 25(2):326, 329, 338, 342; George D. Breck (1st NY Light Artillery) letter, May 6, 1863, typescript at FSNMP.

53. OR, 25(1):566, 810.

54. Urbanus Dart (26th GA Infantry) letter, May 13, 1863, *Brunswick (GA) News*, May 4, 1963; Newell, "Ours," 203; Moore, *Story of a Cannoneer under Stonewall Jackson*, 171–72.

55. Halsey, *Brother against Brother*, 126–27; George D. Breck (1st NY Light Artillery) letter, May 11, 1863, typescript at FSNMP; Sewell Gray (6th ME Infantry) diary, May 1, 1863, Maine State Archives, typescript, copy at FSNMP; Soldier (13th MS Infantry) letter, May 1, 1863, *Mobile (AL) Advertiser and Register*, May 22, 1863.

56. OR, 25(2):328, 331.

57. OR, 25(1):354, 25(2):333; Thomas Beath (19th ME Infantry) diary, May 1–2, 1863, copy at FSNMP.

58. OR, 25(2):327, 331.

59. OR, 25(2):331, 333.

60. OR, 25(1):351.

61. OR, 25(1):351–52, 25(2):302; Sears, *Chancellorsville*, 216–17.

62. OR, 25(1):854–55; Patterson, *Yankee Rebel*, 99.

63. OR, 25(1)855.

4. May 2

1. Henry, *Turn Them Out to Die like a Mule*, 218; *Windham County Monitor* (Brattleboro, VT), Sept. 15, 1893.

2. OR, 25(1):765.

3. Howard, "Eleventh Corps a Chancellorsville," 194.

4. Sears, *Chancellorsville*, 232.

5. Sears, 239.

6. OR, 25(1):558.

7. OR, 25(2):329; Fishel, *Secret War for the Union*, 403. Fishel indicates that the date on the referenced OR document is mistakenly written as May 1. The operative who discovered that information had made his way to Baltimore and relayed the intelligence from there. The copy sent to Colonel Sharpe has a date of May 2.

8. Bigelow, *Campaign of Chancellorsville*, 274.

9. OR, 25(1):219–20, 235–38.

10. OR, 25(1):220, 229.

11. OR, 25(1):855, 25(2):352; McClelen, *I Saw the Elephant*, 35; Banes, *Philadelphia Brigade*, 160.

12. OR, 25(1):254, 558, 25(2):361.

13. OR, 25(1):254, 25(2):351.

14. OR, 25(1):811.

15. OR, 25(1):811; Early, *Autobiographical Sketch and Narrative*, 199–200.

16. James P. Williams (Chesapeake Artillery) letter, May 7, 1863, UVA, copy at FSNMP; Newell, "Ours," 204; Smith, *Richard Snowden Andrews*, 83.

17. James S. Wadsworth letter, May 4, 1863, James S. Wadsworth Family Papers, LC, copy at FSNMP.

18. Daniel D. Andrews (7th MA Infantry) article, *Fall River (MA) Evening News*, Jan. 13, 1912.

19. Andrews article, Jan. 13, 1912.

20. Quiner Scrapbooks: Correspondence of Wisconsin Volunteers, 1861–1865, comp. Edwin B. Quiner, WHS, 8:297, 301, copy at FSNMP; Jacob W. Haas (96th PA Infantry) letter, May 12, 1863, HCWRT, USAMHI, copy at FSNMP.

21. OR, 25(1):259.

22. George D. Breck (Battery L, 1st NY Light Artillery) letter, May 3, 1863, *Rochester (NY) Union and Advertiser*, May 11, 1863.

23. Breck letter, May 3, 1863.

24. OR, 25(1):259; James P. Williams (Chesapeake Artillery) letters, May 2, 7, 1863, UVA, copies at FSNMP.

25. OR, 25(1):215, 622, 25(2):362; OR Supplement, 4:632; Breck letter, May 3, 1863; Benham, "Report to Major General Joseph Hooker, May 20, 1863."

26. Curtis, *Twenty-Fourth Michigan*, 128; OR, 25(1):1034; Soldier (Shaler's brigade) letter, May 5, 1863, *Providence (RI) Daily Evening Press*, May 13, 1863.

27. Sullivan, *Irishman in the Iron Brigade*, 77; John Gibbon letter, May 2, 1863, typescript at FSNMP.

28. OR, 25(2):254–55, 354, 368–69.

29. OR, 25(1):811; Charles Richardson, "Fredericksburg to Salem Church," *Richmond (VA) Times Dispatch*, June 3, 1906. There is a single surviving gun pit on a hill just north of William Street (the historic Orange Plank Road). Earthworks once extended across the ridge now occupied by the University of Mary Washington campus.

30. Bigelow, *Campaign of Chancellorsville*, 272.

31. Bigelow, 276–77, 279–80, 282; Sears, *Chancellorsville*, 247, 254, 256–57; OR, 25(1):772.

32. Bigelow, *Campaign of Chancellorsville*, 283–85; Sears, *Chancellorsville*, 254–57, 262.

33. Bigelow, *Campaign of Chancellorsville*, 285, 294; Sears, *Chancellorsville*, 262.

34. Early, *Autobiographical Sketch and Narrative*, 200; OR, 25(1):811–12.

35. Early, *Autobiographical Sketch and Narrative*, 201; Sears, *To the Gates of Richmond*, 268, 317, 323; "Chilton, Robert Hall," in Boatner, *Civil War Dictionary*, 154.

36. OR, 25(1):812.

37. OR, 25(1):812.

38. Early, *Autobiographical Sketch and Narrative*, 202.

39. OR, 25(1):812, 842; Martin, *Fluvanna Artillery*, 71–72.

40. OR, 25(1):845; Smith, *Richard Snowden Andrews*, 84. Both the Leach and the Cox houses were dwellings along the Telegraph Road (modern Lafayette Boulevard). The Leach house stood on the east side of the road in the vicinity of modern Longstreet Avenue. The surrounding area is developed, but the overall terrain is still evident as a large plateau that would have been attractive for farming as well as for marshaling troops. The Cox house is identified by a state-highway marker on the east side of the road, but the actual structure stood in the southeast quadrant of what is today Lafayette Boulevard and Fleming Street.

41. "Recollections of Fredericksburg," *New Orleans (LA) Times Picayune*, June 23, 1883.

42. "Recollections of Fredericksburg"; "Memoir of Genl. Benjamin Grubb Humphreys," Mississippi Dept. of Archives and History, typescript, chap. 13, copy at FSNMP.

43. OR, 25(2):367; Smith, *Richard Snowden Andrews*, 83–84.

44. Lt. Col. H. C. Jones (57th NC Infantry) report, Alphonso Calhoun Avery Papers, SHC, UNC, copy at FSNMP; *Mobile (AL) Advertiser and Register*, May 22, 1863.

45. OR, 25(1):224, 25(2):354–55, 358, 367; OR, ser. 3, 3:314; Sears, *Chancellorsville*, 264.

46. OR, 25(2):354.

47. OR, 25(2):354.

48. Sears, *Chancellorsville*, 249.

49. OR, 25(1):220.

50. Maj. Rufus W. Wharton (1st Btn. NC Sharpshooters) report, May 13, 1863, Perry Family Papers, copy at FSNMP; OR Supplement, pt. 3, 4:692.

51. OR, 25(1):567, 580; "Second Battle of Fredericksburg," *Vermont Watchman and State Journal* (Montpelier), May 8, 1863; Soldier (Hays's Brigade) letter, May 13, 1863, *Mobile (AL) Advertiser and Register*, May 21, 1863; Alexander B. Sumner (6th ME Infantry) letter, May 11, 1863, typescript at FSNMP; Seymour, *Civil War Memoirs*, 51; Daniel B. Bidwell (49th NY Infantry) letter, May 5, 1863, *Buffalo (NY) Advocate*, May 14, 21, 1863; Chet Campbell (5th WI Infantry) letter, May 20, 1863, typescript at FSNMP; Smith G. Bailey (5th ME Infantry) diary, May 2, 1863, Rauner Special Collections Library, Dartmouth College, copy at FSNMP.

52. Jacob W. Hass (96th PA Infantry) letter, May 12, 1863, HCWRT, USAMHI, copy at FSNMP; Soldier (6th VT Infantry) letter, May 7, 1863, *Burlington (VT) Daily Times*, May 16, 1863; Robert Pratt (5th VT Infantry) letter, typescript at FSNMP; Taylor, *Civil War Letters*, 111.

53. OR, 25(1):567, 812; "Memoir of Genl. Benjamin Grubb Humphreys," Mississippi Dept. of Archives and History, typescript, chap. 13, copy at FSNMP; Harrison, *Fredericksburg Civil War Sites*, 2:211–12. Hazel Hill is no longer standing; an apartment complex with the same name now occupies the prominent hilltop. The Ferneyhough house is also gone, with another dwelling occupying that site but incorporating a portion of the earlier building's foundation.

54. OR, 25(1):813; "Memoir of Genl. Benjamin Grubb Humphreys," Mississippi Dept. of Archives and History, typescript, chap. 13, copy at FSNMP.

55. OR, 25(1):812–13, 25(2):356–57.

56. OR, 25(1):812–13.

57. Soldier (13th MS Infantry) letter, May 6, 1863, *Mobile (AL) Advertiser and Register*, May 22, 1863.

58. Early, *Autobiographical Sketch and Narrative*, 202–3.

59. Lt. Col. Robert F. Webb (6th NC Infantry) report, May 14, 1863, Avery Papers, SHC, UNC, copy at FSNMP; Wharton (1st Btn. NC Sharpshooters) report, May 13, 1863, Perry Family Papers, copy at FSNMP; Charles W. McArthur (61st GA Infantry) letter, May 23, 1863, Kennesaw Mountain National Military Park, copy at FSNMP; Urbanus Dart (26th GA Infantry) letter, May 13, 1863, *Brunswick (GA) News*, May 4, 1963; "Recollections of Fredericksburg," *New Orleans Times Picayune*, June 23, 1883;

William C. Mathews (38th GA Infantry) letter, May 8, 1863, *Sandersville (GA) Central Georgian*, June 3, 1863.

60. OR, 25(1):813–14.

61. OR, 25(2):356; Fairchild, *27th Regiment N.Y. Vols.*, 167; Brooke-Rawle et al., *Third Pennsylvania Cavalry*, 232–33.

62. Halsey, *Brother against Brother*, 127.

63. OR, 25(2):363.

64. OR, 25(1):626; Marker (27th NY Infantry), "The 27th in the Late Battles," *Rochester (NY) Daily Union and Advertiser*, May 11, 1863; George H. Hamilton, "The 5th Maine in the Late Battles," *Lewiston (ME) Daily Evening Journal*, May 18, 1863; Abraham T. Hilands (49th PA Infantry) letter, May 8, 1863, Ottawa County (KS) Museum, typescript, copy at FSNMP; Soldier (27th NY Infantry) letter, *Union (NY) News*, June 4, 1863.

65. OR, 25(2):364–65.

66. OR, 25(1):201, 25(2):365–66; Daniel Butterfield dispatch, May 2, 1863, Box 45, Vol. 64, Gouverneur K. Warren Papers, Special Collections, New York State Library, copy at FSNMP.

67. OR, 25(2):357, 363.

68. OR, 25(1):201–3, 25(2):359.

69. OR, 25(1):814.

5. May 2-3

1. OR, 25(1):573.

2. OR, 25(1):580, 613; OR Supplement, 4:628, 639–40.

3. OR, 25(1):558, 25(2):365.

4. OR, 25(2):366.

5. "From the Fourth Regiment," *Vermont Watchman and State Journal* (Montpelier), May 22, 1863; OR, 25(1):617.

6. OR, 25(1):220, 240.

7. OR, 25(1):220, 25(2):368; John Gibbon letter, May 3, 1863, typescript at FSNMP; Lt. Lemuel B. Norton requisition book, copy at FSNMP.

8. OR, 25(2):396.

9. OR, 25(2):396.

10. OR, 25(1):214, 25(2):360, 368; "From the 127th Regiment," *Lebanon (PA) Courier*, May 21, 1863.

11. OR, 25(1):352–53, 357.

12. "Memoir of Genl. Benjamin Grubb Humphreys," Mississippi Dept. of Archives and History, typescript, chap. 13, copy at FSNMP.

13. OR, 25(1):800; Malone, *Diary*, 32; Maj. William S. Rankin (21st NC Infantry) report, May 14, 1863, and Lt. Col. H. C. Jones Jr. (57th NC Infantry) report, n.d., Alphonso Calhoun Avery Papers, SHC, UNC, copies at FSNMP.

14. OR, 25(2):358–59; Early, *Autobiographical Sketch and Narrative*, 204.

15. OR, 25(1):814.

16. OR, 25(1):842, 845, 847. The positions occupied by the Troup and Pulaski Batteries are within the Fredericksburg and Spotsylvania National Military Park but not interpreted for the events of May 1863.

17. Jonathan T. Scharf (Dement's MD Battery) memoir, Special Collections, New York State Library, typescript, copy at FSNMP.

18. Smith, *Richard Snowden Andrews*, 83–84; OR, 25(1):811, 814.

19. Smith, *Richard Snowden Andrews*, 85.

20. OR, 25(1):609; Lt. John P. Einsfeld (49th NY Infantry) letter, May 9, 1863, *Buffalo (NY) Morning Explorer*, May 19, 1863; "From the 49th Regiment," *Jamestown (NY) Journal*, May 22, 1863; Soldier (49th NY Infantry) letter, May 9, 1863, *Buffalo (NY) Evening Courier and Republic*, May 15, 1863; Capt. Charles Hickhott (49th NY Infantry) letter, May 12, 1863, *Buffalo (NY) Advocate*, May 21, 1863.

21. "Memoir of Genl. Benjamin Grubb Humphreys," Mississippi Dept. of Archives and History, typescript, chap. 13, copy at FSNMP; *New Orleans Times Picayune*, June 23, 1883.

22. "Memoir of Genl. Benjamin Grubb Humphreys," chap. 13.

23. OR, 25(1):558, 563, 573.

24. OR, 25(1):558, 563, 573; "Second Battle of Fredericksburg," *Vermont Watchman and State Journal* (Montpelier), May 8, 1863.

25. OR Supplement, 4:640; Bigelow, "Battle of Marye's Heights and Salem Church," 241.

26. Soldier (2nd RI Infantry) letter, May 14, 1863, *Providence (RI) Daily Evening Press*, May 16, 1863; Brewster, *When This Cruel War Is Over*, 224.

27. Samuel S. Kissinger (65th NY Infantry/1st US Chasseurs) letter, May 5, 1863, *Tiffin (OH) Weekly Tribune*, May 22, 1863; Swinfen, *Ruggles' Regiment*, 19.

28. Jackson, "Sedgwick at Fredericksburg and Salem Heights," 225; Soldier (2nd RI Infantry) letter, May 14, 1863, *Providence (RI) Daily Evening Press*, May 16, 1863; Soldier (2nd RI Infantry) letter, May 5, 1863, ibid., May 13, 1863; Tsouras, *George H. Sharpe*, 463.

29. "Memoir of Genl. Benjamin Grubb Humphreys," Mississippi Dept. of Archives and History, typescript, chap. 13, copy at FSNMP.

30. Tsouras, *George H. Sharpe*, 463. The modern road, Virginia 2/17, runs along a causeway elevated twenty-five feet above the Hazel Run bottomlands.

31. Soldier (2nd RI Infantry) letter, May 5, 1863, *Providence (RI) Daily Evening Press*, May 13, 1863; "Sketch of Battlefield by Joseph Hamblin," in Edward J. Alexander, "The Night March into Fredericksburg, May 2–3, 1863," Emerging Civil War, May 2, 2019, https://emergingcivilwar.com/2019/05/02/the-night-march-into-fredericksburg-may-2-3-1863/ (accessed June 23, 2019).

32. Samuel S. Kissinger (65th NY Infantry/1st US Chasseurs) letter, May 5, 1863, *Tiffin (OH) Weekly Tribune*, May 22, 1863; *Birney's Zouaves*, 144.

33. Jackson, "Sedgwick at Fredericksburg and Salem Heights," 225–26.

34. OR, 25(2):383; OR Supplement, 4:632, 640, 645; Jackson, "Sedgwick at Fredericksburg and Salem Heights," 227; *Birney's Zouaves*, 144.

35. OR, 25(2):366, 384; Sears, *Chancellorsville*, 305, 310.
36. OR, 25(2):385.
37. OR, 25(1):201.
38. OR, 25(2):366.
39. OR, 25(1):220, 25(2):384–85.
40. John Gibbon letter, May 3, 1863, typescript at FSNMP; Committee of Regimental Association, *127th Regiment Pennsylvania Volunteers*, 168–69.
41. OR, 25(2):385; Haskell, *Haskell of Gettysburg*, 70.
42. "Memoir of Genl. Benjamin Grubb Humphreys," Mississippi Dept. of Archives and History, typescript, chap. 13, copy at FSNMP.
43. OR, 25(1):356, 358; Chapin, *Thirty-Fourth Regiment, NYSV*, 91.
44. OR, 25(1):358; Harrison, *Fredericksburg Civil War Sites*, 1:80–84. Harrison references a two-story building, but contemporary photos make clear the Woolen Mills was a four-story structure. The nearby Bridgewater Mill was the two-story industrial building. Woolen Mills is a three-story building today, its upper story knocked off after a postwar fire.
45. "Memoir of Genl. Benjamin Grubb Humphreys," Mississippi Dept. of Archives and History, typescript, chap. 13, copy at FSNMP.
46. *History of the Nineteenth Regiment Massachusetts Volunteer Infantry*, 203; Chapin, *Thirty-Fourth Regiment, NYSV*, 91.
47. Rhodes, *Battery B, First Regiment Rhode Island Light Artillery*, 169–70.
48. Rhodes, 169–70.
49. OR Supplement, 4:645.
50. Sylvester F. Hildebrand (139th PA Infantry) account, *Apollo (PA) Sentinel*, Apr. 21, 1911; Brewster, *When This Cruel War Is Over*, 224–25; OR Supplement, 4:632.
51. OR, 25(1):617. The described terrain has since become a residential neighborhood. The swale, approximately 250 yards from the Sunken Road, is on the east side of Littlepage Street. The terrain drops off again on the east side of Spottswood Street. Federal troops could find cover between what is now Spotswood Street and the low-lying drainage that is covered today by Kenmore Avenue.
52. Stevens, *Three Years in the Sixth Corps*, 193; *Birney's Zouaves*, 32, 34, 302; Soldier (23rd PA Infantry) letter, May 11, 1863, *Columbia (PA) Spy*, May 23, 1863. One account mentions the regiment receiving fire at twenty yards; another specifies fifty yards. The author has averaged these as thirty to forty yards.
53. OR, 25(1):558, 617; OR Supplement, 4:632–33, 641; "The Attack on Fredericksburg," *Albany (NY) Evening Journal*, May 20, 1863; Hyde, *Civil War Letters by General Thomas W. Hyde*, 71.
54. Bigelow, "Battle of Marye's Heights and Salem Church," 245–46.
55. OR, 25(1):617; Rhodes, *All for the Union*, 105; OR Supplement, 4:652.
56. OR, 25(1):563. The modern location of this position is the Cobblestone Square traffic circle near Lafayette Boulevard.
57. OR, 25(1):563; OR Supplement, 4:655–56. The slight knoll on which McCarthy's guns deployed is near modern-day Lafayette Boulevard and Jackson Street.
58. OR, 25(1):622.

59. OR Supplement, 4:652.

60. Edgar P. Ackerman (2nd NJ Infantry), "Fredericksburg Heights Stormed and Carried," *Newark (NJ) Daily Advertiser*, May 6, 1863; Soldier (139th PA Infantry) letter, May 11, 1863, *Pittsburg Evening Chronicle*, May 16, 1863; Brewster, *When This Cruel War Is Over*, 225; Ralph Happel, notes on Douglas H. Gordon to Ann Eliza Gordon, Feb. 2, 1863, copy at FSNMP.

61. OR Supplement, 4:641.

62. OR, 25(1):352–53; Douglas H. Gordon letters, Jan. 31, Feb. 2, 1863, copies at FSNMP.

63. OR, 25(1):350; Rhodes, *Battery B, First Regiment Rhode Island Light Artillery*, 170.

64. Morse, *Personal Experiences*, 22; John Gibbon letter, May 3, 1863, typescript at FSNMP.

65. OR, 25(1):567; Stevens, "In Battle and In Prison," 215; Jacob W. Haas (96th PA Infantry) letter, May 12, 1863. Rigby's position was on what is now Shannon Airport. McCartney deployed on ground that now has been acquired by battlefield preservation groups and will eventually become part of the Fredericksburg and Spotsylvania National Military Park.

66. Alexander, *Fighting for the Confederacy*, 208.

67. OR, 25(1):567, 580; OR Supplement, 4:624.

68. Richardson, *Chancellorsville Campaign*, 29. The historical fields of fire for these batteries are currently blocked by a neighborhood and mature trees along a rail spur.

69. Early, *Autobiographical Sketch and Narrative*, 205; "Memoir of Genl. Benjamin Grubb Humphreys," Mississippi Dept. of Archives and History, typescript, chap. 13, copy at FSNMP.

70. OR, 25(1):842, 846; Smith, *Richard Snowden Andrews*, 81–82, 85. The earthworks occupied by Carlton's Troup Artillery are preserved within the Fredericksburg and Spotsylvania National Military Park, but they are grown up in trees, so its historical field of fire is not evident.

71. Early, *Autobiographical Sketch and Narrative*, 205–6.

72. Memoirs of Eli S. Coble, Dec. 1862–June 1863, Greensboro (NC) Historical Museum Archives, 2, copy at FSNMP; Buck, *With the Old Confederates*, 78.

73. Jonathan T. Scharf (Dement MD Artillery) memoir, Special Collections, New York State Library, transcript, copy at FSNMP.

74. OR, 25(1):580, 590; William A. Lessig, "The Ninety-Sixth Reg., P.V., in the Late Battles," *Pottsville (PA) Miner's Journal*, June 6, 1863; Jacob W. Haas (96th PA Infantry) letter, May 12, 1863, HCWRT, USAMHI, copy at FSNMP.

75. Lessig, "Ninety-Sixth Reg., P.V., in the Late Battles."

76. Jacob W. Haas (96th PA Infantry) letter, May 12, 1863, HCWRT, USAMHI, copy at FSNMP; Col. Isaac E. Avery (6th NC Infantry) report for Hoke's Brigade, n.d. [May 13 or 14, 1863?], Alphonso Calhoun Avery Papers, SHC, UNC, typescript, copy at FSNMP.

77. OR, 25:(1)580; Jacob W. Haas (96th PA Infantry) letter, May 12, 1863, HCWRT, USAMHI, copy at FSNMP; M. Bricksill, "The Ninety-Sixth Regt., P. V. at the Second Battle of Fredericksburg," *Pottsville (PA) Miner's Journal*, May 22, 1863.

78. Smith G. Bailey (5th ME Infantry) diary, May 3, 1863, Rauner Special Collections Library, Dartmouth College, copy at FSNMP; Bicknell, *Fifth Regiment Maine Volunteers*, 217–19.

79. OR, 25(1):584; George H. Hamilton, "The Fifth Maine in the Late Battles," *Lewiston (ME) Daily Evening Journal*, May 18, 1863; Capt. Frank Lindley Lemont (5th WI Infantry) letter, May 13, 1863, copy at FSNMP.

80. Clark S. Edwards (5th ME Infantry), "War Reminiscences," Bethel Historical Society; Bicknell, *Fifth Regiment Maine Volunteers*, 220.

81. OR, 25(1):580, 584, 588, 590; William A. Lessig, "The Ninety-Sixth Reg., P.V., in the Late Battles," *Pottsville (PA) Miner's Journal*, June 6, 1863; Clark S. Edwards (5th ME Infantry) report to Adjutant General, State of Maine, Jan. 27, 1864, Maine State Archives.

82. OR, 25(1):598; Smith, *Richard Snowden Andrews*, 85.

83. James P. Williams (Chesapeake Artillery) letter, May 7, 1863, Manuscripts Collection, UVA, typescript at FSNMP; David E. Moore (Rockbridge Artillery) letter, n.d., John Warwick Daniel Papers, UVA.

84. James P. Williams (Chesapeake Artillery) letter, May 7, 1863, Manuscripts Collection, UVA, typescript at FSNMP; David E. Moore (Rockbridge Artillery) letter, n.d., John Warwick Daniel Papers, UVA; Jonathan T. Scharf (Dement MD Artillery) memoir, Special Collections, New York State Library, transcript, copy at FSNMP.

85. OR, 25(1):592–93, 595–96, 598; Francis E. Pinto, "History of the 32nd Regiment, New York Volunteers in the Civil War, 1861 to 1863, and Personal Recollections during That Period," Brooklyn, NY, 1895, typescript, WHS, copy at FSNMP, 139; Smith, *Richard Snowden Andrews*, 87.

86. OR, 25(1):570, 575; Haines, *Fifteenth Regiment, New Jersey Volunteers*, 51.

87. Smith, *Richard Snowden Andrews*, 87; Soldier (Rockbridge Artillery) letter, May 9, 1863, William McCauley Papers, SHC, UNC, copy at FSNMP.

88. Buck, *With the Old Confederates*, 78–79.

89. Buck, 78–79.

90. Soldier (Battery A, MA Light Artillery) letter, May 7, 1863, *Cambridge (MA) Chronicle*, May 16, 1863.

91. OR, 25(1):593–94; Marshall B. Stull, "From the Fifteenth Regiment," *Sussex (NJ) Register*, May 22, 1863; OR Supplement, 4:625.

92. Halsey, *Brother against Brother*, 128.

93. OR, 25(1):594; Soldier (Rockbridge Artillery) letter, May 9, 1863, McCauley Papers; Soldier (Battery A, MA Light Artillery) letter, May 7, 1863, *Cambridge (MA) Chronicle*, May 16, 1863.

94. OR, 25(1):581, 586, 588: Fairchild, *27th Regiment N.Y. Vols.*, 167; Marker (27th NY Infantry), "The 27th in the Late Battles," *Rochester (NY) Daily Union and Advertiser*, May 11, 1863; Morse, *Personal Experiences*, 23.

95. OR, 25(2):383; Newton T. Hartshorn (US Engineers) diary, May 3, 1863, Rauner Special Collections Library, Dartmouth College, typescript, copy at FSNMP; Gilbert Thompson, "U.S. Engineer Battalion," *National Tribune*, Aug. 16, 1888. Brig. Gen. Henry Benham's report claims that the relocated bridges were in use earlier in the

morning, but he was at Banks' Ford during that evolution. The time indicated here is from men who were on the ground.

96. OR, 25(1):214; Gilbert Thompson, "My Journal, 1861–1865, U.S. Engineers Battalion Army of the Potomac," May 3, 1863, copy at FSNMP.

97. Hartshorn diary, May 3, 1863; Gilbert Thompson, "U.S. Engineer Battalion," *National Tribune*, Aug. 16, 1888.

98. "Memoir of Genl. Benjamin Grubb Humphreys," Mississippi Dept. of Archives and History, typescript, chap. 13, copy at FSNMP.

99. "Memoir of Genl. Benjamin Grubb Humphreys," chap. 13.

6. Morning of May 3

1. Gallagher, "East of Chancellorsville," 40–41; Bigelow, *Campaign of Chancellorsville*, 136, 138.

2. Harrison, *Fredericksburg Civil War Sites*, 2:207–11.

3. Harrison, 1:57; Virginia Historic Landmarks Commission, "Federal Hill," National Register of Historic Places reference 75002110, Mar. 26, 1975, Virginia Department of Historic Resources, Richmond. Federal Hill was built in 1795. In the early twentieth century, Elizabeth Lanier acquired the home and undertook a substantial renovation, including repair of visible battle damage. The Lanier investment also included installation of the dormers, an adaptation not unusual in the 1920s and 1930s, when Colonial Revival architecture was in vogue and people of means made their historic homes look as colonial as possible. Federal Hill was within the extreme range of the infantry weapons wielded by Confederate troops at Marye's Heights, and the twentieth-century renovation uncovered dozens of Minié balls embedded in the wood framing around one of the second-floor windows. Confederate riflemen are said to have targeted a Federal sharpshooter there in December 1862, but given the need to plan a battle on the morning of May 3, 1863, those bullets probably came from Confederates firing at someone studying the Southern position with binoculars or a telescope.

4. "Recollections of Fredericksburg," *New Orleans (LA) Times Picayune*, June 23, 1883; "Memoir of Genl. Benjamin Grubb Humphreys," Mississippi Dept. of Archives and History, typescript, chap. 13, copy at FSNMP. The ditch once known as Marye's Canal remains an important drainage for that part of town but is now covered. Kenmore Avenue roughly delineates its route.

5. OR, 25(1):840.

6. OR, 25(1):235; Sears, *Chancellorsville*, 312–13, 319–20.

7. Bigelow, *Campaign of Chancellorsville*, 350–52; Sears, *Chancellorsville*, 331–33.

8. Bigelow, *Campaign of Chancellorsville*, 366–67; Sears, *Chancellorsville*, 337–39.

9. Sears, *Chancellorsville*, 346; Bigelow, *Campaign of Chancellorsville*, 375–77.

10. OR, 25(2):387.

11. OR, 25(2):386.

12. OR, 25(2):386.

13. OR, 25(2):386.

14. OR, 25(2):386.

15. OR, 25(2):386.
16. OR, 25(2):387.
17. OR, 25(2):387.
18. Fishel, *Secret War for the Union*, 402, 405–6.
19. OR, 25(2):385; Fishel, *Secret War*, 402, 405–6.
20. OR, 25(2):388.
21. OR Supplement, 4:649; Bigelow, "Battle of Marye's Heights and Salem Church," 247.
22. Gamache, "Preliminary Historic Structures Report: Fredericksburg City Cemetery Stone Gateway," 34–35; Perry, "West Wall Soldiers," 82–83.
23. OR, 25(1):220, 225–26, 243; Mann, *Bells and Belfries*, 43. The courthouse bell was cast at the Revere Foundry, Boston, in 1828.
24. OR, 25(1):201, 352; Ford, *Fifteenth Regiment Massachusetts Volunteer Infantry*, 249; Harrison, "Southern Exposure," 179–83. The captured Confederate map described in Harrison's article shows Federal columns moving straight out of Fredericksburg, which would have been along Princess Anne Street.
25. OR, 25(1):201; Harrison, *Fredericksburg Sites*, 2:120–25. While most of the river mansions have succumbed to time and neglect, the hilltop mansions remain intact. Braehead, Brompton, and Fall Hill are well-maintained homes. Snowden sustained substantial damage from a fire in 1926 but was rebuilt; it is now used as corporate offices.
26. OR, 25(1):201–2, 350, 358–59; Rhodes, *All for the Union*, 105.
27. OR, 25(1):202, 358. The stone walls lining the old road are long gone, and the modern Fall Hill Avenue runs straighter than the old route. From about modern Progress Street to Hanson Avenue, the old road coursed along a slight depression just to the north of the modern one. The character of this historic terrain is most evident where Fall Hill intersects Hanson. Modern US Route 1 crosses the canal where the old bridge stood. A stone abutment remains visible on the north side of the waterway, adjacent to the highway bridge.
28. OR, 25(1):201–2.
29. OR, 25(1):839; "Memoir of Genl. Benjamin Grubb Humphreys," Mississippi Dept. of Archives and History, typescript, chap. 13, copy at FSNMP. The three companies Colonel Humphreys left with the Eighteenth Mississippi were C, F, and L. The substantial earthworks on top of the hill adjacent to Hanover Street have since disappeared under a university building, but the property is still called Trench Hill. A portion of its supporting infantry trench remains faintly evident as a shelf on the grassy slope. The hill south of William Street was obliterated during construction of an apartment building.
30. OR Supplement, 4:633, 649; Soldier (2nd RI Infantry) letter, May 14, 1863, *Providence (RI) Daily Evening Press*, May 16, 1863; Brewster, *When This Cruel War Is Over*, 225.
31. OR, 25(1):358, 814; "Second Battle of Fredericksburg," *Vermont Watchman and State Journal* (Montpelier), May 8, 1863; Harrison, *Tour of Civil War Sites on the University of Mary Washington*, 15.
32. OR, 25(1):358; Ambrose F. Cole (59th NY Infantry) letter, May 8, 1863, typescript at FSNMP.

33. Abbott, *Fallen Leaves*, 174; Holmes, *Touched with Fire*, 92.

34. OR, 25(1):814–15; John Gibbon letter, May 3, 1863, typescript at FSNMP.

35. OR, 25(1):814; "Memoir of Genl. Benjamin Grubb Humphreys," Mississippi Dept. of Archives and History, typescript, chap. 13, copy at FSNMP; William I. Bishop (10th MA Infantry) letter, May 6, 1863, *Hampshire (MA) Gazette*, May 19, 1863.

36. OR, 25(1):839; Seymour, *Civil War Memoirs*, 52; "First Louisiana Brigade," *Mobile (AL) Advertiser and Register*, May 21, 1863.

37. OR, 25(1):202, 355–57. This bridge was located where modern Fall Hill Avenue crosses over the Rappahannock Canal. A stone abutment remains visible on the east side of the canal. Prior to construction of the existing bridge, a search on the west side of the canal found no evidence of a similar abutment, which was likely obliterated during construction of an earlier bridge.

38. OR, 25(1):350, 355; Chapin, *Thirty-Fourth Regiment, NYSV*, 92; Bruce, *Twentieth Regiment of Massachusetts Volunteer Infantry*, 253.

39. Rhodes, *All for the Union*, 105; OR Supplement, 4:582–83; *History of the Nineteenth Regiment Massachusetts Volunteer Infantry*, 204. This description of Battery G's position appears to coincide with the area in the vicinity of modern Forbes and Princess Anne Streets.

40. OR, 25(1):358–59; OR Supplement, 4:649; Rhodes, *All for the Union*, 105; Newell, *"Ours,"* 205.

41. OR, 25(1):855.

42. OR, 25(1):855, 885.

43. OR, 25(1):855–56.

44. OR, 25(1):884–85. The Pittsylvania Artillery had been organized with two 3-inch Ordnance Rifles and two 10-pounder Parrotts. At Gettysburg it had two 12-pounder Napoleons in place of the Parrott rifles. It is not clear from available documentation if the battery already had the Napoleons at Fredericksburg in the spring of 1863.

45. OR, 25(1):354–55, 358, 856; *History of the First Regiment Minnesota Volunteer Infantry*, 296, 298.

46. OR, 25(1):856; Oden, "End of Oden's War," 81–82 (May 3, 1863).

47. OR, 25(1):844. The distances stated are measured from existing earthworks.

48. OR, 25(1):856.

49. Col. John C. C. Sanders (11th AL Infantry) report, May 10, 1863, LC, copy at FSNMP; "Wilcox's Brigade," *Richmond (VA) Sentinel*, May 30, 1863.

50. OR, 25(1):856.

51. OR, 25(1):202.

52. OR, 25(1):599.

53. OR, 25(1):612, 614; OR Supplement, 4:628. The battery positions are now part of a Fredericksburg neighborhood called Mayfield.

54. Michler, *Fredericksburg [Dec. 1862]*, 1867, map, color, 1:21,120 scale; Bicknell, *Fifth Regiment Maine Volunteers*, 221.

55. William Stowe (2nd VT Infantry) letter, May 15, 1863, typescript at FSNMP; Robert Pratt (5th VT Infantry) letter, May 13, 1863, typescript at FSNMP.

56. OR, 25(1):599.

57. Bilby, "Through Hades with His Hat Off," 14–15.

58. Bigelow, "Marye's Heights and Salem Church," 256; Joseph C. Felton (2nd VT Infantry) letter, May 18, 1863, typescript at FSNMP.

59. Sewell Gray (6th ME Infantry) diary, May 3, 1863, Maine State Archives, typescript at FSNMP; Soldier (5th WI Infantry) letter, May 8, 1863, *Dunn County Lumberman* (Menomonie, WI), May 23, 1863; Cushing, "Charge of the Light Division at Marye's Heights," 339; Quiner Scrapbooks: Correspondence of Wisconsin Volunteers, 1861–1865, comp. Edwin B. Quiner, WHS, 8:298, 301, copy at FSNMP; Report of the Proceedings of 5th Wisconsin Vol. Infantry, Fifteenth Annual Reunion Held at Milwaukee, July 23–24, 1901, WHS, 4, copy at FSNMP.

60. OR, 25(1):558; OR Supplement, 4:642; Lt. A. W. Hathaway (5th WI Infantry) letter, May 7, 1863, *Janesville (WI) Daily Gazette*, May 13, 1863; Proceedings at the Annual Meeting of the Association of Fifth Wisconsin Volunteer Infantry, Held at Milwaukee, June 27–28, 1900, WHS, 12, copy at FSNMP; Report of the Proceedings of 5th Wisconsin (1901), 4, 8, copy at FSNMP; Quiner Scrapbooks: Correspondence of Wisconsin Volunteers, 8:307, copy at FSNMP.

61. OR, 25(1):622.

62. Sears, *Chancellorsville*, 353.

63. OR, 25(1):558.

64. D. D. Andrews (7th MA Infantry) memoir, *Fall River (MA) Evening News*, Jan. 13, 1912.

65. OR, 25(1):558.

66. Brewer, *Sixty-First Regiment Pennsylvania Volunteers*, 53.

67. Brewer, 54.

68. Gallagher, "East of Chancellorsville," 40–41.

69. OR, 25(1):814.

70. OR, 25(1):812, 846.

71. OR, 25(1):812; "Memoir of Genl. Benjamin Grubb Humphreys," Mississippi Dept. of Archives and History, typescript, chap. 13, copy at FSNMP.

72. OR, 25(1):839; Quinn, *History of the City of Fredericksburg*, 97.

73. "Hyde, Thomas Worcester," in Boatner, *Civil War Dictionary*, 421; Hyde, *Civil War Letters by General Thomas W. Hyde*, 71 (May 7, 1863).

74. Cushing, "Charge of the Light Division at Marye's Heights," 338.

75. OR, 25(1):626; OR Supplement, 4:641; Cushing, "Charge of the Light Division at Marye's Heights," 339.

76. Dr. Edwin D. Buckman (98th PA Infantry) letter, May 9, 1863, copy at FSNMP.

77. David Burhans (43rd NY Infantry) letter, May 5, 1863, *Albany (NY) Evening Journal*, May 12, 1863.

78. Burhans letter, May 5, 1863; William H. Terrell (43rd NY Infantry) letter, May 3, 1863, *Albany (NY) Evening Journal*, May 12, 1863; Harrison, *Fredericksburg Sites*, 1:56–61.

79. John Newman (43rd NY Infantry) letter, May 4, 1863, copy at FSNMP; Stevens, *Three Years in the Sixth Corps*, 199.

80. OR Supplement, 4:636; Brewer, *Sixty-First Regiment Pennsylvania Volunteers*, 54; David Burhans (43rd NY Infantry) letter, May 5, 1863, *Albany (NY) Evening Journal*, May 15, 1863.

81. OR Supplement, 4:646.

82. William A. Moore (3rd Battery, NY Light Artillery) memoirs, n.d., Civil War Miscellaneous Collection, USAMHI, 35.

83. Lowell M. Maxham (7th MA Infantry), "A Famous Charge," *Boston Journal*, May 1893; Newell, *"Ours,"* 206; Hutchinson, *Seventh Massachusetts Volunteer Infantry*, 125.

84. Hutchinson, *Seventh Massachusetts Volunteer Infantry*, 125; Maxham, "Famous Charge," *Boston Journal*, May 1893.

85. Cushing, "Charge of the Light Division at Marye's Heights," 338–39; Soldier (5th WI Infantry) letter, May 6, 1863, *Wabasha County Herald* (Wabasha, MN), May 21, 1863; Alexander B. Sumner (6th ME Infantry) letter, May 11, 1863, typescript at FSNMP; Judd, *Thirty-Third N.Y.S. Vols.*, 294; Trask, *Fire Within*, 172; Report of the Proceedings of 5th Wisconsin (1901), 4, copy at FSNMP; Clark, *Campaigning with the Sixth Maine*, 33.

86. Alexander B. Sumner letter, May 11, 1863; Clark, *Campaigning with the Sixth Maine*, 33.

87. Alexander B. Sumner letter, May 11, 1863; Clark, *Campaigning with the Sixth Maine*, 33; Quiner Scrapbooks: Correspondence of Wisconsin Volunteers, 8:283, copy at FSNMP.

88. Benjamin R. J. Thaxter (6th ME Infantry) letter, May 21, 1863, USAMHI, transcript, copy at FSNMP; Clark, *Campaigning with the Sixth Maine*, 33; Quiner Scrapbooks: Correspondence of Wisconsin Volunteers, 8:298, copy at FSNMP.

89. Cushing, "Charge of the Light Division at Marye's Heights," 339.

90. Lowell M. Maxham (7th MA Infantry), "A Famous Charge," *Boston Journal*, May 1893; D. D. Andrews (7th MA Infantry) memoir, *Fall River (MA) Evening News*, Jan. 13, 1912.

91. Report of the Proceedings of 5th Wisconsin (1901), 4–5, copy at FSNMP; "Justice to a Wisconsin Regiment," *Wisconsin State Journal* (Madison), May 26, 1863; Soldier (5th WI Infantry) letter, May 14, 1863, *Grant County Witness* (Lancaster, WI), May 28, 1863.

92. Mundy, *No Rich Men's Sons*, 110, 117; Quiner Scrapbooks: Correspondence of Wisconsin Volunteers, 8:298, copy at FSNMP.

93. "Justice to a Wisconsin Regiment," *Wisconsin State Journal* (Madison), May 26, 1863; Proceedings at the Annual Meeting of the Association of Fifth Wisconsin (1900), 23, copy at FSNMP; Quiner Scrapbooks: Correspondence of Wisconsin Volunteers, 8:307, copy at FSNMP.

94. Correspondence of *Whig and Courier*, May 23, 1863, *Bangor (ME) Daily Whig and Courier*, May 25, 1863; Anderson, *Papers*, 207–8 (letter, May 4, 1863).

95. *Birney's Zouaves*, 142. The Ebert house was the structure closest to where the Twenty-Third Pennsylvania took fire before dawn.

96. Stevens, *Three Years in the Sixth Corps*, 198; Hutchinson, *Seventh Massachusetts Volunteer Infantry*, 125; Harrison, *Fredericksburg Sites*, 2:172–74.

97. Hutchinson, *Seventh Massachusetts Volunteer Infantry*, 126; Lowell M. Maxham (7th MA Infantry), "A Famous Charge," *Boston Journal*, May 1893; D. D. Andrews (7th MA Infantry) memoir, *Fall River (MA) Evening News*, Jan. 13, 1912.

98. Brewer, *Sixty-First Regiment Pennsylvania Volunteers*, 55.

99. OR Supplement, 4:646; George B. Lincoln (67th NY Infantry), "The First Long Island Regiment at Fredericksburg," *Brooklyn (NY) Eagle*, May 18, 1863.

100. OR, 25(1):814.

101. OR Supplement, 4:646; Lincoln, "First Long Island Regiment at Fredericksburg"; Nelson Cross (67th NY Infantry) account, *Brooklyn (NY) Standard Union*, June 9, 1888.

102. Clark, *Campaigning with the Sixth Maine*, 33; Proceedings at the Annual Meeting of the Association of Fifth Wisconsin (1900), 23, copy at FSNMP; Quiner Scrapbooks: Correspondence of Wisconsin Volunteers, 8:298, copy at FSNMP.

103. "Justice to a Wisconsin Regiment," *Wisconsin State Journal* (Madison), May 26, 1863.

104. Quiner Scrapbooks: Correspondence of Wisconsin Volunteers, 8:292, copy at FSNMP; Report of the Proceedings of 5th Wisconsin (1901), 12, copy at FSNMP.

105. William Stowe (2nd VT Infantry) letter, May 15, 1863, typescript at FSNMP.

106. OR, 25(1):599, 611.

107. OR, 25(1):602–3; Selden Connor (7th ME Infantry) letter, May 10, 1863, Brown Univ. Library, typescript, copy at FSNMP.

108. Lt. Col. Winsor B. French (77th NY Infantry) letter, May 19, 1863, MS 16278, Special Collections, New York State Library, typescript at FSNMP.

109. OR, 25(1):812.

110. OR, 25(1):599, 612, 614.

111. Orin P. Rugg (77th NY Infantry) letter, May 11, 1863, Sarasota Springs Historical Society, typescript, copy at FSNMP; OR, 25(1):602–3, 608.

112. Hiram H. Tilley (2nd VT Infantry) letter, May 6, 1863, Pearce Collection, Navarro College, typescript at FSNMP; Bilby, "Through Hades with His Hat Off," 15; Fisk, *Hard Marching*, 78.

113. Tilley letter, May 6, 1863.

114. Tilley letter, May 6, 1863; OR, 25(1):602–3; Lt. Col. Winsor B. French (77th NY Infantry) letter, May 19, 1863, MS 16278, Special Collections, New York State Library, typescript at FSNMP; George T. Stevens (77th NY Infantry) letter, May 11, 1863, *Saratogian* (Saratoga, NY), May 21, 1863.

115. Soldier (6th VT Infantry) letter, May 7, 1863, *Burlington (VT) Daily Times*, May 16, 1863.

116. Soldier (6th VT Infantry) letter, May 7, 1863.

7. Afternoon of May 3

1. Jackson, "Sedgwick at Fredericksburg and Salem Heights," 229–30.

2. OR Supplement, 4:634; Edward S. Duffey (Parker's VA Battery) diary, May 3, 1863, Virginia Historical Society, copy at FSNMP.

3. Cushing, "Charge of the Light Division at Marye's Heights," 340; William M. Owen, *In Camp and Battle with the Washington Artillery of New Orleans* (Boston: Ticknor and Company, 1885), 222–23; Sears, *Chancellorsville*, 494.

4. Krick, *Parker's Virginia Battery*, 142; Thomas J. Lutman (Washington Artillery) diary, War Library and Museum, Philadelphia, copy at FSNMP.

5. Duffey diary, May 3, 1863; Krick, *Parker's Virginia Battery*, 142–43.

6. Krick, *Parker's Virginia Battery*, 143.

7. Hutchinson, *Seventh Massachusetts Volunteer Infantry*, 127; Proceedings at the Annual Meeting of the Association of Fifth Wisconsin Volunteer Infantry, Held at Milwaukee, June 27–28, 1900, WHS, 21, copy at FSNMP. An outbuilding on that slope still has bullet holes in its weatherboards.

8. "The First Long Island Regiment at Fredericksburg," *Brooklyn (NY) Daily Eagle*, May 18, 1863.

9. Harrison, *Tour of Civil War Sites on the University of Mary Washington*, 15; OR, 25(1):626; Owen, *Washington Artillery*, 223. The Confederate gun pits were in the vicinity of what is now the University of Mary Washington's Monroe and Willard Halls. The earthworks are gone, but the deep gully is still evident.

10. OR, 25(1):626–27; OR Supplement, 4:642; "Our Army Correspondence," *Pittsburg Evening Chronicle*, May 18, 1863; "Gallant Conduct of the Thirty-Third," *Penn-Yan (NY) Democrat*, June 5, 1863.

11. "Memoir of Genl. Benjamin Grubb Humphreys," Mississippi Dept. of Archives and History, typescript, chap. 13, copy at FSNMP.

12. *Birney's Zouaves*, 147–48; OR Supplement, 4:647.

13. OR, 25(1):617, 620, 622, 624; Soldier (6th VT Infantry) letter, May 7, 1863, *Burlington (VT) Times*, May 16, 1863.

14. OR, 25(1):617; OR Supplement, 4:653, 660.

15. OR, 25(1):847.

16. David T. Morrell, "From the Twenty-Sixth Regiment," *Newark (NJ) Daily Advertiser*, May 19, 1863.

17. OR, 25(1):599, 842, 846; William P. Wright (1st NY Independent Battery) diary, May 3, 1863, Osborne Family Papers, Dept. of Special Collections, Syracuse Univ. Library, typescript, copy at FSNMP; "The Troup Artillery," *Athens (GA) Southern Banner*, May 27, 1863.

18. Henry J. Gifford (33rd NY Infantry) letter, May 7, 1863, *New York Daily Union and Advertiser*, May 13, 1863; Selden Connor (7th ME Infantry) letter, May 10, 1863, Brown Univ. Library, typescript, copy at FSNMP; Soldier (6th ME Infantry) letter, May 7, 1863, *Gardiner (ME) Home Journal*, May 14, 1863.

19. Stevens, *Three Years in the Sixth Corps*, 195; "The Storming of the Heights of Fredericksburg" (Colonel Grant's supplementary report), *Rutland (VT) Weekly Herald*, May 28, 1863; Lt. Col. Winsor B. French (77th NY Infantry) letter, May 19, 1863, MS 16278, Special Collections, New York State Library, copy at FSNMP.

20. Fisk, *Hard Marching*, 78; Early, *Autobiographical Sketch and Narrative*, 206; "First Louisiana Brigade," *Mobile (AL) Advertiser and Register*, May 21, 1863; "The Second Regiment at Mayre's [sic] Heights," *Orleans County Monitor* (Barton, VT), Feb. 25, 1889.

21. OR, 25(1):602, 612; Lt. Col. Winsor B. French (77th NY Infantry) letter, May 6, 1863, *Saratogian* (Saratoga, NY), May 14, 1863, copy at FSNMP; "The Storming of the Heights of Fredericksburg" (Colonel Grant's supplementary report), *Rutland (VT) Daily Herald*, May 28 1863; Stevens, *Three Years in the Sixth Corps*, 206; "The

Second Regiment at Mayre's [sic] Heights," *Orleans County Monitor* (Barton, VT), Feb. 25, 1889; Fisk, *Hard Marching*, 79, 86; Peter S. Chase (2nd VT Infantry) diary, May 3, 1863, *Windham County Monitor* (Brattleboro, VT), Sept. 15, 1893.

22. William Stowe (2nd VT Infantry) letter, May 15, 1863, typescript at FSNMP; "Storming of Mayre's [sic] Heights," *St. Johnsbury (VT) Caledonian*, Apr. 23, 1885.

23. Fisk, *Hard Marching*, 86; Stowe letter, May 15, 1863; Judd, *Thirty-Third N.Y.S. Vols.*, 298; Selden Connor (7th ME Infantry) letter, May 10, 1863, Brown Univ. Library, typescript, copy at FSNMP.

24. OR, 25(1):847.

25. OR, 25(1):847; Smith, *A Savannah Family*, 85, 165–66.

26. OR, 25(1):842.

27. Fisk, *Hard Marching*, 79.

28. John J. Toffey (21st NJ Infantry) letter, May 9, 1863, typescript at FSNMP; Fisk, *Hard Marching*, 80.

29. OR, 25(1):610–11; Stevens, *Three Years in the Sixth Corps*, 197.

30. OR, 25(1):609–11; Soldier (6th CT Infantry) letter, May 7, 1863, *Burlington (VT) Times*, May 16, 1863; Orin P. Rugg (77th NY Infantry) letter, May 11, 1863, Sarasota Springs Historical Society, typescript, copy at FSNMP; "Storming Mayre's [sic] Heights," *St. Johnsbury (VT) Caledonian*, Apr. 23, 1885; Lt. Col. Winsor B. French (77th NY Infantry) letter, May 19, 1863, MS 16278, Special Collections, New York State Library, copy at FSNMP.

31. William Stowe (2nd VT Infantry) letter, May 15, 1863, typescript at FSNMP.

32. OR, 25(1):603.

33. OR, 25(1):815; "Storming of Mayre's [sic] Heights," *St. Johnsbury (VT) Caledonian*, Apr. 23, 1885.

34. OR, 25(1):815.

35. OR, 25(1):603; "The Storming of the Heights of Fredericksburg" (Colonel Grant's supplementary report), *Rutland (VT) Daily Herald*, May 28, 1863.

36. "Storming of Mayre's [sic] Heights," *St. Johnsbury (VT) Caledonian*, Apr. 23, 1885.

37. Early, *Autobiographical Sketch and Narrative*, 209.

38. Early, 209.

39. Early, 209–10; OR, 25(1):1001.

40. OR, 25(1):816.

41. Early, *Autobiographical Sketch and Narrative*, 209–10; "Memoir of Genl. Benjamin Grubb Humphreys," Mississippi Dept. of Archives and History, typescript, chap. 13, copy at FSNMP; *New Orleans Times Picayune*, June 23, 1883.

42. OR, 25(1):614; OR Supplement, 4:629, 653.

43. OR, 25(1):564; OR Supplement, 4:629.

44. OR, 25(1):816, 842–43; OR Supplement, 4:653; Anderson W. Reese (Troup Artillery) letter, May 11, 1863, *Athens (GA) Southern Banner*, May 27, 1863.

45. OR, 25(1):815–16, 1001; Reese letter, May 11, 1863; Early, *Autobiographical Sketch and Narrative*, 210.

46. Smith, *Richard Snowden Andrews*, 88; Early, *Autobiographical Sketch and Narrative*, 210–11.

47. OR, 25(1):846; Malone, *Diary*, 33.

48. Alex B. Sumner (6th ME Infantry) letter, May 11, 1863, copy at FSNMP; Correspondence from Shaler's brigade, May 7, 1863, *Providence (RI) Daily Evening Press*, May 25, 1863.

49. Quiner Scrapbooks: Correspondence of Wisconsin Volunteers, 1861–1865, comp. Edwin B. Quiner, WHS, 8:288, copy at FSNMP; Stewart, *Camp, March, and Battlefield*, 315; Anderson, *Papers*, 210 (letter, May 9, 1863).

50. OR, 25(1):816; Cyrus B. Stone (16th NY Infantry) letter, May 6, 1863, copy at FSNMP; "Headquarters 1st Brigade (Shaler's), 3d Div., 6th Corps, [illegible] near Banks' Ford, May 5, '63," *Providence (RI) Daily Evening Press*, May 13, 1863; Quiner Scrapbooks: Correspondence of Wisconsin Volunteers, 8:298, copy at FSNMP; Robert Yard (1st NJ Infantry) letter, May 6, 1863, *Monmouth (NJ) Democrat*, May 14, 1863.

51. OR, 25(1):856; Handerson, *Yankee in Gray*, 56; Newell, "*Ours*," 206; Haskell, *Haskell of Gettysburg*, 72.

52. OR, 25(1):856.

53. OR, 25(1):856–57.

54. Chapin, *Thirty-Fourth Regiment, NYSV*, 92; OR, 25(1):188, 350, 359; Handerson, *Yankee in Gray*, 56.

55. OR, 25(1):188, 350, 615; OR, Supplement, 4:575; Rhodes, *All for the Union*, 106.

56. OR, 25(1):359; Soldier letter, May 20, 1863, *Bangor (ME) Daily Whig and Courier*, May 22, 1863.

57. OR, 25(1):618; Soldier (31st NY Infantry) letter, May 9, 1863, in "31st New York Infantry Regiment's Civil War Newspaper Clippings," New York State Military Museum and Veterans Research Center, https://museum.dmna.ny.gov/index.php/?cID=2113.

58. Soldier (6th VT Infantry) letter, May 7, 1863, *Burlington (VT) Times*, May 16, 1863; "From the Fourth Regiment," May 11, 1863, *Vermont Watchman and State Journal* (Montpelier), May 22, 1863; "Storming of Mayre's [sic] Heights," *St. Johnsbury (VT) Caledonian*, Apr. 23, 1885.

59. Lt. Col. Robert F. Webb (6th NC Infantry) report, May 14, 1863, Alphonso Calhoun Avery Papers, SHC, UNC, copy at FSNMP. The Military Road extended from Hamilton's Crossing to Fredericksburg and was used to move supplies. Remnants are still visible within the national park.

60. "Memoir of Genl. Benjamin Grubb Humphreys," Mississippi Dept. of Archives and History, typescript, chap. 13, copy at FSNMP. The farm road still exists opposite Oakwood Street.

61. Harrison, *Chancellorsville Battlefield Sites*, 191–92. The house site sits under a new road called Idlewild Boulevard, just east of Evelyn Court.

62. OR, 25(1):856–57, 885; Herbert, "Eighth Alabama," 97–98. The two-gun redoubt is extant on the Mary Washington Hospital campus. The section of guns that Penick deployed on the Orange Plank Road were in the northwest quadrant of State Route 3 and Westwood Drive.

63. OR, 25(1):615. Rose Hill remains extant, as is the road that intersected William Street just to the east. Modern Augustine Avenue begins three hundred feet north of William Street.

64. OR Supplement, 4:575.

65. OR, 25(1):615, 885; OR Supplement, 4:635, 642; Rhodes, *All for the Union*, 106.
66. Col. John C. C. Sanders (11th AL Infantry) report, May 10, 1863, LC, copy at FSNMP; Sears, *Chancellorsville*, 493.
67. OR, 25(1):359; Herbert, "Eighth Alabama," 97.
68. Patterson, *Yankee Rebel*, 100.
69. OR, 25(1):857; Herbert, "Eighth Alabama," 97; Sears, *Chancellorsville*, 493, 498.
70. OR, 25(1):857; Harrison, *Chancellorsville Sites*, 194–95. The referenced thicket was located in the area now covered by the State Route 3–Interstate 95 interchange.
71. Happel, *Salem Church Embattled*, 41, OR, 25(1):884. Bulldozers have since flattened the terrain to accommodate modern development, but the knoll on which the tollgate once stood had been where modern Task Force Drive (VA 710) intersects State Route 3.
72. OR, 25(1):387–88.
73. Sears, *Chancellorsville*, 331; Bigelow, *Campaign of Chancellorsville*, 348, 356, 364–65.
74. OR, 25(2):377.
75. OR, 25(2):377–78.
76. Sears, *Chancellorsville*, 332–33, 343, 346, 378.
77. Bigelow, *Campaign of Chancellorsville*, 370–72.
78. OR, 25(2):385, 387–88.
79. OR, 25(2):389–91.
80. OR, 25(2):391–92.
81. OR, 25(2):377.
82. OR, 25(2):378.
83. OR, 25(2):378, 393.
84. OR, 25(2):393.
85. OR, 25(2):379.
86. OR, 25(2):378.
87. OR, 25(2):394.
88. OR, 25(2):394.
89. OR, 25(2):394.
90. Sears, *Chancellorsville*, 365–66; Gallagher, "East of Chancellorsville," 48.
91. OR, 25(1):826.
92. James R. Edwards (9th AL Infantry), "Sketch of Dr. James Randle Edwards Wartime Experiences, 1861–1865," comp. W. Robert Rucker, copy at FSNMP; Clark, "Chancellorsville and Salem Church"; William H. Terrell (43rd NY Infantry) letter, May 3, 1863, *Albany (NY) Evening Journal*, May 12, 1863.
93. Gilbert Thompson, "My Journal, 1861–1865, U.S. Engineer Battalion, Army of the Potomac," May 3, 1863, copy at FSNMP.
94. OR, 25(1):203, 581; Harrison, *Chancellorsville Sites*, 187.
95. OR, 25(1):567–68, 581.
96. OR, 25(2):397; Chapin, *Thirty-Fourth Regiment, NYSV*, 92.
97. OR, 25(1):359, 25(2):396; *History of the Nineteenth Regiment Massachusetts Volunteer Infantry*, 205; "From the 127th Regiment," *Lebanon (PA) Courier*, May 14, 21, 1863.

98. OR, 25(1):353–55; OR Supplement, 4:583.

99. OR, 25(1):213, 25(2):379–80.

100. OR, 25(2):381; Benham, "Report to Major General Joseph Hooker, May 20, 1863."

101. Early, *Autobiographical Sketch and Narrative*, 211.

102. Bradwell, "31st Georgia at Chancellorsville."

103. OR Supplement, 4:630.

104. OR, 25(1):613; Soldier (J.W.C., 1st NY Independent Battery) letter, May 6, 1863, *Auburn (NY) Advertiser and Union*, n.d., in "1st Veteran Independent Battery's Civil War Newspaper Clippings," New York State Military Museum and Veterans Research Center, https://museum.dmna.ny.gov/index.php/?cID=2113.

105. OR Supplement, 4:630–31; William P. Wright (1st NY Independent Artillery) diary, May 3, 1863, Osborne Family Papers, Dept. of Special Collections, Syracuse Univ. Library, typescript, copy at FSNMP; Soldier (J.W.C., 1st NY Artillery) letter, May 6, 1863.

8. Late Afternoon of May 3

1. OR, 25(1):826.

2. Bigelow, *Campaign of Chancellorsville*, 380.

3. OR, 25(1):202, 25(2):379; Jackson, "Sedgwick at Fredericksburg and Salem Heights," 231.

4. OR, 25(2):383–84; Sears, *Chancellorsville*, 373. The trenches and gun positions extended along high hills and were anchored on the Rappahannock River. The position was exceptionally strong.

5. Jacob W. Haas (96th PA Infantry) letter, May 12, 1863, HCWRT, USAMHI, copy at FSNMP; Hartwell, *To My Beloved Wife and Boy at Home*, 87; Harrison, *Chancellorsville Battlefield Sites*, 194; Happel, *Salem Church Embattled*, 41. Harrison notes that the Guest house, called Altoona in the postwar years, was demolished in 1985 to make way for the Gateway Village shopping center. Happel indicates from his own observation that the knoll at the tollgate was located at what is now the intersection of VA 710 and State Route 3.

6. OR, 25(1):600.

7. OR, 25(1):567–68, 570, 574, 617.

8. OR Supplement, 4:642.

9. Harrison, *Chancellorsville Battlefield Sites*, 167–68.

10. OR, 25(1):857, 884; William L. Fagan (8th AL Infantry), "Battle of Salem Church," *Philadelphia Weekly Times*, July 7, 1883; Col. John C. C. Sanders (11th AL Infantry) report, May 10, 1863, LC, copy at FSNMP.

11. OR Supplement, 4:675; "Wilcox's Brigade," *Richmond (VA) Sentinel*, May 30, 1863.

12. OR, 25(1):564, 570–71, 574, 576, 581; OR Supplement, 4:625.

13. OR, 25(1):596, 857, 25(2):393; Stevens, "In Battle and in Prison," 216; Soldier (27th NY Infantry) letter, May 6, 1863, *Rochester (NY) Daily Union and Advertiser*, May 11, 1863.

14. OR, 25(1):595; OR Supplement, 4:625–26; Hyde, *Civil War Letters by General Thomas W. Hyde*, 73. On the modern landscape, Rigby's guns went into battery somewhere between Carl D. Silver Boulevard and Interstate 95.

15. OR, 25(1):595–96, 863, 884; OR Supplement, 4:675.

16. OR, 25(1):827; OR Supplement, 4:674; Harrison, *Chancellorsville Battlefield Sites*, 164–65. The William Perry house was located north of the Orange Plank Road between modern Routes 707 and 708.

17. OR, 25(2):380, 392; Benham, "Report to Major General Joseph Hooker, May 20, 1863"; Ward, *One Hundred and Sixth Regiment Pennsylvania Volunteers*, 163. The stone foundation for Scott's Mill measures thirty by sixty feet. The road to the ferry landing extends around the mill to a point slightly downstream, but river bluffs preclude it extending any farther downstream. Part of the antebellum road to the uplands is obliterated by a storm-water pond established for modern development. The rest of the route, however, clearly follows the contours on the east side of the ravine until the steep slopes preclude further passage. At that point the road is clearly visible across the creek and continues to the river on the west side of the ravine. The extension of the road to the uplands, on the west side of the ravine, is wide and steep, useful to quickly move pontoons from the uplands to the river but difficult for loaded wagons to negotiate going uphill. The ravine has a north–south orientation, which conveniently screened it from view.

18. OR, 25(1):214–15; Benham, "Report to Major General Joseph Hooker, May 20, 1863."

19. OR, 25(1):589, 595, 858; William Remmel (121st NY Infantry) letter, May 5, 1863, Univ. of Arkansas Libraries, copy at FSNMP.

20. OR, 25(1):248, 25(2):379–80, 387.

21. OR, 25(1):248; Banes, *Philadelphia Brigade*, 161.

22. OR, 25(1):221, 236.

23. OR, 25(1):221, 236.

24. OR, 25(1):250, 25(2):392; Banes, *Philadelphia Brigade*, 161; Benham, "Report to Major General Joseph Hooker, May 20, 1863."

25. OR, 25(1):824; McGlashan, "Battle of Salem Church," 91.

26. OR, 25(1):858, 863.

27. OR, 25(1):827, 844; OR Supplement, 4:675.

28. OR, 25(1):827, 857, 863; McGlashan, "Battle of Salem Church," 91; William L. Fagan (8th AL Infantry), "Battle of Salem Church," *Philadelphia Weekly Times*, July 7, 1883.

29. McGlashan, "Battle of Salem Church," 91.

30. OR, 25(1):835; Soldier (GA staff officer) letter, *Montgomery (AL) Weekly Advertiser*, May 27, 1863.

31. OR, 25(1):863; Soldier (61st VA Infantry) letter, May 8, 1863, *Savannah (GA) Republican*, May 20, 1863; John G. Wallace (61st VA Infantry) diary, May 3, 1863, typescript at FSNMP.

32. Soldier (61st VA Infantry) letter, May 8, 1863.

33. OR, 25(1):863; Soldier (61st VA Infantry) letter, May 8, 1863.

34. Morse, *Personal Experiences*, 25.

35. OR, 25(1):581; Stevens, "In Battle and in Prison," 216.

36. OR, 25(1):584–85; Jacob W. Haas (96th PA Infantry) letter, May 12, 1863, HCWRT, USAMHI, copy at FSNMP.

37. OR, 25(1):574, 589–90; William A. Lessig, "The Ninety-Sixth Reg., P.V., in the Late Battles," *Pottsville (PA) Mining Journal*, June 6, 1863.

38. Haskell, *Haskell of Gettysburg*, 74; US Naval Observatory, Astronomical Observations Dept., Sun and Moon data for May 3, 1863, https://aa.usno.navy.mil (accessed May 28, 2014).

39. Hall, *Personal Experience*, 16.

40. OR, 25(1):858; R. G. Firman (121st NY Infantry) letter, May 4, 1863, and Capt. Henry M. Galpin (121st NY Infantry) letter, May 6, 1863, in "121st New York Infantry Regiment's Civil War Newspaper Clippings," New York State Military Museum and Veterans Research Center, https://museum.dmna.ny.gov/index.php/?cID=2761.

41. McClelen, *I Saw the Elephant*, 36–37.

42. Jacob W. Haas (96th PA Infantry) letter, May 12, 1863, HCWRT, USAMHI, copy at FSNMP; Hartwell, *To My Beloved Wife and Boy at Home*, 87; OR, 25(1):589.

43. OR, 25(1):844; Herbert, "Eighth Alabama," 101.

44. Stewart, *Camp, March, and Battlefield*, 317; Jacob W. Haas (96th PA Infantry) letter, May 12, 1863, HCWRT, USAMHI, copy at FSNMP.

45. OR, 25(1):579, 884; John S. Kidder (121st NY Infantry) letter, May 4, 1863, typescript at FSNMP.

46. OR, 25(1):581, 586; Unidentified Soldier (16th NY Infantry), "Fredericksburg during the Civil War," n.d., Schoff Civil War Collection, Clements Library, Univ. of Michigan, copy at FSNMP.

47. OR, 25(1):569; Cyrus Stone (16th NY Infantry) letter, May 6, 1863, copy at FSNMP; Curtis, *From Bull Run to Chancellorsville*, 263–64.

48. Rice, *Letters and other Writings*, 72–73; Holt, *Surgeon's Civil War*, 103; OR, 25(1):589; Morse, *Personal Experiences*, 25.

49. Herbert, "Eighth Alabama," 101. A postwar reminiscence states that two companies swung back to help keep the regiment line intact, but reports closer to the events indicate that three companies executed a rear wheel. *Montgomery (AL) Advertiser*, Apr. 20, 1918.

50. Patterson, *Yankee Rebel*, 101–2; Herbert, "Eighth Alabama," 101; Col. John C. C. Sanders (11th AL Infantry) report, May 10, 1863, LC, copy at FSNMP.

51. OR, 25(1):590; Jacob W. Haas (96th PA Infantry) letter, May 12, 1863, HCWRT, USAMHI, copy at FSNMP; William A. Lessig, "The Ninety-Sixth Reg., P.V., in the Late Battles," *Pottsville (PA) Mining Journal*, June 6, 1863.

52. OR, 25(1):590; Lessig, "Ninety-Sixth Reg., P.V., in the Late Battles."

53. Samuel Lemont letter, May 9, 1863, Special Collections, Univ. of Maine, Orono, copy at FSNMP; Bicknell, *Fifth Regiment Maine Volunteers*, 226; Clark S. Edwards (5th ME Infantry), "War Reminiscences," Bethel Historical Society.

54. Edwards, "War Reminiscences."

55. George Hamilton (5th ME Infantry) letter, May 9, 1863, *Lewiston (ME) Daily Evening Journal*, May 18, 1863.
56. OR, 25(1):584–85.
57. OR Supplement, 4:677.
58. OR Supplement, 4:677; Herbert, "Eighth Alabama," 102; "Virginius" (soldier, 5th ME Infantry) letter, *Portland (ME) Transcript*, June 6, 1863; Soldier (8th AL Infantry) letter, May 25, 1863, *Mobile (AL) Advertiser and Register*, June 3, 1863.
59. OR, 25(1):838; Soldier (16th GA Infantry) letter, May 15, 1863, *Macon (GA) Telegraph*, May 26, 1863; Frederick H. West (51st GA Infantry) letter, May 18, 1863, typescript at FSNMP.
60. McGlashan, "Battle of Salem Church," 91–93; William M. Jones (50th GA Infantry) memoir, United Daughters of the Confederacy Bound Typescripts, vol. 5, Civil War Miscellany, Personal Papers, Georgia Dept. of Archives and History.
61. Soldier (50th GA Infantry) letter, May 18, 1863, *Savannah (GA) Republican*, May 28, 1863.
62. OR, 25(1):575–76, 593; George Hamilton (5th ME Infantry) letter, May 9, 1863, *Lewiston (ME) Daily Evening Journal*, May 18, 1863; P. M. Senderling (1st NJ Infantry) letter, May 12, 1863, copy at FSNMP.
63. OR, 25(1):584–85, 592–93; Maier, *Rough and Regular*, 49–50.
64. Maier, *Rough and Regular*, 51–52.
65. Soldier (16th NY Infantry) letter, May 6, 1863, copy at FSNMP; OR, 25(1):586.
66. Col. John C. C. Sanders (11th AL Infantry) report, May 10, 1863, LC, copy at FSNMP.
67. OR, 25(1):568, 571.
68. OR, 25(1):571, 574; Halsey, *Brother against Brother*, 130.
69. Halsey, *Brother against Brother*, 129; William L. Fagan (8th AL Infantry), "Battle of Salem Church," *Philadelphia Weekly Times*, July 7, 1883; OR, 25(1):572; Marshall B. Stull (15th NJ Infantry), "From the Fifteenth Regiment," May 11, 1863, *Sussex (NJ) Register*, May 22, 1863.
70. Halsey, *Brother against Brother*, 129.
71. OR Supplement, 4:650.
72. OR, 25(1):595–96, 598; OR Supplement, 4:626.
73. OR, 25(1):596, 598.
74. OR, 25(1):598; Frederick H. West (51st GA Infantry) letter, May 5, 1863, *Atlanta Southern Confederacy*, May 19, 1863; Edward Bancroft Williston (2nd US Artillery) memoir, c. 1897, Norwich Univ. Archives, Kreitsberg Library.
75. Fairchild, *27th Regiment N.Y. Vols.*, 169; OR, 25(1):588.
76. OR, 25(1):619; OR Supplement, 4:636, 650; Newell, *"Ours,"* 208; D. D. Andrews (7th MA Infantry) memoir, *Fall River (MA) Evening News*, Jan. 13, 1912; John Dunbar (37th MA Infantry) letter, May 6, 1863, typescript at FSNMP; Hutchinson, *Seventh Massachusetts Volunteer Infantry*, 127–28.
77. OR Supplement, 4:650; Newell, *Tenth Regiment, Massachusetts Volunteers*, 207–8; Edward Mahogany (37th MA Infantry) letter, May 5, 1863, copy at FSNMP.

78. OR, 25(1):574.

79. OR, 25(1):615–16; Woodbury, *Second Rhode Island*, 169.

80. OR, 25(1):616; Rhodes, *All for the Union*, 106.

81. OR, 25(1):615–16; Rhodes, *All for the Union*, 107; Soldier (2nd RI Infantry) letter, May 13, 1863, *Providence (RI) Daily Evening Press*, May 18, 1863.

82. OR, 25(1):574; McGlashan, "Battle of Salem Church," 92; Reuben T. Roberds (50th GA Infantry) article, *Milledgeville (GA) Southern Recorder*, May 26, 1863; Lucian A. Vorhees (15th NJ Infantry) letter, *Hunterdon (NJ) Republican*, May 15, 1863. The confused fighting led to errors in the reporting. Peter McGlashan, for instance, claims he and the Fiftieth Georgia fought a New York regiment, but in fact it was a New Jersey unit. Reuben Roberds claimed capture of a New Jersey flag, but no Federal units lost their colors that day.

83. OR, 25(1):616; OR Supplement, 4:650; Woodbury, *Second Rhode Island*, 170; Halsey, *Brother against Brother*, 130.

84. Rhodes, *All for the Union*, 106, 109–10.

85. Andrew J. McBride memoir, Civil War Unit File, 10th GA, Box 283, Drawer 59, Civil War Miscellany, Personal Papers, Georgia Dept. of Archives and History; OR, 25(1):838.

86. McGlashan, "Battle of Salem Church," 92.

87. McGlashan, 92.

88. OR, 25(1):827.

89. OR, 25(1):833; McGlashan, "Battle of Salem Church," 93.

90. OR, 25(1):835–36.

91. Robertson Tayler (VA soldier) letter, July 18, 1905, Civil War Miscellaneous Collection, USAMHI, copy at FSNMP.

92. OR, 25(1):618, 620.

93. Uhler, *Camps and Campaigns of the 93d Regiment, Penna Vols.*, 15.

94. Soldier (139th PA Infantry) letter, May 7, 1863, *Pittsburgh Daily Gazette and Advertiser*, May 13, 1863.

95. OR, 25(1):618; OR Supplement, 4:635; Mark, *Red, White, and Blue Badge*, 203; US Naval Observatory, Astronomical Applications Dept., Sun and Moon data for May 3, 1863, https://aa.usno.navy.mil (accessed May 28, 2014).

96. OR Supplement, 4:642; Newell, *"Ours,"* 208.

97. OR, 25(1):618, 624; OR Supplement, 4:636; Brig. Gen. William T. H. Brooks quoted in Bilby, "Seeing the Elephant," 11; Rokus, "Daniel D. Wheeler," 132, 137. Wheeler moved to Fredericksburg after a career in the Regular Army, married a local woman named Nannie Phillips Smith, and resided at 213 Caroline Street. He is buried in the Fredericksburg Cemetery.

98. OR, 25(1):568; Westbrook, *49th Pennsylvania*, 145.

99. Westbrook, *49th Pennsylvania*, 145; Abraham T. Hilands (49th PA Infantry) letter, May 8, 1863, Ottawa County (KS) Museum, typescript, copy at FSNMP.

100. OR, 25(1):618; John J. Toffey (21st NJ Infantry) letter, May 9, 1863, typescript at FSNMP.

101. OR Supplement, 4:656, 660.

102. OR, 25(1):612; OR Supplement, 4:629.

103. William P. Wright (1st NY Independent Artillery) diary, May 3, 1863, Osborne Family Papers, Dept. of Special Collections, Syracuse Univ. Library, typescript, copy at FSNMP.

104. OR, 25(1):602–3; Fisk, *Hard Marching*, 81.

105. OR Supplement, 4:629; Harrison, *Chancellorsville Battlefield Sites*, 187. The Confederate winter encampment extended from the Idlewild plateau to Hazel Run. A profusion of hut holes and some chimney remnants are still visible. The ground has been extensively searched by relic hunters, but the land has since been placed under an open-space easement.

106. OR, 25(2):383–84, 395; Williams, *From the Cannon's Mouth*, 200.

107. OR, 25(2):379.

108. Sears, *Chancellorsville*, 385; Soldier (GA staff officer) letter, *Montgomery (AL) Weekly Advertiser*, May 27, 1863.

109. OR, 25(1):582, 589.

110. Sears, *Chancellorsville*, 493; OR, 25(1):838, 861; McGlashan, "Battle of Salem Church," 93.

111. Herbert, "Eighth Alabama," 106.

112. John F. L. Hartwell (121st NY Infantry) diary, May 3, 1863, LC, typescript at FSNMP.

9. May 4

1. Soldier (Shaler's brigade) letter, May 13, 1863, *Providence (RI) Daily Evening Press*, May 20, 1863.

2. John F. L. Hartwell (121st NY Infantry) letter, May 5, 1863, LC, typescript at FSNMP.

3. OR, 25(1):618; William A. Lessig, "The Ninety-Sixth Reg., P.V., in the Late Battles," *Pottsville (PA) Mining Journal*, June 6, 1863.

4. OR, 25(1):618; Lessig, "Ninety-Sixth Reg., P.V., in the Late Battles"; US Naval Observatory, Astronomical Applications Dept., Sun and Moon data for May 4, 1863, https://aa.usno.navy.mil (accessed May 28, 2014).

5. Westervelt, *Lights and Shadows of Army Life*, 42.

6. OR, 25(2):379–80, 382, 553–55.

7. OR, 25(1):203.

8. OR, 25(1):827; Early, *Autobiographical Sketch and Narrative*, 220.

9. OR, 25(2):769–70.

10. OR, 25(1):827.

11. OR, 25(2):402.

12. William P. Wright (1st NY Independent Artillery) diary, May 4, 1863, Osborne Family Papers, Dept. of Special Collections, Syracuse Univ. Library, typescript, copy at FSNMP; Francis E. Pinto, "History of the 32nd Regiment, New York Volunteers in the Civil War, 1861 to 1863, and Personal Recollections during That Period," Brooklyn, NY,

1895, WHS, typescript, 141, copy at FSNMP; John F. Hartwell (121st NY Infantry) diary, May 4, 1863, LC, typescript at FSNMP; John G. Wallace (61st VA Infantry) diary, May 4, 1863, typescript at FSNMP.

13. Pinto, "32nd Regiment, New York Volunteers," 142–43.
14. OR, 25(1):612, 860–61; OR Supplement, 4:656.
15. OR, 25(1):840, 1001; Smith, *Richard Snowden Andrews*, 89.
16. Jubal Early to Robert E. Lee, Nov. 20, 1868, Box 25, Collection 158, UVA, copy at FSNMP; Early, *Autobiographical Sketch and Narrative*, 222.
17. Faust, *Historical Times Illustrated Encyclopedia of the Civil War*, 315.
18. OR, 25(2):204; Henry C. Walker (13th GA Infantry) letter, May 9, 1863, Civil War Miscellany, Personal Papers, Georgia Dept. of Archives and History, copy at FSNMP; Urbanus Dart (26th GA Infantry) letter, May 13, 1863, *Brunswick (GA) News*, May 4, 1963.
19. Bradwell, "31st Georgia at Chancellorsville"; Soldier (13th GA Infantry) letter, May 17, 1863, *Savannah (GA) Daily Morning News*, May 29, 1863.
20. Bradwell, "31st Georgia at Chancellorsville."
21. Bradwell; William C. Mathews (38 GA Infantry) letter, May 8, 1863, *Sandersville (GA) Central Georgian*, June 3, 1863.
22. OR, 25(1):817; Early, *Autobiographical Sketch and Narrative*, 224.
23. Soldier (6th VT Infantry) letter, May 6, 1863, *Rutland (VT) Weekly Herald*, May 14, 1863; Judd, *Thirty-Third N.Y.S. Vols.*, 304; Robert Pratt (5th VT Infantry) letter, May 13, 1863, typescript at FSNMP; Soldier (7th ME Infantry) letter, May 7, 1863, *Portland (ME) Daily Press*, May 15, 1863.
24. OR Supplement, 4:657; Bradwell, "31st Georgia at Chancellorsville"; Smith, *Richard Snowden Andrews*, 90.
25. OR, 25(1):221, 225–26, 240, 242–43, 245, 407.
26. Judd, *Thirty-Third N.Y.S. Vols.*, 303–4, 307; John J. Toffey (21st NJ Infantry) letter, May 11, 1863, typescript at FSNMP; Soldier (7th ME Infantry) letter, May 7, 1863, *Gardiner (ME) Home Journal*, May 14, 1863; Henry J. Gifford (33rd NY Infantry) letter, May 7, 1863, *Rochester (NY) Daily Union and Advertiser*, May 14, 1863.
27. Soldier (49th NY Infantry) letter, May 9, 1863, *Buffalo (NY) Morning Express*, May 19, 1863; Bradwell, "31st Georgia at Chancellorsville"; Early, *Autobiographical Sketch and Narrative*, 224; Smith, *Richard Snowden Andrews*, 90; Soldier (33rd NY Infantry) letter, May 5, 1863, *Palmyra (NY) Courier*, May 16, 1863; "The Maine Seventh," *Gardiner (ME) Home Journal*, May 28, 1863.
28. OR Supplement, 4:629; Smith, *Richard Snowden Andrews*, 90; Early, *Autobiographical Sketch and Narrative*, 224.
29. OR, 25(1):594; Jubal Early, *Autobiographical Sketch and Narrative*, 224; Smith, *Richard Snowden Andrews*, 90.
30. OR, 25(1):594; Soldier (Battery A, MA Light Artillery) letter, May 9, 1863, *Cambridge (MA) Chronicle*, May 16, 1863.
31. Tate, "Chancellorsville Debut," 45, 51.
32. Tate, 53.
33. OR, 25(1):594.

34. Dodd, *Song of the Rappahannock*, 25.

35. OR, 25(1):1001; Soldier (13th MS Infantry) letter, May 6, 1863, *Mobile (AL) Advertiser and Register*, May 22, 1863; Gordon, *Reminiscences of the Civil War*, 100–101.

36. Soldier (13th GA Infantry) letter, May 9, 1863, Harrison Wells Papers, UNC, copy at FSNMP; Lt. Col. H. C. Jones Jr. (57th NC Infantry) report, May 13, 1863, Alphonso Calhoun Avery Papers, SHC, UNC, copy at FSNMP.

37. OR, 25(1):565, 827; William P. Wright (1st NY Independent Battery) diary, May 4, 1863, Osborne Family Papers, Dept. of Special Collections, Syracuse Univ. Library, typescript, copy at FSNMP.

38. OR, 25(2):412; Abbott, *Fallen Leaves*, 175; William H. Pohlman (59th NY Infantry) letter, May 13, 1863, Special Collections, New York State Library, typescript at FSNMP; Adams, *Reminiscences of the Nineteenth Massachusetts*, 64.

39. Soldier (127th PA Infantry) letter, May 3, 1863, *Lebanon (PA) Courier*, May 14, 1863; Soldier (127th PA Infantry) letter, May 6, 1863, ibid., May 21, 1863.

40. OR Supplement, 620, 622; Edgar P. Ackerman (2nd NJ Infantry) letter, May 4, 1863, *Newark (NJ) Daily Advertiser*, May 8, 1863; Dr. Edwin D. Buckman (98th PA Infantry) letter, May 9, 1863, copy at FSNMP.

41. OR, 25(2):403.

42. OR, 25(2):402–3.

43. OR, 25(2):226, 405.

44. OR, 25(1):226, 240–41, 25(2):410.

45. OR, 25(1):220, 224.

46. OR, 25(2):224, 226, 384, 406.

47. OR, 25(1):235, 237–38. The house in question shows up as Downman on the 1867 Michler map of the Fredericksburg area. Located west of Smith Run, it should not be confused with the more prominent Downman house south of the Orange Plank Road. Michler, *Fredericksburg [Dec. 1862]*, map, color, 1:21,120 scale.

48. OR, 25(2):221, 406.

49. OR, 25(1):203, 25(2):403, 404, 406.

50. OR, 25(2):396.

51. OR, 25(2):407.

52. OR, 25(2):407.

53. OR, 25(2):408.

54. OR, 25(2):408.

55. OR, 25(2):408. The reference to Benham's brigade is actually Owen's Philadelphia Brigade of the Second Corps.

56. OR, 25(2):408.

57. OR, 25(1):568, 594; OR Supplement, 4:654.

58. OR, 25(1):568, 595; OR Supplement, 4:626; Hall, *Personal Experience*, 18. The ravine is now a storm-water drain between two commercial sites about 110 yards east of the intersection of State Route 3 and the Carl D. Silver Parkway.

59. OR, 25(1):565.

60. OR Supplement, 4:636–37; William H. Terrell (43rd NY Infantry) letter, May 4, 1863, *Albany (NY) Evening Journal*, May 12, 1863.

61. OR Supplement, 4:636–37; "What the 43d Did in the Late Battles," *Albany (NY) Evening Journal*, May 15, 1863; John G. Wallace (61st VA Infantry) diary, May 4, typescript at FSNMP.

62. OR, 25(1):560, 565; OR Supplement, 4:629; Soldier (49th NY Infantry) letter, May 9, 1863, *Jamestown (NY) Journal*, May 22, 1863.

63. OR, 25(1):614; OR Supplement, 4:629.

64. OR, 25(1):1001.

65. "Smith, William. (Extra Billy.)," in Boatner, *Civil War Dictionary*, 774–75; Faust, *Historical Times Illustrated Encyclopedia of the Civil War*, 698.

66. OR, 25(1):1002; Early, *Autobiographical Sketch and Narrative*, 225; Buck, *With the Old Confederates*, 81.

67. OR, 25(1):1002; Bradwell, "31st Georgia at Chancellorsville"; John William Ford Hatten (1st MD Artillery) memoir, copy at FSNMP.

68. OR, 25(1):1002; Riggs, *13th Virginia Infantry*, 32.

69. OR, 25(1):565, 600, 614; Selden Connor (7th ME Infantry) letter, May 10, 1863, Brown Univ. Library, typescript, copy at FSNMP; Stevens, *Three Years in the Sixth Corps*, 203.

70. OR, 25(1):1002; Early, *Autobiographical Sketch and Narrative*, 226; Buck, *With the Old Confederates*, 81–82; Driver, *58th Virginia Infantry*, 45–46; Adam W. Karsh (52nd VA Infantry) letter, May 15, 1863, typescript at FSNMP.

71. OR, 25(1):1002; Soldier (7th ME Infantry) letter, May 7, 1863, *Portland (ME) Daily Press*, May 15, 1863.

72. Harrison, *Chancellorsville Battlefield Sites*, 184–85.

73. OR, 25(1):609–10, 1002; Samuel D. Buck (13th VA Infantry), "At and around Fredericksburg," *Richmond (VA) Times Dispatch*, June 25, 1864; Buck, *With the Old Confederates*, 82; Soldier (49th NY Infantry) letter, May 12, 1863, *Buffalo (NY) Advocate*, May 21, 1863; Soldier (49th NY Infantry) letter, May 9, 1863, *Buffalo (NY) Evening Courier and Republic*, May 15, 1863.

74. Soldier (49th NY Infantry) letter, May 9, 1863, *Buffalo (NY) Morning Express*, May 19, 1863; Soldier (33rd NY Infantry) letter, *Palmyra (NY) Courier*, May 16, 1863.

75. Early, *Autobiographical Sketch and Narrative*, 226.

76. OR, 25(2):409; Foster, *New Jersey and the Rebellion*, 493; Judd, *Thirty-Third N.Y.S. Vols.*, 308.

77. OR, 25(2):405, 409; OR, ser. 3, 3:316.

78. OR, 25(1):213, 236; Benham, "Report to Major General Joseph Hooker, May 20, 1863."

79. OR, 25(2):401.

80. OR, 25(2):409; OR, ser. 3, 3:316.

81. OR, 25(2):409–10.

82. OR, 25(2):410.

83. OR, 25(2):410.

84. Richard W. York (6th NC Infantry) letter, Nov. 28, 1872, copy at FSNMP.

85. OR, 25(1):827; Early, *Autobiographical Sketch and Narrative*, 227; "Fredericksburg to Salem Church," *Richmond (VA) Times Dispatch*, June 3, 1906.

86. Alexander, *Fighting for the Confederacy*, 213.
87. Early, *Autobiographical Sketch and Narrative*, 222.
88. Early, 221–22.
89. Early, 227.
90. Handerson, *Yankee in Gray*, 56.
91. Col. Isaac E. Avery (6th NC Infantry) report for Hoke's Brigade, n.d. [May 13 or 14, 1863?], Alphonso Calhoun Avery Papers, SHC, UNC, typescript, copy at FSNMP; Memoirs of Eli S. Coble, Greensboro (NC) Historical Museum Archives, copy at FSNMP.
92. OR, 25(1):869; Soldier (3rd GA Infantry) letter, May 8, 1863, *Athens (GA) Southern Watchman*, May 27, 1863.
93. OR, 25(1):876; Anderson J. Peeler (5th FL Infantry) article, *Tallahassee Floridian and Journal*, n.d., copy of typescript.
94. Lemon, *Feed Them the Steel!*, 41; William L. Fagan (8th AL Infantry), "Battle of Salem Church," *Philadelphia Weekly Times*, July 7, 1883.
95. OR, 25(1):831; Frederick Reipschlager (8th AL Infantry) letter, May 25, 1863, *Mobile (AL) Advertiser & Register*, June 3, 1863; William Hood (1st SC Infantry), "The Battle of Salem Church and Its Episodes," n.d., McCain Library, Erskine College.
96. OR, 25(1):817.
97. OR, 25(1):879, 882; OR Supplement, 4:675.
98. OR, 25(1):879–80, 1000; Wise, *Long Arm of Lee*, 536.
99. Bigelow, *Campaign of Chancellorsville*, 406; OR, 25(1):880.
100. OR, 25(1):827, 880.
101. OR, 25(1):880.
102. OR, 25(1):821, 845, 848, 880–81.
103. Soldier (27th NY Infantry) letter, May 6, 1863, *Rochester (NY) Daily Union and Advertiser*, May 11, 1863.
104. Handerson, *Yankee in Gray*, 56; Tyler, *Recollections of the Civil War*, 87; Pinto, "32nd Regiment, New York Volunteers," 143.
105. OR, 25(1):600, 604.
106. Soldier (6th VT Infantry) letter, May 9, 1863, *Vermont Watchman and State Journal* (Montpelier), May 22, 1863.
107. Patrick, *Inside Lincoln's Army*, 242; William H. Terrell (43rd NY Infantry) letter, May 4, 1863, *Albany (NY) Evening Journal*, May 12, 1863; William Paynton (21st NJ Infantry) letter, May 5, 1863, copy at FSNMP.
108. William B. Jennings (22nd GA Infantry) memoir, copy at FSNMP.
109. OR, 25(2):400, 412.
110. OR, 25(1):351, 361; William Plumer (15th MA Infantry) letter, May 10, 1863, typescript at FSNMP.
111. OR, 25(1):359; Ambrose F. Cole (59th NY Infantry) letter, May 8, 1863, typescript at FSNMP; Committee of Regimental Association, *127th Regiment Pennsylvania Volunteers*, 174–77.
112. OR, 25(1):359; *History of the Nineteenth Regiment Massachusetts Volunteer Infantry*, 206; Newton T. Hartshorn (US Engineers) diary, May 4, 1863, Rauner Special

Collections Library, Dartmouth College, transcript, copy at FSNMP; Gilbert Thompson, "My Journal, 1861–1865, U.S. Engineer Battalion, Army of the Potomac," May 6, 1863, copy at FSNMP.

113. "The Vermonters in the Recent Battles," *St. Albans (VT) Messenger*, May 21, 1863; Selden Connor (7th ME Infantry) letter, May 10, 1863, Brown Univ. Library, typescript, copy at FSNMP.

10. May 4

1. David G. Moore (1st Rockbridge Artillery) letter, n.d. (postwar), Folder 1907, Box 22, John Warwick Daniel Papers, UVA.

2. OR, 25(1):782–84; Soldier (8th PA Cavalry) letter, May 22, 1863, *West Jersey Pioneer* (Bridgeton NJ), June 13, 1863.

3. Francis E. Pinto, "History of the 32nd Regiment, New York Volunteers in the Civil War, 1861 to 1863, and Personal Recollections during That Period," Brooklyn, NY, 1895, WHS, typescript, 143, copy at FSNMP; Hyde, *Following the Greek Cross*, 130; Soldier (49th NY Infantry) letter, May 9, 1863, *Buffalo (NY) Morning Express*, May 19, 1863.

4. Sears, *Chancellorsville*, 402.

5. OR, 25(1):876; Owen Keenan (3rd GA Infantry), "Letter from Keenan," *Macon (GA) Telegraph*, May 15, 1863; Snead, *Address;* Francis L. Hillyer (3rd GA Infantry) letter, May 7, 1863, Special Collections, Univ. of Georgia, copy at FSNMP.

6. OR, 25(1):568–69, 582, 586, 588; Fox, *Regimental Losses*, 197; Hall, *Personal Experiences*, 18–19; Unidentified Soldier (16th NY Infantry), "Fredericksburg during the Civil War," n.d., Schoff Civil War Collection, Clements Library, Univ. of Michigan, copy at FSNMP.

7. OR, 25(1):582, 594–95; Soldier (Battery A, MA Light Artillery) letter, May 7, 1863, *Cambridge (MA) Chronicle*, May 16, 1863; Owen Keenan (3rd GA Infantry), "Letter from Keenan," *Macon (GA) Telegraph*, May 15, 1863.

8. OR, 25(1):869; Soldier (Battery A, 1st MA Light Artillery) letter, May 7, 1863, *Cambridge (MA) Chronicle*, May 16, 1863; Jacob W. Hass (96th PA Infantry) letter, May 12, 1863, HCWRT, USAMHI, copy at FSNMP.

9. Hall, *Personal Experiences*, 19–20; Martin (2nd Battalion, GA Infantry), "Chancellorsville: A Soldier's Letter [May 8, 1863]," 227.

10. OR, 25(1):869; Early, *Autobiographical Sketch and Narrative*, 228.

11. OR, 25(1):852.

12. OR, 25(1):565, 568, 594, 846; OR Supplement, 4:626.

13. OR, 25(1):872, 876.

14. OR, 25(1):876; Jacob W. Hass (96th PA Infantry) letter, May 12, 1863, HCWRT, USAMHI, copy at FSNMP; Hall, *Personal Experiences*, 19; OR Supplement, 4:626.

15. OR, 25(1):876; Lemon, *Feed Them the Steel!*, 41–42.

16. OR, 25(1):592, 831; OR Supplement, 4:658.

17. OR, 25(1):828, 848, 880–81.

18. OR, 25(1):881, 884.

19. OR, 25(1):881.

20. OR, 25(1):248, 881. There are three sets of extant Federal earthworks in the area described north of Banks' Ford, but it is not clear how the Union batteries were distributed in them.

21. OR, 25(1):848.

22. OR, 25(1):881.

23. OR, 25(1):1002; Early, *Autobiographical Sketch and Narrative*, 230.

24. Soldier (6th LA Infantry) letter, May 30, 1863, *Mobile (AL) Advertiser and Register*, June 4, 1863.

25. Soldier (6th LA Infantry) letter, May 30, 1863; Clark, *Histories of the Several Regiments and Battalions from North Carolina*, 410.

26. Handerson, *Yankee in Gray*, 57.

27. Ruth Graham, *Combat Map No. 9, Second Battle of Fredericksburg, Chancellorsville Campaign* (1935), FSNMP. This, one of several maps for the battle, accompanied the "Report on Field Investigation of the Chancellorsville Campaign, Aug. 12, 1935," and the "Report on Field Investigation, Aug. 26–Sept. 2, 1935."

28. Seymour, *Civil War Memoirs*, 54.

29. Early, *Autobiographical Sketch and Narrative*, 229.

30. Maj. Rufus W. Wharton (1st Btn. NC Sharpshooters) report, May 13, 1863, Perry Family Papers, SHC, UNC.

31. Lt. Col. Hamilton C. Jones (57th NC Infantry) report, May 13, 1863, Alphonso Calhoun Avery Papers, SHC, UNC, copy at FSNMP.

32. Early, *Autobiographical Sketch and Narrative*, 228; Jones (57th NC Infantry) report, May 13, 1863; Memoirs of Eli S. Coble, Greensboro (NC) Historical Museum Archives, Manuscripts Collection 16, 13.4, copy at FSNMP.

33. Col. Isaac E. Avery (6th NC Infantry) report for Hoke's Brigade, n.d. [May 13 or 14, 1863?], Avery Papers, typescript, copy at FSNMP.

34. Jones (57th NC Infantry) report, May 13, 1863.

35. Soldier (49th NY Infantry) letter, May 9, 1863, *Buffalo (NY) Morning Express*, May 19, 1863.

36. Lt. Col. Kenneth M. Murchison (54th NC Infantry) report, May 13, 1863, Avery Papers; obituary of Col. J. C. S. McDowell, *Fayetteville (NC) Observer*, June 4, 1863.

37. Early, *Autobiographical Sketch and Narrative*, 229; Seymour, *Civil War Memoirs*, 54; John Emmerson (57th NC Infantry) letter, May 6, 1863, *Carolina Watchman* (Salisbury, NC), May 18, 1863.

38. Handerson, *Yankee in Gray*, 57.

39. Handerson, 57.

40. OR, 25(1):604; Robert Pratt (5th VT Infantry) letter, May 14, 1863, typescript at FSNMP; "Vermont Brigade in Battle," *Montpelier (VT) Argus and Patriot*, May 21, 1863.

41. Handerson, *Yankee in Gray*, 58.

42. OR, 25(1):560.

43. OR, 25(1):618–19; OR Supplement, 4:637.

44. OR, 25(1):618; Sylvester F. Hildebrand (139th PA Infantry) account, *Apollo (PA) Sentinel*, Apr. 21, 1911.

45. OR, 25(1):601, 626; OR Supplement, 4:637; Proceedings at the Annual Meeting of the Association of Fifth Wisconsin Volunteer Infantry, Held at Milwaukee, June 27-28, 1900, WHS, 13, copy at FSNMP; Soldier (5th WI Infantry) letter, May 14, 1863, *Grant County Witness* (Lancaster, WI), May 28, 1863.

46. OR, 25(1):619, 621-22; Handerson, *Yankee in Gray*, 58.

47. OR, 25(1):619; Jones (57th NC Infantry) report, May 13, 1863; Soldier (6th LA Infantry) letter, May 30, 1863, *Mobile (AL) Advertiser and Register*, June 4, 1863.

48. OR, 25(1):622.

49. Handerson, *Yankee in Gray*, 58; Soldier (6th LA Infantry) letter, May 30, 1863, *Mobile (AL) Advertiser and Register*, June 4, 1863.

50. Jones (57th NC Infantry) report, May 13, 1863.

51. Avery (6th NC Infantry) report for Hoke's Brigade, n.d. [May 13 or 14, 1863?].

52. Henry C. Walker (13th GA Infantry) letter, May 9, 1863, Civil War Miscellany, Personal Papers, Georgia Dept. of Archives and History, copy at FSNMP; Soldier (13th GA Infantry) letter, May 17, 1863, *Savannah (GA) Daily Morning News*, May 29, 1863.

53. William C. Mathews (38th GA Infantry) letter, May 8, 1863, *Sandersville (GA) Central Georgian*, June 3, 1863.

54. Soldier (127th PA Infantry) letter, May 6, 1863, *Lebanon (PA) Courier*, May 21, 1863; *History of the Nineteenth Regiment Massachusetts Volunteer Infantry*, 207.

55. William C. Mathews (38th GA Infantry) letter, May 8, 1863, *Sandersville (GA) Central Georgian*, June 3, 1863.

56. OR Supplement, 4:692; Maj. Rufus W. Wharton (1st Btn. NC Sharpshooters) report, May 13, 1863, Perry Family Papers, SHC, UNC, copy at FSNMP.

57. Early, *Autobiographical Sketch and Narrative*, 230.

58. Isiah Fogleman (8th AL Infantry) diary, May 4, 1863, typescript copy at FSNMP.

59. OR, 25(1):600-601.

60. Selden Connor (7th ME Infantry) letter, May 10, 1863, Brown Univ. Library, typescript, copy at FSNMP; Pinto, "32nd Regiment, New York Volunteers," 135A; Soldier (7th ME Infantry) letter, May 20, 1863, *Bangor (ME) Daily Whig and Courier*, May 22, 1863; Soldier (6th VT Infantry) letter, May 1, 1863, *Burlington (VT) Times*, May 6, 1863; James M. McNair (33rd NY Infantry) letter, May 6, 1863, *Nunda (NY) News*, May 16, 1863. Hugh Mercer School sits on that ground today. The terrain is cut by modern Cowan Boulevard, which was built on cuts and fills to create a level roadway. The hills and ravines are intact on either side, though, which makes evident the contours of the battleground.

61. OR, 25(1):560; Soldier (VT Brigade) account, *Lamoille (VT) Newsdealer*, May 28, 1863, 2.

62. OR, 25(1):610-11.

63. Stevens, *Three Years in the Sixth Corps*, 203; Selden Connor (7th ME Infantry) letter, May 10, 1863, Brown Univ. Library, typescript, copy at FSNMP.

64. OR, 25(1):610; Stevens, *Three Years in the Sixth Corps*, 204; Foster, *New Jersey and the Rebellion*, 492; Theodore F. Applegate (21st NJ Infantry) letter, May 10, 1863, *Trenton (NJ) Daily State Gazette*, May 21, 1863 (also in *Gardiner (ME) Home Journal*, May 28, 1863); Hyde, *Following the Greek Cross*, 131.

65. Hyde, *Civil War Letters by General Thomas W. Hyde,* 75; Soldier (7th ME Infantry) diary, May 4, 1863, and Soldier (7th ME Infantry) letter, May 20, 1863, *Bangor (ME) Daily Whig and Courier,* May 22, 1863; James M. McNair (33rd NY Infantry) letter, May 5, 1863, *Nunda (NY) News,* May 16, 1863.

66. Judd, *Thirty-Third N.Y.S. Vols.,* 310.

67. OR, 25(1):611; Orrin P. Rugg (77th NY Infantry) letter, May 11, 1863, Sarasota Springs Historical Society, typescript, copy at FSNMP; Lt. Col. Winsor B. French (77th NY Infantry) letter, May 6, 1863, MS 16278, Special Collections, New York State Library, typescript at FSNMP; Selden Connor (7th ME Infantry) letter, May 10, 1863, Brown Univ. Library, typescript, copy at FSNMP; Soldier (7th ME Infantry) letter, May 5, 1863, *Palmyra (NY) Courier,* May 16, 1863.

68. William L. Ingraham (33rd NY Infantry) letter, May 24, 1863, *Rochester (NY) Democrat & American,* May 30, 1863.

69. OR, 25(1):596, 604, 608; Robert Pratt (5th VT Infantry) letter, May 14, 1863, typescript at FSNMP; Albert A. Crane (6th VT Infantry) letter, May 7, 1863, *Rutland (VT) Weekly Herald,* May 16, 1863.

70. Hyde, *Following the Greek Cross,* 131; Hyde, *Letters,* 75; "Death on Every Side," *Yazoo (MS) Sentinel,* June 11, 1891.

71. Beyer and Keydel, *Deeds of Valor,* 166.

72. Fisk, *Hard Marching,* 82; "Storming of Mayre's [sic] Heights," *St. Johnsbury (VT) Caledonian,* Apr. 23, 1885. The men of the Third Vermont dashed about 550 yards to get into position.

73. Fisk, *Hard Marching,* 82; Soldier (7th ME Infantry) letter, May 20, 1863, *Bangor (ME) Daily Whig and Courier,* May 22, 1863; Soldier (33rd NY Infantry) letter, May 11, 1863, *Ontario (NY) Repository,* May 20, 1863.

74. Selden Connor (7th ME Infantry) letter, May 10, 1863, Brown Univ. Library, typescript, copy at FSNMP; Soldier (5th WI Infantry) letter, May 14, 1863, *Grant County Witness* (Lancaster, WI), May 28, 1863.

75. Soldier (7th ME Infantry) letter, May 7, 1863, *Gardiner (ME) Home Journal,* May 14, 1863; Andrew W. Brazee (49th NY Infantry) letter, May 9, 1863, *Buffalo (NY) Morning Express,* May 13, 1863.

76. OR, 25(1):561, 565; OR Supplement, 4:656.

77. OR, 25(1):565; OR Supplement, 4:656.

78. OR, 25(1):614; OR Supplement, 4:630.

79. OR, 25(1):604; Soldier (2nd VT Infantry) letter, May 9, 1863, *Rutland (VT) Courier,* May 22, 1863.

80. OR Supplement, 4:656.

81. Kelly A. Nolin, trans. and ed., "S. E. and S. M. Pingree Civil War Letters, 1861–1865," 1994, Vermont Historical Society, copy at FSNMP.

82. OR, 25(1):607; Fisk, *Hard Marching,* 82.

83. OR, 25(1):605; Dodd, *Song of the Rappahannock,* 32–33; "Death on Every Side," *Yazoo (MS) Sentinel,* June 11, 1891.

84. "Storming of Mayre's [sic] Heights," *St. Johnsbury (VT) Caledonian,* Apr. 23, 1885.

85. Fisk, *Hard Marching,* 83.

86. OR, 25(1):605.

87. Soldier (5th WI Infantry) letter, May 14, 1863, *Grant County Witness* (Lancaster, WI), May 28, 1863.

88. OR, 25(1):605.

89. OR, 25:(1)605, 609; Dodd, *Song of the Rappahannock*, 35–36; Albert A. Crane (6th VT Infantry) letter, May 7, 1863, *Rutland (VT) Weekly Herald*, May 16, 1863; "Storming of Mayre's [sic] Heights," *St. Johnsbury (VT) Caledonian*, Apr. 23, 1885; Soldier (6th VT Infantry) letter, May 9, 1863, *Vermont Watchman and State Journal* (Montpelier), May 22, 1863.

90. OR, 25(1):597; Crane (6th VT Infantry) letter, May 7, 1863.

91. OR, 25(1):597.

92. OR, 25(1):609; Beyer and Keydel, *Deeds of Valor*, 168; Soldier (6th VT Infantry) letter, May 6, 1863, *Rutland (VT) Daily Herald*, May 14, 1863; Soldier (6th VT Infantry) letter, May 6, 1863, *Vermont Watchman and State Journal* (Montpelier), May 15, 1863; Dodd, *Song of the Rappahannock*, 35.

93. OR, 25(1):605; Fisk, *Hard Marching*, 86; "A Private Letter from Sergeant Camp," *Vermont Journal* (Windsor), May 16, 1863.

94. OR, 25(1):607; William Stowe (2nd VT Infantry) letter, May 10, 1863, transcript at FSNMP; Soldier (6th VT Infantry) letter, May 7, 1863, *Rutland (VT) Weekly Herald*, May 21, 1863; Albert A. Crane (6th VT Infantry) letter, May 7, 1863, *Rutland (VT) Weekly Herald*, May 16, 1863; Soldier (6th VT Infantry) letter, May 6, 1863, *Burlington (VT) Times*, May 15, 1863; "A Private Letter from Sergeant Camp," *Vermont Journal* (Windsor), May 16, 1863; Soldier (1st Louisiana Brigade) letter, May 13, 1863, *Mobile (AL) Advertiser and Register*, May 21, 1863; Seymour, *Civil War Memoirs*, 54.

95. OR, 25(1):597, 607; Soldier (6th VT Infantry) letter, May 6, 1863, *Rutland (VT) Daily Herald*, May 14, 1863; Robert Pratt (5th VT Infantry) letter, May 14, 1863, typescript at FSNMP; Soldier (6th VT Infantry) letter, May 9, 1863, *Vermont Watchman and State Journal* (Montpelier), May 22, 1863.

96. Soldier (6th VT Infantry) letter, May 6, 1863, *Burlington (VT) Times*, May 15, 1863.

97. Henry C. Walker (13th GA Infantry) letter, May 9, 1863, Civil War Miscellany, Personal Papers, Georgia Dept. of Archives and History; Fisk, *Hard Marching*, 83.

98. Edwin Forbes sketch, *Attack on Gen Sedwick's [sic] Corps. Banks Ford near Chancellorsville, seen from the north bank of the Rappahannock River*, Morgan Collection of Civil War Drawings, Prints and Photographs Division, LC, https://loc.gov/item/2004661431.

99. William C. Mathews (38th GA Infantry) letter, May 8, 1863, *Sandersville (GA) Central Georgian*, June 3, 1863; Urbanus Dart (26th GA Infantry) letter, May 13, 1863, *Brunswick (GA) News*, May 4, 1963.

100. William C. Mathews (38th GA Infantry) letter, May 8, 1863, *Sandersville (GA) Central Georgian*, June 3, 1863; Soldier (13th GA Infantry) letter, May 17, 1863, *Savannah (GA) Daily Morning News*, May 29, 1863; Capt. John B. Colding (60th GA Infantry) letter, May 29, 1863, Colding Family Papers, South Carolina State Library; Urbanus Dart (26th GA Infantry) letter, May 13, 1863, *Brunswick (GA) News*, May 4, 1963.

101. OR, 25(1):605; 1st Sgt. L. W. Kendall to Mr. Bush, May 6, 1863, copy at FSNMP; Soldier (6th VT Infantry) letter, *Newark (NJ) Journal*, May 16, 1863.

102. OR, 25(1):610; Soldier (6th VT Infantry) letter, May 6, 1863, *Burlington (VT) Times*, May 15, 1863. Colonel Van Houten succumbed to his wounds on May 6. Sgt. Maj. George W. Fielder buried him nearby and then waited with hundreds of other captured men to be paroled.

103. OR, 25(1):606; Fisk, *Hard Marching*, 84; Soldier (6th VT Infantry) letter, May 6, 1863, *Burlington (VT) Times*, May 15, 1863.

104. OR Supplement, 4:630; Soldier (8th PA Cavalry) letter, May 22, 1863, *West Jersey Pioneer* (Bridgeton, NJ), June 13, 1863.

105. OR, 25(1):606; OR Supplement, 4:657.

106. Soldier (7th ME Infantry) letter, May 7, 1863, *Gardiner (ME) Home Journal*, May 14, 1863; Soldier (49th NY Infantry) letter, May 12, 1863, *Buffalo (NY) Advocate*, May 21, 1863; Soldier (49th NY Infantry) letter, May 9, 1863, *Jamestown (NY) Journal*, May 22, 1863; Soldier (49th NY Infantry) letter, May 9, 1863, *Buffalo (NY) Morning Express*, May 19, 1863.

107. Soldier (33rd NY Infantry) letter, May 7, 1863, *Rochester (NY) Daily Union and Advertiser*, May 13, 1863; John J. Toffey (21st NJ Infantry) letter, May 11, 1863, typescript at FSNMP; Judd, *Thirty-Third N.Y.S. Vols.*, 313.

108. G. M. Bandy (60th GA Infantry) letter, May 15, 1863, typescript at FSNMP; Fisk, *Hard Marching*, 84.

109. OR, 25(1):608; William C. Mathews (38th GA Infantry) letter, May 8, 1863, *Sandersville (GA) Central Georgian*, June 3, 1863; Capt. John B. Colding (60th GA Infantry) letter, May 24, 1863, Colding Family Papers, South Carolina State Library; Fisk, *Hard Marching*, 84; Soldier (6th VT Infantry) letter, May 6, 1863, *Burlington (VT) Times*, May 15, 1863.

110. OR, 25(2):379, 411.

111. US Naval Observatory, Astronomical Applications Dept., Sun and Moon data for May 4, 1863, http://aa.usno.navy.mil (accessed May 28, 2014).

11. May 4–5

1. "Storming of Mayre's [sic] Heights," *St. Johnsbury (VT) Caledonian*, Apr. 23, 1885.

2. Soldier (49th NY Infantry) letter, May 9, 1863, *Buffalo (NY) Evening Courier and Republic*, May 15, 1863.

3. OR, 25(1):582, 592.

4. OR, 25(1):588; Unidentified Soldier (16th NY Infantry), "Fredericksburg during the Civil War," n.d., Schoff Civil War Collection, Clements Library, Univ. of Michigan, typescript, copy at FSNMP.

5. OR, 25(1):582, 585, 588; William H. Morse (5th ME Infantry) diary, May 4, 1863, Androscoggin Historical Society, transcript, copy at FSNMP.

6. OR, 25(1):582; Unidentified Soldier (16th NY Infantry), "Fredericksburg during the Civil War," n.d., Schoff Collection, copy at FSNMP; Fairchild, *27th Regiment N.Y. Vols.*, 171–72; Evan M. Gery (96th PA Infantry) diary, copy at FSNMP.

7. Fairchild, *27th Regiment N.Y. Vols.*, 172; Unidentified Soldier (16th NY Infantry), "Fredericksburg during the Civil War," n.d., Schoff Collection, copy at FSNMP.

8. OR, 25(1):612; OR Supplement, 4:661.

9. OR Supplement, 4:627, 661; Soldier (Battery A, MA Light Artillery) letter, May 7, 1863, *Cambridge (MA) Chronicle,* May 16, 1863.

10. OR, 25(1):627.

11. OR, 25(1):613; Westbrook, *49th Pennsylvania,* 146.

12. Westbrook, *49th Pennsylvania,* 146; Abraham T. Hilands (49th PA Infantry) letter, May 8, 1863, Ottawa County (KS) Museum, typescript, copy at FSNMP.

13. OR, 25(1):613.

14. OR, 25(1):569, 572, 575–76; Stephen W. Gordon (15th NJ Infantry) diary, May 4, 1863, Spotsylvania County Museum; Halsey, *Brother against Brother,* 132.

15. OR, 25(1):619.

16. OR, 25(1):619, 622–23; Stewart, *Camp, March, and Battlefield,* 318–19.

17. OR, 25(1):619, 623; Stewart, *Camp, March, and Battlefield,* 320.

18. OR, 25(1):623; Soldier (102nd PA Infantry) letter, May 7, 1863, *Pittsburgh Gazette and Advertiser,* May 13, 1863; John W. Patterson (102nd PA Infantry) letter, May 25, 1863, copy at FSNMP.

19. OR, 25(1):623; Soldier (102nd PA Infantry) letter, May 7, 1863, *Pittsburgh Gazette and Advertiser,* May 13, 1863; Soldier (102nd PA Infantry) letter, May 13, 1863, ibid., May 14, 1863.

20. OR, 25(1):621, 625; Soldier (139th PA Infantry) letter, May 7, 1863, *Pittsburgh Gazette and Advertiser,* May 13, 1863; Sylvester F. Hildebrand (139th PA Infantry) account, *Apollo (PA) Sentinel,* Apr. 21, 1911.

21. OR Supplement, 4:651; Brewster, *When This Cruel War Is Over,* 227; Tyler, *Recollections of the Civil War,* 88; John Dunbar (37th MA Infantry) letter, May 6, 1863, typescript at FSNMP.

22. OR Supplement, 4:643, 648; Soldier (Shaler's brigade) letter, May 7, 1863, *Providence (RI) Evening Press,* May 15, 1863.

23. Newspaper correspondent's letter, May 23, 1863, *Bangor (ME) Whig and Courier,* May 25, 1863; G. F. A. Hill (6th ME Infantry) diary, May 4, 1863, Curatorial Collection, Gettysburg National Military Park, copy at FSNMP; Mundy, *No Rich Men's Sons,* 131.

24. OR, 25(1):860–61, 872, 876; US Naval Observatory, Astronomical Applications Dept., Sun and Moon data for May 4, 1863, http://aa.usno,navy.mil (accessed May 28, 2014); Early, *Autobiographical Sketch and Narrative,* 232; Soldier (Wright's GA Brigade) letter, May 5, 1863, *Southern Confederacy* (Atlanta), May 13, 1863.

25. OR, 25(1):828.

26. William R. Montgomery (2nd SC Infantry) letter, May 7, 1863, Univ. of South Carolina, copy at FSNMP.

27. OR, 25(1):831.

28. OR, 25(1):802; Early, *Autobiographical Sketch and Narrative,* 232.

29. OR, 25(1):831; Edgar P. Alexander (2nd NJ Infantry) letter, May 4, 1863, *Newark (NJ) Daily Advertiser,* May 8, 1863.

30. William L. Fagan (8th AL Infantry), "Battle of Salem Church," *Philadelphia Weekly Times,* July 7, 1883; Soldier (2nd RI Infantry) letter, May 13, 1863, *Providence (RI) Daily Evening Press,* May 18, 1863.

31. Fagan, "Battle of Salem Church."

32. OR, 25(1):831.

33. Mundy, *No Rich Men's Sons*, 131; "What the 43d Did in the Late Battles," *Albany (NY) Evening Journal*, May 15, 1863.

34. Stevens, *Three Years in the Sixth Corps*, 205; David Burhans (43rd NY Infantry) letter, May 5, 1863, *Albany (NY) Evening Journal*, May 12, 1863; "What the 43d Did in the Late Battles," *Albany (NY) Evening Journal*, May 15, 1863.

35. OR, 25(1):860; Mundy, *No Rich Men's Sons*, 132–33; Alexander B. Sumner (6th ME Infantry) letter, May 11, 1863, typescript at FSNMP; Clark, *Campaigning with the Sixth Maine*, 35–36.

36. Clark, *Campaigning with the Sixth Maine*, 36.

37. Clark, 36; Mundy, *No Rich Men's Sons*, 134.

38. Clark, *Campaigning with the Sixth Maine*, 37.

39. Mundy, *No Rich Men's Sons*, 212; Clark, *Campaigning with the Sixth Maine*, 37.

40. OR, 25(1):626; Brewer, *Sixty-First Regiment Pennsylvania Volunteers*, 57; Quiner Scrapbooks: Correspondence of Wisconsin Volunteers, 1861–1865, comp. Edwin B. Quiner, WHS, 8:283–84, copy at FSNMP.

41. OR, 25(1):828; Lemon, *Feed Them the Steel!*, 42.

42. OR, 25(1):881.

43. Frederick M. Colston, "What I Saw of the Battle of Chancellorsville," 1912, Virginia Historical Society, copy at FSNMP.

44. OR, 25(1):1002–3; Early, *Autobiographical Sketch and Narrative*, 232; Adam W. Kersh (52nd VA Infantry) letter, May 15, 1863, copy at FSNMP; Lt. Col. Hamilton C. Jones (57th NC Infantry) report, May 13, 1863, Alphonso Calhoun Avery Papers, SHC, UNC.

45. OR, 25(1):215, 356, 25(2):405–6; Soldier (127th PA Infantry) letter, May 6, 1863, *Lebanon (PA) Courier*, May 21, 1863.

46. OR Supplement, 4:576; Ford, *Fifteenth Regiment Massachusetts Volunteer Infantry*, 249.

47. OR, 25(1):359; Soldier (127th PA Infantry) letter, May 6, 1863, *Lebanon (PA) Courier*, May 21, 1863; Abbott, *Fallen Leaves*, 176; Soldier (Shaler's brigade) letter, May 13, 1863, *Providence (RI) Daily Evening Press*, May 20, 1863.

48. OR, 25(1):359.

49. Newton T. Hartshorn (US Engineers) diary, Rauner Special Collections Library, Dartmouth College, transcript, copy at FSNMP.

50. OR, 25(1):881–82.

51. OR, 25(1):881–82.

52. OR, 25(1):881–82.

53. OR, 25(1):882.

54. OR, 25(1):821; Alexander, *Fighting for the Confederacy*, 214.

55. This gun pit sits at the edge of a bluff, down which the old Banks' Ford Road extends just to the west. The natural ford is visible, as was the Federal pontoon bridge at the Scott's Ferry landing. The old road provided a negotiable grade across an otherwise steep slope. There is a switchback close to the river, below which the road has been obliterated by a century and a half of river flooding.

56. James E. Phillips (12th VA Infantry) journal, May 4, 1863, Virginia Historical Society, copy at FSNMP.

57. OR, 25(1):845; OR Supplement, 4:675; "The Vermonters in the Recent Battles," *St. Albans (VT) Messenger,* May 21, 1863; Luther C. Furst (139th PA Infantry) diary, Apr. 29–May 18, 1863, HCWRT, USAMHI, copy at FSNMP; Basil Manly (NC Artillery) report, *Fayetteville (NC) Observer,* May 28, 1863.

58. Early, *Autobiographical Sketch and Narrative,* 231–32.

59. Benham, "Report to Major General Joseph Hooker, May 20, 1863."

60. OR, 25(1):216; Benham, "Report to Major General Joseph Hooker, May 20, 1863."

61. OR, 25(1):219–20, 25(2):408–10; Benham, "Report to Major General Joseph Hooker, May 20, 1863."

62. OR, 25(2):407, 411.

63. OR, 25(2):412.

64. Benham, "Report to Major General Joseph Hooker, May 20, 1863."

65. OR, 25(2):418.

66. OR, 25(2):418.

67. OR, 25(2):418.

68. OR, 25(2):418.

69. Unidentified Soldier (16th NY Infantry), "Fredericksburg during the Civil War," n.d., Schoff Civil War Collection, Clements Library, Univ. of Michigan, typescript, copy at FSNMP; Fisk, *Hard Marching,* 84.

70. OR Supplement, 4:620.

71. Benham, "Report to Major General Joseph Hooker, May 20, 1863."

72. OR, 25(1):561; Benham, "Report to Major General Joseph Hooker, May 20, 1863."

73. OR, 25(2):419.

74. OR, 25(2):419.

75. OR, 25(1):214.

76. OR, 25(1):248; OR Supplement, 4:550.

77. Holt, *Surgeon's Civil War,* 92–94.

78. Mark, *Red, White, and Blue Badge,* 204.

79. OR, 25(1):784; J. Edward Carpenter, "The Cavalry at Chancellorsville," *Philadelphia Weekly Times,* June 29, 1878; Whitman and True, *Maine in the War for the Union,* 182.

80. OR, 25(1):412–13.

81. OR, 25(1):360; *History of the Nineteenth Regiment Massachusetts Volunteer Infantry,* 207–8; Soldier (127th PA Infantry) letter, May 6, 1863, *Lebanon (PA) Courier,* May 21, 1863.

82. *History of the Nineteenth Regiment Massachusetts Volunteer Infantry,* 208.

83. Ford, *Fifteenth Regiment Massachusetts Volunteer Infantry,* 250.

84. OR Supplement, 4:576; *History of the Nineteenth Regiment Massachusetts Volunteer Infantry,* 208.

85. Benham, "Report to Major General Joseph Hooker, May 20, 1863."

86. Albert A. Crane (6th VT Infantry) letter, May 6, 1863, *Burlington (VT) Times,* May 15, 1863.

87. OR, 25(1):606; Crane letter, May 6, 1863; "Storming of Mayre's [sic] Heights," *St. Johnsbury (VT) Caledonian*, Apr. 23, 1885.

88. OR, 25(2):419.

89. OR, 25(1):625; Sylvester F. Hildebrand (139th PA Infantry) account, *Apollo (PA) Sentinel*, Apr. 21, 1911.

90. Urbanus Dart (26th GA Infantry) letter, May 13, 1863, *Brunswick (GA) News*, May 4, 1963.

91. Soldier (13th GA Infantry) letter, May 17, 1863, *Savannah (GA) Daily Morning News*, May 29, 1863.

92. OR, 25(1):853.

93. OR, 25(1):841; Seymour, *Civil War Memoirs*, 55; Soldier (13th MS Infantry) letter, May 6, 1863, *Mobile (AL) Advertiser and Register*, May 22, 1863.

94. OR Supplement, 4:671; Early, *Autobiographical Sketch and Narrative*, 233.

95. Statement by Maj. Robert T. Harper, June 1890, Ladies Memorial Association of Fredericksburg, copy at FSNMP. Robert Harper and some comrades found Matthew Harper's remains at Salem Church and reburied him in a location where the grave would not likely be disturbed by farming. Robert returned in 1868 with a stone to mark the site but learned that the Ladies Memorial Association had moved Lieutenant Harper to Fredericksburg. He found the new grave and placed the stone, the first one to mark a grave in the Confederate Cemetery in Fredericksburg.

96. OR, 25(1):204; Soldier (8th PA Cavalry) letter, May 22, 1863, *West Jersey Pioneer* (Bridgeton, NJ), June 13, 1863.

97. OR, 25(1):215; Rhodes, *All for the Union*, 107; Benham, "Report to Major General Joseph Hooker, May 20, 1863."

98. Rhodes, *All for the Union*, 107; Jacob W. Haas (96th PA Infantry) letter, May 12, 1863, HCWRT, USAMHI, copy at FSNMP; William A. Lessig, "The Ninety-Sixth Reg., P.V., in the Late Battles," *Pottsville (PA) Mining Journal*, June 6, 1863.

99. Charles W. McArthur (61st GA Infantry) letter, May 23, 1863, Kennesaw Mountain National Military Park, typescript, copy at FSNMP; Soldier (31st NY Infantry) letter, May 9, 1863, *Brooklyn (NY) Daily Times*, May 15, 1863.

100. OR, 25(1):569, 583; *History of Clinton and Franklin Counties*, 73; William Hastings (43rd NY Infantry) letter, n.d., *Albany (NY) Evening Journal*, May 20, 1863.

101. Holt, *Surgeon's Civil War*, 97, 100; Patterson, *Yankee Rebel*, 103.

102. OR, 25(1):831, 25(2):795; Soldier (6th VT Infantry) letter, May 16, 1863, *Burlington (VT) Times*, May 22, 1863.

12. An Assessment

1. Coddington, *Gettysburg Campaign*, 480–81.

2. Sears, *Chancellorsville*, 477–79, 484–87.

3. Sears, 493–94, 497–98.

4. Sears, 492–94. Breaking out the casualties sustained at Salem Church and Banks' Ford for units that also fought at Chancellorsville is a challenge. Brig. Gen.

Ambrose R. Wright reported his casualties day by day, but he is the exception. Using Wright's losses as a percentage to calculate the casualties in other brigades would not provide a valid number because the various units did not experience the same level of fighting as his.

5. Letter, May 14, 1863, in Leonard, "Letters of a 5th Wisconsin Volunteer," 73–74; William H. Pohlman (59th NY Infantry) letter, May 13, 1863, Special Collections, New York State Library, copy at FSNMP.
6. OR, 25(2):171.
7. OR, 25(2):438, 440.
8. OR, 25(2):438; Burlingame, *Abraham Lincoln*, 2:499.
9. OR, 25(2):438.
10. Coddington, *Gettysburg Campaign*, 36.
11. OR, 27(1):114, 27(3):374.
12. Welcher, *Union Army*, 2:246–51, 325–30.
13. OR, 29(2):409.
14. OR, 29(1):11–12, 29(2):412.
15. "Army of the Potomac: General Hooker," in Congress, *Report of the Joint Committee on the Conduct of the War*, xlix.
16. "Army of the Potomac: General Hooker," xlix.
17. "Army of the Potomac: General Hooker," xlviii.
18. "Army of the Potomac: General Hooker," 21.
19. "Army of the Potomac: General Hooker," 40.
20. "Army of the Potomac: General Hooker," 76.
21. Gouverneur K. Warren letter, May 11, 1863, Warren Papers, Special Collections, New York State Library, copy at FSNMP.
22. "Army of the Potomac: General Hooker," 47.
23. "Army of the Potomac: General Hooker," 48.
24. "Army of the Potomac: General Hooker," 87.
25. "Army of the Potomac: General Hooker," 87.
26. "Army of the Potomac: General Hooker," xlix.
27. Bates, "Hooker's Comments on Chancellorsville," 217.
28. Strother, *Virginia Yankee in the Civil War*, 191.
29. Fremantle, *Three Months in the Southern States*, 129.

Appendix 3

1. OR, 25(1):840.
2. OR, 25(1):839.
3. OR, 25(1):840.
4. OR, 25(1):840.
5. OR, 25(1):840.
6. OR, 25(1):840.
7. OR, 25(1):1000; Early to Barksdale, May 14, 1863, *Daily Richmond (VA) Enquirer*, June 15, 1863.

8. OR, 25(1):1001.
9. OR, 25(1):1001.
10. Early to Editors, May 11, 1863, *Daily Richmond (VA) Enquirer,* May 13, 1863.
11. Barksdale to Editors, May 13, 1863, *Daily Richmond (VA) Enquirer,* May 18, 1863. These letters got picked up by other papers.
12. Early to Editors, May 19, 1863, *Daily Richmond (VA) Enquirer,* May 27, 1863.
13. Barksdale to Editors, May 31, 1863, *Daily Richmond (VA) Enquirer,* June 15, 1863.
14. Early to Barksdale, May 14, 1863, *Daily Richmond (VA) Enquirer,* June 15, 1863.
15. Early to Lee, Nov. 20, 1868, Box 25, Collection 158, UVA; OR, 25(1):801.
16. Barksdale to Editors, May 31, 1863, *Daily Richmond (VA) Enquirer,* June 15, 1863.
17. Early, *Autobiographical Sketch and Narrative,* 207.

BIBLIOGRAPHY

Manuscripts

Androscroggin Historical Society, Auburn, ME
    William H. Morse diary
Bethel Historical Society, Bethel, ME
    Clark S. Edwards, "War Reminiscences"
Brown University Library, Providence, RI
    Selden Connor letters
Connecticut Historical Society, Hartford
    Virgil W. Mattoon letter
Dartmouth College, Rauner Special Collections Library, Hanover, NH
    Smith G. Bailey diary
    Newton T. Hartshorn diary
Erskine College, McCain Library, Due West, SC
    William Hood, "The Battle of Salem Church and Its Episodes"
Fredericksburg and Spotsylvania National Military Park, Fredericksburg, VA
    G. M. Bandy letter
    Thomas Beath diary
    Benham, Henry W. "Gen'l H. W. Benham's Reports No. 3, being Part I, of Report of Services with Army of the Potomac from March 1863, until March 1864, Brigadier General H. W. Benham; including Benham's Report to Major General Joseph Hooker, May 20, 1863," June 22, 1876. National Archives, M1098, Roll 6, typescript
    George D. Breck letters, typescript
    Dr. Edwin D. Buckman letter
    Chet Campbell letter, typescript
    Ambrose F. Cole letters, typescript

John P. Carter diary, copy
Thomas M. Crowder, "One Month in the Northern States: The Civil War Diary of Lieutenant Colonel Thomas M. Crowder, 1863," annotated transcript
David D. Davies diary
John Dunbar letter, typescript
James R. Edwards, "Sketch of Dr. James Randle Edwards, Wartime Experiences, 1861–1865," compiled by Robert Rucker, copy
Joseph C. Felton letter, typescript
Isaiah Fogleman diary
Fredericksburg and Spotsylvania County Battle Fields Memorial Commission, *Report on Inspection of Battle Fields in and around Fredericksburg and Spotsylvania Court House, Virginia*, Dec. 1, 1935.
Evan M. Gery diary, copy
John Gibbon letters, typescript
Douglas H. Gordon letters, edited by Ralph Happel
Ruth Graham, *Combat Map No. 9, Second Battle of Fredericksburg, Chancellorsville Campaign* (1935)
John William Ford Hatten memoir, copy
Inspection report of Light Division, Sixth Corps, Apr. 26, 1863, copy
William B. Jennings, memoir
Adam W. Karsh letter, typescript
L. W. Kendall letter
John S. Kidder letters, typescript
Frank Lindley Lemont letter, copy
Edward Mahogany letter, copy
Bailey G. McClelen memoir, typescript copy
John McDonald letters
John Newman letter, copy
Lt. Lemuel B. Norton requisition book, copy
Sebastion N. Page, copy
John W. Patterson letter, copy
William Paynton letter, copy
Anderson J. Peeler article, copy of typescript
William Plumer letter, typescript
Robert Pratt letter, typescript
Philip M. Senderling letter, typescript
Cyrus Stone letter, copy
William Stowe letter, transcript
James Robert Strong letter
Alexander B. Sumner letter, typescript
Gilbert Thompson, "My Journal, 1861–1865, U.S. Engineer Battalion, Army of the Potomac," copy
John J. Toffey letter, typescript
John G. Wallace diary, typescript

Frederick H. West letter, typescript
Richard W. York letter, copy
Georgia Department of Archives and History, Atlanta
    Civil War Miscellany, Personal Papers
    William M. Jones memoir
    Andrew J. McBride memoir
    Henry C. Walker letter
Gettysburg National Military Park, Gettysburg, PA
    Curatorial Collection
    G. F. A. Hill diary
Greensboro Historical Museum Archives, Greensboro, NC
    Memoirs of Eli S. Coble, Dec. 1862–June 1863
Huntington Library, San Marino, CA
    Robert E. Lee to J. E. B. Stuart, May 5, 1863, copy at FSNMP
Kennesaw Mountain National Military Park, Marietta, GA
    Charles W. McArthur letter
Ladies Memorial Association of Fredericksburg, Fredericksburg, VA
    Robert T. Harper statement, June 1890
Mississippi Department of Archives and History, Jackson
    Memoir of Genl. Benjamin Grubb Humphreys, 1878
Library of Congress, Manuscripts Collection, Washington, DC
    John F. L. Hartwell letters and diary
    Thaddeus Lowe Papers
    N. Michler. *Fredericksburg*. NY Lithographing, Engraving, & Printing, 1867. Map, color, 1:21, 120 scale.
    Col. John C. C. Sanders report
    James S. Wadsworth Family Papers
Maine State Archives, Augusta
    Clark S. Edwards report to the Adjutant General, Jan. 27, 1864.
    Sewell Gray diary
Navarro College, Corsicana, TX
    Pearce Collection
    Hiram H. Tilley letter
New York State Library, Albany
    Special Collections
    Uberto A. Burnham Papers
    Winsor B. French letter, MS 16278
    William H. Pohlman letter
    Jonathan T. Scharf memoir
    Gouverneur K. Warren Papers
Norwich University Archives, Kreitsberg Library, Northfield, VT
    Edward Bancroft Williston memoir, c. 1897
Ottawa County Museum, Minneapolis, Kansas

    Abraham T. Hilands letter, typescript
Sarasota Springs Historical Society, Sarasota Springs, NY
    Orrin P. Rugg letter, typescript
South Carolina State Library, Columbia
    Colding Family Papers
Spotsylvania County Museum, Spotsylvania Court House, VA
    Stephen W. Gordon diary
Syracuse University Library, Dept. of Special Collections, Syracuse, NY
    Osborne Family Papers
US Army Military History Institute, Carlisle Barracks, PA
    Civil War Miscellaneous Collection
    William A. Moore memoirs
    Robertson Tayler letter
    Marion H. Fitzpatrick letter
    Harrisburg (PA) Civil War Round Table Collection
    Luther C. Furst diary
    Jacob W. Haas letter
    Edmund D. Halsey Collection
    Benjamin R. J. Thaxter letter, typescript
University of Arkansas Libraries, Fayetteville
    William Remmel letter
University of Alabama, Tuscaloosa
    John C. C. Sanders letters
University of Georgia, Special Collections, Athens
    Francis L. Hillyer letter
University of Michigan, Clements Library, Ann Arbor
    Schoff Civil War Collection
    William Speed letter
    Unidentified soldier, "Fredericksburg during the Civil War"
University of North Carolina at Chapel Hill
    William R. Redding letter
    Southern Historical Collection
    Alphonso Calhoun Avery Papers
    William McCauley Papers
    William N. Pendleton Papers
    Perry Family Papers
    Harrison Wells Papers
University of South Carolina, Columbia
    William R. Montgomery letter
University of Virginia Library, Manuscripts Department Charlottesville
    Early to Lee letter, Collection 158
    James Peter Williams letters
    John Warwick Daniel Papers

Vermont Historical Society, Montpelier
"S. E. and S. M. Pingree Civil War Letters, 1861–1865," transcribed and edited by Kelly A. Nolin (1994)
Virginia Historical Society, Richmond
Frederick M. Colston, "What I Saw of the Battle of Chancellorsville," 1912
Edward S. Duffey diary
James E. Phillips journal
Alfred Lewis Scott, "Memoir of Service in the Confederate Army," 1910
War Library and Museum, Philadelphia
Thomas J. Lutman diary
Wisconsin Historical Society, Madison
Francis E. Pinto, "History of the 32nd Regiment, New York Volunteers in the Civil War, 1861 to 1863, and Personal Recollections during That Period," Brooklyn, NY, 1895, typescript
Proceedings at the Annual Meeting of the Association of Fifth Wisconsin Volunteer Infantry, Held at Milwaukee, June 27–28, 1900
Quiner Scrapbooks: Correspondence of Wisconsin Volunteers, 1861–1865, Vol. 8, compiled by Edwin B. Quiner
Report of the Proceedings of 5th Wisconsin Vol. Infantry, Fifteenth Annual Reunion Held at Milwaukee, July 23–24, 1901

Newspapers and Periodicals

Albany (NY) Evening Journal
Apollo (PA) Sentinel
Athens (GA) Southern Banner
Athens (GA) Southern Watchman
Atlanta Journal
Auburn (NY) Advertiser and Union
Bangor (ME) Daily Whig and Courier
Boston Journal
Brooklyn (NY) Daily Times
Brooklyn (NY) Eagle
Brooklyn (NY) Standard Union
Brunswick (GA) News
Buffalo (NY) Advocate
Buffalo (NY) Evening Courier and Republic
Buffalo (NY) Morning Express
Burlington (VT) Times
Cambridge (MA) Chronicle
Carolina Watchman (Salisbury, NC)
Columbia (PA) Spy
Daily Richmond (VA) Dispatch

Daily Richmond (VA) Enquirer
Dunn County Lumberman (Menomonie, WI)
Fall River (MA) Evening News
Fayetteville (NC) Observer
Flemington (NJ) Hunterdon Republican
Fredericksburg (VA) Free Lance–Star
Gardiner (ME) Home Journal
Grant County Witness (Lancaster, WI)
Hampshire (MA) Gazette
Jamestown (NY) Journal
Janesville (WI) Daily Gazette
Lamoille (VT) Newsdealer
Lancaster (PA) Daily Evening Express
Lebanon (PA) Courier
Lewiston (ME) Daily Evening Journal
Macon (GA) Telegraph
Malone (NY) Palladium
Milwaukee Sunday Telegraph
Mobile (AL) Advertiser & Register
Montpelier (VT) Argus and Patriot
Morristown (NJ) Daily Record
National Tribune (Washington, DC)
Newark (NJ) Daily Advertiser
Newark (NJ) Journal
Newburgh (NY) Telegraph
New Orleans Times Picayune
New York Daily Union and Advertiser
Nunda (NY) News
Ontario (NY) Repository
Orleans County Monitor (Barton, VT)
Orleans Independent Standard (Barton, VT)
Palmyra (NY) Courier
Penn-Yan (NY) Democrat
Philadelphia Weekly Times
Pittsburg Evening Chronicle
Pittsburg Gazette and Advertiser
Portland (ME) Daily Press
Pottsville (PA) Miner's Journal
Providence (RI) Daily Evening Press
Richmond (VA) Daily Dispatch
Richmond (VA) Sentinel
Richmond (VA) Times Dispatch
Rochester (NY) Daily Union and Advertiser
Rochester (NY) Democrat & American

Rockland County Messenger (Haverstraw, NY)
Rutland (VT) Courier
Rutland (VT) Daily Herald
Rutland (VT) Weekly Herald
St. Albans (VT) Messenger
St. Johnsbury (VT) Caledonian
Sandersville (GA) Central Georgian
Saratogian (Saratoga, NY)
Savannah (GA) Daily Morning News
Savannah (GA) Republican
Southern Confederacy (Atlanta)
Sumter (GA) Republican
Sussex (NJ) Register
Tiffin (OH) Weekly Times
Trenton (NJ) Daily State Gazette
Vermont Journal (Windsor)
Vermont Watchman and State Journal (Montpelier)
Virginia Herald (Fredericksburg)
Wabasha County Herald (Wabasha, MN)
West Jersey Pioneer (Bridgeton, NJ)
Winchester (VA) Evening Star
Windham County Monitor (Brattleboro, VT)
Wisconsin State Journal (Madison)
Yazoo (MS) Sentinel

Books and Articles

Abbott, Henry L. *Fallen Leaves: The Civil War Letters of Major Henry Livermore Abbott*. Edited by Robert Garth Scott. Kent, OH: Kent State Univ. Press, 1991.

Adams, John G. B. *Reminiscences of the Nineteenth Massachusetts Regiment*. Boston: Wright & Potter Printing, 1899.

Alexander, Edward P. *Fighting for the Confederacy: The Personal Recollections of General Edward Porter Alexander*. Edited by Gary W. Gallagher. Chapel Hill: Univ. of North Carolina Press, 1989.

Anderson, James S. *The Papers of James S. Anderson: Civil War Diaries and Letters of James Anderson Company A, 5th Wis. Volunteers, Manitowoc Wis.* Edited by Dennis R. Moore. Manitowoc, WI: Bivouac, 1996.

Banes, Charles H. *History of the Philadelphia Brigade*. Philadelphia: J. B. Lippincott, 1876.

Bates, Samuel P. *The Battle of Chancellorsville*. Meadville, PA: Edward T. Bates, 1882.

———. "Hooker's Comments on Chancellorsville." In Johnson and Buel, *Battles and Leaders of the Civil War*, vol. 3.

Beyer, W. F., and O. F. Keydel, eds. *Deeds of Valor*. Vol. 1. Detroit: Perrien-Deydel, 1907.

Bicknell, George W. *History of the Fifth Regiment Maine Volunteers.* 1871. Reprint, Farmington, ME: Knowlton and McLeary, 1988.

Bidwell, Frederick David, comp. *History of the Forty-Ninth New York Volunteers.* Albany, NY: J. B. Lyon, 1916.

Bigelow, John, Jr. *The Campaign of Chancellorsville: A Strategic and Tactical Study.* New Haven, CT: Yale Univ. Press, 1910. Reprint, Dayton: Morningside House, n.d.

———. "The Battle of Marye's Heights and Salem Church." In *Campaigns in Virginia, Maryland, and Pennsylvania, 1862–1863,* vol. 3 of *Papers of the Military Historical Society of Massachusetts.* Boston: Griffith-Stillings, 1903.

Bilby, Joseph G. "Seeing the Elephant: The 15th New Jersey Infantry at the Battle of Salem Church." *Military Images* 5, no. 4 (Jan.–Feb. 1984).

———. "Through Hades with His Hat Off: The Strange Career of A. J. Morrison." *Military Images* 11, no. 4 (Mar.–Apr. 1990).

Blackford, Charles M. *Memories of Life in and out of the Army in Virginia during the War between the States.* Edited by Susan Leigh Blackford. 2 vols. Lynchburg, VA: J. P. Bell, 1896.

Blight, David W. *A Slave No More: Two Men Who Escaped to Freedom.* New York: Harcourt, 2007.

Boatner, Mark M., III. *The Civil War Dictionary.* New York: David McKay, 1959.

Bradwell, I. G. "The 31st Georgia at Chancellorsville." *Confederate Veteran* 23, no. 10 (Oct. 1915).

Brainerd, Wesley. *Bridge Building in Wartime: Colonel Wesley Brainerd's Memoir of the 50th New York Volunteer Engineers.* Edited by Ed Malles. Knoxville: Univ. of Tennessee Press, 1997.

Brewer, A. T. *History of the Sixty-First Regiment Pennsylvania Volunteers, 1861–1865.* Pittsburg: Art Engraving & Printing, 1911.

Brewster, Charles Harvey. *When This Cruel War Is Over: The Civil War Letters of Charles Harvey Brewster.* Edited by David W. Blight. Amherst: Univ. of Massachusetts Press, 1992.

Brooke-Rawle, William, et al. *History of the Third Pennsylvania Cavalry, Sixtieth Regiment Pennsylvania Volunteers, in the American Civil War, 1861–1865.* Philadelphia: Franklin Printing, 1905.

Bruce, George A. *The Twentieth Regiment of Massachusetts Volunteer Infantry, 1861–1865.* New York: Houghton Mifflin, 1906.

Buck, Samuel D. *With the Old Confederates: Actual Experiences of a Captain in the Line.* Baltimore: H. E. Houck, 1925.

Burlingame, Michael. *Abraham Lincoln: A Life.* 2 vols. Baltimore: Johns Hopkins Univ. Press, 2008.

Caldwell, Mary G. "'It Does Appear as if Our Soldiers Were Made Altogether of Patriotism': The Civil War Diary of Mary Gray Caldwell." Edited by Russel P. Smith. *Fredericksburg History and Biography* 11 (2012).

Chapin, L. N. *A Brief History of the Thirty-Fourth Regiment, NYSV.* New York: 1903.

Cheek, Philip, and Mair Pointon. *History of the Sauk County Riflemen Known as Company "A," Sixth Wisconsin Veteran Volunteer Infantry, 1861–1865.* 1909. Reprint, Salem, MA: Higginson Book, 1998.

Clark, Charles A. *Campaigning with the Sixth Maine: A Paper Read before the Iowa Commandery, Military Order of the Loyal Legion of the United States.* Des Moines: Kenyon, 1897.

Clark, George. "Chancellorsville and Salem Church: Special Features of the Latter." *Confederate Veteran* 18, no. 8 (Mar. 1910).

Clark, Walter, ed. *Histories of the Several Regiments and Battalions from North Carolina in the Great War 1861–65.* Vol. 3. 1901. Reprint, Wendell, NC: Broadfoot's Bookmark, 1982.

Coddington, Edwin B. *The Gettysburg Campaign: A Study in Command.* 1968. Reprint, Dayton, OH: Morningside Bookshop, 1979.

Cole, Jacob Henry. *Under Five Commanders; or, A Boy's Experience with the Army of the Potomac.* Patterson, NJ: News Printing, 1906.

Committee of Regimental Association. *History of the 127th Regiment Pennsylvania Volunteers.* Lebanon, PA: Report Publishing, 1902.

Congress. *Report of the Joint Committee on the Conduct of the War, at the Second Session Thirty-Eighth Congress.* Vol. 1. Washington, DC: Government Printing Office, 1865.

Couch, Darius N. "The Chancellorsville Campaign." In Johnson and Buel, *Battles and Leaders of the Civil War,* vol. 3.

Curtis, Newton Martin. *From Bull Run to Chancellorsville: The Story of the Sixteenth New York Infantry together with Personal Reminiscences.* New York: G. P. Putnam's Sons, 1906.

Curtis, O. B. *History of the Twenty-Fourth Michigan.* 1891. Reprint, Gaithersburg, MD: Olde Soldier Books, 1988.

Cushing, Wainwright. "Charge of the Light Division at Marye's Heights, May 3, 1863." In *War Papers Read before the Commandery of the State of Maine, Military Order of the Loyal Legion of the United States,* vol. 3. Portland, ME: Lefavor-Tower, 1908.

Dawes, Rufus R. *Service with the Sixth Wisconsin Volunteers.* 1890. Reprint, Dayton, OH: Morningside Bookshop, 1996.

Dodd, Ira Seymour. *The Song of the Rappahannock: Sketches of the Civil War.* New York: Dodd, Mead, 1898.

Dodge, Theodore A. *The Campaign of Chancellorsville.* Boston: J. R. Osgood, 1881.

Donaldson, Francis A. *Inside the Army of the Potomac: The Civil War Experience of Captain Francis Adams Donaldson.* Edited by J. Gregory Acken. Mechanicsburg, PA: Stackpole Books, 1998.

Doubleday, Abner. *Chancellorsville and Gettysburg.* New York: Charles Scribner's Sons, 1882.

Driver, Robert J., Jr. *52nd Virginia Infantry.* Lynchburg, VA: H. E. Howard, 1986.

———. *58th Virginia Infantry.* Lynchburg, VA: H. E. Howard, 1990.

Early, Jubal A. *Lieutenant General Jubal Anderson Early, C.S.A.: Autobiographical Sketch and Narrative of the War between the States.* 1912. Reprint, Wilmington, NC: Broadfoot, 1989.

Evans, Charles M. *War of the Aeronauts: A History of Ballooning in the Civil War.* Mechanicsburg, PA: Stackpole Books, 2002.

Fairchild, Charles Bryant, comp. *History of the 27th Regiment N.Y. Vols.* 1888. Reprint, Salem, MA: Higginson Book, 1998.

Faust, Patricia L., ed. *Historical Times Illustrated Encyclopedia of the Civil War*. New York: Harper & Row, 1986.

Fishel, Edwin C. *The Secret War for the Union: The Untold Story of Military Intelligence in the Civil War*. New York: Houghton Mifflin, 1996.

Fisk, Wilbur. *Hard Marching Every Day: The Civil War Letters of Private Wilbur Fisk, 1861–1865*. Edited by Emil and Ruth Rosenblatt. 1983. Reprint, Lawrence: Univ. Press of Kansas, 1992.

Ford, Andrew E. *The Story of the Fifteenth Regiment Massachusetts Volunteer Infantry in the Civil War 1861–1864*. 1898. Reprint, Salem, MA: Higginson Book, 1997.

Fortescue, Louis R. *Service with the Signal Corps: The Civil War Memoir of Captain Louis R. Fortescue*. Edited by J. Gregory Acken. Knoxville: Univ. of Tennessee Press, 2015.

Foster, John Y. *New Jersey and the Rebellion: A History of the Service of the Troops and People of New Jersey in Aid of the Union Cause*. Newark, NJ: Martin R. Dennis, 1868.

Fox, William F. *Regimental Losses in the American Civil War, 1861–1865*. 1898. Reprint, Dayton, OH: Morningside Bookshop, 1985.

Freeman, Douglas Southall. *Lee's Lieutenants: A Study in Command*. Vol. 2. New York: Charles Scribner's Sons, 1944.

———. *R. E. Lee: A Biography*. Vols. 2–3. New York: Charles Scribner's Sons, 1934–35.

Fremantle, Arthur J. *Three Months in the Southern States: April, June, 1863*. Mobile: S. H. Goetzel, 1864.

Furgurson, Ernest B. *Chancellorsville 1863: The Souls of the Brave*. New York: Alfred A. Knopf, 1992.

Gallagher, Gary W. "East of Chancellorsville: Jubal A. Early at Second Fredericksburg and Salem Church." In *Chancellorsville: The Battle and Its Aftermath* edited by Gary W. Gallagher. Chapel Hill: Univ. of North Carolina Press, 1996.

Gamache, Claudette M. "Preliminary Historic Structures Report: Fredericksburg City Cemetery Stone Gateway." Paper for Individual Study in Architectural Conservation, Mary Washington College, 1994.

Geary, James W. *We Need Men: The Union Draft in the Civil War*. De Kalb: Northern Illinois Univ. Press, 1991.

Gibbon, John. *Personal Recollections of the Civil War*. New York: G. P. Putnam's Sons, 1928.

Gordon, John B. *Reminiscences of the Civil War*. New York: Charles Scribner's Sons, 1903.

Greene, A. Wilson. "Morale, Maneuver, and Mud: The Army of the Potomac, December 16, 1862–January 26, 1863." In *The Fredericksburg Campaign: Decision on the Rappahannock*, edited by Gary Gallagher. Chapel Hill: Univ. of North Carolina Press, 1995.

Hagerman, Edward. *The American Civil War and the Origins of Modern Warfare: Ideas, Organization, and Field Command*. 1988. Reprint, Bloomington: Indiana Univ. Press, 1992.

Haight, Theron W. "Among the Pontoons at Fitzhugh's Crossing." In *War Papers Read before the Commandery of the State of Wisconsin, Military Order of the Loyal Legion of the United States*, vol. 1. Milwaukee: Burdick, Armitage, & Allen, 1891.

Haines, Alanson A. *History of the Fifteenth Regiment, New Jersey Volunteers*. New York: Jenkins & Thomas, Printers, 1883.

Hall, H. Seymour. *Personal Experience under Generals Burnside and Hooker, in the Battles of Fredericksburg and Chancellorsville. . . .* [Leavensworth]: Kansas Commandery, Military Order of the Loyal Legion of the United States, 1894.

Halsey, Edmund D. *Brother against Brother: The Lost Civil War Diary of Lt. Edmund Halsey*. Edited by Bruce Chadwick. Secaucus, NJ: Carol Publishing Group, 1997.

Handerson, Henry E. *Yankee in Gray: The Civil War Memoirs of Henry E. Handerson with a Selection of His Wartime Letters*. Cleveland: Press of Western Reserve Univ., 1962.

Happel, Ralph. *Salem Church Embattled*. Philadelphia: Eastern National Park and Monument Assoc., 1980.

Harrison, Noel G. *Chancellorsville Battlefield Sites*. Lynchburg, VA: H. E. Howard, 1990.

———. *Fredericksburg Civil War Sites*. 2 vols. 1. Lynchburg, VA: H. E. Howard, 1995.

———. "Southern Exposure: A Rare Map of the Second Battle of Fredericksburg." *Fredericksburg History and Biography* 16 16 (2017).

———. *A Tour of Civil War Sites on the University of Mary Washington Central Grounds*. Fredericksburg, VA: Center for Historic Preservation, Univ. of Mary Washington, 2008.

Hartwell, John F. L. *To My Beloved Wife and Boy at Home: The Letters and Diaries of Orderly Sergeant John F. L. Hartwell*. Edited by Ann Hartwell Britton and Thomas J. Reed. Madison, WI: Fairleagh Dickinson Univ. Press, 1997.

Haskell, Frank A. *Haskell of Gettysburg: His Life and Civil War Papers*. Edited by Frank L. Byrne and Andrew T. Weaver. Madison: State Historical Society of Wisconsin, 1970.

Hennessy, John J. *Return to Bull Run: The Campaign and Battle of Second Manassas*. New York: Simon & Shuster, 1983.

Herbert, Hilary A. "History of the Eighth Alabama Volunteer Regiment, C.S.A." Edited by Maurice S. Fortin. *Alabama Historical Quarterly* 39, nos. 1–4 (1977).

Hebert, Walter H. *Fighting Joe Hooker*. 1944. Reprint, Lincoln: Univ. of Nebraska Press, 1999.

Henry, John N. *Turn Them Out to Die like a Mule: The Civil War Letters of John N. Henry, 49th New York, 1861–1865*. Edited by John Michael Priest. Leesburg, VA: Gauley Mount, 1995.

Hewett, Janet B., Noah Andre Trudeau, and Bryce A. Suderow, eds. *Supplement to the Official Records of the Union and Confederate Armies*. 4 pts. in 100 vols. Wilmington, NC: Broadfoot, 1994–2000.

History of Clinton and Franklin Counties. New York. Philadelphia: J. W. Lewis, 1880.

History of the First Regiment Minnesota Volunteer Infantry, 1861–1864. Stillwater, MN: Easton & Masterman, 1916.

History of the Nineteenth Regiment Massachusetts Volunteer Infantry, 1861–1865. Salem, MA: Salem Press, 1906.

History of the Twenty Third Pennsylvania Volunteer Infantry, Birney's Zouaves: Three Months and Three Years Service. 1903–4. Reprint, Salem, MA: Higginson Book, 1998.

Holmes, Oliver Wendell, Jr. *Touched with Fire: Civil War Letters and Diary of Oliver Wendell Holmes, Jr., 1861–1864.* Edited by Mark DeWolfe Howe. New York: Da Capo, 1969.

Holt, Daniel M. *A Surgeon's Civil War: The Letters and Diary of Daniel M. Holt, MD.* Edited by James M. Greiner, Janel L. Coryell, and James R. Smither. Kent, OH: Kent State Univ. Press, 1994.

Hotchkiss, Jedediah. *Make Me a Map of the Valley: The Civil War Journal of Stonewall Jackson's Topographer.* Edited by Archie P. McDonald. Dallas: Southern Methodist Univ. Press, 1973.

Hotchkiss, Jedediah, and William Allan. *The Battlefields of Virginia: Chancellorsville.* New York: D. Van Nostrand, 1867.

Howard, Oliver O. "The Eleventh Corps at Chancellorsville." In Johnson and Buel, *Battles and Leaders of the Civil War*, vol. 3.

Hutchinson, Nelson V. *History of the Seventh Massachusetts Volunteer Infantry.* 1890. Reprint, Salem, MA: Higginson Book, 1997.

Hyde, John H., ed. *Civil War Letters by General Thomas W. Hyde.* Privately printed, 1933.

Hyde, Thomas W. *Following the Greek Cross; or, Memories of the Sixth Army Corps.* Boston: Houghton Mifflin, 1894.

Jackson, Huntington W. "Sedgwick at Fredericksburg and Salem Church." In Johnson and Buel, *Battles and Leaders of the Civil War*, vol. 3.

Johnson, Robert C., and Clarence C. Buel, eds, *Battles and Leaders of the Civil War.* 4 vols. 1887–88. Reprint, New York: Thomas Yoseloff, 1956.

Judd, David W. *The Story of the Thirty-Third N.Y.S. Vols.; or, Two Years Campaigning in Virginia and Maryland.* Rochester, NY: Benton & Andrews, 1864.

Krick, Robert K. *Civil War Weather in Virginia.* Tuscaloosa: Univ. of Alabama Press, 2007.

———. *Parker's Virginia Battery, CSA.* Wilmington, NC: Broadfoot, 1975.

Lemon, James Lile. *Feed Them the Steel!: Being the Wartime Recollections of Capt. James Lile Lemon, Co. A, 18th Georgia Infantry, C.S.A.* Edited by Mark Lemon. Privately printed, 2013.

Leonard, James H. "Letters of a 5th Wisconsin Volunteer." Edited by R. G. Plumb. *Wisconsin Magazine of History* 3 (Sept. 1919–June 1920).

Library of Congress. *Report of the Librarian of Congress, for the Fiscal Year Ending June 30, 1934.* Washington, DC: Government Printing Office, 1934.

Livermore, Thomas L. *Numbers and Losses in the Civil War in America.* 1900. Reprint, Dayton, OH: Morningside, 1986.

Lonn, Ella. *Desertion during the Civil War.* New York: Century, 1928.

Mackowski, Chris, and Kristopher D. White. *Chancellorsville's Forgotten Front: The Battles of Second Fredericksburg and Salem Church, May 3, 1863.* El Dorado Hills, CA: Savas Beatie, 2013.

Maier, Larry B. *Rough and Regular: A History of Philadelphia's 119th Regiment of Pennsylvania Volunteer Infantry, the Gray Reserves.* Shippensburg, PA: Burd Street, 1997.

Malone, Bartlett Yancey. *The Diary of Bartlett Yancey Malone.* North Carolina Historical Society, Chapel Hill, NC: James Sprunt Historical Publications, 1919.

Mann, J. William. *Bells and Belfries and Some of Neither*. Fredericksburg, VA: J. W. Mann, 1993.

Mark, Penrose G. *Red, White, and Blue Badge: Pennsylvania Veteran Volunteers: A History of the 93rd Regiment, Known as the "Lebanon Infantry."* . . . 1911. Reprint, Baltimore: Butternut and Blue, 1993.

Martin, David G. *The Fluvanna Artillery*. Lynchburg, VA: H. E. Howard, 1992.

Martin, Micajah D. "Chancellorsville: A Soldier's Letter." *Virginia Magazine of History and Biography* 37, no. 3 (July 1929).

Matrau, Henry. *Letters Home: Henry Matrau of the Iron Brigade*. Lincoln: Univ. of Nebraska Press, 1993.

McClelen, Bailey George. *I Saw the Elephant: The Civil War Experiences of Bailey George McClelen, Company D, 10th Alabama Infantry Regiment*. Edited by Norman E. Rourke. Shippensburg, PA: Burd Street, 1995.

McGlashan, Peter A. "Battle of Salem Church." *Addresses and President's Annual Report, 1893, of the Confederate Veterans Association of Savannah, Georgia*. Savannah: Briad & Hutton, 1893.

McPherson, James M. *Battle Cry of Freedom*. New York: Oxford Univ. Press, 1988.

Meade, George. *The Life and Letters of George Gordon Meade*. Vol. 1. New York: Charles Scribner's Sons, 1913.

Moore, Edward A. *The Story of a Cannoneer under Stonewall Jackson*. 1907. Reprint, Alexandria, VA: Time-Life Books, 1983.

Morse, Francis W. *Personal Experiences in the War of the Great Rebellion, from December, 1862, to July, 1865*. Albany, NY: Munsell, Printer, 1866.

Mundy, James H. *No Rich Men's Sons: The Sixth Maine Volunteer Infantry*. Cape Elizabeth, ME: Harp, 1994.

Naisawald, L. VanLoan. *Grape and Canister: The Story of the Field Artillery of the Army of the Potomac, 1861–1865*. 2nd ed. Mechanicsburg, PA: Stackpole Books, 1999.

Nelson, Erik F. "Each Man His Own Supply Train: A Federal Success at Chancellorsville." *Fredericksburg History and Biography* 10 (2011).

Newell, Joseph Keith, ed. *"Ours": Annals of the Tenth Regiment, Massachusetts Volunteers, in the Rebellion*. Springfield, MA: C. A. Nichols, 1875.

Nichols, Samuel Edmund. *"Your Soldier Boy Samuel": Civil War Letters of Lieut. Samuel Edmund Nichols, Amherst '65 of the 37th Regiment Massachusetts Volunteers*. Edited by Charles Sterling Underhill. Buffalo, NY: Privately printed, 1929.

Nolan, Alan T. *The Iron Brigade: A Military History*. 1961. Reprint, Bloomington: Indiana Univ. Press, 1994.

Oden, John P. "The End of Oden's War: A Confederate Captain's Diary." Edited by Michael Barton. *Alabama Historical Quarterly* 43, no. 2 (Summer 1981).

O'Reilly, Francis Augustín. *The Fredericksburg Campaign: Winter War on the Rappahannock*. Baton Rouge: Louisiana State Univ. Press, 2003.

Owen, William M. *In Camp and Battle with the Washington Artillery of New Orleans*. Boston: Ticknor and Company, 1885.

Patterson, Edmund DeWitt. *Yankee Rebel: The Civil War Journal of Edmund DeWitt Patterson*. Edited by John G. Barrett. Chapel Hill: Univ. of North Carolina Press, 1966.

Patrick, Marsena R. *Inside Lincoln's Army: The Diary of General Marsena Rudolph Patrick, Provost Marshal General, Army of the Potomac.* Edited by David S. Sparks. New York: Thomas Yoseloff, 1964.

Perry, Roy B., Jr. "West Wall Soldiers." *Fredericksburg History and Biography* 13, 2014).

Plum, William B. *The Military Telegraph during the Civil War in the United States.* Vol. 1. Chicago: Janson, McClurg, 1882.

Quinn, Sylvanus J. *The History of the City of Fredericksburg, Virginia.* Richmond, VA: Hermitage, 1908.

Rhodes, Elisha Hunt. *All for the Union: The Civil War Diary & Letters of Elisha Hunt Rhodes.* Edited by Robert Hunt Rhodes. Lincoln, RI: Andrew Mowbrey, 1985.

Rhodes, John H. *The History of Battery B, First Regiment Rhode Island Light Artillery.* Providence, RI: Snow & Farnham, Printers, 1894.

Rice, Adam Clarke. *The Letters and Other Writings of the Late Lieut. Adam Clarke Rice of the 121st Regiment, N.Y. Volunteers.* Edited by C. E. Rice. Little Falls, NY: Journal & Courier Book and Job Printing, 1864.

Richardson, Charles. *The Chancellorsville Campaign: Fredericksburg to Salem Church.* New York: Neale, 1907.

Riggs, David F. *13th Virginia Infantry.* Lynchburg, VA: H. E. Howard, 1988.

Robertson, James I., Jr. *Stonewall Jackson: The Man, the Soldier, the Legend.* New York: Macmillan, 1997.

Rokus, Josef W. "Daniel D. Wheeler: Medal of Honor Recipient Returns to Fredericksburg." *Fredericksburg History and Biography* 8 (2009).

Sears, Stephen W. *Chancellorsville.* New York: Houghton Mifflin, 1996.

———. *To the Gates of Richmond: The Peninsula Campaign.* New York: Ticknor & Fields, 1992.

Sedgwick, John. *Correspondence of John Sedgwick Major General.* 2 vols. New York: DeVinne, 1902–3.

Seymour, William J. *The Civil War Memoirs of Captain William J. Seymour: Reminiscences of a Louisiana Tiger.* Edited by Terry L. Jones. Baton Rouge: Louisiana Univ. Press, 1991.

Smith, Abram P. *History of the Seventy-Sixth Regiment New York Volunteers.* Cortland, NY: Privately published, 1867.

Smith, Anna Habersham Wright, ed. *A Savannah Family, 1830–1901: Papers from the Clermont Huger Lee Collection.* Milledgeville, GA: Boyd, 1999.

Smith, James Power. "Stonewall Jackson's Last Battle." In Johnson and Buel, *Battles and Leaders of the Civil War,* vol. 3.

Smith, John Day. *The History of the Nineteenth Regiment of Maine Volunteer Infantry, 1862–1865.* Minneapolis: Great Western Printing, 1909.

Smith, Timothy B. *The Golden Age of Battlefield Preservation: The Decade of the 1890s and the Establishment of America's First Five Military Parks.* Knoxville: Univ. of Tennessee Press, 2008.

Smith, Tunstall, ed. *Richard Snowden Andrews, Lieutenant-Colonel, Commanding the First Maryland Artillery (Andrews' Battalion), Confederate States Army: A Memoir.* Baltimore: Sun Job Printing Office, 1910.

Snead, Clayborne. *Address by Col. Claiborne Snead at the Reunion of the Third Georgia Regiment.* Augusta, GA: Chronicle and Sentinel Job Printing, 1874.

Stackpole, Edward J. *Chancellorsville: Lee's Greatest Victory.* Harrisburg, PA: Stackpole, 1958.

Stevens, George T. *Three Years in the Sixth Corps.* Albany, NY: S. R. Gray, 1866.

Stevens, William E. "In Battle and in Prison." *Granite Monthly* 2 (Apr. 1879).

Stewart, A. M. *Camp, March, and Battlefield; or, Three Years and a Half with the Army of the Potomac.* Philadelphia: Jas. B. Rodgers, Printer, 1865.

Strother, David H. *A Virginia Yankee in the Civil War: The Diaries of David Hunter Strother.* Edited by Cecil D. Eby Jr. Chapel Hill: Univ. of North Carolina Press, 1961.

Sullivan, James P. *An Irishman in the Iron Brigade: The Civil War Memoirs of James P. Sullivan, Sergt. Company K, 6th Wisconsin Volunteers.* Edited by William J. K. Beaudot and Lance J. Herdegon. New York: Fordham Univ. Press, 1993.

Sweet, Palmer, and David Trimble. *Virginia Gold—Resource Data.* Publication 45. Charlottesville: Virginia Division of Minerals, 1983.

Swinfen, David B. *Ruggles' Regiment: The 122nd New York Volunteers in the American Civil War.* Hanover, NH: Univ. Press of New England, 1982.

Tate, Thomas K. "A Chancellorsville Debut: The McEvoy Fuse-Igniter." *Fredericksburg History and Biography* 16 (2017).

Taylor, Joseph K. *The Civil War Letters of Joseph K. Taylor of the Thirty-Seventh Massachusetts Volunteer Infantry.* Edited by Kevin C. Murphy. Lewiston, NY: Edwin Mellen, 1998.

Thompson, George Raynor. "Civil War Signals." *Military Affairs* 18, no. 4 (Winter 1954).

Trask, Kerry A. *Fire Within: A Civil War Narrative from Wisconsin.* Kent, OH: Kent State Univ. Press, 1995.

Tsouras, Peter G. *Major General George H. Sharpe and the Creation of American Military Intelligence in the Civil War.* Philadelphia: Casemate, 2018.

Tyler, Mason Whiting. *Recollections of the Civil War.* Edited by William S. Tyler. New York: G. P. Putnam's Sons, 1912.

Uhler, George H. *Camps and Campaigns of the 93d Regiment, Penna. Vols.* Harrisburg: State Library of Pennsylvania, 1898.

Ward, Joseph R. C. *History of the One Hundred and Sixth Regiment Pennsylvania Volunteers, 2nd Brigade, 2nd Division, 2nd Corps, 1861–1865.* Philadelphia: F. McManus Jr., 1906.

War Department. *The War of the Rebellion: A Compilation of Official Records of the Union and Confederate Armies.* 128 vols. Washington, DC: Government Printing Office, 1890–1901.

Weigley, Russell F. *A Great Civil War: A Military and Political History, 1861–1865.* Bloomington: Indiana Univ. Press, 2000.

———. *Quartermaster General of the Union Army: A Biography of M. C. Meigs.* New York: Columbia Univ. Press, 1959.

Welcher, Frank J. *The Union Army, 1861–1865: Organization and Operations.* 2 vols. Bloomington: Indiana Univ. Press, 1989–93.

Westbrook, Robert S. *History of the 49th Pennsylvania Volunteers*. Altoona, PA: Altoona Times Print, 1898.

Westervelt, William B. *Lights and Shadows of Army Life as Seen by a Private Soldier*. Marlboro, NY: C. H. Cochrane, 1886.

Weymouth, James Edward. *The Civil War Letters of James Edward Weymouth*. Edited by Edith L. Macdonald. Viera, FL: Whitestone, 2002.

White, Wyman S. *The Civil War Diary of Wyman S. White*. Edited by Russell C. White. Baltimore: Butternut & Blue, 1993.

Whitman, William E. S., and Charles M. True. *Maine in the War for the Union*. Lewiston, ME: Nelson Dingley Jr., 1865.

Williams, Alpheus S. *From the Cannon's Mouth: The Civil War Letters of General Alpheus Williams*. Edited by Milo M. Quaife. Detroit: Wayne State Univ. Press, 1959.

Willsey, Berea M. *The Civil War Diary of Berea M. Willsey*. Edited by Jessica H. DeMay. Bowie, MD: Heritage Books, 1995.

Winslow, Richard Elliott, III. *General John Sedgwick: The Story of a Union Corps Commander*. Novato, CA: Presidio, 1982.

Wise, Jennings Cooper. *The Long Arm of Lee: The History of the Artillery of the Army of Northern Virginia*. Vol. 2. 1915. Reprint, Lincoln: Univ. of Nebraska Press, 1973.

Woodbury, Augustus. *The Second Rhode Island Regiment*. Providence, RI: Valpey, Angell, 1875.

Internet Sources

Cady, Rush P., to Gustavus Palmer, Apr. 25, 1863. American Civil War Collection, Digital Collections, Hamilton College Library. https://litsdigital.hamilton.edu/collections/letter-written-rush-p-cady-lieutenant-97th-new-york-volunteer-infantry-regiment-47.

Houghton, Henry H. "Recollections of the War: A Personal Account of the Civil War." http:www.vermontcivilwar.org/1bgd/3houghton.shtml.

Mink, Eric J. "Armament in the Army of the Potomac during the Chancellorsville Campaign." Fredericksburg VA: Fredericksburg and Spotsylvania National Military Park, 2018. https://npsfrsp.wordpress.com/2018/05/armament-aop-chancellorsville2.pdf.

Mysteries and Conundrums: Exploring the Civil War–Era Landscape in the Fredericksburg and Spotsylvania Region (blog). http://npsfrsp.wordpress.com.

US Naval Observatory, Astronomical Applications Department, Sun and Moon Data. https://aa.usno.navy.mil.

Zenzen, Joan M. *At the Crossroads of Preservation and Development: A History of Fredericksburg and Spotsylvania National Military Park: Administrative History*. Washington, DC: National Park Service, 2011. https://www.govinfo.gov/app/details/GOVPUB-I29-PURL-gpo81859.

INDEX

Acquia Landing: Lincoln and Halleck meeting with Hooker (May 7), 273; Ninth Corps departs from, 9
Adams, Alexander D., 185, 250
Adams, George W., 100, 122, 154, 164
Alabama Artillery, Hurt's Battery: at Fredericksburg, 41; at Smith Hill, 224, 258
Alabama Infantry Regiments: 8th, 156, 173, 177–79, 255; 9th, 72, 173, 177, 178, 181; 10th, 50, 75, 123, 124, 152, 171, 173, 177, 178, 181; 11th, 156, 173, 177, 183; 14th, 173
Alexander, E. Porter: at Chancellorsville (May 3), 105; at Fredericksburg (April 29), 39; replaces underperforming officer, 69; at Salem Church, 214, 217, 218; at Smith Hill, 224, 260, 261; at Zoan Church (May 1), 49
Alexander, Edgar P., 255
Alfred Bernard house (The Bend), 36
Allen, Ezra S., 65
Allen, Thomas S., 126, 133, 139, 231
Alum Springs Mill, Confederates deploy near, 196, 215, 227
Amsden, Frank P., 20, 67
Anderson, Richard H.: arrives at Salem Church with Lee, 214; at Chancellorsville (April 29), 42; at Zoan Church, 49, 50, 62. *See also* Anderson's Division
Anderson's Division: attack executed poorly (May 4), 223, 224; attack on Orange Turnpike (May 1), 63; deploys along Hazel Run (May 4), 216, 222; detached from Chancellorsville front (May 4), 214; entrenches at Zoan Church, 49, 50, 62; follows Federal retreat, 254
Andrews, R. Snowden: with Early on Telegraph Road, 196, 199; at Fredericksburg bridgehead, 68, 69, 76, 93; at Massaponax Church, 51; pulled off the line in error, 81; supports Deep Run fighting, 109, 110
Anthony, Oliver P., 181
Apps, George E., 79
Army of Northern Virginia: Barksdale reflects fighting spirit of, 93; doctrine, 144; Early's strength on May 3, 114; strength after May 3 fighting, 167; strength when campaign opens, 42
Army of the Potomac: absentees, 2; atrocities alleged, 143; Burnside departs, 9; enlistment crises, 2, 3; generals struggle with scope of war, 1, 8; Hooker assumes command, 1; Hooker breaks up grand divisions, 7; Hooker rebuilds, 2–5; Hooker's strength after Chancellorsville defeat, 166; Meade assumes command, 274; mutinies, 11; short-term soldiers, 10
Arthur Bernard house. *See* Mannsfield (Arthur Bernard house)
Artillery, Confederate: Early's assets at Fredericksburg, 51; getting to Fredericksburg, 40, 47; night firing at Smith Hill, 258, 260; organized effectively, 7; park at Massaponax Church, 47; worn-out horses, 40, 47
Artillery, Union, organized poorly, 7, 20
Atkins, Theodore, 165, 190
Avery, Isaac E., 228–30, 232, 235; assumes brigade command, 229

Babcock, John C., 5; forms intelligence team with Sharpe, 6
Babcock, Paul H., 198, 199, 203

Index

Baker, Benjamin F., 128, 132
Banks' Dam, 58; Hardaway reconnoiters after May 4, 260
Banks' Ford, description of, 58, 59
Banks' Ford Road, as Union retreat route, 248
Barksdale, William: analysis of official report, 295–301; concerned about inadequate manpower, 93; misdirects reinforcements to Rappahannock Canal, 121; with Pendleton on Telegraph Road, 86; returns to Fredericksburg without orders, 85; scrambles to deploy effectively at Fredericksburg, 113; at Stansbury house, 124. *See also* Barksdale's Brigade
Barksdale Brigade: close ties to Fredericksburg, 38; at Fredericksburg bridgehead, 70; pushes into Fredericksburg, 268; rallies on Telegraph Road, 150; reoccupies old positions at Fredericksburg, 201, 208; stretched too thin to defend Marye's Heights, 128
Barney, Elisha L., 219, 237, 242–44
Bartlett, Joseph J.: advances toward Salem Church, 167; brings up reinforcements at Salem Church, 185; orders assault at Deep Run, 106; at river crossing, 25, 26. *See also* Bartlett's brigade
Bartlett's brigade: assault at Deep Run, 106, 108, 109, 112; assault at Franklin's Crossing, 25, 26; assault at Salem Church, 167, 169, 175–79, 183, 185; attacked on May 4, 228–30, 242; on Plank Road, 206, 219; pulls back night of May 4–5, 246, 248, 249, 250–53
Bassett, Isaac C., 128, 132
Bates, Samuel P., 280
Beardslee, George W., 5
Beardslee Patent Magneto Electric Field Telegraph Machine, 60; limits of, 5, 37
Beers, Edmund O., 29, 36, 91, 112
Belle Plain (Union supply depot), 28, 37
Bend, The. *See* Alfred Bernard house (The Bend)
Benham, Henry W., 13, 36, 53, 71, 171; at Banks' Ford, 71, 75, 164, 212, 261; builds bridge at Banks' Ford, 169; commands bridge builders, 10; coordinates May 4–5 messages between Sedgwick and army headquarters, 262; drinking problem, 23, 24; at Franklin's Crossing, 22–24; holds back bridging materials, 170; at Pollock's Mill Creek, 27, 28, 31; waits to dismantle bridges at Banks' Ford, 264
Bernard, Arthur, 27, 34
Bernard, Matthew, 34
Bidwell, Daniel B., 238
Birney's Zouaves. *See* Pennsylvania Infantry Regiments: 23rd (Birney's Zouaves)
Bissell, George E., 134, 151, 257
Board, Francis H., 209
Bowling Green Road: description of, 36; no bridges at Hazel or Deep Runs, 95
Braehead. *See* Howison house (Braehead)
Bragg, Edward S., 32, 34
Brandy Station, 16, 18

Bridge at Kelly's Ford: built April 28, 18; materials transported expeditiously, 15
Bridges at Banks' Ford: Benham holds back part of bridge train sent to US Ford, 170; bridges removed (May 5), 266; crossing key to Hooker's plan, 43, 45; first bridge built (May 3), 164, 194; planned bridges not built (May 1), 75; second bridge built (May 4), 212; two bridge trains staged on uplands (May 1), 55, 56
Bridges at Franklin's Crossing: last bridge removed, 125; one bridge removed for use at Banks' Ford, 53, 55; preparations (April 28), 21, 22; river assault (April 29), 25, 26; second bridge removed for use in Fredericksburg, 112; three bridges constructed (April 29), 26, 27
Bridges in Fredericksburg: engineers stage equipment near Lacy house, 91; first bridge at Lacy house built (May 3), 100; at Lacy house and railway bridge, 112; last bridge at Lacy house removed, 266; pontoon bridge built at railway bridge, 112; pontoon bridge at railway bridge removed, 258; railway bridge materials removed, 258; railway bridge to be rebuilt, 163; railway bridge repairs abandoned, 219; second bridge at Lacy house built (May 3), 112
Bridges at Pollock's Mill Creek: one bridge damaged (May 2), 76; one bridge removed for use at Banks' Ford, 55; preparations (April 28), 23; river assault (April 29), 30, 31, 34; river assault timetable unravels, 22, 27–29; second bridge removed (May 2), 78; two bridges constructed (April 29), 36
Bridges at US Ford: bridges removed May 6, 268; engineers struggle to deliver bridge materials during night of April 29–30, 45; Hooker orders second bridge at Banks' Ford brought to US Ford, 170; two bridges built on April 30, 48; third bridge built on May 4, 264, 265
Briggs, Ephraim A., 60
Brooker, Albert F., 16, 67, 226
Brooklyn Zouaves, 14th. *See* New York Infantry Regiments: 84th
Brooks, William T. H., 14, 21, 22, 24, 35, 36, 43, 89, 125, 164, 184; conflict with Benham, 23; disappointed in Salem Church fighting, 189; observes Deep Run fight, 112; orders advance up Deep Run, 106; praises 16th New York Infantry at end of campaign, 269. *See also* Brooks's division
Brooks's division: advances on Salem Church, 168; on Bowling Green Road, 87, 93; in bridgehead, 35, 36, 70, 84, 104, 159; dispositions on May 4, 206; at Franklin's Crossing, 24–26; march from Deep Run to Guest house, 167; retreat to Banks' Ford Road, 250; at Salem Church, 163, 167, 175–78, 182–86
Brown, Henry W., at Salem Church, 163, 168. *See also* Brown's brigade
Brown, J. Thompson, Jr., 69, 79
Brown, R. S., 254

Brown, Robert, 144
Brown, T. Frederick, 100, 104, 154, 164
Brown, William D., 68, 76, 81, 93, 109
Browne, William H.: description of, 77; supports Gibbon, 120; wounded, 185. *See also* Browne's brigade
Browne's brigade: Eustis takes command, 185; into Fredericksburg, 94, 101, 117; on Plank Road, 155; at Salem Church, 168, 184, 185, 188
Brown's brigade: into bridgehead, 89; on Bowling Green Road, 110
Buck, Samuel D., 110, 111, 211
Buck, Samuel L., 206, 251
Buckman, Edwin, 131
Burnham, Hiram, 12, 22, 23, 84, 89, 133, 154, 168, 206, 253, 257; fails to retrieve division's knapsacks, 190; at Scott's Ferry bridge, 257. *See also* Light Division
Burnham's Light division. *See* Light Division
Burnside, Ambrose E., 1–2, 9
Bush, Henry, 245
Butler, John H., 94, 103, 129, 190, 195, 206, 224, 239
Butterfield, Daniel, 41, 66, 164, 198, 199, 212, 219; apprises Hooker of Sixth Corps progress, 116, 117, 158, 160, 161, 191; at Chancellorsville, 247, 262; committee testimony, 277; directs field guns to Falmouth Ford, 259; disparages Sedgwick, 265; dispatches to Lincoln, 159, 191; efficiency hindered by Hooker's secretiveness, 60, 61; at Falmouth, 18, 38, 97; ignorant of upriver terrain, 79; interferes with signal teams, 98, 99, 117, 202, 203; orders to Gibbon, 55; questions need for second bridge at Banks' Ford, 170; urgent communications with Sedgwick, 87, 90, 117, 157

Cabell, Henry C., 39, 51, 81
Calloway, William, 149, 150
Campbell, Edward L., 112
Canal Ditch. *See* Marye's Canal (Canal Ditch)
Carlton, Henry H., 41, 51, 145; on Howison Hill, 68, 84, 92, 138; at Leach house, 81, 147; march to Fredericksburg, 47; supports Wright's attack (May 4), 223
Carpenter, Charles, 77
Carpenter, Joseph, 68, 93, 106, 109
Carter, James W., 129, 150
Carter, William P., 224, 226
Cassin, Walter L., 26, 112
Casualties: bridgehead comparison, 34; for campaign overall, 272; at Salem Church, 191, 192
Catherine (Wellford's) Furnace, fighting (May 2) distracts Union command, 74, 79, 80
Cavalry, Confederate, shadows flanking columns, 40
Chandler, Zachariah, 275–79
Charles Street, Union assault columns visible to one another, 131
Chatham. *See* Lacy house (Chatham)
Chilton, Robert H., 80, 81, 90
Clark, Charles A., 133, 256, 257
Clark, George W., 156
Clarke, George J., 90

Clarke, Robert, 67
Cluney, Thomas, 246
Cobb, James S., 157, 168
Cogbill, William B., 143
Colgate, Clinton G., 27, 170, 264, 265
Collet, Mark W., 168
Collier, Frederick H., 188
Collins, Charles R., 156, 168, 169
Colston, Frederick M., 258
Colston, Raleigh E., 167, 176, 213
Comstock, Cyrus B., 6, 15
Connecticut Artillery: 1st Heavy, Battery B, 16, 67, 226; 1st Heavy, Battery M, 19, 27, 52
Cook, John B., 265
Cooper, James H., 20
Costin, Ellison L., 194
Couch, Darius N., 66, 115
Cowan, Andrew, 19, 26, 165; in bridgehead, 89, 105, 125; covers retreat, 251; at Marye house, 150; on Plank Road, 190; supports May 3 assault, 138, 145
Cox house, 82, 155, 194; Early's division spends night of May 3–4, 165; Early's fallback position, 150
Cross, Nelson, 101, 128, 143
Crutchfield, Stapleton, 39
Cummings, Amos J., 243
Cushing, Samuel T., 48, 60, 90, 98, 118, 199, 203; keeps Phillips house station open, 10
Cutts, Allen S., 165

Dawson, George W., 231
DeBlanc, Aleibiades, 243
Decker house, 262
Deep Run: Federals follow ravine to Confederate line (May 2), 84; fighting (May 3), 108, 109; five miles to Guest house, 163
Dement, William F., 68, 76, 81, 92, 93, 106, 108
Denicke, Martin, 171, 203
de Peyster, J. Watts, 89, 125, 150
Devereux, Arthur F., 220, 266
Dodsley, William R., 78
Donath, Harmon, 266
Doull, Alexander, 16, 170
Downman, William, 191, 200
Downman house (Idlewild): description of, 191; family abandons, 200; Federal artillery fires on Lee's Hill (May 4), 199; fighting near (May 4), 223; Howe's headquarters, 191; Lee's headquarters, 254
Downman house (north of Plank Road), 245
Dozier, Woody, 181
Duffey, Sam, 143

Early, Jubal A., 51, 105, 157, 164, 224, 229, 268; artillery at Fredericksburg, 69, 76; Chilton's interference, 80–82; coordinates with McLaws, 212; correspondence with Barksdale, 295–301; exasperated with Chilton's incompetence, 92; on Lee's Hill (May 4), 227; miscalculates where Federal attack will occur, 128, 149, 150; on Plank Road, 85, 91, 92; prepares to attack Sixth Corps, 196; reports crossing to Jackson, 28. *See also* Early's Division

Index

Early's Division, 80, 157, 167, 176, 208, 213, 228; assault on Plank Road, 227, 232, 234, 235; assault at Smith Run, 235–40, 242–45; at Cox farm, 165, 194; deploys against river crossing, 38; deploys for battle (May 4), 215; entrenches at bridgehead, 56; rallies on Telegraph Road, 155; redeploys night of May 4–5, 258, 261; retakes Marye's Heights, 196, 201; scattered along Plank Road, 91, 92; strength at Fredericksburg, 114
Edgell, Frederick M., 20
Edwards, Clark S., 108, 175, 176
Ellmaker, Peter C., 168, 189
Ely, John, 101, 126, 144
Ely's Ford, 18; Fifth Corps crosses, 40, 41
Embrey Mill (on Golin Run), 255
Eustis, Henry L., 120, 185, 188, 253
Evans, James M., 109

Fall Hill. *See* Taylor house (Fall Hill)
Fall Hill (topographical feature), 114, 169, 215, 235; Alabama pickets, 82; Confederate artillery occupies gun pits, 123, 124; Federals take position night of May 4–5, 245; Gordon's Brigade ascends and occupies, 246
Falmouth Ford: Federal artillery sent to guard, 259; potential crossing night of May 2–3, 90
Federal Hill: location, 115; Sedgwick and Newton watch May 3 attacks, 141
Ferneyhough house (Sligo): Confederate pickets, 50, 84; Federal batteries, 105, 129, 145
Ferrell, George A., 258
Ferris, John J., 99
Fielder, George W., 245
Fieldhouse, William, 110
First Long Island Regiment. *See* New York Infantry Regiments: 67th
First US Chasseurs. *See* New York Infantry Regiments: 65th
Fisher, French W., 211
Five Mile Fork, 169, 171
Flag of truce at stone wall, 115; analysis of, 295–301
Forest Hall (signal station), 48
Forney, William H., 124, 178
Forno, Henry, 227, 232
Fowler, Edward B., 30
Fraser, John C., 41, 51, 68, 92, 129, 138, 145, 147, 151
Fredericksburg Baptist Church: signal station dismantled, 199; signal station established, 118
Fredericksburg Cemetery: Confederate graves, 118; description of, 117; Federal stronghold, 220
Fredericksburg Court House (signal station), 118
French, Winsor B., 138, 146
Fry, Charles W., 226
Fryer, John, 132
Furst, Luther C., 261

Garnett, John J., 39
Garrett, Henry H., 265
Gaston, George F., 227, 234
Georgia Artillery: Pulaski Battery, 41, 51, 68, 92, 129, 138, 145, 147, 150; Troup Artillery, 41, 47, 51, 68, 84, 92, 106, 108, 121, 129, 138, 145, 150, 223
Georgia Infantry Regiments: 3rd, 216; 10th, 181, 187; 13th, 27, 29, 32, 196; 26th, 196; 31st, 196, 198, 199, 209; 38th, 196, 247; 50th, 173, 181, 187; 51st, 181, 182, 187; 53rd, 173, 181, 187; 60th, 246
General Orders, from Hooker: No. 44, 11; No. 47, 45; No. 48, 46
Germanna Ford/Mills: Federals capture and cross, 40
Gibbon, John, 55, 61, 90, 98, 114, 132, 198; committee testimony, 278, 279; greets old brigade near Falmouth, 78; handles mutiny, 72; holds Fredericksburg, 259; ordered to join pursuit on Plank Road, 152; ordered to turn Confederate right at Fredericksburg, 118. *See also* Gibbon's division
Gibbon's division: advances on Plank Road, 156; crosses into Fredericksburg, 98, 99, 104; departs Fredericksburg, 266; draws Confederates away from Fredericksburg, 128; in Falmouth during flank march, 87; on Marye's Heights, 154, 155; mutiny within, 72; at Rappahannock Canal, 120–22; returns to Fredericksburg, 163
Gibson, Jonathan C., 209
Gloskoski, Joseph, 118, 198, 199, 203
Godwin, Archibald C., 228, 232
Goggin, James M., 173
Gold mining, 58, 59
Golin Run, 254; Hardaway reconnoiters past night of May 4, 260
Gooch, Daniel W., 278, 279
Gordon, John B., 196; leadership, 208, 196, 245; ordered to Telegraph Road, 150; returns to Fredericksburg without orders, 75; scouts Telegraph Road, 165. *See also* Gordon's Brigade
Gordon's Brigade: advances to Smith Run, 201; ascends and occupies Fall Hill, 246; flanks Sedgwick's Smith Run line, 244, 245; joins fight (May 4), 234, 235; reoccupies Fredericksburg lines, 91, 106; retakes Marye's Heights, 196, 198; skirmishing (May 4), 227, 232; on Telegraph Road, 151, 155
Gosline's Zouaves. *See* Pennsylvania Infantry Regiments: 95th (Gosline's Zouaves)
Graham, Archibald: on Lee's Hill, 198; on Prospect Hill, 37, 51, 68, 76, 106; redeploys section to Latimer's sector, 109; retreat and return, 81, 93; signals May 4 assault, 221
Grant, Lewis A.: assault (May 3), 125, 139, 146; directed to Downman farm, 190; reports prisoners taken at Smith Run, 243. *See also* Grant's brigade
Grant, Ulysses S., 8
Grant's brigade: assault (May 3), 138, 139, 146–48; crosses into bridgehead, 89; fighting at Smith Run, 239, 240, 241–44; at Smith Run, 208, 219, 235; takes position at Downman farm, 190, 191
Griffin, Thomas M., 115, 129, 148, 295–97
Grogan, John, 78
Groner, Virginius D., 175
Grubb, E. Burd, Jr., 169
Guest, George, 167

Guest house: Federals pause in pursuit of Wilcox, 157; Sedgwick departs, 250; Sedgwick's headquarters, 163, 164

Hale, Samuel, Jr., 28
Hall, H. Seymour, 176
Hall, James A., 19
Hall, James S., 10, 62, 90
Hall, Norman J., 118, 220; pulls out of Fredericksburg, 266. *See also* Hall's brigade
Halleck, Henry W., 8, 273; speaks with corps commanders, 274
Hall's brigade: defends Fredericksburg, 220, 234; deploys to defend Fredericksburg, 201; into Fredericksburg, 100; on Marye's Heights, 154, 156; moves back to help evacuate Fredericksburg, 163, 164; provides 50-man storming party (May 3), 99; at Rappahannock Canal, 118, 120–22
Halsey, Edmund D., 111, 112, 251
Halsted, Richard F., 23
Hamblin, Joseph E., 94, 97, 189
Hamilton, George, 181
Hamilton, Samuel P., 169
Hamilton, Theodore B., 101, 231
Hamilton's Crossing, railroad activity observed, 37
Hancock, Winfield Scott, 65
Hanlon, Joseph, 33
Hanover Street, avenue of advance (May 3), 127
Hardaway, Robert A.: reports fuzing problem, 226; shells US Ford night of May 3–4, 217; on Smith Hill, 258, 259; to Smith Hill, 218
Harlow, Franklin P., 135, 136
Harman, Michael G., 209
Harn, William A.: covers retreat, 250; at crossing, 19, 26; in Fredericksburg, 103, 145, 150–51; at Salem Church, 190, 195, 206
Harper, Matthew, 268
Harper, Robert T., 268
Harris, Benjamin F., 126, 256
Hart, Patrick, 20, 27, 67
Hartshorn, Newton T., 259
Haupt, Herman, 219
Hawke Street, pontoon bridge site, 98, 220
Haycock, Joel A., 133
Hays, Harry T.: declines to deploy on Plank Road, 152; leadership, 208; remains in Fredericksburg (May 2), 88, 92; at Stansbury house, 124. *See also* Hays's Brigade
Hays's Brigade: assault on Plank Road (May 4), 227, 230, 232, 234; assault at Smith Run, 235–40, 243, 244; deploys and redeploys (May 4), 196, 201, 212, 215; must detour to rally on Telegraph Road, 155; recovers two cannons, 268; remains in Fredericksburg (May 2), 81, 82, 84; supports Mississippi brigade (May 3), 93, 106, 121, 123
Hazel Hill. *See* Slaughter house (Hazel Hill)
Healy, Henry G., 95
Heath, Francis E., 71
Herbert, Hilary, 156, 178
Hero, Andrew J., 79, 121, 154

Hickox, Charles R., 239
Hill, A. P., 37
Hill, Henry F., 236
Hill, William H., 118, 198, 199
Hoke, Robert: leadership, 208, 212; wounded, 229. *See also* Hoke's Brigade
Hoke's Brigade: assault on Plank Road (May 4), 228, 229, 232, 234; assault at Smith Run (May 4), 235, 240, 243, 244; Avery takes command, 232; at Deep Run, 108; deploys and redeploys (May 4), 196, 201, 215, 216; at Fredericksburg (May 3), 106; rallies on Telegraph Road, 155; retreat and return night of May 2–3, 82, 85, 91
Holder, William D., 82, 129, 150
Holmes, Oliver Wendell, Jr., 121
Holt, Daniel M., 265, 269
Holt, William C., 181
Hooker, Joseph, 9, 18, 24, 43, 52, 63, 64, 74, 88, 202, 212, 247; abandons Chancellorsville crossroads, 158; assessment of, 271, 273, 274; assures Sedgwick will reach Fredericksburg on May 1, 53, 57; authorizes Sedgwick to withdraw, 263; believes Confederates in retreat, 79, 80; blames Sedgwick for defeat, 160, 273; clarifies orders to Sedgwick, 61; committee testimony, 275–76; confusing orders to Sedgwick, 53; delays at Chancellorsville, 49, 53; directs Sedgwick to remain south of river, 204, 205, 206, 213; at Falmouth headquarters, 41; foregoes mobility for telegraph link at US Ford, 48, 60; has no plan for Sixth Corps, 214; headquarters at Mt. Holly Church, 18; inactive after injury, 160; injured, 115, 157; inspects lines at Chancellorsville, 79; mismanages artillery, 20, 115; neglects to inform Sedgwick when suspends advance (May 1), 70; orders Sedgwick to Chancellorsville, 87, 157; plan of campaign, 4, 13, 36, 43, 57; postwar visit to Sedgwick's May 4 battleground, 280; rebuilds Army of the Potomac, 2–5; remains passive during campaign, 45, 117; rescinds order allowing Sedgwick to withdraw, 264; supervises flanking columns, 18; suspends advance (May 1), 66, 71
Hotchkiss, Jedediah, 39, 47
Howard, Oliver O., 73, 79, 80; Hooker blames for defeat, 275, 279; at Kelly's Ford, 18; lax leadership, 16, 79
Howe, Albion P., 12, 125, 159, 163, 221; committee testimony, 276; headquarters at Downman house, 191. *See also* Howe's division
Howe's division: assault (May 3), 137–39, 145, 147; into bridgehead, 89; into Fredericksburg, 94; inadequate manpower to hold Smith Run line, 219, 235; on Plank Road, 164, 167; prepares for attack (May 3), 126, 127; redeploys (May 4), 208, 219; retreat to Fall Hill, 245, 246; returns to Bowling Green Road to retrieve knapsacks, 154; at Smith Run, 235, 237–44
Howison, John, 68
Howison house (Braehead): description of, 68; Federals overrun (May 3), 138

Index

Howison's Mill, Gordon's Brigade passes by retaking Marye's Heights, 198
Hubbell, Wilson, 231
Hudson, Henry W., 72, 91
Huey, Pennock, 221
Huger, Frank, 217
Hulings, Thomas M., 251
Humphreys, Benjamin G., 81, 92, 85, 99, 113, 129, 144; fighting (May 3), 120; at Hazel Hill, 84; rallies on Telegraph Road, 155
Hunt, Henry J., 16, 20, 71, 75, 87, 164, 170, 226; assigned administrative duties, 7; directs ordnance train to Banks' Ford, 194
Huntington, Howard J., 30
Hurkamp, John, 114, 132
Hurkamp house, description of Sedgwick's headquarters, 114, 115
Hurt, William P., 41, 224
Husted, Charles, 78
Hyde, Thomas W., 129, 137, 236, 237

Idlewild. *See* Downman house (Idlewild)
Indiana Infantry, 19th, 31, 32, 36
Ingalls, Rufus, 48, 63; develops system for field mobility, 4; directs Haupt to remove railway bridge repair materials, 219; helps move pontoon bridge trains, 45, 55; reports battle progress to Butterfield, 157
Ingraham, Frank, 144
Iron Brigade, 36; assault at Pollock's Mill Creek, 3–34; greets Gibbon on march upriver, 78, 79

Jackson, Huntington W., 97
Jackson, Thomas J. "Stonewall," 7, 28, 56, 59, 61, 64, 105; flank march, 80; opinion of Early, 51; orders advance on Hooker, 63; plans attack with Lee, 73; reconnoiters bridgehead, 37, 38, 47; wounded, 87; at Zoan Church, 62
James, William E., 78
Jerome, Aaron B., 171
Johns, Thomas D., 127, 133; committee testimony, 276, 277; wounded, 135
Johnston, Samuel R., 217
Joint Committee of the Conduct of the War, 275–79
Jones, Frank, 84, 126
Jones, Hamilton C., Jr., 232
Jordan, Tyler C., 226
Joslin, George C., 220

Kearse, Francis, 181, 187, 188
Keegan, M., 144
Kelly's Ford, Federals cross (April 28), 18
Kendall, Luke W., 245
Kennedy, John D., 254
Kershaw, Joseph B.: arrives at Salem Church, 173; detached from Chancellorsville front, 166. *See also* Kershaw's Brigade
Kershaw's Brigade, 161, 166, 171, 216, 224; advance (May 4), 201; captures New York troops near Banks' Ford, 256; on Plank Road, 254; at Salem Church, 179, 195

King Farm, Hooker's Falmouth headquarters, 2
Kinkead, Joseph M., 101, 126, 127, 231, 252
Kinzie, David H., 67
Kissinger, Samuel S., 94
Koonz, George R. 132
Kusserow, Charles F., 228

Lacy house (Chatham), Gibbon marshals forces night of May 2, 91
Laflin, Byron, 99, 121–23, 156; assumes brigade command, 91. *See also* Laflin's brigade
Laflin's brigade: crosses to north side of river, 164; into Fredericksburg, 100; on Marye's Heights, 154, 156; moves back to Fredericksburg, 163; provides 100-man storming party, 99; at Rappahannock Canal, 121–23
Lamar, G. B., 255
Landram house, 155
Lansdowne valley, description of, 106
Latimer, Joseph W., 68, 76, 106, 108, 110
Leach house: Confederate rally point, 149, 150; description of, 82
Lee, Robert E., 105, 157, 160, 195, 258, 268; arrives at Salem Church (May 4), 214; at Fredericksburg crossing, 18, 19, 28, 37; headquarters in Downman house, 254, 255; informed of Sixth Corps breakthrough, 194; informed of upriver crossings, 41; must operate without Longstreet, 38, 39, 46; plans attack on Sixth Corps (May 4), 215, 217; plans flank attack with Jackson, 73, 74; probes Hooker's left flank (May 3), 167; pulls several brigades from Chancellorsville to reinforce Wilcox, 161, 166; responds to Hooker's movements, 42, 50, 56; returns to Fredericksburg, 67; understanding of operational art, 8
Lee, W. H. Fitzhugh "Rooney," 16, 18
Lemont, Frank L., 108
Leonard, James H., 273
Lessig, William H., 106, 108, 175, 179, 193
Lewis, John R., 219, 230, 237, 242
Lewis, Trevanian D., 227, 243
Light Division, 14, 77, 89, 231, 242; advance toward Salem Church, 168; assault (May 3), 133–35; carries pontoons at Franklin's Crossing, 22–24; crosses river (May 1), 70; on far-right flank (May 4), 206, 253; forms atop Marye's Heights, 154; into Fredericksburg (May 3), 94, 100; prepares to attack Marye's Heights, 126, 127
Lincoln, Abraham: confers with Hooker, 10; grants amnesty for absent troops, 2; irritated by inadequate dispatches, 160, 213; meets with Hooker postbattle, 273; receives dispatches, 157, 159, 160, 191; reviews army, 9; seeks competent army commander, 1, 7
Lodge, Douglas, 132
Logistics: attaining field mobility, 4–5; retrieving knapsacks after May 3 assaults, 154, 190; Sixth Corps replenishes ammunition after Salem Church, 194; status of rations (April 30), 49; status of rations (May 1), 66; status of rations (May 2), 83

Long, John S., 231, 265
Longstreet, James, detached from Army of Northern Virginia, 9. *See also* Longstreet's Corps
Longstreet's Corps: disposition (May 3), 117; two divisions at Fredericksburg (May 4), 218
Louisiana Artillery, Washington Battalion, 47; arrives at Fredericksburg, 51; Eshelman's Fourth Company, 120; history of, 69; on Marye's Heights, 79, 92, 129; Miller's Third Company, 120, 129, 144; Richardson's Second Company, 81, 92, 106, 149, 150; Squires's First Company, 129
Louisiana Infantry Regiments: 5th, 35, 82, 121, 227; 6th, 29, 31, 35, 37, 82, 121, 129, 146, 150, 227; 7th, 82, 84, 87, 121, 227, 243; 8th, 82, 121, 227, 243; 9th, 82, 121, 227, 243
Lowe, Thaddeus, 6, 37, 56
Lubey, Timothy, 9; gets pontoons to Kelly's Ford, 15
Lutman, Thomas J., 143
Lyon, Isaac S., 60, 203
Lyon, Samuel, 228, 234

Mahone, William, arrives at Salem Church, 171. *See also* Mahone's Brigade
Mahone's Brigade: detached from Chancellorsville front, 161, 166; at Salem Church, 173, 187, 188
Maine Artillery, 2nd, 19
Maine Infantry: 5th, 105, 108–9, 112, 175–79, 181, 183, 185, 250; 6th, 22, 84, 133–35, 137, 141–43, 151, 253, 256, 257; 7th, 138, 139, 145, 146, 149, 199, 209, 235–38, 246; 19th, 71, 99, 164
Manly, Basil C., 41, 51, 168, 169, 255
Mannsfield (Arthur Bernard house), 34, 35, 84, 105; description of, 27
Marsten, Frank W., 118, 198
Martin, Edward T., 143
Martin, Joseph W., 52
Martin, Leonard, 89, 105, 125, 138, 145, 150, 151, 191, 199, 208, 239
Martindale, Edward, 139, 146, 238, 240
Marye, Edward A., 224
Marye house (Brompton): Federal artillery, 145, 150; overrun (May 3), 137
Marye's Canal (Canal Ditch): blocks Gibbon's advance, 118; description of, 94; intact bridges at William and Hanover Streets, 132, 133
Maryland Artillery: 1st Battery, 68, 76, 92, 106; 4th Battery, Chesapeake, 68, 76, 93, 110; Light, Battery A, 19, 104–6, 109, 110, 169, 184, 190, 208, 219, 237, 239, 242, 251
Mary Washington grave: Federal artillery, 154; unfinished monument, 104
Massachusetts Artillery, Light, Battery A, 105, 106, 109, 112, 199, 206, 222, 250
Massachusetts Infantry Regiments: 1st Company of Sharpshooters, 220; 7th, 117, 118, 127, 133–35, 184, 185, 188, 189; 10th, 120–22, 154, 156, 184–86, 188, 189, 253; 15th, 72, 99, 122, 123, 220; 19th, 99, 120, 121, 123, 201, 220, 259, 266; 20th, 99, 121, 201; 37th, 184, 185, 224, 248, 253

Massaponax Church, Confederate artillery park, 47
Massie, John L., 69
McAlpine, Charles R., 260
McCarthy, Edward S., 41, 51, 169, 224, 258; guns overlook Banks' Ford, 261
McCarthy, Jeremiah, 19, 26, 94, 103, 145, 150, 151, 206
McCartney, William H., 105, 106, 111, 199, 200, 206, 222, 250
McClellan, George B., 1, 2, 5
McDonald, Alexander J., 239
McDowell, James C. S., 228, 229
McKay, Thomas M., 99
McLaws, Lafayette: detached from Chancellorsville front, 161; follows Union retreat, 254; hesitates to attack (May 4), 212; holds Kershaw back, 258; during May 1 fighting, 65; positions troops at Salem Church, 187; professionally negligent (May 4), 214; at river crossing, 42; senior officer at Salem Church, 194, 195; at Zoan Church, 62. *See also* McLaws's Division
McLaws Division, 82, 160, 218, 222, 224; departs Fredericksburg, 51, 56; minor probe (May 4), 201, 226
McMahon, Martin T., 103
McVean, John P., 211
Meade, George G.: at Chancellorsville, 48, 49; at Ely's Ford, 40; on River Road, 63, 65, 66; succeeds Hooker as army commander, 274
Meigs, Montgomery C., 4
Meinell, Henry, 67
Meredith, Solomon, 28
Michigan Infantry Regiments: 7th, 121, 201; 24th, 30–32, 36, 78
Miller, Merritt B., 120, 121, 129, 132
Milne, Joseph S., 259
Miner, Brinkerhoff N., 171, 203
Minnesota Infantry, 1st, 99, 122, 123, 164, 259
Mississippi Infantry Regiments: 13th, 50, 93, 129, 146, 150; 17th, 50, 93, 129, 146, 147, 150; 18th, 50, 93, 129, 144, 148, 150; 21st, 50, 81, 84, 85, 91, 93, 95, 99, 113, 120, 129, 144, 150, 155
Monaghan, William, 31, 37, 121, 129, 146, 227
Moore, Joseph D., 123, 155, 156, 169
Morrison, Andrew J., 125, 139
Morse, Francis W., 175
Morse, William H., 250
Murchison, Kenneth M., 229
Murray, Thomas A., 145

Neill, Thomas H.: confronts Confederates cutting off Sixth Corps (May 4), 199; prepares for assault (May 3), 125; Smith Run line untenable, 236. *See also* Neill's brigade
Neill's brigade: assailed at Smith Run (May 4), 238, 239; assault on May 3, 138; in bridgehead, 89, 93; destroys Confederate attack morning of May 4, 209; position near Smith Run, 219, 235; retreat to River Road, 246
Nelson, William, 69, 81

New Hampshire Artillery, 1st, Battery A, 20, 52
New Jersey Artillery, Light, Battery A, 105, 109, 110, 169, 184, 190, 206, 222, 223, 229, 250
New Jersey Infantry Regiments: 1st, 168, 182, 183, 185, 186; 2nd, 168, 183; 3rd, 168, 182–86; 15th, 110–12, 183–86; 21st, 125, 138, 139, 146, 147, 199, 212, 219, 235–37, 239; 23rd, 110, 169, 176–79, 182; 26th, 125, 138, 139, 146, 238–40, 244, 245
Newton, John, 12; at Federal Hill during May 3 assaults, 141; in Fredericksburg, 103, 115; at Guest house, 163; meets with Benham, 15; on Plank Road (May 4), 231; plans May 3 assault, 117; at Salem Church, 185, 188, 206; supports Gibbon, 120. *See also* Newton's division
Newton's division: in bridgehead, 89, 93; covers retreat, 248; at crossing, 70, 87; on Plank Road (May 4), 218; at Salem Church, 168, 184, 185
New York Artillery: 1st Independent Light, 19, 89, 105, 125, 138, 145, 149, 150, 165, 190, 206, 250; 1st Light, Battery L, 19, 52, 77; 3rd Independent Light, 19, 103, 145, 150, 190, 195, 206, 250; 5th Independent Light, 20, 52, 227, 234; 15th Independent Light, 20, 27, 67; 29th Independent Light, 16, 67, 78; 30th Independent Light, 19; 32nd Independent Light, 20, 228, 234
New York Engineers: 15th, 9, 16, 26, 27, 112, 265, 268; 50th, 19, 23, 29, 36, 45, 47, 53, 55, 91, 112, 164, 169, 266, 268
New York Infantry Regiments: 16th, 25, 105, 108, 176, 178, 179, 182, 183, 185, 222, 250, 269; 18th, 24, 26, 189; 20th, 235, 236, 238; 24th, 29; 27th, 11, 105, 108, 109, 112, 185, 206, 218, 222, 224, 250; 31st, 84, 126, 134, 135, 137, 253, 256, 257; 32nd, 11, 24–26, 36, 110, 189, 195; 33rd, 138, 139, 145, 146, 148–49, 199, 235–38; 34th, 72, 91, 99, 122, 123, 163; 36th, 76, 77, 127, 132, 135, 184, 185, 224, 248; 42nd, 201; 43rd, 35, 128, 132, 136–37, 143, 144, 206, 219, 253, 256, 257; 49th, 121, 199, 209, 211, 235, 236, 238, 240, 246; 59th, 121, 201, 220; 62nd, 101, 103, 144, 188, 231, 252, 253; 65th, 94, 95, 189, 253; 67th, 101, 128, 132, 136–37, 143, 253; 76th, 31, 59; 77th, 137–39, 146, 148–49, 219, 236; 82nd, 72, 99, 156; 84th, 32, 34; 95th, 36; 121st, 105, 108, 163, 175–77, 179, 181, 183, 185, 191; 122nd, 94, 156, 189, 253
Norcom, Joseph, 120, 132, 154
North Carolina Artillery, 1st Battery, 41, 47, 51, 168–69, 255
North Carolina Infantry Regiments: 1st Battalion, Sharpshooters, 216, 228, 231, 234; 6th, 216, 228, 231, 232; 21st, 106, 110, 111, 216, 228, 231, 243; 54th, 27, 35, 216, 228, 229, 231, 243; 57th, 35, 216, 228, 231, 232, 243

Odell, Moses F., 278, 279
O'Kane, Dennis, 60
Ordnance, fuze igniter problems, 200, 226
Owen, Joshua T., 60, 75, 170; directed to move bridge trains to Banks' Ford, 55. *See also* Owen's Brigade

Owen's Brigade, 67; at Banks' Ford, 71, 75, 87; crosses river to link with Sedgwick, 170, 171; holds ground on Confederate flank, 188; moves bridge trains to Banks' Ford, 55, 60

Parker, Dexter F., 185
Parker, William, 47, 69, 224
Parsons, Augustus N., 105, 169, 190, 206, 222
Patrick, Marsena R., 5; arms Sixth Corps stragglers, 259; at Chancellorsville with Hooker (April 30), 53
Patterson, Edmund D., 270
Patterson, George M., 68, 148, 151
Pendleton, William N., 9, 39, 69; artillery park at Massaponax Church, 47, 51; confronts May 3 assault, 120, 145, 149; at crossing, 69, 76; failure on William Street, 121, 136; in Fredericksburg, 79, 80, 82, 84, 86, 88; with Lee, 67, 68; on Telegraph Road, 150, 151
Penick, Nathan, 122, 152, 168, 169, 173, 177, 224
Penn, Davidson B., 227
Pennington, Alexander C. M., 226
Pennsylvania Artillery: 1st Light, Battery C-D, 19, 94, 103, 145, 150, 206; 1st, Battery B, 20; 1st, Battery F, 20, 52; 1st, Battery G, 20, 67; 4th, Battery C, 20, 52
Pennsylvania Cavalry, 8th, 48–49, 53, 221, 245, 252, 265
Pennsylvania Infantry Regiments: 23rd (Birney's Zouaves), 101, 126, 134, 135, 144, 253; 49th, 24, 25, 36, 189, 251; 61st, 22, 84, 128, 132, 136, 144, 231, 238, 242, 254, 257; 69th, 55, 60, 61, 67; 71st, 55, 164, 170, 171; 72nd, 55, 67; 82nd, 128, 132, 136, 137, 143, 144, 253; 93rd, 103, 144, 188, 231, 265; 95th (Gosline's Zouaves), 24–25, 36, 167, 168, 182, 183, 185, 189; 96th, 56, 105, 106, 109, 112, 175–77, 179, 185, 250, 269; 98th, 78, 103, 144, 188, 231, 253; 102nd, 78, 101, 103, 126, 144, 188, 231, 252, 268; 106th, 55, 67; 119th, 24, 25, 36, 167, 168, 182, 183, 185, 189; 127th, 98, 121, 163, 220, 266; 139th, 103, 144, 188, 231, 253, 261, 267
Penrose, William H., 183
Perrin, William, 155
Perry, Edward A.: does not advance after dark, 254; prepares for May 4 assault, 216. *See also* Perry's Brigade
Perry's Brigade, 214; assault cut off by Wright's advance (May 4), 216; deployed for May 1 fighting, 65; at Falmouth, 63
Pettes, William H., 15, 23, 36, 266
Philadelphia Brigade. *See* Owen's Brigade
Phillips house, signal station, 37, 198, 203
Pickett, George E., 59
Pierce, Seymour, 90
Pingree, Samuel E., 239
Pinkerton, Alan, 5
Pinto, Francis E., 11, 195
Pitzer, Andrew L., 161, 212
Plumer, William, 220
Pohlman, William H., 273

Posey, Carnot, prepares for May 4 assault, 214. *See also* Posey's Brigade
Posey's Brigade: advances to Plank Road (May 4), 254; assault cut off by Wright (May 4), 216; at US Ford, 19
Pratt, Franklin A., 19, 27
Pratt, Thomas, 34
Pratt house. *See* Smithfield (Pratt house)
Prince Edward Street, edge of town for Hanover Street assault column, 133
Princess Anne Street: assault columns stack knapsacks, 128; road cut in front of Fredericksburg Cemetery, 131

Raine, Charles J., 68, 76, 81, 93, 106, 108
Rankin, William S., 228
Ransom, Dunbar R., 20, 31, 46
Rappahannock Canal: Confederates dismantle bridges, 118; Federals dismantle bridges, 259
Rappahannock Navigation System, 59
Razderichin, Valerian, 97
Read, Theodore, 169
Reese, Chauncey B., 14, 23, 24, 112
Reynolds, John A., 19, 77
Reynolds, John F., 13; at bridgehead, 43, 52, 57, 70; departs bridgehead, 76, 78; mishandles crossing, 30, 31, 35; ordered to Chancellorsville, 75; preparations for crossing, 23, 28; reinforces bridgehead with artillery, 46
Rhett, Andrew B., 51, 68, 81
Rhode Island Artillery: 1st, Battery B, 100, 104, 120, 122, 154, 156, 164, 259, 266; 1st, Battery G, 100, 104, 120, 122, 124, 154, 164, 228
Rhode Island Infantry, 2nd, 121, 122, 154, 156, 184, 186, 188, 269
Rice, Edmund, 220, 259, 266
Richard's Ford, 18
Richardson, John B., 81, 149
Richardson, John M., 69, 106
Richmond Stage Road. *See* Bowling Green Road
Ricketts, R. Bruce, 20
Rigby, James H., 19; covers retreat, 251; at Franklin's Crossing, 26; at Salem Church, 169, 190; at Smith Run, 208, 219, 237, 242, 243; supports Deep Run fight, 104–6
Robb, James, 132
Robinson, William H., 32
Rogers, Horatio, Jr., 120, 185
Rogers, James A., 27
Royston, Young L., 177
Russell, David A., 21–22; at crossing, 24; at Salem Church, 167, 189. *See also* Russell's brigade
Russell's brigade, 163; assault at Franklin's Crossing, 24, 27; in bridgehead, 89; covers retreat, 248; position (May 4), 206; at Salem Church, 167, 189
Ryan, William W., 33
Ryerson, George W., 99, 156

Salem Church: battleground burns, 193; battleground description, 167, 168, 176, 191; Confederates hinder recovery of wounded, 195; intensity of fighting compared to Gaines' Mill, 186
Sanders, John C. C., 183
Sands house, 20, 27
Saye, Richard W., 145
Scott, Winfield, 1
Scott house (Stafford County), telegraph station, 10, 171, 203
Scott's Mill and Ferry, 19, 75, 170, 203, 221; bridge removed (May 5), 266; retreat route, 263; suitable place to anchor pontoon bridge, 164
Seabury, Robert S., 164
Sears, William, 165
Seaver, Joel J., 176, 178, 250, 269
Seaver, Thomas O., 148, 149, 237, 238
Seddon house, 41
Sedgwick, John, 9, 11, 15, 18, 78, 83, 157, 164, 213, 230, 264, 279; consolidates Sixth Corps on Plank Road, 157, 164; coordinates Fredericksburg assaults, 125, 129, 137; departs Guest house, 250; disengages to march west, 151, 155; faces reinforced Confederates at Salem Church, 176; headquarters at Guest house, 163, 167; headquarters at Hurkamp house, 114, 127; informs Hooker will hold south of river, 263; knows Hooker will blame him for failed campaign, 279; meets with division commanders at Banks' Ford, 261; ordered to Chancellorsville, 87; orders rescinded for march to Chancellorsville, 204; plans crossing with Benham, 14; plans May 3 assaults with Newton, 115, 117, 118; prepares to march to Chancellorsville, 89, 90; received orders unclear, 61, 75, 98; reports operations concluded, 267; reports Salem Church fight to Hooker, 195; requests permission to withdraw, 262; seeks instructions (May 4), 202, 204, 205; takes position south of river, 206; watches Fredericksburg assaults from Federal Hill, 141
Seeley, Francis W., 19
Semmes, Paul J., 181, 191; arrives at Salem Church, 173; detached from Chancellorsville front, 166. *See also* Semmes's brigade
Semmes's brigade: at Salem Church, 175, 181, 187; casualties, 191; en route to Salem Church, 171
Seymour, William J., 15
Shaler, Alexander, 253; description of under fire, 136; on Marye's Heights, 143, 144, 156; rallies William Street column, 132; reconnoiters Marye's Heights, 101. *See also* Shaler's brigade
Shaler's brigade: assault in Fredericksburg, 128; into Fredericksburg, 94, 100; gathers prisoners, 104; at Salem Church, 168
Sharpe, George H., 5, 6; determines Longstreet not on field, 61; discovers Lee's strength, 74
Sickles, Daniel E., 13, 14, 50, 52, 57, at Chancellorsville, 79, 80
Slaughter house (Hazel Hill), occupied by Confederate pickets, 84, 95
Slocum, Henry W., 18, 63, 65
Smallwood, Charley, 135

Smith, James Power, 28, 56
Smith, R. Penn, 171
Smith, William, 268
Smith, William F. "Extra Billy": avoids reproach as governor-elect, 211; political background, 208. *See also* Smith's Brigade
Smithfield (Pratt house), 82; cache found, 35; description of, 34
Smith Hill, artillery position on, 224, 226, 258, 260, 268
Smith's Brigade: at crossing, 35; helps retake Marye's Heights, 196, 201, 209; march out Plank Road and back, 85, 91; not engaged (May 3), 106, 110; probes Union line (May 4), 209, 211; in reserve (May 4), 215, 234, 235; on Telegraph Road, 155
Snowden. *See* Stansbury house (Snowden)
South Carolina Artillery: Brooks Battery, 51, 68, 81, 129; Sumter Battery B, 68, 148, 149
South Carolina Infantry Regiments: 2nd, 254; 3rd, 179, 255; 7th, 255; 15th, 255
Spaulding, Ira, 45, 47
Spear, George C., 128, 131, 132
Squires, Charles W., 79, 129, 143
Stafford, Leroy A., 15, 227, 243
Stansbury house (Snowden), 118, 120, 122, 152, 244; Confederate artillery in nearby redoubt, 155, 156; Confederate brigade commanders meet (May 3), 124; Confederate infantry in trenches, 123
Stanton, Edwin M., 159; controls US Military Telegraph, 5
Stevenson, James M., 253
Stewart, James, 46
Stoneman, George, 9, 160, 275, 279
Stoughton, Charles B., 148, 242
Strickler, William L., 70
Strong, Lewis A., 135
Strother, David H., Hooker's limitations, 280
Stuart, Charles B., 23, 55, 164, 266
Stuart, J. E. B., 16; commands at Chancellorsville, 115; reconnoiters Union position, 73–74; shadows Federal flanking columns, 40
Sully, Alfred, 72
Sykes, George, 63–65

Taft, Elijah D., 20, 227, 234
Tannery, on William Street, 128, 132, 136
Tate, Samuel M., 232
Taylor, Peter A., 90
Taylor, Robert F., 146, 237
Taylor house (Fall Hill), 72, 123, 213, 215
Taylor house (Rose Hill), 113, 155
Taylor's Dam, part of Rappahannock Navigation system, 269
Taylor's Hill. *See* Fall Hill (topographical feature)
Telegraph Road, lined by stone walls at Marye's Heights, 135
Terrill, James B., 27, 111, 209
Terrill, William H., 219
Terry, Thomas M., 244
Thoman, Max A., 220

Thomas, Lorenzo, Jr., 67, 226, 265
Thompson, James, 20
Titus, Silas, 156, 189
Tompkins, John A., 19, 250; in Fredericksburg, 150; headquarters at Sands house, 20; at Salem Church, 184, 190; stops May 4 assault, 224
Town, Gustavus W., 168, 182
Town, Thomas J., 182
Travellers Rest, 20, 38, 52, 67
Trumbull, Hoel W., 33
Tullis, John W., 41, 68, 81
Tyler, James M., 141
Tyler, Robert O., 205

Unfinished railway: in Fredericksburg, 103, 126, 139, 145; near Landram house, 155, 196; part of battleground (May 1), 64
Union Cavalry Corps, initiates campaign (April 13), 9
Union Eleventh Corps: at Germanna Ford, 40; at Kelly's Ford, 18, 19; on the march, 13, 16; overwhelmed by Confederate attack, 86; poorly deployed (May 2), 79
Union Fifth Corps: at Chancellorsville, 40; at Ely's Ford, 40; at Kelly's Ford, 18, 19; on the march, 13, 16; on River Road, 63
Union First Corps: departs Fredericksburg bridgehead, 76; ordered to Chancellorsville, 74, 75; at Pollock's Mill Creek, 28, 30–34; prepares for river crossing, 21; at US Ford, 86
Union Ninth Corps, division sent to Suffolk, 9
Union Second Corps: fighting (May 1), 65, 66; one division at Fredericksburg, 13, 98, 99, 104; two divisions at US Ford, 47, 48
Union Sixth Corps: combined strength in bridgehead, 36; composition of, 11, 12; at crossing, 69, 76; orders unclear (May 4), 205; strength on May 3, 204; victory at Fredericksburg only battlefield success, 213
Union Third Corps: at Catherine Furnace, 74, 79, 80; at Chancellorsville, 79; ordered to Chancellorsville, 50; overwhelmed by Confederate attack, 86; in reserve at Fredericksburg crossings, 14
Union Twelfth Corps: fighting (May 1), 63–65; at Germanna Ford, 40; at Kelly's Ford, 18, 19; on the march, 13, 16
United States Military Railroad, 63
United States Military Telegraph: contends with poor wires, 48; controlled by Stanton, 5; new wires strung (May 2), 75; replaces inadequate Beardslee equipment, 60
Upton, Emory, 175, 177
US Artillery: 1st US, Battery K, 67, 226, 265; 2nd, Battery D, 19, 36, 105, 109, 110, 184, 190, 206, 251; 2nd US, Battery G, 94, 103, 129, 190, 195, 206, 224, 231, 239, 246; 2nd US, Battery M, 67, 226; 3rd US, Battery C, 67; 4th US, Battery B, 46, 52; 4th US, Battery K, 19; 5th US, Battery C, 20, 31, 46; 5th US, Battery F, 89, 105, 125, 145, 149–51, 191, 199, 208, 209, 223, 239; 5th, Battery K, 67

US Ford: interim crossing to reinforce flanking columns, 48; strategic limitations, 60, 66

Van Houten, J. Gilliam, 236, 245
Vermont Infantry Regiments: 2nd, 138, 139, 146, 147, 149, 238–40, 242, 266; 3rd, 148, 149, 237–40, 242; 4th, 148, 149, 240, 242; 5th, 149, 219, 228, 230, 232, 235, 237, 242; 6th, 137–39, 143–45, 219, 242–44, 246, 266
Virginia Artillery: 1st Rockbridge Artillery, 37, 41, 51, 68, 70, 76, 93, 106, 198, 199, 209, 221, 227; Alleghany Battery, 68, 93, 106; Bedford Battery, 226; Fluvanna Battery, 47, 69; Fredericksburg Battery, 224; King William Battery, 224, 259; Lee Battery, 68, 93, 106; Norfolk Battery, 124, 155, 156, 169; Orange Battery, 226, 259; Pittsylvania Battery, 122, 123, 152, 156, 157, 168, 177, 224; Richmond Battery, 47, 69, 79, 85, 129, 143, 224; Richmond Howitzers, 1st Company, 41, 51, 169, 224, 258, 261, 265
Virginia Cavalry, 15th, 156, 168, 169
Virginia Infantry Regiments: 12th, 261; 13th, 35, 106, 110, 112, 208, 209, 211; 41st, 260; 49th, 209, 211, 234, 258; 52nd, 209, 211, 234, 258; 58th, 209, 211; 61st, 175, 208
Voegelee, Adolph, 19
von Blucher, Gustav, 16, 67, 78
von Vegesack, Ernst, 236

Wade, Benjamin W., 275, 279
Wadsworth, James S., 23, 35; failure at crossing, 28; inexperienced, 15, 29; joins river assault, 33; ordered upriver, 75. *See also* Wadsworth's division
Wadsworth's division: collapses and abandons bridgehead, 75–78; at crossing, 30–33
Wainwright, Charles S., 19, 52, 77, 78
Walbridge, James H., 139, 146, 238
Walsh, James J., 77, 127, 133
Walton, James B., 51, 69, 79, 92
Warner, Edward R., 20, 52
Warren, Gouverneur K., 88; authorizes Sedgwick to withdraw, 214; committee testimony, 277, 278; messages to Hooker, 159, 161; messages to Sedgwick, 204, 205; on Orange Turnpike (May 1), 65; at Rappahannock Canal, 118, 120, 121; reports to Sedgwick, 98; at US Ford (April 30), 45, 47, 48
Washington farm, 164, 228, 234
Wells, Harrison, 30
Wendell, Nelson O., 178
Wharton, Rufus W., 228, 234
Wheaton, Frank: assault in Fredericksburg (May 3), 144, 145, 155; on Plank Road, 231, 232; at Salem Church, 189, 193. *See also* Wheaton's brigade
Wheaton's brigade, 100, 103, 117; into Fredericksburg, 94; on Plank Road, 231, 232; reconnoiters Marye's Heights, 101; retreat, 251, 252; at Salem Church, 168, 185, 188
Wheeler, Daniel D., 189
White Oak Church, Federal reserve artillery nearby, 67

Whitworth rifle, 41, 52, 68, 112, 224, 258
Wilcox, Cadmus M., 59; blocks Federal advance on Plank Road, 152, 155, 156; brings artillery to bluffs at Banks' Ford, 261; decides to leave Banks' Ford to reinforce Lee, 122; identifies Salem Church as rally point, 156; leaves Banks' Ford to defend Fredericksburg, 123, 124; on Plank Road, 255; reinforcements arrive at Salem Church, 168, 171, 173; at Salem Church, 157, 161; at Stansbury house, 124. *See also* Wilcox's Brigade
Wilcox's Brigade, 184, 187; at Banks' Ford, 19, 65, 82; casualties, 191; follows Federal retreat, 255, 256; at Rappahannock Canal, 128, 152; at Salem Church, 168, 171, 176–78, 181
Wilderness Church, 74, 90
William Perry house, Confederate artillery rally point, 169
Williams, Alpheus S., 191
Williams, Henry L. N., 243
Williams, James P., 109
Williams, Jeremiah H. J., 178
Williams, Seth, 247
William S. Williams house: apex of Union line (May 4), 206; Federal rally point, 181
Willis Cemetery, Confederate battery position, 129, 141
Willis Hill (part of Marye's Heights): occupied by Confederate artillery, 129; Federals overrun (May 3), 137
Williston, Edward B., 19, 206; at Franklin's Crossing, 26, 27, 36, 105; retreat, 251; at Salem Church, 184, 185, 190
Wilson, Fountain, 90
Wilson, John, 132
Wisconsin Infantry Regiments: 2nd, 31, 32, 36, 126; 5th, 22, 29, 77, 84, 126, 134, 137, 139, 143, 145, 151, 231, 238, 242, 253, 257; 6th, 30, 31, 34, 36; 7th, 31–33, 36
Wofford, William T.: advances brigade after dark (May 4), 257; detached from Chancellorsville front, 161; furious when held back from Banks' Ford, 258. *See also* Wofford's Brigade
Wofford's Brigade: arrives at Salem Church, 173, 187; at Salem Church (May 4), 195, 201, 216, 224, 254
Woodbury, Daniel P., 10
Woolen Mills, 118; description of, 99
Wormsley, John, 169
Wright, Ambrose R. "Rans": botched attack (May 4), 223, 224, 229; detached from Chancellorsville front, 161; follows Federal retreat, 254. *See also* Wright's Brigade
Wright, William W., 63
Wright's Brigade: arrives at Salem Church, 214, 216; assault (May 4), 222–24
Wyckoff, William, 195
Wynkoop, George, 231

Zoan Church, 49, 50, 56; description of, 62, 69, 171